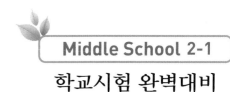

Middle School 2-1
학교시험 완벽대비

1학기 전과정

적중 100 plus

영어 기출문제집

중 2

동아 | 윤정미

Best Collection

구성과 특징

교과서의 주요 학습 내용을 중심으로 학습 영역별 특성에 맞춰 단계별로 다양한 학습 기회를 제공하여
단원별 학습능력 평가는 물론 중간 및 기말고사 시험 등에 완벽하게 대비할 수 있도록 내용을 구성

Words & Expressions

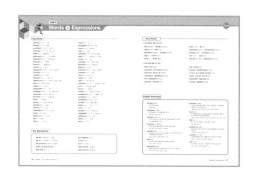

Step1   Key Words 단원별 핵심 단어 설명 및 풀이
Key Expression 단원별 핵심 숙어 및 관용어 설명
Word Power 반대 또는 비슷한 뜻 단어 배우기
English Dictionary 영어로 배우는 영어 단어

Step2   실력평가 단원별 수시평가 대비 주관식, 객관식 문제풀이

Step3   서술형 대비 학업성취도 및 수행능력평가 대비 서술형 문제풀이

Conversation

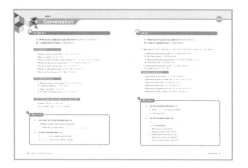

Step1   핵심 의사소통 소통에 필요한 주요 표현 방법 요약
핵심 Check 기본적인 표현 방법 및 활용능력 확인

Step2   대화문 익히기 교과서 대화문 심층 분석 및 확인

Step3   교과서 확인학습 빈칸 채우기를 통한 문장 완성 능력 확인

Step4   기본평가 시험대비 기초 학습 능력 평가

Step5   실력평가 단원별 수시평가 대비 주관식, 객관식 문제풀이

Step6   서술형 대비 학업성취도 및 수행능력평가 대비 서술형 문제풀이

Grammar

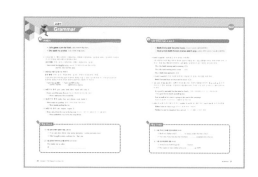

Step1   주요 문법 단원별 주요 문법 사항과 예문을 알기 쉽게 설명
핵심 Check 기본 문법사항에 대한 이해 여부 확인

Step2   기본평가 시험대비 기초 학습 능력 평가

Step3   실력평가 단원별 수시평가 대비 주관식, 객관식 문제풀이

Step4   서술형 대비 학업성취도 및 수행능력평가 대비 서술형 문제풀이

Reading

Step1   구문 분석 단원별로 제시된 문장에 대한 구문별 분석과 내용 설명
확인문제 문장에 대한 기본적인 이해와 인지능력 확인

Step2   확인학습A 빈칸 채우기를 통한 문장 완성 능력 확인

Step3   확인학습B 제시된 우리말을 영어로 완성하여 작문 능력 키우기

Step4   실력평가 단원별 수시평가 대비 주관식, 객관식 문제풀이

Step5   서술형 대비 학업성취도 및 수행능력평가 대비 서술형 문제풀이
교과서 구석구석 교과서에 나오는 기타 문장까지 완벽 학습

Composition

|영역별 핵심문제|

단어 및 어휘, 대화문, 문법, 독해 등 각 영역별 기출문제의
출제 유형을 분석하여 실전에 대비하고 연습할 수 있도록 문
제를 배열

|단원별 예상문제|

기출문제를 분석한 후 새로운 시험 출제 경향을 더하여 새롭
게 출제될 수 있는 문제를 포함하여 시험에 완벽하게 대비할
수 있도록 준비

|서술형 실전 및 창의사고력 문제|

학교 시험에서 점차 늘어나는 서술형 시험에 집중 대비하고
고득점을 취득하는데 만전을 기하기 위한 학습 코너

|단원별 모의고사|

영역별, 단계별 학습을 모두 마친 후 실전 연습을 위한
모의고사

교과서 파헤치기

- **단어Test1~3** 영어 단어 우리말 쓰기, 우리말을 영어 단어로 쓰기, 영영풀이에 해당하는 단어와 우리말 쓰기
- **대화문Test1~2** 대화문 빈칸 완성 및 전체 대화문 쓰기
- **본문Test1~5** 빈칸 완성, 우리말 쓰기, 문장 배열연습, 영어 작문하기 복습 등 단계별 반복 학습을 통해 교
  과서 지문에 대한 완벽한 습득
- **구석구석지문Test1~2** 지문 빈칸 완성 및 전문 영어로 쓰기

Contents

Lesson 1

My Happy Everyday Life

🎤 의사소통 기능

- 여가 활동 묻기

  A: What do you usually do in your free time?

  B: I usually listen to music.

- 정보 묻기

  A: What kind of music do you listen to?

  B: I listen to classical music.

🎤 언어 형식

- 4형식 동사

  You can also **show me some pictures**.

- 상관 접속사 both A and B

  Both my father **and** I like to sleep under the tree.

교과서
Words & Expressions

Key Words

- **almost** [ɔ́:lmoust] 부 거의
- **animal** [ǽnəməl] 명 동물
- **architect** [á:rkətèkt] 명 건축가
- **around** [əráund] 부 약, ~쯤, ~경
- **bake** [beik] 동 (빵을) 굽다
- **because** [bikɔ́:z] 접 ~이기 때문에
- **between** [bitwíːn] 전 사이[중간]에
- **boring** [bɔ́:riŋ] 형 지루한
- **brush** [brʌʃ] 동 솔질을 하다
- **carrot** [kǽrət] 명 당근
- **classical** [klǽsikəl] 형 고전적인, 클래식의
- **country** [kʌ́ntri] 명 나라
- **culture** [kʌ́ltʃər] 명 문화
- **dessert** [dizə́:rt] 명 디저트, 후식
- **detective** [ditéktiv] 형 탐정의 명 탐정, 수사관
- **end** [end] 동 끝나다, 마치다
- **enjoy** [indʒɔ́i] 동 즐기다
- **especially** [ispéʃəli] 부 특히
- **exciting** [iksáitiŋ] 형 신나는, 흥미진진한
- **exercise** [éksərsàiz] 동 운동하다
- **favorite** [féivərit] 형 가장 좋아하는
- **free** [fri:] 형 자유로운
- **funny** [fʌ́ni] 형 웃기는, 재미있는
- **garden** [gá:rdn] 명 정원
- **horror** [hɔ́:rər] 명 공포
- **important** [impɔ́:rtənt] 형 중요한
- **kind** [kaind] 명 종류
- **library** [láibrèri] 명 도서관
- **lie** [lai] 명 거짓말
- **like** [laik] 전 ~와 같은

- **meat** [mi:t] 명 고기
- **Mongolia** [maŋgóuliə] 명 몽골
- **most** [moust] 형 대부분의
- **nap** [næp] 명 낮잠
- **national** [nǽʃənl] 형 국가의, 국립의
- **near** [niər] 전 ~가까이에(서) 형 가까운
- **novel** [návəl] 명 소설
- **outside** [áutsàid] 부 밖에서, 밖에
- **peaceful** [píːsfəl] 형 평화로운
- **place** [pleis] 명 장소
- **practice** [prǽktis] 명 연습 동 연습하다
- **present** [préznt] 명 선물
- **race** [reis] 명 경주, 경기
- **really** [ríːəli] 부 정말로
- **ride** [raid] 동 (탈 것을) 타다
- **romantic** [roumǽntik] 형 로맨틱한, 낭만적인
- **sci-fi** 명형 공상 과학 소설(의)
- **show** [ʃou] 동 보여주다
- **siesta** [siéstə] 명 낮잠[휴식], 시에스타
- **sometimes** [sʌ́mtàmz] 부 때때로, 가끔
- **southern** [sʌ́ðərn] 형 남쪽의
- **strawberry** [strɔ́:bèri] 명 딸기
- **sunset** [sʌ́nset] 명 일몰, 해질녘
- **times** [taimz] 명 ~배
- **truth** [tru:θ] 명 진실
- **usually** [júːʒuəli] 부 보통, 대개
- **vegetable** [védʒətəbl] 명 야채, 채소
- **weekend** [wíːkend] 명 주말
- **when** [hwən] 접 ~할 때
- **win** [win] 동 이기다

Key Expressions

- **be like** ~처럼 되다, ~와 같다
- **be on** ~의 일원이다, ~의 소속이다
- **be proud of** ~을 자랑스러워하다
- **both A and B** A와 B 둘 다
- **free time** 여가 시간

- **get together** 모이다
- **in fact** 사실은
- **live in** ~에 살다
- **take care of** ~을 돌보다
- **what kind of** 어떤 종류의 ~

Word Power

※ 서로 반대되는 뜻을 가진 단어

- like (좋아하다) ↔ dislike (싫어하다)
- many (많은) ↔ few (적은)
- peaceful (평화로운) ↔ warlike (호전적인)
- big (큰) ↔ small (작은)
- long (긴) ↔ short (짧은)

- near (가까운) ↔ far (먼)
- important (중요한) ↔ unimportant (하찮은)
- boring (지루한) ↔ exciting (흥미로운)
- win (이기다) ↔ lose (지다)
- proud (자랑스러운) ↔ ashamed (부끄러운)

※ 서로 비슷한 뜻을 가진 단어

- kind : sort (종류)
- peaceful : nonviolent (평화로운)
- exercise : work out (운동하다)
- important : significant (중요한)
- fun : enjoyable (재미있는)
- practice : training (훈련)

- nap : siesta (낮잠)
- boring : uninteresting (지루한)
- in fact : as a matter of fact (사실은)
- many : a lot of : lots of (많은)
- especially : specially (특히)
- sunset : nightfall (해질녘)

English Dictionary

- **boring** 지루한
  → not interesting
  흥미롭지 않은

- **classical** 고전적인
  → belonging to a traditional style
  전통적인 양식에 속해 있는

- **dessert** 디저트, 후식
  → sweet food served after the main part of a meal
  식사 후에 제공되는 단 음식

- **favorite** 가장 좋아하는
  → liked more than others of the same kind
  같은 종류의 다른 것들보다 더 좋아하는

- **garden** 정원
  → an area of ground where plants such as flowers or vegetables are grown
  꽃이나 채소같은 식물을 재배하는 지역

- **nap** 낮잠
  → a short sleep, especially during the day
  특히 낮 동안의 짧은 수면

- **peaceful** 평화로운
  → quiet and calm without any worry or excitement
  걱정이나 자극이 없이 조용하고 차분한

- **practice** 연습하다
  → to do a particular thing, often regularly, in order to improve your skill at it
  기술을 향상시키기 위해 종종 규칙적으로 특정한 일을 하다

- **race** 경주
  → a competition in which people or animals compete to run fastest and finish first
  사람이나 동물이 가장 빨리 달려서 먼저 끝을 내기 위해 겨루는 경쟁

- **ride** 타다
  → to sit on an animal, especially a horse
  동물, 특히 말을 타다

- **sunset** 일몰, 해질녘
  → the time of day when the sun disappears and night begins
  해가 사라지고 밤이 시작되는 시간

- **usually** 대개, 보통
  → talking about what happens on most occasions
  대부분의 경우에 일어나는 일에 관해 말하는

- **win** 이기다
  → to achieve victory in a fight, contest, game, etc.
  싸움, 시합, 경기 등에서 승리를 거두다

서답형

01 다음 짝지어진 단어의 관계가 같도록 빈칸에 알맞은 말을 쓰시오.

> sunset : sunrise =
>
> interesting : _____

중요

02 다음 빈칸에 공통으로 알맞은 것은?

> • When is your favorite time _____ the day?
> • I take good care _____ my horse.

① at　　　　　　② of
③ on　　　　　　④ out
⑤ in

[03~04] 다음 빈칸에 알맞은 말이 바르게 짝지어진 것을 고르시오.

03

> • I am so proud _____ them.
> • What do you usually do _____ your free time?

① of – at　　　　　② in – in
③ out – on　　　　④ of – in
⑤ to – on

중요

04

> • Diego's family gets _____ and has a big long lunch.
> • Musa is _____ the school's soccer team.

① together – on　　② on – on
③ off – in　　　　④ to – to
⑤ together – off

[05~06] 다음 영영 풀이에 해당하는 단어를 고르시오.

05

> a short sleep, especially during the day

① rest　　　　　　② nap
③ cheer　　　　　④ change
⑤ soup

중요

06

> a competition in which people or animals compete to run fastest and finish first

① sports　　　　　② sunset
③ game　　　　　④ fight
⑤ race

07 다음 밑줄 친 단어의 우리말 뜻이 잘못된 것은?

① My favorite time of the day is our running practice time. 가장 좋아하는
② My school usually ends around 2 p.m. ~경, 대략
③ Horses are important in our culture. 문화
④ I often brush him and give him some carrots. 솔
⑤ Everything is peaceful. 평화로운

서답형

08 다음 우리말에 맞게 빈칸에 알맞은 말을 쓰시오.

> Tamu와 나는 둘 다 그들처럼 되고 싶어한다.
> ➡ _____ Tamu _____ I want to _____ them.

01 다음 빈칸에 들어갈 말을 〈보기〉에서 찾아 쓰시오.

┌─ 보기 ├─
won   boring   care   take

(1) After lunch, we usually _____ a siesta, a short nap.
(2) Many runners from Kenya _____ races.
(3) I take good _____ of my horse.
(4) Our English class isn't _____.

02 다음 빈칸에 공통으로 들어갈 말을 〈보기〉에서 골라 쓰시오.(대·소문자 무시)

┌─ 보기 ├─
like   both   when

(1) • I'm happy _____ I eat candy.
    • _____ is your favorite time of the day?
(2) • This country has many national parks with animals _____ lions, zebras, and giraffes.
    • I especially _____ listening to rap music.
(3) • I like _____ math and science.
    • _____ Tom and Joe were late for school.

03 다음 괄호 안의 단어를 문맥에 맞게 알맞은 형태로 고쳐 쓰시오.

(1) The sky is blue, and everything is _____. (peace)
(2) Our practice time isn't _____ because we can see many animals. (bore)
(3) What do you _____ do in your free time? (usual)

04 다음 우리말과 같은 뜻이 되도록 주어진 단어를 알맞은 순서로 배열하시오.

(1) 민수는 축구와 야구를 둘 다 좋아한다.
(likes / soccer / Minsu / both / and / baseball)
➡ _____

(2) 나는 친구들과 함께 놀 때 가장 행복하다.
(I'm / when / I / with / my friends / happiest / play)
➡ _____

(3) 너는 어떤 종류의 음악을 듣니?
(what / to / of / music / do / kind / you / listen)
➡ _____

05 다음 영영풀이에 해당하는 단어를 주어진 철자로 시작하여 쓰고 아래 문장에 알맞은 단어를 채우시오.

┌──────────────────────────────┐
│ • p_____: to do something again and again in order to become better at it
│ • c_____: belonging to a traditional style
│ • g_____: an area of ground where plants such as flowers or vegetables are grown
│ • d_____: sweet food served after the main part of a meal
└──────────────────────────────┘

(1) I listen to _____ music when I have free time.
(2) You should _____ playing the piano.
(3) My family has a _____ like churros after having breakfast.
(4) She will plant roses in her _____ this year.

Conversation

① 여가 활동 묻기

A What do you usually do in your free time? 너는 보통 여가 시간에 무엇을 하니?
B I usually listen to music. 나는 보통 음악을 들어.

여가 활동 묻기

- What do you do in your free time? 너는 여가 시간에 무엇을 하니?
- What's your hobby? 너의 취미가 뭐니?
- What do you like to do when you have free time? 여가 시간이 있을 때 무엇을 하는 것을 좋아하니?
- What do you like to do in your free time? 여가 시간에 무엇을 하는 것을 좋아하니?
- How do you spend your free time? 너는 여가 시간을 어떻게 보내니?
- What do you like doing for fun? 너는 재미로 무엇을 하는 것을 좋아하니?
- What's your free time activity? 여가 활동으로 무엇을 하니?

여가 활동 묻고 답할 때

- A: What do you do in your free time? 너는 여가 시간에 무엇을 하니?
  B: I usually go shopping. 나는 보통 쇼핑하러 가.
- A: What's your hobby? 너의 취미는 뭐니?
  B: My hobby is listening to music. 내 취미는 음악 감상이야.

여가 시간을 어떻게 보내는지 물을 때 주로 답하는 표현

- I usually + 일반 동사. 나는 보통 ～을 해.
- I like + 동사원형 + -ing ～. 나는 ～하는 것을 좋아해.

핵심 Check

1. 다음 두 문장의 의미가 같도록 빈칸에 알맞은 말을 쓰시오.

   - What do you do when you have free time?

     = What do you like to do in _____ _____ _____?

2. 다음 대화의 빈칸에 알맞은 말을 쓰시오.

   A: _____ do you spend your free time?

   B: I _____ play soccer with my friends.

② 정보 묻기

A What kind of music do you listen to? 어떤 종류의 음악을 듣니?

B I listen to classical music. 나는 클래식 음악을 들어.

■ 'What kind of+명사?'는 '어떤 종류의 ~?'라는 의미로 특정한 종류를 물어볼 때 쓸 수 있는 표현이다.

• A: What kind of movies do you like? 너는 어떤 종류의 영화를 좋아하니?
  B: I like horror movies. 나는 공포 영화를 좋아해.

• A: What kind of pets do you want to have? 너는 어떤 종류의 애완동물을 갖고 싶니?
  B: I want to have cats. 나는 고양이를 갖고 싶어.

• A: What kind of exercise do you do? 너는 어떤 종류의 운동을 하니?
  B: I usually swim. 나는 보통 수영을 해.

정보를 묻는 다양한 표현

• What kind of car do you like? 너는 어떤 종류의 차를 좋아하나?
• What kind of fish do you usually eat? 너는 보통 어떤 종류의 생선을 먹니?
• What kind of soup is this? 이것은 어떤 종류의 수프니?
• What kind of book is this? 이것은 어떤 종류의 책이니?
• What kind of vegetables do you like? 너는 어떤 종류의 채소를 좋아하니?
• What kind of fruit do you like? 너는 어떤 종류의 과일을 좋아하니?

핵심 Check

3. 다음 대화의 빈칸에 들어갈 알맞은 말을 쓰시오.

   A: What _____ of music do you like?

   B: I like pop music.

4. 다음 대화의 빈칸에 들어갈 알맞은 것은?

   A: _____

   B: I like pineapples.

   ① Why don't you like fruit?
   ② Would you like to have fruit?
   ③ What kind of fruit do you like?
   ④ What did you have for dessert?
   ⑤ Are you going to buy some fruit?

A. Listen and Talk A-1

> G: Hajun, ❶what do you usually do in your free time?
> B: I ❷like playing games with my dad.
> G: ❸What kind of games do you play?
> B: I ❹usually ❺play baduk.

G: 하준아, 너는 여가 시간에 보통 무엇을 하니?
B: 나는 아버지와 게임을 하는 걸 좋아해.
G: 어떤 종류의 게임을 하니?
B: 나는 주로 바둑을 둬.

❶ what do you usually do in your free time?: 여가 시간에 주로 무엇을 하니? / free time: 여가 시간
❷ like -ing: ~하는 것을 좋아하다
❸ what kind of 명사: 어떤 종류의 ~
❹ usually는 빈도부사로 일반동사 앞에 위치한다.
❺ play baduk: 바둑을 두다 / 스포츠나 운동경기 앞에는 정관사 the를 붙이지 않는다. play baseball, play basketball, play chess 등.

Check(√) True or False

(1) Hajun likes playing baduk with his dad.　　　　　　　T ☐ F ☐

(2) The girl knows about Hajun's hobby.　　　　　　　　T ☐ F ☐

B. Listen and Talk A

> B: Subin, what do you usually do in your free time?
> G: I exercise outside.
> B: What kind of exercise do you do?
> G: I ❶play badminton with my brother. I'm on the school's badminton team. What do you usually do in your free time, Andy?
> B: I ❷like watching movies.
> G: What kind of movies do you like?
> B: I like action movies. ❸They're fun.
> G: Oh, I ❹sometimes watch action movies, too. ❺Why don't we go see an action movie this weekend?
> B: Sure. That sounds great.

B: 수빈아, 너는 여가 시간에 주로 무엇을 하니?
G: 나는 밖에서 운동을 해.
B: 어떤 종류의 운동을 하니?
G: 나는 남동생과 배드민턴을 쳐. 난 학교 배드민턴 팀이야. 너는 여가 시간에 주로 무엇을 하니, Andy?
B: 나는 영화보는 것을 좋아해.
G: 어떤 종류의 영화를 좋아하니?
B: 나는 액션 영화를 좋아해. 액션 영화는 재미있어.
G: 오, 나도 가끔 액션 영화를 봐. 이번 주말에 액션 영화 보러 갈래?
B: 그래. 좋아.

❶ play badminton: 운동이나 스포츠경기 앞에는 관사 the를 사용하지 않는다.
❷ like는 목적어로 watching(동명사)이나 to watch(부정사)를 취할 수 있다.
❸ They's action movies를 가리킨다.
❹ sometimes는 빈도부사로 일반동사 watch 앞에 위치한다.
❺ Why don't we + 동사원형 ~?: '~하는 게 어때?'라는 의미다. 같은 표현으로 How[What] about + -ing? = Shall we + 동사원형 ~? = What do you say to + -ing? = Let's + 동사원형 ~. 등이 있다.

Check(√) True or False

(3) Subin plays badminton with her brother on weekends.　　T ☐ F ☐

(4) Subin and Andy are going to see a movie this weekend.　　T ☐ F ☐

Listen and Talk A-2

G: Hey, Eric. What do you usually do in your free time?

B: ❶I go to the library and read books.

G: What kind of books do you read?

B: I ❷like reading detective stories. I ❸really like ❹Sherlock Holmes' stories.

❶ I go ~ and read books.: go와 read가 접속사 and로 연결되어 있는 동사 병렬구조다.

❷ like -ing: ~하는 것을 좋아하다 / detective story: 탐정 소설

❸ really는 '정말로'의 뜻으로 쓰인 부사로 동사 like를 꾸며주는 역할을 한다.

❹ Sherlock Holmes' stories: -s로 끝나는 명사의 소유격은 '(apostrophe)만 사용한다.

Listen and Talk A-3

G: Seho, ❶what do you do in your free time?

B: I ❷listen to music.

G: ❸What kind of music do you listen to?

B: Rock music.

❶ what do you do ~?: '무엇을 하니?'의 의미로 일반적인 사실을 물어보는 현재형을 사용한다.

❷ listen to ~: ~을 듣다

❸ What kind of music do you listen to?: 어떤 종류의 음악을 듣니? / '~을 듣다'의 의미일 때는 listen to를 사용한다.

Listen and Talk A-4

G: Chris, what do you do ❶when you have free time?

B: I make cookies. I ❷enjoy baking.

G: What kind of cookies do you make?

B: I ❸usually make strawberry cookies. I love strawberries.

❶ when you have free time: 여기서 when은 부사절을 이끄는 접속사로 '~할 때'의 의미다.

❷ enjoy는 '동사원형+ing(동명사)'를 목적어로 가진다.

❸ usually는 빈도부사로 일반동사 make 앞에 사용한다.

Listen and Talk B

A: Minji, ❶what do you usually do in your free time?

B: I usually listen to music.

A: ❷What kind of music do you listen to?

B: I listen to classical music.

❶ what do you usually do in your free time?: 여가 시간에 주로 무엇을 하니? / free time: 여가 시간

❷ what kind of 명사: 어떤 종류의 ~

Review 1

B: Emma, what do you usually do in your free time?

G: I usually listen to music. ❶How about you, Chris?

B: I read books. I like detective stories.

❶ '너는 어때?'의 의미로 What about you?와 같은 표현이다.

Review 2

G: Jiho, ❶what do you usually do when you have free time?

B: I usually watch movies.

G: ❷What kind of movies do you watch?

B: I like action movies. Bruce Lee is my favorite movie star.

❶ what do you usually do in your free time?: 여가 시간에 주로 무엇을 하니? / free time 여가 시간

❷ what kind of 명사: 어떤 종류의 ~

Review 3

1. W: What does Minho usually do in his free time?

2. W: What kind of games does Sewon play?

● 다음 우리말과 일치하도록 빈칸에 알맞은 말을 쓰시오.

Listen and Talk A-1

G: Hajun, _____ _____ you _____ _____ in your free time?

B: I _____ _____ games with my dad.

G: _____ _____ _____ games do you play?

B: I usually _____ _____.

Listen and Talk A-2

G: Hey, Eric. What do you usually do _____ _____ _____ _____?

B: I go to the library and read books.

G: _____ _____ _____ _____ do you read?

B: I _____ _____ detective stories. I really like Sherlock Holmes' stories.

Listen and Talk A-3

G: Seho, what do you do in your free time?

B: I _____ _____ music.

G: What kind of music _____ _____ _____ _____?

B: Rock music.

Listen and Talk A-4

G: Chris, what do you do _____ you have free time?

B: I make cookies. I enjoy _____.

G: _____ _____ _____ cookies do you make?

B: I _____ make strawberry cookies. I love strawberries.

Listen and Talk B

A: Minji, _____ do you _____ _____ in your free time?

B: I _____ _____ _____ music.

A: _____ _____ _____ music do you listen to?

B: I _____ _____ _____ music.

해석

G: 하준아, 여가 시간에 보통 무엇을 하니?
B: 나는 아버지와 게임을 하는 걸 좋아해.
G: 어떤 종류의 게임을 하니?
B: 나는 주로 바둑을 둬.

G: 이봐, Eric, 넌 여가 시간에 보통 무엇을 하니?
B: 나는 도서관에 가서 책을 읽어.
G: 어떤 종류의 책을 읽니?
B: 나는 탐정 소설을 읽는 것을 좋아해. 난 Sherlock Holmes의 이야기를 정말 좋아해.

G: 세호야, 너는 여가 시간에 무엇을 하니?
B: 나는 음악을 들어.
G: 어떤 종류의 음악을 듣니?
B: 록 음악.

G: Chris, 넌 여가 시간이 있을 때 무엇을 하니?
B: 쿠키를 만들어. 나는 베이킹을 좋아해.
G: 어떤 종류의 쿠키를 만드니?
B: 나는 보통 딸기 쿠키를 만들어. 난 딸기를 좋아해.

A: 민지야, 넌 여가 시간에 보통 무엇을 하니?
B: 나는 보통 음악을 들어.
A: 어떤 종류의 음악을 듣니?
B: 나는 클래식 음악을 들어.

Listen and Talk C

B: Subin, what do you _____ _____ in your free time?

G: I exercise _____.

B: What kind of exercise _____ _____ _____?

G: I _____ badminton with my brother. I'm _____ the school's badminton team. What do you usually do in your free time, Andy?

B: I like _____ movies.

G: _____ _____ _____ movies do you like?

B: I like action movies. They're _____.

G: Oh, I _____ watch action movies, too. _____ _____ _____ _____ see an action movie this weekend?

B: Sure. _____ _____ great.

Review 1

B: Emma, what do you usually do in your free time?

G: I usually listen to music. _____ _____ _____, Chris?

B: I read books. I like _____ _____.

Review 2

G: Jiho, what do you usually do _____ _____ _____ free time?

B: I _____ _____ movies.

G: What _____ of movies do you watch?

B: I like action movies. Bruce Lee is my _____ movie star.

Review 3

1. W: What _____ Minho usually do in his _____ _____?

2. W: _____ kind _____ games does Sewon play?

해석

B: 수빈아, 너는 여가 시간에 주로 무엇을 하니?

G: 나는 밖에서 운동을 해.

B: 어떤 종류의 운동을 하니?

G: 나는 남동생과 배드민턴을 쳐. 난 학교 배드민턴 팀이야. 너는 여가 시간에 주로 무엇을 하니, Andy?

B: 나는 영화 보는 것을 좋아해.

G: 어떤 종류의 영화를 좋아하니?

B: 나는 액션 영화를 좋아해. 액션 영화는 재미있어.

G: 오, 나도 가끔 액션 영화를 봐. 이번 주말에 액션 영화 보러 갈래?

B: 그래. 좋아.

B: Emma, 너는 여가 시간에 보통 무엇을 하니?

G: 나는 보통 음악을 들어. 너는 어떠니, Chris?

B: 나는 책을 읽어. 탐정 소설을 좋아해.

G: 지호야, 너는 여가 시간이 있을 때 보통 무엇을 하니?

B: 나는 보통 영화를 봐.

G: 어떤 종류의 영화를 보니?

B: 나는 액션 영화를 좋아해. Bruce Lee는 내가 가장 좋아하는 영화배우야.

1. W: 민호는 여가 시간에 주로 무엇을 하니?

2. W: 세원이는 어떤 종류의 게임을 하니?

01 다음 대화의 빈칸에 알맞은 것은?

> A: What kind of movies do you like?
>
> B: _____

① I like action movies.

② I enjoy listening to classical music.

③ I want to watch a horror movie.

④ I like making bread.

⑤ I want to be a movie star.

02 다음 대화의 밑줄 친 부분과 바꾸어 쓸 수 <u>없는</u> 것은?

> A: <u>Why don't we watch</u> a movie together?
>
> B: Sure. That sounds good.

① How about watching   ② What about watching

③ Shall we watch   ④ What do you say to watching

⑤ Why do we watch

[03~04] 다음 대화의 빈칸에 알맞은 것을 고르시오.

03

> B: Emma, _____ in your free time?
>
> G: I usually listen to music. How about you, Chris?
>
> B: I read books. I like detective stories.

① whcrc did you go

② what do you usually do

③ what kind of music do you listen to

④ what do you say to doing

⑤ what do you want to do

04

> A: _____
>
> B: I eat Korean food.

① What are you cooking now?

② What food do you cook?

③ What kind of food do you eat?

④ Why don't we cook Korean food?

⑤ What food do you want?

[01~02] 다음 대화를 읽고, 물음에 답하시오.

G: Hey, Eric. _____ⓐ_____

B: I go to the library and read books.

G: ⓑ어떤 종류의 책을 읽니?

B: I like reading detective stories. I really like Sherlock Holmes' stories.

01 위 대화의 빈칸 ⓐ에 들어갈 말로 알맞은 것은?

① What do you do in your free time?

② What are you doing now?

③ What book do you like?

④ Where are you going?

⑤ How often do you go to the library?

서답형

02 위 대화의 밑줄 친 ⓑ의 우리말에 맞게 주어진 단어를 이용하여 영어로 쓰시오.

```
what / kind / books / you / read
```

➡ _____

중요

03 다음 대화의 빈칸에 들어갈 말로 알맞은 것은?

G: Hajun, what do you usually do in your free time?

B: I like playing games with my dad.

G: _____

B: I usually play baduk.

① How often do you play baduk?

② What kind of games do you play?

③ Do you like playing baduk?

④ What do you do when you have free time?

⑤ What are you going to do?

[04~06] 다음 대화를 읽고, 물음에 답하시오.

B: Subin, (A)너는 여가 시간에 주로 무엇을 하니?

G: I exercise outside. (a)

B: What kind of exercise do you do? (b)

G: I play badminton with my brother. I'm on the school's badminton team. (c)

B: I like watching movies.

G: What kind of movies do you like? (d)

B: I like action movies. They're fun. (e)

G: Oh, I sometimes watch action movies, too. (B)Why don't we go see an action movie this weekend?

B: Sure. That sounds great.

서답형

04 위 대화의 밑줄 친 (A)의 우리말에 맞게 주어진 문장의 빈칸을 채우시오.

```
_____ _____ _____ usually
_____ in your _____ _____?
```

서답형

05 위 대화의 밑줄 친 (B)를 다음과 같이 바꾸어 쓸 때, 빈칸에 알맞은 말을 쓰시오.

```
• _____ _____ go see an action movie
  this weekend?
• _____ _____ going to see an action
  movie this weekend?
```

06 위 대화의 (a)~(e) 중, 다음 주어진 문장이 들어갈 위치로 알맞은 것은?

```
What do you usually do in your free time,
Andy?
```

① (a) ② (b) ③ (c) ④ (d) ⑤ (e)

[07~09] 다음 대화를 읽고, 물음에 답하시오.

> G: Chris, what do you do _____ⓐ_____ you have free time?
> B: I make cookies. I enjoy _____ⓑ_____.
> G: What kind of cookies do you make?
> B: I usually make strawberry cookies. I love strawberries.

07 위 대화의 빈칸 ⓐ에 들어갈 말로 알맞은 것은?

① what   ② where
③ how   ④ when
⑤ that

08 위 대화의 빈칸 ⓑ에 들어갈 말로 알맞은 것은?

① bake   ② baking
③ to bake   ④ baked
⑤ to baking

09 위 대화의 주된 목적으로 알맞은 것은?

① 음식 선호 묻기   ② 권유하기
③ 약속 정하기   ④ 여가 활동 묻기
⑤ 충고하기

[10~11] 다음 대화를 읽고, 물음에 답하시오.

> G: Jiho, _____
> B: I usually watch movies.
> G: What kind of movies do you watch?
> B: I like action movies. Bruce Lee is my favorite movie star. How about you, Ann?
> G: I read books. I like detective stories.

10 위 대화의 빈칸에 들어갈 말로 어색한 것은?

① What do you like to do when you have free time?
② What do you like to do for fun?
③ What do you want to do?
④ How do you spend your free time?
⑤ What's your free time activity?

11 위 대화를 통해 유추할 수 없는 것은?

① Jiho and Ann are talking about free time activity.
② Jiho must enjoy watching the action movie 'The Bourne Identity'.
③ Bruce Lee is an action movie star.
④ Ann may like Sherlock Holmes' stories.
⑤ Ann must like Bruce Lee.

12 다음 대화의 밑줄 친 우리말에 맞게 주어진 단어를 알맞게 배열하시오.

> A: Minji, what do you usually do in your free time?
> B: 나는 보통 음악을 들어.
> A: What kind of music do you listen to?
> B: I listen to classical music.

> usually / music / listen / I / to

➡ _____

[01~02] 다음 대화를 읽고, 물음에 답하시오.

G: Jiho, (A)너는 여가 시간에 보통 무엇을 하니?
B: I usually watch movies.
G: _____(B)_____
B: I like action movies. Bruce Lee is my favorite movie star.

01 위 대화의 밑줄 친 (A)의 우리말에 맞게 주어진 단어를 이용하여 영어로 쓰시오.

| what / do / usually / when / have / free time |

➡ _____

02 위 대화의 빈칸 (B)에 들어갈 말을 다음 조건에 맞게 영어로 쓰시오.

┤ 조건 ├
1. 의문문으로 쓸 것
2. 아래 제시된 단어를 이용할 것

| what / kind / movies / you / watch |

➡ _____

03 그림을 보고, 다음 질문에 대한 답을 완전한 문장의 영어로 쓰시오. (빈도부사를 사용할 것)

Q: What does she usually do in her free time?
A: _____

04 다음 대화의 빈칸 (1)은 주어진 단어를 이용하고, 빈칸 (2)는 사진을 참고하여 빈칸을 완성하시오.

Ted: Emma, what do you usually do in your free time?
Emma: I exercise outside.
Ted: (1)_____(kind, exercise, do)?
Emma: I enjoy (2)_____.

(1) _____
(2) _____

05 사진을 참고하여, 다음 대화의 빈칸에 알맞은 말을 넣어 완성하시오.

A: What do you usually do in your free time?
B: I usually _____ with my friends in my free time.

➡ _____

교과서

Grammar

1 수여동사

> • Julie **gave** a pen **to** Mark. Julie는 Mark에게 펜을 주었다.
> • She **sent** me a letter. 그녀는 나에게 편지를 보냈다.

■ 수여동사란 두 개의 목적어로 간접목적어(~에게)와 직접목적어(…을/를)를 취하는 동사이며 수여동사 가 쓰인 문장을 보통 4형식 문장이라고 한다.

문장 형태: 주어＋동사＋간접목적어(~에게)＋직접목적어(…을/를)

• Jason made his daughter a toy. Jason은 그의 딸에게 장난감을 만들어 주었다.
간접목적어(~에게)＋직접목적어(~을/를)

■ 4형식을 3형식 문장으로 바꾸기

문장 형태: 주어＋동사＋직접목적어(…을/를)＋전치사＋간접목적어(~에게)

간접목적어 앞에 전치사를 붙여 목적어의 위치를 바꿀 수 있다. 동사에 따라 쓰는 전치사가 달라지며 목적어의 위치를 바꾸면 문장의 형식이 4형식에서 3형식으로 바뀐다.

• I gave her an MP3. → I gave an MP3 to her.
간접목적어＋직접목적어   직접목적어＋전치사＋간접목적어

(1) **to**를 쓰는 동사: give, pass, send, show, teach, tell, write 등

• Henry sent Ella some flowers. Henry는 Ella에게 꽃 몇 송이를 보냈다.
→ Henry **sent** some flowers **to** Ella.

(2) **for**를 쓰는 동사: make, buy, get, choose, cook, build 등

• Mom made me gimbap. 엄마는 나에게 김밥을 만들어 주셨다.
→ Mom **made** gimbap **for** me.

(3) **of**를 쓰는 동사: ask, inquire, require 등

• Bruce asked him the way to the bus stop. Bruce는 그에게 버스 정류장으로 가는 길을 물었다.
→ Bruce **asked** the way to the bus stop **of** him.

핵심 Check

1. 다음 괄호 안에서 알맞은 것을 고르시오.

(1) You can also show (me some pictures / some pictures me).

(2) She bought some cookies (to / for) me.

2. 다음 문장의 목적어의 순서를 바꾸어 다시 쓰시오.

He made me a cake.

➡ _____

② 상관 접속사 both A and B

- **Both** Emily **and** Tana like music. Emily와 Tana 둘 다 음악을 좋아한다.
- Melina likes **both** Korean dramas **and** K-pop. Melina는 한국 드라마와 K-pop 둘 다 좋아한다.

■ both A and B는 'A와 B 둘 다'의 의미를 나타낸다.

2개 이상의 단어가 짝을 이루어 하나의 접속사 역할을 하는 것을 상관접속사라고 하며 단어와 단어, 구와 구, 절과 절을 대등하게 연결한다. A와 B에는 문법적으로 같은 성질의 것이 와야 한다.

- They like **both** running **and** swimming. (○)

  They like both running and to swim.　　(X)
- She is **both** kind **and** pretty. (○)

  ■ both A and B가 주어 자리에 오면 복수 취급하므로 동사는 복수형을 써야 한다.

- **Both** Clint **and** Sean are interested in soccer. (○)

■ 'not only A but also B'는 'A뿐만 아니라 B도'라는 의미의 상관접속사이며, 'B as well as A'로 바꾸어 쓸 수 있다. A와 B는 문법적으로 대등해야 하며, 주어로 쓰일 경우 동사의 수는 B에 일치시켜야 한다.

- It is good for **not only** him **but also** his family. 그것은 그에게 뿐만 아니라 그의 가족에게도 좋다.

  = It is good for his family **as well as** him.
- Kate **as well as** her sisters is going to take part in the campaign.

  Kate의 언니들 뿐만 아니라 Kate도 그 캠페인에 참가할 것이다.

■ either A or B: A 또는 B 둘 중 하나 / neither A nor B: A도 B도 아닌 / not A but B: A가 아니라 B

- **Either** Yuna **or** I have to go. 유나나 나 둘 중 하나는 가야 한다.
- **Neither** he **nor** his daughters have arrived. 그도 그의 딸들도 도착하지 않았다.

핵심 Check

3. 다음 주어진 단어를 빈칸에 알맞게 쓰시오.

　(1) Both my father and I _____ to sleep under the tree. (like)

　(2) Not only Sora but also her brothers _____ smartphones. (have)

4. 다음 빈칸에 알맞은 말을 쓰시오.

　(1) Andy loves both English _____ history.

　(2) He wants to have either a bicycle _____ an MP3.

01 다음 문장에서 어법상 <u>어색한</u> 부분을 바르게 고쳐 쓰시오.

vegetables 야채
golden hair 금발

(1) She sent a letter for him.

_____ ➡ _____

(2) She bought cookies to me.

_____ ➡ _____

(3) She bought both meat or vegetables.

_____ ➡ _____

(4) Both Miranda and her sister has golden hair.

_____ ➡ _____

02 다음 빈칸에 알맞지 <u>않은</u> 것은?

> Donald _____ pictures to Aria.

① gave　　　　　　　② showed

③ brought　　　　　④ bought

⑤ sent

03 다음 빈칸에 들어갈 알맞은 것은?

> I as well as you and Mina _____ wrong.

① be　　　　② am　　　　③ are

④ is　　　　⑤ were

04 다음 빈칸에 알맞은 말이 바르게 짝지어진 것은?

messy 어질러진, 더러운
tidily 말쑥하게, 단정하게

> Her room was both _____ and _____.

① cute – clean　　　　② cutely – cleanly

③ cute – cleanly　　　④ cutely – clean

⑤ messy – tidily

중요

01 다음 중 어법상 어색한 문장은?

① She showed me her pictures.
② The man gave her a toy.
③ He told them a funny story.
④ She sent an email her friend.
⑤ Dad bought a pen for me.

서답형

02 다음 괄호 안에서 알맞은 것을 고르시오.

(1) My dad is teaching (them math / math them).
(2) I (bought / gave) a new computer for my daughter.
(3) Both Tamu (and / or) I want to be like them.

03 다음 중 문장 전환이 어색한 것은?

① He will give me a book written by Hobbes.
  → He will give a book written by Hobbes to me.
② She bought her a dress with a pretty little red ribbon.
  → She bought a dress with a pretty little red ribbon for her.
③ He made her pizza while she was watching TV.
  → He made pizza for her while she was watching TV.
④ Anna showed him her pictures taken at the party.
  → Anna showed her pictures taken at the party for him.
⑤ In class, she asked them a difficult question.
  → In class, she asked a difficult question of them.

서답형

04 다음 우리말에 맞게 주어진 단어를 이용하여 문장을 완성하시오.

(1) Margaret은 그녀의 아들에게 새 컴퓨터를 사 주었다. (buy, her son)
  ➡ Margaret _____ _____ _____ a new computer.
(2) 당신의 사랑을 부모님께 말하세요. (tell)
  ➡ _____ your love _____ your parents.
(3) 엄마는 나에게 예쁜 옷을 만들어 주셨다. (make)
  ➡ Mom _____ a pretty dress _____ me.
(4) 그와 그의 안내인 둘 다 사라졌다. (and)
  ➡ _____ he _____ his guide disappeared.

서답형

05 다음 두 문장이 같은 뜻이 되도록 빈칸에 알맞은 말을 쓰시오.

My father bought me a bike.
= My father bought _____ _____
_____ _____.

중요

06 다음 중 어법상 올바른 문장은?

① When night came, Robert told an interesting story me.
② My mother bought a pretty red dress to me.
③ Dad asked a strange question for me.
④ I'd like to show some pictures of my friends for you.
⑤ She chose the book written by Hemingway for me.

07 다음 문장을 같은 의미로 바꿔 쓸 때 바르게 바꾼 것은?

> Not only the games but also the cheering is fun.

① The cheering as well as the games is fun.
② The games as well as the cheering is fun.
③ The games or the cheering is fun.
④ The games and the cheering is fun.
⑤ Both the games and the cheering is fun.

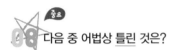

08 다음 중 어법상 틀린 것은?

① Matilda asked a very difficult question of me.
② David bought a new cell phone for his daughter.
③ She wrote a letter written in symbols to him.
④ Tony gave a beautiful doll to her.
⑤ Sharon sent a pretty long email her friend.

09 다음 우리말에 맞도록 빈칸에 순서대로 알맞은 것은?

> 그는 책과 공책 둘 다 샀다.
> ➡ She bought _____ a book _____ a notebook.

① both – or
② both – and
③ either – or
④ either – and
⑤ neither – nor

10 다음 밑줄 친 부분의 쓰임이 나머지와 다른 하나는?

① He <u>gave</u> me a nice new pen.
② She <u>made</u> her daughter a doctor.
③ Stephanie <u>told</u> us a very interesting story.
④ His mom <u>showed</u> her some of his photos.
⑤ Emily will <u>send</u> her parents some flowers.

11 다음 두 문장을 같은 의미의 한 문장으로 바꿀 때 빈칸에 알맞은 말이 바르게 짝지어진 것은?

> • Jennifer received birthday gifts from her parents.
> • Jennifer received birthday gifts from her friends, too.
> ➡ Jennifer received birthday gifts _____ from her parents _____ from her friends.

① not – nor
② not – but
③ both – and
④ either – or
⑤ neither – nor

12 다음 문장의 빈칸에 들어갈 수 없는 것은?

> Clara _____ Simon a letter.

① wrote
② brought
③ gave
④ wanted
⑤ sent

13 다음 문장을 같은 의미로 바꿔 썼을 때 바르게 바꾼 것은?

> My son likes social science as well as music.

① My son likes not social science but music.

② My son likes not only social science and music.

③ My son likes not only social science but music.

④ My son likes not only music but also social science.

⑤ My son likes either social science or music.

서답형

14 다음 빈칸에 공통으로 들어갈 말을 쓰시오.

> • Harry bought a birthday present _____ his dad.
> • Delilah chose a beautiful dress _____ her sister.

중요

15 다음 중 어법상 바르지 않은 것은?

① Yesterday, it snowed as well as windy.

② The shirts will be sent not only to nursing homes but also to kindergartens.

③ Both the manager and the workers will take part in the campaign.

④ Sarah saw not a lion but a tiger.

⑤ Not only my brother but also my sisters enjoy tennis.

서답형

16 다음 주어진 문장을 〈보기〉와 같이 한 문장으로 바꿔 쓰시오.

> ┤ 보기 ├
> • Miranda likes oranges.
> • Her sister likes oranges, too.
> ➡ Both Miranda and her sister like oranges.

(1) • James wants to visit London.
   • He wants to visit Paris, too.
   ➡ James wants to visit _____.

(2) • Emily doesn't want to visit China.
   • She doesn't want to visit Japan, either.
   ➡ Emily wants to visit _____.

서답형

17 다음 문장의 빈칸에 알맞은 전치사를 쓰시오.

> • Clark will send some flowers _____ Vivian.
> • The reporter asked some questions _____ Nicholas.
> • Mom cooked *samgyupsal* _____ us yesterday.

서답형

18 다음 두 문장을 한 문장으로 바꿔 쓸 때 빈칸에 알맞은 말을 쓰시오.

(1) • Jacob doesn't want to study math.
   • Abe doesn't want to study math, either.
   ➡ _____ wants to study math.

(2) • Her room was very clean.
   • And it was very cute.
   ➡ Her room was _____.

Grammar 서술형 시험대비

01 다음 두 문장을 한 문장으로 바꾸어 쓸 때, 빈칸에 알맞은 단어를 쓰시오.

> • Mike likes to hang out with his friends.
> • Bob likes to hang out with his friends, too.

➡ _____ _____ _____ Bob _____
to hang out with their friends.

02 다음 문장을 3형식 문장으로 바꿔 쓰시오.

(1) Gilbert bought his daughter some candies.
➡ _____
(2) George sent Mary a card on her birthday.
➡ _____
(3) Sophie asked Nick the way to the library.
➡ _____

03 다음 괄호 안의 말을 이용하여 우리말에 맞게 빈칸을 완성하시오.

(1) 그녀는 장미와 튤립 둘 다 샀다.
➡ She bought _____.
(roses, tulips)
(2) Bonnie는 호랑이뿐만 아니라 치타도 보았다.
➡ Bonnie saw _____.
(not, tigers, cheetahs)

04 다음 문장에서 어법상 잘못된 부분을 찾아 바르게 고쳐 쓰시오.

(1) He will buy a dress to his mom as her birthday present.
_____ ➡ _____
(2) Both Tom and Joe was late for school.
_____ ➡ _____
(3) Natalie asked many questions the math teacher during math class.
_____ ➡ _____

05 다음 우리말에 맞도록 괄호 안의 단어들을 순서대로 배열하시오.

> 나는 너에게 쿠키를 좀 만들어 주겠다.
> (I'll / cookies / you / some / for / make)

➡ _____

06 다음 문장을 어법에 맞게 고쳐 쓰시오.

(1) Minhee as well as her sisters are very kind and cool.
➡ _____
(2) Annabel likes not only studying history but also to play the computer games.
➡ _____

07 다음 두 문장을 not only A but (also) B와 B as well as A를 써서 한 문장으로 바꾸시오.

(1) • Matthew thought of going to the amusement park.

　• Matthew thought of enjoying the rides.

➡ _____

_____

➡ _____

_____

(2) • Emily made a pancake for me.

　• Emily made some chocolate cookies for me.

➡ _____

_____

➡ _____

_____

(3) • Anna enjoyed riding a bike.

　• Anna had a delicious ice cream.

➡ _____

_____

➡ _____

_____

08 다음 우리말과 일치하도록 주어진 어휘에 한 단어를 추가하여 알맞은 순서로 배열하시오.

(1) 엄마는 우리에게 맛있는 저녁을 요리해 주셨다.
(mom, a, us, delicious, cooked, dinner)

➡ _____

(2) Emma는 그에게 언제 오는지 물었다.
(Emma, he, him, inquired, come, would, when)

➡ _____

09 다음 우리말을 괄호 안에 주어진 단어를 사용해 영작하시오.

(1) 너뿐만 아니라 나도 그 문제를 풀 수 있다.
(as well as, able, solve)

➡ _____

(2) 너와 Grace 둘 다 예쁘고 현명하다.
(pretty, wise)

➡ _____

(3) Sheryll이 아니라 네가 그것이 틀렸다는 것을 알고 있다. (wrong, it)

➡ _____

10 다음 두 문장의 의미가 같도록 빈칸에 알맞은 말을 쓰시오.

(1) Dad promised to buy me a nice birthday gift.
➡ Dad promised to buy _____ _____ me.

(2) Imelda wrote Kyle a letter.
➡ Imelda wrote _____ Kyle.

11 다음 빈칸에 알맞은 말을 〈보기〉에서 모두 고르시오.

보기
gave / brought / wanted / sent / had / bought / made / wasted / showed

Melanie _____ her a delicious pizza.

➡ _____

Reading

Teen Talk: My Favorite Time of the Day

Somin

Hello! I'm Somin. I'm 15 years old, and I live in Korea. Please tell
= Hi!   = My name is Somin.   in+넓은 장소

me about your favorite time of the day. You can also show me some
~에 관하여   매우 좋아하는   ~(가운데)의, ~ 중의   also는 be동사, 조동사 뒤에 위치

pictures.
show(4형식 동사)+간접목적어+직접목적어 = some pictures to me(3형식)

Diego

Hi, my name is Diego, and I live in Seville, Spain. My favorite time
= Hello. I'm Diego.   '도시, 나라'의 어순

of the day is lunch time. My school usually ends around 2 p.m. On
점심시간   빈도부사(주로 일반동사 앞에 위치)   ~경, ~쯤   on+요일, 날짜

most days, my family gets together and has a big, long lunch. We
get together: 모이다   먹다(=eats)

usually have soup, vegetables, and meat. We also have a dessert like
먹다(= eat)   ~와 같은(전치사)

churros. After lunch, we usually take a siesta, a short nap. Both my
~ 후에 (전치사)   동격   both A and B: A와 B 둘 다

father and I like to sleep under the tree in our garden.
명사(목적어) 역할을 하는 to부정사

teen 십대의
most 대부분의
usually 보통
vegetables 채소
meat 고기
dessert 디저트, 후식
nap 낮잠

확인문제

● 다음 문장이 본문의 내용과 일치하면 T, 일치하지 <u>않으면</u> F를 쓰시오.

1 Somin's favorite time of the day is lunch time. ☐

2 Diego lives in Seville, Spain. ☐

3 Diego's school usually ends around 2 p.m. ☐

4 Diego's family seldom take a siesta, a short nap. ☐

Tabin

Hi! My name is Tabin, and I live near the Gobi Desert in Mongolia.
= Hello! I'm Tabin.   ∼의 가까이에

I'm happy when I ride my horse. Horses are important in our culture.
         ∼할 때(접속사)   우리 문화에서

Almost everyone can ride a horse in Mongolia. In fact, we say, "We
거의   ∼할 수 있다(능력을 나타내는 조동사)   사실

ride horses before we can walk." I take good care of my horse. I often
         ∼하기 전에(접속사)   ∼을 돌보다

brush him and give him some carrots. I enjoy riding especially in
    my horse   give(4형식 동사)+간접목적어+직접목적어   enjoy -ing: ∼하는 것을 즐기다

the evening before the sunset. Then the sky is red, and everything is
         ∼전에(전치사)   = In the evening before the sunset

peaceful.

Musa

Hi! I'm Musa, and I live in Nairobi, Kenya. My favorite time of
Hello! My name is Musa.   '도시, 나라'의 어순

the day is our running practice time. My friend, Tamu, and I are on
                           연습   동격

the school's running team. I'm happiest when I run with Tamu. Our
    ∼ 팀에 속해 있다   happy의 최상급   ∼와 함께

practice time isn't boring because we can see many animals. Many
                        ∼이기 때문에(이유의 접속사)   = a lot of   many+복수명사

runners from Kenya won races in the Olympics. I'm so proud of them.
    ∼ 출신의   win의 과거형   = many runners from Kenya who won races in the Olympics

Both Tamu and I want to be like them.
both A and B: A와 B 둘 다   ∼처럼

near ∼ 가까이에
desert 사막
Mongolia 몽골
important 중요한
culture 문화
take care of ∼을 돌보다
brush 솔: 솔질하다
carrot 당근
especially 특히
sunset 일몰, 해질녘
peaceful 평화로운
practice 연습
race 경주

확인문제

● 다음 문장이 본문의 내용과 일치하면 T, 일치하지 <u>않으면</u> F를 쓰시오.

1 Tabin is happy when she rides her horse. ☐

2 Everyone can ride a horse in Mongolia. ☐

3 Tabin gives some apples to her horse. ☐

4 Tabin enjoys riding especially in the evening before the sunset. ☐

5 Musa's favorite time of the day is his running practice time. ☐

6 Musa is happiest when he runs with Tamu. ☐

7 Tamu and Musa are on the school's running team. ☐

8 Musa is so proud that he won races in the Olympics. ☐

● 우리말을 참고하여 빈칸에 알맞은 말을 쓰시오.

1 Teen Talk: My _____ _____ of the Day

2 Hello! _____ Somin.

3 I'm _____ _____ _____, and I live in Korea.

4 Please tell me _____ _____ _____ _____ of the day.

5 You can also _____ _____ _____ _____.

6 Hi, _____ _____ is Diego, and I live in Seville, Spain.

7 My favorite time _____ _____ _____ is lunch time.

8 My school _____ _____ _____ 2 p.m.

9 _____ _____ _____, my family gets together and has a big, long lunch.

10 We usually have _____, _____, and _____.

11 We also _____ _____ _____ like churros.

12 After lunch, we usually take a siesta, _____ _____ _____.

13 _____ my father _____ I like to sleep under the tree in our garden.

14 Hi! My name is Tabin, and I _____ _____ the Gobi Desert in Mongolia.

15 I'm happy _____ I ride my horse.

16 Horses are important _____ _____ _____.

1 십대들의 이야기: 하루 중 내가 가장 좋아하는 시간

2 안녕! 나는 소민이야.

3 나는 15살이고 한국에 살아.

4 너희들이 하루 중 가장 좋아하는 시간에 대해 말해 줘.

5 나에게 사진 몇 장을 보여 줘도 좋아.

6 안녕. 내 이름은 Diego이고, 나는 스페인의 세비야에서 살아.

7 내가 하루 중 가장 좋아하는 시간은 점심시간이야.

8 우리 학교는 보통 오후 2시경에 끝나.

9 대부분의 날에는, 가족들이 모여서 푸짐하고 긴 점심 식사를 해.

10 우리는 보통 수프, 채소 그리고 고기를 먹어.

11 우리는 또한 추로스와 같은 후식도 먹어.

12 점심 식사 후에는 우리는 보통 시에스타, 즉 짧은 낮잠을 자.

13 아빠와 나는 둘 다 우리 정원에 있는 나무 밑에서 자는 것을 좋아해.

14 안녕! 내 이름은 Tabin이고 나는 몽골에 있는 고비 사막 근처에 살아.

15 나는 내 말을 탈 때 행복해.

16 말은 우리 문화에서 중요해.

17 _____ _____ can ride a horse in Mongolia.

18 _____ _____, we say, "We ride horses before we can walk."

19 I _____ _____ _____ _____ my horse.

20 I _____ _____ him and _____ _____ _____ _____.

21 I _____ _____ especially in the evening before the sunset.

22 _____ the sky is red, and everything is _____.

23 Hi! I'm Musa, and I live _____ _____, _____.

24 My favorite time of the day is _____ _____ _____ _____.

25 My friend, Tamu, and I are _____ _____ _____.

26 I'm _____ when I run with Tamu.

27 Our practice time isn't _____ because we can see many animals.

28 Many runners _____ Kenya won races in the Olympics.

29 I'm so _____ of them.

30 _____ Tamu _____ I want to _____ _____ them.

17 몽골에서는 거의 모든 사람이 말을 탈 수 있어.

18 실제로 우리는 "우리는 걸을 수 있기 전에 말을 탄다."라고 말해.

19 나는 내 말을 잘 돌봐.

20 나는 종종 내 말의 털을 빗겨 주고 당근을 줘.

21 나는 특히 해가 지기 전 저녁에 말 타는 것을 즐겨.

22 그 무렵엔 하늘은 붉고 모든 것이 평화로워.

23 안녕! 나는 Musa이고, 케냐의 나이로비에 살아.

24 내가 하루 중 가장 좋아하는 시간은 달리기 연습 시간이야.

25 내 친구 Tamu와 나는 학교의 달리기 팀이야.

26 나는 Tamu와 달리기를 할 때 가장 행복해.

27 우리의 연습 시간은 지루하지 않아, 왜냐하면 우리는 많은 동물들을 볼 수 있기 때문이야.

28 케냐의 많은 달리기 선수들이 올림픽의 육상 경기에서 우승을 했어.

29 나는 그들이 매우 자랑스러워.

30 Tamu와 나 둘 다 그들처럼 되고 싶어해.

● 우리말을 참고하여 본문을 영작하시오.

1 십대들의 이야기: 하루 중 내가 가장 좋아하는 시간
➡ _____

2 안녕! 나는 소민이야.
➡ _____

3 나는 15살이고 한국에 살아.
➡ _____

4 너희들이 하루 중 가장 좋아하는 시간에 대해 말해 줘.
➡ _____

5 나에게 사진 몇 장을 보여 줘도 좋아.
➡ _____

6 안녕, 내 이름은 Diego이고, 나는 스페인의 세비야에서 살아.
➡ _____

7 내가 하루 중 가장 좋아하는 시간은 점심시간이야.
➡ _____

8 우리 학교는 보통 오후 2시경에 끝나.
➡ _____

9 대부분의 날에는, 가족들이 모여서 푸짐하고 긴 점심 식사를 해.
➡ _____

10 우리는 보통 수프, 채소 그리고 고기를 먹어.
➡ _____

11 우리는 또한 추로스와 같은 후식도 먹어.
➡ _____

12 점심 식사 후에는 우리는 보통 시에스타, 즉 짧은 낮잠을 자.
➡ _____

13 아빠와 나는 둘 다 우리 정원에 있는 나무 밑에서 자는 것을 좋아해.
➡ _____

14 안녕! 내 이름은 Tabin이고 나는 몽골에 있는 고비 사막 근처에 살아.
➡ _____

15 나는 내 말을 탈 때 행복해.
➡ _____

16 말은 우리 문화에서 중요해.
➡ _____

17 몽골에서는 거의 모든 사람이 말을 탈 수 있어.

➡ _____

18 실제로 우리는 "우리는 걸을 수 있기 전에 말을 탄다."라고 말해.

➡ _____

19 나는 내 말을 잘 돌봐.

➡ _____

20 나는 종종 내 말의 털을 빗겨 주고 당근을 줘.

➡ _____

21 나는 특히 해가 지기 전 저녁에 말 타는 것을 즐겨.

➡ _____

22 그 무렵엔 하늘은 붉고 모든 것이 평화로워.

➡ _____

23 안녕! 나는 Musa이고, 케냐의 나이로비에 살아.

➡ _____

24 내가 하루 중 가장 좋아하는 시간은 달리기 연습 시간이야.

➡ _____

25 내 친구 Tamu와 나는 학교의 달리기 팀이야.

➡ _____

26 나는 Tamu와 달리기를 할 때 가장 행복해.

➡ _____

27 우리의 연습 시간은 지루하지 않아, 왜냐하면 우리는 많은 동물들을 볼 수 있기 때문이야.

➡ _____

28 케냐의 많은 달리기 선수들이 올림픽의 육상 경기에서 우승을 했어.

➡ _____

29 나는 그들이 매우 자랑스러워.

➡ _____

30 Tamu와 나 둘 다 그들처럼 되고 싶어해.

➡ _____

[01~03] 다음 글을 읽고, 물음에 답하시오.

Hello! I'm Somin. I'm 15 years old, and I live in Korea. Please tell me about your favorite time of the day. You can also show me some pictures.

01 위 글의 종류로 알맞은 것을 고르시오.

① e-mail ② article
③ essay ④ SNS posting
⑤ diary

서답형

02 다음 빈칸 (A)와 (B)에 알맞은 단어를 넣어 소민이에 대한 소개를 완성하시오.

> Somin is a 15- __(A)__ -old girl, and she __(B)__ in Korea.

(A)_____ (B)_____

서답형

03 소민이가 사람들에게 요청하고 있는 것 두 가지를 우리말로 쓰시오.

(1) _____
(2) _____

[04~06] 다음 글을 읽고, 물음에 답하시오.

Diego: Hi, my name is Diego, and I live __ⓐ__ Seville, Spain. My favorite time of the day is lunch time. My school usually ends around 2 p.m. __ⓑ__ most days, my family gets together and has a big, long lunch. We usually have soup, vegetables, and meat. We also have a dessert like churros. After lunch, we usually take a siesta, a short __ⓒ__ . Both my father and I like to sleep under the tree in our garden.

중요

04 위 글의 빈칸 ⓐ와 ⓑ에 들어갈 전치사가 바르게 짝지어진 것은?

① at – Of ② in – On
③ in – At ④ at – At
⑤ from – On

서답형

05 위 글의 빈칸 ⓒ에 주어진 영영풀이를 참고하여 철자 n으로 시작하는 단어를 쓰시오.

> a short sleep, usually during the day

➡ _____

06 위 글을 읽고 대답할 수 없는 질문은?

① Where does Diego live?
② When is Diego's favorite time of the day?
③ When does Diego's school usually start?
④ Does Diego's family have dessert after lunch?
⑤ Where does Diego's father like to sleep after lunch?

[07~09] 다음 글을 읽고, 물음에 답하시오.

Tabin: Hi! My name is Tabin, and I live (A) [near / nearly] the Gobi Desert in Mongolia. I'm happy when I ride my horse. Horses are important in our culture. Almost everyone can ride a horse in Mongolia. In fact, we say, " _____ⓐ_____ "

I take good care of my horse. I often brush him and give him some carrots. I enjoy riding (B)[especially / probably] in the evening before the sunset. (C)[Than / Then] the sky is red, and everything is peaceful.

서답형

07 위 글의 괄호 (A)~(C)에서 문맥상 알맞은 것을 골라 쓰시오.

(A)_____ (B)_____ (C)_____

08 위 글의 빈칸 ⓐ에 들어갈 알맞은 말을 고르시오.

① We can walk before we ride horses.

② It's not easy to ride horses.

③ We like to feed the horses.

④ We ride horses before we can walk.

⑤ To walk is easier than to ride horses.

중요

09 위 글의 내용과 일치하지 <u>않는</u> 것은?

① Tabin은 몽골 고비 사막 근처에 산다.

② Tabin은 말을 탈 때 행복하다.

③ 말은 몽골 문화에서 중요하다.

④ Tabin은 자신의 말을 잘 돌본다.

⑤ Tabin은 해가 뜨기 전에 말 타는 것을 즐긴다.

[10~12] 다음 글을 읽고, 물음에 답하시오.

Musa: Hi! (①) I'm Musa, and I live in Nairobi, Kenya. (②) My favorite time of the day is our running practice time. (③) My friend, Tamu, and I are on the school's running team. (④) Our practice time isn't ____ⓐ____ because we can see many animals.

(⑤) Many runners from Kenya won races in the Olympics. I'm so proud of ⓑ<u>them</u>. Both Tamu and I want to be like ⓒ<u>them</u>.

10 위 글의 흐름으로 보아, 주어진 문장이 들어가기에 가장 적절한 곳은?

I'm happiest when I run with Tamu.

① ② ③ ④ ⑤

중요

11 위 글의 빈칸 ⓐ에 들어갈 알맞은 말을 고르시오.

① interesting ② important

③ tired ④ funny

⑤ boring

서답형

12 위 글의 밑줄 친 ⓑ와 ⓒ의 them이 공통으로 가리키는 것을 쓰시오.

➡ _____

[13~15] 다음 글을 읽고, 물음에 답하시오.

Diego: Hi, my name is Diego, and I live in Seville, Spain. My favorite time of the day is lunch time. My school usually ends ⓐ around 2 p.m. On most days, my family gets together and (A)[have / has] a big, long lunch. We usually have soup, vegetables, and meat. We also have a dessert like churros. After (B)[lunch / a lunch], we usually take a siesta, a short nap. Both my father and (C)[I / me] like to sleep under the tree in our garden.

13 위 글의 Diego에 관한 내용으로 적절하지 <u>않은</u> 것은?

① 스페인의 세비야에 살고 있다.
② 학교가 대체로 오후 2시경에 끝난다.
③ 대부분의 날에 가족들과 함께 점심을 먹는다.
④ 추로스와 같은 후식도 먹는다.
⑤ 짧게 낮잠을 잔 후에 점심을 먹는다.

서답형
14 위 글의 괄호 (A)~(C)에서 어법상 알맞은 것을 골라 쓰시오.

(A)_____ (B)_____ (C)_____

중요
15 위 글의 밑줄 친 ⓐaround 2 p.m.과 바꿔 쓸 수 <u>없는</u> 말을 <u>모두</u> 고르시오.

① across 2 p.m.
② approximately 2 p.m.
③ round 2 p.m.
④ about 2 p.m.
⑤ 2 p.m. or so

[16~18] 다음 글을 읽고, 물음에 답하시오.

Tabin: Hi! My name is Tabin, and I live near the Gobi Desert in Mongolia. ①I'm bored when I ride my horse. ②Horses are important in our culture. ③Almost everyone can ride a horse in Mongolia. ④In fact, we say, "We ride horses before we can walk."
⑤I take good care of my horse. I often brush him and give him some carrots. I enjoy ⓐriding especially in the evening before the sunset. Then the sky is red, and everything is peaceful.

16 위 글을 읽고 알 수 <u>없는</u> 것을 고르시오.

① Tabin이 사는 곳
② 고비 사막이 있는 나라
③ Tabin이 말을 돌보는 방법
④ Tabin의 말 이름
⑤ 하루 중 Tabin이 말 타기를 즐기는 때

서답형
17 위 글의 밑줄 친 ①~⑤에서 문맥상 낱말의 쓰임이 적절하지 <u>않은</u> 것을 찾아 알맞게 고치시오.

➡ _____

_____

중요
18 위 글의 밑줄 친 ⓐriding과 문법적 쓰임이 같은 것을 고르시오.

① Jane is <u>running</u> on the playground.
② We sat <u>watching</u> TV in the room.
③ <u>Walking</u> in the heavy rain is difficult.
④ The boy <u>sleeping</u> there is my son.
⑤ I saw him <u>entering</u> the room.

[19~21] 다음 글을 읽고, 물음에 답하시오.

Musa: Hi! I'm Musa, and I live in Nairobi, Kenya. My (A)[favorite / terrible] time of the day is our running practice time. My friend, Tamu, and I are ___ⓐ___ the school's running team. I'm happiest when I run with Tamu. Our practice time isn't boring (B)[because / because of] we can see many animals.

　Many runners from Kenya won races in the Olympics. I'm so proud of them. Both Tamu and I want to be (C)[like / different from] them.

19 위 글의 내용과 일치하는 것을 고르시오.

① Musa는 나이로비의 케냐에 산다.

② Musa는 하루 중 달리기 시합을 할 때를 매우 좋아한다.

③ Musa의 친구와 Tamu는 학교 달리기 팀에 소속되어 있다.

④ Musa는 달리기 연습을 할 때 많은 동물들을 볼 수 있다.

⑤ Tamu는 케냐 출신의 달리기 선수들이 올림픽에 출전한 것에 관심이 없다.

20 위 글의 빈칸 ⓐ에 들어갈 알맞은 전치사를 고르시오.

① from　　② by　　③ with

④ to　　⑤ on

서답형

21 위 글의 괄호 (A)~(C)에서 문맥과 어법상 알맞은 것을 골라 쓰시오.

(A)_____　(B)_____　(C)_____

[22~24] 다음 글을 읽고, 물음에 답하시오.

Diego: Hi, my name is Diego, I live in Seville, Spain. My favorite time of the day is lunch time. (①) My school usually ends around 2 p.m. (②) On most days, my family gets together and has a big, long lunch. (③) ⓐWe usually have soup, vegetables, and meat. (④) After lunch, we usually take a siesta, a short nap. (⑤) Both my father and I like ⓑto sleep under the tree in our garden.

22 위 글의 흐름으로 보아, 주어진 문장이 들어가기에 가장 적절한 곳은?

| We also have a dessert like churros. |

①　　②　　③　　④　　⑤

서답형

23 위 글의 밑줄 친 ⓐWe가 가리키는 것을 영어로 쓰시오.

➡ _____

24 위 글의 밑줄 친 ⓑto sleep과 부정사의 용법이 같은 것을 고르시오.

① He tried to solve the problem.

② This book is easy to read.

③ I want something cold to drink.

④ He must be mad to say so.

⑤ I have no friends to help me.

25 주어진 글 다음에 이어질 글의 순서로 가장 적절한 것은?

> I take good care of my horse.

> (A) I enjoy riding especially in the evening before the sunset.
> (B) I often brush him and give him some carrots.
> (C) Then the sky is red, and everything is peaceful.

① (A) – (C) – (B)   ② (B) – (A) – (C)
③ (B) – (C) – (A)   ④ (C) – (A) – (B)
⑤ (C) – (B) – (A)

[26~28] 다음 글을 읽고, 물음에 답하시오.

Tabin: Hi! My name is Tabin, and I live near the Gobi Desert in Mongolia. I'm happy ___ⓐ___ I ride my horse. Horses are important in our culture. (①) Almost everyone can ride a horse in Mongolia. (②) In fact, we say, "ⓑWe ride horses after we can walk." (③) I take good care of my horse. (④) I often brush him and give him some carrots. (⑤) Then the sky is red, and everything is peaceful.

26 위 글의 빈칸 ⓐ에 들어갈 가장 알맞은 말을 고르시오.

① though   ② if
③ so   ④ when
⑤ but

27 위 글의 흐름으로 보아, 주어진 문장이 들어가기에 가장 적절한 곳은?

> I enjoy riding especially in the evening before the sunset.

①   ②   ③   ④   ⑤

28 위 글의 밑줄 친 ⓑ에서 흐름상 어색한 부분을 찾아 고치시오.

_____ ➡ _____

[29~32] 다음 글을 읽고, 물음에 답하시오.

Musa: Hi! I'm Musa, and I live in Nairobi, Kenya. My favorite time of the day is our running practice time. My friend, Tamu, and I are on the school's running team. I'm happiest when I ___ⓐ___ with Tamu. Our practice time isn't boring because we can see many animals.

Many runners from Kenya won races in the Olympics. ⓑI'm so proud of them. Both Tamu and I want to be ⓒlike them.

29 위 글을 읽고 대답할 수 없는 질문은?

① Where does Musa live?
② How long does Musa practice running every day?
③ Does Musa like his running practice time?
④ What team is Musa on?
⑤ Can Musa see many animals during his running practice time?

30 위 글의 빈칸 ⓐ에 들어갈 가장 알맞은 말을 고르시오.

① eat
② travel
③ play
④ run
⑤ talk

31 위 글의 밑줄 친 ⓑ를 다음과 같이 바꿔 쓸 때 빈칸에 알맞은 말을 쓰시오.

I take _____ in them very much.

32 위 글의 밑줄 친 ⓒlike와 같은 의미로 쓰인 것을 고르시오.

① Which tie do you like best?
② She doesn't like ice cream.
③ I like a hobby like painting.
④ Would you like to come with us?
⑤ You don't look like her at all.

[33~35] 다음 글을 읽고, 물음에 답하시오.

Tabin: Hi! ⓐMy name is Tabin, and I live near to the Gobi Desert in Mongolia. I'm happy when I ride my horse. Horses are important in our culture. Almost everyone can ride a horse in Mongolia. In fact, we say, "We ride horses before we can walk."
I take good care __ⓑ__ my horse. I often brush him and give him some carrots. I enjoy riding especially in the evening before the sunset. Then the sky is red, and everything is peaceful.

33 위 글의 밑줄 친 ⓐ에서 어법상 틀린 부분을 찾아 고치시오.

_____ ➡ _____

34 위 글의 빈칸 ⓑ에 알맞은 것을 고르시오.

① of
② to
③ at
④ for
⑤ with

35 다음 질문에 대한 알맞은 대답을 주어진 단어로 시작하여 쓰시오. (4단어)

Q: What does Tabin give to her horse?
A: She _____.

➡ _____

36 주어진 글 다음에 이어질 글의 순서로 가장 적절한 것은?

Hi, my name is Diego, and I live in Seville, Spain. My favorite time of the day is lunch time. My school usually ends around 2 p.m.

(A) After lunch, we usually take a siesta, a short nap. Both my father and I like to sleep under the tree in our garden.
(B) We usually have soup, vegetables, and meat. We also have a dessert like churros.
(C) On most days, my family gets together and has a big, long lunch.

① (A) – (C) – (B)
② (B) – (A) – (C)
③ (B) – (C) – (A)
④ (C) – (A) – (B)
⑤ (C) – (B) – (A)

[01~02] 다음 글을 읽고, 물음에 답하시오.

Somin: Hello! I'm Somin. I'm 15 years old, and I live in Korea. Please tell me about ⓐ너희들이 가장 좋아하는 시간 of the day. ⓑYou can also show me some pictures.

01 위 글의 밑줄 친 ⓐ의 우리말을 세 단어로 쓰시오. (time을 사용할 것.)

➡ _____

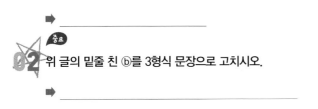

02 위 글의 밑줄 친 ⓑ를 3형식 문장으로 고치시오.

➡ _____

[03~04] 다음 글을 읽고, 물음에 답하시오.

Diego: Hi, my name is Diego, and I live in Seville, Spain. My favorite time of the day is lunch time. My school usually ends around 2 p.m. On most days, my family gets together and has a big, long lunch. We usually have soup, vegetables, and meat. We also have a dessert ___ⓐ___ churros. After lunch, we usually take a siesta, a short nap. Both my father and I like to sleep under the tree in our garden.

03 위 글의 빈칸 ⓐ에 들어갈 알맞은 말을 본문에서 찾아 쓰시오.

➡ _____

04 다음 빈칸 (A)와 (B)에 알맞은 단어를 넣어 Diego의 가족에 대한 소개를 완성하시오.

> Almost every day, Diego's family has ___(A)___ together. After lunch, Diego and his father usually take a ___(B)___ nap under the tree in their garden.

(A)_____ (B)_____

[05~07] 다음 글을 읽고, 물음에 답하시오.

Tabin: Hi! My name is Tabin, and I live near the Gobi Desert in Mongolia. I'm happy when I ride my horse. Horses are important in our culture. ⓐ몽골에서는 거의 모든 사람들이 말을 탈 수 있어. In fact, we say, "We ride horses before we can walk."
  ⓑI take good care of my horse. I often brush him and give him some carrots. I enjoy ___ⓒ___ especially in the evening before the sunset. Then the sky is red, and everything is peaceful.

05 위 글의 밑줄 친 ⓐ의 우리말에 맞게 한 단어를 보충하여, 주어진 어휘를 알맞게 배열하시오.

> ride / everyone / horse / can / Mongolia / a / in

➡ _____
_____

06 위 글의 밑줄 친 ⓑ를 다음과 같이 바꿔 쓸 때 빈칸에 알맞은 말을 쓰시오.

> I _____ _____ my horse well.
> = I _____ _____ my horse well.

07 위 글의 빈칸 ⓒ에 ride를 알맞은 형태로 쓰시오.

➡ _____

[08~10] 다음 글을 읽고, 물음에 답하시오.

Musa: Hi! I'm Musa, and I live in Nairobi, Kenya. My favorite time of the day is our running practice time. ⓐMy friend, Tamu, and I am on the school's running team. I'm happiest when I run with Tamu. Our practice time isn't boring because we can see many animals.

Many runners from Kenya won races in the Olympics. I'm so proud of them. ⓑTamu와 나는 둘 다 그들처럼 되고 싶어한다.

08 다음 질문에 대한 알맞은 대답을 주어진 단어로 시작하여 쓰시오. (10단어)

> Q: When is Musa's favorite time of the day?

➡ His _____

_____ .

09 위 글의 밑줄 친 ⓐ에서 어법상 틀린 부분을 찾아 고치시오.

_____ ➡ _____

10 위 글의 밑줄 친 ⓑ의 우리말에 맞게 주어진 어휘를 이용하여 9 단어로 영작하시오.

> both, like

➡ _____

[11~12] 다음 글을 읽고, 물음에 답하시오.

Diego: Hi, my name is Diego, and I live in Seville, Spain. My favorite time of the day is lunch time. My school usually ends around 2 p.m. ⓐ대부분의 날에는, 가족들이 모여서 푸짐하고 긴 점심 식사를 해. We usually have soup, vegetables, and meat. We also have a dessert like churros. After lunch, we usually take a siesta, a short nap. ⓑBoth my father and I like to sleep under the tree in our garden.

11 위 글의 밑줄 친 ⓐ의 우리말에 맞게 주어진 어휘를 이용하여 13 단어로 영작하시오.

> most, gets together, has, big

➡ _____

_____

12 위 글의 밑줄 친 ⓑ를 다음과 같이 바꿔 쓸 때 빈칸에 알맞은 말을 쓰시오.

> Both my father and I like _____ under the tree in our garden.

Before You Read

This country is in <u>southern</u> Europe. People here usually <u>take a short nap</u> in the
남쪽의, 남쪽에 있는 　　　　　　　　　　　　　　　　짧은 낮잠을 자다

afternoon.

This country is in East Asia. <u>Almost</u> everyone can <u>ride a horse</u> here.
　　　　　　　　　　　　　거의　　　　　　　　말을 타다

This country is in East Africa. <u>There are</u> <u>many</u> great runners from here.
　　　　　　　　　　　　　　　　　～가 있다　　many+복수명사

구문해설 · nap: 낮잠 · almost: 거의

이 나라는 유럽 남부에 있다. 이곳의 사람들은 보통 오후에 짧은 낮잠을 잔다.

이 나라는 동아시아에 있다. 이곳의 거의 모든 사람들은 말을 탈 수 있다.

이 나라는 동아프리카에 있다. 이곳 출신의 훌륭한 달리기 선수들이 많이 있다.

Around the World

Some people in this country don't live in one place <u>for long</u>. <u>They move</u>
　　　　　　　　　　　　　　　　　　　　　　오랫동안　　= Some people

around with their animals.
여기저기 이동하다

People in this country usually eat four or five times a day. They eat tapas

<u>between</u> meals.
둘 사이에 (셋 이상의 사이: among)

This country has many national parks <u>with</u> animals <u>like</u> lions, zebras,
　　　　　　　　　　　　　　　　　　～이 있는　　～와 같은(= such as)

elephants, and giraffes.

구문해설 · ~ times: ~ 번 · national park: 국립공원 · zebra: 얼룩말 · giraffe: 기린

이 나라의 몇몇 사람들은 한 장소에서 오랫동안 살지 않는다. 그들은 그들의 동물들과 이동한다.

이 나라의 사람들은 보통 하루에 네 번 또는 다섯 번의 식사를 한다. 그들은 식사 사이에 타파스를 먹는다.

이 나라에는 사자, 얼룩말, 코끼리, 그리고 기린과 같은 동물들이 있는 국립공원이 많이 있다.

Think and Write

I'm <u>happiest</u> when I read <u>exciting</u> novels.
　　　happy의 최상급　　감정을 나타내는 말이 사물을 수식할 때는 현재분사형의 형용사를 쓴다.

I'm happiest <u>when</u> I eat candy.
　　　　　～할 때

I'm happiest when my brother <u>tells me funny jokes</u>.
　　　　　　　　　　　　　　tells funny jokes to me(3형식)

I'm happiest when I play <u>with</u> my friends <u>after school</u>.
　　　　　　　　　　　　～와 함께　　　　　방과 후에

구문해설 · happiest: 가장 행복한 · exciting: 흥미진진한 · novel: 소설 · candy: 사탕
· funny: 웃기는 · joke: 농담

나는 흥미 있는 소설을 읽을 때 가장 행복해.

나는 사탕을 먹을 때 가장 행복해.

나는 내 남동생이 나에게 재미있는 농담을 할 때 가장 행복해.

나는 방과 후에 내 친구들과 놀 때 가장 행복해.

01 다음 주어진 두 단어의 관계가 같도록 빈칸에 알맞은 단어를 쓰시오.

> long : short = far : _____

[02~03] 다음 영영 풀이에 해당하는 것을 고르시오.

02

> the beliefs, way of life, art, and customs that are shared and accepted by people in a particular society

① nap   ② sunset
③ picture   ④ culture
⑤ history

03

> to look after someone or something

① look at   ② get together
③ live in   ④ be proud of
⑤ take care of

04 다음 빈칸에 들어갈 말로 알맞게 짝지어진 것은?

> • My friend, Tamu, and I are _____ the school's running team.
> • A club should be _____ a big family.

① off – as   ② in – to
③ on – like   ④ at – like
⑤ on – both

05 다음 빈칸에 알맞은 동사가 바르게 짝지어진 것은?

> • You can also _____ me some pictures.
> • I _____ baduk with my dad after school.

① tell – show   ② show – go
③ give – make   ④ send – take
⑤ show – play

06 다음 밑줄 친 부분의 뜻이 잘못된 것은?

① You should be proud of yourself.
　　자랑스러워하다
② They move around with their animals.
　　돌아다니다
③ People in this country usually eat four or five times a day. 네다섯 시간
④ What kind of books do you read?
　　종류
⑤ Almost everyone in this country can ride a horse. 말을 타다

07 다음 주어진 문장에 이어질 대화의 순서로 알맞은 것은?

> Hajun, what do you usually do in your free time?

> (A) What kind of games do you play?
> (B) I usually play baduk.
> (C) I like playing games with my dad.

① (A) – (C) – (B)   ② (B) – (A) – (C)
③ (B) – (C) – (A)   ④ (C) – (A) – (B)
⑤ (C) – (B) – (A)

08 다음 중 짝지어진 대화가 어색한 것은?

① A: What do you usually do in your free time?
　 B: I usually listen to music.
② A: What kind of movies do you watch?
　 B: I like action movies.
③ A: Why don't we go see an action movie this weekend?
　 B: Sure. That sounds great.
④ A: How do you spend your free time?
　 B: I usually play badminton.
⑤ A: What kind of cookies do you make?
　 B: I love strawberries.

[09~11] 다음 대화를 읽고, 물음에 답하시오.

B: Subin, what do you usually do in your free time?
G: I exercise outside.
B: What kind of exercise do you do?
G: I play badminton with my brother. (A)나는 학교 배드민턴 팀이야. What do you usually do in your free time, Andy?
B: I like watching movies.
G: ＿＿＿＿＿＿ (B)
B: I like action movies. They're fun.
G: Oh, I sometimes watch action movies, too. Why don't we go see an action movie this weekend?
B: Sure. That sounds great.

09 위 대화의 밑줄 친 (A)의 우리말을 영어로 옮길 때 문장의 빈칸에 들어갈 알맞은 말을 쓰시오.

I'm ＿＿＿＿＿ the ＿＿＿＿＿ badminton team.

10 위 대화의 빈칸 (B)에 들어갈 말로 알맞은 것은?

① When do you usually go to the movies?
② What are you going to do tomorrow?
③ What kind of movies do you like?
④ What do you usually do in your free time?
⑤ How about you?

11 위 대화의 내용과 일치하지 않는 것은?

① Subin plays badminton with her brother.
② Subin exercises outside in her free time.
③ Andy likes watching action movies because they're fun.
④ Subin and Andy plan to see an action movie.
⑤ Andy prefers exercising to watching movies.

12 다음 대화의 순서를 바르게 배열한 것은?

(A) I usually make strawberry cookies. I love strawberries.
(B) Chris, what do you do when you have free time?
(C) What kind of cookies do you make?
(D) I make cookies. I enjoy baking.

① (A) – (B) – (C) – (D)
② (B) – (A) – (C) – (D)
③ (B) – (D) – (C) – (A)
④ (C) – (A) – (B) – (D)
⑤ (C) – (B) – (D) – (A)

Grammar

13 다음 두 문장이 같은 뜻이 되도록 빈칸을 채우시오.

(1) I want to give my mom a scarf.

⇒ I want to give _____ _____ _____ my mom.

(2) Her mom made her a nice dress.

⇒ Her mother made _____ _____ _____ _____ her.

14 다음 우리말을 괄호 안에 주어진 단어를 이용하여 영작하시오. (2가지)

> Paul은 Michelle에게 생일 케이크를 하나 만들어 주었다. (a birthday cake)

⇒ _____

⇒ _____

15 다음 문장을 as well as를 이용하여 바꿔 쓰시오.

(1) Not only humans but also animals need water and air.

⇒ _____

(2) Mom bought not only beef but pork.

⇒ _____

16 다음 중 문장 형식이 나머지 넷과 다른 것은?

① Ella made her son a doctor.
② Jane gave me a present.
③ Yuna showed her father a picture.
④ Minsu told me a lie.
⑤ Jinho sent her some cookies.

17 다음 우리말을 영어로 바르게 옮긴 것은?

> 그녀는 며칠 동안 먹지도 마시지도 않았다.

① She not only ate but also drank for days.
② She neither ate nor drank for days.
③ She either ate or drank for days.
④ She ate as well as drank for days.
⑤ She did not ate not drank for days.

18 다음 중 문장의 전환이 올바르지 않은 것은?

① We threw her a birthday party.
→ We threw a birthday party for her.
② Bill showed Jenny his old pictures.
→ Bill showed his old pictures to Jenny.
③ Camila asked me an interesting question.
→ Camila asked an interesting question to me.
④ Jane's mom made her a new bag.
→ Jane's mom made a new bag for her.
⑤ Sam gave me a present.
→ Sam gave a present to me.

19 다음 문장에서 틀린 것을 고치시오.

> Both humans or animals are living creatures.

_____ ⇒ _____

20 다음 중 어법상 바르지 않은 문장은 몇 개인가?

> • Not only I but also Elizabeth are poor at singing.
> • Both Eric and Tom are good at math.
> • Neither she nor her kids were at home.
> • Sujin likes both pizza and fruit.
> • Alexander likes math as well as music.

① 1개　　② 2개　　③ 3개
④ 4개　　⑤ 5개

21 다음 문장의 빈칸에 들어갈 단어의 형태로 알맞은 것은?

> Minsu likes both _____ soccer and to play baseball.

① play　　② plays　　③ played
④ to play　　⑤ playing

22 다음 문장에서 틀린 곳을 찾아 바르게 고쳐 쓰시오.

(1) I will give my pen of you.

➡ _____

(2) Alicia bought a toy robot to her son last weekend.

➡ _____

➡ _____

(3) The stranger asked the way to the police officer.

➡ _____

23 다음 중 어법상 바르지 않은 것은?

① I like both math and science.
② Both Eric and Tom live in New York City.
③ Stevenson not only read the book but also took a picture of the book.
④ Either you or Ethan is wrong.
⑤ Ann likes both reading books and to watch movies.

24 다음 중 어법상 올바른 문장을 고르시오.

① Eva bought for her daughter a new smartphone.
② My grandfather told to us a funny story.
③ Mr. Kim sent an email me.
④ Leah wrote him a letter.
⑤ Yuna made a cake to her mom.

Reading

[25~27] 다음 글을 읽고, 물음에 답하시오.

Diego: Hi, my name is Diego, I live in Seville, Spain. My favorite time of the day is lunch time. My school usually ends ⓐaround 2 p.m. On most days, my family gets together and has a big, long lunch. We usually have soup, vegetables, and meat. We also have a dessert like churros. After lunch, we usually take a siesta, a short nap. ⓑ_____ my father ⓒ_____ I like to sleep under the tree in our garden.

25 위 글의 목적으로 알맞은 것을 고르시오.

① to introduce the culture of Spain
② to explain the reason why Diego's family gets together on most days
③ to introduce what Diego's family eats for lunch
④ to introduce Diego's favorite time of the day
⑤ to introduce what Diego's family does after lunch

26 위 글의 밑줄 친 ⓐaround와 같은 의미로 쓰인 것을 고르시오.

① I could hear laughter all around.
② He can make the wheels go around.
③ It happened around ten years ago.
④ I will show you around.
⑤ There was no one around.

27 위 글의 빈칸 ⓑ와 ⓒ에 문맥상 알맞은 상관접속사를 쓰시오. (한 칸에 한 단어씩 쓰시오.)

ⓑ _____　　ⓒ _____

[28~30] 다음 글을 읽고, 물음에 답하시오.

Tabin: Hi! My name is Tabin, and I live near the Gobi Desert in Mongolia. I'm happy when I ride my horse. Horses are important in our culture. (A)[Almost / Most] everyone can ride a horse in Mongolia. ⓐIn fact, we say, "We ride horses (B)[before / after] we can walk."

 I take good care of my horse. I often brush him and ⓑgive him some carrots. I enjoy (C)[riding / to ride] especially in the evening before the sunset. Then the sky is red, and everything is peaceful.

28 위 글의 괄호 (A)~(C)에서 문맥과 어법상 알맞은 낱말을 골라 쓰시오.

(A)＿＿＿ (B)＿＿＿ (C)＿＿＿

29 위 글의 밑줄 친 ⓐIn fact와 바꿔 쓸 수 있는 말을 모두 고르시오.

① Therefore　　② Instead
③ Actually　　④ In other words
⑤ As a matter of fact

30 위 글의 밑줄 친 ⓑ를 3형식으로 고치시오.

➡ ＿＿＿＿＿＿＿＿＿＿＿＿＿

[31~33] 다음 글을 읽고, 물음에 답하시오.

Musa: Hi! I'm Musa, and I live in Nairobi, Kenya. ①My favorite time of the day is our running practice time. ②My friend, Tamu, and I are on the school's running team. I'm happiest when I run ＿ⓐ＿ Tamu. ③Our practice time is boring because we can see many animals.

 Many runners ＿ⓑ＿ Kenya won races in the Olympics. ④I'm so proud of them. ⑤Both Tamu and I want to be like them.

31 위 글을 읽고 알 수 <u>없는</u> 것을 고르시오.

① Musa가 사는 곳
② Musa가 속해 있는 운동 팀의 종류
③ Musa가 가장 행복한 때
④ 올림픽의 육상 경기에서 이긴 케냐 선수들의 이름
⑤ 올림픽의 육상 경기에서 이긴 케냐 출신의 선수들에 대한 Musa의 생각

32 위 글의 밑줄 친 ①~⑤에서 흐름상 어색한 부분을 찾아 고치시오.

➡ ＿＿＿＿＿＿＿＿＿＿＿＿＿

33 위 글의 빈칸 ⓐ와 ⓑ에 들어갈 전치사가 바르게 짝지어진 것은?

① with – from　　② by – in
③ in – for　　④ with – to
⑤ by – from

01 출제율 95%

다음 짝지어진 단어의 관계가 같도록 빈칸에 알맞은 말을 쓰시오.

> boring : exciting = _____ : ashamed

02 출제율 90%

다음 설명에 해당하는 단어는?

> to talk about what happens on most occasions

① always ② never ③ usually
④ really ⑤ seldom

03 출제율 90%

다음 빈칸에 들어갈 말로 알맞게 짝지어진 것은?

> • What _____ of movies do you like?
> • What do you usually do in your _____ time?
> • _____ don't we go see an action movie this weekend?

① kind – free – How
② sort – own – What
③ do – kind – How
④ kind – free – Why
⑤ are – own – How

04 출제율 85%

다음 대화의 빈칸에 들어갈 말로 알맞은 것은?

> A: What do you usually do when you have free time?
> B: _____

① I want to travel to Europe.
② Let's play together sometime.
③ I like detective stories.
④ I usually watch movies.
⑤ That sounds great.

05 출제율 100%

다음 문장의 빈칸에 들어갈 알맞은 단어를 주어진 단어를 이용하여 쓰시오.

> • This country is in _____ Europe. (south)
> • I enjoy _____ especially in the evening. (ride)
> • Many _____ from Kenya won races in the Olympics. (run)

[06~07] 다음 대화를 읽고, 물음에 답하시오.

> B: Subin, (1)_____?
> G: I exercise outside.
> B: What kind of exercise do you do?
> G: I play badminton with my brother. I'm on the school's badminton team. (A)What do you usually do in your free time, Andy?
> B: I like watching movies.
> G: What kind of movies do you like?
> B: I like action movies. They're fun.
> G: Oh, I sometimes watch action movies, too. (2)_____ this weekend?
> B: Sure. That sounds great.

06 출제율 95%

위 대화의 빈칸 (1)과 (2)에 들어갈 말로 알맞은 것을 〈보기〉에서 찾아 쓰시오.

> ┌─ 보기 ─┐
> • how do you spend your free time
> • what do you want to do in your free time
> • Why don't we go see an action movie
> • Why did you go see an action movie

(1) _____
(2) _____

07 위 대화의 밑줄 친 (A)와 같은 의미로 사용될 수 있는 것은?

① What do you think of having a hobby, Andy?

② Why don't you exercise outside, Andy?

③ What's your hobby, Andy?

④ What do you want to do in your free time, Andy?

⑤ Let's watch movies, Andy.

[08~09] 다음 대화를 읽고, 물음에 답하시오.

G: Jiho, what do you usually do when you have free time?

B: (A)I watch usually movies.

G: What kind of movies do you watch?

B: (B) _____ Bruce Lee is my favorite movie star.

08 위 대화의 밑줄 친 (A)를 어법에 맞게 고쳐 쓰시오.

➡ _____

09 위 대화의 빈칸 (B)에 들어갈 말로 알맞은 것은?

① I usually watch TV. How about you?

② I think I need to go to watch movies.

③ I want to see *Fantastic Beasts*.

④ I like playing badminton.

⑤ I like action movies.

10 다음 대화에서 Jenny가 Chris에 관해 궁금해하는 것은?

Jenny: Chris, what do you do when you have free time?

Chris: I make cookies. I enjoy baking.

Jenny: What kind of cookies do you make?

Chris: I usually make strawberry cookies. I love strawberries.

① why he makes cookies

② what he likes

③ with whom he makes cookies

④ what he does in his free time

⑤ how often he makes cookies in his free time

11 다음 중 어법상 올바른 문장을 모두 고르시오.

① I give some carrots my horse.

② Mary wrote a letter to him.

③ She bought flowers to me.

④ Both Minsu and Sujin likes pizza.

⑤ I like not only math but science.

12 다음 빈칸에 들어갈 말이 바르게 짝지어진 것은?

- _____ Tom and Joe were late for school.
- _____ the girls or the boy has to do the dishes.

① Both – Either   ② Either – Both

③ Both – Neither   ④ Neither – Both

⑤ Not – Every

출제율 90%

13 다음 빈칸에 알맞은 말이 순서대로 짝지어진 것은?

> • Give _____ a big hug for me.
> • Nora bought a gift _____.

① him – to me
② him – for me
③ to him – to me
④ to him – for me
⑤ for him – to me

출제율 95%

14 다음 중 어법상 어색한 것은?

① Both Yuna and June are good at drawing.
② Not only Jean but also I want to have something hot to drink.
③ Marion as well as I am from Finland.
④ Neither you nor your sister is able to go to the amusement park.
⑤ Either you or she has to put out the trash.

[15~17] 다음 글을 읽고, 물음에 답하시오.

Diego: Hi, my name is Diego, and I live in Seville, Spain. My favorite time of the day is lunch time. My school usually ends around 2 p.m. On (A)[most / almost] days, my family gets together and has a big, long lunch. We usually have (B)[soap / soup], vegetables, and meat. We also have a (C)[desert / dessert] like churros. After lunch, we usually ⓐtake a siesta, a short nap. Both my father and I like ⓑto sleep under the tree in our garden.

출제율 90%

15 위 글의 괄호 (A)~(C)에서 문맥과 어법상 알맞은 낱말을 골라 쓰시오.

(A)_____ (B)_____ (C)_____

출제율 85%

16 위 글의 밑줄 친 ⓐtake와 바꿔 쓸 수 있는 단어를 고르시오.

① bring
② give
③ make
④ put
⑤ have

출제율 95%

17 위 글의 밑줄 친 ⓑto sleep과 부정사의 용법이 다른 것을 고르시오.

① It is fun to sleep under the tree.
② He decided to sleep under the tree.
③ I was happy to sleep under the tree.
④ My dream is to sleep under the tree.
⑤ Do you want to sleep under the tree?

[18~20] 다음 글을 읽고, 물음에 답하시오.

Tabin: Hi! My name is Tabin, and I live near the Gobi Desert in Mongolia. I'm happy when I ride my horse. Horses are important in our culture. Almost everyone can _____ⓐ_____ in Mongolia. In fact, we say, "We ride horses before we can walk."

I take good care of my horse. I often brush ⓑhim and give him some carrots. I enjoy riding especially in the evening before the sunset. Then the sky is red, and everything is peaceful.

출제율 95%

18 위 글의 빈칸 ⓐ에 들어갈 알맞은 말을 고르시오.

① feed the horses
② bet on horse racing
③ brush the horses
④ ride a horse
⑤ do stunt on horseback

19 위 글의 밑줄 친 ⓑ가 가리키는 것을 본문에서 찾아 쓰시오.

➡ _____

20 위 글을 읽고 대답할 수 <u>없는</u> 질문은?

① Does Tabin live in the city?

② Why are horses important in Mongolian culture?

③ When is Tabin happy?

④ Does Tabin look after her horse well?

⑤ When does Tabin enjoy riding a horse?

[21~23] 다음 글을 읽고, 물음에 답하시오.

Musa: Hi! I'm Musa, and I live in Nairobi, Kenya. My favorite time of the day is our running practice time. My friend, Tamu, and I are on the school's running team. ① I'm happiest when I run with Tamu. ②Our practice time isn't boring because we can see many animals.
  ③Many runners from Kenya won ⓐraces in the Olympics. ④I'm so proud of them. ⑤I run faster than Tamu. <u>ⓑNeither Tamu nor I want to be like them.</u>

21 위 글의 ①~⑤ 중에서 전체 흐름과 관계 <u>없는</u> 문장은?

①   ②   ③   ④   ⑤

22 위 글의 밑줄 친 ⓐraces와 같은 의미로 쓰인 것을 고르시오.

① This custom is found in people of all <u>races</u> throughout the world.

② She <u>races</u> for the senior team this year.

③ We like to have <u>races</u> with them.

④ Let's find the similarities between African and European <u>races</u>.

⑤ My heart <u>races</u> with excitement.

23 위 글의 밑줄 친 ⓑ에서 낱말의 쓰임이 문맥상 적절하지 않은 것을 찾아 알맞게 고치시오.

_____ ➡ _____

[24~25] 다음 글을 읽고, 물음에 답하시오.

Diego: My favorite time of the day is lunch time. ①We usually have soup, vegetables, and meat.
Tabin: ②I'm happiest when I ride my horse. ③ I enjoy riding especially in the evening before the sunset.
Musa: ④My favorite time of the day is our running practice time. ⑤Our practice time isn't boring though we can see many animals.

24 위 글의 제목으로 알맞은 것을 고르시오.

① What Does Diego Eat for Lunch?

② Tabin's Happiest Time of the Day

③ When Is the Best Time to Ride?

④ Favorite Time of the Day

⑤ Musa's Practice Time Isn't Boring!

25 위 글의 밑줄 친 ①~⑤ 중 흐름상 어색한 부분을 찾아 고치시오.

➡ _____

01 다음 대화의 밑줄 친 (1)과 같은 의미를 가진 문장으로 쓰려고 한다. 주어진 단어를 보고 알맞게 배열하시오.

> G: Seho, (1)what do you do in your free time?
> B: I listen to music.
> G: What kind of music do you listen to?
> B: Rock music.

> what / you / to do / like / when / do / you, free / have / time

➡ _____

02 ⭐ 다음은 Minji와 Subin이의 여가 시간의 활동에 관한 내용이다. 표를 보고 다음 대화를 완성하시오

Free Time Activity	
Minji	watch movies / action movies
Subin	exercise outside / badminton

> M: Subin, what do you usually do in your free time?
> S: I (1)_____.
> M: (2)_____ exercise do you do?
> S: I (3)_____ with my brother. What do you usually do in your free time, Minji?
> M: I like (4)_____.
> S: What kind of movies do you like?
> M: I like (5)_____. They're fun.

03 다음 글을 참고하여 아래의 대화를 완성하시오.

> I'm Minho. My favorite time of the day is night. I love to see the moon and the stars.

> A: _____ is your _____ time of the day?
> B: I like night most _____ I can see the moon and the stars.

04 다음 주어진 단어를 이용하여 빈칸에 들어갈 알맞은 말을 쓰시오. (시제는 과거로 하고 필요시 단어를 변형할 것.)

(1) Melanie _____ _____ _____ _____. (buy, he, a necktie)
(2) Ariana _____ some candies _____ _____. (give, they)
(3) Ellie _____ a funny question _____ me last night. (ask)

05 ⭐ 다음 문장에서 어법상 틀린 부분을 찾아 바르게 고쳐 쓰시오.

(1) Both Benjamin and Bella works happily.
   _____ ➡ _____
(2) Hannah is both kindly and wise.
   _____ ➡ _____

06 다음 문장을 3형식으로 고치시오.

(1) Liam bought his family some meat.
   ➡ _____
(2) Luna showed me some post cards.
   ➡ _____

07 ⭐ 다음 문장에서 어법상 틀린 부분을 찾아 바르게 고쳐 쓰시오. (두 가지로 쓸 것)

> Lucas gave to her a piece of advice.

➡ _____
➡ _____

[08~10] 다음 글을 읽고, 물음에 답하시오.

Musa: Hi! I'm Musa, and I live in Nairobi, Kenya. My favorite time of the day is our running practice time. My friend, Tamu, and I are on the school's running team. ⓐ나는 Tamu와 달리기를 할 때 가장 행복해. Our practice time isn't boring because we can see many animals.

Many ___ⓑ___ from Kenya won races in the Olympics. I'm so proud of them. Both Tamu and I want to be like them.

08 위 글의 밑줄 친 ⓐ의 우리말에 맞게 7단어로 영작하시오.

➡ _____

🌟 중요
09 위 글의 내용과 일치하도록 다음 빈칸에 알맞은 단어를 쓰시오. (본문의 단어를 변형할 것.)

> Musa and Tamu aren't _____ during their running practice time because they can see many animals.

➡ _____

10 본문의 한 단어를 변형하여 위 글의 빈칸 ⓑ에 들어갈 알맞은 말을 쓰시오.

➡ _____

[11~13] 다음 글을 읽고, 물음에 답하시오.

Diego: Hi, my name is Diego, and I live in Seville, Spain. My favorite time of the day is lunch time. My school usually ends around 2 p.m. On most days, my family gets together and has a big, long lunch. We usually have soup, vegetables, and meat. We also have a dessert ⓐlike churros. ⓑ점심 식사 후에는 우리는 보통 시에스타, 즉 짧은 낮잠을 자. Both my father and I like to sleep under the tree in our garden.

11 위 글의 내용과 일치하도록 다음 빈칸에 들어갈 알맞은 단어를 쓰시오.

> Diego is Spanish and his favorite time of the day is _____.

➡ _____

🌟 중요
12 위 글의 밑줄 친 ⓐlike를 두 단어로 바꿔 쓰시오.

➡ _____

13 위 글의 밑줄 친 ⓑ의 우리말에 맞게 한 단어를 보충하여, 주어진 어휘를 알맞게 배열하시오.

> nap / take / short / lunch / siesta / we / a / after / a

➡ _____

01 다음 주어진 단어를 이용하여 4개의 의문문 문장을 만드시오.

(A)	(B)	(C)
Why don't	you usually do	an action movie this weekend?
What do you do	of cookies	free time?
What kind	we go see	do you make?
What do	when you have	in your free time?

(1) _____

(2) _____

(3) _____

(4) _____

02 Chloe가 이번 생일에 받은 선물 목록을 보고 수여동사를 이용한 문장을 3개 쓰시오.

a new computer from Dad, some flowers from Jack, a nice wallet from Lily

(1) _____

(2) _____

(3) _____

03 동영상 촬영하기: 하루 중 가장 행복한 시간에 관해 동영상 촬영을 위한 스토리보드를 만드시오.

> 보기
>
> We're going to show you our favorite time of the day.
> • I'm Jinsu. I'm happiest when I play soccer.
> • I'm Sumi. My favorite time of the day is lunch time. I love eating lunch at school.

(1) _____

(2) _____

단원별 모의고사

01 다음 짝지어진 단어의 관계가 같도록 빈칸에 알맞은 단어를 쓰시오.

> important : unimportant = win : _____

[02~03] 다음 영영풀이에 해당하는 단어를 고르시오.

02

> the time of day when the sun disappears and night begins

① night   ② morning
③ sunset   ④ dawn
⑤ noon

03

> quiet and calm without any worry or excitement

① peaceful   ② boring
③ noisy   ④ free
⑤ favorite

04 다음 빈칸에 들어갈 말로 알맞은 것은?

> G: Jiho, what do you usually do _____ you have free time?
> B: I usually watch movies.

① what   ② how
③ why   ④ where
⑤ when

05 다음 문장의 빈칸에 공통으로 들어갈 말은?

> • She took care _____ her baby.
> • His mother is proud _____ her son.

① at   ② for
③ of   ④ in
⑤ to

06 다음 대화의 빈칸에 들어갈 말로 알맞은 것은?

> A: _____
> B: I listen to classical music.

① What are you going to do this weekend?
② How often do you listen to music?
③ Where do you usually go in your free time?
④ What kind of music do you listen to?
⑤ What are you doing?

07 다음 대화의 빈칸에 들어갈 말로 알맞은 것은?

> G: Chris, what do you do when you have free time?
> B: _____ I enjoy baking.
> G: What kind of cookies do you make?
> B: I usually make strawberry cookies. I love strawberries.

① I usually listen to music.
② I love strawberries.
③ I make cookies.
④ I go to the library and read books.
⑤ I like watching movies.

08 다음 주어진 문장에 이어질 대화의 순서를 바르게 배열하시오.

> Jiho, what do you usually do when you have free time?
> (A) I like action movies.
> (B) What kind of movies do you watch?
> (C) I usually watch movies.
> (D) Bruce Lee is my favorite movie star.

➡ _____

[09~12] 다음 대화를 읽고, 물음에 답하시오.

B: Subin, what do you usually do in your free time?
G: I exercise outside. ①
B: (A) 어떤 종류의 운동을 하니?
G: I play badminton with my brother. ② I'm ____ⓐ____ the school's badminton team. ③ What do you usually do in your free time, Andy?
B: I like watching movies.
G: ④ What kind of movies do you like?
B: I like action movies. ⑤
G: Oh, I sometimes watch action movies, too. ____ⓑ____ go see an action movie this weekend?
B: Sure. That sounds great.

09 위 대화의 ①~⑤ 중, 주어진 말이 들어갈 위치로 알맞은 것은?

> They're fun.

①　　　②　　　③　　　④　　　⑤

10 위 대화의 밑줄 친 (A)의 우리말에 맞게 주어진 단어를 이용하여 영어로 쓰시오.

> kind　exercise　do

➡ _____

11 위 대화의 빈칸 ⓐ에 들어갈 말로 알맞은 것은?

① at　　　② in　　　③ with
④ on　　　⑤ off

12 위 대화의 빈칸 ⓑ에 들어갈 말로 알맞은 것은?

① How about　　② Why don't we
③ How do you　　④ What do you
⑤ Why did you

13 다음 우리말을 괄호 안에 주어진 단어를 이용하여 영작하시오. (2가지)

> 나는 너에게 뭐 좀 물어보고 싶어.
> (ask, something)

➡ _____
➡ _____

14 다음 문장에서 틀린 부분을 찾아 바르게 고쳐 다시 쓰시오.

(1) Jeremy could neither read or to write.
➡ _____

(2) Both Jessie and I am studying English.
➡ _____

(3) Angelina not only had a hamburger but also an ice cream.
➡ _____
_____

15 다음 중 문장의 전환이 올바르지 <u>않은</u> 것은?

① Grandma read us a funny story.
→ Grandma read a funny story to us.
② Ken asked me a favor.
→ Ken asked a favor of me.
③ We threw Amy a birthday party.
→ We threw a birthday party for Amy.
④ Mel sent her some beautiful roses.
→ Mel sent some beautiful roses to her.
⑤ She chose her sister a pretty skirt.
→ She chose a pretty skirt to her sister.

16 다음 중 어법상 어색한 것은?

① Both Tamu and I want to be like them.
② Victoria as well as I likes singing.
③ Either you or she is to go.
④ Not only Seho but Jinsu wear glasses.
⑤ Neither you nor he plans to attend the school festival.

17 다음 중 어법상 옳은 문장은?

① Charlotte made a cake to her sister.
② Mia sent a text for me.
③ Eric gave Olivia to some books.
④ Jonathan showed Eveline a few pictures.
⑤ Tom bought a ring Amelia.

[18~19] 다음 글을 읽고, 물음에 답하시오.

Diego: On most days, my family gets together and has a big, long lunch. We usually have soup, vegetables, and meat. We also have a dessert ⓐlike churros. After lunch, we usually take a siesta, a short nap. ⓑBoth my father and I like to sleep under the tree in our garden.

18 위 글의 밑줄 친 ⓐlike와 같은 의미로 쓰인 것을 고르시오.

① She's wearing a dress <u>like</u> mine.
② I like a novel <u>like</u> 'Hamlet.'
③ She is just <u>like</u> her mother.
④ Do you <u>like</u> their new house?
⑤ He ran <u>like</u> the wind.

19 위 글의 밑줄 친 ⓑ와 바꿔 쓸 수 있는 말을 <u>모두</u> 고르시오.

① At once my father and I
② Either my father or I
③ Not my father but I
④ My father and I alike
⑤ Neither my father nor I

[20~22] 다음 글을 읽고, 물음에 답하시오.

Tabin: Hi! My name is Tabin, and I live near the Gobi Desert ⓐ Mongolia. (A) I'm happy when I ride my horse. Horses are important ⓑ our culture. Almost everyone can ride a horse ⓒ Mongolia. (B) , we say, "We ride horses before we can walk."
  I take good care of my horse. I often brush him and give him some carrots. I enjoy riding especially ⓓ the evening before the sunset. Then the sky is red, and everything is peaceful.

20 위 글의 빈칸 ⓐ~ⓓ에 공통으로 들어갈 알맞은 전치사를 쓰시오.

➡ _____

21 위 글의 밑줄 친 (A)를 다음과 같이 바꿔 쓸 때 빈칸에 철자 f로 시작하는 알맞은 단어를 쓰시오.

> My _____ time of the day is my horse riding time.

22 위 글의 빈칸 (B)에 들어갈 알맞은 말을 고르시오.

① Instead   ② However

③ In fact   ④ At last

⑤ By contrast

23 주어진 글 다음에 이어질 글의 순서로 가장 적절한 것은?

> Hi! I'm Musa, and I live in Nairobi, Kenya. My favorite time of the day is our running practice time.

> (A) I'm so proud of them. Both Tamu and I want to be like them.
> (B) My friend, Tamu, and I are on the school's running team. I'm happiest when I run with Tamu.
> (C) Our practice time isn't boring because we can see many animals. Many runners from Kenya won races in the Olympics.

① (A) – (C) – (B)   ② (B) – (A) – (C)

③ (B) – (C) – (A)   ④ (C) – (A) – (B)

⑤ (C) – (B) – (A)

[24~25] 다음 글을 읽고, 물음에 답하시오.

Musa: Hi! I'm Musa, and I live in Nairobi, Kenya. My favorite time of the day is our running practice time. My friend, Tamu, and I are on the school's running team. I'm happiest when I run with Tamu. Our practice time isn't (A)[boring / bored] because we can see many animals.

Many runners from Kenya (B)[gave up / won] races in the Olympics. I'm so (C)[ashamed / proud] of them. Both Tamu and I want ⓐto be like them.

24 위 글의 괄호 (A)~(C)에서 문맥상 알맞은 낱말을 골라 쓰시오.

(A)_____ (B)_____ (C)_____

25 위 글의 밑줄 친 ⓐto be와 to부정사의 용법이 같은 것을 고르시오.

① He is the last man to tell a lie.

② She can't be honest to say so.

③ I need a chair to sit on.

④ She hoped to go shopping alone.

⑤ He grew up to be a scientist.

Lesson 2

Enjoying Local Culture

🗣 의사소통 기능

- 길 묻고 답하기 1

  A: Where is the school?

  B: It's across from the hospital.

- 길 묻고 답하기 2

  A: How do I get there?

  B: Go straight three blocks and turn left.

🗣 언어 형식

- have to

  They **have to** be healthy.

- to부정사의 부사적 용법(목적)

  They have to produce a lot of milk **to win** a prize.

Words & Expressions

Key Words

- **across** [əkrɔ́ːs] 부 가로질러, 건너서
- **amazing** [əméiziŋ] 형 놀라운
- **bakery** [béikəri] 명 빵집
- **big** [big] 형 큰
- **bee** [biː] 명 모임
- **blanket** [blǽŋkit] 명 담요
- **block** [blɑk] 명 구역, 블록
- **bookstore** [búkstɔ̀ːr] 명 서점
- **cancel** [kǽnsəl] 동 취소하다
- **city hall** 시청
- **collect** [kəlékt] 동 모으다, 수집하다
- **colorful** [kʌ́lərfəl] 형 형형색색의, 다채로운
- **combination** [kàmbənéiʃən] 명 조합, 결합
- **contest** [kántest] 명 대회
- **enter** [éntər] 동 참가하다, 들어가다
- **exciting** [iksáitiŋ] 형 흥미진진한
- **expensive** [ikspénsiv] 형 비싼(↔ cheap)
- **fabric** [fǽbrik] 명 직물, 천
- **fair** [fɛər] 명 박람회, 품평회
- **fasten** [fǽsn] 동 매다
- **favorite** [féivərit] 형 가장 좋아하는
- **follow** [fálou] 동 따르다
- **gate** [geit] 명 문, 대문, 출입구
- **get** [get] 동 도착하다
- **goat** [gout] 명 염소
- **healthy** [hélθi] 형 건강한
- **main gate** 정문

- **movie theater** 영화관
- **mud** [mʌd] 명 진흙
- **museum** [mjuːzíəm] 명 박물관
- **near** [niər] 전 ~ 근처에 형 가까운(↔ far)
- **north** [nɔːrθ] 명 북쪽
- **over** [óuvər] 전 ~ 이상, ~을 넘어
- **past** [pæst] 명 과거
- **piece** [piːs] 명 조각
- **police station** 경찰서
- **prize** [praiz] 명 상
- **produce** [prədjúːs] 동 생산하다, 만들다
- **quilt** [kwilt] 명 퀼트, 누비이불
- **scared** [skɛərd] 형 겁먹은, 무서운
- **sew** [sou] 동 깁다, 바느질하다
- **spicy** [spáisi] 형 매운, 양념이 강한
- **stage** [steidʒ] 명 무대
- **state** [steit] 명 (미국의) 주
- **straight** [streit] 부 똑바로, 곧장, 곧바로
- **train station** 기차역
- **tasty** [téisti] 형 맛있는(= delicious)
- **third** [θəːrd] 형 세 번째의
- **tradition** [trədíʃən] 명 전통
- **turn** [təːrn] 동 돌다
- **unique** [juːníːk] 형 독특한, 특별한
- **view** [vjuː] 명 전망, 경관
- **wheel** [hwiːl] 명 바퀴
- **win** [win] 동 (상을) 타다, (경기에서) 이기다

Key Expressions

- **across from** ~의 맞은편에
- **be famous for** ~로 유명하다
- **be going to**+동사원형 ~할 예정이다
- **be proud of** ~을 자랑스러워하다
- **between A and B** A와 B 사이에
- **don't have to**+동사원형 ~할 필요가 없다
- **get**+형용사 ~가 되다
- **get to** ~에 도착하다
- **had to**+동사원형 ~해야 했다
- **have to**+동사원형 ~해야 한다

- **look at** ~을 보다
- **look for** ~을 찾다
- **move on to** ~로 이동하다
- **next to** ~ 옆에
- **on one's right** ~ 오른편에
- **some day** 언젠가
- **take care of** ~을 돌보다
- **taste**+형용사 ~한 맛이 나다
- **wait for** ~을 기다리다
- **work on** ~에 공들이다, 애쓰다

Word Power

※ 서로 반대되는 뜻을 가진 단어

- [ ] **right** (오른쪽) ↔ **left** (왼쪽)
- [ ] **right** (옳은) ↔ **wrong** (틀린)
- [ ] **straight** (똑바른) ↔ **curved** (굽은)
- [ ] **big** (큰) ↔ **small** (작은)
- [ ] **follow** (따르다) ↔ **precede** (앞서다)
- [ ] **young** (어린) ↔ **old** (나이 많은)
- [ ] **reach** (도착하다) ↔ **leave** (떠나다)

- [ ] **healthy** (건강한) ↔ **ill** (아픈)
- [ ] **win** (이기다) ↔ **lose** (지다)
- [ ] **expensive** (비싼) ↔ **cheap** (값싼)
- [ ] **exciting** (흥미진진한) ↔ **boring** (지루한)
- [ ] **popular** (인기 있는) ↔ **unpopular** (인기 없는)
- [ ] **famous** (유명한) ↔ **unknown** (알려지지 않은)
- [ ] **catch** (잡다) ↔ **miss** (놓치다)

※ 서로 비슷한 뜻을 가진 단어

- [ ] **spicy** : **hot** (매운)
- [ ] **unique** : **special** (특별한)
- [ ] **amazing** : **surprising** (놀라운)
- [ ] **tasty** : **delicious** (맛있는)
- [ ] **fasten** : **tie** (매다)

- [ ] **collect** : **gather** (모으다)
- [ ] **famous** : **well-known** (유명한)
- [ ] **healthy** : **well** (건강한)
- [ ] **scared** : **afraid** (두려운)
- [ ] **cancel** : **call off** (취소하다)

English Dictionary

- [ ] **straight** 똑바로
  - → in a line or direction that is not curved or bent
  - 곡선이거나 구부러지지 않은 선이나 방향으로

- [ ] **healthy** 건강한
  - → physically strong and not likely to become ill or weak
  - 신체적으로 강하고 아프거나 허약해지지 않는

- [ ] **produce** 만들다, 생산하다
  - → to make something to be bought, used, or enjoyed by people
  - 사람들이 구입하거나 사용하고 즐기는 것을 만들다

- [ ] **museum** 박물관
  - → a building where important cultural, historical, or scientific objects are kept
  - 중요한 문화적, 역사적, 과학적인 물건들이 보관되어 있는 건물

- [ ] **combination** 조합, 결합
  - → two or more different things that exist together or put together
  - 둘 또는 그 이상의 다른 것들이 함께 있거나 조립되는 것

- [ ] **gate** 문, 출입구
  - → a structure like a door which is used at the entrance to a field, a garden, or the grounds of a building
  - 들, 정원 또는 건물의 구내의 입구로 사용되는 문과 같은 구조물

- [ ] **spicy** 매운, 양념이 강한
  - → strongly flavored with spices
  - 향신료로 강한 맛이 나는

- [ ] **tradition** 전통
  - → a belief, custom, or way of doing something that has existed for a long time
  - 오랜 시간 동안 존재해 온 것을 행하는 방식이나 믿음, 관습

- [ ] **expensive** 비싼
  - → costing a lot of money
  - 많은 비용이 드는

- [ ] **collect** 모으다, 수집하다
  - → to get things of the same type from different places and bring them together
  - 다른 곳으로부터 같은 종류의 물건들을 얻어서 함께 모으다

- [ ] **sew** 바느질하다
  - → to use a needle and thread to make or repair clothes
  - 옷을 만들거나 수선하기 위해 실과 바늘을 사용하다

- [ ] **scared** 무서운, 두려워하는
  - → frightened of or nervous about something
  - 무언가에 놀라거나 초조해하는

서답형

01 다음 짝지어진 두 단어의 관계가 같도록 빈칸에 알맞은 단어를 쓰시오.

> tasty : delicious = _____ : hot

02 다음 빈칸에 공통으로 들어갈 말은?

> • How do I get _____ the police station?
> • They have _____ produce a lot of milk to win a prize.

① on
② of
③ for
④ to
⑤ in

03 다음 중 밑줄 친 단어의 우리말 뜻이 잘못된 것은?

① The goats in the show don't have to be big. ~해서는 안 된다
② Tex-Mex food is a combination of food from Texas and Mexico. 결합
③ His face is getting red because his fajita is too spicy. 매운
④ In the past, fabric was expensive. 직물
⑤ My mother taught me how to sew. 바느질하다

[04~05] 다음 영영 풀이에 해당하는 단어를 고르시오.

04

> frightened of or nervous about something

① disappointed
② excited
③ healthy
④ surprised
⑤ scared

05

> to make something to be bought, used, or enjoyed by people

① sew
② produce
③ enter
④ sell
⑤ collect

서답형

06 다음 우리말에 맞게 빈칸에 알맞은 단어를 쓰시오.

> 역사박물관은 Green Street에 있습니다.
> ➡ The History Museum is _____ Green Street.

[07~08] 다음 빈칸에 들어갈 말이 알맞게 짝지어진 것을 고르시오.

07

> • There is a bookstore _____ from the school.
> • I'm looking _____ Green Park.

① next to – at
② cross – for
③ across – for
④ between – at
⑤ around – on

08

> • He _____ work next weekend.
> • This state is famous _____ butter.

① have to – for
② has to – in
③ must – on
④ has to – for
⑤ don't have to – for

01 다음 짝지어진 두 단어의 관계가 같도록 빈칸에 알맞은 단어를 쓰시오.

(1) win : lose = exciting : _____

(2) unique : special = _____ : gather

02 다음 빈칸에 들어갈 말을 〈보기〉에서 찾아 쓰시오. (필요하면 변형하여 쓰시오.)

┌─ 보기 ├─
tradition   bee   move   unique   sew
└────────────────

(1) My mom and her friends have a quilting _____ every week.

(2) They _____ on to the next town last night.

(3) The company has a long _____ of fine design.

(4) She looked for a needle and thread to _____ the button.

03 다음 문장에 어울리는 단어를 〈보기〉에서 찾아 알맞은 형태로 고쳐 쓰시오.

┌─ 보기 ├─
piece   taste   color   amaze   look
└────────────────

(1) I'm scared, but the view is _____!

(2) Eddie saw his grandma and her friends' _____ quilt at the quilt contest.

(3) People had to collect small _____ of fabric and sew them together.

(4) People can eat many _____ cheese dishes.

04 다음 우리말과 같은 뜻이 되도록 주어진 단어를 알맞은 순서로 배열하시오.

(1) 우체국은 빵집과 학교 사이에 있다.
(between, the post office, and, the school, the bakery, is)
➡ _____

(2) 경찰서에 어떻게 가나요?
(get, do, I, how, to, police, the, station)
➡ _____

(3) Jane은 이번 주말까지 숙제를 끝내야 한다.
(Jane, finish, her, has, by, to, this, weekend, homework)
➡ _____

05 다음 빈칸에 공통으로 들어갈 말을 〈보기〉에서 골라 알맞은 형태로 고쳐 쓰시오.

┌─ 보기 ├─
have to   go   get   take   move
└────────────────

(1) Dad's face is _____ red.

(2) The African Music Concert is _____ to start at 4 p.m. at the Star Concert Stage.

(3) They _____ _____ call off the game as the ground was too wet.

06 다음에 제시된 의미에 맞는 단어를 주어진 철자로 시작하여 빈칸에 쓰시오.

┌──────────────────────┐
• s_____ : in a line or direction that is not curved or bent

• m_____ : a building where important cultural, historical, or scientific objects are kept
└──────────────────────┘

Conversation

① **길 묻고 답하기 1**

A Where is the school? 학교가 어디에 있니?

B It's across from the hospital. 병원 맞은편에 있어.

■ **길 찾아가는 방법을 물어볼 때**

건물의 위치를 묻는 표현으로 의문사 where를 이용하여 '~은 어디에 있니?'라는 의미로 'Where is the 장소?'라고 말한다.

• Where is the library?

• Where is the school?

• Where is the bakery?

• Where is the flower shop?

'How can[do] I get to ~?'도 길을 묻는 표현으로 비슷한 표현으로는 Can[Could / Will] you show[tell] me the way to ~? / Please tell me the way to ~. / I want to know the directions to ~. / Where is ~? / Where can I find ~? / Can you tell me where ~? 등이 있다. Go straight two blocks and turn left.는 '두 블록을 곧장 가서 왼쪽으로 도세요.'라는 의미로 상대방이 길을 물을 때 안내하는 표현이다.

길을 안내하는 표현

• It's just around the corner. 모퉁이를 돌면 바로 있어요.

• Turn right[left]. 오른쪽[왼쪽]으로 도세요.

• Turn around the corner. 모퉁이에서 도세요.

• It's on your right[left]. 당신 오른쪽[왼쪽]에 있어요.

• It's next to the hospital. 병원 옆에 있어요.

• You can't miss it. 꼭 찾을 거예요.

• I'm a stranger here, too. 저도 여기 처음이에요.

핵심 Check

1. 다음 두 문장의 의미가 같도록 빈칸에 알맞은 말을 쓰시오.

    Where is the flower shop?

    = Can you _____ _____ _____ _____ to the flower shop?

2. 다음 대화의 빈칸에 알맞은 말을 쓰시오.

    A: Please _____ me the way _____ the post office.

    B: Go straight two blocks and _____ left. It's _____ your right.

② 길 묻고 답하기 2

A How do I get there? 거기에 어떻게 가니?

B Go straight three blocks and turn left. 세 블록 곧장 가서 왼쪽으로 돌아.

■ 길을 물을 때는 'How do I get to ~?'라는 표현을 사용하는데, 여기에 쓰인 get은 '(장소·위치에) 도착하다[이르다]'를 의미한다. 비슷한 표현으로는 How can I get to ~?(~에 어떻게 갈 수 있나요?), Can you tell me where ~ is?(~가 어디에 있는지 말씀해 주시겠어요?) 등이 있다. 상대방에게 길을 설명할 때는 Go straight ~ block(s).(~ 블록을 직진하세요.), Turn right[left].(우[좌]회전하세요.) 등과 같은 표현을 이용해서 말할 수 있다.

길 묻기

- How do I get to the hospital? 병원에 어떻게 가나요?
- How can I get there? 그곳에 어떻게 갈 수 있나요?
- Can you tell me where the library is? 도서관이 어디에 있는지 말씀해 주시겠어요?
- I want to know the directions to the hospital. 그 병원에 가는 길을 알고 싶어요.

길 묻기에 답하기

- Go straight two blocks. 두 블록을 직진하세요.
- You'll see it on your right[left]. 그것은 당신의 오른편[왼편]에 있을 거예요.
- It's across from the post office. 그것은 우체국 맞은편에 있어요.

핵심 Check

3. 다음 대화의 빈칸에 들어갈 알맞은 말을 쓰시오.

A: Excuse me. _____ can I _____ _____ the museum?

B: Go straight ahead. It's on your right.

4. 다음 대화의 빈칸에 들어갈 말로 적절하지 <u>않은</u> 것은?

A: Can you tell me where the post office is?

B: _____

① It's across from the police station. ② Go straight two blocks.
③ Sorry, I'm a stranger here, too. ④ You can't miss it.
⑤ It's just around the corner.

A. Listen and Talk A-1

B: Excuse me. ❶I'm looking for the Star Mall.

G: ❷Go straight two blocks and turn left. ❸It'll be the first building on your right.

B: Oh, ❹I see. Thank you.

G: You're welcome.

B: 실례합니다. Star Mall을 찾고 있어요.

G: 두 블록을 곧장 가서 왼쪽으로 도세요. 오른쪽에 있는 첫 번째 건물이에요.

B: 오, 알겠어요. 감사해요.

G: 천만에요.

❶ I'm looking for ~: 나는 ~을 찾고 있다
❷ 길을 안내할 때 사용하는 표현이다.
❸ It은 the Star Mall을 가리킨다.
❹ 몰랐던 사실을 알았을 때 사용하는 표현이다.

Check(√) True or False

(1) The boy is looking for the Star Mall.　　　　　　　　　T ☐ F ☐

(2) The girl knows where the Star Mall is.　　　　　　　　T ☐ F ☐

B. Listen and Talk C

B: Hello. ❶May I help you?

G: Yes, please. ❷I'm looking for Green Park.

B: OK. Please look at this map. We are here.

G: Oh, I see. So ❸how do I get to the park?

B: Go straight two blocks and turn left. ❹It's across from the train station.

G: I see. The African Music Concert is there, right?

B: Yes, it is. ❺It's going to start at 4 p.m. at the Star Concert Stage.

G: Right, and where is the stage?

B: It's near the north gate of the park.

G: OK, thank you!

B: 안녕하세요. 도와 드릴까요?

G: 네, 저는 Green 공원을 찾고 있어요.

B: 네. 이 지도를 보세요. 우리는 여기에 있어요.

G: 아, 그렇군요. 그럼 공원에 어떻게 가나요?

B: 두 블록을 곧장 가서 왼쪽으로 도세요. 공원은 기차역 맞은편에 있어요.

G: 알겠어요. 거기서 아프리카 음악 콘서트가 열리죠, 맞나요?

B: 네. 오후 4시에 Star Concert 무대에서 시작할 예정이에요.

G: 맞아요. 그런데 무대는 어디에 있나요?

B: 공원 북문 근처에 있어요.

G: 네, 감사해요!

❶ May I help you? = Can I help you?: 남에게 도움을 주고자 할 때 사용하는 표현이다.
❷ look for ~: '~을 찾다'는 의미로 be동사와 함께 사용이 되어 현재진행형을 사용하고 있다.
❸ how do I get to+장소?: ~에 어떻게 가나요?
❹ across from ~: ~의 맞은편에
❺ be going to+동사원형: ~할 예정이다

Check(√) True or False

(3) The girl wants to go to the African Music Concert.　　　T ☐ F ☐

(4) The boy doesn't know where the Star Concert Stage is.　　T ☐ F ☐

Listen and Talk A-2

B: Excuse me. ❶Where's the bookstore?

G: ❷There's one across from the post office.

B: ❸How do I get there?

G: Go straight one block and turn right. It'll be on your right.

B: Thank you!

❶ 길을 물을 볼 때 사용하는 말로 Where can I find the bookstore?로 바꾸어 쓸 수 있다.

❷ There's는 There is의 줄임말로 '~이 있다'는 뜻이다. one은 a bookstore를 가리키는 부정대명사다. across from은 '~의 맞은편에'의 뜻이다.

❸ '그곳에 어떻게 가나요?'라는 표현으로 How can I get there?로 바꾸어 쓸 수 있다.

Listen and Talk B

A: ❶Where is the school?

B: It's on Green Street. ❷It's across from the hospital.

A: ❸How do I get there?

B: Go straight three blocks and turn left. It'll be on your right.

A: Thank you.

❶ Where is + 장소?: 길을 물어볼 때 사용하는 표현이다.

❷ across from ~: ~의 맞은편에

❸ How do I get there?: 그곳에 어떻게 가나요?

Listen and Talk A-3

B: Excuse me. ❶How do I get to the police station?

G: ❷Walk straight three blocks and turn left. It'll be on your right.

B: Oh, I see.

G: It's ❸between the bakery and the school. ❹ You can't miss it.

B: Thank you!

❶ get to는 '~에 도착하다'는 의미이다.

❷ straight는 부사로 '곧장'의 뜻이다.

❸ between A and B는 'A와 B 사이에'라는 뜻이다.

❹ '꼭 찾을 거예요.'라는 표현이다.

Review 1

M: Excuse me. ❶How do I get to the bookstore?

W: Walk straight two blocks and turn left. ❷It'll be on your right.

M: ❸That sounds easy. Thank you.

❶ How do I get to+장소?: ~에 어떻게 가나요?

❷ It'll be on your right.는 '오른쪽에 있을 거예요'라는 뜻이다.

❸ sound+형용사: '~처럼 들리다'는 뜻으로 '쉽네요.'라는 뜻으로 사용되었다.

Listen and Talk A-4

B: Excuse me. ❶Where is the History Museum?

G: It's ❷on Green Street.

B: ❸How do I get there?

G: Go straight three blocks and turn right. You'll see it on your right. ❹It's next to the bank.

B: Thank you so much.

❶ Where is + 장소?: 길을 물어볼 때 사용하는 표현이다.

❷ 도로상에 있다는 표현으로 전치사 on을 사용한다.

❸ get+부사 = get to+명사: ~에 도착하다

❹ next to ~: 전치사구로 '~ 옆에'라는 뜻이다.

Review 2

G: Excuse me. ❶Where's Tom's Bakery?

B: It's on Main Street. ❷It's next to the bank.

G: Thanks.

❶ Where is + 장소?: 길을 물어볼 때 사용하는 표현이다.

❷ next to ~: 전치사구로 '~ 옆에'라는 뜻이다.

● 다음 우리말과 일치하도록 빈칸에 알맞은 말을 쓰시오.

Listen and Talk A-1

B: Excuse me. I'm _____ _____ the Star Mall.

G: Go _____ two blocks and _____ left. It'll be the first building _____ your right.

B: Oh, _____ _____. Thank you.

G: You're welcome.

해석

B: 실례합니다. Star Mall을 찾고 있어요.
G: 두 블록을 곧장 가서, 왼쪽으로 도세요. 오른쪽 첫 건물일 거예요.
B: 오, 알겠어요. 감사해요.
G: 천만에요.

Listen and Talk A-2

B: Excuse me. _____ the bookstore?

G: There's one _____ _____ the post office.

B: _____ do I _____ there?

G: _____ straight one block and turn right. It'll _____ _____ your right.

B: Thank you!

B: 실례합니다. 서점이 어디 있나요?
G: 우체국 맞은편에 하나 있어요.
B: 그곳에 어떻게 가나요?
G: 한 블록을 곧장 가서 오른쪽으로 도세요. 오른쪽에 있을 거예요.
B: 감사합니다!

Listen and Talk A-3

B: Excuse me. _____ do I _____ _____ the police station?

G: _____ _____ three blocks and turn left. It'll be on your right.

B: Oh, I see.

G: It's _____ the bakery _____ the school. You _____ miss it.

B: Thank you!

B: 실례합니다. 경찰서에 어떻게 가나요?
G: 세 블록을 곧장 걸어가서 왼쪽으로 도세요. 오른쪽에 있을 거예요.
B: 오, 알겠어요.
G: 경찰서는 빵집과 학교 사이에 있어요. 꼭 찾을 거예요.
B: 감사합니다!

Listen and Talk A-4

B: Excuse me. _____ is the Histroy Museum?

G: It's _____ Green Street.

B: _____ do I _____ there?

G: Go straight three blocks _____ turn right. You'll see it on your right. It's _____ _____ the bank.

B: Thank you so much.

B: 실례합니다. 역사박물관은 어디에 있나요?
G: Green가에 있어요.
B: 거기에 어떻게 가나요?
G: 세 블록 곧장 가서 오른쪽으로 도세요. 오른쪽에 보일 거예요. 은행 옆에 있어요.
B: 정말 감사합니다.

Listen and Talk B

A: _____ is the school?

B: It's _____ Green Street. It's _____ _____ the hospital.

A: _____ _____ _____ get there?

B: _____ _____ three blocks and turn left. It'll be on your right.

A: Thank you.

Listen and Talk C

B: Hello. May I help you?

G: Yes, please. I'm _____ _____ Green Park.

B: OK. Please _____ _____ this map. We are here.

G: Oh, I see. So how do I _____ _____ the park?

B: Go _____ two blocks and turn left. It's _____ _____ the train station.

G: I see. The African Music Concert is there, right?

B: Yes, it is. It's _____ to start at 4 p.m. at the Star Concert Stage.

G: Right, and _____ is the stage?

B: It's _____ the north gate of the park.

G: OK, thank you!

Review 1

M: Excuse me. _____ do I _____ to the bookstore?

W: Walk straight two blocks and _____ left. It'll be on your right.

M: That _____ _____. Thank you.

Review 2

G: Excuse me. Where's Tom's Bakery?

B: It's _____ Main Street. It's _____ _____ the bank.

G: Thanks.

해석

A: 학교가 어디 있니?
B: Green가에 있어. 병원 맞은편에 있어.
A: 거기에 어떻게 가니?
B: 세 블록을 곧장 가서 왼쪽으로 돌아. 오른쪽에 있을 거야.
A: 고마워.

B: 안녕하세요. 도와 드릴까요?
G: 네, 저는 Green 공원을 찾고 있어요.
B: 네. 이 지도를 보세요. 우리는 여기에 있어요.
G: 아, 그렇군요. 그럼 공원에 어떻게 가나요?
B: 두 블록을 곧장 가서 왼쪽으로 도세요. 공원은 기차역 맞은편에 있어요.
G: 알겠어요. 거기서 아프리카 음악 콘서트가 열리죠, 맞나요?
B: 네. 오후 4시에 Star Concert 무대에서 시작할 예정이에요.
G: 맞아요, 그런데 무대는 어디에 있나요?
B: 공원 북문 근처에 있어요.
G: 네, 감사해요!

M: 실례합니다. 서점에 어떻게 가나요?
W: 두 블록을 곧장 걸어가서 왼쪽으로 도세요. 오른쪽에 있을 거예요.
M: 쉽네요. 고마워요.

G: 실례합니다. Tom's Bakery는 어디에 있나요?
B: Main가에 있어요. 은행 옆에 있어요.
G: 감사합니다.

01 다음 질문의 의도로 알맞은 것을 고르시오.

> Q. Excuse me. How can I get to the post office?

① 길 묻기   ② 안부 묻기
③ 허락 요청하기   ④ 반복 요청하기
⑤ 확인 요청하기

02 다음 대화를 바르게 배열한 것은?

> (A) Walk straight three blocks and turn right. It's on your left.
> (B) How do I get there?
> (C) Thanks.
> (D) There's one across from the post office.
> (E) Where is a bookstore?

① (B) – (A) – (C) – (D) – (E)
② (B) – (A) – (D) – (E) – (C)
③ (E) – (A) – (C) – (D) – (B)
④ (E) – (B) – (C) – (A) – (D)
⑤ (E) – (D) – (B) – (A) – (C)

03 다음 질문에 대한 대답으로 알맞은 것을 고르시오.

> Q. Excuse me. Where is the bank?

① I'm looking for the bank.
② Go straight two blocks and turn left.
③ Hurry up.
④ I don't go to the bank.
⑤ I work at a bank.

04 다음 우리말에 해당하는 표현을 주어진 단어를 이용하여 영어로 쓰시오.

> 은행에 가는 방법을 알려주시겠어요?
> (how, do, get, the bank)

➡ _____

[01~02] 다음 대화를 읽고, 물음에 답하시오.

G: Excuse me. _____ ⓐ _____
B: It's on Main Street. ⓑ그것은 은행 옆에 있어요.
G: Thanks.

01 위 대화의 빈칸 ⓐ에 들어갈 말로 알맞은 것은?

① Where did you go?
② What are you doing now?
③ Where's Tom's Bakery?
④ Where are you going?
⑤ How can I help you?

서답형
02 위 대화의 밑줄 친 ⓑ의 우리말에 맞게 주어진 단어를 이용하여 영어로 쓰시오.

> it, next, the bank

➡ _____

03 다음 대답이 나올 수 있는 질문으로 알맞은 것을 고르시오.

> Go straight one block and turn left.

① Are you going to the library?
② How can I get to the library?
③ Do you like to go to the library?
④ How often do you go to the library?
⑤ What do you usually do in the library?

[04~05] 다음 대화를 읽고, 물음에 답하시오.

B: Excuse me. (A)Where is the History Museum?
G: It's _____ ⓐ _____ Green Street.
B: How do I get there?
G: Go straight three blocks and turn right. You'll see it _____ ⓑ _____ your right. It's next to the bank.
B: Thank you so much.

04 위 대화의 밑줄 친 (A)와 바꾸어 쓸 수 없는 것은?

① I'm looking for the History Museum.
② How do I get to the History Museum?
③ Can you show me the way to the History Museum?
④ Shall we go to the History Museum?
⑤ Can you tell me where the History Museum is?

05 위 대화의 빈칸 ⓐ, ⓑ에 공통으로 들어갈 말로 알맞은 것은?

① in　　　② of　　　③ about
④ for　　　⑤ on

[06~07] 다음 대화를 읽고, 물음에 답하시오.

A: Where is the school?
B: It's on Green Street. It's ⓐ맞은편에 the hospital.
A: _____
B: Go straight three blocks and turn left. It'll be on your right.
A: Thank you.

06 위 대화의 빈칸에 들어갈 말로 알맞은 것은?

① Where is Green Street?
② How do I get there?
③ Thank you so much.
④ Can you go to the school?
⑤ May I help you?

서답형
07 위 대화의 밑줄 친 ⓐ의 우리말에 맞는 표현을 영어로 쓰시오.

➡ _____

08 다음 문장이 자연스러운 대화가 되도록 알맞은 순서대로 배열한 것을 고르시오.

> (A) Go straight one block and turn right.
> (B) Thanks a lot.
> (C) How can I get to the police station?

① (A) – (B) – (C)   ② (B) – (A) – (C)
③ (B) – (C) – (A)   ④ (C) – (A) – (B)
⑤ (C) – (B) – (A)

서답형

09 다음 대화의 괄호 안에서 알맞은 것을 고르시오.

> A: I'm (looking for / looking at) Green Park.
> B: OK. Please (look for / look at) this map. We are here.

[10~11] 다음 대화를 읽고, 물음에 답하시오.

> B: Excuse me. (A)_____
> G: Walk straight three blocks and turn left. It'll be on your right.
> B: Oh, I see.
> G: It's between the bakery and the school. (B)_____
> B: Thank you!

중요

10 위 대화의 빈칸 (A)에 들어갈 질문을 주어진 단어를 이용하여 영어로 쓰시오.

> how, I, get, the police station

➡ _____

11 위 대화의 빈칸 (B)에 들어갈 말로 알맞은 것을 모두 고르시오.

① That sounds easy.
② It's easy to find.
③ This is my first time here.
④ I'm sorry. I can't help you.
⑤ You can't miss it.

중요

12 다음 중 짝지어진 대화가 어색한 것을 고르시오.

① A: How can I get to the bank?
   B: Go straight two blocks.
② A: Where is the hospital?
   B: It's on Pine Street.
③ A: Where is the stage?
   B: It's near the north gate of the park.
④ A: How do I get to the airport?
   B: You arrived too late.
⑤ A: Where are you now?
   B: I'm in front of the pet shop.

13 다음 대화의 빈칸에 알맞은 것은?

> B: Excuse me. Where's the bookstore?
> G: There's one across from the post office.
> B: How do I _____ there?
> G: Go straight one block and turn right. It'll be on your right.
> B: Thank you!

① take   ② reach   ③ get
④ catch   ⑤ come

서답형

14 다음 우리말에 맞게 주어진 단어를 이용하여 영어로 쓰시오.

> 꽃가게 옆에 하나 있어요.
> (there, one, next, the flower shop)

➡ _____

01 다음 그림을 보고 질문에 알맞은 답을 쓰시오.

M: How do I get to the bookstore?

W: _____

_____

02 다음 그림을 보고 문장을 완성하시오.

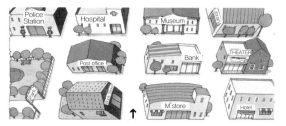

(1) The bank is _____ _____ the store.

(2) The hospital is _____ the police station _____ the museum.

(3) The theater is _____ _____ the bank.

03 다음 대화를 읽고 질문에 답하시오.

Boy: Excuse me. Where is the History Museum?

Girl: It's on Green Street.

Boy: How do I get there?

Girl: Go straight three blocks and turn right. You'll see it on your right. It's next to the bank.

Boy: Thank you so much.

Q: What is the boy looking for? Answer in Korean.

➡ _____

04 다음 대화의 밑줄 친 우리말에 맞게 주어진 단어를 이용하여 빈칸을 채우시오.

B: Excuse me. (A)경찰서에 어떻게 가나요? (how, get to, the police station)

G: Walk straight three blocks and turn left. (B)오른쪽에 있을 거예요. (it, be, on)

B: Oh, I see.

G: (C)빵집과 학교 사이에 있어요. (between, the bakery, the school) You can't miss it.

B: Thank you!

(A) _____

(B) _____

(C) _____

05 다음 그림을 보고 〈보기〉를 참고하여 대화를 완성하시오.

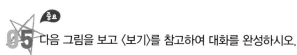
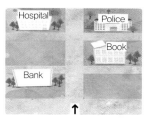

┤ 보기 ├

A: Excuse me. I'm looking for the bank.

B: Go straight one block and turn left. It's on your left.

A: Thanks a lot.

A: Excuse me. I'm _____ _____ the hospital.

B: Go straight _____ _____ and turn _____. It's on your _____.

A: Thanks a lot.

Grammar

① have to

> • You **have to** be patient. 너는 인내심을 가져야 한다.
> • She **has to** be kind to her friends. 그녀는 친구들에게 친절해야 한다.

- 'have to + 동사원형'은 '~해야 한다'라는 뜻으로 의무를 나타내며, 'must + 동사원형'으로 바꿔 쓸 수 있다.
  - I **have to** finish the work today. 나는 오늘 그 일을 끝내야만 한다.
    = I **must** finish the work today.

- **have to의 부정문**
  have to의 부정문은 'do/does/did not+have to'로 하며 '~할 필요가 없다'라는 의미를 갖는다. 또한 'need not+동사원형'으로 바꿔 쓸 수 있다. 반면에 must not은 '~하면 안 된다'라는 의미로 '금지'를 나타낸다.
  - You **don't have to** finish the work today. 너는 그 일을 오늘 끝낼 필요가 없다.
  - You **must not** finish the work today. 너는 그 일을 오늘 끝내서는 안 된다.

- **have to의 의문문**
  have to의 의문문은 do 동사를 이용하여 'do/does/did+주어+have to'의 형태로 쓴다.
  - **Does** he **have to** buy a ticket? 그는 표를 사야 합니까?

- must는 '~임에 틀림없다'라는 의미로 강한 추측을 나타낼 수도 있다.
  - He **must** be a fool to say such a foolish thing. 그는 그런 바보같은 말을 하다니 바보임에 틀림없다.

핵심 Check

1. 다음 두 문장이 같은 뜻이 되도록 빈칸에 알맞은 말을 쓰시오.

   You have to take a bath.

   ➡ You _____ take a bath.

2. 다음 괄호 안에서 알맞은 것을 고르시오.

   (1) Roger (have / has) to do it right now.

   (2) We (had / have) to wait almost an hour for our food last night.

② to부정사의 부사적 용법(목적)

- She worked hard **to help** her family. 그녀는 가족을 돕기 위해 열심히 일했다.
- He went to France **to study** French. 그는 프랑스어를 공부하기 위해 프랑스에 갔다.

■ 'to+동사원형' 형태의 to부정사가 부사처럼 쓰여, 목적의 의미를 나타내어 '~하기 위해서, ~하러'라는 의미를 가진다. 이외에도 부사적 용법의 to부정사는 (감정의) 원인, 조건, 결과, 이유나 판단의 근거 등을 나타낸다.

■ 목적의 뜻을 보다 분명하게 하기 위하여 to부정사 앞에 in order나 so as를 쓰기도 한다.

■ **to부정사의 부사적 용법**

(1) 원인

 • He was pleased **to hear** the news. 그는 그 소식을 듣고 기뻤다.

 (to hear the news가 was pleased의 원인을 나타낸다.)

(2) 판단의 근거

 • He must be stupid **to say** such a silly thing. 그는 그런 바보 같은 것을 말하다니 멍청함에 틀림없다.

 (to say such a silly thing이 be stupid로 판단하는 근거를 나타낸다.)

(3) 결과

 • She grew up **to be** a novelist. 그녀는 자라서 소설가가 되었다.

 (to be a novelist가 grew up의 결과를 나타낸다.)

(4) 형용사 수식

 • This problem is a little too hard **to solve**. 이 문제는 풀기가 좀 까다롭다.

 (to solve가 형용사 hard를 수식한다.)

핵심 Check

3. 다음 괄호 안에서 알맞은 것을 고르시오.

 (1) They have to produce a lot of milk (to win / winning) a prize.

 (2) He used his computer (find / to find) the information.

 (3) Jordan came to Korea to (learn / learns) *taegwondo*.

4. 다음 우리말에 맞게 괄호 안의 단어를 바르게 배열하시오.

 그는 사과를 좀 사려고 그 가게에 갔다.

 (he, to, buy, the shop, to, some apples, went)

 ➡ _____

01 다음 문장에서 어법상 <u>어색한</u> 부분을 바르게 고쳐 쓰시오.

(1) She have to clean her room.

_____ ➡ _____

(2) Study hard getting a good grade.

_____ ➡ _____

(3) Sunny have to finish her homework last night.

_____ ➡ _____

(4) He went to the station took the train.

_____ ➡ _____

02 다음 우리말과 일치하도록 주어진 단어를 이용하여 빈칸에 알맞은 말을 쓰시오.

take a taxi 택시를 타다
take care of ~을 돌보다

(1) 그는 지난 일요일에 택시를 타야만 했다.

➡ He _____ _____ _____ a taxi last Sunday. (take)

(2) Minsu는 어제 그 일을 끝낼 필요가 없었다.

➡ Minsu _____ _____ _____ _____ the work yesterday.
(finish)

(3) 우리는 살기 위해서 먹는다.

➡ We eat _____ _____. (live)

(4) 그는 배우가 되기 위해 Hollywood로 갔다.

➡ He went to Hollywood _____ _____ an actor. (be)

(5) 그녀는 아이들을 돌보기 위해 많은 일을 해야 했다.

➡ She _____ _____ _____ lots of work _____ _____
care of her children. (do, take)

03 다음 중 어법상 알맞은 것을 고르면?

essay 수필, 평론

① Karen has to clean the house.

② Is Mina have to water the plant?

③ Sonya must walks the dog.

④ Cathy doesn't have to wash the dishes yesterday.

⑤ She must have to read the essay.

01 다음 중 어법상 옳은 것은?

① Sera have to take an umbrella as it is raining.
② Jessica hasn't to finish the report today.
③ When we cross the road, have we to stop at the red light?
④ You don't have to start right from the beginning.
⑤ Visitors have not to park their cars in front of the gate.

02 다음 중 어법상 어색한 문장은?

① I need a bike to ride.
② Harry went to the gallery to watch the works of Gogh.
③ I never thought him to be capable of passing the exam.
④ I exercise every day to stay healthy.
⑤ Elise bought some toys in order to gave them to her daughter.

03 Choose a grammatically incorrect dialogue.

① A: Why did Suji go to the shopping mall?
   B: She went to the shopping mall to have a snack.
② A: Do you have to return the book to the library today?
   B: Yes, I had to return it today.
③ A: What did you do last Sunday?
   B: We went to the park to take a walk.
④ A: Did you go to the shopping mall last night?
   B: Yes, I had to go there. I had nothing to eat.
⑤ A: Why did Mina come here yesterday?
   B: She came here to meet her sister.

04 다음 밑줄 친 부분의 쓰임이 나머지 넷과 다른 것은?

① Marianne studied hard to pass the math test.
② I'm saving money to buy an electric bike.
③ My mom wants me to be a fashion designer.
④ He waited in line to enjoy the rides in the amusement park.
⑤ She went to the store to buy some cookies.

05 다음 우리말에 맞게 영작한 것을 고르시오.

> Stephanie는 내일 일찍 일어날 필요가 없다.

① Stephanie doesn't have to get up early tomorrow.
② Stephanie has to get up early tomorrow.
③ Stephanie must get up early tomorrow.
④ Stephanie mustn't get up early tomorrow.
⑤ Stephanie need to get up early tomorrow.

06 다음 문장의 의미가 가장 자연스러운 것은?

① Scarlet went to the bus stop to have lunch.
② James went to the library to take the plane.
③ Jennifer went to the store to buy some bread.
④ Emma went to the gym to get some sleep.
⑤ Bruce went to the theater to take the train.

서답형

07 다음 문장에서 어법상 잘못된 것을 바르게 고치시오.

(1) Susie have to always work from morning to night.

_____ ➡ _____

(2) Are you have to finish the work by five today?

_____ ➡ _____

(3) We haven't to go to school on Saturdays.

_____ ➡ _____

(4) We have to wait for long to buy the concert ticket yesterday.

_____ ➡ _____

중요

08 다음 괄호 안에서 알맞은 말을 고르시오.

(1) People eat (to live / live), not live (to eat / eat).

(2) She turned on the computer (to find / finding) the information.

(3) Ulrich went to England (to study / to studying) English.

(4) What could she do (to celebrate / celebrate) her mother's birthday?

09 다음 밑줄 친 부분이 바르게 쓰인 것은?

① They have to are healthy.

② To earn more money, Johnson had to have two jobs at that time.

③ Kyle and his brother has to walk fast to get there in time.

④ Sharon have to brush her teeth morning and night.

⑤ I has to go to school right now.

중요

10 다음 밑줄 친 부분의 쓰임이 다른 하나를 고르시오.

① Mike went to the shopping mall to buy shoes.

② We need the map to find the right direction.

③ Eugene got up early to take the first train.

④ Jack was very glad to do it again in front of everyone.

⑤ Chloe went to the library to read some books.

11 다음 중 밑줄 친 부분의 쓰임이 〈보기〉와 같은 것은?

┌─ 보기 ─┐
Jane studied very hard to succeed as an animal scientist.
└────────┘

① I often listen to music to relax.

② Samson is not the kind of man to be trusted.

③ To be fair and truthful is important to me.

④ What do you want to do this weekend?

⑤ Few live to be one hundred years old.

12 다음 빈칸에 알맞은 것은?

┌──────────────────────────────┐
│ Matilda studies hard _____ a good grade. │
└──────────────────────────────┘

① get   ② gets

③ got   ④ getting

⑤ to get

서답형

13 have to를 이용하여 다음 두 문장이 같은 의미가 되도록 빈칸에 알맞은 말을 쓰시오.

(1) Wayne must solve the math problems before he goes back home.

➡ Wayne ＿＿＿＿＿＿＿＿ the math problems before he goes back home.

(2) You need not go to hospital.

➡ You ＿＿＿＿＿＿＿＿ go to hospital.

중요

14 다음 중 빈칸에 to를 쓸 수 있는 것을 모두 고르시오.

① Dave was surprised ＿＿＿＿ the news.

② They were happy ＿＿＿＿ get one more chance.

③ William is fond ＿＿＿＿ drawing comic cartoons.

④ The players practiced hard ＿＿＿＿ prepare for the World Cup games.

⑤ I apologize ＿＿＿＿ bothering you.

서답형

15 다음 두 문장을 한 문장으로 만들 때 빈칸을 알맞게 채우시오.

> • Famela went to the shopping mall.
> • Famela wanted to buy a skirt.

➡ Famela went to the shopping mall ＿＿＿＿

＿＿＿＿＿＿＿＿＿＿＿.

16 다음 대화의 빈칸에 알맞은 대답을 모두 고르시오.

> A: Do I have to do it over again?
> B: ＿＿＿＿＿＿＿＿＿＿＿

① Yes, you do.

② Yes, you have.

③ Yes, I have to.

④ No, you don't have to.

⑤ No, you don't have.

서답형

17 다음 문장을 부정문으로 바꿀 때 빈칸에 알맞은 말을 쓰시오.

> Jane has to finish her homework by this Friday.
> ➡ Jane ＿＿＿＿＿＿＿＿＿＿＿ her homework by this Friday.

서답형

18 다음 우리말에 맞도록 괄호 안에 주어진 어휘를 이용하여 과거시제로 영작하시오.

(1) Bob은 첫 버스를 타려고 일찍 일어났다.
(get, catch, the first)

➡ ＿＿＿＿＿＿＿＿＿＿＿＿

(2) Joe는 파티에서 그녀를 만나서 기뻤다.
(glad, meet)

➡ ＿＿＿＿＿＿＿＿＿＿＿＿

중요

19 다음 중 밑줄 친 부분의 쓰임이 나머지 넷과 다른 것은?

① He ran to catch the train.

② Mia wants to have a guinea pig.

③ She lived to be 90.

④ I used the computer to find information on the Internet.

⑤ Jim was glad to reach home.

01 다음 밑줄 친 말을 대신할 수 있는 것을 쓰시오.

> You <u>must</u> relax and quit smoking.

➡ _____

02 다음 두 문장을 to부정사를 써서 한 문장으로 만드시오.

(1) • Amy was pleased.
　　• She got A⁺ on the math test.

➡ _____

(2) • Nicole went to France.
　　• She wanted to learn French.

➡ _____

(3) • I study science very hard.
　　• I wish to be an animal doctor.

➡ _____

03 have to를 이용해서 내일 자신이 하지 않아도 되는 일을 하나 쓰시오.

➡ _____
　_____

04 다음 주어진 문장과 같은 뜻이 되도록 빈칸을 적절히 채우시오.

> I use my smartphone to send texts to my friends.

(1) I use my smartphone _____ _____ _____ send texts to my friends.
(2) I use my smartphone _____ _____ _____ send texts to my friends.
(3) I use my smartphone _____ _____ _____ I _____ send texts to my friends.

05 다음 문장에서 어법상 <u>잘못된</u> 것을 고쳐 문장을 다시 쓰시오.

(1) Susan doesn't had to clean her house yesterday.

➡ _____

(2) Nick and Dick has to do some more exercise losing weight.

➡ _____
　_____

(3) Has she to go see a doctor?

➡ _____

06 다음 〈보기〉의 동사를 골라 어법에 맞게 빈칸을 채우시오.

┤ 보기 ├
> get　　take　　give

(1) I bought a pretty dress _____ _____ it to my daughter.
(2) I had to wait almost an hour _____ _____ the ticket.
(3) Mike had to hurry _____ _____ the 9:30 train to London.

07 다음 문장과 같은 의미가 되도록 빈칸에 알맞은 말을 쓰시오.

> We don't have to cancel the picnic.

(1) We don't _____ _____ cancel the picnic.
(2) We _____ _____ cancel the picnic.

08 다음 문장을 to부정사를 이용한 문장으로 바꿔 쓰시오.

(1) • I went to Sophie's house.
   • I studied with her.

   ➡ _____

(2) • Amy went to the theater.
   • She watched the movie, *Avatar*.

   ➡ _____

(3) • Her grandmother lived.
   • She was 100 when she died.

   ➡ _____

09 다음 문장을 해석하고 must not과 don't have to의 차이를 설명하시오.

(1) You <u>must not</u> attend the meeting.
(2) You <u>don't have</u> to attend the meeting.

(해석) (1) _____
       (2) _____
(차이) _____
      _____

10 다음 문장을 to부정사를 이용하여 바꿔 쓸 때 빈칸에 알맞은 말을 쓰시오.

(1) Jiho went to the shopping mall for a shirt.
   ➡ Jiho went to the shopping mall _____ _____ a shirt.

(2) Wesley ran to his office because he didn't want to be late for the meeting.
   ➡ Wesley ran to his office _____ _____ _____ _____ for the meeting.

(3) We sat down at the table for breakfast.
   ➡ We sat down at the table _____ _____ breakfast.

11 다음 우리말을 괄호 안에 주어진 어휘를 이용하여 영작하시오.

(1) 어려움에 처한 사람들을 돕기 위해 네가 부자일 필요는 없다. (have, rich, help, people in need)

   ➡ _____

(2) Linda는 그녀의 친구들을 만나려고 그 쇼핑 몰로 갔다. (the shopping mall, meet)

   ➡ _____

(3) Eddie는 얼마나 오래 병원에 있어야 하니? (long, have, be)

   ➡ _____

(4) Abigail은 숙제를 하기 위하여 그 컴퓨터를 사용해야만 했다. (have, use)

   ➡ _____

12 다음 문장에서 어법상 잘못된 것을 찾아 고쳐 다시 쓰시오. (6 군데)

> The goats in the show doesn't have to be big, but they had to be healthy. They had to producing a lots of milk winning a prize.

➡ _____
_____
_____

Reading

Fun at the State Fair of Texas!

Hi, I'm Eddie Parker. I live in Dallas, Texas. Now, my family and I are at the State Fair of Texas. The fair is over 130 years old, and it's the biggest fair in the USA. I'll show you around. Follow me! Look at the goats here! This is a goat show. My younger brother, Steve, entered it. The goats in the show don't have to be big, but they have to be healthy. They have to produce a lot of milk to win a prize. Steve took good care of his goat, Bonnie. Wow! Steve and Bonnie won a white ribbon, third prize! I'm so proud of them! Now it's lunch time, so we're eating fair food. Mom and Dad are eating nachos and fajitas. They are Tex-Mex food. Tex-Mex food is a combination of food from Texas and Mexico. Dad's face is getting red because his fajita is too spicy. Steve and I are eating corn dogs. They taste great.

state 주
fair 품평회, 박람회
enter 참가하다
healthy 건강한
produce 생산하다
prize 상
combination 조합, 결합
corn dog 콘도그
spicy 양념 맛이 강한, 매운

확인문제

● 다음 문장이 본문의 내용과 일치하면 T, 일치하지 않으면 F를 쓰시오.

1 Eddie Parker lives in Dallas, Texas. ☐

2 The State Fair of Texas is the biggest fair in the world. ☐

3 The goats in the show must be big. ☐

4 Eddie is so proud of Steve and Bonnie. ☐

5 Eddie's mom and dad are eating Tex-Mex food. ☐

6 Tex-Mex food is Mexican food. ☐

7 Eddie's dad's fajita is too spicy, so his face is getting red. ☐

8 Steve and Eddie are eating nachos. ☐

Let's move on to the quilt contest. Quilting has a long tradition. In the
~로 이동하다

past, fabric was expensive. To make a blanket, people had to collect
과거(↔ future)   비싼(↔ cheap) 목적을 나타내는 to부정사

small pieces of fabric and sew them together. Grandma and her friends
= small pieces of fabric

had a quilting bee every week. They had to work on the quilt for the
누비이불을 만드는 모임   매주   노력을 들이다, 일하다

contest for over six months. Look! It's very colorful and unique.
= the quilt

The most exciting part of the day is riding the Texas Star. It's a tall
exciting의 최상급   보어로 쓰인 동명사(= to ride)

Ferris wheel. Wow! Steve and I are now on the top. I'm scared, but the
회전식 관람차   = on the top of Ferris wheel

view is amazing! I love living in Texas and going to the fair.
              love -ing: ~하는 것을 아주 좋아하다   = the State Fair of Texas

Come to the fair some day!
= the State Fair of Texas

quilt 퀼트, 누비이불

contest 대회, 시합

tradition 전통, 관습

fabric 직물, 천

blanket 담요

sew 바느질하다, 꿰매다

unique 독특한, 특별한

Ferris wheel 대회전 관람차

scared 무서워하는, 겁먹은

view 광경, 시야

amazing 놀랄 만한

확인문제

● 다음 문장이 본문의 내용과 일치하면 T, 일치하지 않으면 F를 쓰시오.

1   The quilt contest has a long tradition. ☐

2   In the past, people had to sew small pieces of fabric together to make a blanket. ☐

3   The most exciting part of the day is watching the Texas Star. ☐

4   The Texas Star is a tall Ferris wheel. ☐

● 우리말을 참고하여 빈칸에 알맞은 말을 쓰시오.

1 Fun _____ the State Fair of Texas!

2 Hi, _____ Eddie Parker.

3 I _____ _____ Dallas, Texas.

4 Now, my family and I _____ _____ the State Fair of Texas.

5 The fair _____ _____ 130 years old, and it's _____ _____ _____ in the USA.

6 I'll _____ you _____ .

7 _____ me!

8 _____ _____ the goats here!

9 This is _____ _____ _____ .

10 My younger brother, Steve, _____ _____ .

11 The goats in the show _____ _____ _____ _____ big, but they _____ _____ _____ healthy.

12 They have to produce a lot of milk _____ _____ _____ _____ .

13 Steve _____ _____ _____ _____ _____ his goat, Bonnie.

14 Wow! Steve and Bonnie _____ a white ribbon, _____ _____ !

15 I'm so _____ _____ them!

16 Now it's lunch time, so we're eating _____ _____ .

17 Mom and Dad _____ _____ nachos and fajitas.

1 Texas의 주 품평회를 즐겨요!

2 안녕, 나는 Eddie Parker야.

3 나는 Texas주의 Dallas에 살아.

4 지금, 우리 가족과 나는 텍사스 주 품평회에 와 있어.

5 이 품평회는 130년이 넘었고, 미국에서 가장 큰 품평회야.

6 내가 구경시켜 줄게.

7 따라와!

8 여기 염소들을 봐!

9 이건 염소 쇼야.

10 내 남동생 Steve가 이 쇼에 참가했어.

11 이 쇼의 염소들은 클 필요는 없지만 건강해야 해.

12 염소들은 상을 타기 위해서 많은 우유를 생산해야 해.

13 Steve는 자신의 염소인 Bonnie를 잘 돌봤어.

14 와! Steve와 Bonnie는 3등상인 흰색 리본을 탔어.

15 나는 그들이 매우 자랑스러워!

16 지금은 점심시간이어서 우리는 품평회 음식을 먹고 있어.

17 엄마와 아빠는 나초와 파히타를 먹고 있어.

18 They are _____ _____ .

19 Tex-Mex food is _____ _____ _____ _____ from Texas and Mexico.

20 Dad's face _____ _____ _____ because his fajita is too spicy.

21 Steve and I _____ _____ corn dogs.

22 They _____ _____ .

23 Let's _____ _____ _____ the quilt contest.

24 Quilting has a long _____ .

25 _____ _____ _____ , fabric was _____ .

26 To make a blanket, people _____ _____ _____ small pieces of fabric and _____ them together.

27 Grandma and her friends had _____ _____ _____ every week.

28 They had to _____ _____ the quilt for the contest _____ _____ _____ _____ .

29 Look! It's very _____ and _____ .

30 _____ _____ _____ part of the day is riding the Texas Star.

31 It's a tall _____ _____ .

32 Wow! Steve and I are now _____ _____ _____ .

33 I'm _____ , but the view is _____ !

34 I love _____ in Texas and _____ to the fair.

35 Come to the fair _____ _____ !

18 그것들은 Tex-Mex 음식이야.

19 Tex-Mex 음식은 텍사스 음식과 멕시코 음식이 혼합된 거야.

20 아빠는 파히타가 너무 매워서 얼굴이 빨개지고 있어.

21 Steve와 나는 콘도그를 먹고 있어.

22 맛이 매우 좋아.

23 퀼트 대회로 이동하자.

24 퀼트 만들기는 오랜 전통을 가지고 있어.

25 과거에는 천이 비쌌어.

26 담요를 만들기 위해서 사람들은 작은 천 조각들을 모아서 꿰매 붙여야 했지.

27 할머니와 할머니의 친구들은 매주 퀼트를 만드는 모임을 가지셨어.

28 그분들은 이 대회를 위해서 6개월 이상 퀼트를 만드는 작업을 하셔야 했어.

29 봐! 그 퀼트는 매우 색깔이 화려하고 독특해.

30 오늘의 가장 신나는 부분은 Texas Star를 타는 거야.

31 Texas Star는 높은 회전 관람차야.

32 우와! Steve와 나는 지금 꼭대기에 있어.

33 무섭긴 하지만 전망이 멋져!

34 나는 Texas에 살고 품평회에 가는 것이 매우 좋아.

35 언젠가 품평회에 와라!

● 우리말을 참고하여 본문을 영작하시오.

1 Texas의 주 품평회를 즐겨요!
➡ _____

2 안녕, 나는 Eddie Parker야.
➡ _____

3 나는 Texas주의 Dallas에 살아.
➡ _____

4 지금, 우리 가족과 나는 텍사스 주 품평회에 와 있어.
➡ _____

5 이 품평회는 130년이 넘었고, 미국에서 가장 큰 품평회야.
➡ _____

6 내가 구경시켜 줄게.
➡ _____

7 따라와!
➡ _____

8 여기 염소들을 봐!
➡ _____

9 이건 염소 쇼야.
➡ _____

10 내 남동생 Steve가 이 쇼에 참가했어.
➡ _____

11 이 쇼의 염소들은 클 필요는 없지만 건강해야 해.
➡ _____

12 염소들은 상을 타기 위해서 많은 우유를 생산해야 해.
➡ _____

13 Steve는 자신의 염소인 Bonnie를 잘 돌봤어.
➡ _____

14 와! Steve와 Bonnie는 3등상인 흰색 리본을 탔어.
➡ _____

15 나는 그들이 매우 자랑스러워!
➡ _____

16 지금은 점심시간이어서 우리는 품평회 음식을 먹고 있어.
➡ _____

17 엄마와 아빠는 나초와 파히타를 먹고 있어.
➡ _____

18 그것들은 Tex-Mex 음식이야.

➡ _____

19 Tex-Mex 음식은 텍사스 음식과 멕시코 음식이 혼합된 거야.

➡ _____

20 아빠는 파히타가 너무 매워서 얼굴이 빨개지고 있어.

➡ _____

21 Steve와 나는 콘도그를 먹고 있어.

➡ _____

22 맛이 매우 좋아.

➡ _____

23 퀼트 대회로 이동하자.

➡ _____

24 퀼트 만들기는 오랜 전통을 가지고 있어.

➡ _____

25 과거에는 천이 비쌌어.

➡ _____

26 담요를 만들기 위해서 사람들은 작은 천 조각들을 모아서 꿰매 붙여야 했지.

➡ _____

27 할머니와 할머니의 친구들은 매주 퀼트를 만드는 모임을 가지셨어.

➡ _____

28 그분들은 이 대회를 위해서 6개월 이상 퀼트를 만드는 작업을 하셔야 했어.

➡ _____

29 봐! 그 퀼트는 매우 색깔이 화려하고 독특해.

➡ _____

30 오늘의 가장 신나는 부분은 Texas Star를 타는 거야.

➡ _____

31 Texas Star는 높은 회전 관람차야.

➡ _____

32 우와! Steve와 나는 지금 꼭대기에 있어.

➡ _____

33 무섭긴 하지만 전망이 멋져!

➡ _____

34 나는 Texas에 살고 품평회에 가는 것이 매우 좋아.

➡ _____

35 언젠가 품평회에 와라!

➡ _____

[01~03] 다음 글을 읽고, 물음에 답하시오.

Hi, I'm Eddie Parker. I live in Dallas, Texas. Now, my family and I are at the State Fair of Texas. The fair is over 130 years old, and ⓐ it's the biggest fair in the USA. I'll show you around. Follow me!

서답형

01 위 글의 밑줄 친 ⓐit이 가리키는 것을 본문에서 찾아 영어로 쓰시오.

➡ _____

서답형

02 다음 빈칸 (A)와 (B)에 알맞은 어구를 넣어 the State Fair of Texas에 대한 소개를 완성하시오.

> It started _____(A)_____ 130 years ago and it is _____(B)_____ than any other fair in the USA.

(A) _____ (B) _____

03 위 글의 뒤에 올 내용으로 가장 알맞은 것을 고르시오.

① 세계의 유명한 품평회를 소개하는 글
② 텍사스 주 품평회에 참가하는 방법
③ 품평회에 대한 사람들의 관심
④ 텍사스 주 품평회를 소개하는 글
⑤ 품평회의 역사와 유래

[04~06] 다음 글을 읽고, 물음에 답하시오.

Look at the goats here! This is a goat show. My younger brother, Steve, entered it. The goats in the show don't have to be big, but they have to be healthy. They have to produce a lot of milk to win a prize. Steve took good care of his goat, Bonnie. Wow! Steve and Bonnie won a white ribbon, third prize! I'm so proud of them!

I = Eddie

위 글의 내용과 일치하지 <u>않는</u> 것은?

① Eddie's younger brother entered the goat show.
② To enter the show, the goats must be big.
③ To enter the show, the goats must be healthy.
④ To win a prize, the goats must produce a lot of milk.
⑤ Eddie's younger brother won third prize.

05 위 글의 목적으로 알맞은 것을 고르시오.

① to introduce Steve and Bonnie
② to advertise the State Fair of Texas
③ to describe Steve's goat, Bonnie
④ to discuss the State Fair of Texas
⑤ to introduce a goat show

서답형

06 다음 문장에서 위 글의 내용과 <u>다른</u> 부분을 찾아서 고치시오.

> Eddie is so proud of the goat show.

➡ _____

[07~08] 다음 글을 읽고, 물음에 답하시오.

Now ⓐit's lunch time, so we're eating fair food. Mom and Dad are eating nachos and fajitas. They are Tex-Mex food. Tex-Mex food is a combination of food from Texas and Mexico. Dad's face is getting red (A) [because / because of] his fajita is too spicy. Steve and I (B)[am / are] eating corn dogs. They taste (C)[great / greatly].

I = Eddie

중요

07 위 글의 밑줄 친 ⓐit과 문법적 쓰임이 같은 것을 고르시오.

① Did you see it?
② It's impossible to get there in time.
③ It was there that I met her yesterday.
④ It's two miles from here to the beach.
⑤ I make it a rule to get up early.

서답형

08 위 글의 괄호 (A)~(C)에서 어법상 알맞은 것을 골라 쓰시오.

(A)_____ (B)_____ (C)_____

[09~11] 다음 글을 읽고, 물음에 답하시오.

Let's move on to the quilt contest. (①) Quilting has a long tradition. (②) To make a blanket, people had to collect small pieces of fabric and sew ⓐthem together.

(③) Grandma and her friends had a quilting bee every week. (④) They had to work on the quilt for the contest for over six months. (⑤) Look! It's very colorful and unique.

09 위 글의 흐름으로 보아, 주어진 문장이 들어가기에 가장 적절한 곳은?

In the past, fabric was expensive.

① ② ③ ④ ⑤

10 위 글을 읽고 대답할 수 없는 질문은?

① Was fabric cheap in the past?
② To make a blanket, what did people have to collect?
③ How often did Grandma and her friends have a quilting bee?
④ How long did Grandma and her friends have to work on the quilt for the contest?
⑤ Did Grandma and her friends win the quilt contest?

서답형

11 위 글의 밑줄 친 ⓐthem이 가리키는 것을 본문에서 찾아 쓰시오.

➡ _____

[12~14] 다음 글을 읽고, 물음에 답하시오.

The most ⓐexcited part of the day is (A) riding the Texas Star. ⓑIts a tall Ferris wheel. Wow! Steve and I are now on the top. I'm ⓒscaring, but the view is ⓓamazed!

I love living in Texas and ⓔto go to the fair. Come to the fair some day!

12 위 글의 밑줄 친 ⓐ~ⓔ 중 어법상 틀린 개수를 고르시오.

① 1개 ② 2개 ③ 3개 ④ 4개 ⑤ 5개

13 위 글의 마지막 부분에서 알 수 있는 'I'의 심경으로 가장 알맞은 것을 고르시오.

① bored ② afraid
③ nervous ④ disappointed
⑤ satisfied

14 위 글의 밑줄 친 (A)riding과 문법적 쓰임이 다른 것을 모두 고르시오.

① Was she playing the piano then?
② Washing the dishes isn't easy.
③ She finished reading the book.
④ I saw him entering the room.
⑤ He is good at making model cars.

[15~18] 다음 글을 읽고, 물음에 답하시오.

(A)Seochon is full of fun things. You can go to Tongin Market. ⓐIt's famous for oil Tteokbokki, so you have to go there (B)to try ⓑit. There are also many traditional Korean houses. You can walk around to see ⓒthem.
Come visit us in Seochon. You'll have so much fun!

15 위 글의 밑줄 친 (A)를 다음과 같이 바꿔 쓸 때 빈칸에 알맞은 말을 쓰시오.

> Seochon _____ _____ _____ fun things.

16 위 글의 밑줄 친 ⓐ, ⓑ, ⓒ가 가리키는 것을 본문에서 찾아 각각 쓰시오.

ⓐ _____ ⓑ _____
ⓒ _____

17 서촌의 명소 두 곳을 다음과 같이 정리하고자 한다. 빈칸 ①과 ②에 들어갈 알맞은 단어를 본문에서 찾아 쓰시오.

- You can enjoy oil Tteokbokki at ① _____ _____.
- You can walk around to see lots of ② _____ _____ _____.

18 위 글의 밑줄 친 (B)to try와 용법이 다른 것을 모두 고르시오.

① He worked hard to pass the test.
② She tried to solve the problem.
③ My sister came to see me yesterday.
④ She went abroad to study physics.
⑤ I want something to write with.

[19~20] 다음 글을 읽고, 물음에 답하시오.

Look at the goats here! This is a goat show. My younger brother, Steve, (A)[entered / entered into] it. The goats in the show (B)[doesn't / don't] have to be big, but they have to be healthy. They have (C)[produced / to produce] ⓐa lot of milk to win a prize. Steve took good care of his goat, Bonnie. Wow! Steve and Bonnie won a white ribbon, third prize! I'm so proud of them!

I = Eddie

19 위 글의 괄호 (A)~(C)에서 어법상 알맞은 것을 골라 쓰시오.

(A)_____ (B)_____ (C)_____

20 위 글의 밑줄 친 ⓐa lot of와 바꿔 쓸 수 없는 말을 모두 고르시오.

① lots of ② many

③ a number of ④ plenty of

⑤ much

[21~22] 다음 글을 읽고, 물음에 답하시오.

Now it's lunch time, so we're eating (A)[fair / fare] food. Mom and Dad are eating nachos and fajitas. (B)[It is / They are] Tex-Mex food. Tex-Mex food is a (C)[combination / communication] of food from Texas and Mexico. Dad's face is getting red because his fajita is too spicy. Steve and I are eating corn dogs. They taste great.

I = Eddie

21 위 글의 제목으로 알맞은 것을 고르시오.

① The Biggest Fair in the USA!

② Enjoy Tex-Mex Food

③ Customs from Texas and Mexico

④ Come to the State Fair of Texas!

⑤ How to Enjoy Spicy Food

22 위 글의 괄호 (A)~(C)에서 문맥이나 어법상 알맞은 것을 골라 쓰시오.

(A)_____ (B)_____ (C)_____

[23~25] 다음 글을 읽고, 물음에 답하시오.

Let's move on to the quilt contest. Quilting has a long tradition. In the past, fabric was expensive. ⓐTo make a blanket, people had to collect small pieces of fabric and sew it together.

①Grandma and her friends had a quilting bee every week. ②There are many quilting bees in America. ③They had to work on the quilt for the contest for over six months. ④ Look! ⑤It's very colorful and unique.

23 위 글의 밑줄 친 ⓐ에서 어법상 틀린 부분을 찾아 고치시오.

_____ ➡ _____

24 위 글의 ①~⑤ 중에서 전체 흐름과 관계 없는 문장은?

① ② ③ ④ ⑤

25 퀼트 담요의 유래를 다음과 같이 정리하고자 한다. 빈칸 (A)와 (B)에 들어갈 알맞은 단어를 본문에서 찾아 쓰시오. (필요한 경우 형태를 바꾸시오.)

In the past, people ___(A)___ small pieces of fabric together to make a blanket because fabric was ___(B)___ .

(A)_____ (B)_____

[26~27] 주어진 글 다음에 이어질 글의 순서로 가장 적절한 것을 고르시오.

26 Now it's lunch time, so we're eating fair food.

(A) Mom and Dad are eating nachos and fajitas. They are Tex-Mex food.

(B) Dad's face is getting red because his fajita is too spicy. Steve and I are eating corn dogs. They taste great.

(C) Tex-Mex food is a combination of food from Texas and Mexico.

① (A) – (C) – (B) ② (B) – (A) – (C)
③ (B) – (C) – (A) ④ (C) – (A) – (B)
⑤ (C) – (B) – (A)

27 Look at the goats here! This is a goat show. My younger brother, Steve, entered it.

(A) They have to produce a lot of milk to win a prize. Steve took good care of his goat, Bonnie.

(B) Wow! Steve and Bonnie won a white ribbon, third prize! I'm so proud of them!

(C) The goats in the show don't have to be big, but they have to be healthy.

① (A) – (C) – (B) ② (B) – (A) – (C)
③ (B) – (C) – (A) ④ (C) – (A) – (B)
⑤ (C) – (B) – (A)

[28~30] 다음 글을 읽고, 물음에 답하시오.

Hi, I'm Eddie Parker. I live in Dallas, Texas. Now, my family and I (A)[am / are] at the State Fair of Texas. The ⓐfair is over 130 years old, and (B)[it's / its] the biggest fair in the USA. I'll (C)[see / show] you around. Follow me!

서답형

28 위 글의 괄호 (A)~(C)에서 문맥과 어법상 알맞은 낱말을 골라 쓰시오.

(A)_____ (B)_____ (C)_____

29 위 글의 밑줄 친 ⓐfair와 같은 의미로 쓰인 것을 고르시오.

① She has always been fair.
② Let's take the kids to the fair.
③ She has long fair hair.
④ It's a fair and beautiful day.
⑤ My hometown is a fair-sized town.

서답형

30 다음 질문에 대한 알맞은 대답을 완전한 문장으로 쓰시오. (6단어)

Q: What is the biggest fair in the USA?

➡ _____

[31~32] 다음 글을 읽고, 물음에 답하시오.

Look at the goats here! This is a goat show. My younger brother, Steve, entered it. ⓐ쇼에 참가하는 염소들은 클 필요는 없지만, 건강해야만 한다. They have to produce a lot of milk ⓑto win a prize. Steve took good care of his goat, Bonnie. Wow! Steve and Bonnie won a white ribbon, third prize! I'm so proud of them!

I = Eddie

서답형

31 위 글의 밑줄 친 @의 우리말에 맞게 주어진 어구를 이용하여 16 단어로 영작하시오.

> in the show, big, but, healthy

➡ _____

_____

32 위 글의 밑줄 친 ⓑto win과 to부정사의 용법이 같은 것을 고르시오.

① He ran fast to catch the bus.
② I'm glad to meet her.
③ He awoke to find himself famous.
④ She must be rich to buy the bag.
⑤ He would be happy to pass the test.

[33~35] 다음 글을 읽고, 물음에 답하시오.

@Now it's lunch time, as we're eating fair food. Mom and Dad are eating nachos and fajitas. ⓑThey are Tex-Mex food. Tex-Mex food is a combination of food from Texas and Mexico. ⓒ파히타의 양념 맛이 너무 강해서 아빠의 얼굴이 빨개지고 계셨다. Steve and I are eating corn dogs. They taste great.

I = Eddie

서답형

33 위 글의 밑줄 친 @에서 문맥상 낱말의 쓰임이 적절하지 않은 것을 찾아 알맞게 고치시오.

_____ ➡ _____

서답형

34 위 글의 밑줄 친 ⓑThey가 가리키는 것을 본문에서 찾아 쓰시오.

➡ _____

서답형

35 위 글의 밑줄 친 ⓒ의 우리말에 맞게 주어진 어구를 이용하여 11 단어로 영작하시오.

> get, too spicy

➡ _____

_____

[36~38] 다음 글을 읽고, 물음에 답하시오.

Let's move on to the quilt contest. @ Quilting has a short tradition. In the past, fabric was expensive. To make a blanket, ⓑ 사람들은 작은 천 조각들을 모아 그것들을 함께 꿰매어야 했다.

Grandma and her friends had a quilting bee every week. They had to work on the quilt for the contest for over six months. Look! It's very colorful and unique.

서답형

36 위 글의 밑줄 친 @에서 문맥상 어색한 부분을 찾아 고치시오.

_____ ➡ _____

서답형

37 위 글의 밑줄 친 ⓑ의 우리말에 맞게 한 단어를 보충하여, 주어진 어휘를 알맞게 배열하시오.

> and / pieces / had to / together / small / collect / fabric / them / people / of

➡ _____

_____

서답형

38 다음 빈칸 (A)와 (B)에 알맞은 단어를 넣어 할머니와 할머니의 친구들이 만든 퀼트 작품에 대한 소개를 완성하시오.

> Every week Grandma and her friends had (A)_____ _____ _____ and worked on the very colorful and (B)_____ quilt for the contest for over half a year.

[01~03] 다음 글을 읽고, 물음에 답하시오.

Look at the goats here! This is a goat show. My younger brother, Steve, entered it. The goats in the show don't have to be big, but they have to be healthy. They have to produce a lot of milk to win a prize. Steve _____ ⓐ _____ his goat, Bonnie. Wow! Steve and Bonnie won a white ribbon, third prize! I'm so proud of ⓑthem!

I = Eddie

01 다음 문장의 빈칸 (A)와 (B)에 알맞은 단어를 넣어 염소 쇼에 출전할 수 있는 염소의 자격에 대한 설명을 완성하시오.

Though the goats in the show __(A)__ not be big, they __(B)__ not be unhealthy.

(A)_____ (B)_____

02 아래 주어진 문장의 밑줄 친 부분과 같은 뜻이 되도록 위 글의 빈칸 ⓐ에 알맞은 말을 쓰시오.

Steve looked after his goat, Bonnie, well.

➡ _____

03 위 글의 밑줄 친 ⓑthem이 가리키는 것을 본문에서 찾아 쓰시오.

➡ _____

[04~06] 다음 글을 읽고, 물음에 답하시오.

Now it's lunch time, so we're eating _____ ⓐ _____ food. Mom and Dad are eating nachos and fajitas. They are Tex-Mex food. ⓑTex-Mex 음식은 텍사스 음식과 멕시코 음식이 혼합된 거야. Dad's face is getting red because his fajita is too spicy. Steve and I are eating corn dogs. They taste great.

I = Eddie

04 주어진 영영풀이를 참고하여 빈칸 ⓐ에 철자 f로 시작하는 단어를 쓰시오.

an event where there are, for example, displays of goods and animals, and amusements, games, and competitions

➡ _____

05 위 글의 밑줄 친 ⓑ의 우리말에 맞게 한 단어를 보충하여, 주어진 어휘를 배열하시오.

of / Texas and Mexico / a / is / from / food / Tex-Mex food

➡ _____
_____

06 위 글의 내용을 다음과 같이 정리하고자 한다. 빈칸에 들어갈 알맞은 단어를 본문에서 찾아 쓰시오.

Eddie's family are eating _____ like nachos and fajitas for lunch.

➡ _____

[07~09] 다음 글을 읽고, 물음에 답하시오.

Let's move on to the quilt contest. Quilting has a long tradition. In the past, fabric was expensive. ⓐTo make a blanket, people had to collect small pieces of fabric and sew them together.

Grandma and her friends had a quilting bee every week. ⓑ그분들은 이 대회를 위해서 6개월 이상 퀼트를 만드는 작업을 하셔야 했어. Look! It's very ⓒcolor and unique.

07 위 글의 밑줄 친 ⓐ를 다음과 같이 바꿔 쓸 때 빈칸에 알맞은 말을 쓰시오.

> People had to collect small pieces of fabric and sew them together _____ _____ _____ they _____ make a blanket.

08 위 글의 밑줄 친 ⓑ의 우리말에 맞게 주어진 어휘를 이용하여 14 단어로 영작하시오.

> work on the quilt, over

➡ _____

_____

09 위 글의 밑줄 친 ⓒ를 알맞은 형으로 고치시오.

➡ _____

[10~12] 다음 글을 읽고, 물음에 답하시오.

Look at the goats here! This is a goat show. My younger brother, Steve, entered it. ⓐ The goats in the show have to be big, but ⓑ they don't have to be healthy. They have to produce a lot of milk to win a prize. ⓒSteve는 자신의 염소인 Bonnie를 잘 돌봤어. Wow! Steve and Bonnie won a white ribbon, third prize! I'm so proud of them!   I = Eddie

10 위 글의 밑줄 친 ⓐ와 ⓑ에서 문맥상 낱말의 쓰임이 적절하지 않은 것을 찾아 알맞게 고치시오.

> ⓐ _____ ➡ _____
> ⓑ _____ ➡ _____

11 위 글의 밑줄 친 ⓒ의 우리말에 맞게 한 단어를 보충하여, 주어진 어휘를 알맞게 배열하시오.

> care / Steve / , / his / of / goat / took / Bonnie

➡ _____

12 다음 질문에 대한 알맞은 대답을 쓰시오. (5단어)

> Q: What was the third prize of the goat show?

➡ _____

After You Read

COME TO THE STATE FAIR OF TEXAS!

Goat Show

To win a prize, the goats have to be healthy and produce a lot of milk.
부사적 용법(목적)　　　　　　= must　　　　　　　　= much

Fair Food

Enjoy Tex-Mex food, a combination of food from Texas and Mexico. Try the

nachos and fajitas!

Quilt Contest

Come and see the beautiful quilts! Quilting has a long tradition.
= Come to see

Texas Star

The view is amazing from the top of this Ferris wheel.

구문해설　• prize: 상　• healthy: 건강한　• produce: 생산하다　• combination: 조합

• tradition: 전통　• amazing: 놀라운

Around the World

1. Maryland State Fair: Horse racing is popular in this state. At the fair in this

   state, people can see horse races.

2. Iowa State Fair: This state is famous for butter. For the fair in this state,

   people make a butter cow from about 272 kg of butter.
   　　　　　　　　　　　　　　　～으로 액(= around)

3. Wisconsin State Fair: This state produces the most cheese in the USA. At
   　　　　　　　　　　　　　　　　　　　　much의 최상급

   the fair in this state people can eat many tasty cheese dishes.

구문해설　• horse racing: 경마　• be famous for: ~으로 유명하다　• produce: 생산하다

Think and Write

Seochon is full of fun things. You can go to Tongin Market. It's famous for oil
= be filled with　　　　　　　　　　　　　　　　　　　　　～로 유명하다

Tteokbokki, so you have to go there to try it. There are also many traditional
　　　　　　　　　= must　　부사적 용법(목적)

Korean houses. You can walk around to see them.

Come visit us in Seochon. You'll have so much fun!
= Come to visit = Come and visit

구문해설　• be full of = be filled with: ~로 가득 차 있다　• be famous for: ~로 유명하다

• traditional: 전통적인

해석

STATE FAIR OF TEXAS
로 오세요!
염소 쇼
상을 받기 위해서, 염소들은
건강하고 많은 우유를 생산해
야 합니다.
품평회 음식
Texas와 Mexico에서 온
음식들의 조합인 Tex-Mex
음식을 즐겨요. 나초와 파히
타를 먹어 보세요.
퀼트 대회
오셔서 아름다운 퀼트를 구경
하세요. 퀼트를 만드는 것은
오랜 전통을 가지고 있습니다.
Texas Star
이 대회전 관람차의 정상에서
보는 전망은 정말 멋집니다.

1. Maryland State Fair
이 주에서는 경마가 인기가
있다. 이 주의 품평회에서 사
람들은 경마를 볼 수 있다.

2. Iowa State Fair
이 주는 버터로 유명하다. 이
주의 품평회를 위해서 사람들
은 272kg의 버터로 소를 만
든다.

3. Wisconsin State Fair
이 주는 미국에서 가장 많은
치즈를 생산한다. 이 주의 품
평회에서 사람들은 많은 맛있
는 치즈 요리를 먹을 수 있다.

서촌은 재미있는 것들로 가득
차 있어. 너는 통인 시장에 갈
수 있어. 그곳은 기름 떡볶이
로 유명해서 너는 거기에 그
것을 먹으러 가야 해. 또한 많
은 한국의 전통 가옥이 있어.
너는 그것들을 보기 위해 주
변을 걸을 수 있어. 서촌에 와
서 우리를 방문해. 정말 재미
있을 거야!

영역별 핵심문제

01 다음 주어진 두 단어의 관계가 같도록 빈칸에 알맞은 단어를 쓰시오.

> amazing : surprising = _____ : delicious

02 다음 대화의 빈칸에 들어갈 알맞은 단어를 고르시오.

> B: Excuse me. How do I get to the police station?
> G: Walk straight three blocks and turn left. It'll be on your right. You can't _____ it.
> B: Thank you!

① find   ② catch
③ bring   ④ look
⑤ miss

[03~04] 다음 영영 풀이에 해당하는 것을 고르시오.

03

> costing a lot of money

① cheap   ② high
③ fair   ④ expensive
⑤ amazing

04

> two or more different things that exist together or put together

① combination   ② blanket
③ unique   ④ prize
⑤ culture

05 다음 빈칸에 들어갈 말이 알맞게 짝지어진 것은?

> • How do I _____ the police station?
> • It's across _____ the hospital.

① get – with   ② take – in
③ get to – from   ④ show – from
⑤ get to – with

06 다음 밑줄 친 부분의 뜻이 잘못된 것은?

① Let's move on to the quilt contest. ~로 이동하다
② I'm so proud of them. 매우 자랑스럽다
③ You have to fasten your seat belt. 매다
④ Quilting has a long tradition. 문화
⑤ It's very colorful and unique. 독특한

07 다음 대화의 빈칸에 들어갈 말로 알맞은 것은?

> M: Excuse me. How do I get to the bookstore?
> W: Walk straight two blocks and turn left. It'll be on your right.
> M: _____ Thank you.

① It is interesting.
② How surprising!
③ It's my pleasure.
④ That sounds easy.
⑤ Excuse me?

[08~10] 다음 대화를 읽고, 물음에 답하시오.

Ben: Hello. May I help you?
Jenny: Yes, please. I'm looking for Green Park.
Ben: OK. Please look at this map. We are here. (①)
Jenny: Oh, I see. (②)
Ben: Go straight two blocks and turn left. It's across from the train station.
Jenny: I see. The African Music Concert is there, right? (③)
Ben: Yes, it is. (A)It's going to start at 4 p.m. at the Star Concert Stage. (④)
Jenny: Right, and where is the stage? (⑤)
Ben: It's near the north gate of the park.
Jenny: OK, thank you!

08 위 대화의 ①~⑤ 중 주어진 문장이 들어갈 위치로 알맞은 것은?

> So how do I get to the park?

①   ②   ③   ④   ⑤

09 위 대화의 밑줄 친 (A)가 가리키는 것을 찾아 쓰시오.

➡ _____

10 위 대화의 내용으로 알맞지 <u>않은</u> 것은?

① Ben은 Green Park로 가는 길을 알고 있다.
② Jenny는 Green Park로 가기 위해 두 블록 곧장 가서 왼쪽으로 돌아야 한다.
③ Jenny는 Green Park로 가기 위해 기차역에서 길을 건너야 한다.
④ Jenny가 Green Park로 가는 목적은 아프리카 음악 콘서트를 보기 위해서이다.
⑤ Jenny는 Ben과 콘서트를 같이 보러 가기로 했다.

11 다음 중 짝지어진 대화가 <u>어색한</u> 것은?

① A: Where's the bookstore?
   B: There's one across from the post office.
② A: How do I get to the bank?
   B: Go straight one block and turn right.
③ A: How do I get to the post office?
   B: It'll be on your right.
④ A: Can you show me the way to the police station?
   B: Sorry, but this is my first time here.
⑤ A: I'm looking for the bank.
   B: Go straight three blocks and you'll see it on your left.

12 다음 대화의 내용과 일치하지 <u>않는</u> 것은?

G: Is there a bookstore here?
W: No, there isn't, but there's one on Green Street.
G: How do I get there?
W: Look at this map. You're here. Go straight two blocks and turn right. It'll be on your right.
G: OK, thanks.

① The girl wants to know where a bookstore is.
② There is a bookstore on Green Street.
③ They are looking at a map.
④ The woman gives the girl directions to the bookstore.
⑤ The woman wants to give the girl the map.

13 다음 중 어법상 어색한 것을 고르면?

① Kate have to walk the dog.
② You have to fasten your seat belt.
③ Harry went to the theater to watch a movie.
④ Does Sam have to hand in the science report today?
⑤ I didn't have to get up early in the morning yesterday.

14 다음 두 문장이 의미가 같도록 빈칸에 알맞은 것을 고르시오.

> Karen was disappointed because she heard you were absent.
> = Karen was disappointed _____ you were absent.

① hear   ② hears   ③ heard
④ hearing   ⑤ to hear

15 다음 괄호 안에서 알맞은 것을 고르시오.

(1) He (hasn't to / doesn't have to) work on weekends.
(2) Bella (had to / has to) help her mom last week.
(3) (Is / Does) Rob have to solve the problem by himself?

16 다음 밑줄 친 부분의 쓰임이 나머지 넷과 다른 것은?

① They have to produce a lot of milk to win a prize.
② Eric was very sad to hear the sad news from her.
③ Mike must be a fool to say such a stupid thing.
④ Sean went to Europe never to return home.
⑤ She needed some books to read while traveling by train.

17 다음 문장을 지시대로 바꿔 쓰시오.

(1) You have to bring your lunch to the picnic. (부정문으로)
    ➡ _____

(2) Melanie has to make a speech in front of other students. (의문문으로)
    ➡ _____
       _____

18 다음 〈보기〉의 밑줄 친 부분과 쓰임이 같은 것은?

> ┤ 보기 ├
> I get up early to jog for my health.

① I want to visit Tibet someday.
② I'm thirsty. Please give me something to drink.
③ He ran very fast in order not to miss the bus.
④ Andy grew up to be a doctor.
⑤ My plan is to visit Jejudo this winter.

19 다음 밑줄 친 부분과 바꿔 쓸 수 있는 것은?

> Tomorrow is Saturday. You <u>don't need</u>
> <u>to</u> get up early.

① cannot   ② need not   ③ will not

④ must not   ⑤ should not

20 다음 그림을 참고하고 주어진 어휘를 이용하여 빈칸을 알맞게 채우시오.

> You _____ _____
> _____ paper and
> glass in different
> boxes. (put)

21 다음 중 어법에 맞는 것은?

① Cathy visited the library borrowing some books.

② She went to the store to buy some drink.

③ Minsu goes to the park plays badminton with his friend.

④ Emma got up early to catching the first train.

⑤ I use my smartphone make a call.

22 다음 문장에서 어법상 어색한 것을 바르게 고치시오.

> Chris has to be foolish to cancel the nice party.

_____ ➡ _____

[23~25] 다음 글을 읽고, 물음에 답하시오.

> Look at the goats here! This is a goat show. My younger brother, Steve, entered it. The goats in the show don't have to be big, but they have to be (A)[health / healthy]. They have to produce (B)[a little / a lot of] milk to win a prize. Steve took good care of his goat, Bonnie. Wow! Steve and Bonnie won a white ribbon, (C)[three / third] prize! I'm so ⓐ of them!
>
> I = Eddie

23 위 글의 괄호 (A)~(C)에서 문맥이나 어법상 알맞은 것을 골라 쓰시오.

(A)_____ (B)_____ (C)_____

24 위 글의 빈칸 ⓐ에 들어갈 알맞은 말을 고르시오.

① ashamed   ② nervous

③ proud   ④ anxious

⑤ scared

25 위 글을 읽고 대답할 수 <u>없는</u> 질문은?

① Where is Eddie now?

② Do the goats have to be big in the show?

③ Do the goats have to be healthy in the show?

④ How many times has Steve entered the goat show?

⑤ Did Steve care for Bonnie well?

[26~29] 다음 글을 읽고, 물음에 답하시오.

Now it's lunch time, so we're eating fair food. Mom and Dad are eating nachos and fajitas. They are Tex-Mex food. Tex-Mex food is a combination of food from Texas and Mexico. ⓐDad's face is getting red because his fajita is too sweet. Steve and I are eating corn dogs. ⓑThey taste great.

I = Eddie

26 위 글의 내용과 일치하지 않는 것은?

① Eddie의 가족은 품평회 음식을 먹고 있다.
② Eddie는 나초와 파히타를 먹고 있다.
③ 나초와 파히타는 Tex-Mex 음식이다.
④ 아빠의 얼굴이 빨개지고 있다.
⑤ Steve와 Eddie는 콘도그를 먹고 있다.

27 위 글의 밑줄 친 ⓐ에서 문맥상 낱말의 쓰임이 적절하지 않은 것을 찾아 알맞게 고치시오.

_____ ➡ _____

28 위 글의 밑줄 친 ⓑThey가 가리키는 것을 본문에서 찾아 쓰시오.

➡ _____

29 위 글의 분위기로 가장 알맞은 것을 고르시오.

① boring   ② calm
③ serious   ④ disappointing
⑤ festive

[30~32] 다음 글을 읽고, 물음에 답하시오.

Let's move ___ⓐ___ to the quilt contest. Quilting has a long tradition. In the past, ⓑfabric was expensive. To make a blanket, people had to collect small pieces of fabric and sew them together.

Grandma and her friends had a quilting bee every week. They had to work ___ⓐ___ the quilt ___ⓒ___ the contest ___ⓒ___ over six months. Look! It's very colorful and unique.

30 위 글의 빈칸 ⓐ와 ⓒ에 들어갈 단어가 바르게 짝지어진 것은?

① to – from   ② on – for
③ in – for   ④ to – on
⑤ on – by

31 위 글의 밑줄 친 ⓑ와 바꿔 쓸 수 있는 단어를 철자 c로 시작하여 쓰시오.

➡ _____

32 다음 질문에 대한 알맞은 대답을 쓰시오. (5단어)

> Q: How often did Grandma and her friends have a quilting bee?

➡ _____

01 다음 빈칸에 들어갈 말이 알맞게 짝지어진 것은?

> • His face is getting red because his food is too _____.
> • This state is _____ for butter.

① cold – care

② hot – proud

③ sweet – smelly

④ spicy – famous

⑤ delicious – look

[02~03] 다음 대화를 읽고, 물음에 답하시오.

B: Hello. May I help you?

G: Yes, please. _____ (A) _____

B: OK. Please look at this map. We are here.

G: Oh, I see. So how do I get to the park?

B: 두 블록 곧장 가서 왼쪽으로 도세요. It's across from the train station.

G: I see. The African Music Concert is there, right?

B: Yes, it is. It's going to start at 4 p.m. at the Star Concert Stage.

G: Right, and _____ (B) _____

B: It's near the north gate of the park.

G: OK, thank you!

02 위 대화의 빈칸 (A)와 (B)에 들어갈 알맞은 것을 〈보기〉에서 찾아 쓰시오. (대·소문자 무시)

> ┤ 보기 ├
> • Where can I find them?
> • Where is the stage?
> • How do I get there?
> • I'm looking for Green Park.
> • It'll be on your right.
> • How do you go there?

(A) _____

(B) _____

03 위 대화의 밑줄 친 우리말에 맞게 주어진 단어를 이용하여 영어로 쓰시오.

> straight, block, left

➡ _____

04 다음 대화의 빈칸에 들어갈 말로 알맞지 <u>않은</u> 것은?

B: Excuse me. Where is the History Museum?

G: It's on Green Street.

B: _____

G: Go straight three blocks and turn right. You'll see it on your right. It's next to the bank.

B: Thank you so much.

① How do I get there?

② Can you show me the way to the History Museum?

③ How can I get to the History Museum?

④ Can you tell me the name?

⑤ Do you know how to go there?

05 다음 문장의 빈칸에 들어갈 알맞은 단어를 주어진 단어를 이용하여 쓰시오.

> • This state produces the most cheese in the USA. People can eat many ⓐ _____ cheese dishes. (taste)
> • There are many ⓑ _____ Korean houses. (tradition)

06 다음 짝지어진 단어의 관계가 같도록 빈칸에 알맞은 말을 쓰시오.

famous : unknown = ill : _____

07 다음 영영 풀이에 해당하는 단어는?

to use a needle and thread to make or repair clothes

① collect　　② design　　③ sew
④ quilt　　　⑤ ride

[08~09] 다음 대화를 읽고, 물음에 답하시오.

A: Where is the school?
B: It's on Green Street.
A: (A)How do I get to there?
B: Go straight three blocks and turn left.
　　　　　　(B)
A: Thank you.

08 위 대화의 밑줄 친 (A)를 어법상 어색한 것을 고쳐 쓰시오.

➡ _____

09 위 대화의 빈칸 (B)에 들어갈 말로 어색한 것은?

① You can't miss it.
② It's between the bank and the police station.
③ It's on the third floor.
④ It's across from the hospital.
⑤ It'll be on your right.

10 다음 대화에서 Bony가 서점을 어떻게 찾아가는지 우리말로 구체적으로 쓰시오.

Bony: Excuse me. Where's the bookstore?
Sori: There's one across from the post office.
Bony: How do I get there?
Sori: Walk straight one block and turn right. It'll be on your right.
Bony: Thank you.

➡ _____
_____

11 다음 밑줄 친 부분의 쓰임이 나머지 넷과 다른 것은?

① Natalie is going to the library to read some science books.
② I went to the park to play basketball with my friends.
③ I would be happy to be with you.
④ David studied really hard not to fail the exam.
⑤ To stay healthy, I exercise every day.

12 다음 중 어법상 어색한 것을 고르시오.

① I don't have to wear my school uniform during the vacation.
② Is Lilian have to hurry up?
③ Emma has to get up early tomorrow.
④ Diana had to study all day long yesterday.
⑤ Jenny and Kate have to clean their room together.

13 다음 중 의미가 다른 하나는? [출제율 90%]

① Elizabeth got up early so that she could catch the first plane.

② Elizabeth got up early so as to catch the first plane.

③ Elizabeth got up early in order to catch the first plane.

④ Elizabeth got up too early to catch the first plane.

⑤ Elizabeth got up early to catch the first plane.

14 다음 우리말에 맞게 괄호 안의 단어를 알맞게 배열하시오. [출제율 95%]

(1) Vivian은 Mike의 무례함을 참을 필요가 없었다.
(Vivian, rudeness, need, stand, didn't, Mike's, to)

➡ _____

(2) Steve는 무엇을 포기해야만 하는가?
(Steve, what, have, give, does, up, to)

➡ _____

15 주어진 두 문장을 한 문장으로 만들 때, 빈칸에 알맞은 말을 쓰시오. [출제율 95%]

• Edward uses his smartphone.
• He sends messages to his friends.
➡ Edward uses his smartphone _____
_____ messages to his friends.

[16~19] 다음 글을 읽고, 물음에 답하시오.

①Now it's lunch time, so we're eating fair food. ②Mom and Dad are eating nachos and fajitas. ③Some Tex-Mex food is very hot. ④ They are Tex-Mex food. ⑤Tex-Mex food is a combination of food ___ⓐ___ Texas and Mexico. ⓑDad's face is getting red because his fajita is too spice. Steve and I are eating corn dogs. They ⓒtaste great.

I = Eddie

16 위 글의 ①~⑤ 중에서 전체 흐름과 관계 없는 문장은? [출제율 95%]

①   ②   ③   ④   ⑤

17 위 글의 빈칸 ⓐ에 들어갈 알맞은 전치사를 고르시오. [출제율 95%]

① from   ② by   ③ in
④ for   ⑤ on

18 위 글의 밑줄 친 ⓑ에서 어법상 틀린 부분을 찾아 고치시오. [출제율 95%]

_____ ➡ _____

19 위 글의 밑줄 친 ⓒtaste와 문법적 쓰임이 같은 것을 고르시오. [출제율 95%]

① I'd like to taste this tea.
② I didn't taste food today.
③ These cakes taste nice.
④ Can you taste anything strange in it?
⑤ Please taste the joy of life!

[20~22] 다음 글을 읽고, 물음에 답하시오.

Look at the goats here! (①) This is a goat show. (②) My younger brother, Steve, entered it. (③) The goats in the show ⓐdon't have to be big, but they have to be healthy. (④) Steve took good care of his goat, Bonnie. (⑤) Wow! Steve and Bonnie won a white ribbon, third prize! I'm so proud of them!

I = Eddie

출제율 90%

20 위 글의 흐름으로 보아, 주어진 문장이 들어가기에 가장 적절한 곳은?

They have to produce a lot of milk to win a prize.

①   ②   ③   ④   ⑤

출제율 90%

21 위 글의 밑줄 친 ⓐ와 바꿔 쓸 수 있는 말을 쓰시오.

➡ _____

출제율 95%

22 다음 빈칸 (A)와 (B)에 알맞은 단어를 넣어 Steve에 대한 소개를 완성하시오.

Steve is Eddie's (A)_____ _____ and he entered a goat show. He took good care of his goat, Bonnie, and they won (B)_____ prize.

(A)_____ (B)_____

[23~26] 다음 글을 읽고, 물음에 답하시오.

Let's move on to the quilt contest. Quilting has a long tradition. ⓐIn the past, fabric was cheap. ⓑTo make a blanket, people (A)[have to / had to] collect small pieces of fabric and (B)[sew / sewed] them together.

Grandma and her friends had a quilting ____ⓒ____ every week. They had to work on the quilt for the contest (C)[during / for] over six months. Look! It's very colorful and unique.

출제율 95%

23 위 글의 밑줄 친 ⓐ에서 문맥상 낱말의 쓰임이 적절하지 않은 것을 찾아 알맞게 고치시오.

_____ ➡ _____

출제율 90%

24 위 글의 밑줄 친 ⓑTo make와 to부정사의 용법이 다른 것을 고르시오.

① To make a blanket was difficult.
② He went to the station to see her off.
③ She stopped to listen to music.
④ I use my computer to do the work.
⑤ She saved money to take a trip.

출제율 95%

25 위 글의 괄호 (A)~(C)에서 어법상 알맞은 것을 골라 쓰시오.

(A)_____ (B)_____ (C)_____

출제율 90%

26 위 글의 빈칸 ⓒ에 들어갈 알맞은 말을 고르시오

① bird   ② bug
③ bat   ④ bee
⑤ butterfly

서술형 실전문제

[01~02] 다음 그림을 보고, 물음에 답하시오.

You are here.

01 위의 그림을 보고 아래의 대화를 완성하시오.

B: Excuse me. _____ _____
_____ _____ to the bookstore?
G: Walk _____ _____ blocks and
_____ _____. It'll be _____
your _____.
B: Oh, I see.
G: It's _____ _____ the hospital.
You can't _____ it.
B: Thank you!

02 위의 그림을 보고 A의 빈칸에 들어갈 알맞은 질문을 주어진 단어를 활용하여 두 문장의 영어로 쓰시오.

A: _____ (look for,
how, get, there)
B: Well, Go straight one block and turn
right. You'll see it on your left.
A: Thank you.

➡ _____

03 다음 문장을 우리말에 맞게 부정문으로 바꿀 때 빈칸에 알맞은 말을 쓰시오.

You have to be afraid of darkness.

(1) You _____ _____ be afraid of
darkness.
(너는 어둠을 두려워해서는 안 된다.)
(2) You _____ _____ _____ be
afraid of darkness.
(너는 어둠을 두려워할 필요가 없다.)

04 다음 우리말을 괄호 안에 주어진 어구를 이용하여 영작하시오.

(1) 나는 학교를 가기 위해 지하철을 탔다.
(take, the subway)
➡ _____
(2) Anne은 그녀의 개를 산책시키러 공원에 갔다.
(walk)
➡ _____

05 다음 문장에서 어법상 어색한 부분을 바르게 고쳐 문장을 다시 쓰시오.

(1) Hugh has not to clean his room today.
➡ _____
(2) Had Bridget to put off the meeting
yesterday?
➡ _____

06 다음 주어진 두 문장을 한 문장으로 만들 때, 빈칸에 알맞은 말을 쓰시오.

(1) • You can walk around.
    • You want to see them.
    ➡ You can walk around _____
        _____ them.

(2) • You have to go there and try it.
    • Because it is famous for oil Tteokbokki.
    ➡ It's famous for oil Tteokbokki, so you have to go there _____ _____ it.

[07~09] 다음 글을 읽고, 물음에 답하시오.

Now it's lunch time, so we're eating fair food. Mom and Dad are eating nachos and fajitas. They are Tex-Mex food. Tex-Mex food is a ___ⓐ___ of food from Texas and Mexico. ⓑDad's face is getting red because his fajita is too spicy. Steve and I are eating corn dogs. They taste great.
        I = Eddie

07 주어진 영영풀이를 참고하여 빈칸 ⓐ에 철자 c로 시작하는 단어를 쓰시오.

a mixture of things

➡ _____

08 위 글의 밑줄 친 ⓑ를 다음과 같이 바꿔 쓸 때 빈칸에 알맞은 말을 쓰시오.

Dad's face is _____ red

09 위 글의 내용과 일치하도록 다음 빈칸에 들어갈 알맞은 단어를 쓰시오.

Dad's face is getting red _____ _____ his too spicy fajita.

➡ _____

[10~12] 다음 글을 읽고, 물음에 답하시오.

Seochon is full of ⓐfun things. You can go to Tongin Market. It's famous for oil Tteokbokki, so you have to go ___ⓑ___ to try it. ___ⓒ___ are also many traditional Korean houses. You can walk around to see them. ⓓCome visit us in Seochon. You'll have so much fun!

10 위 글의 밑줄 친 ⓐfun things의 예 두 가지를 본문에서 찾아 우리말로 쓰시오.

① _____
② _____

11 위 글의 빈칸 ⓑ와 ⓒ에 공통으로 들어갈 알맞은 말을 쓰시오. (대・소문자 무시)

➡ _____

12 위 글의 밑줄 친 ⓓ를 다음과 같이 바꿔 쓸 때 빈칸에 들어갈 알맞은 한 단어를 쓰시오.

Come _____ visit

창의사고력 서술형 문제

01 다음 주어진 어구를 이용하여 길을 물어보는 4개의 문장을 만드시오.

(A)	(B)	(C)
How do I	looking for	to the hospital
Could you	how to	the way to the school
I am	show me	the tourist information center
Do you know	get	get there

(1) _____

(2) _____

(3) _____

(4) _____

02 다음 조건에 맞게 영작하시오.

조건

ⓐ to부정사의 부사적 용법을 이용해서 자신의 경우에 맞게 두 가지 이상씩.

ⓑ 자신이 집에서

(1) 해야 하는 일과 (2) 하지 않아도 되는 일을 두 개씩.

ⓐ (1) _____

 (2) _____

ⓑ (1) _____

 (2) _____

03 축제 기획하기: 축제의 이름, 시간, 장소 등을 정한 후, 축제를 홍보하는 홍보 자료를 만드시오.

보기

Festival Name: _____

Date/Time: _____

Place: _____

Activities: Swimming and Playing in the Sand

Slogan: _____

단원별 모의고사

01 다음 짝지어진 단어의 관계와 같도록 빈칸에 알맞은 단어를 쓰시오.

> fasten : tie = _____ : afraid

[02~03] 다음 영영풀이에 해당하는 단어를 고르시오.

02

> in a line or direction that is not curved or bent

① tidy   ② strange   ③ straight
④ excellent   ⑤ healthy

03

> frightened of or nervous about something

① scared   ② boring   ③ spicy
④ tasty   ⑤ favorite

04 다음 그림을 보고 Jenny의 질문에 대한 답을 완성하시오.

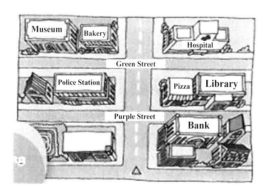

> Jenny: Excuse me. How can I get to the museum?
> ➡ Go straight _____ _____ and turn _____. It's on your _____.

05 다음 중 길을 묻는 표현으로 나머지와 의미가 <u>다른</u> 하나는?

① Where can I find the bookstore?
② How can I get to the bookstore?
③ How long does it take to the bookstore?
④ Can you tell me the way to the bookstore?
⑤ Will you show me the way to the bookstore?

06 다음 그림을 참고하여 대화의 빈칸에 들어갈 말로 알맞은 말을 쓰시오.

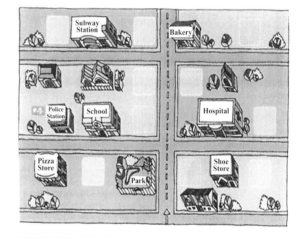

> B: Excuse me. How do I get to the police station?
> G: Walk straight _____ _____ and _____ _____. It'll be _____ _____ _____.
> B: Oh, I see.
> G: It's _____ _____ the school. You can't miss it.
> B: Thank you!

[07~08] 다음 그림의 A~E의 건물 중에서 대화에서 언급한 건물과 그에 해당하는 알파벳을 쓰시오.

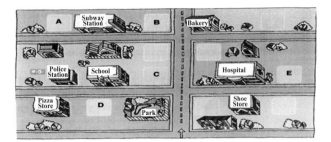

07

A: How do I get to the school?
B: Go straight one block and turn left. It'll be on your right. It's between the police station and the City Hall.
A: Thank you.

➡ _____

08

B: Excuse me. I'm looking for the Star Mall.
G: Go straight two blocks and turn left. It'll be the first building on your right.
B: Oh, I see. Thank you.
G: You're welcome.

➡ _____

[09~11] 다음 대화를 읽고, 물음에 답하시오.

B: Hello. May I help you?
G: Yes, please. I'm ___(A)___ Green Park.
B: OK. Please ___(B)___ this map. We are here.
G: Oh, I see. So how do I get to the park?
B: Go straight two blocks and turn left. 그것은 기차역 맞은편에 있습니다.
G: I see. The African Music Concert is there, right?

B: Yes, it is. It's going to start at 4 p.m. at the Star Concert Stage.
G: Right, and _____(C)_____
B: It's near the north gate of the park.
G: OK, thank you!

09 위 대화의 빈칸 (A)와 (B)에 들어갈 말로 알맞게 짝지어진 것은?

① look for – looking at
② looking at – look for
③ look at – look for
④ looking for – look for
⑤ looking for – look at

10 위 대화의 빈칸 (C)에 들어갈 말로 알맞은 것은?

① when does it start?
② where is the stage?
③ how can I get to the African Music Concert?
④ is there the stage in Green Park?
⑤ do you know if the African Music Concert will be held?

11 위 대화의 밑줄 친 우리말에 맞게 영작하시오.

➡ _____

12 다음 대화의 순서를 알맞게 쓰시오.

(A) Walk straight two blocks and turn left. It'll be on your right.
(B) That sounds easy. Thank you.
(C) Excuse me. How do I get to the bookstore?

➡ _____

13 다음 우리말에 맞게 괄호 안의 단어를 알맞게 배열하시오.

(1) 엄마는 나를 깨우려고 내 방으로 들어오셨다.
(mom, room, entered, wake, my, me, up, to)

➡ _____

(2) 모든 일이 잘 되고 있다는 소식을 들으니 기쁘다.
(I, everything, is, am, hear, pleased, going, that, well, to)

➡ _____

(3) Violet은 자라서 의사가 되었다.
(Violet, a doctor, be, grew, to, up)

➡ _____

14 다음 문장을 부정문으로 바르게 고쳐 쓰시오.

Tim has to go to work this Sunday.

➡ _____

15 다음 밑줄 친 부분의 쓰임이 나머지 넷과 <u>다른</u> 것은?

① It started <u>to rain</u> cats and dogs.
② I study hard <u>to get</u> a good grade.
③ Julie visited the hospital <u>to see</u> a doctor.
④ Robinson went to the store <u>to buy</u> something cold to drink.
⑤ I use my smartphone <u>to find</u> the information on the Internet.

16 다음 중 어법상 <u>어색한</u> 것은?

① Annabel had to wash the dishes.
② Do you have to clean your room?
③ Mel don't have to get up early.
④ Sophie has to finish the work tonight.
⑤ You have to go to bed early.

17 다음 문장에서 어법상 <u>어색한</u> 곳을 찾아 바르게 고치시오.

(1) Rebecca have to wash the dishes for her mom during the vacation.

_____ ➡ _____

(2) Sally went to the park walking her dog.

_____ ➡ _____

(3) Mike was shocked read the accident in the newspaper.

_____ ➡ _____

[18~20] 다음 글을 읽고, 물음에 답하시오.

Look at the goats here! This is a goat show. My younger brother, Steve, entered ⓐit. The goats in the show don't have to be big, but they have to be healthy. ⓑThey have to ___ⓒ___ a lot of milk to win a prize. Steve took good care of his goat, Bonnie. Wow! Steve and Bonnie won a white ribbon, third prize! I'm so proud of them!　　　　I = Eddie

18 위 글의 밑줄 친 ⓐit과 ⓑThey가 가리키는 것을 본문에서 찾아 쓰시오.

ⓐ _____
ⓑ _____

19 위 글의 빈칸 ⓒ에 들어갈 알맞은 말을 고르시오.

① pour　　　　② produce
③ drink　　　　④ heat
⑤ add

20 위 글을 읽고 알 수 <u>없는</u> 것을 고르시오.

① Eddie의 남동생 이름
② 염소 쇼에 출전할 수 있는 염소의 자격
③ Steve의 염소 이름
④ 염소 쇼의 1등상 이름
⑤ Steve가 수상한 상의 등급

[21~22] 다음 글을 읽고, 물음에 답하시오.

Now it's lunch time, so we're eating fair food. (①) Mom and Dad are eating nachos and fajitas. (②) Tex-Mex food is a combination of food from Texas and Mexico. (③) Dad's face is getting red because his fajita is too spicy. (④) Steve and I are ⓐeating corn dogs. (⑤) They taste great.

I = Eddie

21 위 글의 흐름으로 보아, 주어진 문장이 들어가기에 가장 적절한 곳은?

They are Tex-Mex food.

①   ②   ③   ④   ⑤

22 위 글의 밑줄 친 ⓐeating과 문법적 쓰임이 같은 것을 모두 고르시오.

① I like eating corn dogs.
② Eating corn dogs makes me happy.
③ Is he eating corn dogs?
④ My only wish is eating corn dogs.
⑤ Look at the boy eating corn dogs.

23 주어진 글 다음에 이어질 글의 순서로 가장 적절한 것은?

Let's move on to the quilt contest. Quilting has a long tradition.

(A) In the past, fabric was expensive. To make a blanket, people had to collect small pieces of fabric and sew them together.

(B) They had to work on the quilt for the contest for over six months. Look! It's very colorful and unique.

(C) Grandma and her friends had a quilting bee every week.

① (A) – (C) – (B)　② (B) – (A) – (C)
③ (B) – (C) – (A)　④ (C) – (A) – (B)
⑤ (C) – (B) – (A)

[24~25] 다음 글을 읽고, 물음에 답하시오.

Let's move on to the quilt contest. Quilting has a long tradition. In the past, fabric was expensive. To make a blanket, people had to (A)[collect / correct] small pieces of fabric and (B)[saw / sew] them together.

Grandma and her friends had a quilting bee every week. They had to work on the quilt for the contest for over six months. Look! It's very colorful and (C)[common / unique].

24 위 글의 괄호 (A)~(C)에서 문맥상 알맞은 것을 골라 쓰시오.

(A) _____ (B) _____ (C) _____

25 위 글의 내용과 일치하지 않는 것은?

① 퀼트는 오랜 전통을 가지고 있다.
② 과거에는 천이 비쌌다.
③ 할머니는 매주 퀼팅 모임을 가지셨다.
④ 할머니는 6주 동안 퀼트 대회 출품작을 만드셨다.
⑤ 할머니가 출품한 퀼트는 색깔이 매우 다채롭다.

Lesson 3

Ideas for Saving the Earth

의사소통 기능

- 물건 사기 1
  A: How much is this soccer ball?
  B: It's 6 dollars.

- 물건 사기 2
  A: Can I get a discount?
  B: OK. I'll take 1 dollar off.

언어 형식

- 수동태
  This **was made by** Hajun.

- 목적격보어로 to부정사를 취하는 동사
  I **want you to understand** the meaning of "upcycling."

Words & Expressions

교과서

Key Words

- **afraid** [əfréid] 형 두려워하는, 걱정하는
- **almost** [ɔ́ːlmoust] 부 거의
- **anyone** [éniwʌn] 대 누군가, 누가
- **backpack** [bǽkpæk] 명 가방
- **better** [bétər] 형 (good의 비교급) 더 나은
- **blue jeans** 청바지
- **bottom** [bάtəm] 명 아래 부분, 바닥
- **bucket** [bʌ́kit] 명 양동이
- **clock** [klɑk] 명 (벽에 걸거나 실내에 두는) 시계
- **clothes** [klouz] 명 옷, 의복
- **club** [klʌb] 명 동아리, 동호회, 클럽
- **combination** [kὰmbənéiʃən] 명 조합, 결합
- **condition** [kəndíʃən] 명 상태, 조건
- **creative** [kriéitiv] 형 창의적인
- **decorate** [dékərèit] 동 장식하다
- **discount** [dískaunt] 명 할인
- **each** [iːtʃ] 형 각각의 대 각각
- **environment** [inváiərnmənt] 명 환경
- **event** [ivént] 명 행사
- **expensive** [ikspénsiv] 형 비싼
- **explain** [ikspléin] 동 설명하다
- **glasses** [glǽsiz] 명 안경
- **glove** [glʌv] 명 장갑, 글러브
- **help** [help] 동 돕다, 도와주다
- **hold** [hould] 동 개최하다, 열다
- **instrument** [ínstrəmənt] 명 악기
- **interesting** [íntərəstiŋ] 형 흥미로운
- **kit** [kit] 명 (도구장비) 세트, 용구 한 벌

- **knife** [naif] 명 칼
- **large** [lɑːrdʒ] 형 큰
- **lastly** [lǽstli] 부 마지막으로
- **like** [laik] 전 ~처럼, ~와 같이
- **meaning** [míːniŋ] 명 의미
- **musical** [mjúːzikəl] 형 음악의
- **number** [nʌ́mbər] 명 숫자
- **nursing home** 양로원
- **price** [prais] 명 가격
- **purple** [pə́ːrpl] 형 자주색의 명 자주색
- **recycling** [risáikəliŋ] 명 재활용
- **round** [raund] 형 둥근
- **rubber band** 고무 밴드, 고무줄
- **sew** [sou] 동 바느질하다
- **sewing** [sóuiŋ] 명 바느질
- **shoulder** [ʃóuldər] 명 어깨
- **soccer ball** 축구공
- **strap** [stræp] 명 가죽 끈
- **thing** [θiŋ] 명 물건
- **through** [θruː] 전 ~를 통해
- **throw** [θrou] 동 던지다
- **trash** [træʃ] 명 쓰레기
- **T-shirt** 명 티셔츠
- **understand** [ʌndərstǽnd] 동 이해하다
- **upcycle** [ʌ́psaikl] 동 업사이클하다
- **upcycling** [ʌ́psaikliŋ] 명 업사이클링
- **upgrade** [əpgréid] 명 향상, 개선 동 개선하다
- **used** [juːzd] 형 중고의

Key Expressions

- **be about** ~에 관한 것이다
- **become interested in** ~에 관심을 가지다
- **be good for** ~에 좋다
- **be made by** ~에 의해 만들어지다
- **cut off** ~을 자르다
- **for example** 예를 들어
- **get a discount** 할인을 받다
- **hear from** ~로부터 이야기[소식]를 듣다
- **How much+동사+주어 ~?** ~은 얼마예요?
- **I'll take it.** 그것을 살게요.

- **let me think** 잠깐 생각해 볼게
- **let's+동사원형** ~하자
- **look for** ~을 찾다
- **plan to+동사원형** ~할 계획이다
- **sound like+명사** ~처럼 들리다
- **take ~(돈) off** ~을 할인하다, 깎다
- **talk about** ~에 관해 말하다
- **throw away** 버리다
- **want+목적어+to+동사원형** ~가 …하기를 원하다
- **What[How] about+명사 ~?** ~은 어때?

Word Power

※ 서로 반대되는 뜻을 가진 단어

- □ **much** (많은) ↔ **little** (적은)
- □ **afraid** (두려워하는) ↔ **unafraid** (두려워하지 않는)
- □ **expensive** (비싼) ↔ **cheap** (값싼)
- □ **good** (좋은) ↔ **bad** (나쁜)
- □ **used** (중고의) ↔ **new** (새로운)
- □ **interesting** (흥미로운) ↔ **uninteresting** (재미없는)

- □ **large** (큰) ↔ **small** (작은)
- □ **give** (주다) ↔ **take** (받다)
- □ **better** (더 좋은) ↔ **worse** (더 나쁜)
- □ **like** (~와 같이) ↔ **unlike** (~와 달리)
- □ **before** (~ 전에) ↔ **after** (~ 후에)
- □ **upgrade** (개선하다) ↔ **downgrade** (격하시키다)

※ 서로 비슷한 뜻을 가진 단어

- □ **discount** : **reduction** (할인)
- □ **afraid** : **scared** (무서워하는)
- □ **used** : **second-hand** (중고의)
- □ **condition** : **state** (상태)
- □ **understand** : **comprehend** (이해하다)

- □ **trash** : **garbage** (쓰레기)
- □ **fun** : **enjoyable** (재미있는)
- □ **use** : **utilize** (이용하다)
- □ **creative** : **original** (독창적인, 창의적인)
- □ **bucket** : **pail** (양동이)

English Dictionary

- □ **clothes** 옷
  → the things that people wear, such as shirts, coats, trousers, and dresses
  셔츠, 코트, 바지, 드레스와 같은 사람들이 입는 것들

- □ **combination** 조합
  → two or more different things that exist together or put together
  둘 또는 그 이상의 다른 것이 함께 존재하거나 결합되어 있는 것

- □ **creative** 창의적인
  → involving the use of imagination to produce new ideas or things
  새로운 생각이나 물건을 만들기 위해 상상력을 사용하는 것을 포함하는

- □ **decorate** 장식하다
  → to make something look more attractive by putting something pretty on it
  어떤 예쁜 것을 위에 놓음으로써 물건을 더 매력적으로 보이게 만들다

- □ **discount** 할인
  → a reduction in the usual price of something
  어떤 물건의 보통 가격보다 싸진 가격

- □ **environment** 환경
  → the air, water, and land on Earth, which is affected by man's activities
  인간의 활동에 의해 영향을 받는 지구상의 공기, 물과 땅

- □ **explain** 설명하다
  → to tell someone about something in a way that is clear or easy to understand
  이해하기 쉽거나 분명한 방식으로 어떤 것을 말해주다

- □ **instrument** 악기
  → an object used for producing music
  음악을 만들어 내기 위해 사용되는 물건

- □ **interested** 관심 있는
  → giving a lot of attention to something because you want to find out more about it
  더 많이 알고 싶기 때문에 어떤 것에 더 많은 관심을 가지는

- □ **meaning** 의미
  → a particular idea that a word, expression, or sign represents
  어떤 단어나 표현 또는 표시가 나타내는 특정한 생각

- □ **recycling** 재활용
  → the process of treating things that have already been used so that they can be used again
  이미 사용된 것을 다시 사용할 수 있도록 처리하는 과정

- □ **trash** 쓰레기
  → things that you throw away because you no longer want or need them
  당신이 더 이상 원하지 않거나 필요하지 않기 때문에 버리는 것

Step2

서답형

01 다음 짝지어진 두 단어가 관계가 같도록 빈칸에 알맞은 단어를 쓰시오.

> discount : reduction = _____ : state

02 다음 빈칸에 공통으로 들어갈 말은?

> • How do I _____ to the police station?
> • Can I _____ a discount?

① take
② get
③ go
④ make
⑤ look

03 다음 중 밑줄 친 단어의 우리말 뜻이 잘못된 것은?

① I'll take 2 dollars off. 2달러 할인하다
② How about this hat? ~은 어때?
③ I want you to understand the meaning of this word. 의미
④ Students became interested in upcycling. ~에 관심을 가졌다
⑤ We're going to give all the money to a nursing home. 탁아소

[04~05] 다음 영영풀이에 해당하는 단어로 알맞은 것을 고르시오.

04

> an object used for producing music

① meaning
② combination
③ instrument
④ trash
⑤ creative

05

> to make something look more attractive by putting something pretty on it

① sell
② paint
③ sew
④ decorate
⑤ produce

서답형

06 다음 우리말에 맞게 빈칸에 알맞은 단어를 쓰시오.

> 이곳의 모든 것은 오래되었거나 중고다.
> ➡ Everything here is old or _____.

07 다음 빈칸에 들어갈 말로 알맞게 짝지어진 것은?

> • _____ recycling, upcycling is good for the environment.
> • I'm looking _____ a baseball glove.

① Like – for
② Likely – for
③ Unlike – at
④ Unlike – for
⑤ Unlikely – on

08 다음 빈칸에 들어갈 말로 알맞은 것은?

> "Trashion" is a(n) _____ of "trash" and "fashion."

① instrument
② upcycling
③ combination
④ idea
⑤ meaning

01 다음 빈칸에 들어갈 말을 〈보기〉에서 찾아 쓰시오. (필요하면 변형하여 쓰시오.)

┌─── 보기 ───┐
discount   kit   interest   instruments
└──────────┘

(1) Students became _____ in upcycling.
(2) Do you have a sewing _____?
(3) We plan to play the _____ in a concert.
(4) Can I get a _____?

02 다음 제시된 밑줄 친 단어의 철자를 재배열하여 문장의 의미에 맞게 단어를 만든 후, 단어의 뜻을 쓰시오.

(1) My group wants to <u>dohl</u> a trashion show.

  ➡ _____

(2) How <u>chum</u> are the round glasses?

  ➡ _____

(3) Can anyone <u>plainex</u> the meaning of upcycling?

  ➡ _____

(4) Your ideas are so <u>reactive</u>.

  ➡ _____

03 다음 우리말과 같은 표현이 되도록 문장의 빈칸을 채우시오.

(1) 청바지 다리 부분을 잘라라.

  ➡ _____ _____ the legs of the blue jeans.

(2) 트래션 쇼는 재미있을 것 같은데.

  ➡ A trashion show _____ _____ fun!

(3) 나를 버리지 말아줘.

  ➡ Don't _____ me _____!

(4) 그것을 살게요.

  ➡ I'll _____ it.

04 다음 빈칸에 들어갈 말을 〈보기〉에서 골라 알맞은 형태로 고쳐 쓰시오.

┌─── 보기 ───┐
mean   music   take   combine
└──────────┘

(1) My group is going to make _____ instruments from old things.
(2) I want you to understand the _____ of "upcycling."
(3) The word "upcycling" is a _____ of "upgrade" and "recycling."
(4) A: Can I get a discount?
    B: OK. I'll _____ 1 dollar _____.

05 다음 영영풀이에 해당하는 단어를 주어진 철자로 시작하여 쓰시오.

┌──────────────────────────────┐
• t_____ : things that you throw away because you no longer want or need them
• c_____ : two or more different things that exist together or put together
└──────────────────────────────┘

06 다음에 제시된 우리말에 맞는 영어를 쓰고, 각 단어의 첫 글자를 이용하여 단어를 완성하고 그 뜻을 쓰시오.

(1) 다른: _____
(2) 환경: _____
(3) 창의적인: _____
(4) 한 번: _____
(5) 고무: _____
(6) 거의: _____
(7) ~을 통해: _____
(8) 비싼: _____

  ➡ _____

Conversation

1 물건 사기 1

> **A** How much is this soccer ball? 이 축구공은 얼마입니까?
> **B** It's 6 dollars. 6달러예요.

■ 가격 묻고 말하기

"How much is[are] ~?"는 '~은 얼마입니까?'라는 뜻으로, 물건의 가격을 물을 때 사용하는 표현이다. 대답은 "It is[They are] 10 dollars."처럼 구체적인 가격을 넣어 답한다. 가격을 묻는 다른 표현은 How much does it cost?, What's the price?, I want to know the price., Can you tell me the price? 등이 있다.

상점에서 점원이 손님에게 도움이 필요한지 물을 때

- May[Can] I help you? 도와 드릴까요?
  = How may I help you? 도와 드릴까요?
  = What can I do for you? 무엇을 도와 드릴까요?

상점에서 점원이 손님에게 물건을 추천할 때

- How about this[that] one? 이건[저건] 어떠세요?

상점에서 손님이 점원에게 찾는 물건을 말할 때

- I'm looking for ~. 저는 ~을 찾고 있어요. • I'd like to buy ~. 저는 ~을 사고 싶어요.

상점에서 손님이 점원에게 가격을 물어볼 때

- How much is it[are they]? 그것은 얼마입니까?
- What's the price (of it[them])? (그것의) 가격은 얼마입니까?

상점에서 손님이 물건의 구입 의사를 말할 때

- I'll take it[them]. 그것을 살게요.

핵심 Check

1. 다음 대화의 빈칸에 알맞은 말을 쓰시오.

   A: _____ _____ is this blue T-shirt?

   B: It's 10 dollars.

2. 다음 주어진 문장과 같은 의미가 되도록 빈칸에 알맞은 말을 쓰시오.

   How much does it cost? = What's the _____ of it?

② 물건 사기 2

A Can I get a discount? 할인을 받을 수 있나요?

B OK. I'll take 1 dollar off. 네. 1 달러 깎아 드릴게요.

■ 물건을 사면서 할인을 원할 때 사용하는 표현으로 Is[Are] ~ on sale?(~은 할인 판매 중인가요?)
을 사용할 수 있다. 또 어느 정도 할인이 되는지에 대해 언급할 때는 '~달러 할인하여'라는 의미의
~dollar[dollars] off라는 표현을 쓴다.

손님이 점원에게 할 수 있는 표현

• Is this computer on sale? 이 컴퓨터는 할인 판매 중인가요?

• 40% off? 40% 할인하나요?

• (That's) Great! I'll take[buy] it. 좋아요. 그것을 살게요.

점원이 손님에게 할 수 있는 표현

• I'll take 15 dollars off. 15달러 할인해 드릴게요.

• They're 30% off. 그것들은 30% 할인 판매 중입니다.

• It's 40% off the regular price. 정상 가격에서 40% 할인해 드려요.

• It was 100 dollars before, but now it's only 60 dollars. 전에 100달러였는데 지금은 단지 60달러입니다.

• The regular price is 100 dollars, so it's 50 dollars now. 정상 가격이 100달러이니까 지금은 50달러입니다.

핵심 Check

3. 다음 우리말에 맞게 빈칸에 들어갈 알맞은 말은?

이 가방은 할인 판매 중입니다.

= This backpack is _____.

① on sale   ② for sale   ③ sale   ④ to sell   ⑤ selling

4. 다음 빈칸에 들어갈 알맞은 것은?

This red shirt is 50% _____. The regular price is 100 dollars, so it's 50 dollars now.

① up   ② at   ③ out   ④ on   ⑤ off

A. Listen and Talk A-1

G: Excuse me. ❶How much are the round glasses?

M: ❷They're 18 dollars.

G: Hmm. ❸Can I get a discount?

M: No, ❹I'm afraid not. Sorry.

G: ❺That's OK. ❻I'll take them.

G: 실례합니다. 저 동그란 안경은 얼만가요?
M: 그것은 18달러예요.
G: 음. 할인을 받을 수 있을까요?
M: 아니요. 안 될 것 같아요. 미안합니다.
G: 괜찮아요. 그것을 살게요.

❶ How much are ~?는 가격을 물어볼 때 사용하는 표현으로 '~은 얼마입니까?'라는 뜻이다.
❷ They는 복수형 대명사로 the round glasses를 가리킨다.
❸ Can I ~?는 '~할 수 있을까요?'라는 뜻이고, get a discount는 '할인을 받다'는 뜻이다.
❹ 상대방에게 정중하게 미안함을 나타낼 때 사용하는 표현이다.
❺ Sorry에 대한 대답으로 '괜찮아요.'라는 뜻이다. It's okay.를 사용할 수 있다.
❻ take는 '선택하다, 사다'라는 의미다.

Check(√) True or False

(1) The girl is able to get a discount. T ☐ F ☐

(2) The girl will buy the round glasses. T ☐ F ☐

B. Listen and Talk C

B: Wow! There are so many interesting things here.

W: ❶Everything here is old or used. What are you looking for?

B: ❷I'm looking for a clock.

W How about this red clock?

B: How much is it?

W: It's 15 dollars.

B: That's too expensive for me. Can I get a discount?

W: No, ❸I'm afraid not. It's only one year old. It's ❹almost new.

B: Then, how much is this blue clock with the large numbers?

W: It's 10 dollars.

B: Then, I'll take the blue one. Thank you.

B: 와. 여기에는 흥미로운 것들이 많이 있네요.
W: 여기 있는 모든 물건들은 오래되었거나 이미 사용한 물건들입니다. 무엇을 찾고 있나요?
B: 시계를 찾고 있어요.
W: 이 빨간색 시계는 어때요?
B: 얼마예요?
W: 15달러예요.
B: 저에게 너무 비싸군요. 깎아주실 수 있어요?
W: 미안하지만 안 돼요. 그건 일 년밖에 안된 거예요. 거의 새 것입니다.
B: 그럼 숫자가 큰 이 파란 시계는 얼마예요?
W: 10달러예요.
B: 그럼 파란색을 살게요. 감사합니다.

❶ Everything은 단수 취급한다. used는 '중고의'란 뜻으로 second-hand로 바꾸어 쓸 수 있다.
❷ look for ~: '~을 찾다'는 의미로 be동사와 함께 사용되어 현재진행형 구문이다.
❸ 상대방에게 정중하게 미안함을 나타낼 때 사용하는 표현으로 '유감스럽지만 안 됩니다.'란 의미다.
❹ almost는 부사로 '거의'란 뜻이며 형용사 new를 꾸며주고 있다.

Check(√) True or False

(3) The boy can buy the red clock at a discount. T ☐ F ☐

(4) The boy will take the blue clock. T ☐ F ☐

Listen and Talk A-2

M: Hello. ❶May I help you?

G: Yes. ❷I'm looking for a backpack for school.

M: ❸What about this red one? ❹It's 12 dollars.

G: Can I get a discount?

M: OK. ❺I'll take 2 dollars off.

G: ❻That sounds good. I'll take it.

❶ 매장에 손님이 들어올 때 점원이 사용하는 말이다. Can I help you?, What can I do for you?, Do you need any help? 등의 표현이 있다.
❷ '~을 찾고 있다'는 표현으로 'I'm looking for ~'를 사용한다.
❸ 'What about ~?'은 '~은 어떤가요?'라는 표현이고, one은 a backpack을 받는 부정대명사이다.
❹ 가격을 말할 때 사용하는 표현으로 It은 this red backpack을 가리킨다.
❺ take off는 '할인하다'는 뜻이다.
❻ 'sound+형용사'는 '~처럼 들리다'라는 의미로 대화에서 '좋아요', '좋은 생각이야'의 의미로 사용된다.

Listen and Talk A-3

G: Excuse me. ❶How much is this purple T-shirt?

M: ❷It's 10 dollars.

G: That's expensive. Can I get a discount?

M: OK. ❸I'll take 1 dollar off. That'll be 9 dollars.

G: I'll take it, then. Thank you!

❶ How much is[are] ~?는 가격을 물어볼 때 사용하는 표현으로 '~은 얼마입니까?'라는 뜻이다.
❷ It은 this purple T-shirt를 가리킨다.
❸ take off는 '할인하다'는 뜻이다.

Listen and Talk A-4

M: Hello. ❶May I help you?

G: I'm looking for a baseball glove.

M: ❷This one is 15 dollars and it's in good condition.

G: Can I get a discount?

M: OK. I'll take 2 dollars off.

G: Then it's 13 dollars. I'll take it.

❶ Can I help you?, What can I do for you?, Do you need any help? 등의 표현으로 바꾸어 쓸 수 있다.
❷ one은 a baseball glove를 가리키는 부정대명사다. in good condition은 '상태가 좋은'의 의미다.

Listen and Talk B

A: May I help you?

B: Yes. How much is this soccer ball?

A: It's 6 dollars.

B: ❶Can I get a discount?

A: OK. ❷I'll take 1 dollar off.

B: Then that'll be 5 dollars. ❸I'll take it.

❶ '할인해 주시겠습니까?'라는 뜻이다.
❷ take off는 '할인하다'는 뜻이다.
❸ take는 '선택하다, 사다'는 의미다.

Review 1

G: Excuse me. How much is this yellow backpack?

M: It's 18 dollars.

G: Hmm. ❶That's expensive for me. ❷How about this red one?

M: It's 15 dollars.

G: That's a good price. I'll take it.

❶ '그것은 나에게 비싸다'는 뜻이다.
❷ 'How about+명사 ~?'는 '~은 어때요?'라는 뜻이다.

Review 2

W: May I help you?

B: Yes. How much is this blue T-shirt?

W: It's 10 dollars.

B: Can I get a discount?

W: OK. ❶I'll take 2 dollars off.

B: That sounds good. I'll take it.

❶ take off는 '할인하다'는 뜻으로, '2달러 할인해 드리겠습니다.'는 의미다.

Review 3

M: Hello. May I help you?

G: I'm looking for a clock.

M: ❶This one is 15 dollars and it's in good condition.

G: Can I get a discount?

M: OK. I'll take 2 dollars off.

G: Then it's 13 dollars. I'll take it.

❶ one은 a clock을 가리키는 부정대명사다.

● 다음 우리말과 일치하도록 빈칸에 알맞은 말을 쓰시오.

Listen and Talk A-1

G: Excuse me. _____ _____ are the round glasses?

M: They're 18 dollars.

G: Hmm. Can I _____ _____ _____?

M: No, _____ _____ _____. Sorry.

G: That's OK. I'll _____ them.

Listen and Talk A-2

M: Hello. May I help you?

G: Yes. I'm _____ _____ a backpack for school.

M: _____ _____ this red _____? It's 12 dollars.

G: Can I _____ a discount?

M: OK. I'll _____ 2 dollars _____.

G: That sounds good. I'll _____ it.

Listen and Talk A-3

G: Excuse me. _____ _____ _____ this purple T-shirt?

M: It's 10 dollars.

G: That's _____. Can I get a _____?

M: OK. I'll _____ 1 dollar _____. That'll be 9 dollars.

G: I'll _____ _____, then. Thank you!

Listen and Talk A-4

M: Hello. _____ I help you?

G: I'_____ _____ _____ a baseball glove.

M: This _____ is 15 dollars and it's _____ good _____.

G: Can I get a discount?

M: OK. I'll _____ _____ _____ _____.

G: Then it's 13 dollars. I'll take it.

Listen & Talk B

A: May I help you?

B: Yes. _____ _____ is this soccer ball?

A: It's 6 dollars.

B: Can I _____ _____ _____?

A: OK. I'll _____ 1 dollar _____.

B: Then that'll be 5 dollars. I'll _____ _____.

G: 실례합니다. 저 동그란 안경은 얼만가요?
M: 그것은 18달러예요.
G: 음. 할인을 받을 수 있을까요?
M: 아니요, 안 될 것 같아요. 미안합니다.
G: 괜찮아요. 그것을 살게요.

M: 안녕하세요. 도와드릴까요?
G: 네. 저는 학교 갈 때 쓸 배낭을 찾고 있어요.
M: 이 빨간색은 어때요? 12달러입니다.
G: 할인을 받을 수 있을까요?
M: 네. 2달러 깎아 드릴게요.
G: 좋군요. 그것을 살게요.

G: 실례합니다. 이 보라색 티셔츠는 얼마인가요?
M: 10달러예요.
G: 비싸군요. 할인을 받을 수 있을까요?
M: 네. 1달러 깎아 드릴게요. 9달러예요.
G: 그럼 그것을 살게요. 감사해요.

M: 안녕하세요. 도와드릴까요?
G: 저는 야구 글러브를 찾고 있어요.
M: 이건 15달러고, 상태가 좋아요.
G: 할인을 받을 수 있을까요?
M: 네. 2달러 깎아드릴게요.
G: 그럼 13달러네요. 그것을 살게요.

A: 도와드릴까요?
B: 네. 이 축구공은 얼마인가요?
A: 6달러예요.
B: 할인을 받을 수 있을까요?
A: 네. 1달러 깎아 드릴게요.
B: 그러면 5달러겠네요. 그것을 살게요.

Listen and Talk C

B: Wow! There are so many _____ things here.

W: Everything here is old or _____ . What are you _____ _____?

B: I'm looking for a clock.

W: _____ _____ this red clock?

B: How much is it?

W: It's 15 dollars.

B: That's _____ _____ _____ me. Can I get a discount?

W: No, I'm _____ not. It's only one year old. It's almost new.

B: Then, how much is this blue clock _____ the large numbers?

W: It's 10 dollars.

B: Then, I'll _____ the blue _____ . Thank you.

Review 1

G: Excuse me. _____ _____ is this yellow backpack?

M: It's 18 dollars.

G: Hmm. That's _____ _____ me. _____ _____ this red _____?

M: It's 15 dollars.

G: That's a good _____ . I'll take _____ .

Review 2

W: May I help you?

B: Yes. _____ _____ is this blue T-shirt?

W: It's 10 dollars.

B: Can I _____ a discount?

W: OK. I'll _____ 2 dollars _____ .

B: That sounds good. I'll take it.

Review 3

M: Hello. May I help you?

G: I'm _____ _____ a clock.

M: This _____ is 15 dollars and it's _____ _____ _____ .

G: Can I _____ a discount?

M: OK. I'll _____ 2 dollars _____ .

G: Then it's 13 dollars. I'll _____ it.

해석

B: 와! 여기에는 흥미로운 것들이 많이 있네요.

W: 여기 있는 모든 물건들은 오래되었거나 이미 사용한 물건들입니다. 무엇을 찾고 있나요?

B: 시계를 찾고 있어요.

W: 이 빨간색 시계는 어때요?

B: 얼마예요?

W: 15달러예요.

B: 저에게 너무 비싸군요. 깎아주실 수 있어요?

W: 미안하지만 안 돼요. 그건 일 년밖에 안된 거예요. 거의 새 것입니다.

B: 그럼 숫자가 큰 이 파란 시계는 얼마예요?

W: 10달러예요.

B: 그럼 파란색을 살게요. 감사합니다.

G: 실례합니다. 이 노란색 배낭은 얼마인가요?

M: 18달러예요.

G: 음. 그건 저에게 비싸네요. 이 빨간색은 어떤가요?

M: 그건 15달러예요.

G: 좋은 가격이네요. 그것을 살게요.

W: 도와드릴까요?

B: 네. 이 파란 티셔츠는 얼마인가요?

W: 10달러예요.

B: 할인을 받을 수 있을까요?

W: 네. 2달러 깎아 드릴게요.

B: 좋아요. 그것을 살게요.

M: 안녕하세요. 도와드릴까요?

G: 저는 시계를 찾고 있어요.

M: 이것은 15달러이고 상태가 좋아요.

G: 할인을 받을 수 있을까요?

M: 좋아요. 2달러 깎아 드릴게요.

G: 그럼 13달러군요. 그것을 살게요.

01 다음 우리말에 맞도록 빈칸에 들어갈 알맞은 말을 쓰시오.

> 시계를 하나 사려고 합니다.
> ➡ I'm _____ _____ a clock.

02 다음 대화의 밑줄 친 부분과 의미가 같은 것은?

> A: How much are these shoes?
> B: They're 13 dollars.

① What are your favorite shoes?
② What is the size of these shoes?
③ What color are these shoes?
④ Which shoes are the best?
⑤ What is the price of these shoes?

03 다음 대화의 빈칸에 들어갈 말로 가장 적절한 것은?

> W: May I help you?
> B: Yes. How much is this blue T-shirt?
> W: It's 10 dollars.
> B: Can I get a discount?
> W: OK. I'll take 2 dollars off.
> B: That sounds good. _____

① Show me another.   ② I'll take it.
③ Hurry up.   ④ Here you are.
⑤ It's too expensive.

04 다음 우리말에 해당하는 표현에 맞게 주어진 문장의 빈칸을 채워 쓰시오.

> 깎아 줄 수 있어요?
> ➡ Can I _____ a discount?

[01~02] 다음 대화를 읽고, 물음에 답하시오.

G: Excuse me. _____(A)_____ the round glasses?

M: They're 18 dollars.

G: Hmm. Can I get a discount?

M: No, _____(B)_____ Sorry.

G: That's OK. I'll take them.

01 위 대화의 빈칸 (A)에 들어갈 말로 알맞은 것은?

① How much is
② What are for
③ How much are
④ Why are there
⑤ Where are

02 위 대화의 빈칸 (B)에 들어갈 말로 알맞은 것은?

① I want to know the price.
② That's too expensive.
③ You can get a discount.
④ You should buy them.
⑤ I'm afraid not.

03 다음 대답이 나올 수 있는 질문으로 알맞지 <u>않은</u> 것은?

> It's 5,000 won.

① How much does this book cost?
② How much is this book?
③ I want to know the price of this book.
④ Is this book on sale?
⑤ What's the price of this book?

[04~05] 다음 대화를 읽고, 물음에 답하시오.

M: Hello. May I help you?

G: Yes. (A)I'm looking for a backpack for school.

M: What about this red one? It's 12 dollars.

G: Can I get a discount?

M: OK. I'll take 2 dollars ___(B)___.

G: That sounds good. I'll take it.

04 위 대화의 밑줄 친 (A)와 바꾸어 쓸 수 <u>없는</u> 말은?

① I want to buy a backpack for school.
② Where can I get a backpack for school?
③ I'm trying to find a backpack for school.
④ I'd like to buy a backpack for school.
⑤ Do you have any backpacks for school?

05 위 대화의 빈칸 (B)에 들어갈 말로 알맞은 것은?

① in   ② of   ③ about
④ for   ⑤ off

06 다음 주어진 문장에 이어질 대화의 순서로 알맞은 것은?

> May I help you?

> (A) They're 13 dollars.
> (B) Can I get a discount?
> (C) OK. I'll take 2 dollars off.
> (D) Yes. How much are these shoes?

① (A) – (B) – (C) – (D)
② (B) – (A) – (C) – (D)
③ (B) – (C) – (A) – (D)
④ (D) – (A) – (B) – (C)
⑤ (D) – (B) – (A) – (C)

[07~08] 다음 대화를 읽고, 물음에 답하시오.

G: Excuse me. How much is this yellow backpack?
M: It's 18 dollars.
G: Hmm. (A)저에게는 비싸네요. How about this red (B)one?
M: It's 15 dollars.
G: That's a good price. I'll take it.

서답형

07 위 대화의 밑줄 친 (A)의 우리말에 맞게 주어진 단어를 이용하여 영어로 쓰시오.

> that / expensive / for

➡ _____

서답형

08 위 대화의 밑줄 친 (B)의 one이 가리키는 것을 찾아 쓰시오.

➡ _____

09 다음 중 짝지어진 대화가 <u>어색한</u> 것을 고르시오.

① A: How much is it?
   B: It's 15 dollars.
② A: Can I get a discount?
   B: OK. I'll take 1 dollar off.
③ A: Hello. May I help you?
   B: Yes. I'm looking for a backpack.
④ A: Excuse me. How much are these sneakers?
   B: They are $15.
⑤ A: What are you looking for?
   B: I'm looking at a clock.

[10~12] 다음 대화를 읽고, 물음에 답하시오.

B: Wow! There are so many interesting things here.
W: Everything here is old or ___(A)___ . What are you looking for?

B: I'm looking for a clock.
W: How about this red clock?
B: How much is it?
W: It's 15 dollars.
B: That's too expensive for me. Can I get a discount?
W: _____(B)_____ It's only one year old. It's almost new.
B: Then, how much is this blue clock with the large numbers?
W: It's 10 dollars.
B: Then, I'll take the blue one. Thank you.

서답형

10 위 대화의 빈칸 (A)에 들어갈 단어에 대한 영어 설명을 보고 알맞은 단어를 쓰시오.

> dirty or not in good condition any longer as a result of being used

➡ _____

11 위 대화의 빈칸 (B)에 들어갈 말로 알맞은 것은?

① That sounds good.
② No, I'm afraid not.
③ Of course.
④ How about this one?
⑤ This is on sale.

12 위 대화의 내용과 일치하지 <u>않는</u> 것은?

① 두 사람은 중고가게에서 대화중이다.
② B는 시계를 사려고 한다.
③ 15달러는 B가 사기에 비싼 가격이다.
④ 가게 주인은 5달러를 깎아주었다.
⑤ B는 파란색 시계를 10달러에 구입했다.

[01~02] 다음 대화를 읽고, 물음에 답하시오.

Man: Hello. May I help you?

Girl: Yes. I'm looking for a backpack for school.

Man: What about this red one? It's 12 dollars.

Girl: (A)깎아 줄 수 있어요? (can, I)

Man: OK. I'll take 2 dollars off.

Girl: That sounds good. I'll take it.

01 위 대화의 밑줄 친 (A)의 우리말에 맞게 주어진 단어를 이용하여 영어로 쓰시오.

➡ _____

02 Q: How much will the girl pay? (Write a full sentence in English.)

➡ _____

03 다음 대화의 밑줄 친 우리말에 맞게 주어진 단어를 이용하여 빈칸을 채우시오.

> G: Excuse me. (A)이 노란색 배낭은 얼마인가요? (how)
>
> M: It's 18 dollars.
>
> G: Hmm. That's expensive for me. (B)이 빨간색은 어떤가요? (about, one)
>
> M: It's 15 dollars.
>
> G: That's a good price. (C)그걸로 살게요. (take)

(A) _____

(B) _____

(C) _____

04 다음 그림을 참고하여 두 사람이 나누는 대화의 빈칸을 완성하시오.

> B: Wow! There are so many interesting things here.
>
> W: Everything here is old or _____. What are you looking for?
>
> B: I'm looking for a clock.
>
> W: How about this red clock?
>
> B: _____ _____ _____ _____?
>
> W: It's 15 dollars.
>
> B: That's too expensive for me. Can I _____ _____ _____?
>
> W: No, I'm _____ not. It's only one year old. It's almost new.
>
> B: Then, how much is this blue clock with the _____ _____?
>
> W: It's 10 dollars.
>
> B: Then, I'll take the blue one. Thank you.

05 다음 대화의 밑줄 친 우리말에 맞게 영어로 쓰시오.

> G: Can I get a discount?
>
> M: OK. 3달러를 깎아줄게요.
>
> G: Then it's 13 dollars. I'll take it.

➡ _____

Grammar

1 목적격보어로 to부정사를 취하는 동사

> • Sue wants her father **to come** home early. Sue는 아빠가 집에 일찍 오기를 원한다.
> • She asked me **to wait** for her. 그녀는 내게 그녀를 기다리라고 요청했다.

■ 동사(want) 다음에 목적어와 to부정사가 쓰여 '~가 …하는 것을 (원)한다'라는 의미를 나타낸다. 이때 목적어 다음의 to부정사를 목적격보어라고 하고 이런 문장 유형을 5형식이라고 한다.

■ to부정사를 목적격보어로 취하는 동사에는 advise, allow, ask, cause, enable, encourage, expect, force, get, help, order, persuade, teach, tell, want, would like 등이 있다.

   • Mom wants Jane **to study** harder. 엄마는 Jane이 더 열심히 공부하기를 원한다.
   • Mom asked me **to wash** the dishes. 엄마는 내게 설거지를 부탁하셨다.

■ 목적격보어로 쓰인 to부정사의 부정형은 'not to+동사원형'으로 쓴다.

   • I told him **not to go**. 나는 그에게 가지 말라고 말했다.

핵심 Check

1. 다음 괄호 안에서 알맞은 것을 고르시오.

   (1) She wanted me (to buy / buy) her a bag.

   (2) I expected him (to be / being) a soccer player.

   (3) He asked them (to be / be) quiet.

2. 다음 우리말에 맞게 빈칸에 알맞은 말을 쓰시오.

   그는 자기 아이들에게 천천히 걸으라고 말했다.

   ➡ He told his children _____ _____ slowly.

② 수동태

- People planted many trees. 사람들이 많은 나무를 심었습니다. 〈능동태〉
- Many trees **were planted** by people. 많은 나무가 사람들에 의해 심겨졌습니다. 〈수동태〉

■ 수동태는 '주어+be동사+동사의 과거분사+by+행위자'의 형식을 가지며 수동태 문장의 주어 자리에는 능동태 문장의 목적어가 오고, by 다음에는 능동태 문장의 주어를 쓴다. 누가 그 동작을 했는지 중요하지 않거나 잘 모를 때, 수동태 문장으로 표현한다. 수동태는 현재, 과거, 미래 시제로 쓸 수 있고, 'be동사+동사의 과거분사'에서 be동사로 시제를 표현한다.
  - The pizza **was cooked** by my mother. 그 피자는 우리 엄마에 의해 요리되었다.

■ 4형식 문장의 수동태는 간접목적어와 직접목적어 각각을 주어로 하는 수동태가 가능하다. 직접목적어를 주어로 한 수동태에서는 간접목적어 앞에 특정한 전치사를 써야 한다. 전치사 to를 쓰는 동사는 'give, send, tell, teach, show, bring' 등이고, 전치사 for를 쓰는 동사는 'buy, make, choose, cook, get' 등이며, 전치사 of를 쓰는 동사는 'ask, inquire' 등이 있다. 또한 make, buy, read, write 등은 직접목적어를 주어로 하는 수동태만 가능하다.
  - Stella **was given** a book by me. Stella는 나에게서 책 한 권을 받았다.
  - A book **was given** to Stella by me. 책 한 권이 나에 의해 Stella에게 주어졌다.

■ 조동사가 있는 문장의 수동태는 '조동사+be+p.p.' 형식을 갖는다.
  - A flower pot **can be made** by us. 화분이 우리에 의해 만들어질 수 있다.

■ 목적격보어가 원형부정사인 경우, 수동태 문장에서는 to부정사로 바뀐다.
  - He **was made** to do the dishes by his mom. 그는 엄마에 의해 설거지를 하도록 시켜졌다.

■ **by** 이외의 전치사를 사용하는 수동태
  - be interested in ~에 흥미가 있다
  - be covered with ~로 덮여 있다
  - be made of ~로 만들어지다(물리적 변화)
  - be satisfied with ~에 만족하다
  - be filled with ~로 가득 차다
  - be surprised at ~에 놀라다
  - be made from ~로 만들어지다(화학적 변화)
  - be pleased with ~에 기뻐하다

핵심 Check

3. 다음 우리말에 맞게 빈칸에 알맞은 말을 쓰시오.

(1) 그 건물은 10년 전에 지어졌다.

➡ The building _____ _____ 10 years ago.

(2) 이메일이 Andrew에 의해 나에게 보내졌다.

➡ An email _____ _____ _____ me by Andrew.

01 다음 문장에서 어법상 어색한 부분을 바르게 고쳐 쓰시오.

(1) The floor cleans once a week.

_____ ➡ _____

(2) A letter is sent to me yesterday.

_____ ➡ _____

(3) They asked everyone sit down.

_____ ➡ _____

(4) Mom told me to not play computer games.

_____ ➡ _____

02 다음 빈칸에 알맞은 것은?

> The book _____ by Roald Dahl.

① writes ② writing

③ to write ④ was writing

⑤ was written

03 다음 괄호 안의 동사를 어법에 맞게 빈칸에 쓰시오.

(1) They _____ _____ in a car accident. (injure)

(2) The vase _____ _____ by Bill. (break)

(3) I want you _____ _____ happy. (be)

(4) He advised me _____ _____ regularly. (exercise)

04 다음 우리말에 맞게 빈칸에 알맞은 말을 쓰시오.

(1) 나는 엄마가 그것에 관해 아시는 것을 원하지 않아.

➡ I don't want my mom _____ _____ about it.

(2) 그 방은 Jenny에 의해 청소되었다.

➡ The room _____ _____ by Jenny.

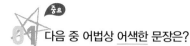

01 다음 중 어법상 어색한 문장은?

① Two parrots were bought by Jane.
② The picture was taken by Morris.
③ The old building was build about 200 years ago.
④ *Romeo and Juliet* was written by Shakespeare.
⑤ The letter was sent to her yesterday.

02 다음 우리말을 바르게 영작한 것은?

> 그는 Christine에게 집에 조금 일찍 도착하라고 요청했다.

① He asked Christine arrive home a little early.
② He asked Christine arrives home a little early.
③ He asked Christine arrived home a little early.
④ He asked Christine to arrive home a little early.
⑤ He asked Christine arriving home a little early.

서답형

03 다음 괄호 안에서 알맞은 것을 고르시오.

(1) Math was taught (to / for) them by Mr. Lee.
(2) A beautiful dress was bought (to / for) me by my mom.
(3) Some interesting questions were asked (to / of) me by Sally.

04 다음 빈칸에 알맞은 것은?

> She told me _____ careful when I crossed the road.

① be   ② was   ③ is
④ being   ⑤ to be

05 다음 중 수동태로의 전환이 어색한 것은?

① Roald Dahl wrote the book, *Charlie and the Chocolate Factory*.
  → The book, *Charlie and the Chocolate Factory*, was written by Roald Dahl.
② They make a lot of wonderful smartphones in Korea.
  → A lot of wonderful smartphones are made in Korea.
③ He made her a pizza while she was studying.
  → A pizza was made for her by him while she was studying.
④ Mary showed me her pictures taken at the party.
  → Her pictures shown to me were taken at the party by Mary.
⑤ Thomas Edison invented the light bulb.
  → The light bulb was invented by Thomas Edison.

06 다음 문장의 빈칸에 알맞지 <u>않은</u> 것은?

> Yuna _____ him to follow her advice.

① made   ② wanted
③ asked   ④ expected
⑤ advised

[07~08] 다음 중 어법상 옳은 것을 고르시오.

07 ① A difficult question was asked to her by them.
② Who built this bridge hundreds years ago?
③ These books was sent to you tomorrow morning.
④ The window will be broken by Mike yesterday.
⑤ The telephone invented Alexander Bell in 1876.

08 ① I asked my friend to help me.
② The coach told us did our best in the game.
③ His father advised him join the science club.
④ My mom wanted me reading many books.
⑤ I expected him goes there with me as it was getting dark.

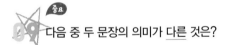

09 다음 중 두 문장의 의미가 다른 것은?

① Amy told me that I must not forget to bring some sandwiches.
→ Amy told me not to forget to bring some sandwiches.
② Her parents expected that she would study English very hard.
→ Her parents expected her to study English very hard.
③ Dan asked that he should come over at once.
→ Dan asked him to come over at once.
④ Mom advised me that I should be cautious when driving.
→ Mom advised me to be cautious when driving.
⑤ The doctor hoped that Harry would get well soon.
→ Harry wanted the doctor to get well soon.

10 다음 빈칸에 공통으로 들어갈 말로 가장 적절한 것은?

- His shoes were covered _____ dust.
- He was pleased _____ the result.

① by　　② for　　③ in
④ with　　⑤ of

서답형

11 다음 우리말을 주어진 단어를 이용하여 영어로 쓰시오.

(1) *The Mona Lisa*는 Leonardo da Vinci에 의해 그려졌다. (paint)
➡ _____

(2) 그 유명한 선수는 그녀의 움직임에 깜짝 놀랐다. (famous, surprise, movements)
➡ _____

(3) 그 집은 토네이도에 의해 부서지지 않았다. (break, the tornado)
➡ _____

(4) Ms. Jackson은 Tom에게 창문을 청소하라고 말했다. (clean the windows)
➡ _____

(5) 그 선생님은 그의 학생들이 최선을 다하길 기대했다. (expect, do)
➡ _____

12 다음 문장을 수동태로 바르게 바꾼 것은?

Jane turned on the TV.

① The TV turned Jane.
② The TV turned on by Jane.
③ The TV was turned on Jane.
④ The TV was turned by Jane.
⑤ The TV was turned on by Jane.

서답형

13 다음 괄호 안에 주어진 동사를 어법에 맞게 빈칸에 쓰시오.

- Jane wants Tom _____ _____ a computer club. (join)
- Computers allow him _____ _____ the work quickly. (do)

[14~15] 다음 두 문장이 같은 의미가 되도록 빈칸에 알맞은 말을 고르시오.

중요
14

Cinderella made her daughter a doll.
= A doll _____ her daughter by Cinderella.

① was making
② was made
③ was made for
④ was made to
⑤ made to

15

Chuck saw Wendy flying high above the sky.
= Wendy _____ high above the sky by Chuck.

① was seen flying
② was seen fly
③ was seen to fly
④ is seen fly
⑤ is seen flying

16 다음 중 어법상 어색한 부분을 찾아 바르게 고친 것은?

Mom wants Tom come home by 5:30.

① wants → want
② Tom → Tom's
③ come → to come
④ home → to home
⑤ by → to

중요
17 다음 빈칸에 들어갈 괄호 안에 주어진 동사의 형태가 다른 하나는?

① I want you _____ the dishes. (wash)
② Mom made me _____ playing the computer games. (stop)
③ They got him _____ a new contract. (sign)
④ She asked him _____ to the movies together. (go)
⑤ My parents didn't allow me _____ camping. (go)

서답형
18 다음 문장을 수동태는 능동태로, 능동태는 수동태로 고치시오.

(1) The picture was painted by Sujin.
➡ _____

(2) Antonio Gaudi built Casa Mila.
➡ _____

(3) My father made me a model plane.
➡ _____

(4) Kate will finish her homework by the end of this week.
➡ _____
_____

(5) Who built the house?
➡ _____

01 다음 문장을 수동태로 바꿔 쓰시오. (두 가지로 쓸 것.)

> Williams taught Angelina English last year.

(1) _____

(2) _____

02 다음 두 문장이 비슷한 의미를 갖도록 빈칸을 알맞은 말로 채우시오.

(1) The teacher said to her, "Draw pictures. You can do it!"
  ➡ The teacher encouraged her _____ _____ pictures.

(2) His daughter said to him, "Please read me a story book."
  ➡ His daughter told him _____ _____ her a story book.

(3) My dad ordered that I should solve the math problems.
  ➡ My dad ordered me _____ _____ the math problems.

(4) Vivian said to her son, "Don't drive too fast."
  ➡ Vivian warned her son _____ _____ _____ too fast.

(5) Mom asked that I should clean my room every Sunday.
  ➡ Mom asked me _____ _____ my room every Sunday.

03 다음 우리말을 괄호 안에 주어진 어휘를 이용하여 영작하시오.

(1) 그 마루는 아름다운 카펫으로 덮여 있었다. (floor, cover, a carpet)
  ➡ _____

(2) 그 책은 한글로 쓰여져 있지 않았다. (write)
  ➡ _____

(3) 그곳의 동물들은 사람들에 의해 잘 돌보아지고 있었다. (there, good care, take)
  ➡ _____

(4) 그 시계는 이년 전에 아버지에 의해 나에게 주어진 것이다. (watch, give)
  ➡ _____
  _____

(5) 그녀는 나에게 책 한 권을 사주었다. (buy) (수동태로 쓸 것.)
  ➡ _____

04 다음 문장을 수동태는 능동태로, 능동태는 수동태로 고치시오.

(1) A basket was made by me.
  ➡ _____

(2) Marc Chagall painted *I and the Village* in 1911.
  ➡ _____
  _____

(3) The dentist pulled out a rotten tooth.
  ➡ _____

(4) The way to the National Museum was kindly shown to me by Matthew.
  ➡ _____
  _____

(5) He was covered with dust while he was walking along the road.
  ➡ _____
  _____

05 다음 문장에서 어법상 어색한 부분을 찾아 바르게 고쳐 다시 쓰시오.

(1) She wants Steve coming home early.

➡ _____

(2) He believed his students be diligent.

➡ _____

(3) He asked me drive a car very carefully.

➡ _____

(4) My boss forced me signed the agreement.

➡ _____

(5) The doctor told me to not do exercise too much.

➡ _____

06 다음 문장에서 어법상 어색한 부분을 찾아 바르게 고쳐 다시 쓰시오.

(1) The airplane invented the Wright brothers.

➡ _____

(2) The house was build by him in 1963.

➡ _____

(3) Handerson is not interested by playing the guitar.

➡ _____

(4) He is told of the news by his sister tomorrow.

➡ _____

(5) Soup was cooked to Christina by John.

➡ _____

07 괄호 안에 주어진 단어를 사용해 다음을 영작하시오.

(1) 그 여자는 그 남자에게 그녀의 가방을 들어달라고 요청했다. (ask, carry)

➡ _____

(2) Emma는 나에게 내일까지 기다리라고 충고했다. (advise, till)

➡ _____

(3) Peter는 Sylvia에게 그와 함께 춤을 추자고 말했다. (tell, dance)

➡ _____

(4) 그들은 그가 축제에 참가할 것으로 기대했다. (expect, participate, the festival)

➡ _____

(5) 좋은 건강이 그가 그 계획을 마칠 수 있도록 했다. (good, enable, finish)

➡ _____

08 다음 괄호 안에 주어진 동사를 어법에 맞게 빈칸에 쓰시오.

(1) Linda had her son _____ science. (study)

(2) I would like you _____ _____ me when you arrive there. (call)

Reading

Let's Talk about Upcycling

Mr. Brown: Hello, club members. As you know, this year's Environment
Day is about upcycling. Before we talk about each group's
event idea for that day, I want you to understand the meaning of
"upcycling." Can anyone explain upcycling?

Sumi: Yes. The word "upcycling" is a combination of "upgrade" and
"recycling."

Eric: Like recycling, upcycling is good for the environment. When you
upcycle, you make new and better things from old things.

Mr. Brown: Good. Now, let's talk about each group's idea for the event.
Let's start with Pei's group.

Pei: My group wants to hold a trashion show. "Trashion" is a
combination of "trash" and "fashion." We'll use trash to make
clothes. We want other students to become interested in upcycling
through the show.

Mr. Brown: A trashion show sounds like fun! What about your group,
Eric?

환경 environment 환경
upcycling 업사이클링
event 행사
meaning 뜻
explain 설명하다, 알려주다
upgrade 개선하다
recycling 재활용
trash 쓰레기
through ~을 통해

확인문제

● 다음 문장이 본문의 내용과 일치하면 T, 일치하지 않으면 F를 쓰시오.

1 Mr. Brown wants the club members to understand the meaning of "upcycling." ☐

2 Sumi says the word "upcycling" is a combination of "upgrade" and "reusing." ☐

3 Mr. Brown says upcycling is good for the environment. ☐

4 When you upcycle, you make old things into new and better things. ☐

5 Pei's group wants to hold a trashion show. ☐

6 Other students became interested in upcycling through the trashion show. ☐

Eric: My group is going to make musical instruments from old things.
be going to: ~할 예정이다   악기

We'll make drums from old plastic buckets. We'll also make a
플라스틱(으로 만들어진) 양동이

guitar from old boxes and rubber bands. We plan to play the
plan to+동사원형: ~할 계획이다

instruments in a mini-concert.
작은, 소규모의

Mr. Brown: Thank you, Eric. Now, let's hear from Sumi's group.

Sumi: My group will make bags from old clothes. For example, we'll
예를 들면

use blue jeans. Look at this bag. This was made by Hajun, one of
수동태(be동사+과거분사 ~+by+행위자)

our group members. Isn't it nice? We'll make more bags and sell
= the bag made by Hajun

them on Environment Day. We're going to give all the money to
= bags   = give a nursing home all the money(4형식 문장)

a nursing home.

Mr. Brown: That's a great idea. Your ideas are all so creative. I want
5형식 문장(want+

everyone to work hard for Environment Day.
목적어+to부정사)

Blue Jeans Bag

You Need: old blue jeans, sewing kit, scissors, pins and buttons

Step: 1 Cut off the legs of the blue jeans. 2 Sew the bottom together.
자르다

3 Make shoulder straps from one of the legs. 4 Sew the straps to

the top of the jeans. 5 Decorate the bag with pins and buttons.
청바지의 위쪽   ~을 사용하여(도구)   단추

instrument 기구, 악기
bucket 양동이
rubber band 고무 밴드, 고무줄
example 예
sell 팔다
nursing home 양로원
creative 창의적인
kit 도구 세트
bottom 맨 아래
strap 끈, 줄
decorate 장식하다, 꾸미다
button 단추

📎 **확인문제**

● 다음 문장이 본문의 내용과 일치하면 T, 일치하지 않으면 F를 쓰시오.

1   Eric's group will make drums from old boxes and rubber bands. ☐

2   Eric's group plans to play the instruments in a mini-concert. ☐

3   Sumi's group will make bags from old clothes. ☐

4   Hajun made blue jeans from old bags. ☐

5   Sumi's group will make more bags and send them to a nursing home on Environment

Day. ☐

6   Sumi's group is going to give all the money to a nursing home. ☐

● 우리말을 참고하여 빈칸에 알맞은 말을 쓰시오.

1 Let's Talk _____ _____

2 Hello, _____ _____.

3 _____ _____ _____, this year's Environment Day is about upcycling.

4 Before we talk about _____ _____ _____ _____ for that day, I want _____ _____ _____ the meaning of "upcycling."

5 Can anyone _____ _____?

6 Yes. The word "upcycling" is _____ _____ _____ "upgrade" and "recycling."

7 _____ _____, upcycling _____ _____ _____ the environment.

8 When you upcycle, you make new and better things _____ _____ _____.

9 Good. Now, let's talk about each group's idea _____ _____ _____.

10 _____ _____ _____ Pei's group.

11 My group wants _____ _____ _____ _____ _____.

12 "Trashion" is _____ _____ _____ "trash" and "fashion."

13 _____ _____ _____ to make clothes.

14 We want other students to _____ _____ _____ upcycling through the show.

15 A trashion show _____ _____ _____!

16 _____ _____ your group, Eric?

17 My group is going to _____ _____ _____ from old things.

1	업사이클링에 대해 이야기해 봅시다
2	동아리 회원 여러분, 안녕하세요.
3	여러분도 알다시피 올해의 환경의 날은 업사이클링에 관한 것입니다.
4	각 그룹이 그날에 할 행사 아이디어를 이야기하기 전에 여러분이 '업사이클링'의 의미를 이해하기를 바랍니다.
5	누가 업사이클링의 뜻을 설명해 줄 수 있나요?
6	네. '업사이클링'이란 단어는 "upgrade"와 "recycling"이 결합한 것입니다.
7	재활용과 마찬가지로 업사이클링도 환경에 좋아요.
8	업사이클링을 하면, 여러분은 오래된 것들로 새롭고 더 좋은 것을 만들어요.
9	좋아요. 이제 각 그룹의 행사 아이디어에 대해 이야기해 봅시다.
10	Pei의 그룹부터 시작하죠.
11	저희 그룹은 트래션 쇼를 하고 싶습니다.
12	"트래션(Trashion)"은 "trash"와 "fashion"이 결합한 말입니다.
13	저희는 옷을 만들기 위해 쓰레기를 이용할 것입니다.
14	저희는 이 쇼를 통해서 다른 학생들이 업사이클링에 관심을 갖게 되기를 바랍니다.
15	트래션 쇼라니 멋지겠구나!
16	너희 그룹은 어떠니, Eric?
17	저희 그룹은 낡은 물건으로 악기를 만들려고 합니다.

18 We'll _____ drums _____ old plastic buckets.

19 We'll also make a guitar _____ _____ _____ and _____

_____.

20 We _____ _____ _____ _____ _____ in a mini-

concert.

21 Thank you, Eric. Now, _____ _____ _____ Sumi's

group.

22 My group will _____ _____ _____ old clothes.

23 _____ _____, we'll use blue jeans.

24 _____ _____ this bag.

25 This _____ _____ _____ Hajun, one of our group members.

26 _____ _____ nice?

27 We'll make more bags and _____ _____ _____ _____

_____.

28 We're going to give all the money _____ _____ _____

_____.

29 That's _____ _____ _____.

30 Your ideas are _____ _____ _____.

31 I want everyone _____ _____ _____ for Environment

Day.

32 _____ _____ the legs of the blue jeans.

33 _____ the bottom _____.

34 _____ _____ _____ from one of the legs.

35 Sew the straps _____ _____ _____ _____ the jeans.

36 _____ the bag _____ pins and buttons.

18 낡은 플라스틱 양동이로 드럼을 만들 겁니다.

19 또한 저희는 낡은 상자와 고무 줄로 기타를 만들 겁니다.

20 저희는 소규모 음악회를 열어 그 악기들로 연주할 계획입니다.

21 고맙다, Eric. 그럼 이제 수미의 그룹 의견을 들어 보자.

22 저희 그룹은 낡은 옷으로 가방 을 만들 거예요.

23 예를 들어 청바지를 이용할 거 예요.

24 이 가방을 보세요.

25 이것은 저희 모둠원 중 한 명인 하준이가 만들었어요.

26 멋지지 않나요?

27 우리는 가방을 더 많이 만들어 서 환경의 날에 팔 거예요.

28 번 돈을 모두 양로원에 줄 예정 이에요.

29 훌륭한 생각이구나.

30 너희들의 발상은 모두 아주 창 의적이구나.

31 너희들 모두 환경의 날을 위해 열심히 노력하길 바란다.

32 청바지의 다리 부분을 잘라낸다.

33 아래쪽을 붙여서 바느질한다.

34 다리 한 짝으로 어깨끈을 만든다.

35 청바지의 윗부분에 어깨끈을 바 느질한다.

36 핀이나 단추로 가방을 장식한다.

● 우리말을 참고하여 본문을 영작하시오.

1 업사이클링에 대해 이야기해 봅시다

➡ _____

2 동아리 회원 여러분, 안녕하세요.

➡ _____

3 여러분도 알다시피 올해의 환경의 날은 업사이클링에 관한 것입니다.

➡ _____

4 각 그룹이 그날에 할 행사 아이디어를 이야기하기 전에 여러분이 '업사이클링'의 의미를 이해하기를 바랍니다.

➡ _____

_____

5 누가 업사이클링의 뜻을 설명해 줄 수 있나요?

➡ _____

6 네. '업사이클링'이란 단어는 "upgrade"와 "recycling"이 결합한 것입니다.

➡ _____

7 재활용과 마찬가지로 업사이클링도 환경에 좋아요.

➡ _____

8 업사이클링을 하면, 여러분은 오래된 것들로 새롭고 더 좋은 것을 만들어요.

➡ _____

9 좋아요. 이제 각 그룹의 행사 아이디어에 대해 이야기해 봅시다.

➡ _____

10 Pei의 그룹부터 시작하죠.

➡ _____

11 저희 그룹은 트래션 쇼를 하고 싶습니다.

➡ _____

12 "트래션(Trashion)"은 "trash"와 "fashion"이 결합한 말입니다.

➡ _____

13 저희는 옷을 만들기 위해 쓰레기를 이용할 것입니다.

➡ _____

14 저희는 이 쇼를 통해서 다른 학생들이 업사이클링에 관심을 갖게 되기를 바랍니다.

➡ _____

15 트래션 쇼라니 멋지겠구나!

➡ _____

16 너희 그룹은 어떠니, Eric?

➡ _____

17 저희 그룹은 낡은 물건으로 악기를 만들려고 합니다.

➡ _____

18 낡은 플라스틱 양동이로 드럼을 만들 겁니다.

➡ _____

19 또한 저희는 낡은 상자와 고무줄로 기타를 만들 겁니다.

➡ _____

20 저희는 소규모 음악회를 열어 그 악기들로 연주할 계획입니다.

➡ _____

21 고맙다, Eric. 그럼 이제 수미의 그룹 의견을 들어 보자.

➡ _____

22 저희 그룹은 낡은 옷으로 가방을 만들 거예요.

➡ _____

23 예를 들어 청바지를 이용할 거예요.

➡ _____

24 이 가방을 보세요.

➡ _____

25 이것은 저희 모둠원 중 한 명인 하준이가 만들었어요.

➡ _____

26 멋지지 않나요?

➡ _____

27 우리는 가방을 더 많이 만들어서 환경의 날에 팔 거예요.

➡ _____

28 번 돈을 모두 양로원에 줄 예정이에요.

➡ _____

29 훌륭한 생각이구나.

➡ _____

30 너희들의 발상은 모두 아주 창의적이구나.

➡ _____

31 너희들 모두 환경의 날을 위해 열심히 노력하길 바란다.

➡ _____

32 청바지의 다리 부분을 잘라낸다.

➡ _____

33 아래쪽을 붙여서 바느질한다.

➡ _____

34 다리 한 짝으로 어깨끈을 만든다.

➡ _____

35 청바지의 윗부분에 어깨끈을 바느질한다.

➡ _____

36 핀이나 단추로 가방을 장식한다.

➡ _____

[01~03] 다음 글을 읽고, 물음에 답하시오.

Mr. Brown: Hello, club members. As you know, this year's Environment Day is about upcycling. Before we talk about each group's event idea for that day, I want you ⓐto understand the meaning of "upcycling." Can anyone explain upcycling?

Sumi: Yes. The word "upcycling" is a combination of "upgrade" and "recycling."

Eric: Like recycling, upcycling is good for the environment. When you upcycle, you make new and better things ⓑ old things.

Mr. Brown: Good. Now, let's talk about each group's idea for the event. Let's start with Pei's group.

01 위 글의 내용과 일치하지 <u>않는</u> 것은?

① 올해의 환경의 날은 업사이클링에 관한 것이다.
② '업사이클링'이란 단어는 "upgrade"와 "recycling" 이 결합한 것이다.
③ recycling과는 달리 upcycling은 환경에 좋다.
④ 업사이클을 하면 오래된 것들로 새롭고 더 좋은 것들을 만들게 된다.
⑤ Brown 선생님은 각 그룹의 행사 아이디어에 대해 이야기해 보자고 한다.

중요

02 위 글의 밑줄 친 ⓐto understand와 용법이 같은 것을 고르시오.

① He worked hard to pass the test.
② I want a chair to sit on.
③ She went out to buy some snacks.
④ Show me the way to go to the park.
⑤ Mom told me to wash the dishes.

03 위 글의 빈칸 ⓑ에 들어갈 알맞은 전치사를 고르시오.

① for   ② from   ③ by
④ to   ⑤ on

[04~06] 다음 글을 읽고, 물음에 답하시오.

Pei: My group wants to hold a trashion show. "Trashion" is a combination of "trash" and "fashion." We'll use trash to make clothes. We want (A)[another / other] students to become interested in upcycling (B)[though / through] the show.

Mr. Brown: A trashion show sounds (C)[like / alike] fun! What about your group, Eric?

Eric: My group is going to make musical instruments from old things. We'll make drums from old plastic buckets. We'll also make a guitar from old boxes and rubber bands. We plan to play the instruments in a mini-concert.

서답형

04 위 글의 괄호 (A)~(C)에서 문맥이나 어법상 알맞은 낱말을 골라 쓰시오.

(A)_____ (B)_____ (C)_____

05 위 글을 읽고 알 수 <u>없는</u> 것을 고르시오.

① "Trashion"의 뜻
② 트래션 쇼에 출품되는 옷의 재료
③ 트래션 쇼를 통해 Pei의 그룹이 바라는 것
④ Eric의 그룹이 만드는 악기들의 재료
⑤ Eric의 그룹이 소규모 음악회를 여는 장소

06 위 글의 제목으로 알맞은 것을 고르시오.

① How to Hold a Trashion Show
② Use Trash to Make Clothes
③ Event Ideas of Two Groups
④ Musical Instruments from Old Things
⑤ Play the Instruments in a Mini-concert

[07~09] 다음 글을 읽고, 물음에 답하시오.

Sumi: My group will make bags from old clothes. ___ⓐ___, we'll use blue jeans. Look at this bag. This was made by Hajun, one of our group members. Isn't it nice? We'll make more bags and sell ⓑthem on Environment Day. We're going to give all the money to a nursing home.

07 위 글의 빈칸 ⓐ에 들어갈 알맞은 말을 고르시오.

① However   ② For example
③ Therefore   ④ In addition
⑤ As a result

08 위 글의 밑줄 친 ⓑthem이 가리키는 것을 본문에서 찾아 쓰시오.

➡ _____

09 다음 문장에서 위 글의 내용과 다른 부분을 찾아서 고치시오.

> Sumi's group will make bags from old clothes and sell them. They will give the bags to a nursing home.

_____ ➡ _____

[10~12] 다음 글을 읽고, 물음에 답하시오.

Step: 1 Sew the bottom together.
2 Decorate the bag ___ⓐ___ pins and buttons.
3 Make shoulder straps from one of the legs.
4 Cut off the legs of the blue jeans.
5 Sew the straps ___ⓑ___ the top of the jeans.

10 위 글은 Blue Jeans Bag을 만드는 법을 설명하는 글이다. 알맞은 순서대로 배열하시오.

➡ _____

11 위 글의 빈칸 ⓐ와 ⓑ에 들어갈 알맞은 전치사를 쓰시오.

ⓐ_____   ⓑ_____

12 위 글을 읽고, 다음 질문에 대한 대답을 완성하시오.

> **Q:** What do you need to make shoulder straps of the Blue Jeans Bag?
> ➡ We need _____ _____ _____
> _____ of the blue jeans.

[13~15] 다음 글을 읽고, 물음에 답하시오.

Mr. Brown: ①Hello, club members. ②As you know, this year's Environment Day is about upcycling. ③Before we talk about each group's event idea for that day, I want you to understand the meaning of "upcycling." ④"Upcycling" is the use of waste materials to make new things. ⑤Can anyone explain upcycling?

Sumi: Yes. The word "upcycling" is a combination of " ⓐ " and " ⓑ ."

Eric: ⓒLike recycling, upcycling is good at the environment. When you upcycle, you make new and better things from old things.

13 위 글의 ①~⑤ 중에서 전체 흐름과 관계 없는 문장은?

① ② ③ ④ ⑤

⭐중요
14 위 글의 빈칸 ⓐ와 ⓑ에 들어갈 알맞은 말을 고르시오.

① recycling – reusing
② update – reducing
③ upgrade – recycling
④ repairing – update
⑤ upgrade – repairing

서답형
15 위 글의 밑줄 친 ⓒ에서 흐름상 어색한 부분을 찾아 고치시오.

_____ ➡ _____

[16~19] 다음 글을 읽고, 물음에 답하시오.

Pei: My group wants ⓐto hold a trashion show. "Trashion" is a combination of "trash" and "fashion." We'll use trash to make clothes. We want other students to become interested ① upcycling through the show.

Mr. Brown: A trashion show sounds ⓑ fun! What about your group, Eric?

Eric: My group is going to make musical instruments ② old things. We'll make drums ③ old plastic buckets. We'll also make a guitar ④ old boxes and rubber bands. We plan to play the instruments in a mini-concert.

Mr. Brown: Thank you, Eric. Now, let's hear ⑤ Sumi's group.

16 위 글의 밑줄 친 ⓐto hold와 to부정사의 용법이 다른 것을 고르시오.

① To know oneself is important.
② My goal is to become a scientist.
③ It isn't easy for me to learn English.
④ She awoke to find herself famous.
⑤ He continued to solve the problem.

서답형
17 위 글의 빈칸 ①~⑤ 중에서 들어갈 전치사가 나머지 넷과 다른 것을 고른 후, 그곳에 들어 갈 전치사를 쓰시오.

_____ 번, 들어갈 전치사: _____

⭐중요
18 위 글에서 알 수 있는 'Mr. Brown'의 심경으로 가장 알맞은 것을 고르시오.

① bored   ② satisfied
③ depressed   ④ ashamed
⑤ disappointed

서답형
19 위 글의 빈칸 ⓑ에 들어갈 알맞은 말을 쓰시오.

➡ _____

[20~22] 다음 글을 읽고, 물음에 답하시오.

Sumi: My group will make bags from old clothes. (①) For example, we'll use blue jeans. (②) This was made by Hajun, one of our group members. (③) Isn't it nice? (④) We'll make more bags and sell them on Environment Day. (⑤) We're going to give all the money to a nursing home.

Mr. Brown: That's a great idea. Your ideas are all so creative. ⓐ너희들 모두 환경의 날을 위해 열심히 노력하길 바란다.

20 위 글의 흐름으로 보아, 주어진 문장이 들어가기에 가장 적절한 곳은?

> Look at this bag.

①   ②   ③   ④   ⑤

서답형

21 위 글의 밑줄 친 ⓐ의 우리말에 맞게 주어진 어휘를 이용하여 9단어로 영작하시오.

> want / hard

➡ _____

서답형

22 다음 빈칸 (A)와 (B)에 알맞은 단어를 넣어 upcycling을 위한 수미의 아이디어 노트를 완성하시오.

> Sumi's Group: For Environment Day
> • make bags from _____(A)_____
> • sell the bags on _____(B)_____ and give a nursing home _____(C)_____

(A)_____
(B)_____
(C)_____

[23~25] 다음 글을 읽고, 물음에 답하시오.

Creative Upcycling Idea: Blue Jeans Basket

There are many great upcycling ideas. Here is ____ⓐ____ example. I made a basket from my old blue jeans. Do you want to make ____ⓑ____, too? Then I want you to follow these ____ⓒ____.

You Need: old blue jeans, sewing kit, scissors, and pins and buttons

First, ①_____.
Second, ②_____.
Third, ③_____.
Lastly, ④_____.

Upcycling is good for the environment. I want you to become interested in upcycling.

서답형

23 위 글의 빈칸 ⓐ와 ⓑ에 공통으로 들어갈 알맞은 단어를 쓰시오.

➡ _____

서답형

24 주어진 영영풀이를 참고하여 빈칸 ⓒ에 철자 d로 시작하는 단어를 쓰시오.

> instructions that tell you what to do, how to do something, or how to get somewhere

➡ _____

서답형

25 위 글의 빈칸 ①~④에 들어갈 알맞은 말을 〈보기〉에서 골라 쓰시오.

┌─ 보기 ├─
- cut out a piece to make the bottom of the basket
- decorate with pins and buttons
- cut off a leg of the old blue jeans
- sew the bottom to the leg
└─

① _____.

② _____.

③ _____.

④ _____.

중요

26 주어진 글 다음에 이어질 글의 순서로 가장 적절한 것은?

My group is going to make musical instruments from old things.

(A) We'll make drums from old plastic buckets.

(B) We plan to play the instruments in a mini-concert.

(C) We'll also make a guitar from old boxes and rubber bands.

① (A) – (C) – (B)   ② (B) – (A) – (C)

③ (B) – (C) – (A)   ④ (C) – (A) – (B)

⑤ (C) – (B) – (A)

[27~30] 다음 글을 읽고, 물음에 답하시오.

Sumi: My group will make bags from old clothes. ⓐFor example, we'll use blue jeans. Look ___ⓑ___ this bag. ⓒThis was made by Hajun, one of our group members. Isn't it nice? We'll make more bags and sell them ___ⓓ___ Environment Day. ⓔWe're going to give all the money for a nursing home.

서답형

27 위 글의 밑줄 친 ⓐ와 바꿔 쓸 수 있는 말을 쓰시오.

➡ _____

28 위 글의 빈칸 ⓑ와 ⓓ에 알맞은 말이 바르게 짝지어진 것은?

① at – in   ② for – at

③ in – at   ④ at – on

⑤ for – during

서답형

29 위 글의 밑줄 친 ⓒ를 능동태로 고치시오.

➡ _____

서답형

30 위 글의 밑줄 친 ⓔ에서 어법상 틀린 부분을 찾아 바르게 고쳐 쓰시오.

_____ ➡ _____

[31~33] 다음 글을 읽고, 물음에 답하시오.

How can we make a bag from old blue jeans? First, cut off the legs of the blue jeans. Second, sew the bottom together. Third, make shoulder straps from one of the legs. Fourth, sew the straps to the top of the jeans. _____ⓐ_____, decorate the bag with pins and buttons.

서답형

31 위 글의 빈칸 ⓐ에 들어갈 알맞은 말을 L로 시작하여 쓰시오.

➡ _____

서답형

32 위 글에서 다음 영영풀이에 해당하는 단어를 찾아 쓰시오.

> to make something look more attractive by putting things on it

➡ _____

서답형

33 다음 질문에 대한 알맞은 대답을 영어로 쓰시오. (6 단어)

> Q: After making shoulder straps, where do you have to sew them?

➡ _____

[34~37] 다음 글을 읽고, 물음에 답하시오.

Pei: My group wants to ___ⓐ___ a trashion show. "Trashion" is a ①combination of "trash" and "fashion." We'll use ②trash to make clothes. We want other students ⓑ become interested in ③upgrading through the show.

Mr. Brown: A trashion show sounds like fun! What about your group, Eric?

Eric: My group is going to make ④musical instruments from old things. We'll make drums from old plastic buckets. We'll also make a ⑤guitar from old boxes and rubber bands. We plan to play the instruments in a mini-concert.

중요

34 위 글의 빈칸 ⓐ에 알맞은 것을 모두 고르시오. (정답 2개)

① hold   ② take
③ have   ④ bring
⑤ catch

35 위 글의 밑줄 친 ①~⑤ 중 문맥상 쓰임이 어색한 것은?

①   ②   ③   ④   ⑤

서답형

36 위 글의 밑줄 친 ⓑ를 알맞은 형태로 고쳐 쓰시오.

➡ _____

서답형

37 What kind of musical instrument will Eric's group make from old things? Answer in English.

➡ _____

[01~03] 다음 글을 읽고, 물음에 답하시오.

Mr. Brown: Hello, club members. As you know, this year's Environment Day is about upcycling. Before we talk about each group's event idea for that day, I want you ⓐ the meaning of "upcycling." Can anyone explain upcycling?

Sumi: Yes. ⓑ'업사이클링'이란 단어는 "upgrade" 와 "recycling"이 결합한 것입니다.

Eric: Like recycling, upcycling is good for the environment. ⓒWhen you upcycle, you make old and better things from new things.

01 위 글의 빈칸 ⓐ에 understand를 알맞은 형태로 쓰시오.

➡ _____

02 위 글의 밑줄 친 ⓑ의 우리말에 맞게 주어진 어구를 이용하여 10 단어로 영작하시오.

The word / combination

➡ _____

_____

03 위 글의 밑줄 친 ⓒ에서 흐름상 어색한 부분을 찾아 고치시오.

_____ ➡ _____

_____ ➡ _____

[04~06] 다음 글을 읽고, 물음에 답하시오.

Pei: My group wants to hold a trashion show. "Trashion" is a combination of "___ⓐ___" and "fashion." We'll use ⓐ to make clothes. We want other students to become interested in upcycling through the show.

Mr. Brown: A trashion show sounds like fun! ⓑWhat about your group, Eric?

Eric: My group is going to make ⓒmusical instruments from old things. We'll make drums from old plastic buckets. We'll also make a guitar from old boxes and rubber bands. We plan to play the instruments in a mini-concert.

04 주어진 영영풀이를 참고하여 빈칸 ⓐ에 철자 t로 시작하는 단어를 쓰시오.

unwanted things or waste material such as used paper, empty bottles, and waste food

➡ _____

05 위 글의 밑줄 친 ⓑ와 바꿔 쓸 수 있는 말을 쓰시오.

➡ _____

06 위 글의 밑줄 친 ⓒ의 재료를 악기별로 각각 우리말로 쓰시오.

드럼: _____

기타: _____

[07~08] 다음 글을 읽고, 물음에 답하시오.

Sumi: My group will make bags from old clothes. For example, we'll use blue jeans. Look at this bag. This was made by Hajun, one of our group members. Isn't it nice? We'll make more bags and sell them on Environment Day. ⓐ We're going to give all the money to a nursing home.

Mr. Brown: That's a great idea. Your ideas are all so creative. ⓑI want everyone to work hardly for Environment Day.

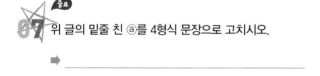

07 위 글의 밑줄 친 ⓐ를 4형식 문장으로 고치시오.

➡ _____

08 위 글의 밑줄 친 ⓑ에서 문맥상 낱말의 쓰임이 적절하지 않은 것을 찾아 알맞게 고치시오.

_____ ➡ _____

[09~10] 다음 글을 읽고, 물음에 답하시오.

Mr. Brown: Hello, club members. As you know, this year's Environment Day is about upcycling. ⓐBefore we talk about each groups' event idea for that day, I want you to understand the meaning of "upcycling." Can anyone explain upcycling?

09 다음 문장에서 위 글의 내용과 다른 부분을 찾아 고치시오.

> Mr. Brown wants to understand the meaning of "upcycling."

_____ ➡ _____

10 위 글의 밑줄 친 ⓐ에서 어법상 틀린 것을 찾아 고치시오.

_____ ➡ _____

[11~12] 다음 글을 읽고, 물음에 답하시오.

Pei: My group wants to hold a trashion show. "Trashion" is a combination of "trash" and "fashion." We'll use trash to make clothes. We want other students to become interested in upcycling through the show.

Mr. Brown: A trashion show sounds like fun! What about your group, Eric?

Eric: My group is going to make musical instruments from old things. We'll make drums from old plastic buckets. We'll also make a guitar from old boxes and rubber bands. We plan to play the instruments in a mini-concert.

11 다음 빈칸 (A)와 (B)에 알맞은 단어를 넣어 upcycling을 위한 Pei 그룹의 아이디어 노트를 완성하시오.

> Pei's Group: For Environment Day
> • use trash to _____(A)_____
> • hold a _____(B)_____

(A)_____ (B)_____

12 다음 빈칸 (A)와 (B)에 알맞은 단어를 넣어 Eric의 그룹이 만들 악기들에 대한 소개를 완성하시오.

> Eric's group is going to make _____(A)_____ from old plastic buckets and _____(B)_____ from old boxes and rubber bands.

(A)_____ (B)_____

구석구석

Talk and play

A: May I help you?
손님을 맞이할 때 '어서 오세요'라는 표현이다.

B: Yes. How much is this T-shirt?
가격을 묻는 표현으로 How much is[are] ~?를 사용한다.

A: It's 20 dollars.

B: Can I get a discount?
할인을 받다

A: OK. I'll take 3 dollars off.
할인 금액을 말할 때 사용한다.

B: Great. I'll take it.

구문해설 · discount: 할인 · take off: 할인하다 · take: 사다, 선택하다

Around the World

Kids, I want to give music lessons to you. But we don't have any musical instruments. I can help you. I have a good idea. Oh, thank you! I can make musical instruments from trash. The world sends us trash. We send back music. This is the power of upcycling.

구문해설 · give lessons: 수업하다 · musical instrument: 악기 · send back: 되돌려주다

Think and Write

Creative Upcycling Idea: Blue Jeans Basket

You Need: old blue jeans, sewing kit, scissors, buttons and pins

Step:

1 Cut off a leg of the old blue jeans.
자르다

2 Cut out a piece to make the bottom of the basket.
바구니의 바닥

3 Sew the bottom to the leg.

4 Decorate with buttons and pins.

구문해설 · creative: 창의적인 · sewing kit: 바느질 도구 세트 · bottom: 밑부분, 바닥
· decorate: 장식하다

해석

A: 도와 드릴까요?
B: 이 티셔츠는 얼마인가요?
A: 20달러예요.
B: 할인을 받을 수 있을까요?
A: 네. 3달러 깎아 드릴게요.
B: 좋아요. 그걸 살게요.

얘들아, 너희에게 음악 수업을 해주고 싶구나. 하지만 우리는 악기가 하나도 없어. 내가 도와줄 수 있어. 나에게 좋은 생각이 있어. 오, 고마워! 나는 쓰레기로 악기를 만들 수 있어. 세상은 우리에게 쓰레기를 보내줬어. 우리는 음악으로 되돌려준다. 이것이 업사이클링의 힘이란다.

창의적인 업사이클링 아이디어: 청바지 바구니

준비물: 낡은 청바지, 바느질 도구 세트, 가위, 단추와 장식 핀

단계

1. 낡은 청바지의 다리를 자른다.
2. 바구니의 바닥을 만들기 위해 한 조각을 자른다.
3. 바닥을 다리 부분과 꿰맨다.
4. 단추와 핀으로 장식한다.

Words & Expressions

01 다음 주어진 두 단어의 관계가 같도록 빈칸에 알맞은 단어를 쓰시오.

> expensive : cheap = _____ : worse

02 다음 대화의 빈칸 ⓐ와 ⓑ에 들어갈 단어가 바르게 짝지어진 것은?

> G: How much is this yellow backpack?
> M: It's 18 dollars.
> G: Hmm. That's expensive for me. How ___ⓐ___ this red one?
> M: It's 15 dollars.
> G: That's a good price. I'll ___ⓑ___ it.

① in – catch   ② about – bring
③ in – buy   ④ about – take
⑤ on – miss

[03~04] 다음 영영풀이에 해당하는 것을 고르시오.

3

> an object used for producing music

① machine   ② bucket
③ instrument   ④ backpack
⑤ event

04

> giving a lot of attention to something because you want to find out more about it

① interested   ② excited
③ worse   ④ used
⑤ creative

05 다음 빈칸에 공통으로 들어갈 말로 알맞은 것은?

> • Nancy held the _____ of her beach bag.
> • She pulled the _____ of her nightgown onto her shoulder.

① button   ② strap
③ trash   ④ bucket
⑤ meaning

06 다음 밑줄 친 부분의 뜻이 <u>잘못된</u> 것은?

① Let's <u>hear from</u> Sumi's group.
  ~로부터 이야기를 듣다
② A trashion show <u>sounds like</u> fun.
  ~하게 들리다
③ Upcycling <u>is good for</u> the environment.
  ~에 좋다
④ We <u>plan to play</u> the instruments in a mini-concert. 연주할 계획이다
⑤ He runs <u>like</u> a horse.
  좋아하다

Conversation

07 다음 대화의 빈칸에 알맞은 것은?

> G: Excuse me. How much is this purple T-shirt?
> M: It's 10 dollars.
> G: That's expensive. Can I get a discount?
> M: _____ That'll be 9 dollars.

① I'm afraid not.
② I'm sorry but you can't.
③ This purple T-shirt is for sale.
④ I'll take 1 dollar off.
⑤ That sounds good.

[08~10] 다음 대화를 읽고, 물음에 답하시오.

B: Wow! There are so many interesting things here.

W: Everything here is ⓐold or used. What are you looking for? (1)

B: I'm looking for a clock.

W: How about this red clock? (2)

B: How much is it? (3)

W: It's 15 dollars.

B: That's too ⓑexpensive for me. (4)

W: No, ⓒI'm afraid not. It's only one year old. It's almost ⓓused.

B: Then, how much is this blue clock with the large numbers? (5)

W: It's 10 dollars.

B: Then, I'll ⓔtake the blue (A)one. Thank you.

08 주어진 문장이 들어갈 위치로 알맞은 것은?

> Can I get a discount?

① (1) ② (2) ③ (3) ④ (4) ⑤ (5)

09 위 대화의 밑줄 친 (A)가 가리키는 것을 찾아 쓰시오.

➡ _____

10 위 대화의 흐름상 밑줄 친 ⓐ~ⓔ 중, 어휘의 쓰임이 어색한 것은?

① ⓐ ② ⓑ ③ ⓒ ④ ⓓ ⑤ ⓔ

11 다음 중 짝지어진 대화가 어색한 것은?

① A: What are you looking for?
   B: I'm looking for a clock.
② A: What will you do?
   B: Hmm. Let me think.
③ A: Can I get a discount?
   B: No, I'm afraid not.
④ A: May I help you?
   B: Yes. How much is this T-shirt?
⑤ A: How much is this soccer ball?
   B: I'll take 1 dollar off.

12 다음 대화의 내용과 일치하지 <u>않는</u> 것은?

> Woman: May I help you?
> Andy: Yes. How much is this soccer ball?
> Woman: It's 6 dollars.
> Andy: Can I get a discount?
> Woman: OK. I'll take 1 dollar off.
> Andy: Then that'll be 5 dollars. I'll take it.

① Andy is looking for a soccer ball.
② Andy buys a soccer ball for 6 dollars.
③ Andy gets a discount.
④ The woman takes one dollar off.
⑤ Andy decides to buy the soccer ball.

13 다음 대화의 빈칸에 들어갈 말을 <u>모두</u> 고르시오.

> A: May I help you?
> B: Yes. _____
> A: They're 13 dollars.
> B: Can I get a discount?
> A: OK. I'll take 2 dollars off.
> B: Then that'll be 11 dollars. I'll take them.

① How much are these shoes?
② What are you looking for?
③ How much do these shoes cost?
④ What is the price of these shoes?
⑤ How about this one?

Grammar

14 다음 중 어법상 올바른 것은?

① We want you join our club.

② The cookies was cooked by Eric.

③ Mr. Gilbert would like his students doing their best.

④ The airplane invented by the Wright brothers.

⑤ The doctor advised me to eat more vegetables.

15 다음 문장을 주어진 말로 시작하는 문장으로 바꿔 쓰시오.

(1) Mom made me a beautiful dress.

➡ A beautiful dress _____

_____ .

(2) Jonathan gave Emily some flowers.

➡ Some flowers _____ .

➡ Emily _____ .

(3) I was made to wash his car by my dad.

➡ My dad _____ .

(4) *Girl in the Woods* was painted by Van Gogh.

➡ Van Gogh _____ .

(5) They put off the game on account of the rain.

➡ The game _____

_____ .

16 주어진 단어들을 바르게 배열하여 문장을 완성하시오.

(1) chocolate cookies, these, baked, me, were, by

➡ _____

(2) you, we, want, wash, our clothes, to

➡ _____

(3) Judy, her sister, care, taken, was, by, of

➡ _____

(4) the police, the thief, caught, be, will, by

➡ _____

(5) dinner, my hands, she, me, told, wash, before, to

➡ _____

17 다음 중 어법상 바르지 <u>않은</u> 것은?

① She allowed me to use her computer.

② Amy had him clean the room.

③ I'd like you to stop playing computer games.

④ I saw Jenny having coffee at the cafe.

⑤ I want my brother play soccer with me.

18 다음 밑줄 친 부분의 형태가 <u>잘못된</u> 것은?

① Hangeul <u>was invented by</u> King Sejong.

② The light <u>turned off by</u> Alex.

③ A book <u>was read to</u> him by his dad.

④ The food here <u>was cooked by</u> a chef.

⑤ She <u>was interested in</u> making Korean food.

19 다음 빈칸에 들어갈 수 <u>없는</u> 것을 고르시오.

> Dad _____ Tom to clean his room.

① allowed ② got ③ asked
④ had ⑤ advised

20 다음 문장에서 어법상 <u>어색한</u> 것을 찾아 바르게 고쳐 다시 쓰시오.

(1) She was made a doll by her mother.

➡ _____

(2) Most of the doors in this building are made from wood.

➡ _____

_____

(3) I was brought up my grandparents.

➡ _____

(4) The teacher warned his students hand in their homework by Friday.

➡ _____

_____

(5) I believe Ella being very smart.

➡ _____

Reading

[21~23] 다음 글을 읽고, 물음에 답하시오.

Mr. Brown: Hello, club members. ⓐ여러분도 알다시피, this year's Environment Day is about upcycling. Before we talk about each group's event idea for that day, I want you to understand the meaning of "upcycling." Can anyone explain upcycling?

Sumi: Yes. The word "upcycling" is a combination of "upgrade" and "recycling."

Eric: ⓑLike recycling, upcycling is good for the environment. When you upcycle, you make new and better things from old things.

Mr. Brown: Good. Now, let's talk about each group's idea for the event. Let's start with Pei's group.

21 위 글을 읽고 알 수 <u>없는</u> 것을 고르시오.

① 올해의 환경의 날의 주제
② "upcycling"의 어원
③ upcycling의 좋은 점
④ recycling과 upcycling의 차이점
⑤ 환경의 날 행사 아이디어에 대해 처음 발표할 그룹

22 위 글의 밑줄 친 ⓐ의 우리말을 세 단어로 쓰시오.

➡ _____

23 위 글의 밑줄 친 ⓑLike와 같은 의미로 쓰인 것을 고르시오.

① You can do it like this.
② How did you like the movie?
③ He enjoys jazz, rock and the like.
④ Do you like your new house?
⑤ I like tropical fruits like bananas and pineapples.

[24~26] 다음 글을 읽고, 물음에 답하시오.

Pei: My group wants to hold a trashion show. "Trashion" is a combination of "trash" and "fashion." We'll use trash to make clothes. We want other students to become interested in upcycling through the show.

Mr. Brown: A trashion show sounds like fun! What about your group, Eric?

Eric: My group is going to make ___ⓐ___ from old things. We'll make drums from old plastic buckets. We'll also make a guitar from old boxes and rubber bands. We plan to play the instruments in a mini-concert.

Mr. Brown: Thank you, Eric. Now, let's hear from Sumi's group.

24 위 글의 내용과 일치하지 <u>않는</u> 것은?

① Pei의 그룹은 트래션 쇼를 열 것이다.
② Pei의 그룹은 옷을 만들기 위해 쓰레기를 사용할 것이다.
③ Eric의 그룹은 낡은 양철 양동이로 드럼을 만들 것이다.
④ Eric의 그룹은 낡은 상자와 고무줄로 기타를 만들 것이다.
⑤ Eric의 그룹은 소규모 음악회를 열 것이다.

25 위 글의 빈칸 ⓐ에 들어갈 알맞은 말을 고르시오.

① experiment equipment
② motor vehicles
③ communication instruments
④ construction equipment
⑤ musical instruments

26 위 글을 읽고, 다음 질문에 대한 대답을 완성하시오.

Q: Where will Eric's group play the musical instruments?
➡ They will play them _____.

[27~28] 다음 글을 읽고, 물음에 답하시오.

Sumi: My group will make bags ①from old clothes. For example, we'll use blue jeans. Look ②at this bag. This was made ③of Hajun, one of our group members. Isn't it nice? We'll make more bags and sell them ④on Environment Day. We're going to give all the money to a nursing home.

Mr. Brown: That's a great idea. Your ideas are all so ___ⓐ___. I want everyone to work hard ⑤for Environment Day.

27 위 글의 밑줄 친 ①~⑤에서 전치사의 쓰임이 적절하지 않은 것을 찾아 알맞게 고치시오.

➡ _____

28 위 글의 빈칸 ⓐ에 들어갈 알맞은 말을 고르시오.

① dull   ② creative
③ common   ④ boring
⑤ old-fashioned

출제율 90%

01 다음 짝지어진 두 단어의 관계가 같도록 빈칸에 철자 c로 시작하는 단어를 쓰시오.

> trash : garbage = original : _____

출제율 95%

02 다음 영영풀이에 해당하는 단어는?

> particular idea that a word, expression, or sign represents

① instrument   ② discount
③ meaning   ④ condition
⑤ combination

출제율 90%

03 다음 빈칸에 우리말에 맞게 알맞은 단어를 쓰시오.

> • 아래쪽을 붙여서 바느질해라.
>   ___(A)___ the bottom together.
> • 핀과 단추로 가방을 장식해라.
>   ___(B)___ the bag with pins and buttons.

(A)_____ (B)_____

출제율 100%

04 다음의 Upcycling에 관한 글을 읽고, 괄호 (A)~(C)에 알맞은 단어가 바르게 짝지어진 것을 고르시오.

> The word "upcycling" is a (A)[combination / meaning] of "upgrade" and "recycling." (B)[Unlike / Like] recycling, upcycling is good for the environment. When you upcycle, you make new and better things from (C)[old / new] things.

① combination – Like – new
② combination – Unlike – old
③ meaning – Like – new
④ combination – Like – old
⑤ meaning – Unlike – new

[05~06] 다음 대화를 읽고, 물음에 답하시오.

> M: Hello. May I help you?
> G: _____(A)_____
> M: This one is 15 dollars and it's in good condition.
> G: Can I get a discount?
> M: OK. I'll take 2 dollars off.
> G: Then it's 13 dollars. (B)그것을 살게요.

출제율 85%

05 위 대화의 빈칸 (A)에 들어갈 말로 알맞은 것은?

① Is this clock on sale?
② I'm looking for a baseball glove.
③ How much money do you have?
④ How much are these shoes?
⑤ That's good.

출제율 95%

06 위 대화의 (B)의 우리말에 맞게 영어로 쓰시오.

➡ _____

[07~09] 다음 대화를 읽고, 물음에 답하시오.

> B: Wow! There are so ⓐmany interesting things here.
> W: Everything here ⓑare old or used. What are you looking for?
> B: I'm looking for a clock.
> W: _____(A)_____
> B: How much is it?
> W: It's 15 dollars.
> B: That's ⓒtoo expensive for me.
>   _____(B)_____
> W: No, I'm afraid not. It's only one year old. It's ⓓalmost new.
> B: Then, 숫자가 큰 이 파란색 시계는 얼마예요?
> W: It's 10 dollars.
> B: Then, I'll take the blue ⓔone. Thank you.

07 위 대화의 빈칸 (A)와 (B)에 들어갈 말로 알맞은 것을 〈보기〉에서 찾아 쓰시오.

> ┤ 보기 ├
> - Where can I find them?
> - How about this red clock?
> - What can I do for you?
> - Can I get a discount?
> - How much is it?

(A) _____

(B) _____

08 위 대화의 밑줄 친 우리말에 맞게 주어진 단어를 이용하여 영어로 쓰시오.

> how / this blue / with / numbers

➡ _____

09 위 대화의 밑줄 친 부분 중 어법상 <u>어색한</u> 것은?

① ⓐ　　② ⓑ　　③ ⓒ　　④ ⓓ　　⑤ ⓔ

10 다음 대화의 빈칸에 들어갈 말로 알맞은 것은?

> A: May I help you?
> B: Yes. How much is this scarf?
> A: It's 6 dollars.
> B: Can I get a discount?
> A: _____
> B: Then, I don't think I'll take it.

① OK. I'll take 2 dollars off.
② Sounds good.
③ No, I'm afraid not. Sorry.
④ It is on sale.
⑤ I got it.

11 다음 중 어법상 올바른 것은?

① The key was stole by Bill.
② Presents were given for all the children.
③ The pictures were taken by Jerry.
④ Did her homework finished by her?
⑤ The spaghetti made my dad.

12 다음 중 어법상 올바르지 <u>않은</u> 것은?

① They asked me to stay longer.
② Sujin, do you want me to dance?
③ I made her clean her room.
④ Tell them coming to my birthday party.
⑤ Mom didn't allow me to go camping.

13 다음 문장을 수동태로 고쳐 쓰시오.

(1) Did Emma teach the students English?
(두 가지로)

➡ _____

➡ _____

(2) We can send a lot of data through the Internet.

➡ _____

(3) Edgar Degas painted *The Dance Class*.

➡ _____

14 다음 문장에서 어법상 잘못된 것을 고치시오. (출제율 95%)

(1) They asked him give a speech.

_____ ➡ _____

(2) Clara made him to wait for her for an hour outside.

_____ ➡ _____

15 다음 질문에 맞는 답을 빈칸을 알맞게 채워 완성하시오. (출제율 85%)

(1) Who painted *The Walk*?

➡ *The Walk* _____ Marc Chagall.

(2) Who invented Hangeul?

➡ Hangeul _____ King Sejong.

(3) Who was pleased to hear the news?

➡ Jake _____ the news.

[16~18] 다음 글을 읽고, 물음에 답하시오.

Mr. Brown: Hello, club members. ⓐAs you know, this year's Environment Day is about upcycling. Before we talk ⓑ_____ each group's event idea ⓒ_____ that day, I want you to understand the meaning of "upcycling." Can anyone explain upcycling?

Sumi: Yes. The word "upcycling" is a combination of "upgrade" and "recycling."

Eric: Like recycling, upcycling is good for the _____ⓓ_____ . When you upcycle, you make new and better things from old things.

16 위 글의 밑줄 친 ⓐAs와 같은 의미로 쓰인 것을 고르시오. (출제율 90%)

① I respect him as a doctor.

② As you can see, I have no money.

③ She doesn't play as well as her sister.

④ As he was busy, he couldn't go there.

⑤ As he grew older, he became faster.

17 위 글의 빈칸 ⓑ와 ⓒ에 들어갈 전치사가 바르게 짝지어진 것은? (출제율 100%)

① about – to
② for – from
③ to – for
④ with – by
⑤ about – for

18 위 글의 빈칸 ⓓ에 들어갈 알맞은 말을 본문에서 찾아 쓰시오. (출제율 90%)

➡ _____

[19~21] 다음 글을 읽고, 물음에 답하시오.

Pei: My group wants to _____ⓐ_____ a trashion show. "Trashion" is a combination of "trash" and "fashion." We'll use trash ⓑto make clothes. We want other students to become interested in upcycling through the show.

19 위 글의 빈칸 ⓐ에 들어갈 알맞은 말을 고르시오. (출제율 95%)

① bring
② hold
③ find
④ take
⑤ get

20 위 글의 밑줄 친 ⓑto make와 to부정사의 용법이 다른 것을 고르시오. (출제율 90%)

① This river is dangerous to swim in.

② I was sad to lose the game.

③ He ran fast to catch the bus.

④ She must be careless to do so.

⑤ Pei's group plans to make clothes.

21 본문의 내용과 일치하도록 다음 빈칸 (A)~(C)에 알맞은 단어를 쓰시오.

> Pei's group will make ___(A)___ by using trash and prepare a ___(B)___ . They want other students to become interested in ___(C)___ through the show.

(A)_____ (B)_____ (C)_____

[22~24] 다음 글을 읽고, 물음에 답하시오.

Sumi: My group will make bags from old clothes. For example, we'll use blue jeans. Look at this bag. ⓐThis was made by Hajun, one of our group members. Isn't it nice? We'll make more bags and sell them on Environment Day. We're going to give all the money to a nursing home.

Mr. Brown: That's a great idea. Your ideas are all so creative. I want everyone to work hard for Environment Day.

22 위 글을 읽고 대답할 수 없는 질문은?

① What will Sumi's group make?
② When will Sumi's group sell more bags?
③ How much money does Sumi's group expect to earn?
④ How will Sumi's group use the money from the sale?
⑤ What does Mr. Brown want everyone to do?

23 위 글의 밑줄 친 ⓐThis가 가리키는 것을 본문에서 찾아 쓰시오.

➡ _____

24 위 글을 읽고, 다음 빈칸에 들어갈 말로 가장 적절한 것을 고르시오.

> Sumi's group will sell more bags and _____ all the money to a nursing home.

① save
② donate
③ keep
④ store
⑤ recycle

[25~26] 다음 그림을 보고, 물음에 답하시오.

Blue Jeans Bag

You Need: old blue jeans, sewing kit, scissors, pins and buttons

Step
1 ___ the legs of the blue jeans.
2 ___ the bottom together.
3 Make shoulder straps ___ one of the legs.
4 ___ the straps to the top of the jeans.
5 ___ the bag with pins and buttons.

25 위 그림의 Step 1~5의 빈칸에 들어갈 알맞은 단어를 쓰시오.

(1)_____ (2)_____ (3)_____
(4)_____ (5)_____

26 위 글의 Blue Jeans Bag을 만드는 데 필요한 재료가 <u>아닌</u> 것을 고르시오.

① 낡은 청바지
② 바느질 도구 세트
③ 가위
④ 지퍼
⑤ 핀과 단추들

서술형 실전문제

01 다음 대화를 읽고, 아래 문장의 빈칸을 채우고 질문에 영어로 답하시오.

> B: Wow! There are so many interesting things here.
> W: Everything here is old or used. What are you looking for?
> B: I'm looking for a clock.
> W: How about this red clock?
> B: How much is it?
> W: It's 15 dollars.
> B: That's too expensive for me. Can I get a discount?
> W: No, I'm afraid not. It's only one year old. It's almost new.
> B: Then, how much is this blue clock with the large numbers?
> W: It's 10 dollars.
> B: Then, I'll take the blue one. Thank you.

 Price: _____
It's only _____ old.

 Price: _____
It has _____ .

> Q: What is the boy going to buy?
> ➡ _____

 02 다음 그림을 보고 대화를 완성하시오.

 black bag
$15 → $13

> A: (A) _____
> B: It's 15 dollars.
> A: Can I get a discount?
> B: OK. (B) _____
> A: Then it's 13 dollars. I'll take it.

03 다음 그림을 보고, Jenny가 점원과 나누는 대화의 빈칸을 완성하시오.

 $18

> Jenny: Excuse me. How much are the _____ _____ ?
> Man: They're _____ _____ .
> Jenny: Hmm. Can I get a discount?
> Man: No, _____ _____ _____ . Sorry.
> Jenny: That's OK. I'll take them.

04 다음 주어진 문장을 같은 뜻을 갖는 문장으로 바꾸어 쓰시오.

(1) Ms. Brown asked that the students should clean the classroom.
➡ _____

(2) His parents expected that he would win the contest.
➡ _____

(3) The boss warned that the driver should drive very carefully.
➡ _____

05 다음 우리말을 영작하시오.

> 그 책은 한국어로 쓰이지 않았다.

➡ _____

06 다음 상황에 알맞은 말을 어법에 맞게 빈칸에 쓰시오.

(1) This morning he was late for school. The teacher said to him, "Don't be late."
➡ The teacher told him _____ _____ _____ _____ for school.

(2) Mr. White said to me, "Don't give up."
➡ Mr. White encouraged me _____ _____ _____ _____ .

Pei: My group wants to hold a trashion show. "Trashion" is a combination of "trash" and "fashion." We'll use trash to make clothes. ⓐWe want other students to become interesting in upcycling through the show.

Mr. Brown: ⓑ트래션 쇼라니 멋지겠구나! What about your group, Eric?

Eric: My group is going to make musical instruments from old things. We'll make drums from old plastic buckets. We'll also make a guitar from old boxes and rubber bands. We plan to play the instruments in a mini-concert.

07 위 글의 밑줄 친 ⓐ에서 어법상 틀린 부분을 찾아 고치시오.

_____ ➡ _____

08 위 글의 밑줄 친 ⓑ의 우리말에 맞게 주어진 어휘를 이용하여 6 단어로 영작하시오.

like / fun

➡ _____

09 다음 빈칸 (A)~(D)에 알맞은 단어를 넣어 upcycling을 위한 Eric의 아이디어를 완성하시오.

Eric's Group: For Environment Day
- make (A)_____ _____ from old things
- make drums from (B)_____ _____ _____
- make a guitar (C)_____ old boxes and rubber bands
- play (D)_____ _____ in a mini-concert

Sumi: My group will make bags from old (A)[cloths / clothes]. For example, we'll use blue jeans. Look at this bag. This was made by Hajun, one of our group members. (B)[Is / Isn't] it nice? We'll make more bags and sell them on Environment Day. We're going to give all the money (C)[for / to] a nursing home.

Mr. Brown: ⓐThat's a great idea. Your ideas are all so creative. I want everyone to work hard for Environment Day.

10 위 글의 괄호 (A)~(C)에서 문맥이나 어법상 알맞은 낱말을 골라 쓰시오.

(A)_____ (B)_____ (C)_____

11 위 글의 밑줄 친 ⓐThat이 가리키는 내용을 우리말로 쓰시오.

➡ _____
_____

12 다음 문장에서 위 글의 내용과 다른 부분을 찾아서 고치시오.

Mr. Brown wants to work hard for Environment Day.

_____ ➡ _____

창의사고력 서술형 문제

01 다음 연결된 말을 보고 두 개의 대화를 완성하시오. (할인을 받는 경우는 I'll take it.으로, 할인을 받지 못하는 경우는 Then, I don't think I'll take it.으로 대화를 끝내시오.)

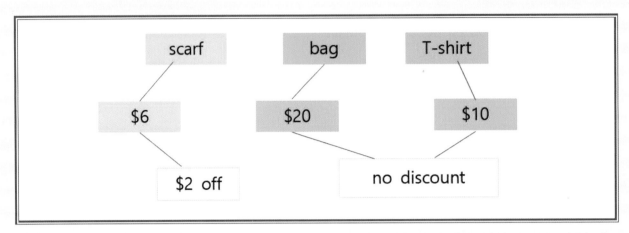

02 다음 메모 내용과 일치하도록 want를 이용하여 어법에 맞게 쓰시오.

To-do List
(1) Minsu – clean your room
(2) Mina – do the dishes
(3) me – walk the dog
               - Mom -

(1) _____

(2) _____

(3) _____

03 다음 빈칸 (A)~(D)에 알맞은 단어를 넣어 낡은 청바지를 이용하여 바구니를 만드는 방법을 설명하는 글을 완성하시오.

Creative Upcycling Idea: Blue Jeans Basket

   There are many great upcycling ideas. Here is one example. I made a basket from my old blue jeans. Do you want to make one, too? Then I want you to follow these (A)_____.

   You Need: old blue jeans, sewing kit, scissors, and pins and buttons

First, (B)_____ off a leg of the old blue jeans.

(C)_____, cut out a piece to make the bottom of the basket.

Third, sew the bottom to the leg.

Lastly, (D)_____ with pins and buttons.

Upcycling is good for the environment. I want you to become interested in upcycling.

단원별 모의고사

01 다음 단어에 대한 영어 설명이 <u>어색한</u> 것은?

① decorate: to make something look nice by adding pretty things to it
② environment: the natural world, including water, air, land, and plants
③ discount: the amount of money that you have to pay in order to buy something
④ bucket: a deep round container with a handle on the top
⑤ instrument: something such as a piano, guitar, or drum that you play in order to make music

02 다음 짝지어진 두 단어의 관계가 같도록 빈칸에 알맞은 말을 쓰시오.

expensive : cheap = downgrade : _____

03 다음 영영풀이에 해당하는 단어를 고르시오.

to tell someone about something in a way that is clear or easy to understand

① explain   ② sell
③ know   ④ understand
⑤ throw

04 다음 대화의 빈칸에 공통으로 들어갈 말은?

M: This backpack is 15 dollars.
G: Can I get a discount?
M: OK. I'll _____ 2 dollars off. So it'll be 13 dollars.
G: I'll _____ it, then.

① get   ② buy   ③ make
④ turn   ⑤ take

05 다음 그림을 보고, 대화의 빈칸을 완성하시오.

W: May I help you?
B: Yes. (A)_____ _____ is this blue T-shirt?
W: (B)_____ _____.
B: Can I get a discount?
W: OK. I'll (C)_____ _____ _____.
B: That sounds good. I'll take it.

06 다음 그림을 참고하여 대화의 빈칸에 들어갈 알맞은 말을 쓰시오.

clock
$15
$3 off

M: Hello. May I help you?
G: I _____ _____ _____ a clock.
M: This one is 15 dollars and it's in good condition.
G: Can I _____ _____ _____?
M: OK. I'll _____ 3 dollars _____.
G: Then it's _____ dollars. I'll take it.

07 다음 그림을 보고, 대화의 빈칸을 완성하시오.

pink skirt
$10 → $9

A: (1)_____
B: It's 10 dollars.
A: Can I get a discount?
B: OK. (2)_____

08 다음 밑줄 친 ⓐ와 ⓑ가 가리키는 것으로 알맞게 짝지어진 것은?

G: Excuse me. How much is this yellow backpack?
M: It's 18 dollars.
G: Hmm. That's expensive for me. How about this red ⓐone?
M: It's 15 dollars.
G: That's a good price. I'll take ⓑit.

① yellow backpack – the red backpack
② red backpack – the red backpack
③ backpack – the yellow backpack
④ backpack – the red backpack
⑤ yellow backpack – the backpack

09 다음 두 사람의 대화가 <u>어색한</u> 것은?

① A: What are you looking for?
　 B: I'm looking for a clock.
② A: How much is this red clock?
　 B: It's 15 dollars.
③ A: What's the price of this hat?
　 B: It's 15 dollars.
④ A: Can I get a discount?
　 B: No, I'm afraid not.
⑤ A: May I help you?
　 B: That sounds good. I'll take it.

10 다음 대화의 밑줄 친 ⓐ와 쓰임이 같은 것은?

M: Hello. May I help you?
G: I'm looking for a clock.
M: This ⓐone is 15 dollars and it's in good condition.

① Do you want one biscuit or two?
② There's only one thing we can do
③ He has only one dollar in his wallet.
④ It cost one hundred and fifty pounds.
⑤ I don't like this color. Do you have a red one?

[11~12] 다음 대화를 읽고, 물음에 답하시오.

Ben: Wow! There are so many interesting things here.
Woman: Everything here is old or used. What are you looking for?
Ben: I'm looking for a clock.
Woman: How about this red clock?
Ben: How much is it?
Woman: It's 15 dollars.
Ben: That's too expensive for me. Can I get a discount?
Woman: No, I'm afraid not. It's only one year old. It's almost new.
Ben: Then, how much is this blue clock with the large numbers?
Woman: It's 10 dollars.
Ben: Then, 그 파란색을 살게요(take, one). Thank you.

11 위 대화를 읽고 답할 수 <u>없는</u> 질문은?

① Where does the conversation probably take place?
② How much is the red clock?
③ How old is the blue clock?
④ Did Ben get a discount?
⑤ What is Ben going to buy?

12 위 대화의 밑줄 친 우리말에 맞게 주어진 단어를 이용하여 영어로 쓰시오.

➡ _____

13 다음 능동태는 수동태로, 수동태는 능동태로 바꾸어 쓰시오.

(1) This flower pot was made from an ice cream bowl.

➡ _____

(2) The Beatles wrote the song, *Yesterday*.

➡ _____

(3) She cooked us some cookies.

➡ _____

(4) People laughed at Picasso at first.

➡ _____

14 다음 중 밑줄 친 부분의 쓰임이 바르지 못한 것은?

① Jack wants Jane to water the plants.
② He asked her teach math to his son.
③ He made her do her work right now.
④ We saw him singing in the rain.
⑤ He advised me not to smoke.

15 다음 문장과 같은 의미가 되도록 빈칸에 알맞은 말을 쓰시오.

I heard her open the window.

➡ She _____ .

16 다음 문장에서 어법상 어색한 것을 찾아 고치시오.

Tom asked him close the window.

_____ ➡ _____

17 다음 우리말을 to부정사를 써서 영작하시오.

나는 그녀가 친절하다고 믿는다.

➡ _____

[18~20] 다음 글을 읽고, 물음에 답하시오.

Mr. Brown: Hello, club members. As you know, this year's Environment Day is about upcycling. Before we talk about each group's event idea for ⓐthat day, I want you to understand the meaning of "upcycling." Can anyone explain upcycling?

Sumi: Yes. The word "upcycling" is a combination of "upgrade" and "recycling."

Eric: Like recycling, upcycling is good for the environment. When you upcycle, you make new and better things from old things.

Mr. Brown: Good. Now, let's talk about each group's idea for the event. Let's start ⓑ _____ Pei's group.

18 위 글의 밑줄 친 ⓐthat day가 가리키는 것을 본문에서 찾아 쓰시오.

➡ _____

19 위 글의 빈칸 ⓑ에 들어갈 알맞은 전치사를 고르시오.

① with   ② by   ③ in
④ for   ⑤ on

20 다음 빈칸 (A)와 (B)에 알맞은 단어를 넣어 위 글의 다음에 올 내용을 완성하시오.

> (A)_____ will talk about the event idea for (B)_____.

(A) _____ (B) _____

[21~22] 다음 글을 읽고, 물음에 답하시오.

Pei: My group wants to hold a trashion show. "Trashion" is a combination of "trash" and "fashion." We'll use trash to make clothes. We want other students to become interested in upcycling through the show.

Mr. Brown: A trashion show sounds ⓐlike fun! What about your group, Eric?

Eric: My group is going to make musical instruments from old things. We'll make drums from old plastic buckets. We'll also make a guitar from old boxes and rubber bands. We plan to play the instruments in a mini-concert.

Mr. Brown: Thank you, Eric. Now, let's hear from Sumi's group.

21 위 글을 읽고 대답할 수 없는 질문은?

① Who wants to hold a trashion show?
② How many students are interested in upcycling?
③ What does Mr. Brown think about Pei's idea?
④ From what is Eric's group going to make musical instruments?
⑤ Who will talk about the idea for the event after Eric?

22 위 글의 밑줄 친 ⓐlike와 쓰임이 다른 것을 고르시오.

① She looks like a serious person.
② It smells like coffee.
③ I don't like the way he talks to me.
④ It tastes like tomato juice.
⑤ That sounds like a good plan.

[23~25] 다음 글을 읽고, 물음에 답하시오.

Sumi: My group will make bags from old clothes. For example, we'll use blue jeans. Look at this bag. ⓐThis was made by Hajun, one of our group member. Isn't it nice? We'll make more bags and sell them on Environment Day. We're going to give all the money to a nursing home.

Mr. Brown: That's a great idea. ⓑ너희들의 아이디어들은 모두 아주 창의적이다. I want everyone to work hard for Environment Day.

23 위 글의 내용과 일치하지 않는 것은?

① 수미의 그룹은 낡은 옷으로 가방을 만들 예정이다.
② 하준이는 수미의 그룹에 속해 있다.
③ 수미의 그룹은 더 많은 가방을 만들어 그것들을 환경의 날에 팔 것이다.
④ 수미의 그룹은 모든 돈을 양로원에 드릴 것이다.
⑤ Mr. Brown은 환경의 날을 위해 열심히 일하고 싶어 한다.

24 위 글의 밑줄 친 ⓐ에서 어법상 틀린 부분을 찾아 고치시오.

_____ ➡ _____

25 위 글의 밑줄 친 ⓑ의 우리말에 맞게 주어진 어휘를 이용하여 6 단어로 영작하시오.

> so

➡ _____
_____

The Amazing World of Animals

 의사소통 기능

- 외모 묘사하기
  A: What does your cat look like?
  B: It's small and it has grey hair.

- 정보 묻기
  A: Can you tell me more about it?
  B: It has a long tail.

 언어 형식

- 주격 관계대명사
  Scientists **who** were studying crows did an experiment.

- 접속사 if
  If you think this bird is special, you are wrong.

Words & Expressions

Key Words

- **also** [ɔ́ːlsou] 부 또한
- **announcement** [ənáunsmənt] 명 발표, 소식
- **carry** [kǽri] 동 휴대하다
- **coconut** [kóukənʌt] 명 코코넛 열매
- **coin purse** 동전 지갑
- **cotton** [kátn] 명 면
- **crow** [krou] 명 까마귀
- **drop** [drap] 동 떨어뜨리다
- **else** [els] 부 또 다른
- **example** [igzǽmpl] 명 예, 예제
- **experiment** [ikspérəmənt] 명 실험, 시험
- **fable** [féibl] 명 우화, 동화
- **female** [fíːmeil] 형 여성의, 암컷의
- **float** [flout] 동 [물체가] (액체 면에) 뜨다, 떠다니다
- **floss** [flɔːs] 동 치실질을 하다 명 치실
- **gorilla** [gərílə] 명 고릴라
- **hide** [haid] 동 숨다, 감추다
- **imagine** [imǽdʒin] 동 상상하다
- **jar** [dʒaːr] 명 병, 단지
- **leave** [liːv] 동 ~을 두고 가다, 떠나다
- **level** [lévəl] 명 높이, 정도, 수준
- **lucky** [lʌ́ki] 형 운이 좋은
- **male** [meil] 형 남자의, 수컷의
- **navy** [néivi] 명 남색
- **octopus** [áktəpəs] 명 문어
- **once** [wʌns] 부 한때, 한동안
- **parrot** [pǽrət] 명 앵무새

- **pattern** [pǽtərn] 명 무늬, 도안
- **photograph** [fóutəgræf] 명 사진
- **pile** [pail] 동 쌓다, 포개다
- **protection** [prətékʃən] 명 보호
- **record** [rikɔ́ːrd] 동 기록하다, 등록하다 명 기록
- **restroom** [restruːm] 명 화장실
- **round-shaped** 형 둥근 모양의
- **shell** [ʃel] 명 (딱딱한) 껍데기, 껍질
- **sign** [sain] 명 몸짓, 신호, 표시
- **slowly** [slóuli] 부 천천히
- **snake** [sneik] 명 뱀
- **solve** [salv] 동 해결하다, 풀다
- **store** [stɔːr] 명 가게 동 저장하다
- **stripe** [straip] 명 줄무늬
- **succeed** [səksíːd] 동 성공하다
- **surprise** [sərpráiz] 동 놀라게 하다
- **tail** [teil] 명 꼬리
- **talent** [tǽlənt] 명 재능
- **temple** [témpl] 명 절, 사원
- **tool** [tuːl] 명 도구, 수단
- **unique** [juːníːk] 형 독특한
- **usually** [júːʒuəli] 부 대개, 보통
- **way** [wei] 명 방법, 방식
- **wear** [wɛər] 동 입다, 신다, 쓰다
- **whale** [hweil] 명 고래
- **while** [hwail] 접 ~하는 동안에
- **worm** [wəːrm] 명 벌레

Key Expressions

- **be good at** ~을 잘하다, ~에 능숙하다
- **dance to music** 음악에 맞춰 춤추다
- **find out** 알아보다
- **just as** 꼭 ~처럼
- **look for** ~을 찾다
- **look like** ~처럼 보이다, ~와 닮다
- **more than** ~ 이상(의)

- **not A but B** A가 아니고 B
- **on top of** ~의 위에
- **pull out** ~을 뽑다
- **take a rest** 휴식하다
- **talk with** ~와 이야기하다
- **watch out for** ~에 대해 조심하다, 경계하다
- **what else** 그 밖에, 그 외에

Word Power

※ 서로 반대되는 뜻을 가진 단어

□ **female**(여성의) ↔ **male**(남성의)

□ **slowly**(천천히) ↔ **fast**(빨리)

□ **float**((액체 면에) 뜨다, 떠다니다) ↔ **sink**(가라앉다)

□ **hide**(숨다, 감추다) ↔ **find**(찾다)

※ 서로 비슷한 뜻을 가진 단어

□ **lucky**(운이 좋은) : **fortunate**(운이 좋은, 행운의)

□ **pile**(쌓다, 포개다) : **stack**(쌓다, 포개다)

□ **pattern**(무늬, 도안) : **design**(디자인, 무늬)

□ **photograph**(사진) : **picture**(그림, 사진)

□ **record**(기록하다, 등록하다; 기록) : **document**(기록하다; 기록(물))

□ **solve**(해결하다, 풀다) : **deal with**(~을 해결하다)

□ **surprise**(놀라게 하다) : **amaze**(몹시 놀라게 하다)

□ **talent**(재능) : **gift**(타고난 재능), **capacity**(재능)

□ **unique**(독특한) : **special**(특별한)

□ **way**(방법) : **method**(방법, 방식)

English Dictionary

□ **announcement** 발표, 소식
→ something important that someone tells people
사람들에게 말하는 중요한 어떤 것

□ **coconut** 코코넛 열매
→ a large brown nut with a hairy shell
털이 있는 껍질을 가진 큰 갈색 견과

□ **cotton** 면
→ a type of cloth made from soft fibres from a particular plant
어떤 특별한 식물의 부드러운 섬유로 만들어지는 천의 일종

□ **experiment** 실험, 시험
→ a scientific test you do to learn about something, or to show if an idea is true
무엇인가 배우기 위해 또는 생각이 맞는지 보여주기 위해 하는 과학적 검사

□ **fable** 우화
→ a story that teaches us something
무엇인가를 우리에게 가르쳐 주는 이야기

□ **floss** 치실질을 하다; 치실
→ to clean between your teeth with dental floss/special string that you use to clean between your teeth
치실로 이 사이를 닦다 / 이 사이를 닦기 위해 사용하는 특별한 실

□ **level** 정도, 수준
→ the amount or degree of something
어떤 것의 양이나 정도

□ **navy** 남색
→ a very dark blue color
매우 진한 파란색

□ **pattern** 무늬, 도안
→ a set of lines, shapes, or colours that are repeated regularly
규칙적으로 반복되는 일련의 선, 모양, 색깔

□ **photograph** 사진
→ a picture you take using a camera
카메라를 사용하여 찍는 사진

□ **pile** 쌓다, 포개다
→ to put a lot of things on top of each other
차곡차곡 많은 것을 놓다

□ **record** 기록하다, 등록하다
→ to write down information or store it on a computer
컴퓨터에 정보를 적거나 저장하다

□ **shell** (딱딱한) 껍데기, 껍질
→ the hard outside part of a nut or egg
견과류나 알의 딱딱한 겉부분

□ **surprise** 놀라게 하다
→ to make someone have a feeling of surprise
누군가를 놀라움의 감정을 갖게 하다

□ **talent** 재능
→ an ability to do something well
어떤 것을 잘하는 능력

□ **tool** 도구, 수단
→ a thing that you use for making or doing something
어떤 것을 하거나 만들기 위해 사용하는 것

01 다음 문장의 빈칸에 들어갈 말로 알맞은 것은?

> Children have to wear helmets for _____
> when they ride bikes.

① helper   ② control
③ function   ④ equipment
⑤ protection

02 다음 밑줄 친 부분과 의미가 가장 가까운 것을 고르시오.

> I need to <u>take a rest</u> a little.

① be tired   ② take care of
③ make a mistake   ④ sleep
⑤ relax

03 다음 문장의 빈칸에 알맞은 것은?

> Pull _____ the flag around the corner.

① up   ② out
③ off   ④ from
⑤ with

04 다음 중 밑줄 친 부분의 뜻풀이가 바르지 <u>않은</u> 것은?

① The scientists did a new <u>experiment</u> to learn more about monkeys. (실험)
② Do you need anything <u>else</u>? (또 다른)
③ She <u>piled</u> the boxes. (보관하다)
④ The <u>crow</u> flew up into a high tree. (까마귀)
⑤ We should use dental <u>floss</u> every day. (치실)

05 다음 빈칸에 공통으로 들어갈 말로 알맞은 것은?

> • I _____ my glasses and broke them.
> • He _____ his plate into the sink.

① dropped   ② dried
③ carried   ④ decreased
⑤ drank

06 다음 빈칸에 들어갈 알맞은 단어를 〈보기〉에서 찾아 쓰시오. (형태 변화 가능)

> ┤ 보기 ├
> unique   fable   carry

(1) I like reading Aesop's _____. They are fun.
(2) Karen was a woman of _____ talent.
(3) He always _____ a gun at that time.

07 다음 제시된 단어를 사용하여 자연스러운 문장을 만들 수 <u>없는</u> 것은? (형태 변화 가능)

> photograph   parrot   jar   floss

① To keep your teeth healthy, you have to _____ your teeth.
② There is water in the _____.
③ The man in this _____ is my grandfather.
④ The river is at its highest _____ for several years.
⑤ You can teach some _____ to say words.

08 다음 영영풀이에 해당하는 것은?

> a story that teaches us something

① fiction   ② fable
③ myth   ④ legend
⑤ language

Words & Expressions 서술형 시험대비

01 다음 짝지어진 두 단어의 관계가 같도록 빈칸에 알맞은 말을 쓰시오. (주어진 철자가 있는 경우, 주어진 철자로 시작할 것)

(1) subtract : add = sink : f_____

(2) stupid : smart = male : _____

(3) good : nice = special : u_____

(4) soft : smooth = fortunate : _____

02 다음 빈칸에 알맞은 단어를 〈보기〉에서 골라 쓰시오. (형태 변화 가능)

┌─ 보기 ─┐
leave   floss   succeed   hide
└─────┘

(1) The little goats cry out and _____ around the house.

(2) People brush and _____ their teeth.

(3) They were happy that they _____ in finishing the project in time.

(4) I _____ my key in the car, so I can't open it.

03 다음 〈보기〉에서 빈칸에 공통으로 들어갈 단어를 골라 쓰시오.

┌─ 보기 ─┐
like   take   do   talk   look
└─────┘

(1) • We started to _____ for a house with a garden.

• Koalas _____ like bears.

(2) • I just wanted to _____ to you.

• He had a chance to _____ with a new student called Christina.

04 다음 우리말에 맞게 주어진 단어를 바르게 배열하시오.

(1) 그녀는 뱀을 보고 놀랐다.

(surprised, see, snake, she, a, was, to)

➡ _____

(2) 나는 남색 정장을 입었다.

(dressed, suit, a, was, in, I, navy)

➡ _____

(3) 사원은 소나무 사이에 위치하고 있다.

(is, trees, the, located, the, pine, temple, among)

➡ _____

05 다음 주어진 우리말에 맞게 빈칸을 채우시오.

(1) 우리는 이 실험을 위해 물 한 컵이 필요하다.

➡ We need _____ _____ _____ water for this _____.

(2) 수컷 새들은 그들의 짝을 찾기 위해 노래를 부른다.

➡ The _____ birds sing to _____ their mates.

[06~07] 다음 영영풀이에 해당하는 말을 주어진 철자로 시작하여 쓰시오.

06 t_____ : an ability to do something well

07 n_____ : a very dark blue color

Conversation

1 외모 묘사하기

> **A** What does your cat look like? 너의 고양이는 어떻게 생겼니?
> **B** It's small and it has grey hair. 작고 회색 털을 가지고 있어.

■ 'What does ~ look like?'는 '~는 어떻게 생겼니?'라는 의미로 주어의 외모나 생김새를 묻는 질문이다. 이 문장에서 like는 '~처럼'이라는 의미의 전치사이다.

■ 외모를 묘사할 때에는 'be동사 + 형용사' 혹은 'have + 형용사 + 명사'의 표현을 사용할 수 있다.

외모 묻기

- What does ~ look like? ~는 어떻게 생겼니?
- How does ~ look?
- How do you describe ~?
- Tell me what ~ looks like. ~는 어떻게 생겼는지 말해 줘.

like의 쓰임

- (동사) ~을 좋아하다 ex) She likes pizza.
- (전치사) ~와 비슷한 ex) She's wearing a dress like mine.
- (전치사) ~처럼　　　ex) Don't look at me like that.

핵심 Check

1. 다음 우리말과 일치하도록 빈칸에 알맞은 말을 쓰시오.

A: _____ _____ it _____ like? (그것은 어떻게 생겼나요?)

B: It's _____ _____ _____. (그것은 길고 검은색이에요.)

2. 다음 대화의 순서를 바르게 배열하시오.

(A) Yes. I'm looking for my cap.　　(B) It's red.

(C) May I help you?　　(D) What does it look like?

_____ ➡ _____ ➡ _____ ➡ _____

② 정보 묻기

A Can you tell me more about it? 그것에 대해 더 말해 줄래?

B It has a long tail. 그것은 긴 꼬리를 가지고 있어.

■ 상대방에게 무엇인가에 대한 좀 더 많은 정보를 물어보기 위해서 'tell' 동사를 사용할 수 있다. 이때 tell 은 4형식 동사로 간접목적어와 직접목적어를 가질 수 있다. 'Can you tell me more about it?'에서 간접 목적어는 'me'이며, 직접목적어는 'more'이다. 'tell' 대신에 'explain', 'describe' 등의 동사로 바꾸어 쓸 수 있고, 이에 대해 모양, 무늬, 크기 등 여러 가지 특징의 정보로 대답할 수 있다.

정보를 묻는 표현

- Can[Could/Would] you tell me more about it? 그것에 대해 더 말해 줄래?
- Can[Could/Would] you explain more about it? 그것에 대해 더 설명해 줄래?
- Can[Could/Would] you describe it? 그것 좀 (자세히) 설명해 줄래?
- Can[Could/Would] you explain a little bit more? 좀 더 설명해 줄래?
- Can[Could/Would] you explain it more clearly? 그것을 더 분명하게 설명해 줄래?

■ 묘사나 정보를 묻는 대답에 사용할 수 있는 어휘

1. 무늬 종류

- stripes, a striped pattern 줄무늬
- check pattern 체크무늬
- polka dots 물방울무늬
- floral design[pattern] 꽃무늬
- a star design 별무늬

2. 모양

- round-shaped 둥근 모양의
- ring-shaped 고리 모양의
- heart-shaped 하트 모양의
- be shaped like+명사 ~의 모양을 하고 있다
- look like+명사 ~처럼 보이다. ~와 닮다

3. 색깔

- violet 보라색
- navy, Indian blue 남색
- yellow 노란색
- blue 파란색
- red 빨간색
- grey 회색
- Olive green 올리브색

4. 크기

- big, large 큰
- small 작은
- long 긴
- short 짧은

핵심 Check

3. 다음 우리말과 일치하도록 빈칸에 알맞은 말을 쓰시오.

A: _____ _____ _____ more about it (그것에 대해 더 설명해 줄래?)

B: It _____ _____ _____. (그것은 물방울무늬가 있어.)

A. Listen and Talk A 1

B: Excuse me. I'm ❶looking for my scarf.

W: ❷What does it look like?

B: ❸It's a long cotton scarf.

W: ❹Can you tell me more about it?

B: Well, it's grey.

W: OK. ❺I'll go and check.

B: 실례합니다. 저는 제 스카프를 찾고 있어요.
W: 어떻게 생겼는데요?
B: 그것은 긴 면 스카프예요.
W: 그것에 대해 더 말해 줄래요?
B: 음, 회색이에요.
W: 알겠어요. 가서 확인해 볼게요.

❶ look for: ∼을 찾다, look for 다음에는 명사나 동명사가 올 수 있다.
❷ 'What does ∼ look like?'는 '∼는 어떻게 생겼니?'라는 의미로 주어의 외모나 생김새를 묻는 질문이다. 이 문장에서 like는 '∼처럼'이라는 의미의 전치사이다.
❸ It은 scarf를 대신 받아 주는 대명사로 쓰였다. long: 긴 cotton: 면
❹ Can you tell me more about it?은 추가 정보를 얻기 위해 묻는 표현이다.
❺ I'll = I will, go와 check는 등위접속사 and에 의해 병렬 구조로 연결되어 있다.

Check(√) True or False

(1) The boy's scarf is long and grey.　　　　　　　　　　T ☐ F ☐

(2) The boy's scarf is made of cotton.　　　　　　　　　　T ☐ F ☐

B. Listen and Talk C

M: May I help you?

G: Yes. I'm looking for my dog. His name is Prince.

M: ❶What does he look like?

G: ❷He's very small and has short white hair.

M: ❸Can you tell me more?

G: Well, he has a really long tail.

M: I see. And ❹one more thing. ❺Where did you lose him?

G: I lost him ❻near the main gate.

M: OK. I'll go and ❼make an announcement. Can you please wait here?

G: Sure. Thanks a lot.

M: 도와드릴까요?
G: 네. 제 개를 찾고 있어요. 이름은 Prince예요.
M: 그가 어떻게 생겼나요?
G: 매우 작고 짧은 흰 털을 가지고 있어요.
M: 더 얘기해 줄 수 있나요?
G: 음, 그는 무척 긴 꼬리를 가지고 있어요.
M: 알겠습니다. 그리고 한 가지 더요. 어디서 잃어버렸나요?
G: 정문 근처에서 잃어버렸어요.
M: 좋아요. 가서 안내 방송을 하겠습니다. 잠시 여기에서 기다려 주시겠어요?
G: 네. 정말 감사합니다.

❶ What does he look like? = How does he look?: 그가 어떻게 생겼나요?
❷ is very small(매우 작다)와 has short white hair(짧은 흰 털을 가지고 있다)는 등위접속사 and에 의해 병렬 구조로 연결되어 있다.
❸ Can you tell me more (about your dog)?
❹ one more thing: 한 가지 더요.
❺ 의문사 where를 이용하여 장소를 묻는 표현이다.
❻ near는 '∼ 근처에서'란 뜻으로 비슷한 어구로 'close to'가 있다.
❼ announcement: 발표, 소식, make an announcement: 발표하다, 방송을 하다

Check(√) True or False

(3) The girl lost her dog.　　　　　　　　　　　　　　T ☐ F ☐

(4) The man and the girl will make an announcement.　　T ☐ F ☐

Listen and Talk A-2

W: ❶May I help you?

B: Yes. I ❷lost my bag. ❸I think I left it in the restroom.

W: OK. What does it look like?

B: It's small and yellow.

W: ❹What else? ❺Tell me more about it.

B: Let me think. Oh, it has two pockets outside.

❶ May I help you? = Can I help you? = Do you need any help?: 도와드릴까요?

❷ lose – lost – lost: 잃어버리다, 분실하다

❸ I think (that) I left in the restroom. think 다음에 that절인 명사절을 목적어로 받을 수 있는데, 여기서 that은 생략이 가능하다.

❹ what else: 그 밖에, 그 외에

❺ Tell(4형식 동사) + me(간접목적어) + more about it(직접목적어), 여기서 more는 명사로 '더 많은 것'을 의미한다.

Listen and Talk A-3

W: Do you need help?

B: Yes. I lost my umbrella.

W: ❶What does it look like?

B: It's long and navy.

W: ❷Can you tell me more?

B: Yes. ❸It has a star pattern on it.

❶ What does it look like? = How does it look?: 그것은 어떻게 생겼나요?

❷ Can you tell me more (about your umbrella)?

❸ a star pattern: 별무늬

Listen and Talk A-4

W: ❶Do you need help?

B: Yes. ❷I'm looking for my cat.

W: What does it look like?

B: Well, ❸she's not very big and she has black hair.

W: Can you tell me more? Is there ❹anything special about her?

B: She has a short tail.

❶ Do you need (any) help? = Would you like any help? = Is there anything I can do to help you? = Can I do anything to help you?

❷ be + 동사-ing: ~하는 중이다(진행형) look for: ~을 찾다

❸ 여기서 she는 my cat을 가리킨다. hair: 털

❹ anything과 같이 -thing으로 끝나는 대명사는 형용사가 뒤에서 수식한다. ex) nothing special

Listen and Talk B-4

A: May I help you?

B: Yes. I'm looking for my ❶coin purse.

A: What does it look like?

B: It's red and has a ❷smiley face on it.

A: Can you tell me more about it?

B: It has a ❸key chain.

❶ coin purse: 동전 지갑

❷ smiley: 스마일 동그라미 속에 눈 두 개와 웃는 입 모양을 그려 넣은 단순한 얼굴 그림 ☺

❸ key chain: 열쇠 고리

Listen and Talk B

A: May I help you?

B: Yes. I'm looking for my hat.

A: What does it look like?

B: It's pink and ❶round-shaped.

A: Can you tell me more about ❷it?

B: It has a yellow ❸band.

❶ 모양을 나타내는 명사(heart, square 등)와 shaped가 합쳐져서 형용사가 된다. '명사-shaped'는 '~ 모양인'의 의미를 가진다.

❷ it = the hat

❸ band: 끈

Talk and Play

A: ❶What does Amy look like?

B: ❷She's tall and has long brown hair.

A: Can you tell me more?

B: ❸She's wearing short navy pants.

A: I ❹found her!

❶ 'What does ~ look like?'는 외모를 묻는 표현이다. 여기서 like는 '~처럼'이라는 의미의 전치사이다.

❷ 명사를 수식하는 형용사가 여러 개 나왔을 경우 '외형 (크기, 형상/길이) + 신구/색깔 + 재료'의 순서로 명사를 수식할 수 있다.

❸ 'She's wearing(= She is wearing)'은 현재진행형이다. navy: 남색

❹ find-found-found: 발견하다, 찾다

Review 1

G: Hi. ❶I think I lost my umbrella.

M: ❷What does it look like?

G: It's a big navy umbrella.

M: ❸Can you tell me more?

G: ❹It has a white flower pattern on it.

❶ I think (that) + 주어 + 동사 ~: 나는 ~라고 생각한다

❷ What does it look like? = How does it look?: 그것은 어떻게 생겼나요?

❸ Can you tell me more (about your umbrella)?

❹ a white flower pattern: 흰색 꽃무늬

● 다음 우리말과 일치하도록 빈칸에 알맞은 말을 쓰시오.

Listen and Talk A-1

B: Excuse me. I'm _____ _____ my scarf.

W: What does it look _____?

B: It's a long _____ scarf.

W: Can you _____ _____ _____ about it?

B: Well, it's _____.

W: OK. I'll _____ and _____.

Listen and Talk A-2

W: May _____ _____ _____?

B: Yes. I _____ my bag. I think I _____ it in the _____.

W: OK. _____ does it look _____?

B: _____ small and yellow.

W: _____ _____? Tell me _____ about it.

B: Let me think. Oh, it has _____ _____ _____.

Listen and Talk A-3

W: Do you need _____?

B: Yes. I _____ _____ _____.

W: What _____ _____ _____ like?

B: It's _____ _____ _____.

W: Can you _____ me more?

B: Yes. It has _____ _____ _____ _____ it.

Listen and Talk A-4

B: _____ _____ need help?

W: Yes. _____ _____ for my cat.

B: What does _____ _____ _____?

W: Well, she's _____ _____ _____ and she _____ black hair.

B: Can _____ _____ _____ more? Is there _____ _____ about her?

W: She has a _____ _____.

해석

B: 실례합니다. 저는 제 스카프를 찾고 있어요.
W: 어떻게 생겼는데요?
B: 그것은 긴 면 스카프예요.
W: 그것에 대해 더 말해 줄래요?
B: 음, 회색이에요.
W: 알겠어요. 가서 확인해 볼게요.

W: 도와드릴까요?
B: 네. 저는 제 가방을 잃어버렸어요. 제 생각엔 화장실에 두고 온 것 같아요.
W: 알겠어요. 그것은 어떻게 생겼나요?
B: 작고 노란색이에요.
W: 또 다른 건요? 그것에 대해 더 말해 주세요.
B: 어디 보자. 오, 바깥쪽에 두 개의 주머니가 있어요.

W: 도움이 필요하신가요?
B: 네. 저는 제 우산을 잃어버렸어요.
W: 그것은 어떻게 생겼나요?
B: 길고 남색이에요.
W: 더 말해 주시겠어요?
B: 네. 별무늬가 있어요.

B: 도움이 필요하신가요?
W: 네. 저는 고양이를 찾고 있어요.
B: 그것은 어떻게 생겼나요?
W: 음, 그렇게 크지는 않고 털이 검은색이에요.
B: 더 말해 주시겠어요? 특별한 점이 있나요?
W: 그것은 짧은 꼬리를 가지고 있어요.

Listen and Talk B

A: May I help you?
B: Yes. _____ _____ _____ my cat.
A: What _____ _____ _____ _____ ?
B: _____ small and it _____ _____ hair.
A: _____ you tell me more _____ _____ ?
B: It _____ a long tail.

Listen and Talk B-2

A: _____ I help you?
B: Yes. _____ _____ _____ my _____ .
A: _____ does it look _____ ?
B: It's small and red.
A: Can you _____ me more _____ it?
B: _____ _____ _____ _____ in it.

Listen and Talk C

M: May I help you?
G: Yes. I'm looking _____ my dog. _____ _____ is Prince.
M: _____ _____ _____ _____ ?
G: He's very small and _____ _____ _____ hair.
M: _____ _____ tell me more?
G: Well, _____ has a _____ long tail.
M: I see. And _____ _____ _____ . _____ did you lose him?
G: I _____ him near the _____ gate.
M: OK. _____ go and _____ _____ _____ . Can you please _____ here?
G: Sure. Thanks a lot.

Talk and Play

A: What does Amy _____ _____ ?
B: She's _____ and has long _____ hair.
A: _____ _____ _____ _____ _____ ?
B: She's _____ short navy _____ .
A: I _____ her.

Review

G: Hi. I think I _____ my _____ .
M: What _____ _____ look like?
G: It's a _____ _____ _____ .
M: Can you _____ _____ ?
G: It _____ a white _____ _____ _____ it.

해석

A: 도와드릴까요?
B: 네. 저는 제 고양이를 찾고 있어요.
A: 그것은 어떻게 생겼나요?
B: 그것은 작고 회색 털을 가지고 있어요.
A: 그것에 대해 더 말해 주실 수 있나요?
B: 그것은 긴 꼬리를 가지고 있어요.

A: 도와드릴까요?
B: 네. 저는 제 지갑을 찾고 있어요.
A: 그것은 어떻게 생겼나요?
B: 그것은 작고 빨간색이에요.
A: 그것에 대해 더 말해 주실 수 있나요?
B: 그것 안에는 카드가 있어요.

M: 도와드릴까요?
G: 네. 제 개를 찾고 있어요. 이름은 Prince 예요.
M: 그가 어떻게 생겼나요?
G: 매우 작고 짧은 흰 털을 가지고 있어요.
M: 더 얘기해 줄 수 있나요?
G: 음, 그는 무척 긴 꼬리를 가지고 있어요.
M: 알겠습니다. 그리고 한 가지 더요. 어디서 잃어버렸나요?
G: 정문 근처에서 잃어버렸어요.
M: 좋아요. 가서 안내 방송을 하겠습니다. 잠시 여기에서 기다려 주시겠어요?
G: 네. 정말 감사합니다.

A: Amy는 어떻게 생겼니?
B: 그녀는 키가 크고 긴 갈색 머리야.
A: 더 말해 주겠니?
B: 그녀는 짧은 남색 바지를 입고 있어.
A: 그녀를 찾았어.

G: 안녕하세요. 제 우산을 잃어버린 것 같아요.
M: 그것은 어떻게 생겼나요?
G: 그것은 큰 남색 우산이에요.
M: 더 말해 주시겠어요?
G: 흰색 꽃무늬가 있어요.

[01~02] 다음 대화의 빈칸에 알맞은 것을 고르시오.

01

B: _____ does Amy look like?

G: She's tall and has long brown hair.

① What shape   ② How   ③ Where

④ What look   ⑤ What

02

M: What does it look like?

G: It's a big navy umbrella.

M: _____

G: It has a white flower pattern on it.

① Can you talk with me more?

② Do you need help?

③ Can you tell me more?

④ Can you talk to me?

⑤ Can you find my umbrella?

03 다음 대화의 빈칸에 들어갈 말로 적절하지 <u>않은</u> 것은?

A: What does it look like?

B: It's _____.

① long and navy   ② big and black

③ heart-shaped   ④ smart and kind

⑤ like a really big ball

04 주어진 문장의 앞에 나올 대화의 순서를 알맞게 쓰시오.

(A) What does it look like?

(B) Excuse me. I'm looking for my scarf.

(C) Can you tell me more about it?

(D) It's a long cotton scarf.

Well, it's grey.

➡ _____

[01~04] 다음 대화를 읽고, 물음에 답하시오.

W: May I help you?

B: Yes. (①) I think I left it in the restroom. (②)

W: OK. What does it look like?

B: It's small and yellow. (③)

W: What else? __(A)__ me more about it.

B: (④) Let me think. Oh, it has two pockets outside. (⑤)

01 위 대화의 ①~⑤ 중 주어진 문장이 들어갈 알맞은 곳은?

> I lost my bag.

①   ②   ③   ④   ⑤

02 Where are they?

① the restroom   ② the restaurant

③ the shop   ④ the cafeteria

⑤ the Lost and Found

03 위 대화의 빈칸 (A)에 들어갈 말로 적절한 것은?

① Show   ② Buy   ③ Tell

④ Talk   ⑤ Look

04 위 대화의 내용과 일치하지 않는 것을 고르시오.

① The woman helps the boy to find his bag.

② The boy's bag is small and has a pocket outside.

③ The woman wants to know more about the boy's bag.

④ The boy lost his bag.

⑤ The boy's bag is yellow.

[05~06] 다음 대화를 읽고, 물음에 답하시오.

A: __(A)__ I help you?

B: Yes. ①I'm looking my scarf.

A: ②What does it look like?

B: ③It's blue.

A: ④Can you tell me more about it?

B: ⑤It has a star pattern on it.

05 위 대화의 빈칸 (A)에 들어갈 말로 적절하지 않은 것은?

① May   ② Could   ③ Can

④ Should   ⑤ How may

06 위 대화의 ①~⑤ 중 어색한 곳을 고르고 고치시오.

_____ ➡ _____

[07~09] 다음 대화를 읽고, 물음에 답하시오.

W: ①Do you need help?

B: Yes. ②I'm looking for my cat.

W: ③What does it look like?

B: Well, she's not very big and she __(A)__ black hair.

W: ④Can you tell me more? ⑤Is there special anything about her?

B: She __(B)__ a short tail.

07 위 대화의 빈칸 (A)와 (B)에 들어갈 말로 적절한 것은?

① is – has   ② is – is

③ has – is   ④ has – has

⑤ has – looks

서답형

08 위 대화의 ①~⑤ 중 어색한 곳을 고르고 고치시오.

_____ ➡ _____

09 위 대화의 내용과 일치하지 <u>않는</u> 것을 고르시오.

① The boy is looking for his cat.
② The cat is black.
③ The boy lost his cat.
④ The cat's tail is long.
⑤ The cat is female.

[10~13] 다음 대화를 읽고, 물음에 답하시오.

M: May I help you? (①)
G: Yes. 제 개를 찾고 있어요. His name is Prince.
M: What does he look like?
G: He's very small and has short white hair. (②)
M: Can you tell me more? (③)
G: Well, he has a really long tail.
M: I see. And one more thing. (④)
G: I lost him near the main gate. (⑤)
M: OK. I'll go and ___(A)___ an announcement. Can you please wait here?
G: Sure. Thanks a lot.

중요

10 위 대화의 ①~⑤ 중 주어진 문장이 들어갈 알맞은 곳은?

Where did you lose him?

①　　　②　　　③　　　④　　　⑤

서답형

11 위 대화의 밑줄 친 우리말을 영작하시오.

➡ _____

중요

12 위 대화의 빈칸 (A)에 들어갈 말로 적절한 것은?

① take　　② make　　③ do
④ let　　⑤ hear

13 위 대화의 내용과 일치하지 <u>않는</u> 것을 고르시오.

① 개는 짧은 털을 가지고 있다.
② 개의 꼬리는 길다.
③ 여자아이는 개를 후문 근처에서 잃어버렸다.
④ 남자는 개를 찾는 방송을 할 것이다.
⑤ 개의 이름은 Prince이다.

[14~15] 다음 대화를 읽고, 물음에 답하시오.

A: What does Amy look like?
B: She's tall and ___(A)___ brown hair. (2단어)
A: Can you tell me more?
B: She's ___(B)___ navy pants. (2단어)
A: I ___(C)___ her!

서답형

14 다음 Amy의 사진을 보고 (A)와 (B)를 완성하시오.

(A) _____
(B) _____

서답형

15 위 대화의 빈칸 (C)에 들어갈 말로 적절한 것을 주어진 철자로 시작하여 쓰시오.

➡ f_____

[01~02] 다음 대화를 읽고, 물음에 답하시오.

G: Hi. (A)(lost, my, think, I, I, umbrella)
M: What does it look like?
G: It's a big navy umbrella.
M: Can you tell me more?
G: (B)흰색 꽃무늬가 있어요.(a, pattern, on)

01 위 대화의 (A)에 주어진 단어를 알맞게 배열하시오.

➡ _____

02 위 대화의 (B)의 밑줄 친 우리말을 영어로 옮기시오.

➡ _____

[03~06] 다음 대화를 읽고, 물음에 답하시오.

W: May I help you?
B: Yes. I lost my bag. I think I left it ___(A)___ the restroom.
W: OK. What does it look ___(B)___ ?
B: It's small and ___(C)___ .
W: What else? ⓐTell me more about it.
B: Let me think. Oh, ___(D)___ .

03 위 대화의 빈칸 (A)와 (B)에 알맞은 전치사를 쓰시오.

(A) _____ (B) _____

04 위 그림을 참고하여 (C)에 알맞은 말을 쓰시오.

➡ _____

05 위 대화의 밑줄 친 ⓐ와 의미가 같게 주어진 단어를 이용해 문장을 쓰시오.

(can)

➡ _____

06 그림을 참고하여, 주어진 단어를 이용해 (D)에 들어갈 문장을 완성하시오.

(outside, pockets)

➡ _____

07 주어진 문장 앞에 나올 대화의 순서를 바르게 배열하시오.

(A) Yes. I'm looking for my wallet. (B) It's small and red. (C) May I help you? (D) Can you tell me more about it? (E) What does it look like?

There is a card in it.

➡ _____

08 다음 표를 보고 대화를 완성하시오.

Lost Pet Report	
type of animal	cat
color	black hair
size	not very big
anything special	short tail

W: Do you need help?
B: Yes. I'm looking for _____ _____ .
W: What does it look like?
B: Well, she's _____ _____ _____ and she has _____ _____ .
W: Can you tell me more? Is there anything special about her?
B: She _____ _____ _____ _____ .

Grammar

교과서

① 주격 관계대명사

- Scientists **who** were studying crows did an experiment.
  까마귀를 연구하던 과학자들이 실험을 했다.

- We'll go to a restaurant **that** has a kids' menu. 우리는 아이들 식단이 있는 식당에 갈 것이다.

■ 관계대명사는 접속사와 대명사의 역할을 한다. 관계대명사절은 명사를 수식해 주는 절의 한 종류로 관계대명사절이 꾸며 주는 말을 선행사라고 하고 관계대명사는 앞의 선행사와 같은 대상을 가리킨다. 관계대명사절이 되기 전의 문장에서 주어로 쓰였으면 주격 관계대명사로, 소유격으로 쓰였으면 소유격 관계대명사로, 목적격으로 쓰였으면 목적격 관계대명사가 된다. 주격 관계대명사는 관계대명사절에서 주어 역할을 하므로 그 다음에는 동사가 온다.

- He is the man. He(=The man) met Mary yesterday.
  = He is the man **who** met Mary yesterday.

- He is the man. Mary met him(=the man) yesterday.
  = He is the man **whom** Mary met yesterday.

■ 관계대명사는 선행사에 따라 다음과 같이 사용되며, 목적격 관계대명사는 생략할 수 있다.

	주격	소유격	목적격
사람	who / that	whose	whom[who] / that
동물, 사물	which / that	whose / of which	which / that

- I'm looking for the man **who[that]** sent me the present. 나는 나에게 그 선물을 보낸 남자를 찾고 있다.

- I went to the concert **which** was free of charge. 나는 무료인 그 콘서트에 갔다.

■ 관계대명사 that은 who, whom과 which 대신 사용할 수 있으며 소유격은 없다. 또한 선행사가 '사람+동물[사물]'인 경우에는 반드시 that을 써야 한다.

- Look at the boy and his dog **that** are playing in the park. 공원에서 놀고 있는 소년과 그의 개를 보아라.

핵심 Check

1. 다음 우리말에 맞게 빈칸에 알맞은 말을 쓰시오.

(1) 그가 새 도서관을 디자인한 남자이다.

➡ He's the man _____ designed the new library.

(2) 나는 말을 할 수 있는 로봇을 가지고 싶다.

➡ I want to have a robot _____ can talk.

2 접속사 if

- **If** you think this bird is special, you are wrong.
  만약 당신이 이 새가 특별하다고 생각한다면, 당신이 틀렸다.

- Your English will improve **if** you study hard.
  네가 열심히 공부한다면, 너의 영어 실력이 향상될 것이다.

■ if는 '만약 ~한다면'이라는 뜻의 접속사로 문장 앞에 쓰여 그 문장을 다른 문장에 연결해 준다. if절은 조건을 나타내는 부사절이다. 접속사가 사용된 문장에서 접속사가 붙은 절을 종속절, 접속사가 붙지 않은 나머지 절을 주절이라고 하는데, 주절이 먼저 나올 수도 있고 종속절이 먼저 나올 수도 있다.

- You can come to the party **if** you want. 너는 네가 원하면 그 파티에 올 수 있어.

■ 접속사 unless는 '만약 ~하지 않는다면'의 뜻으로 'if ~ not'과 같은 의미이다.

- We won't go to the party **unless** we're invited.
  = We won't go to the party **if** we're **not** invited. 우리는 초대받지 않는다면 그 파티에 가지 않을 것이다.

■ 시간이나 조건의 접속사가 이끄는 부사절에서는 미래의 의미를 갖더라도 will을 쓰지 않고 현재시제를 쓴다.

- **If** it **rains** tomorrow, I won't go swimming. 내일 비가 오면 수영하러 안 갈 거야.

- I will go shopping **after** I **finish** doing my homework. 숙제를 끝낸 후에 나는 쇼핑하러 갈 거야.

■ if절이 명사 역할을 하는 경우도 있으며 (이때 if는 whether와 같은 의미이다.) 이때는 '~인지 아닌지' 로 해석하며 미래를 나타낼 때에는 미래시제를 써야 한다.

- I wonder **if** she will be at home tomorrow. 나는 그녀가 내일 집에 있을지 궁금하다.

핵심 Check

2. 다음 우리말에 맞게 빈칸에 알맞은 말을 쓰시오.

(1) 만약 그들이 지금 떠난다면 기차를 탈 수 있다.

➡ They can catch the train _____ they leave now.

(2) 만약 학교가 일찍 끝난다면, 나는 해변에 갈 것이다.

➡ If school _____ early, I _____ _____ to the beach.

(3) 나는 그가 파티에 참석할 것인지 잘 모르겠다.

➡ I am not sure _____ he _____ take part in the party.

01 다음 빈칸에 들어갈 알맞은 것은?

> The girl _____ is standing next to him is my sister.

① which   ② what   ③ that   ④ whom   ⑤ whose

02 다음 문장에서 어법상 <u>어색한</u> 부분을 바르게 고쳐 쓰시오.

(1) I have a friend which lives in London.

_____ ➡ _____

(2) Read the magazine who is on the desk.

_____ ➡ _____

(3) You don't have to do so unless you don't want to.

_____ , _____ ➡ _____

(4) If it will rain tomorrow, the picnic will be held inside.

_____ ➡ _____

03 다음 우리말에 맞게 괄호 안에 주어진 단어를 빈칸에 바르게 배열하시오.

(1) 만약 네가 내 여동생을 본다면, 이 책을 줘라.

   (see, you, my sister, if)

   ➡ _____ _____ _____ _____ _____ , please give her this book.

(2) 우리는 재미있는 모자를 쓰고 있는 여자를 봤다.

   (was, a, hat, wearing, funny, who)

   ➡ We saw a woman _____ _____ _____ _____ _____ _____ .

04 다음 우리말을 영어로 옮길 때, 빈칸에 알맞은 것이 순서대로 짝지어진 것은?

> 그는 숙제를 끝내면 TV를 볼 것이다.
> ➡ He _____ TV if he _____ his homework.

① will watch – will finish   ② will watch – finishes
③ watches – will finish   ④ watches – finishes
⑤ watched – finished

01 다음 빈칸에 들어갈 수 있는 말이 <u>다른</u> 하나는?

① He wants to meet the woman _____ saved his son.
② I have a friend _____ is good at dancing.
③ There is a house _____ the roof is red.
④ The water _____ was flowing out of the bottle changed into ice.
⑤ Do you know the girl _____ wants to go abroad?

02 다음 중 어법상 바르지 <u>않은</u> 것은?

① If school finishes early tomorrow, I will go to see a movie.
② I forget things unless I take notes.
③ I like the book that has many pictures.
④ Unless we take the subway, we will get there on time.
⑤ Your parents should visit the Louvre Museum if they go to Paris.

03 다음 괄호 안에서 알맞은 말을 고르시오.

(1) Degas loved painting dancers (which / who) were dancing on stage.
(2) Jane likes the *Starry Night* (who / which) Van Gogh painted.
(3) Do you know the girl (that / which) is wearing a red skirt?
(4) We will go on a picnic, (if / unless) it's fine.
(5) If you (will go / go) straight two blocks, you will find the building.

04 주어진 어휘를 이용하여 다음 우리말을 영어로 쓰시오.

당신은 휴식을 취하면 기분이 더 좋아질 거예요.
(feel better, take a rest)

➡ _____

05 다음 밑줄 친 that의 성격이 나머지 넷과 <u>다른</u> 것은?

① The dog <u>that</u> has a long tail belongs to Mr. Jones.
② This is the boy <u>that</u> showed me the way to the library.
③ There are lots of Korean dishes <u>that</u> taste delicious.
④ The book <u>that</u> Merriam bought for me is interesting.
⑤ I knew <u>that</u> you were going to ask this question.

06 다음 밑줄 친 부분의 의미가 <u>다른</u> 하나는?

① I would like a cup of coffee <u>if</u> you don't mind.
② I don't know <u>if</u> you can help me.
③ <u>If</u> you know the answer, please speak loudly.
④ <u>If</u> it's fine tomorrow, we'll go hiking.
⑤ <u>If</u> I sell the eggs, I can make money.

07 다음 문장에서 생략할 수 있는 것을 찾아 쓰시오.

(1) He never touched food which he didn't like.

➡ _____

(2) The man who is talking on the radio is famous.

➡ _____

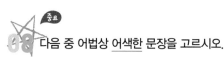 다음 중 어법상 <u>어색한</u> 문장을 고르시오.

① If it will snow tomorrow, I'll go skiing.
② Unless you study hard, you can't pass the exam.
③ If I sell some milk, I can buy a chicken.
④ If you can't fall asleep easily, count numbers.
⑤ It is difficult to do unless you are a professional.

09 다음 중 어법상 옳은 문장을 고르시오.

① Leonardo da Vinch painted *the Mona Lisa* who is a very famous picture.
② I want to make a robot who can do the dishes.
③ This is the boy which she met the other day.
④ Emily likes to take pictures of flowers who are blooming.
⑤ Sam made two chairs that are comfortable to sit on.

10 다음 문장의 빈칸에 들어가기에 의미상 자연스러운 것은? (2개)

> _____, you will get a good grade.

① Unless you listen to your teacher
② Unless you waste your time
③ If you use your cell phone during a class
④ If you pay attention to your teacher carefully
⑤ If you don't study hard

11 다음 두 문장을 한 문장으로 바르게 바꾸면?

> • A koala is an animal.
> • It has a big nose.

① A koala is that an animal has a big nose.
② A koala is an animal which it has a big nose.
③ A koala is an animal which has a big nose.
④ A koala is an animal which a big nose.
⑤ A koala is an animal who has a big nose.

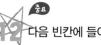 다음 빈칸에 들어갈 알맞은 것은?

> I bought a new camera _____.

① that I like a lot
② who works really well
③ which it looks very expensive
④ that I gave it to my son
⑤ that the shop sold it

13 다음 괄호 안에 주어진 단어들을 바르게 배열하여 문장을 완성하시오.

> (class, there, no, today, if, is), I will go see a movie with my friend.

➡ _____

서답형

14 다음 그림을 보고 괄호 안에 주어진 어휘를 이용하여 빈칸을 알맞게 채우시오.

_____, you must go to the dentist. (have a toothache)

서답형

15 다음 우리말에 맞게 괄호 안의 어구를 바르게 배열하시오.

소년과 함께 잔디 위에 앉아 있는 개를 봐. (boy, the grass, sitting, that, is, on, a, with)
➡ Look at the dog _____.

➡ _____

16 다음 중 밑줄 친 부분의 쓰임이 잘못된 것은?

① What shall we do if it will begin snowing?
② If I travel to Europe, I will visit Oxford University in England.
③ If I have 100,000 won now, I'll buy a new backpack.
④ If you are hungry, you can eat the pizza on the table.
⑤ If I am hungry, I will eat ramyeon.

17 다음 밑줄 친 부분의 쓰임이 어색한 것은?

① I want to buy a bag which has many pockets outside.
② Morris gave me a book which has many pictures.
③ Children who are under 120 cm cannot ride the roller coaster.
④ Mary likes the boy who came from Turkey.
⑤ Summer is the season who comes before fall.

중요

18 다음 빈칸에 들어갈 말을 순서대로 바르게 연결한 것은?

- _____ you go to bed early, you will be late for school tomorrow.
- _____ I get enough sleep, I will feel better.

① If – If
② If – Unless
③ Unless – If
④ Unless – Unless
⑤ When – However

19 다음 주어진 문장의 밑줄 친 부분과 동일한 역할을 하는 것을 두 개 고르시오.

Mike has a brother who plays the guitar very well.

① The lady who you met yesterday is my mom.
② Minsu met a girl who was very kind.
③ There are many girls who want to go swimming.
④ Who are you waiting for?
⑤ Find a friend who you can always depend on.

20 다음 주어진 문장과 의미가 같은 문장은?

You'll be late unless you hurry.

① You'll be late because you don't hurry.
② Hurry, so you will be late.
③ Hurry, and you will be late.
④ Hurry, or you will be late.
⑤ Hurry, but you will be late.

01 다음 두 문장을 관계대명사를 이용하여 한 문장으로 연결하시오.

(1) • This is a great book.

• The book gave hope to many people.

➡ _____

_____

(2) • Pilots are the persons.

• They fly airplanes.

➡ _____

(3) • David has a brother.

• He plays basketball well.

➡ _____

_____

(4) • Kate bought some roses.

• They smelled good.

➡ _____

_____

(5) • Look at the man and his dog.

• They are sleeping under the tree.

➡ _____

_____

02 다음 두 문장의 뜻이 같도록 빈칸에 알맞은 말을 쓰시오.

(1) Eat vegetables, and you can stay healthy.

➡ _____ you eat vegetables, you can stay healthy.

(2) Take the subway, or you'll be late.

➡ _____ you take the subway, you'll be late.

03 다음 문장의 잘못된 부분을 바르게 고쳐 문장을 다시 쓰시오.

(1) This is a bird who can talk.

➡ _____

(2) Look at those musicians which are singing on the street.

➡ _____

_____

(3) Alice lives in a house who has a beautiful garden.

➡ _____

_____

(4) She is drawing two pictures that looks very similar.

➡ _____

(5) I like Cindy who she is very cool.

➡ _____

04 다음 문장을 어법에 맞게 고쳐 쓰시오.

(1) Kathy will go shopping in the afternoon if she will not be busy.

➡ _____

_____

(2) If you will meet Morina tomorrow, can you tell her to call me?

➡ _____

_____

(3) Unless you don't study hard, you won't pass the exam.

➡ _____

_____

(4) Unless the weather is bad, I will not go hiking.

➡ _____

05 다음 〈보기〉의 (A)와 (B)에서 각각 서로 관계있는 문장을 선택한 후 관계대명사 who, whom, which 중 하나를 사용하여 한 문장으로 연결하시오.

> ─┤ 보기 ├─
>
> (A) • Don't take the umbrella.
>   • Do you know the girl?
>   • He is the tour guide.
> (B) • Jack met her in the park.
>   • He will guide us in New York City.
>   • I bought it last weekend.

(1) _____

    _____

(2) _____

    _____

(3) _____

    _____

06 다음 괄호 안에 주어진 어구를 이용하여 문장을 완성하시오.

(1) _____, I will swim in the sea. (go to Jeju-do)

(2) _____, I will let you play the computer games. (finish, your homework)

(3) _____, I will buy a T-shirt for Mom. (go shopping)

07 다음 빈칸을 어법에 맞게 채우시오.

> This is the house. Diana lives in the house.

(1) This is the house _____.

(2) This is the house _____.

(3) This is the house _____.

(4) This is the house _____.

08 다음 주어진 어구를 알맞게 배열하여 문장을 완성하시오.

(1) I, I, my, him, the street, pictures, actor, will, meet, take, favorite, if, with, on

➡ _____

    _____

(2) you, it, the work, will, do, done, not, be, unless

➡ _____

09 두 문장을 관계대명사를 사용하여 한 문장으로 썼을 때, 빈칸에 해당하는 문장을 쓰시오.

(1) I want to get a robot.

_____

➡ I want to get a robot which can clean my room.

(2) _____

She is playing basketball.

➡ The girl who is playing basketball is my friend, Ann.

(3) This is a restaurant.

_____

➡ This is a restaurant that is famous for traditional Korean food.

(4) _____

The friend listens to me carefully.

➡ I want to have a friend that listens to me carefully.

10 다음 우리말을 if로 시작하여 10단어로 영작하시오.

> 오늘 학교가 일찍 끝나면, 나는 책을 읽을 거야.

➡ _____

Reading

교과서

Animals That Use Tools

People once thought that only humans can use tools. Now, scientists
are finding out that many animals can also use tools.

Macaque Monkeys

If you go to a Buddhist temple in Lop Buri, Thailand, watch out for
the Macaque monkeys. They may come to you and pull out your hair.
They use human hair to floss their teeth. If you are lucky, you may see
female monkeys that are teaching flossing to their babies. While the
babies are watching, the female monkeys floss their teeth very slowly.

This way, the baby monkeys learn to floss.
= By watching the female monkeys floss their teeth

tool 도구
once 한때, 예전에
only 오직, 단지
human 인간, 사람
Buddhist 불교의
temple 절, 사원
pull out ～을 뽑다
floss 치실질을 하다; 치실
female 여성의, 암컷의
while ～하는 동안에, ～과 동시에

확인문제

● 다음 문장이 본문의 내용과 일치하면 T, 일치하지 <u>않으면</u> F를 쓰시오.

1 Scientists are finding out that animals can't use tools. ☐

2 The Macaque monkeys may pull out your hair in the Buddhist temple in Lop Buri,
   Thailand. ☐

3 The Macaque monkeys use human hair to floss their teeth. ☐

4 While the babies are watching, the male monkeys floss their teeth very slowly. ☐

Octopuses

People don't usually think <u>that</u> octopuses are smart. <u>However,</u>
접속사   그러나(역접)
octopuses are very smart, and they can also use tools. <u>They</u> use coconut
= Octopuses   코코넛 껍질
<u>shells</u> for protection. <u>When</u> they can't find a good hiding place, they
~을 위해 (목적의 전치사)   ~할 때(접속사) = octopuses
hide under coconut shells. Some octopuses <u>even</u> store coconut shells
심지어
for later <u>use.</u> They pile the coconut shells and carry <u>them</u> to use later.
쓰임, 사용
~을 위해(목적의 전치사)   = Octopuses   = coconut shells 목적을 나타내는 to부정사
How smart!
감탄문(they are가 생략됨)

Crows

In <u>Aesop's fable</u> *The Thirsty Crow*, a crow drops stones into a jar <u>to</u>
이솝 우화   목적을 나타내는 to부정사
raise the level of water. You may think <u>this</u> is just a story, but it is not.
앞 문장 전체를 나타냄 단지
Scientists <u>who</u> were studying crows <u>did</u> an experiment. <u>They</u> put a jar
주격 관계대명사   Scientists ~ 문장의 동사   = Scientists
with water <u>in front of</u> a crow. A worm was floating on top of the water.
~ 앞에
However, the water level was low, so the crow could not eat the worm.
그러나   그래서
The crow solved the problem <u>just as</u> in the fable. It dropped stones into
꼭 ~ 처럼
the jar. If you think <u>this bird</u> is special, you are <u>wrong.</u> Scientists did
a crow in the experiment   ↔ right
the same experiment with other crows, and <u>they</u> all <u>did the same,</u> too.
= other crows = dropped stones into a jar

 확인문제

● 다음 문장이 본문의 내용과 일치하면 T, 일치하지 <u>않으면</u> F를 쓰시오.

1 Octopuses are very smart, and they can use tools. ☐

2 Octopuses use coconut shells to attack others. ☐

3 Octopuses always hide under coconut shells. ☐

4 Some octopuses carry coconut shells to use later. ☐

5 *The Thirsty Crow* is Aesop's fable. ☐

6 In an experiment, scientists put a jar filled with water in front of a crow. ☐

7 In the experiment, a worm was floating on top of the water. ☐

8 The crow in the experiment gave up eating the worm. ☐

octopus 문어
coconut 코코넛 열매
shell (딱딱한) 껍데기, 껍질
protection 보호
hide 숨다, 감추다
store 저장하다
pile 쌓다, 포개다
crow 까마귀
fable 우화, 동화
jar 병, 단지, 항아리
raise 올리다
level 높이, 정도, 수준
experiment 실험, 시험
float 뜨다, 떠오르다
solve 해결하다, 풀다

• 우리말을 참고하여 빈칸에 알맞은 말을 쓰시오.

1 Animals _____ Use _____

2 People _____ _____ that only humans can use tools.

3 Now, scientists _____ _____ _____ that many animals can _____ use tools.

4 If you go to a Buddhist temple in Lop Buri, Thailand, _____ _____ _____ the Macaque monkeys.

5 They may come to you and _____ _____ your hair.

6 They use human hair _____ _____ _____ _____ .

7 If you are lucky, you may see female monkeys _____ _____ _____ _____ to their babies.

8 _____ the babies are watching, the female monkeys _____ _____ _____ very slowly.

9 This way, the baby monkeys _____ _____ _____ .

10 People _____ _____ _____ that octopuses are smart.

11 _____ , octopuses are very smart, and they _____ _____ _____ tools.

12 They use coconut shells _____ _____ .

1	도구를 사용하는 동물들
2	사람들은 한때 인간만이 도구를 사용할 수 있다고 생각했다.
3	이제 과학자들은 많은 동물들 역시 도구를 사용할 수 있다는 것을 밝혀내고 있다.
4	당신이 태국의 롭부리에 있는 절에 간다면, 마카크 원숭이들을 조심해야 한다.
5	그들이 당신에게 다가와 당신의 머리카락을 뽑을 수도 있다.
6	그들은 이빨을 치실질하기 위해서 사람의 머리카락을 사용한다.
7	만약 당신이 운이 좋으면, 당신은 새끼들에게 치실질하는 것을 가르치고 있는 암컷 원숭이들을 볼 수 있을 것이다.
8	새끼들이 지켜보고 있는 동안, 암컷 원숭이들은 아주 천천히 그들의 이빨을 치실질한다.
9	이런 방식으로, 새끼 원숭이들은 치실질을 배운다.
10	사람들은 대개 문어가 영리하다고 생각하지 않는다.
11	하지만, 문어는 매우 영리하고 또한 도구를 사용할 수 있다.
12	그들은 자신을 보호하기 위해 코코넛 껍데기를 사용한다.

13 When they can't find _____ _____ _____ _____, they _____ _____ coconut shells.

14 Some octopuses _____ _____ coconut shells _____ _____ _____.

15 They _____ the coconut shells and carry them _____ _____ _____.

16 _____ smart!

17 In Aesop's fable *The Thirsty Crow*, a crow _____ stones _____ a jar _____ _____ the level of water.

18 You may think _____ _____ _____ _____ _____, but it is not.

19 Scientists who were studying crows _____ _____ _____ _____.

20 They put a jar _____ water _____ _____ _____ a crow.

21 A worm was floating _____ _____ _____ _____ water.

22 _____, the _____ _____ was _____, so the crow could not eat the worm.

23 The crow solved the problem _____ _____ in the fable.

24 It _____ stones _____ the jar.

25 If you think this bird is _____, you are _____.

26 Scientists did the same experiment _____ _____ _____, and they all _____ _____ _____, too.

---

13 그들이 숨을 만한 좋은 장소를 찾지 못했을 때, 그들은 코코넛 껍데기 아래로 숨는다.

14 어떤 문어들은 심지어 코코넛 껍데기를 나중에 쓰기 위해 모은다.

15 그들은 코코넛 껍데기를 쌓아두고 나중에 쓰기 위해서 가지고 다닌다.

16 얼마나 똑똑한가!

17 이솝 우화 '목마른 까마귀'에서 까마귀는 물 높이를 높이기 위해 항아리 안으로 돌을 떨어뜨린다.

18 당신은 이것이 그저 이야기라고 생각할 수 있지만, 그렇지 않다.

19 까마귀를 연구하던 과학자들이 실험을 했다.

20 그들은 까마귀 앞에 물이 든 항아리를 놓았다.

21 물 위에 벌레가 떠다니고 있었다.

22 하지만, 물 높이가 낮아서, 까마귀는 그 벌레를 먹을 수 없었다.

23 그 까마귀는 우화에서처럼 문제를 해결했다.

24 까마귀는 돌을 항아리 안으로 떨어뜨렸다.

25 만약 당신이 이 새가 특별하다고 생각한다면, 당신이 틀렸다.

26 과학자들은 다른 까마귀들에게도 똑같은 실험을 했고, 그들 모두가 똑같이 그렇게 했다.

● 우리말을 참고하여 본문을 영작하시오.

1 도구를 사용하는 동물들

➡ _____

2 사람들은 한때 인간만이 도구를 사용할 수 있다고 생각했다.

➡ _____

3 이제 과학자들은 많은 동물들 역시 도구를 사용할 수 있다는 것을 밝혀내고 있다.

➡ _____

4 당신이 태국의 롭부리에 있는 절에 간다면, 마카크 원숭이들을 조심해야 한다.

➡ _____

5 그들이 당신에게 다가와 당신의 머리카락을 뽑을 수도 있다.

➡ _____

6 그들은 이빨을 치실질하기 위해서 사람의 머리카락을 사용한다.

➡ _____

7 만약 당신이 운이 좋으면, 당신은 새끼들에게 치실질하는 것을 가르치고 있는 암컷 원숭이들을 볼 수 있을 것이다.

➡ _____

8 새끼들이 지켜보고 있는 동안, 암컷 원숭이들은 아주 천천히 그들의 이빨을 치실질한다.

➡ _____

9 이런 방식으로, 새끼 원숭이들은 치실질을 배운다.

➡ _____

10 사람들은 대개 문어가 영리하다고 생각하지 않는다.

➡ _____

11 하지만, 문어는 매우 영리하고 또한 도구를 사용할 수 있다.

➡ _____

12 그들은 자신을 보호하기 위해 코코넛 껍데기를 사용한다.

➡ _____

13 그들이 숨을 만한 좋은 장소를 찾지 못했을 때, 그들은 코코넛 껍데기 아래로 숨는다.

➡ _____

14 어떤 문어들은 심지어 코코넛 껍데기를 나중에 쓰기 위해 모은다.

➡ _____

15 그들은 코코넛 껍데기를 쌓아두고 나중에 쓰기 위해서 가지고 다닌다.

➡ _____

16 얼마나 똑똑한가!

➡ _____

17 이솝 우화 '목마른 까마귀'에서 까마귀는 물 높이를 높이기 위해 항아리 안으로 돌을 떨어뜨린다.

➡ _____

18 당신은 이것이 그저 이야기라고 생각할 수 있지만, 그렇지 않다.

➡ _____

19 까마귀를 연구하던 과학자들이 실험을 했다.

➡ _____

20 그들은 까마귀 앞에 물이 든 항아리를 놓았다.

➡ _____

21 물 위에 벌레가 떠다니고 있었다.

➡ _____

22 하지만, 물 높이가 낮아서, 까마귀는 그 벌레를 먹을 수 없었다.

➡ _____

23 그 까마귀는 우화에서처럼 문제를 해결했다.

➡ _____

24 까마귀는 돌을 항아리 안으로 떨어뜨렸다.

➡ _____

25 만약 당신이 이 새가 특별하다고 생각한다면, 당신이 틀렸다.

➡ _____

26 과학자들은 다른 까마귀들에게도 똑같은 실험을 했고, 그들 모두가 똑같이 그렇게 했다.

➡ _____

[01~03] 다음 글을 읽고, 물음에 답하시오.

Macaque Monkeys

If you go to a Buddhist temple in Lop Buri, Thailand, (A)[to watch / watch] out for the Macaque monkeys. They ⓐmay come to you and pull out your hair. They use human hair (B)[to floss / flossing] their teeth. If you are lucky, you may see female monkeys that (C)[is / are] teaching flossing to their babies. While the babies are watching, the female monkeys floss their teeth very slowly. This way, the baby monkeys learn to floss.

 서답형

01 위 글의 괄호 (A)~(C)에서 어법상 알맞은 낱말을 골라 쓰시오.

(A)_____ (B)_____ (C)_____

02 위 글의 밑줄 친 ⓐmay와 의미가 다른 것을 고르시오.

① It may be true.
② You may go there at any moment.
③ It may rain at any moment.
④ He may be swimming in the pool.
⑤ He may have missed his train.

03 위 글의 내용과 일치하지 않는 것은?

① 태국의 롭부리에 있는 절에 간다면, 마카크 원숭이들을 조심해야 한다.
② 마카크 원숭이들이 당신에게 다가와 당신의 머리카락을 뽑을 수도 있다.
③ 마카크 원숭이들은 이빨을 치실질하기 위해서 사람의 머리카락을 사용한다.
④ 태국의 롭부리에 있는 절에서는 새끼들에게 치실질하는 것을 가르치고 있는 암컷 원숭이들을 항상 볼 수 있다.
⑤ 새끼들이 지켜보고 있는 동안, 암컷 원숭이들은 아주 천천히 그들의 이빨을 치실질한다.

[04~05] 다음 글을 읽고, 물음에 답하시오.

Octopuses

People don't usually think that octopuses are smart. However, octopuses are very smart, and ①they can also use tools. ②They use coconut shells for protection. When they can't find a good hiding place, ③they hide under coconut shells. Some octopuses even store coconut shells for later use. ④They pile the coconut shells and carry ⑤them to use later. How smart!

04 위 글의 밑줄 친 ①~⑤ 중에서 가리키는 대상이 나머지 넷과 다른 것은?

① 　② 　③ 　④ 　⑤

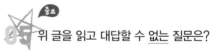

05 위 글을 읽고 대답할 수 없는 질문은?

① Do people usually think that octopuses are smart?
② Can octopuses use tools?
③ What do octopuses use as tools?
④ Where do octopuses hide when they can't find a good hiding place?
⑤ How many coconut shells do octopuses store?

[06~08] 다음 글을 읽고, 물음에 답하시오.

Crows

  In Aesop's fable *The Thirsty Crow*, a crow drops stones into a jar ⓐto raise the level of water. You may think this is just a story, but it is not. Scientists who were studying crows did an experiment. They put a jar with water in front of a crow. A worm was floating on top of the water. However, the water level was (A)[low / high], so the crow could not eat the worm. The crow (B)[solved / gave up] the problem just as in the fable. It dropped stones into the jar. If you think this bird is special, you are (C)[right / wrong]. Scientists did the same experiment with other crows, and they all did the same, too.

06 위 글의 괄호 (A)~(C)에서 문맥상 알맞은 낱말을 골라 쓰시오.

(A)_____ (B)_____ (C)_____

서답형

07 실험에서 까마귀가 도구를 사용했던 이유를 빈칸에 쓰시오. (6단어)

> The crow dropped stones into a jar _____
> _____.

➡ _____

08 위 글의 밑줄 친 ⓐto raise와 to부정사의 용법이 같은 것을 모두 고르시오.

① He grew up to be a brave soldier.
② My plan is to climb Mt. Everest.
③ I need a friend to talk with.
④ I have a lot of homework to do.
⑤ This river is dangerous to swim in.

[09~11] 다음 글을 읽고, 물음에 답하시오.

Macaque Monkeys

  ⓐIf you will go to a Buddhist temple in Lop Buri, Thailand, watch out for the Macaque monkeys. (①) They may come to you and pull out your hair. (②) They use human hair ⓑto floss their teeth. (③) If you are lucky, you may see female monkeys that are teaching flossing to their babies. (④) This way, the baby monkeys learn to floss. (⑤)

09 위 글의 흐름으로 보아, 주어진 문장이 들어가기에 가장 적절한 곳은?

> While the babies are watching, the female monkeys floss their teeth very slowly.

①   ②   ③   ④   ⑤

서답형

10 위 글의 밑줄 친 ⓐ에서 어법상 틀린 부분을 찾아 고치시오.

_____ ➡ _____

11 위 글의 밑줄 친 ⓑto floss와 to부정사의 용법이 다른 것을 모두 고르시오.

① I have no time to waste.
② She visited my house to help me.
③ I went to the library to return the books.
④ My dream is to become a nurse.
⑤ She got up early to catch the train.

[12~14] 다음 글을 읽고, 물음에 답하시오.

Octopuses

People don't usually think that octopuses are smart. ⓐ , octopuses are very smart, and they can also use tools. They use coconut shells ⓑ protection. When they can't find a good hiding place, they hide under coconut shells. Some octopuses even store coconut shells ⓒ later use. They pile the coconut shells and carry them to use later. How smart!

12 위 글의 빈칸 ⓐ에 들어갈 알맞은 말을 고르시오.

① Therefore
② Besides
③ Instead
④ However
⑤ For example

서답형

13 위 글의 빈칸 ⓑ와 ⓒ에 공통으로 들어갈 전치사를 쓰시오.

➡ _____

14 위 글의 내용과 일치하지 않는 것은?

① 사람들은 대개 문어가 영리하다고 생각하지 않는다.
② 문어들은 매우 영리하고 또한 도구를 사용할 수 있다.
③ 문어들은 숨을 만한 좋은 장소를 찾을 수 없을 때, 코코넛 껍데기 아래로 숨는다.
④ 몇몇 문어들은 나중에 사용하기 위해 코코넛 껍데기를 모은다.
⑤ 몇몇 문어들은 코코넛 껍데기를 쌓아 두고 바로 쓰기 위해 그것들을 가지고 다닌다.

[15~16] 다음 글을 읽고, 물음에 답하시오.

Crows

However, the water level was low, so the crow could not eat the worm. The crow solved the problem just as in the ⓐ . It dropped stones into the jar. ⓑIf you think this bird is ordinary, you are wrong. Scientists did the same experiment with other crows, and they all did the same, too.

서답형

15 주어진 영영풀이를 참고하여 빈칸 ⓐ에 철자 f로 시작하는 단어를 쓰시오.

> a story which teaches a moral lesson and sometimes has animals as the main characters

➡ f_____

서답형

16 위 글의 밑줄 친 ⓑ에서 흐름상 어색한 부분을 찾아 고치시오.

_____ ➡ _____

[17~19] 다음 글을 읽고, 물음에 답하시오.

Animals ⓐThat Use Tools

People once thought ⓑthat only humans can use tools. Now, scientists are finding out that many animals can also use tools.

서답형

17 위 글의 밑줄 친 ⓐ, ⓑ와 문법적 쓰임이 같은 것을 각각 아래 〈보기〉에서 모두 골라 쓰시오.

┌─ 보기 ┐
① Look at the bird that is flying there.
② He said that the story was true.
③ I believe that you'll finish it in time.
④ This is the pen that I bought yesterday.
⑤ She told me that I was smart.
└──────┘

ⓐ와 쓰임이 같은 것: _____
ⓑ와 쓰임이 같은 것: _____

18 위 글의 다음에 올 내용으로 가장 알맞은 것을 고르시오.

① 도구를 사용하는 많은 사람들
② 도구 사용에 관한 사람들의 생각
③ 동물의 지능에 관한 과학자들의 연구
④ 도구를 사용할 수 있는 많은 동물들
⑤ 도구를 사용한 과학자들의 연구

서답형
19 위 글의 내용과 일치하도록 다음 빈칸에 알맞은 말을 쓰시오.

> Now, scientists are finding out that not only humans but also many animals can _____ _____.

➡ _____

[20~22] 다음 글을 읽고, 물음에 답하시오.

Octopuses

People don't usually think that octopuses are smart. However, octopuses are very smart, and they can also use tools. ①They use coconut shells for protection. ②The coconut shell is a good place to sleep in. ③When they (A)[can / can't] find a good hiding place, they hide (B)[over / under] coconut shells. ④Some octopuses even store coconut shells for later use. ⑤They (C)[file / pile] the coconut shells and carry them to use later. How smart!

20 위 글의 ①~⑤ 중에서 전체 흐름과 관계 없는 문장은?

①　　②　　③　　④　　⑤

서답형
21 위 글의 괄호 (A)~(C)에서 문맥상 알맞은 낱말을 골라 쓰시오.

(A)_____ (B)_____ (C)_____

서답형
22 다음 질문에 대한 알맞은 대답을 빈칸에 쓰시오. (2단어)

> Q: What do the octopuses use as tools?
> A: They use _____ _____ as tools for protection.

[23~24] 다음 글을 읽고, 물음에 답하시오.

Giant Pandas

• Size: They grow 1.2m to 1.9m long and weigh up to 135kg.
• Food: They eat leaves, fish, and small animals.
• Home: They live in the wild, high up in the mountains of China.
• Amazing Facts: ⓐThey are very good at climbing trees. They take a rest on trees. They even walk from one tree to another.

23 위 글을 읽고 대답할 수 없는 질문은?

① How big are Giant Pandas?
② Where do Giant Pandas live?
③ How fast can Giant Pandas run?
④ What do Giant Pandas eat?
⑤ What is special about Giant Pandas?

서답형
24 위 글의 밑줄 친 ⓐ를 다음과 같이 바꿔 쓸 때 빈칸에 알맞은 말을 쓰시오.

> They climb trees _____ _____.

25 주어진 글 다음에 이어질 글의 순서로 가장 적절한 것은?

People don't usually think that octopuses are smart.

(A) When they can't find a good hiding place, they hide under coconut shells. Some octopuses even store coconut shells for later use.

(B) They pile the coconut shells and carry them to use later. How smart!

(C) However, octopuses are very smart, and they can also use tools. They use coconut shells for protection.

① (A) – (C) – (B)   ② (B) – (A) – (C)
③ (B) – (C) – (A)   ④ (C) – (A) – (B)
⑤ (C) – (B) – (A)

[26~28] 다음 글을 읽고, 물음에 답하시오.

Crows

(①) In Aesop's fable *The Thirsty Crow*, a crow drops stones into a jar to raise the level of water. (②) You may think this is just a story, but it is not. (③) Scientists who were studying crows did an experiment. (④) A worm was floating on top of the water. (⑤) However, the water level was low, so the crow could not eat the worm. ⓐ그 까마귀는 꼭 우화에서처럼 그 문제를 해결했다. It dropped stones into the jar. If you think this bird is special, you are wrong. Scientists did the same experiment with other crows, and they all did the same, too.

26 위 글의 흐름으로 보아, 주어진 문장이 들어가기에 가장 적절한 곳은?

They put a jar with water in front of a crow.

①   ②   ③   ④   ⑤

서답형

27 위 글의 밑줄 친 ⓐ의 우리말에 맞게 주어진 어구를 이용하여 10 단어로 영작하시오.

solved, just as

➡ _____

중요

28 위 글의 요지로 알맞은 것을 고르시오.

① 이솝 우화 '목마른 까마귀'는 단지 이야기일 뿐이다.
② 까마귀는 영리한 동물이고 도구를 사용할 줄 안다.
③ 과학자들은 실험을 통해 까마귀를 연구했다.
④ 까마귀는 벌레를 먹는 것을 좋아한다.
⑤ 항아리의 수위가 낮으면 까마귀는 벌레를 먹을 수 없다.

29 다음 글의 제목으로 알맞은 것을 고르시오.

People don't usually think that octopuses are smart. However, octopuses are very smart, and they can also use tools. They use coconut shells for protection. When they can't find a good hiding place, they hide under coconut shells. Some octopuses even store coconut shells for later use. They pile the coconut shells and carry them to use later. How smart!

① Animals with Special Talents
② The Amazing World of Nature
③ Octopuses Are Cleverer Than Humans!
④ Animals in the Fable
⑤ The Octopus, a Smart Animal!

[30~31] 다음 글을 읽고, 물음에 답하시오.

Crows

In Aesop's fable *The Thirsty Crow*, a crow drops stones into a jar to raise the level of water. You may think this is just a story, but it is not. Scientists who were studying crows did an experiment. ⓐThey put a jar with water in front of a crow. A worm was floating on top of the water. However, the water level was low, so the crow could not eat the worm. ⓑThe crow solved the problem just as in the fable. It dropped stones into the jar. If you think this bird is special, you are wrong. Scientists did the same experiment with other crows, and they all did the same, too.

서답형

30 위 글의 밑줄 친 ⓐ가 가리키는 것을 본문에서 찾아 쓰시오.

➡ _____

서답형

31 다음 빈칸 (A)와 (B)에 알맞은 단어를 넣어 위 글의 밑줄 친 ⓑ에 대한 설명을 완성하시오.

> When the crow could not eat the worm, it (A)_____ stones (B)_____ the jar to raise the level of water just as a crow does in Aesop's fable *The Thirsty Crow*.

[32~33] 주어진 글 다음에 이어질 글의 순서로 가장 적절한 것을 고르시오.

32

> If you go to a Buddhist temple in Lop Buri, Thailand, watch out for the Macaque monkeys.

> (A) While the babies are watching, the female monkeys floss their teeth very slowly. This way, the baby monkeys learn to floss.

> (B) They may come to you and pull out your hair. They use human hair to floss their teeth.

> (C) If you are lucky, you may see female monkeys that are teaching flossing to their babies.

① (A) – (C) – (B) ② (B) – (A) – (C)
③ (B) – (C) – (A) ④ (C) – (A) – (B)
⑤ (C) – (B) – (A)

33

> In Aesop's fable *The Thirsty Crow*, a crow drops stones into a jar to raise the level of water.

> (A) They put a jar with water in front of a crow. A worm was floating on top of the water. However, the water level was low, so the crow could not eat the worm. The crow solved the problem just as in the fable.

> (B) You may think this is just a story, but it is not. Scientists who were studying crows did an experiment.

> (C) It dropped stones into the jar. If you think this bird is special, you are wrong. Scientists did the same experiment with other crows, and they all did the same, too.

① (A) – (C) – (B) ② (B) – (A) – (C)
③ (B) – (C) – (A) ④ (C) – (A) – (B)
⑤ (C) – (B) – (A)

[01~03] 다음 글을 읽고, 물음에 답하시오.

ⓐAnimals That Uses Tools

People once thought that only humans can use tools. ⓑNow, scientists are finding out that many animals can also use tools.

01 위 글의 밑줄 친 ⓐ에서 어법상 틀린 부분을 찾아 고치시오.

_____ ➡ _____

02 위 글의 밑줄 친 ⓑ에서 생략할 수 있는 단어를 찾아 쓰시오.

➡ _____

03 위 글의 내용과 일치하도록 다음 빈칸 (A)와 (B)에 알맞은 말을 쓰시오.

There are many ___(A)___ that can use tools in addition to ___(B)___ .

(A)_____ (B)_____

[04~06] 다음 글을 읽고, 물음에 답하시오.

Macaque Monkeys

If you go to a Buddhist temple in Lop Buri, Thailand, watch out for the Macaque monkeys. They may come to you and (A)[pull / push] out your hair. They use human hair to floss their teeth. If you are (B)[lucky / unlucky], you may see female monkeys that are teaching flossing to ⓐtheir babies. (C)[During / While] the babies are watching, the female monkeys floss their teeth very slowly. This way, the baby monkeys learn to floss.

04 위 글의 괄호 (A)~(C)에서 문맥과 어법상 알맞은 낱말을 골라 쓰시오.

(A)_____ (B)_____ (C)_____

05 위 글의 밑줄 친 ⓐtheir가 가리키는 것을 본문에서 찾아 쓰시오.

➡ _____

06 다음 빈칸에 알맞은 단어를 넣어 Macaque 원숭이가 도구를 구하는 방법을 완성하시오. (본문의 단어를 변형할 것.)

They get the tools to floss their teeth by _____ _____ human hair.

[07~08] 다음 글을 읽고, 물음에 답하시오.

Octopuses

People don't usually think that octopuses are smart. However, octopuses are very smart, and they can also use tools. They use coconut shells for protection. When they can't find a good hiding place, they hide under coconut shells. Some octopuses even store coconut shells for later use. They ⓐ_____ the coconut shells and carry them to use later. How smart!

07 다음 문장에서 위 글의 내용과 다른 부분을 찾아서 고치시오.

Octopuses are very smart, and they use coconut shells to prevent accidents.

_____ ➡ _____

08 주어진 영영풀이를 참고하여 빈칸 ⓐ에 철자 p로 시작하는 단어를 쓰시오.

to lay objects on top of each other

➡ _____

[09~11] 다음 글을 읽고, 물음에 답하시오.

Crows

In Aesop's fable *The Thirsty Crow*, a crow drops stones into a jar to raise the level of water. You may think this is just a story, but it is not. Scientists who were studying crows did an experiment. They put a jar ⓐ____ water in front of a crow. A worm was floating on top of the water. However, the water level was low, so the crow could not eat the worm. The crow solved the problem just as in the fable. It dropped stones into the jar. ⓑIf you think this bird is special, you are wrong. Scientists did the same experiment ⓒ____ other crows, and they all did the same, too.

09 실험에서 까마귀가 사용한 도구가 무엇인지 본문에서 찾아 다음 빈칸에 쓰시오.

When the crow could not eat the worm because of the low water level, it dropped _____ into the jar to raise the level of water.

10 위 글의 빈칸 ⓐ와 ⓒ에 공통으로 들어갈 전치사를 쓰시오.

➡ _____

11 위 글에서 밑줄 친 ⓑ처럼 말한 이유를 우리말로 쓰시오.

➡ _____
_____

[12~14] 다음 글을 읽고, 물음에 답하시오.

Octopuses

People don't usually think that octopuses are smart. However, octopuses are very smart, and they can also use tools. They use coconut shells for protection. When they can't find a good hiding place, they hide under coconut shells. ⓐ어떤 문어들은 심지어 코코넛 껍데기를 나중에 쓰기 위해 모은다. ⓑThey pile the coconut shells and to carry them to use later. How smart!

12 위 글을 읽고, 다음 질문에 대한 대답을 완성하시오. (8단어)

Q: When do octopuses use coconut shells for protection?   A: They use them _____ _____.

13 위 글의 밑줄 친 ⓐ의 우리말에 맞게 한 단어를 보충하여, 주어진 어휘를 알맞게 배열하시오.

store / octopuses / some / use / coconut shells / even / for

➡ _____
_____

14 위 글의 밑줄 친 ⓑ에서 어법상 틀린 부분을 찾아 고치시오.

_____ ➡ _____

Words and Reading

Scientists are now finding out that many animals can use tools. Macaque
　　　　　　　　　　　　　　　　명사절을 이끄는 접속사
monkeys use human hair to floss their teeth. Octopuses hide under coconut
　　　　　　　　　　　부사적 용법(목적)　　　　　　　　　　　　　전 ~ 아래
shells when they can't find a good hiding place. Crows can drop stones into
　　　　접 ~할 때　　　　　　　　　　형 숨기, 은신　　　　　　　　　~ 안으로
a jar to raise the level of water to eat the worm that is floating on top of the
　　　　　　　　　높이　　　　부사적 용법(목적)　　　벌레　　= which(주격 관계대명사)　 ~ 위에
water.

구문해설 • find out: 알아내다　• tool: 도구, 수단　• hide: 숨다, 감추다　• drop: 떨어뜨리다

과학자들은 이제 많은 동물들이 도구를 사용할 수 있다는 것을 알아내고 있다. 마카크 원숭이는 그들의 이빨을 치실질하기 위해 사람의 머리카락을 사용한다. 문어는 그들이 숨을 만한 좋은 장소를 찾지 못할 때 코코넛 껍질 아래 숨는다. 까마귀는 물의 높이를 올려 물 위에 떠 있는 벌레를 먹기 위해 항아리 안에 돌을 떨어뜨린다.

Think and Write

Animals with Special Talents

There are many animals that have special talents. An example is Einstein.
　　~이 있다　　　　　　　　= which(주격 관계대명사)
He is an African Grey Parrot which can use 200 English words to talk with
　　　　　　　　　　　= that(주격 관계대명사)　　　　　　　　　부사적 용법(목적)
people. He can sing the "Happy Birthday" song.

There are many animals that have special talents. An example is Koko. She is
　　~이 있다　　　　선행사가 복수(animals)이므로 has (X)
a female gorilla which lives in America. She can talk with people in American
　　선행사가 단수(a female gorilla)이므로 live(X)　　　　　　　[도구·수단] ~으로
Sign Language. She knows more than 1,000 signs.
　　　　　　　　　more than: ~ 이상

구문해설 • special: 특별한　• talent: 재능　• female: 여성인, 암컷의　• Sign Language: 수화

특별한 재능을 가진 동물들

특별한 재능을 가진 많은 동물들이 있다. 한 예는 Einstein이다. 그는 사람들과 대화를 하기 위해 200개의 영어 단어를 사용할 수 있는 아프리카 회색앵무새이다. 그는 '생일 축하합니다' 노래를 부를 수 있다.

특별한 재능을 가진 많은 동물들이 있다. 한 예는 Koko이다. 그녀는 미국에 살고 있는 암컷 고릴라이다. 그녀는 수화로 사람들과 이야기할 수 있다. 그녀는 1,000개가 넘는 신호를 알고 있다.

Around the World

1. The longest snake ever is Medusa. She is 7.67 meters long.
　최상급 표현: 가장 ~한

2. Alley recorded the longest jump by a cat. Her record was 1.83 meters.

3. The oldest pig ever is Ernestine. He lived for 22 years and 359 days.

구문해설 • jump: 도약, 비약, 뜀, 뛰어오름

1. 지금까지 가장 긴 뱀은 Medusa이다. 그것은 길이가 7.67미터이다.

2. Alley는 가장 멀리 뛰는 고양이로 기록되었다. 그녀의 기록은 1.83 미터였다.

3. 지금까지 가장 오래 산 돼지는 Ernestine이다. 그는 22년 359일을 살았다.

01 다음 〈보기〉와 같은 관계가 되도록 빈칸에 알맞은 말을 쓰시오. (주어진 철자로 시작할 것)

> 보기
>
> speak – talk

(1) stack ➡ p_____

(2) gift ➡ t_____

(3) deal with ➡ s_____

(4) amaze ➡ s_____

02 다음 우리말에 맞게 주어진 단어를 이용해 빈칸을 완성하시오.

> 너는 선생님의 발표를 들었니?
>
> ➡ Did you hear the teacher's _____?
> (announce)

03 다음 제시된 단어를 사용하여 자연스러운 문장을 만들 수 없는 것은? (형태 변화 가능)

> 보기
>
> protection   pattern   whale   shell

① A _____ is the largest animal in the world.

② These are _____ of how to use tools.

③ Such a diet is believed to offer _____ against a number of cancers.

④ I like the shirt with a _____.

⑤ The kids were collecting _____ on the beach.

04 다음 빈칸에 공통으로 들어갈 단어를 쓰시오.

> • It was the lowest _____ of inflation for some years.
> • The water _____ of the Han River is averagely 10 meters.

05 다음 제시된 의미에 맞는 단어를 주어진 철자로 시작하여 빈칸에 쓰고, 알맞은 것을 골라 문장을 완성하시오.

> • c_____ : a large brown nut with a hairy shell
> • t_____ : a thing that you use for making or doing something
> • p_____ : a picture you take using a camera

(1) Her _____ appeared on the front page of The New York Times.

(2) In my town, there are lots of _____ trees.

(3) In present day life, fire is a very useful _____.

06 다음 우리말과 일치하도록 괄호 안의 단어를 바르게 배열하시오.

(1) 문어의 몸은 가방처럼 생겼다.

(like, a, the, bag, body, an, of, octopus, looks)

➡ _____

(2) 고릴라의 팔은 그것의 다리보다 길다.

(of, than, the, a, longer, legs, arms, its, gorilla, are)

➡ _____

Conversation

[07~08] 다음 대화는 그림에서 빨간 동그라미 물건을 찾는 내용이다. 그림과 일치하도록 (A)~(C)에서 알맞은 것을 고르시오.

07

G: Hi. I think I lost my umbrella.

M: What does it look like?

G: It's a (A)[small / big] (B)[pink / navy] umbrella.

M: Can you tell me more?

G: It has a white (C)[cloud / flower] pattern on it.

08

A: May I help you?

B: Yes. I'm looking for my (A)[scarf / bag].

A: What does it look like?

B: It's (B)[blue / grey].

A: Can you tell me more about it?

B: It has a (C)[star / heart] pattern on it.

09 다음 대화의 순서를 바르게 배열한 것은?

> (A) It's a big silver bag.
> (B) Excuse me. I'm looking for my bag. I left it in the restroom.
> (C) OK. What does it look like?
> (D) Alright. I'll go and check.

① (B) – (A) – (C) – (D)
② (B) – (A) – (D) – (C)
③ (B) – (C) – (A) – (D)
④ (C) – (A) – (B) – (D)
⑤ (C) – (B) – (A) – (D)

[10~11] 다음 대화를 읽고, 물음에 답하시오.

A: (A)_____

B: Yes. I'm looking for my bag.

A: (B)_____

B: It's big and orange.

A: (C)_____

B: ⓐIt has one big pocket outside.

10 위 대화의 빈칸 (A)~(C)에 들어갈 말을 <보기>에게 골라 기호를 쓰시오.

┌─── 보기 ───┐

① How does it look like?
② Can you tell me more about it?
③ May I help you?
④ What does it look like?
⑤ Can you help me to find a pocket?
⑥ Can I tell you more about it?
⑦ What are you looking for?

(A) _____ (B) _____ (C) _____

11 위 대화의 밑줄 친 ⓐIt이 가리키는 말을 주어진 단어를 이용해 찾아 쓰시오.

➡ _____ (be, which)

12 다음 중 짝지어진 대화가 <u>어색한</u> 것은?

① A: Do you need help?

　B: I lost my wallet.

② A: What are you looking for?

　B: I'm looking for my cat.

③ A: Can you tell me more?

　B: It has a big blue star on it.

④ A: Where did you lose it?

　B: I'll make an announcement.

⑤ A: Tell me more about it.

　B: I lost it near the bus station.

Grammar

13 다음 밑줄 친 which와 용법이 <u>다른</u> 하나는?

> I went to a shopping mall <u>which</u> was very far from my house.

① Tom is a student <u>who</u> studies art in a college.

② Look at the men <u>who</u> are dancing on the street.

③ I want to live in a house <u>that</u> has many rooms.

④ I don't know the girl <u>who</u> you met yesterday.

⑤ Julie is the girl <u>who</u> is wearing jeans and a white shirt.

14 관계대명사를 이용하여 만든 다음 문장을 원래의 두 문장으로 쓰시오.

> Mr. Kim lives in a house which has many big windows.

➡ _____

15 다음 문장의 밑줄 친 부분과 쓰임이 같은 것은?

> If it rains tomorrow, I will read a book at home.

① I think you should wait and see <u>if</u> the market improves.

② I wonder <u>if</u> I should go there or not.

③ <u>If</u> you take a taxi, you can get there in ten minutes.

④ I'd like to know <u>if</u> the bus has arrived.

⑤ <u>If</u> I were you, I would take part in the meeting.

16 다음 중 어법상 바르지 <u>않은</u> 것은?

> Olivia ①<u>will go</u> ②<u>shopping</u> ③<u>if</u> she ④<u>will have</u> time ⑤<u>in</u> the afternoon.

①　　　②　　　③　　　④　　　⑤

17 다음 중 두 문장을 한 문장으로 만들 때 의미가 <u>다른</u> 하나는?

① I have to catch the train. It leaves at 8:45.

　→ I have to catch the train that leaves at 8:45.

② The boy sent me some flowers. I received them yesterday.

　→ The boy received some flowers yesterday that I sent.

③ I want to be a person. The person is loved by many people.

　→ I want to be a person who is loved by many people.

④ Mariana bought a book. She wanted to read it.

　→ Mariana bought a book that she wanted to read.

⑤ I called Jack yesterday. He lives in Seoul.

　→ I called Jack yesterday who lives in Seoul.

18 다음 우리말과 일치하도록 할 때, 빈칸에 알맞은 것은?

> 조용히 하지 않으면 너는 아이를 깨울 것이다.
> ➡ _____ you do not keep silent, you will wake up the baby.

① Because   ② When   ③ That
④ Unless   ⑤ If

19 다음 중 어법상 바르지 <u>않은</u> 것은?

① Diana has two puppies who are brown and white.
② Look at those birds that are sitting on the tree.
③ I met a girl who has the same name as me.
④ Jane saw a woman that was eating an apple.
⑤ This is an animal which has a long nose.

20 다음 중 어법상 <u>잘못된</u> 문장은?

① He won't pass the test unless he does his best.
② If I sell some milk, I can buy a chicken.
③ If my friend will look sad, I will invite her to dinner.
④ You should clean your room before your parents come tomorrow.
⑤ Is counting sheep helpful if I can't fall asleep?

21 다음 두 문장을 알맞은 관계대명사를 이용하여 하나의 문장으로 쓰시오.

> • This is the snack shop.
> • It is famous for corn dogs.

➡ _____
_____

[22~23] 다음 글을 읽고, 물음에 답하시오.

Macaque Monkeys

If you go to a Buddhist temple in Lop Buri, Thailand, watch out for the Macaque monkeys. They may come to you and pull out your hair. They use human hair to floss their teeth. If you are lucky, you may see female monkeys that are teaching flossing to their babies. While the babies are ⓐwatching, the female monkeys floss their teeth very slowly. This way, the baby monkeys learn to floss.

22 아래 〈보기〉에서 위 글의 밑줄 친 ⓐwatching과 문법적 쓰임이 같은 것의 개수를 고르시오.

> ── 보기 ──
> ① My hobby is <u>making</u> model cars.
> ② He stopped <u>smoking</u>.
> ③ Jane is <u>helping</u> her mom do the dishes.
> ④ <u>Watching</u> TV always makes me happy.
> ⑤ They are <u>cleaning</u> their house now.

① 1개   ② 2개   ③ 3개   ④ 4개   ⑤ 5개

23 다음 빈칸 (A)와 (B)에 알맞은 단어를 넣어 질문에 대한 알맞은 대답을 완성하시오.

> Q: How do the baby monkeys learn to floss?
> A: By (A)_____ the female monkeys (B)_____ their teeth very slowly.

[24~26] 다음 글을 읽고, 물음에 답하시오.

Octopuses

People don't usually think that octopuses are smart. (①) However, octopuses are very smart, and they can also use ____ⓐ____. (②) When they can't find a good hiding place, they hide under coconut shells. (③) Some octopuses even store coconut shells for later use. (④) They pile the coconut shells and carry them ____ⓑ____ later. (⑤) How smart!

24 위 글의 빈칸 ⓐ에 들어갈 알맞은 말을 고르시오.

① machines ② engines ③ systems
④ black ink ⑤ tools

25 위 글의 흐름으로 보아, 주어진 문장이 들어가기에 가장 적절한 곳은?

> They use coconut shells for protection.

①   ②   ③   ④   ⑤

26 위 글의 빈칸 ⓑ에 use를 알맞은 형태로 쓰시오.

➡ _____

[27~28] 다음 글을 읽고, 물음에 답하시오.

Crows

In Aesop's fable *The Thirsty Crow*, ①a crow drops stones into a jar to raise the level of water. You may think this is just a story, but it is not. Scientists who were studying crows did an experiment. They put a jar with water in front of ②a crow. A worm was floating on top of the water. However, the water level was low, so ③the crow could not eat the worm.

The crow solved the problem just as in the fable. ④It dropped stones into the jar. If you think ⑤this bird is special, you are wrong. Scientists did the same experiment with other crows, and they all did the same, too.

27 위 글의 내용과 일치하지 <u>않는</u> 것은?

① 이솝 우화 '목마른 까마귀'에서 까마귀가 물 높이를 높이기 위해 항아리 안으로 돌을 떨어뜨린다.
② 실험에서 과학자들은 까마귀 앞에 물이 든 항아리를 놓았다.
③ 항아리 안의 물 위에 벌레 한 마리가 떠다니고 있었다.
④ 물높이가 낮아서 까마귀는 벌레를 먹을 수 없었다.
⑤ 실험 대상이었던 까마귀는 특별했다.

28 위 글의 밑줄 친 ①~⑤ 중에서 가리키는 대상이 나머지 넷과 <u>다른</u> 것은?

①   ②   ③   ④   ⑤

[29~30] 다음 글을 읽고, 물음에 답하시오.

Animals with Special Talents

There are many animals ____ⓐ____ have special talents. An example is Koko. She is a female gorilla ____ⓑ____ lives in America. She can talk with people in American Sign Language. She knows more than 1,000 signs.

29 위 글의 빈칸 ⓐ와 ⓑ에 공통으로 알맞은 말을 쓰시오.

➡ _____

30 다음 질문에 대한 알맞은 대답을 우리말로 쓰시오.

> Q: What is Koko's special talent?
> A: _____
> _____

01 다음 빈칸에 들어갈 알맞은 표현을 찾아 문장을 완성하시오.

to fix	to carry	suprised
carry	tool	floating
surprise	dropping	fix

(1) He's using a _____ _____ the door.

(2) It _____ me when he shouted in the dark.

(3) A tree branch was _____ down the river.

02 다음 영영풀이에 해당하는 단어를 고르시오.

something important that someone tells people

① management　　② information
③ announcement　　④ activity
⑤ lecture

03 다음 주어진 우리말에 맞게 빈칸을 채우시오.

(1) Let us _____ that dogs can talk _____ us. (개가 우리처럼 말할 수 있다고 상상해 보자.)

(2) This is the best _____ _____ _____ the problem. (이것이 그 문제를 푸는 가장 좋은 방법이다.)

04 다음 밑줄 친 부분과 의미가 가장 가까운 것은?

The computer has become an important teaching tool.

① equipment　　② type
③ object　　④ way
⑤ sign

05 다음 중 의미가 다른 하나를 고르시오.

① What does he look like?
② How does he look?
③ What's he like?
④ How do you describe him?
⑤ Tell me what he looks like.

[06~07] 다음 대화의 밑줄 친 부분에서 어색한 것의 개수를 고르시오.

06

B: Excuse me. ⓐI'm looking like my bag. I ⓑleft it in the restroom.
W: OK. ⓒWhat does it look?
B: ⓓIt's a big silver bag.
W: Alright. ⓔIt'll go and check.

① 1개　② 2개　③ 3개　④ 4개　⑤ 5개

07

B: Excuse me. ⓐI'm looking for my cat.
W: ⓑWhat does it look like?
B: ⓒThey're small and white.
W: ⓓCan you tell me more it?
B: ⓔIt's wearing a T-shirt

① 1개　② 2개　③ 3개　④ 4개　⑤ 5개

[08~10] 다음 대화를 읽고, 물음에 답하시오.

M: May I ____ⓐ____ you?

G: Yes. I'm looking for my dog. His name ____ⓑ____ Prince.

M: What does he ____ⓒ____ like? (①)

G: He's very small and ____ⓓ____ short white hair.

M: Can you tell me more? (②)

G: Well, he (A)has a really long tail. (③)

M: I see. And one more thing. Where did you lose him? (④)

G: I ____ⓔ____ him near the main gate.

M: OK. I'll go and make an announcement. (⑤)

G: Sure. Thanks a lot.

출제율 95%

08 위 대화의 ①~⑤ 중 주어진 문장이 들어갈 알맞은 곳은?

> Can you please wait here?

① ② ③ ④ ⑤

출제율 85%

09 위 대화의 밑줄 친 (A)has와 같은 단어가 들어갈 곳을 고르시오.

① ⓐ ② ⓑ ③ ⓒ ④ ⓓ ⑤ ⓔ

출제율 90%

10 다음 표에서 대화의 내용과 맞지 않는 것을 고르시오.

Lost Pet Report	
① type of animal	dog
② color	short white hair
③ size	not very small
④ something special	long tail
⑤ lost place	near the main gate

[11~12] 다음 글을 읽고, 물음에 답하시오.

A: This is my dog, Coco. (A)Coco는 크진 않지만 다리가 매우 튼튼해. (B)Coco는 두 다리로 서서 음악에 맞춰 춤을 출 수 있어.(music, stand, can, to, on, dance, two, Coco, and, legs) I think she's a great dancer!

출제율 90%

11 (A)의 우리말에 맞게 주어진 단어를 이용해 영작하시오.

> (she, big, but, very)

➡ _____

출제율 100%

12 (B)의 우리말과 일치하도록 괄호 안의 단어를 바르게 배열하시오.

➡ _____

출제율 95%

13 다음 빈칸에 들어갈 알맞은 말을 모두 고르시오.

> Jessica has a brother _____ plays the violin well.

① which ② who

③ whose ④ whom

⑤ that

14 출제율 100%

다음 〈보기〉에서 주어진 표현을 골라 if나 unless를 이용하여 문맥에 맞게 문장을 완성하시오.

┌─── 보기 ───┐
• the weather is nice tomorrow
• you try hard
• you exercise hard
• school finishes early today
└────────────┘

(1) _____, Minsu will go to a movie.

(2) _____, we will go to the beach.

(3) _____, you will become weak.

(4) _____, you can't be a doctor.

15 출제율 95%

다음 문장의 밑줄 친 부분의 쓰임이 어색한 것은?

① She is the woman who works at the nursing home.
② I want to have a robot that can cook.
③ Look at the boy and the dog which are walking together.
④ The boy who came to your birthday party is my cousin.
⑤ The plan that Jim made isn't realistic.

16 출제율 90%

다음 두 문장의 뜻이 같도록 빈칸에 알맞은 말을 쓰시오.

The post office won't accept it if you don't seal it.
➡ The post office won't accept it _____ you seal it.

17 출제율 90%

다음 빈칸에 공통으로 들어갈 단어는?

• Mr. Smith is the teacher _____ came from England.
• My sister likes movies _____ are based on real stories.

① whose   ② who   ③ that
④ which   ⑤ what

18 출제율 95%

다음 중 어법상 바르지 않은 것은?

① You can catch the train if you leave now.
② If I make enough money, I can buy new clothes.
③ If you feel tired, please have a rest.
④ If school will finish early today, Yuri will go swimming.
⑤ If you have a cold, you should go see a doctor.

19 출제율 85%

다음 우리말을 괄호 안에 주어진 어휘를 사용하여 영작하시오. (that 사용 금지)

(1) 매일 운동하는 학생들은 건강하다. (exercise, healthy, 8 단어)
➡ _____

(2) 아이스크림을 먹고 있는 저 소녀는 친절하다. (eat, kind, 10 단어)
➡ _____

(3) 그녀는 솜사탕을 만드는 기계를 가지고 있다. (machine, cotton candy, 8 단어)
➡ _____

(4) 내일 날씨가 좋으면 우리는 공원에 가서 연을 날릴 것이다. (the weather, kites, fly, good, go, and, 14 단어)
➡ _____
_____

[20~22] 다음 글을 읽고, 물음에 답하시오.

Macaque Monkeys

If you go to a Buddhist temple in Lop Buri, Thailand, watch out ___@___ the Macaque monkeys. ①They may come to you and pull out your hair. ②They like to play with people. ③They use human hair to floss their teeth. ④ If you are lucky, you may see female monkeys that are teaching flossing ___ⓑ___ their babies. ⑤While the babies are watching, the female monkeys floss their teeth very slowly. ©This way, the baby monkeys learn to floss.

출제율 90%

20 위 글의 ①~⑤ 중에서 전체 흐름과 관계 없는 문장은?

①   ②   ③   ④   ⑤

출제율 95%

21 위 글의 빈칸 @와 ⓑ에 들어갈 전치사가 바르게 짝지어진 것은?

① for – from   ② to – by
③ in – for   ④ for – to
⑤ on – to

출제율 85%

22 위 글의 밑줄 친 ©This way를 우리말로 설명하시오.

➡ _____

_____

[23~24] 다음 글을 읽고, 물음에 답하시오.

Octopuses

People don't usually think that octopuses are smart. However, octopuses are very smart, and they can also use tools. They use coconut shells for ___@___. When they can't find a good (A)[hide / hiding] place, they hide under coconut shells. Some octopuses even store coconut shells for later use. They pile the coconut shells and (B)[carry / to carry] them to use later. (C)[How / What] smart!

출제율 90%

23 위 글의 빈칸 @에 들어갈 알맞은 말을 고르시오.

① attack   ② prevention
③ protection   ④ repair
⑤ saving

출제율 100%

24 위 글의 괄호 (A)~(C)에서 어법상 알맞은 낱말을 골라 쓰시오.

(A) _____ (B) _____ (C) _____

[25~26] 다음 글을 읽고, 물음에 답하시오.

THE AMAZING ZEBRA

@They are 1 to 1.5m long and weight 200-450kg.
They live in eastern Africa.
They eat grass and leaves.
Every zebra has a unique pattern of black and white stripes.
Zebras stand while they are sleeping.

출제율 95%

25 위 글의 밑줄 친 @에서 어법상 틀린 부분을 찾아 고치시오.

_____ ➡ _____

출제율 90%

26 위 글을 읽고 얼룩말에 대해 알 수 없는 것을 고르시오.

① 크기   ② 서식지
③ 먹이   ④ 수명
⑤ 특징

[01~02] 다음 대화를 읽고, 물음에 답하시오.

> G: Hi. I think I lost my umbrella.
> M: <u>그것은 어떻게 생겼나요?</u>
> G: It's big and navy.
> M: Can you tell me more?
> G: It has a white flower pattern on it.

01 위 대화의 밑줄 친 우리말과 의미가 같도록 주어진 단어를 이용하여 영작하시오.

(1) _____ (what, look)

(2) _____ (how, look)

02 주어진 영영풀이에 해당하는 단어를 대화에서 찾아 쓰시오.

> a set of lines, shapes, or colours that are repeated regularly

➡ _____

03 다음 우리말과 일치하도록 괄호 안의 단어를 바르게 배열하시오.

(1) 나는 고릴라에게 수화를 가르친다.
(sign, gorillas, teach, to, I, language)
➡ _____

(2) 그것들은 날개에 검은색과 하얀색 줄무늬가 있다.
(a black, on, stripe, they, their, white, have, wings, and)
➡ _____

04 다음 괄호 안에 주어진 동사를 알맞은 형태로 빈칸에 써 넣으시오.

(1) Unless you _____ up, you _____ _____ the first class. (hurry, miss)

(2) If it _____ tomorrow, I _____ _____ _____ camping. (rain, not, go)

(3) You _____ _____ able to sleep if you _____ a scary movie. (not, be, see)

05 다음 잘못된 부분을 바르게 고쳐 문장을 다시 쓰시오.

(1) Ann lives in the house who has a beautiful garden.
➡ _____
_____

(2) These are the pictures who were painted by Picasso.
➡ _____

(3) I want to play with the boy whom has a new board game.
➡ _____

06 다음 우리말에 맞게 괄호 안의 단어를 알맞게 배열하시오.

(1) 연세가 80세인 그 할머니는 여전히 건강해 보이신다. (the, years, lady, 80, who, looks, is, still, healthy, old, old)
➡ _____

(2) 그녀는 사람의 말을 따라할 줄 아는 새가 있다. (bird, she, words, can, has, repeat, that, a, people's, after)
➡ _____

(3) 당신이 도와준다면, 나는 행복할 것이다. (I, me, you, be, help, will, if, happy)
➡ _____

07 다음 문장을 어법에 맞게 고쳐 쓰시오.

(1) I will see the doctor unless I don't feel better tomorrow.

➡ _____

(2) If I will get a ticket, I go to the concert.

➡ _____

(3) If it will snow tomorrow, we will go skiing.

➡ _____

[08~10] 다음 글을 읽고, 물음에 답하시오.

Macaque Monkeys

If you go to a Buddhist temple in Lop Buri, Thailand, watch out for the Macaque monkeys. They may come to you and pull out your hair. They use human hair to floss their teeth. If you are lucky, you may see female monkeys ⓐthat are teaching flossing to their babies. ⓑ새끼들이 지켜보고 있는 동안, 암컷 원숭이들은 아주 천천히 그들의 이빨을 치실질한다. This way, the baby monkeys learn to floss.

08 다음 질문에 대한 알맞은 대답을 본문에서 찾아 주어진 단어로 시작하여 쓰시오. (8단어)

Q: Why do the Macaque monkeys come to people and pull out their hair?

A: Because _____ .

09 위 글의 밑줄 친 ⓐthat과 바꿔 쓸 수 있는 단어를 쓰시오.

➡ _____

10 위 글의 밑줄 친 ⓑ의 우리말에 맞게 주어진 어휘를 이용하여 13 단어로 영작하시오.

While, watching, female, slowly

➡ _____

_____

[11~13] 다음 글을 읽고, 물음에 답하시오.

Crows

In Aesop's fable *The Thirsty Crow*, a crow drops stones into a jar to raise the level of water. You may think this is just a story, ⓐ but it is not. Scientists who were studying crows did an experiment. They put a jar with water in front of a crow. A worm was floating on top of the water. However, the water level was low, so the crow could not eat the worm. The crow solved the problem just as in the fable. It dropped stones into the jar. If you think this bird is special, you are wrong. Scientists did the same experiment with other crows, and they all ⓑdid the same, too.

11 위 글의 밑줄 친 ⓐ 문장 뒤에 생략된 말을 쓰시오.

➡ _____

12 다음 질문에 대한 알맞은 대답을 주어진 단어로 시작하여 쓰시오. (5단어)

Q: Why was it impossible for the crow to eat the worm which was floating on top of the water?

A: Because _____ .

13 위 글의 밑줄 친 ⓑ가 가리키는 것을 본문에서 찾아 쓰시오.

➡ _____

01 그림을 보고 표를 채우고, 내용과 일치하도록 대화를 완성하시오.

Lost Pet Report	
① type of animal	_____
② color	_____ hair
③ size	small
④ something special	_____ tail
⑤ lost place	near the library

A: May I help you?

B: Yes. _____

A: What does it look like?

B: _____ hair.

A: Can you tell me more about it?

B: It _____.

A: _____ did you lose it?

B: _____

02 관계대명사를 이용하여 직업을 설명하는 문장을 쓰시오.

(1) A pilot is a person _____.

(2) A painter is a person _____.

(3) A driver is a person _____.

(4) A baker is a person _____.

(5) A teacher is a person _____.

단원별 모의고사

01 다음 짝지어진 두 단어의 관계가 <u>다른</u> 하나를 고르시오.

① pattern – design
② way – method
③ photograph – picture
④ slowly – fast
⑤ record – document

02 다음 밑줄 친 부분과 바꾸어 쓸 수 있는 것을 고르시오.

> He is <u>trying to find</u> the book to read.

① looking at   ② looking for
③ talking with   ④ looking like
⑤ watching out

03 다음 〈보기〉의 어휘를 사용하여 문장을 완성하시오.

> ┤ 보기 ├
> to   at   out   for   of   on

(1) I'm only interested in finding _____ what the fact are.
(2) He is good _____ solving difficult math problems.
(3) He added a lot of whipped cream _____ top _____ hot chocolate.
(4) They started to dance _____ music.

04 다음 우리말과 일치하도록 빈칸에 알맞은 말을 쓰시오.

(1) 너는 여행을 하는 동안 너의 모든 비용을 기록해야 한다.
→ You should _____ all your expenses _____ your trip.
(2) 그는 컴퓨터를 사용하는 동안 먹는 중이다.
→ He's eating _____ he is using a computer.

(3) Jane은 그녀의 학교에서 첫 여성 축구 팀 멤버이다.
→ Jane is _____ _____ _____ soccer team member in her school.
(4) 우리 할머니는 항상 나에게 흥미로운 우화를 들려주셨다.
→ My grandmother always _____ me some interesting _____.

[05~07] 다음 그림에서 빨간 동그라미로 표시된 것을 찾은 다음, 대화를 읽고 물음에 답하시오.

A: May I help you?
B: Yes. I'm looking for my (A)[hat / scarf / coin purse].
A: What does it look like?
B: It's red and has a (smile) face on it.
A: <u>그것에 대해 더 말해 주실 수 있나요?</u>
B: It has (B)[a lock / a key chain / a rock] on it.

05 위 대화의 괄호 (A)와 (B)에서 알맞은 것을 골라 쓰시오.

(A) _____   (B) _____

06 위 대화의 괄호 안의 smile을 알맞게 고치시오.

→ _____

07 위 대화의 밑줄 친 우리말과 의미가 같도록 영작하시오. (7단어)

→ _____

08 그림과 일치하지 <u>않는</u> 대화의 내용을 모두 고르고 알맞게 고치시오.

A: What does Steve look like?
B: He has long brown hair.
A: Can you tell me more?
B: He's wearing glasses and holding a racket.
A: I found her!

Steve

(1) _____ ➡ _____
(2) _____ ➡ _____
(3) _____ ➡ _____

[09~11] 다음 대화를 읽고, 물음에 답하시오.

M: May I ___ⓐ___ you?
G: Yes. I'm looking for my dog. His name ___ⓑ___ Prince.
M: What does he ___ⓒ___ like?
G: He's very small and ___ⓓ___ short white hair.
M: Can you tell me more?
G: Well, he ___ⓔ___ a really long tail.
M: I see. And one more thing. Where did you lose him?
G: 정문 근처에서 잃어버렸어요.
M: OK. _____(A)_____ Can you please wait here?
G: Sure. Thanks a lot.

09 ⓐ~ⓔ의 빈칸을 주어진 동사를 이용해 채우시오. (형태 변화 가능)

be look have help

ⓐ_____ ⓑ_____ ⓒ_____ ⓓ_____ ⓔ_____

10 위 대화의 밑줄 친 우리말을 영작하시오.

➡ _____

11 위 대화의 빈칸 (A)에 알맞은 말을 고르시오.

① He's wearing a T-shirt.
② Tell me more about it.
③ I think I lost it.
④ I'll go and make an announcement.
⑤ It's a long cotton scarf.

12 다음 대화는 그림에서 빨간 동그라미 물건을 찾는 내용이다. 빈칸을 알맞게 채우시오.

G: Hi. I think I _____ my _____.
M: What does it look like?
G: It's a small _____ umbrella.
M: Can you tell me more?
G: It has _____ _____ _____ _____ on it.

13 다음 괄호 안에 주어진 어휘를 이용하여 우리말을 영작하시오.

(1) 나는 11살인 개를 키운다. (have, a dog, old)
➡ _____

(2) 나는 경주에서 우승한 차가 마음에 든다.
(the car, like, win the race)
➡ _____

(3) 머리가 금발인 남자아이는 내 동생이다.
(boy, brother, has blond hair)
➡ _____

(4) 눈이 온다면 우리는 공원에 가지 않겠다.
(snows, won't, the park)
➡ _____

14 다음 두 문장을 한 문장으로 바르게 바꾼 것은?

> • Megan is talking with a girl.
> • The girl is wearing cute earrings.

① Megan is talking with a girl whom is wearing cute earrings.

② Megan is talking with a girl which is wearing cute earrings.

③ Megan is talking with a girl is wearing cute earrings.

④ Megan is talking with a girl who she is wearing cute earrings.

⑤ Megan is talking with a girl who is wearing cute earrings.

15 다음 빈칸에 공통으로 들어갈 단어는?

> • Is it OK _____ I smoke here?
> • I will watch TV _____ I finish my homework.

① if   ② unless   ③ how
④ that   ⑤ which

16 두 문장을 관계대명사를 사용하여 한 문장으로 썼을 때 빈칸에 다른 한 문장을 쓰시오.

(1) My mother bought me a new computer.

_____

➡ My mother bought me a new computer which worked really well.

(2) The man is my uncle.

_____

➡ The man who drove me to school is my uncle.

17 다음 문장의 밑줄 친 부분과 쓰임이 같은 것은?

> If I go to the beach, I'll swim in the sea.

① I'm not sure if I can do it.

② I'll tell her if she comes back.

③ I don't know if there is anything else I can do.

④ How can I tell if someone is my true friend or not?

⑤ I wonder if my child expresses himself well in English.

[18~20] 다음 글을 읽고, 물음에 답하시오.

Macaque Monkeys

If you go to a Buddhist temple in Lop Buri, Thailand, watch out for the Macaque monkeys. They may come to you and pull out your hair. They use human hair to floss their teeth. ⓐIf you are lucky, you may see female monkeys that are teaching flossing to their babies. While the babies are watching, the female monkeys floss their teeth very slowly. This way, the baby monkeys learn ⓑto floss.

18 위 글을 읽고 대답할 수 없는 질문은?

① Why do you have to watch out for the Macaque monkeys in the Buddhist temple in Lop Buri, Thailand?

② What do the Macaque monkeys use to floss their teeth?

③ Can you always see female monkeys teaching flossing to their babies?

④ What do the male monkeys teach to their babies?

⑤ How do the female monkeys teach flossing to their babies?

19 위 글의 밑줄 친 ⓐ에서 생략할 수 있는 것을 쓰시오.

➡ _____

20 위 글의 밑줄 친 ⓑto floss와 to부정사의 용법이 같은 것을 고르시오.

① Please tell me the way to go there.
② It is easy to solve the problem.
③ He must be foolish to believe her.
④ Give me a chair to sit on.
⑤ He practiced hard to win the game.

[21~22] 다음 글을 읽고, 물음에 답하시오.

Octopuses

People don't usually think that octopuses are smart. However, octopuses are very smart, and they can also use tools. They use coconut shells for protection. When they can't find a good hiding place, they hide under coconut shells. Some octopuses even ⓐunderline store coconut shells for later use. They pile the coconut shells and carry them to use later. How smart!

21 위 글의 내용과 일치하도록 다음 빈칸에 공통으로 들어갈 알맞은 단어를 쓰시오.

> When octopuses can't find a good place to _____, they _____ under coconut shells for protection.

➡ _____

22 위 글의 밑줄 친 ⓐstore와 같은 의미로 쓰인 것을 고르시오.

① We can buy candies at a store.
② She has a vast store of knowledge.
③ He doesn't like store clothes.
④ We have a grain store.
⑤ Animals store food for the winter.

[23~24] 다음 글을 읽고, 물음에 답하시오.

Crows

In Aesop's fable *The Thirsty Crow*, a crow drops stones into a jar to raise the level of water. You may think this is just a story, but it is not. Scientists who were studying crows did an experiment. They put a jar with water in front of a crow. A worm was floating on top of the water. _____ⓐ_____, the water level was low, so the crow could not eat the worm. The crow solved ⓑthe problem just as in the fable. It dropped stones into the jar. If you think this bird is special, you are wrong. Scientists did the same experiment with other crows, and they all did the same, too.

23 위 글의 빈칸 ⓐ에 들어갈 알맞은 말을 고르시오.

① For instance   ② Moreover
③ In other words   ④ As a result
⑤ However

24 위 글의 밑줄 친 ⓑ가 가리키는 내용을 우리말로 쓰시오.

➡ _____

_____

Middle School 2-1
학교시험 완벽 대비

1학기 전과정

적중100 plus

영어 기출문제집

영어 중 2

동아 | 윤정미

Best Collection

내용문의 중등영어발전소 적중100 편집부 TEL 070-7707-0457

INSIGHT
on the textbook

교과서 파헤치기

영어 기출 문제집

적중 100 plus
1학기 전과정

영어 중 **2**

동아 | 윤정미

Insight
on the textbook

교과서 파헤치기

※ 다음 영어를 우리말로 쓰시오.

01 important _____

02 nap _____

03 exciting _____

04 boring _____

05 near _____

06 practice _____

07 strawberry _____

08 usually _____

09 weekend _____

10 really _____

11 classical _____

12 architect _____

13 show _____

14 vegetable _____

15 sunset _____

16 romantic _____

17 most _____

18 library _____

19 enjoy _____

20 almost _____

21 country _____

22 place _____

23 sometimes _____

24 carrot _____

25 animal _____

26 end _____

27 meat _____

28 kind _____

29 Mongolia _____

30 win _____

31 truth _____

32 present _____

33 national _____

34 exercise _____

35 detective _____

36 around _____

37 brush _____

38 be proud of _____

39 live in _____

40 free time _____

41 be like _____

42 in fact _____

43 what kind of ~ _____

※ 다음 우리말을 영어로 쓰시오.

01 ~할 때

02 ~배

03 정원

04 가장 좋아하는

05 ~이기 때문에

06 (빵을) 굽다

07 디저트, 후식

08 남쪽의

09 공상 과학 소설(의)

10 경주

11 (탈 것을) 타다

12 평화로운

13 소설

14 문화

15 사이[중간]에

16 탐정의; 탐정

17 특히

18 자유로운

19 ~와 같은

20 밖에서, 밖에

21 고기

22 공포

23 웃기는, 재미있는

24 거짓말

25 일몰, 해질녘

26 지루한

27 진실

28 로맨틱한, 낭만적인

29 고전적인, 클래식의

30 운동하다

31 때때로, 가끔

32 정말로

33 선물

34 건축가

35 거의

36 중요한

37 낮잠[휴식], 시에스타

38 ~을 돌보다

39 모이다

40 A와 B 둘 다

41 ~에 살다

42 ~의 일원이다, ~의 소속이다

43 ~을 자랑스러워하다

※ 다음 영영풀이에 알맞은 단어를 <보기>에서 골라 쓴 후, 우리말 뜻을 쓰시오.

1 _____ : not interesting: _____

2 _____ : a short sleep, especially during the day: _____

3 _____ : to sit on an animal, especially a horse: _____

4 _____ : belonging to a traditional style: _____

5 _____ : a competition in which people or animals compete to run fastest and

    finish first: _____

6 _____ : to do a particular thing, often regularly, in order to improve your skill at

    it: _____

7 _____ : the time of day when the sun disappears and night begins: _____

8 _____ : quiet and calm without any worry or excitement: _____

9 _____ : sweet food served after the main part of a meal: _____

10 _____ : to achieve victory in a fight, contest, game, etc.: _____

11 _____ : liked more than others of the same kind: _____

12 _____ : talking about what happens on most occasions: _____

13 _____ : an area of ground where plants such as flowers or vegetables are grown:

    _____

14 _____ : the true facts about something, rather than the things that have been

    invented or guessed: _____

15 _____ : to do physical activities in order to make yourself stronger and healthier:

    _____

16 _____ : a very strong feeling of fear, dread, and shock: _____

보기			
dessert	truth	exercise	win
horror	classical	garden	practice
ride	nap	favorite	usually
boring	sunset	race	peaceful

대화문 Test

※ 다음 우리말과 일치하도록 빈칸에 알맞은 말을 쓰시오.

Listen and Talk A-1

G: Hajun, what do you _____ do in your _____ _____?

B: I like _____ _____ with my dad.

G: _____ _____ _____ games do you play?

B: I _____ _____ baduk.

G: 하준아, 여가 시간에 보통 무엇을 하니?
B: 나는 아버지와 게임을 하는 걸 좋아해.
G: 어떤 종류의 게임을 하니?
B: 나는 주로 바둑을 둬.

Listen and Talk A-2

G: Hey, Eric. What do you usually do _____ _____ _____ _____?

B: I _____ _____ the library and _____ books.

G: _____ _____ _____ books do you read?

B: I like reading _____ _____. I _____ like Sherlock Holmes' stories.

G: 이봐, Eric, 넌 여가 시간에 보통 무엇을 하니?
B: 나는 도서관에 가서 책을 읽어.
G: 어떤 종류의 책을 읽니?
B: 나는 탐정 소설을 읽는 것을 좋아해. 난 Sherlock Holmes의 이야기를 정말 좋아해.

Listen and Talk A-3

G: Seho, what do you do _____ _____ _____ _____?

B: I _____ _____ music.

G: What _____ _____ music do you _____ _____?

B: _____ music.

G: 세호야, 너는 여가 시간에 무엇을 하니?
B: 나는 음악을 들어.
G: 어떤 종류의 음악을 듣니?
B: 록 음악.

Listen and Talk A-4

G: Chris, what do you do _____ you _____ _____ _____?

B: I make cookies. I _____ _____.

G: What _____ of cookies do you _____?

B: I _____ _____ strawberry cookies. I love _____.

G: Chris, 넌 여가 시간이 있을 때 무엇을 하니?
B: 쿠키를 만들어. 나는 베이킹을 좋아해.
G: 어떤 종류의 쿠키를 만드니?
B: 나는 보통 딸기 쿠키를 만들어. 난 딸기를 좋아해.

Listen and Talk B

A: Minji, what do you _____ _____ in your free time?

B: I _____ _____ _____ music.

A: _____ _____ _____ _____ do you listen to?

B: I _____ _____ _____ music.

A: 민지야, 넌 여가 시간에 보통 무엇을 하니?
B: 나는 보통 음악을 들어.
A: 어떤 종류의 음악을 듣니?
B: 나는 클래식 음악을 들어.

Listen and Talk C

B: Subin, what do you _____ do _____ your free time?

G: I _____ _____.

B: What _____ _____ _____ do you do?

G: I _____ badminton _____ my brother. I'm _____ the school's badminton team. What do you _____ _____ in your _____ _____, Andy?

B: I like _____ _____.

G: _____ _____ _____ movies do you _____?

B: I like _____ _____. They're _____.

G: Oh, I _____ _____ action movies, too. _____ _____ _____ go see an _____ movie this weekend?

B: Sure. That _____ _____.

B: 수빈아, 너는 여가 시간에 주로 무엇을 하니?
G: 나는 밖에서 운동을 해.
B: 어떤 종류의 운동을 하니?
G: 나는 남동생과 배드민턴을 쳐. 난 학교 배드민턴 팀이야. 너는 여가 시간에 주로 무엇을 하니, Andy?
B: 나는 영화 보는 것을 좋아해.
G: 어떤 종류의 영화를 좋아하니?
B: 나는 액션 영화를 좋아해. 액션 영화는 재미있어.
G: 오, 나도 가끔 액션 영화를 봐. 이번 주말에 액션 영화 보러 갈래?
B: 그래. 좋아.

Review 1

B: Emma, what do you _____ do in your _____ _____?

G: I _____ _____ _____ music. _____ _____ you, Chris?

B: I read books. I _____ _____ stories.

B: Emma, 너는 여가 시간에 보통 무엇을 하니?
G: 나는 보통 음악을 들어. 너는 어떠니, Chris?
B: 나는 책을 읽어. 탐정 소설을 좋아해.

Review 2

G: Jiho, what do you _____ do _____ you _____ free time?

B: I usually _____ _____.

G: _____ _____ of movies do you _____?

B: I like _____ movies. Bruce Lee is my _____ movie _____.

G: 지호야, 너는 여가 시간이 있을 때 보통 무엇을 하니?
B: 나는 보통 영화를 봐.
G: 어떤 종류의 영화를 보니?
B: 나는 액션 영화를 좋아해. Bruce Lee는 내가 가장 좋아하는 영화배우야.

Review 3

1. W: What _____ Minho usually do in his _____ _____?

2. W: What kind of _____ does Sewon _____?

1. W: 민호는 여가 시간에 주로 무엇을 하니?
2. W: 세원이는 어떤 종류의 게임을 하니?

※ 다음 우리말에 맞도록 대화를 영어로 쓰시오.

Listen and Talk A-1

G: _____

B: _____

G: _____

B: _____

G: 하준아, 여가 시간에 보통 무엇을 하니?
B: 나는 아버지와 게임을 하는 걸 좋아해.
G: 어떤 종류의 게임을 하니?
B: 나는 주로 바둑을 둬.

Listen and Talk A-2

G: _____

B: _____

G: _____

B: _____

G: 이봐, Eric, 넌 여가 시간에 보통 무엇을 하니?
B: 나는 도서관에 가서 책을 읽어.
G: 어떤 종류의 책을 읽니?
B: 나는 탐정 소설을 읽는 것을 좋아해. 난 Sherlock Holmes의 이야기를 정말 좋아해.

Listen and Talk A-3

G: _____

B: _____

G: _____

B: _____

G: 세호야, 너는 여가 시간에 무엇을 하니?
B: 나는 음악을 들어.
G: 어떤 종류의 음악을 듣니?
B: 록 음악.

Listen and Talk A-4

G: _____

B: _____

G: _____

B: _____

G: Chris, 넌 여가 시간이 있을 때 무엇을 하니?
B: 쿠키를 만들어. 나는 베이킹을 좋아해.
G: 어떤 종류의 쿠키를 만드니?
B: 나는 보통 딸기 쿠키를 만들어. 난 딸기를 좋아해.

Listen and Talk B

A: _____

B: _____

A: _____

B: _____

A: 민지야, 넌 여가 시간에 보통 무엇을 하니?
B: 나는 보통 음악을 들어.
A: 어떤 종류의 음악을 듣니?
B: 나는 클래식 음악을 들어.

Listen and Talk C

B: _____

G: _____

B: _____

G: _____
_____

B: _____

G: _____

B: _____

G: _____
_____

B: _____

B: 수빈아, 너는 여가 시간에 주로 무엇을 하니?

G: 나는 밖에서 운동을 해.

B: 어떤 종류의 운동을 하니?

G: 나는 남동생과 배드민턴을 쳐. 난 학교 배드민턴 팀이야. 너는 여가 시간에 주로 무엇을 하니, Andy?

B: 나는 영화 보는 것을 좋아해.

G: 어떤 종류의 영화를 좋아하니?

B: 나는 액션 영화를 좋아해. 액션 영화는 재미있어.

G: 오, 나도 가끔 액션 영화를 봐. 이번 주말에 액션 영화 보러 갈래?

B: 그래. 좋아.

Review 1

B: _____

G: _____

B: _____

B: Emma, 너는 여가 시간에 보통 무엇을 하니?

G: 나는 보통 음악을 들어. 너는 어떠니, Chris?

B: 나는 책을 읽어. 탐정 소설을 좋아해.

Review 2

G: _____

B: _____

G: _____

B: _____

G: 지호야, 너는 여가 시간이 있을 때 보통 무엇을 하니?

B: 나는 보통 영화를 봐.

G: 어떤 종류의 영화를 보니?

B: 나는 액션 영화를 좋아해. Bruce Lee는 내가 가장 좋아하는 영화배우야.

Review 3

1. W: _____

2. W: _____

1. W: 민호는 여가 시간에 주로 무엇을 하니?

2. W: 세원이는 어떤 종류의 게임을 하니?

※ 다음 우리말과 일치하도록 빈칸에 알맞은 것을 골라 쓰시오.

1 Teen Talk: My _____ Time of the _____

A. Day   B. Favorite

2 _____! _____ Somin.

A. I'm   B. hello

3 I'm 15 _____ _____, and I live _____ Korea.

A. in   B. old   C. years

4 Please _____ me about _____ _____ time of the day.

A. favorite   B. tell   C. your

5 You can also _____ _____ some _____.

A. pictures   B. me   C. show

6 Hi, _____ name is Diego, and I _____ _____ Seville, Spain.

A. in   B. live   C. my

7 _____ favorite time _____ the _____ is lunch time.

A. day   B. of   C. my

8 My school _____ _____ _____ 2 p.m.

A. around   B. ends   C. usually

9 On _____ days, my family _____ _____ and has a big, long lunch.

A. together   B. most   C. gets

10 We _____ _____ soup, _____, and meat.

A. vegetables   B. have   C. usually

11 We _____ _____ a dessert _____ churros.

A. have   B. like   C. also

12 After lunch, we _____ _____ a siesta, a short _____.

A. nap   B. take   C. usually

13 _____ my father _____ I like to sleep _____ the tree in our garden.

A. under   B. and   C. both

14 Hi! My name is Tabin, and I _____ _____ the Gobi Desert _____ Mongolia.

A. in   B. near   C. like

15 I'm happy _____ I _____ _____ horse.

A. ride   B. when   C. my

---

1 십대들의 이야기: 하루 중 내가 가장 좋아하는 시간

2 안녕! 나는 소민이야.

3 나는 15살이고 한국에 살아.

4 너희들이 하루 중 가장 좋아하는 시간에 대해 말해 줘.

5 나에게 사진 몇 장을 보여 줘도 좋아.

6 안녕, 내 이름은 Diego이고, 나는 스페인의 세비야에서 살아.

7 내가 하루 중 가장 좋아하는 시간은 점심시간이야.

8 우리 학교는 보통 오후 2시경에 끝나.

9 대부분의 날에는, 가족들이 모여서 푸짐하고 긴 점심 식사를 해.

10 우리는 보통 수프, 채소 그리고 고기를 먹어.

11 우리는 또한 추로스와 같은 후식도 먹어.

12 점심 식사 후에는 우리는 보통 시에스타, 즉 짧은 낮잠을 자.

13 아빠와 나는 둘 다 우리 정원에 있는 나무 밑에서 자는 것을 좋아해.

14 안녕! 내 이름은 Tabin이고 나는 몽골에 있는 고비 사막 근처에 살아.

15 나는 내 말을 탈 때 행복해.

16 Horses are _____ _____ our _____ .

    A. important   B. in   C. culture

17 _____ _____ can _____ a horse in Mongolia.

    A. ride   B. everyone   C. almost

18 _____ _____ , we say, "We ride horses _____ we can walk."

    A. before   B. fact   C. in

19 I _____ good _____ _____ my horse.

    A. care   B. of   C. take

20 I often _____ him and _____ _____ some carrots.

    A. him   B. brush   C. give

21 I _____ _____ especially in the evening _____ the sunset.

    A. before   B. riding   C. enjoy

22 _____ the sky is red, and everything _____ _____ .

    A. peaceful   B. then   C. is

23 Hi! I'm Musa, and I live _____ _____ , _____ .

    A. in   B. Kenya   C. Nairobi

24 My _____ time of the day is our _____ _____ time.

    A. practice   B. favorite   C. running

25 My friend, Tamu, and I are _____ the _____ _____ team.

    A. running   B. on   C. school's

26 I'm _____ _____ I run _____ Tamu.

    A. with   B. happiest   C. when

27 Our practice time isn't _____ _____ we _____ see many animals.

    A. can   B. because   C. boring

28 Many runners _____ Kenya _____ _____ in the Olympics.

    A. races   B. won   C. from

29 I'm _____ _____ _____ them.

    A. of   B. proud   C. so

30 Both Tamu _____ I want to _____ _____ them.

    A. like   B. be   C. and

---

16 말은 우리 문화에서 중요해.

17 몽골에서는 거의 모든 사람이 말을 탈 수 있어.

18 실제로 우리는 "우리는 걸을 수 있기 전에 말을 탄다."라고 말해.

19 나는 내 말을 잘 돌봐.

20 나는 종종 내 말의 털을 빗겨 주고 당근을 줘.

21 나는 특히 해가 지기 전 저녁에 말 타는 것을 즐겨.

22 그 무렵엔 하늘은 붉고 모든 것이 평화로워.

23 안녕! 나는 Musa이고, 케냐의 나이로비에 살아.

24 내가 하루 중 가장 좋아하는 시간은 달리기 연습 시간이야.

25 내 친구 Tamu와 나는 학교의 달리기 팀이야.

26 나는 Tamu와 달리기를 할 때 가장 행복해.

27 우리의 연습 시간은 지루하지 않아, 왜냐하면 우리는 많은 동물들을 볼 수 있기 때문이야.

28 케냐의 많은 달리기 선수들이 올림픽의 육상 경기에서 우승을 했어.

29 나는 그들이 매우 자랑스러워.

30 Tamu와 나 둘 다 그들처럼 되고 싶어해.

※ 다음 우리말과 일치하도록 빈칸에 알맞은 말을 쓰시오.

1 _____ Talk: _____ _____ Time of the Day

2 Hello! _____ Somin.

3 I'm 15 _____ _____, and I _____ _____ Korea.

4 Please _____ me _____ your _____ time of the day.

5 You can _____ _____ me some _____.

6 Hi, _____ name is Diego, and I _____ _____ Seville, Spain.

7 My _____ time of the day is _____ time.

8 My school _____ ends _____ 2 p.m.

9 _____ most days, my family _____ _____ and has a big, long lunch.

10 We _____ _____ soup, _____, and meat.

11 We also _____ a dessert _____ churros.

12 After lunch, we usually _____ a siesta, a _____ _____.

13 _____ my father _____ I like to sleep _____ the tree in our garden.

14 Hi! My name is Tabin, and I live _____ the Gobi Desert _____ Mongolia.

15 I'm happy _____ _____ _____ my horse.

16 Horses are _____ in our _____.

1 십대들의 이야기: 하루 중 내가 가장 좋아하는 시간

2 안녕! 나는 소민이야.

3 나는 15살이고 한국에 살아.

4 너희들이 하루 중 가장 좋아하는 시간에 대해 말해 줘.

5 나에게 사진 몇 장을 보여 줘도 좋아.

6 안녕, 내 이름은 Diego이고, 나는 스페인의 세비야에서 살아.

7 내가 하루 중 가장 좋아하는 시간은 점심시간이야.

8 우리 학교는 보통 오후 2시경에 끝나.

9 대부분의 날에는, 가족들이 모여서 푸짐하고 긴 점심 식사를 해.

10 우리는 보통 수프, 채소 그리고 고기를 먹어.

11 우리는 또한 추로스와 같은 후식도 먹어.

12 점심 식사 후에는 우리는 보통 시에스타, 즉 짧은 낮잠을 자.

13 아빠와 나는 둘 다 우리 정원에 있는 나무 밑에서 자는 것을 좋아해.

14 안녕! 내 이름은 Tabin이고 나는 몽골에 있는 고비 사막 근처에 살아.

15 나는 내 말을 탈 때 행복해.

16 말은 우리 문화에서 중요해.

17 _____ everyone _____ _____ a horse in Mongolia.

18 _____ _____, we say, "We ride horses _____ we can walk."

19 I _____ good _____ _____ my horse.

20 I _____ _____ him and give him some _____ .

21 I _____ _____ especially in the evening before the _____ .

22 Then the sky is red, and _____ is _____ .

23 Hi! I'm Musa, and I _____ _____ Nairobi, Kenya.

24 My _____ time of the day is our _____ _____ time.

25 My friend, Tamu, and I _____ _____ the school's _____ team.

26 I'm _____ when I _____ Tamu.

27 Our _____ time isn't _____ because we _____ see many animals.

28 Many _____ from Kenya _____ _____ in the Olympics.

29 I'm so _____ _____ them.

30 _____ Tamu _____ I want _____ _____ like them.

17 몽골에서는 거의 모든 사람이 말을 탈 수 있어.

18 실제로 우리는 "우리는 걸을 수 있기 전에 말을 탄다."라고 말해.

19 나는 내 말을 잘 돌봐.

20 나는 종종 내 말의 털을 빗겨 주고 당근을 줘.

21 나는 특히 해가 지기 전 저녁에 말 타는 것을 즐겨.

22 그 무렵엔 하늘은 붉고 모든 것이 평화로워.

23 안녕! 나는 Musa이고, 케냐의 나이로비에 살아.

24 내가 하루 중 가장 좋아하는 시간은 달리기 연습 시간이야.

25 내 친구 Tamu와 나는 학교의 달리기 팀이야.

26 나는 Tamu와 달리기를 할 때 가장 행복해.

27 우리의 연습 시간은 지루하지 않아, 왜냐하면 우리는 많은 동물들을 볼 수 있기 때문이야.

28 케냐의 많은 달리기 선수들이 올림픽의 육상 경기에서 우승을 했어.

29 나는 그들이 매우 자랑스러워.

30 Tamu와 나 둘 다 그들처럼 되고 싶어해.

※ 다음 문장을 우리말로 쓰시오.

1 ▸ Teen Talk: My Favorite Time of the Day

➡ _____

2 ▸ Hello! I'm Somin.

➡ _____

3 ▸ I'm 15 years old, and I live in Korea.

➡ _____

4 ▸ Please tell me about your favorite time of the day.

➡ _____

5 ▸ You can also show me some pictures.

➡ _____

6 ▸ Hi, my name is Diego, I live in Seville, Spain.

➡ _____

7 ▸ My favorite time of the day is lunch time.

➡ _____

8 ▸ My school usually ends around 2 p.m.

➡ _____

9 ▸ On most days, my family gets together and has a big, long lunch.

➡ _____

10 ▸ We usually have soup, vegetables, and meat.

➡ _____

11 ▸ We also have a dessert like churros.

➡ _____

12 ▸ After lunch, we usually take a siesta, a short nap.

➡ _____

13 ▸ Both my father and I like to sleep under the tree in our garden.

➡ _____

14 ▸ Hi! My name is Tabin, and I live near the Gobi Desert in Mongolia.

➡ _____

15 ▸ I'm happy when I ride my horse.

➡ _____

16 ▸ Horses are important in our culture.

➡ _____

17 Almost everyone can ride a horse in Mongolia.

➡ _____

18 In fact, we say, "We ride horses before we can walk."

➡ _____

19 I take good care of my horse.

➡ _____

20 I often brush him and give him some carrots.

➡ _____

21 I enjoy riding especially in the evening before the sunset.

➡ _____

22 Then the sky is red, and everything is peaceful.

➡ _____

23 Hi! I'm Musa, and I live in Nairobi, Kenya.

➡ _____

24 My favorite time of the day is our running practice time.

➡ _____

25 My friend, Tamu, and I are on the school's running team.

➡ _____

26 I'm happiest when I run with Tamu.

➡ _____

27 Our practice time isn't boring because we can see many animals.

➡ _____

28 Many runners from Kenya won races in the Olympics.

➡ _____

29 I'm so proud of them.

➡ _____

30 Both Tamu and I want to be like them.

➡ _____

※ 다음 괄호 안의 단어들을 우리말에 맞도록 바르게 배열하시오.

1 (Talk: / Teen / the / Time / Day / of / Favorite / My)

➡ _____

2 (I'm / Hello! / Somin.)

➡ _____

3 (I / old, / in / 15 / I'm / live / Korea. / years / and)

➡ _____

4 (me / your / of / please / time / the / tell / about / day. / favorite)

➡ _____

5 (show / some / you / also / pictures. / can / me)

➡ _____

6 (name / Seville, / is / and / my / Hi, / live / Spain. / I / Diego, / in)

➡ _____

7 (the / time / is / favorite / lunch / time. / day / my / of)

➡ _____

8 (school / around / my / p.m. / usually / 2 / ends)

➡ _____

9 (days, / most / on / family / big, / and / lunch. / gets / my / long / a / together / has)

➡ _____

10 (we / meat. / usually / vegetables, / have / and / soup,)

➡ _____

11 (like / a / dessert / also / churros. / we / have)

➡ _____

12 (lunch, / after / take / usually / we / siesta, / a / nap. / short / a)

➡ _____

13 (father / and / my / both / sleep / to / like / I / tree / the / under / garden. / in / our)

➡ _____

14 (Tabin, / my / Hi! / and / is / name / I / the / Desert / near / live / in / Mongolia. / Gobi)

➡ _____

15 (my / when / I'm / horse. / ride / happy / I)

➡ _____

1 십대들의 이야기: 하루 중 내가 가장 좋아하는 시간

2 안녕! 나는 소민이야.

3 나는 15살이고 한국에 살아.

4 너희들이 하루 중 가장 좋아하는 시간에 대해 말해 줘.

5 나에게 사진 몇 장을 보여 줘도 좋아.

6 안녕, 내 이름은 Diego이고, 나는 스페인의 세비야에서 살아.

7 내가 하루 중 가장 좋아하는 시간은 점심시간이야.

8 우리 학교는 보통 오후 2시경에 끝나.

9 대부분의 날에는, 가족들이 모여서 푸짐하고 긴 점심 식사를 해.

10 우리는 보통 수프, 채소 그리고 고기를 먹어.

11 우리는 또한 추로스와 같은 후식도 먹어.

12 점심 식사 후에는 우리는 보통 시에스타, 즉 짧은 낮잠을 자.

13 아빠와 나는 둘 다 우리 정원에 있는 나무 밑에서 자는 것을 좋아해.

14 안녕! 내 이름은 Tabin이고 나는 몽골에 있는 고비 사막 근처에 살아.

15 나는 내 말을 탈 때 행복해.

16 (in / horses / our / important / are / culture.)

➡ _____

17 (everyone / a / almost / Mongolia. / horse / can / in / ride)

➡ _____

18 (we / fact, / say, / in / "We / before / walk." / we / can / horses / ride)

➡ _____

19 (care / horse. / take / I / of / good / my)

➡ _____

20 (him / I / brush / often / and / some / give / carrots. / him)

➡ _____

21 (I / especially / riding / the / enjoy / evening / before / the / in / sunset.)

➡ _____

22 (is / the / then / red, / sky / is / and / everything / peaceful.)

➡ _____

23 (Hi! / Musa, / and / I'm / Kenya. / I / live / Nairobi, / in)

➡ _____

24 (time / the / my / favorite / of / day / running / is / time. / practice / our)

➡ _____

25 (friend, / Tamu, / my / and / on / the / team. / I / running / are / school's)

➡ _____

26 (happiest / run / Tamu. / I'm / when / with / I)

➡ _____

27 (practice / our / time / boring / isn't / we / see / animals. / because / can / many)

➡ _____

28 (runners / Kenya / many / races / from / won / the / Olympics. / in)

➡ _____

29 (so / proud / them. / I'm / of)

➡ _____

30 (Tamu / I / want / both / and / be / to / them. / like)

➡ _____

16 말은 우리 문화에서 중요해.

17 몽골에서는 거의 모든 사람이 말을 탈 수 있어.

18 실제로 우리는 "우리는 걸을 수 있기 전에 말을 탄다."라고 말해.

19 나는 내 말을 잘 돌봐.

20 나는 종종 내 말의 털을 빗겨 주고 당근을 줘.

21 나는 특히 해가 지기 전 저녁에 말 타는 것을 즐겨.

22 그 무렵엔 하늘은 붉고 모든 것이 평화로워.

23 안녕! 나는 Musa이고, 케냐의 나이로비에 살아.

24 내가 하루 중 가장 좋아하는 시간은 달리기 연습 시간이야.

25 내 친구 Tamu와 나는 학교의 달리기 팀이야.

26 나는 Tamu와 달리기를 할 때 가장 행복해.

27 우리의 연습 시간은 지루하지 않아, 왜냐하면 우리는 많은 동물들을 볼 수 있기 때문이야.

28 케냐의 많은 달리기 선수들이 올림픽의 육상 경기에서 우승을 했어.

29 나는 그들이 매우 자랑스러워.

30 Tamu와 나 둘 다 그들처럼 되고 싶어해.

Step5

※ **다음 우리말을 영어로 쓰시오.**

1 십대들의 이야기: 하루 중 내가 가장 좋아하는 시간

➡ _____

2 안녕! 나는 소민이야.

➡ _____

3 나는 15살이고 한국에 살아.

➡ _____

4 너희들이 하루 중 가장 좋아하는 시간에 대해 말해 줘.

➡ _____

5 나에게 사진 몇 장을 보여 줘도 좋아.

➡ _____

6 안녕, 내 이름은 Diego이고, 나는 스페인의 세비야에서 살아.

➡ _____

7 내가 하루 중 가장 좋아하는 시간은 점심시간이야.

➡ _____

8 우리 학교는 보통 오후 2시경에 끝나.

➡ _____

9 대부분의 날에는, 가족들이 모여서 푸짐하고 긴 점심 식사를 해.

➡ _____

10 우리는 보통 수프, 채소 그리고 고기를 먹어.

➡ _____

11 우리는 또한 추로스와 같은 후식도 먹어.

➡ _____

12 점심 식사 후에는 우리는 보통 시에스타, 즉 짧은 낮잠을 자.

➡ _____

13 아빠와 나는 둘 다 우리 정원에 있는 나무 밑에서 자는 것을 좋아해.

➡ _____

14 안녕! 내 이름은 Tabin이고 나는 몽골에 있는 고비 사막 근처에 살아.

➡ _____

15 나는 내 말을 탈 때 행복해.

➡ _____

16 말은 우리 문화에서 중요해.

➡ _____

17 몽골에서는 거의 모든 사람이 말을 탈 수 있어.

➡ _____

18 실제로 우리는 "우리는 걸을 수 있기 전에 말을 탄다."라고 말해.

➡ _____

19 나는 내 말을 잘 돌봐.

➡ _____

20 나는 종종 내 말의 털을 빗겨 주고 당근을 줘.

➡ _____

21 나는 특히 해가 지기 전 저녁에 말 타는 것을 즐겨.

➡ _____

22 그 무렵엔 하늘은 붉고 모든 것이 평화로워.

➡ _____

23 안녕! 나는 Musa이고, 케냐의 나이로비에 살아.

➡ _____

24 내가 하루 중 가장 좋아하는 시간은 달리기 연습 시간이야.

➡ _____

25 내 친구 Tamu와 나는 학교의 달리기 팀이야.

➡ _____

26 나는 Tamu와 달리기를 할 때 가장 행복해.

➡ _____

27 우리의 연습 시간은 지루하지 않아, 왜냐하면 우리는 많은 동물들을 볼 수 있기 때문이야.

➡ _____

28 케냐의 많은 달리기 선수들이 올림픽의 육상 경기에서 우승을 했어.

➡ _____

29 나는 그들이 매우 자랑스러워.

➡ _____

30 Tamu와 나 둘 다 그들처럼 되고 싶어해.

➡ _____

※ 다음 우리말과 일치하도록 빈칸에 알맞은 말을 쓰시오.

Before You Read

1. This country is _____ _____ Europe.

2. People here usually _____ _____ _____ _____ in the afternoon.

3. This country _____ _____ _____ Asia.

4. _____ _____ can _____ a horse here.

5. This country is _____ _____ _____.

6. _____ _____ many great runners _____ here.

1. 이 나라는 유럽 남부에 있다.
2. 이곳의 사람들은 보통 오후에 짧은 낮잠을 잔다.
3. 이 나라는 동아시아에 있다.
4. 이곳의 거의 모든 사람들은 말을 탈 수 있다.
5. 이 나라는 동아프리카에 있다.
6. 이곳 출신의 훌륭한 달리기 선수들이 많이 있다.

Around the World

1. Some people _____ this country don't _____ _____ one place _____ _____.

2. They _____ _____ with their animals.

3. People in this country _____ _____ four or five _____ _____ _____.

4. They eat tapas _____ meals.

5. This country has many _____ parks _____ animals _____ lions, zebras, elephants, and giraffes.

1. 이 나라의 몇몇 사람들은 한 장소에서 오랫동안 살지 않는다.
2. 그들은 그들의 동물들과 이동한다.
3. 이 나라의 사람들은 보통 하루에 네 번 또는 다섯 번의 식사를 한다.
4. 그들은 식사 사이에 타파스를 먹는다.
5. 이 나라에는 사자, 얼룩말, 코끼리, 그리고 기린과 같은 동물들이 있는 국립공원이 많이 있다.

Think and Write

1. I'm _____ when I read _____ novels.

2. I'm happiest _____ _____ _____ candy.

3. I'm happiest when my brother _____ _____ _____ _____.

4. I'm happiest _____ _____ _____ my friends after school.

1. 나는 흥미 있는 소설을 읽을 때 가장 행복해.
2. 나는 사탕을 먹을 때 가장 행복해.
3. 나는 내 남동생이 나에게 재미있는 농담을 할 때 가장 행복해.
4. 나는 방과 후에 내 친구들과 놀 때 가장 행복해.

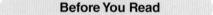

※ 다음 우리말을 영어로 쓰시오.

Before You Read

1. 이 나라는 유럽 남부에 있다.
   ➡ _____

2. 이곳의 사람들은 보통 오후에 짧은 낮잠을 잔다.
   ➡ _____

3. 이 나라는 동아시아에 있다.
   ➡ _____

4. 이곳의 거의 모든 사람들은 말을 탈 수 있다.
   ➡ _____

5. 이 나라는 동아프리카에 있다.
   ➡ _____

6. 이곳 출신의 훌륭한 달리기 선수들이 많이 있다.
   ➡ _____

Around the World

1. 이 나라의 몇몇 사람들은 한 장소에서 오랫동안 살지 않는다.
   ➡ _____

2. 그들은 그들의 동물들과 이동한다.
   ➡ _____

3. 이 나라의 사람들은 보통 하루에 네 번 또는 다섯 번의 식사를 한다.
   ➡ _____

4. 그들은 식사 사이에 타파스를 먹는다.
   ➡ _____

5. 이 나라에는 사자, 얼룩말, 코끼리, 그리고 기린과 같은 동물들이 있는 국립공원이 많이 있다.
   ➡ _____

Think and Write

1. 나는 흥미 있는 소설을 읽을 때 가장 행복해.
   ➡ _____

2. 나는 사탕을 먹을 때 가장 행복해.
   ➡ _____

3. 나는 내 남동생이 나에게 재미있는 농담을 할 때 가장 행복해.
   ➡ _____

4. 나는 방과 후에 내 친구들과 놀 때 가장 행복해.
   ➡ _____

※ 다음 영어를 우리말로 쓰시오.

01 amazing	
02 bookstore	
03 combination	
04 view	
05 train station	
06 scared	
07 healthy	
08 cancel	
09 expensive	
10 unique	
11 win	
12 straight	
13 sew	
14 prize	
15 movie theater	
16 tradition	
17 spicy	
18 police station	
19 mud	
20 main gate	
21 fabric	

22 fasten	
23 produce	
24 follow	
25 collect	
26 bee	
27 wheel	
28 tasty	
29 museum	
30 enter	
31 colorful	
32 blanket	
33 gate	
34 piece	
35 have to+동사원형	
36 be proud of	
37 move on to	
38 don't have to+동사원형	
39 get+형용사	
40 take care of	
41 work on	
42 across from	
43 get to	

※ 다음 우리말을 영어로 쓰시오.

01 가로질러, 건너서

02 염소

03 가장 좋아하는

04 북쪽

05 무대

06 세 번째의

07 (미국의) 주

08 ~ 이상, ~을 넘어

09 시청

10 빵집

11 담요

12 겁먹은, 무서운

13 형형색색의, 다채로운

14 깁다, 바느질하다

15 비싼

16 모으다, 수집하다

17 똑바로, 곧장, 곧바로

18 생산하다, 만들다

19 바퀴

20 취소하다

21 매다

22 문, 대문, 출입구

23 박람회, 품평회

24 대회

25 흥미진진한

26 퀼트, 누비이불

27 구역, 블록

28 과거

29 직물, 천

30 독특한, 특별한

31 조합, 결합

32 전통

33 조각

34 매운, 양념이 강한

35 A와 B 사이에

36 ~로 유명하다

37 ~ 옆에

38 ~을 찾다

39 당신의 오른편에

40 ~을 돌보다

41 ~을 기다리다

42 ~의 맞은편에

43 ~을 보다

※ 다음 영영풀이에 알맞은 단어를 <보기>에서 골라 쓴 후, 우리말 뜻을 쓰시오.

1 _____ : having a good flavor: _____

2 _____ : costing a lot of money: _____

3 _____ : in a line or direction that is not curved or bent: _____

4 _____ : very special or unusual: _____

5 _____ : physically strong and not likely to become ill or weak: _____

6 _____ : strongly flavored with spices: _____

7 _____ : to make something to be bought, used, or enjoyed by people: _____

8 _____ : to get things of the same type from different places and bring them together: _____

9 _____ : two or more different things that exist together or put together: _____

10 _____ : a belief, custom, or way of doing something that has existed for a long time: _____

11 _____ : to use a needle and thread to make or repair clothes: _____

12 _____ : frightened of or nervous about something: _____

13 _____ : a building where important cultural, historical, or scientific objects are kept: _____

14 _____ : a structure like a door which is used at the entrance to a field, a garden, or the grounds of a building: _____

15 _____ : full of bright colors or having a lot of different colors: _____

16 _____ : a place where bread and cakes are made and/or sold: _____

※ 다음 우리말과 일치하도록 빈칸에 알맞은 말을 쓰시오.

Listen and Talk A-1

B: Excuse me. I'm _____ _____ the Star Mall.

G: Go _____ two _____ and _____ _____. It'll be the _____ building _____ your right.

B: Oh, _____ _____. Thank you.

G: You're _____.

B: 실례합니다. Star Mall을 찾고 있어요.
G: 두 블록을 곧장 가서, 왼쪽으로 도세요. 오른쪽 첫 건물일 거예요.
B: 오, 알겠어요. 감사해요.
G: 천만에요.

Listen and Talk A-2

B: _____ me. _____ the bookstore?

G: There's _____ _____ _____ the post office.

B: _____ do I _____ there?

G: _____ _____ one block and _____ right. It'll be _____ _____ _____.

B: Thank you!

B: 실례합니다. 서점이 어디 있나요?
G: 우체국 맞은편에 하나 있어요.
B: 그곳에 어떻게 가나요?
G: 한 블록을 곧장 가서 오른쪽으로 도세요. 오른쪽에 있을 거예요.
B: 감사합니다!

Listen and Talk A-3

B: Excuse me. _____ do I _____ _____ the police station?

G: _____ _____ three blocks and turn left. It'll _____ _____ your _____.

B: Oh, _____ _____.

G: It's _____ the bakery _____ the school. You _____ _____ it.

B: _____ _____!

B: 실례합니다. 경찰서에 어떻게 가나요?
G: 세 블록을 곧장 걸어가서 왼쪽으로 도세요. 오른쪽에 있을 거예요.
B: 오, 알겠어요.
G: 경찰서는 빵집과 학교 사이에 있어요. 꼭 찾을 거예요.
B: 감사합니다!

Listen and Talk A-4

B: Excuse me. _____ is the Histroy _____?

G: It's _____ Green _____.

B: _____ do I _____ there?

G: Go _____ _____ _____ and turn right. You'll see it _____ your right. It's _____ _____ the bank.

B: Thank you _____ _____.

B: 실례합니다. 역사박물관은 어디에 있나요?
G: Green가에 있어요.
B: 거기에 어떻게 가나요?
G: 세 블록 곧장 가서 오른쪽으로 도세요. 오른쪽에 보일 거예요. 은행 옆에 있어요.
B: 정말 감사합니다.

Listen and Talk B

A: _____ _____ the school?

B: It's _____ Green Street. It's _____ _____ the hospital.

A: _____ do I _____ there?

B: _____ _____ three blocks and _____ _____. It'll be _____ your right.

A: _____ you.

A: 학교가 어디 있니?

B: Green가에 있어. 병원 맞은편에 있어.

A: 거기에 어떻게 가니?

B: 세 블록을 곧장 가서 왼쪽으로 돌아. 오른쪽에 있을 거야.

A: 고마워.

Listen and Talk C

B: Hello. _____ I _____ you?

G: Yes, please. I'm _____ _____ Green Park.

B: OK. Please _____ _____ this map. We _____ _____.

G: Oh, I _____. So _____ do I _____ _____ the park?

B: _____ _____ two blocks and turn _____. It's _____ _____ the train station.

G: I see. The _____ Music Concert is there, _____?

B: Yes, _____ is. It's _____ _____ start _____ 4 p.m. at the Star Concert Stage.

G: Right, and _____ is the _____?

B: It's _____ the north _____ of the park.

G: OK, thank you!

B: 안녕하세요. 도와 드릴까요?

G: 네, 저는 Green 공원을 찾고 있어요.

B: 네. 이 지도를 보세요. 우리는 여기에 있어요.

G: 아, 그렇군요. 그럼 공원에 어떻게 가나요?

B: 두 블록을 곧장 가서 왼쪽으로 도세요. 공원은 기차역 맞은편에 있어요.

G: 알겠어요. 거기서 아프리카 음악 콘서트가 열리죠, 맞나요?

B: 네. 오후 4시에 Star Concert 무대에서 시작할 예정이에요.

G: 맞아요. 그런데 무대는 어디에 있나요?

B: 공원 북문 근처에 있어요.

G: 네, 감사해요!

Review 1

M: Excuse me. _____ do I _____ _____ the bookstore?

W: _____ _____ two blocks and trun left. It'll be _____ _____ _____.

M: That _____ easy. Thank you.

M: 실례합니다. 서점에 어떻게 가요?

W: 두 블록을 곧장 걸어가서 왼쪽으로 도세요. 오른쪽에 있을 거예요.

M: 쉽네요. 고마워요.

Review 2

G: _____ me. _____ Tom's Bakery?

B: It's _____ Main Street. It's _____ _____ the bank.

G: _____.

G: 실례합니다. Tom's Bakery는 어디에 있나요?

B: Main가에 있어요. 은행 옆에 있어요.

G: 감사합니다.

※ 다음 우리말에 맞도록 대화를 영어로 쓰시오.

Listen and Talk A-1

B: _____

G: _____

B: _____

G: _____

B: 실례합니다. Star Mall을 찾고 있어요.

G: 두 블록을 곧장 가서, 왼쪽으로 도세요. 오른쪽 첫 건물일 거예요.

B: 오, 알겠어요. 감사해요.

G: 천만에요.

Listen and Talk A-2

B: _____

G: _____

B: _____

G: _____

B: _____

B: 실례합니다. 서점이 어디 있나요?

G: 우체국 맞은편에 하나 있어요.

B: 그곳에 어떻게 가나요?

G: 한 블록을 곧장 가서 오른쪽으로 도세요. 오른쪽에 있을 거예요.

B: 감사합니다!

Listen and Talk A-3

B: _____

G: _____

B: _____

G: _____

B: _____

B: 실례합니다. 경찰서에 어떻게 가나요?

G: 세 블록을 곧장 걸어가서 왼쪽으로 도세요. 오른쪽에 있을 거예요.

B: 오, 알겠어요.

G: 경찰서는 빵집과 학교 사이에 있어요. 꼭 찾을 거예요.

B: 감사합니다!

Listen and Talk A-4

B: _____

G: _____

B: _____

G: _____

B: _____

B: 실례합니다. 역사박물관은 어디에 있나요?

G: Green가에 있어요.

B: 거기에 어떻게 가나요?

G: 세 블록 곧장 가서 오른쪽으로 도세요. 오른쪽에 보일 거예요. 은행 옆에 있어요.

B: 정말 감사합니다.

Listen and Talk B

A: _____

B: _____

A: _____

B: _____

A: _____

A: 학교가 어디 있니?
B: Green가에 있어. 병원 맞은편에 있어.
A: 거기에 어떻게 가니?
B: 세 블록을 곧장 가서 왼쪽으로 돌아. 오른쪽에 있을 거야.
A: 고마워.

Listen and Talk C

B: _____

G: _____

B: _____

G: _____

B: _____

G: _____

B: _____

G: _____

B: _____

G: _____

B: 안녕하세요. 도와 드릴까요?
G: 네, 저는 Green 공원을 찾고 있어요.
B: 네. 이 지도를 보세요. 우리는 여기에 있어요.
G: 아, 그렇군요. 그럼 공원에 어떻게 가나요?
B: 두 블록을 곧장 가서 왼쪽으로 도세요. 공원은 기차역 맞은편에 있어요.
G: 알겠어요. 거기서 아프리카 음악 콘서트가 열리죠, 맞나요?
B: 네. 오후 4시에 Star Concert 무대에서 시작할 예정이에요.
G: 맞아요, 그런데 무대는 어디에 있나요?
B: 공원 북문 근처에 있어요.
G: 네, 감사해요!

Review 1

M: _____

W: _____

M: _____

M: 실례합니다. 서점에 어떻게 가나요?
W: 두 블록을 곧장 걸어가서 왼쪽으로 도세요. 오른쪽에 있을 거예요.
M: 쉽네요. 고마워요.

Review 2

G: _____

B: _____

G: _____

G: 실례합니다. Tom's Bakery는 어디에 있나요?
B: Main가에 있어요. 은행 옆에 있어요.
G: 감사합니다.

※ 다음 우리말과 일치하도록 빈칸에 알맞은 것을 골라 쓰시오.

1 Fun _____ the _____ _____ of Texas!
  A. Fair   B. at   C. State

2 Hi, _____ _____ Parker.
  A. I'm   B. Eddie

3 I live _____ _____, _____.
  A. Texas   B. in   C. Dallas

4 Now, my family and I _____ _____ the State Fair _____ Texas.
  A. of   B. at   C. are

5 The fair _____ _____ 130 years old, and it's the _____ fair in the USA.
  A. biggest   B. over   C. is

6 I'll _____ you _____.
  A. around   B. show

7 _____ _____!
  A. me   B. follow

8 _____ _____ the goats here!
  A. at   B. look

9 This is a _____ _____.
  A. show   B. goat

10 My _____ brother, Steve, _____ it.
  A. entered   B. younger

11 The goats in the show _____ _____ to be big, but they have to _____ _____.
  A. be   B. don't   C. healthy   D. have

12 They have to _____ a _____ of milk to _____ a prize.
  A. lot   B. win   C. produce

13 Steve _____ good _____ _____ his goat, Bonnie.
  A. of   B. care   C. took

14 Wow! Steve and Bonnie _____ a white _____, _____ prize!
  A. third   B. won   C. ribbon

15 I'm _____ _____ _____ them!
  A. of   B. proud   C. so

16 Now _____ lunch time, so we're eating _____ _____.
  A. food   B. it's   C. fair

17 Mom and Dad _____ _____ nachos _____ fajitas.
  A. and   B. eating   C. are

---

1 Texas의 주 품평회를 즐겨요!

2 안녕, 나는 Eddie Parker야.

3 나는 Texas주의 Dallas에 살아.

4 지금, 우리 가족과 나는 텍사스 주 품평회에 와 있어.

5 이 품평회는 130년이 넘었고, 미국에서 가장 큰 품평회야.

6 내가 구경시켜 줄게.

7 따라와!

8 여기 염소들을 봐!

9 이건 염소 쇼야.

10 내 남동생 Steve가 이 쇼에 참가했어.

11 이 쇼의 염소들은 클 필요는 없지만 건강해야 해.

12 염소들은 상을 타기 위해서 많은 우유를 생산해야 해.

13 Steve는 자신의 염소인 Bonnie를 잘 돌봤어.

14 와! Steve와 Bonnie는 3등상인 흰색 리본을 탔어.

15 나는 그들이 매우 자랑스러워!

16 지금은 점심시간이어서 우리는 품평회 음식을 먹고 있어.

17 엄마와 아빠는 나초와 파히타를 먹고 있어.

18 They are _____ _____.
    A. food   B. Tex-Max

19 Tex-Mex food is a _____ _____ food _____ Texas and Mexico.
    A. from   B. of   C. combination

20 Dad's face is _____ red _____ his fajita is too _____.
    A. because   B. spicy   C. getting

21 Steve and I _____ _____ _____ dogs.
    A. corn   B. eating   C. are

22 They _____ _____.
    A. great   B. taste

23 Let's _____ _____ to the _____ contest.
    A. quilt   B. on   C. move

24 Quilting _____ a _____ _____.
    A. tradition   B. long   C. has

25 _____ the _____, fabric was _____.
    A. past   B. expensive   C. in

26 To make a blanket, people _____ _____ small pieces of fabric and _____ them together.
    A. sew   B. to   C. had   D. collect

27 Grandma and her friends had a _____ _____ _____ week.
    A. bee   B. quilting   C. every

28 They had to _____ _____ the quilt for the contest _____ _____ six months.
    A. over   B. on   C. for   D. work

29 Look! It's _____ _____ and _____.
    A. unique   B. colorful   C. very

30 The _____ _____ part of the day is _____ the Texas Star.
    A. riding   B. exciting   C. most

31 It's _____ _____ Ferris _____.
    A. wheel   B. a   C. tall

32 Wow! Steve and I _____ now _____ the _____.
    A. top   B. on   C. are

33 I'm _____, but the _____ is _____!
    A. view   B. scared   C. amazing

34 I love _____ _____ Texas and _____ to the fair.
    A. going   B. in   C. living

35 _____ _____ the fair some _____!
    A. day   B. to   C. come

---

18 그것들은 Tex-Mex 음식이야.

19 Tex-Mex 음식은 텍사스 음식과 멕시코 음식이 혼합된 거야.

20 아빠는 파히타가 너무 매워서 얼굴이 빨개지고 있어.

21 Steve와 나는 콘도그를 먹고 있어.

22 맛이 매우 좋아.

23 퀼트 대회로 이동하자.

24 퀼트 만들기는 오랜 전통을 가지고 있어.

25 과거에는 천이 비쌌어.

26 담요를 만들기 위해서 사람들은 작은 천 조각들을 모아서 꿰매 붙여야 했지.

27 할머니와 할머니의 친구들은 매주 퀼트를 만드는 모임을 가지셨어.

28 그분들은 이 대회를 위해서 6개월 이상 퀼트를 만드는 작업을 하셔야 했어.

29 봐! 그 퀼트는 매우 색깔이 화려하고 독특해.

30 오늘의 가장 신나는 부분은 Texas Star를 타는 거야.

31 Texas Star는 높은 회전 관람차야.

32 우와! Steve와 나는 지금 꼭대기에 있어.

33 무섭긴 하지만 전망이 멋져!

34 나는 Texas에 살고 품평회에 가는 것이 매우 좋아.

35 언젠가 품평회에 와라!

※ 다음 우리말과 일치하도록 빈칸에 알맞은 말을 쓰시오.

1   Fun _____ the _____ _____ of Texas!

2   Hi, _____ _____ _____.

3   I _____ _____ Dallas, Texas.

4   Now, _____ family and I _____ _____ the State Fair of Texas.

5   The fair is _____ 130 years _____, and it's _____ _____ _____ in the USA.

6   I'll _____ _____ _____.

7   _____ me!

8   _____ _____ the goats here!

9   This is _____ _____ _____.

10   My _____ brother, Steve, _____ it.

11   The goats in the show _____ _____ _____ be big, but they _____ _____ be healthy.

12   They have _____ produce a _____ of milk _____ _____ a prize.

13   Steve _____ good _____ _____ his goat, Bonnie.

14   Wow! Steve and Bonnie _____ a white _____, _____ prize!

15   I'm _____ _____ _____ them!

16   Now it's lunch time, _____ we're _____ _____ _____.

17   Mom and Dad _____ _____ nachos and fajitas.

1   Texas의 주 품평회를 즐겨요!

2   안녕, 나는 Eddie Parker야.

3   나는 Texas주의 Dallas에 살아.

4   지금, 우리 가족과 나는 텍사스 주 품평회에 와 있어.

5   이 품평회는 130년이 넘었고, 미국에서 가장 큰 품평회야.

6   내가 구경시켜 줄게.

7   따라와!

8   여기 염소들을 봐!

9   이건 염소 쇼야.

10   내 남동생 Steve가 이 쇼에 참가했어.

11   이 쇼의 염소들은 클 필요는 없지만 건강해야 해.

12   염소들은 상을 타기 위해서 많은 우유를 생산해야 해.

13   Steve는 자신의 염소인 Bonnie를 잘 돌봤어.

14   와! Steve와 Bonnie는 3등상인 흰색 리본을 탔어.

15   나는 그들이 매우 자랑스러워!

16   지금은 점심시간이어서 우리는 품평회 음식을 먹고 있어.

17   엄마와 아빠는 나초와 파히타를 먹고 있어.

18 They are _____ _____ .

19 Tex-Mex food is _____ _____ _____ food _____ Texas and Mexico.

20 Dad's face _____ _____ red _____ his fajita is too _____ .

21 Steve and I _____ _____ corn dogs.

22 They _____ _____ .

23 _____ _____ _____ to the quilt contest.

24 Quilting has _____ _____ _____ .

25 _____ _____ _____ , fabric was _____ .

26 _____ _____ a blanket, people _____ _____ _____ small pieces of fabric and _____ them together.

27 Grandma and her friends had _____ _____ _____ every week.

28 They had to _____ _____ the quilt for the contest _____ _____ six months.

29 Look! It's very _____ and _____ .

30 The _____ _____ part of the day _____ _____ the Texas Star.

31 It's a _____ Ferris _____ .

32 Wow! Steve and I _____ now _____ _____ _____ .

33 I'm _____ , but the _____ is amazing!

34 I _____ _____ in Texas and _____ _____ the fair.

35 Come _____ the _____ some day!

18	그것들은 Tex-Mex 음식이야.
19	Tex-Mex 음식은 텍사스 음식과 멕시코 음식이 혼합된 거야.
20	아빠는 파히타가 너무 매워서 얼굴이 빨개지고 있어.
21	Steve와 나는 콘도그를 먹고 있어.
22	맛이 매우 좋아.
23	퀼트 대회로 이동하자.
24	퀼트 만들기는 오랜 전통을 가지고 있어.
25	과거에는 천이 비쌌어.
26	담요를 만들기 위해서 사람들은 작은 천 조각들을 모아서 꿰매 붙여야 했지.
27	할머니와 할머니의 친구들은 매주 퀼트를 만드는 모임을 가지셨어.
28	그분들은 이 대회를 위해서 6개월 이상 퀼트를 만드는 작업을 하셔야 했어.
29	봐! 그 퀼트는 매우 색깔이 화려하고 독특해.
30	오늘의 가장 신나는 부분은 Texas Star를 타는 거야.
31	Texas Star는 높은 회전 관람차야.
32	우와! Steve와 나는 지금 꼭대기에 있어.
33	무섭긴 하지만 전망이 멋져!
34	나는 Texas에 살고 품평회에 가는 것이 매우 좋아.
35	언젠가 품평회에 와라!

※ 다음 문장을 우리말로 쓰시오.

1 ▶ Fun at the State Fair of Texas!

➡ _____

2 ▶ Hi, I'm Eddie Parker.

➡ _____

3 ▶ I live in Dallas, Texas.

➡ _____

4 ▶ Now, my family and I are at the State Fair of Texas.

➡ _____

5 ▶ The fair is over 130 years old, and it's the biggest fair in the USA.

➡ _____

6 ▶ I'll show you around.

➡ _____

7 ▶ Follow me!

➡ _____

8 ▶ Look at the goats here!

➡ _____

9 ▶ This is a goat show.

➡ _____

10 ▶ My younger brother, Steve, entered it.

➡ _____

11 ▶ The goats in the show don't have to be big, but they have to be healthy.

➡ _____

12 ▶ They have to produce a lot of milk to win a prize.

➡ _____

13 ▶ Steve took good care of his goat, Bonnie.

➡ _____

14 ▶ Wow! Steve and Bonnie won a white ribbon, third prize!

➡ _____

15 ▶ I'm so proud of them!

➡ _____

16 ▶ Now it's lunch time, so we're eating fair food.

➡ _____

17 ▶ Mom and Dad are eating nachos and fajitas.

➡ _____

18 They are Tex-Mex food.

➡ _____

19 Tex-Mex food is a combination of food from Texas and Mexico.

➡ _____

20 Dad's face is getting red because his fajita is too spicy.

➡ _____

21 Steve and I are eating corn dogs.

➡ _____

22 They taste great.

➡ _____

23 Let's move on to the quilt contest.

➡ _____

24 Quilting has a long tradition.

➡ _____

25 In the past, fabric was expensive.

➡ _____

26 To make a blanket, people had to collect small pieces of fabric and sew them together.

➡ _____

27 Grandma and her friends had a quilting bee every week.

➡ _____

28 They had to work on the quilt for the contest for over six months.

➡ _____

29 Look! It's very colorful and unique.

➡ _____

30 The most exciting part of the day is riding the Texas Star.

➡ _____

31 It's a tall Ferris wheel.

➡ _____

32 Wow! Steve and I are now on the top.

➡ _____

33 I'm scared, but the view is amazing!

➡ _____

34 I love living in Texas and going to the fair.

➡ _____

35 Come to the fair some day!

➡ _____

※ 다음 괄호 안의 단어들을 우리말에 맞도록 바르게 배열하시오.

1 (of / State / at / Fun / Texas! / the / Fair)
➡ _____

2 (Hi, / Parker. / I'm / Eddie)
➡ _____

3 (live / Texas. / I / Dallas, / in)
➡ _____

4 (family / now, / and / my / I / the / Fair / at / Texas. / of / State / are)
➡ _____

5 (fair / years / the / over / is / old, / 130 / the / and / fair / the / it's / in / USA. / biggest)
➡ _____

6 (you / around. / I'll / show)
➡ _____

7 (me! / follow)
➡ _____

8 (here! / goats / at / look / the)
➡ _____

9 (a / show. / is / this / goat)
➡ _____

10 (brother, / entered / my / it. / younger / Steve,)
➡ _____

11 (in / the / goats / the / show / big, / have / to / don't / be / have / be / they / but / healthy. / to)
➡ _____

12 (have / they / to / lot / produce / a / of / win / prize. / milk / to / a)
➡ _____

13 (good / took / Steve / of / goat, / care / Bonnie. / his)
➡ _____

14 (wow! / won / Bonnie / white / Steve / third / a / ribbon, / and / prize!)
➡ _____

15 (of / I'm / them! / proud / so)
➡ _____

16 (time, / it's / lunch / now / we're / food / eating / so / fair)
➡ _____

17 (are / Dad / and / nachos / eating / Mom / fajitas. / and)
➡ _____

---

1 Texas의 주 품평회를 즐겨요!

2 안녕, 나는 Eddie Parker야.

3 나는 Texas주의 Dallas에 살아.

4 지금, 우리 가족과 나는 텍사스 주 품평회에 와 있어.

5 이 품평회는 130년이 넘었고, 미국에서 가장 큰 품평회야.

6 내가 구경시켜 줄게.

7 따라와!

8 여기 염소들을 봐!

9 이건 염소 쇼야.

10 내 남동생 Steve가 이 쇼에 참가했어.

11 이 쇼의 염소들은 클 필요는 없지만 건강해야 해.

12 염소들은 상을 타기 위해서 많은 우유를 생산해야 해.

13 Steve는 자신의 염소인 Bonnie를 잘 돌봤어.

14 와! Steve와 Bonnie는 3등상인 흰색 리본을 탔어.

15 나는 그들이 매우 자랑스러워!

16 지금은 점심시간이어서 우리는 품평회 음식을 먹고 있어.

17 엄마와 아빠는 나초와 파히타를 먹고 있어.

18 (Tex-Mex / they / food. / are)

➡ _____

19 (Tex-Mex / of / is / food / a / Texas / from / and / Mexico. / food / combination)

➡ _____

20 (red / Dad's / is / because / face / getting / too / fajita / spicy. / is / his)

➡ _____

21 (I / eating / dogs. / Steve / corn / and / are)

➡ _____

22 (great. / taste / they)

➡ _____

23 (the / contest. / move / quilt / to / let's / on)

➡ _____

24 (tradition. / long / has / a / quilting)

➡ _____

25 (was / past, / the / expensive / in / was / fabric)

➡ _____

26 (blanket, / make / a / to / people / small / of / to / pieces / had / and / collect / fabric / together. / them / sew)

➡ _____

27 (her / grandma / had / and / friends / week. / a / every / bee / quilting)

➡ _____

28 (had / work / they / to / the / quilt / for / on / over / months. / contest / the / for / six)

➡ _____

29 (look! / colorful / it's / and / unique. / very)

➡ _____

30 (part / the / day / of / exciting / the / most / Texas / the / Star. / riding / is)

➡ _____

31 (wheel. / a / tall / it's / Ferris)

➡ _____

32 (wow! / are / on / and / top. / Steve / the / I / now)

➡ _____

33 (scared, / I'm / is / the / amazing! / but / view)

➡ _____

34 (Texas / and / I / going / in / love / to / fair. / living / the)

➡ _____

35 (the / day! / come / some / to / fair)

➡ _____

18 그것들은 Tex-Mex 음식이야.

19 Tex-Mex 음식은 텍사스 음식과 멕시코 음식이 혼합된 거야.

20 아빠는 파히타가 너무 매워서 얼굴이 빨개지고 있어.

21 Steve와 나는 콘도그를 먹고 있어.

22 맛이 매우 좋아.

23 퀼트 대회로 이동하자.

24 퀼트 만들기는 오랜 전통을 가지고 있어.

25 과거에는 천이 비쌌어.

26 담요를 만들기 위해서 사람들은 작은 천 조각들을 모아서 꿰매 붙여야 했지.

27 할머니와 할머니의 친구들은 매주 퀼트를 만드는 모임을 가지셨어.

28 그분들은 이 대회를 위해서 6개월 이상 퀼트를 만드는 작업을 하셔야 했어.

29 봐! 그 퀼트는 매우 색깔이 화려하고 독특해.

30 오늘의 가장 신나는 부분은 Texas Star를 타는 거야.

31 Texas Star는 높은 회전 관람차야.

32 우와! Steve와 나는 지금 꼭대기에 있어.

33 무섭긴 하지만 전망이 멋져!

34 나는 Texas에 살고 품평회에 가는 것이 매우 좋아.

35 언젠가 품평회에 와라!

※ 다음 우리말을 영어로 쓰시오.

1 Texas의 주 품평회를 즐겨요!

➡ _____

2 안녕, 나는 Eddie Parker야.

➡ _____

3 나는 Texas주의 Dallas에 살아.

➡ _____

4 지금, 우리 가족과 나는 텍사스 주 품평회에 와 있어.

➡ _____

5 이 품평회는 130년이 넘었고, 미국에서 가장 큰 품평회야.

➡ _____

6 내가 구경시켜 줄게.

➡ _____

7 따라와!

➡ _____

8 여기 염소들을 봐!

➡ _____

9 이건 염소 쇼야.

➡ _____

10 내 남동생 Steve가 이 쇼에 참가했어.

➡ _____

11 이 쇼의 염소들은 클 필요는 없지만 건강해야 해.

➡ _____

12 염소들은 상을 타기 위해서 많은 우유를 생산해야 해.

➡ _____

13 Steve는 자신의 염소인 Bonnie를 잘 돌봤어.

➡ _____

14 와! Steve와 Bonnie는 3등상인 흰색 리본을 탔어.

➡ _____

15 나는 그들이 매우 자랑스러워!

➡ _____

16 지금은 점심시간이어서 우리는 품평회 음식을 먹고 있어.

➡ _____

17 엄마와 아빠는 나초와 파히타를 먹고 있어.

➡ _____

18 그것들은 Tex-Mex 음식이야.

➡ _____

19 Tex-Mex 음식은 텍사스 음식과 멕시코 음식이 혼합된 거야.

➡ _____

20 아빠는 파히타가 너무 매워서 얼굴이 빨개지고 있어.

➡ _____

21 Steve와 나는 콘도그를 먹고 있어.

➡ _____

22 맛이 매우 좋아.

➡ _____

23 퀼트 대회로 이동하자.

➡ _____

24 퀼트 만들기는 오랜 전통을 가지고 있어.

➡ _____

25 과거에는 천이 비쌌어.

➡ _____

26 담요를 만들기 위해서 사람들은 작은 천 조각들을 모아서 꿰매 붙여야 했지.

➡ _____

27 할머니와 할머니의 친구들은 매주 퀼트를 만드는 모임을 가지셨어.

➡ _____

28 그분들은 이 대회를 위해서 6개월 이상 퀼트를 만드는 작업을 하셔야 했어.

➡ _____

29 봐! 그 퀼트는 매우 색깔이 화려하고 독특해.

➡ _____

30 오늘의 가장 신나는 부분은 Texas Star를 타는 거야.

➡ _____

31 Texas Star는 높은 회전 관람차야.

➡ _____

32 우와! Steve와 나는 지금 꼭대기에 있어.

➡ _____

33 무섭긴 하지만 전망이 멋져!

➡ _____

34 나는 Texas에 살고 품평회에 가는 것이 매우 좋아.

➡ _____

35 언젠가 품평회에 와라!

➡ _____

※ 다음 우리말과 일치하도록 빈칸에 알맞은 말을 쓰시오.

After You Read

1. COME _____ THE _____ _____ OF TEXAS!

2. Goat Show: _____ _____ a prize, the goats _____ _____
   _____ healthy and produce a _____ of milk.

3. Fair Food: Enjoy Tex-Mex food, a _____ _____ _____
   from Texas and Mexico.

4. _____ the nachos and fajitas!

5. Quilt Contest: _____ _____ _____ the beautiful quilts!
   Quilting has a _____ _____.

6. Texas Star: The _____ is amazing _____ _____ _____ of
   this Ferris wheel.

Around the World

1. Maryland State Fair: Horse racing is _____ in this state.

2. _____ the fair in this state, people can see horse _____.

3. Iowa State Fair: This state _____ _____ _____ butter.

4. _____ the fair _____ _____ _____, people make a butter
   cow _____ about 272 kg of butter.

5. Wisconsin State Fair: This state produces _____ _____ cheese
   _____ the USA.

6. At the fair in this state people can eat _____ _____ cheese
   _____.

Think and Write

1. Seochon _____ _____ _____ fun things.

2. You _____ _____ _____ Tongin Market.

3. It's _____ _____ oil Tteokbokki, so you _____ _____
   _____ there to try it.

4. _____ _____ also many _____ Korean houses.

5. You can _____ _____ to see them.

6. Come visit _____ _____ Seochon.

7. You'll have so _____ fun!

※ 다음 우리말을 영어로 쓰시오.

After You Read

1. STATE FAIR OF TEXAS로 오세요!
➡ _____

2. 염소 쇼: 상을 받기 위해서, 염소들은 건강하고 많은 우유를 생산해야 합니다.
➡ _____

3. 품평회 음식: Texas와 Mexico에서 온 음식들의 조합인 Tex-Mex 음식을 즐겨요.
➡ _____

4. 나초와 파히타를 먹어 보세요.
➡ _____

5. 퀼트 대회: 오셔서 아름다운 퀼트를 구경하세요. 퀼트를 만드는 것은 오랜 전통을 가지고 있습니다.
➡ _____

6. Texas Star: 이 대회전 관람차의 정상에서 보는 전망은 정말 멋집니다.
➡ _____

Around the World

1. Maryland State Fair: 이 주에서는 경마가 인기가 있다.
➡ _____

2. 이 주의 품평회에서 사람들은 경마를 볼 수 있다.
➡ _____

3. Iowa State Fair: 이 주는 버터로 유명하다.
➡ _____

4. 이 주의 품평회를 위해서 사람들은 272kg의 버터로 소를 만든다.
➡ _____

5. Wisconsin State Fair: 이 주는 미국에서 가장 많은 치즈를 생산한다.
➡ _____

6. 이 주의 품평회에서 사람들은 많은 맛있는 치즈 요리를 먹을 수 있다.
➡ _____

Think and Write

1. 서촌은 재미있는 것들로 가득 차 있어.
➡ _____

2. 너는 통인 시장에 갈 수 있어.
➡ _____

3. 그곳은 기름 떡볶이로 유명해서 너는 거기에 그것을 먹으러 가야 해.
➡ _____

4. 또한 많은 한국의 전통 가옥이 있어.
➡ _____

5. 너는 그것들을 보기 위해 주변을 걸을 수 있어.
➡ _____

6. 서촌에 와서 우리를 방문해.
➡ _____

7. 정말 재미있을 거야!
➡ _____

※ 다음 영어를 우리말로 쓰시오.

01	round		22	anyone	
02	discount		23	explain	
03	afraid		24	combination	
04	purple		25	upgrade	
05	expensive		26	recycling	
06	condition		27	upcycle	
07	used		28	hold	
08	almost		29	trash	
09	large		30	clothes	
10	price		31	through	
11	throw		32	creative	
12	bucket		33	sewing	
13	strap		34	decorate	
14	instrument		35	get a discount	
15	rubber band		36	take ~(돈) off	
16	upcycling		37	throw away	
17	knife		38	let me think	
18	environment		39	be good for	
19	each		40	be about	
20	understand		41	hear from	
21	meaning		42	for example	
			43	cut off	

※ 다음 우리말을 영어로 쓰시오.

01 안경

02 가방

03 흥미로운

04 음악의

05 청바지

06 행사

07 ~처럼, ~와 같이

08 물건

09 양로원

10 (도구장비) 세트

11 바느질하다

12 아래 부분, 바닥

13 어깨

14 마지막으로

15 ~를 통해

16 조합, 결합

17 가죽 끈

18 이해하다

19 양동이

20 쓰레기

21 할인

22 비싼

23 던지다

24 환경

25 장식하다

26 재활용

27 악기

28 의미

29 칼

30 거의

31 중고의

32 가격

33 설명하다

34 개최하다, 열다

35 ~에 의해 만들어지다

36 ~을 찾다

37 ~처럼 들리다

38 ~을 자르다

39 ~에 좋다

40 예를 들어

41 버리다

42 할인을 받다

43 ~에 관해 말하다

※ 다음 영영풀이에 알맞은 단어를 <보기>에서 골라 쓴 후, 우리말 뜻을 쓰시오.

1 _____ : a reduction in the usual price of something: _____

2 _____ : the things that people wear, such as shirts, coats, trousers, and dresses: _____

3 _____ : particular idea that a word, expression, or sign represents: _____

4 _____ : the air, water, and land on Earth, which is affected by man's activities: _____

5 _____ : two or more different things that exist together or put together: _____

6 _____ : giving a lot of attention to something because you want to find out more about it: _____

7 _____ : an object used for producing music: _____

8 _____ : to tell someone about something in a way that is clear or easy to understand: _____

9 _____ : involving the use of imagination to produce new ideas or things: _____

10 _____ : to make something look more attractive by putting something pretty on it: _____

11 _____ : a bag for carrying things that has two shoulder straps and is carried on the back: _____

12 _____ : things that you throw away because you no longer want or need them: _____

13 _____ : shaped like a circle or a ball: _____

14 _____ : an open container with a handle that is used especially to hold and carry water and other liquids: _____

15 _____ : having the color of blue and red mixed together: _____

16 _____ : the process of treating things that have already been used so that they can be used again: _____

보기			
bucket	combination	trash	creative
discount	recycling	environment	meaning
backpack	clothes	round	decorate
explain	instrument	purple	interested

※ 다음 우리말과 일치하도록 빈칸에 알맞은 말을 쓰시오.

Listen and Talk A-1

G: Excuse me. _____ _____ are the _____ _____ ?

M: _____ 18 dollars.

G: Hmm. Can I _____ _____ _____ ?

M: No, I'm _____ _____ . Sorry.

G: That's OK. I'll _____ them.

G: 실례합니다. 저 동그란 안경은 얼만가요?
M: 그것은 18달러예요.
G: 음. 할인을 받을 수 있을까요?
M: 아니요, 안 될 것 같아요. 미안합니다.
G: 괜찮아요. 그것을 살게요.

Listen and Talk A-2

M: Hello. _____ I _____ you?

G: Yes. I'm _____ _____ a backpack _____ school.

M: _____ _____ this red one? It's 12 dollars.

G: _____ _____ _____ a discount?

M: OK. I'll _____ 2 dollars _____ .

G: That _____ good. I'll _____ it.

M: 안녕하세요. 도와드릴까요?
G: 네. 저는 학교 갈 때 쓸 배낭을 찾고 있어요.
M: 이 빨간색은 어때요? 12달러입니다.
G: 할인을 받을 수 있을까요?
M: 네. 2달러 깎아 드릴게요.
G: 좋군요. 그것을 살게요.

Listen and Talk A-3

G: Excuse me. _____ _____ is this _____ T-shirt?

M: _____ 10 _____ .

G: That's _____ . Can I get a _____ ?

M: OK. I'll _____ 1 dollar _____ . That'll _____ 9 dollars.

G: I'll _____ _____ , then. Thank you!

G: 실례합니다. 이 보라색 티셔츠는 얼마인가요?
M: 10달러예요.
G: 비싸군요. 할인을 받을 수 있을까요?
M: 네. 1달러 깎아 드릴게요. 9달러예요.
G: 그럼 그것을 살게요. 감사해요.

Listen and Talk A-4

M: Hello. _____ _____ _____ you?

G: _____ _____ _____ a baseball glove.

M: This _____ is 15 dollars and it's _____ good _____ .

G: Can I _____ _____ _____ ?

M: OK. I'll _____ 2 dollars _____ .

G: Then it's 13 dollars. I'll _____ _____ .

M: 안녕하세요. 도와드릴까요?
G: 저는 야구 글러브를 찾고 있어요.
M: 이건 15달러고, 상태가 좋아요.
G: 할인을 받을 수 있을까요?
M: 네. 2달러 깎아 드릴게요.
G: 그럼 13달러네요. 그것을 살게요.

Listen and Talk B

A: _____ I help you?

B: Yes. _____ _____ is this soccer ball?

A: _____ 6 dollars.

B: _____ _____ _____ _____ a discount?

A: OK. I'll _____ _____ _____ off.

B: Then that'll _____ 5 dollars. _____ _____ _____ .

A: 도와드릴까요?
B: 네. 이 축구공은 얼마인가요?
A: 6달러예요.
B: 할인을 받을 수 있을까요?
A: 네. 1달러 깎아 드릴게요.
B: 그러면 5달러겠네요. 그것을 살게요.

Listen and Talk C

B: Wow! _____ _____ so _____ interesting things here.

W: Everything here _____ old or _____. What are you _____ _____?

B: I'm _____ _____ a clock.

W: _____ _____ this red clock?

B: _____ _____ is it?

W: _____ 15 dollars.

B: That's too _____ _____ me. Can I get a _____?

W: No, I'm _____ not. It's only one _____ old. It's _____ new.

B: Then, _____ _____ is this blue clock _____ the large numbers?

W: It's 10 dollars.

B: Then, I'll _____ the blue _____. Thank you.

Review 1

G: Excuse me. _____ _____ is this yellow backpack?

M: _____ 18 _____.

G: Hmm. That's _____ _____ me. _____ _____ this red one?

M: It's 15 dollars.

G: That's a _____ _____. I'll _____ _____.

Review 2

W: _____ I _____ you?

B: Yes. _____ _____ is this blue T-shirt?

W: It's _____ _____.

B: _____ _____ _____ a discount?

W: OK. I'll _____ _____ _____ _____.

B: That _____ _____. I'll _____ it.

Review 3

M: Hello. _____ I _____ you?

G: _____ _____ _____ a clock.

M: This _____ is 15 dollars and it's _____ _____ _____.

G: Can I _____ _____ _____?

M: OK. I'll _____ 2 dollars _____.

G: Then it's 13 dollars. _____ _____ _____.

B: 와! 여기에는 흥미로운 것들이 많이 있네요.

W: 여기 있는 모든 물건들은 오래되었거나 이미 사용된 물건들입니다. 무엇을 찾고 있나요?

B: 시계를 찾고 있어요.

W: 이 빨간색 시계는 어때요?

B: 얼마예요?

W: 15달러예요.

B: 저에게 너무 비싸군요. 깎아주실 수 있어요?

W: 미안하지만 안 돼요. 그건 일 년밖에 안된 거예요. 거의 새 것입니다.

B: 그럼 숫자가 큰 이 파란 시계는 얼마예요?

W: 10달러예요.

B: 그럼 파란색을 살게요. 감사합니다.

G: 실례합니다. 이 노란색 배낭은 얼마인가요?

M: 18달러예요.

G: 음. 그건 저에게 비싸네요. 이 빨간색은 어떤가요?

M: 그건 15달러예요.

G: 좋은 가격이네요. 그것을 살게요.

W: 도와드릴까요?

B: 네. 이 파란 티셔츠는 얼마인가요?

W: 10달러예요.

B: 할인을 받을 수 있을까요?

W: 네. 2달러 깎아 드릴게요.

B: 좋아요. 그것을 살게요.

M: 안녕하세요. 도와드릴까요?

G: 저는 시계를 찾고 있어요.

M: 이것은 15달러이고 상태가 좋아요.

G: 할인을 받을 수 있을까요?

M: 좋아요. 2달러 깎아 드릴게요.

G: 그럼 13달러군요. 그것을 살게요.

※ 다음 우리말에 맞도록 대화를 영어로 쓰시오.

Listen and Talk A-1

G: _____

M: _____

G: _____

M: _____

G: _____

G: 실례합니다. 저 동그란 안경은 얼마가
요?
M: 그것은 18달러예요.
G: 음. 할인을 받을 수 있을까요?
M: 아니요, 안 될 것 같아요. 미안합니다.
G: 괜찮아요. 그것을 살게요.

Listen and Talk A-2

M: _____

G: _____

M: _____

G: _____

M: _____

G: _____

M: 안녕하세요. 도와드릴까요?
G: 네. 저는 학교 갈 때 쓸 배낭을 찾고
있어요.
M: 이 빨간색은 어때요? 12달러입니다.
G: 할인을 받을 수 있을까요?
M: 네. 2달러 깎아 드릴게요.
G: 좋군요. 그것을 살게요.

Listen and Talk A-3

G: _____

M: _____

G: _____

M: _____

G: _____

G: 실례합니다. 이 보라색 티셔츠는 얼마
인가요?
M: 10달러예요.
G: 비싸군요. 할인을 받을 수 있을까요?
M: 네. 1달러 깎아 드릴게요. 9달러예요.
G: 그럼 그것을 살게요. 감사해요.

Listen and Talk A-4

M: _____

G: _____

M: _____

G: _____

M: _____

G: _____

M: 안녕하세요. 도와드릴까요?
G: 저는 야구 글러브를 찾고 있어요.
M: 이건 15달러고, 상태가 좋아요.
G: 할인을 받을 수 있을까요?
M: 네. 2달러 깎아 드릴게요.
G: 그럼 13달러네요. 그것을 살게요.

Listen and Talk B

A: _____

B: _____

A: _____

B: _____

A: _____

A: 도와드릴까요?
B: 네. 이 축구공은 얼마인가요?
A: 6달러예요.
B: 할인을 받을 수 있을까요?
A: 네. 1달러 깎아 드릴게요.

Listen and Talk C

B: _____
W: _____
B: _____
W: _____
B: _____
W: _____
B: _____
W: _____
B: _____
W: _____
B: _____

B: 와! 여기에는 흥미로운 것들이 많이 있네요.
W: 여기 있는 모든 물건들은 오래되었거나 이미 사용한 물건들입니다. 무엇을 찾고 있나요?
B: 시계를 찾고 있어요.
W: 이 빨간색 시계는 어때요?
B: 얼마예요?
W: 15달러예요.
B: 저에게 너무 비싸군요. 깎아주실 수 있어요?
W: 미안하지만 안 돼요. 그건 일 년밖에 안된 거예요. 거의 새 것입니다.
B: 그럼 숫자가 큰 이 파란 시계는 얼마예요?
W: 10달러예요.
B: 그럼 파란색을 살게요. 감사합니다.

Review 1

G: _____
M: _____
G: _____
M: _____
G: _____

G: 실례합니다. 이 노란색 배낭은 얼마인가요?
M: 18달러예요.
G: 음. 그건 저에게 비싸네요. 이 빨간색은 어떤가요?
M: 그건 15달러예요.
G: 좋은 가격이네요. 그것을 살게요.

Review 2

W: _____
B: _____
W: _____
B: _____
W: _____
B: _____

W: 도와드릴까요?
B: 네. 이 파란 티셔츠는 얼마인가요?
W: 10달러예요.
B: 할인을 받을 수 있을까요?
W: 네. 2달러 깎아 드릴게요.
B: 좋아요. 그것을 살게요.

Review 3

M: _____
G: _____
M: _____
G: _____
M: _____
G: _____

M: 안녕하세요. 도와드릴까요?
G: 저는 시계를 찾고 있어요.
M: 이것은 15달러이고 상태가 좋아요.
G: 할인을 받을 수 있을까요?
M: 좋아요. 2달러 깎아 드릴게요.
G: 그럼 13달러군요. 그것을 살게요.

※ 다음 우리말과 일치하도록 빈칸에 알맞은 것을 골라 쓰시오.

1 _____ Talk _____ Upcycling
A. about   B. let's

2 Hi, _____ _____.
A. members   B. club

3 _____ you know, this _____ Environment Day is _____ upcycling.
A. about   B. year's   C. as

4 Before we talk about _____ group's event idea for that day, I want you _____ _____ the _____ of "upcycling."
A. to   B. meaning   C. each   D. understand

5 _____ anyone _____ upcycling?
A. explain   B. can

6 Yes. The word "_____" is a _____ of "upgrade" and "_____."
A. combination   B. recycling   C. upcycling

7 _____ recycling, upcycling is _____ for the _____.
A. good   B. environment   C. like

8 _____ you upcycle, you make new and _____ things _____ _____ things.
A. old   B. when   C. from   D. better

9 Good. Now, _____ _____ about _____ group's idea for the event.
A. talk   B. each   C. let's

10 _____ start _____ Pei's group.
A. with   B. let's

11 _____ group wants _____ _____ a trashion show.
A. hold   B. to   C. my

12 "Trashion" is a _____ of "_____" and "_____."
A. fashion   B. combination   C. trash

13 We'll use _____ to make _____.
A. clothes   B. trash

14 We want _____ students to become _____ in upcycling _____ the show.
A. interested   B. through   C. other

15 A trashion show _____ _____ fun!
A. like   B. sounds

16 What _____ your _____, Eric?
A. group   B. about

17 My group is _____ to _____ musical _____ from old things.
A. make   B. going   C. instruments

1 업사이클링에 대해 이야기해 봅시다.

2 동아리 회원 여러분, 안녕하세요.

3 여러분도 알다시피 올해의 환경의 날은 업사이클링에 관한 것입니다.

4 각 그룹이 그날에 할 행사 아이디어를 이야기하기 전에 여러분이 '업사이클링'의 의미를 이해하기를 바랍니다.

5 누가 업사이클링의 뜻을 설명해 줄 수 있나요?

6 네. '업사이클링'이란 단어는 "upgrade"와 "recycling"이 결합한 것입니다.

7 재활용과 마찬가지로 업사이클링도 환경에 좋아요.

8 업사이클링을 하면, 여러분은 오래된 것들로 새롭고 더 좋은 것을 만들어요.

9 좋아요. 이제 각 그룹의 행사 아이디어에 대해 이야기해 봅시다.

10 Pei의 그룹부터 시작하죠.

11 저희 그룹은 트래션 쇼를 하고 싶습니다.

12 "트래션(Trashion)"은 "trash"와 "fashion"이 결합한 말입니다.

13 저희는 옷을 만들기 위해 쓰레기를 이용할 것입니다.

14 저희는 이 쇼를 통해서 다른 학생들이 업사이클링에 관심을 갖게 되기를 바랍니다.

15 트래션 쇼라니 멋지겠구나!

16 너희 그룹은 어떠니, Eric?

17 저희 그룹은 낡은 물건으로 악기를 만들려고 합니다.

18 We'll _____ drums _____ old plastic _____ .
A. buckets   B. from   C. make

19 We'll _____ make a guitar _____ old boxes and _____ bands.
A. from   B. also   C. rubber

20 We _____ to play _____ instruments _____ a mini-concert.
A. the   B. plan   C. in

21 Thank you, Eric. Now, _____ _____ _____ Sumi's group.
A. hear   B. let's   C. from

22 My group _____ make bags _____ old _____ .
A. clothes   B. from   C. will

23 _____ _____ , we'll _____ blue jeans.
A. use   B. example   C. for

24 _____ _____ this bag.
A. at   B. look

25 This was _____ _____ Hajun, one _____ our group members.
A. of   B. made   C. by

26 _____ _____ nice?
A. it   B. isn't

27 We'll make _____ bags and _____ them _____ Environment Day.
A. sell   B. on   C. more

28 We're _____ to give all the money _____ a _____ home.
A. nursing   B. going   C. to

29 _____ a _____ idea.
A. great   B. that's

30 _____ ideas are _____ so _____ .
A. creative   B. your   C. all

31 I _____ everyone _____ _____ hard for Environment Day.
A. work   B. to   C. want

32 _____ _____ the legs _____ the blue jeans.
A. of   B. off   C. cut

33 _____ the bottom _____ .
A. together   B. sew

34 _____ shoulder _____ from one _____ the legs.
A. of   B. straps   C. make

35 _____ the _____ to the _____ of the jeans.
A. top   B. sew   C. straps

36 _____ the bag _____ pins _____ buttons.
A. and   B. decorate   C. with

18 낡은 플라스틱 양동이로 드럼을 만들 겁니다.

19 또한 저희는 낡은 상자와 고무 줄로 기타를 만들 겁니다.

20 저희는 소규모 음악회를 열어 그 악기들로 연주할 계획입니다.

21 고맙다, Eric. 그럼 이제 수미의 그룹 의견을 들어 보자.

22 저희 그룹은 낡은 옷으로 가방을 만들 거예요.

23 예를 들어 청바지를 이용할 거예요.

24 이 가방을 보세요.

25 이것은 저희 모둠원 중 한 명인 하준이가 만들었어요.

26 멋지지 않나요?

27 우리는 가방을 더 많이 만들어서 환경의 날에 팔 거예요.

28 번 돈을 모두 양로원에 줄 예정이에요.

29 훌륭한 생각이구나.

30 너희들의 발상은 모두 아주 창의적이구나.

31 너희들 모두 환경의 날을 위해 열심히 노력하길 바란다.

32 청바지의 다리 부분을 잘라낸다.

33 아래쪽을 붙여서 바느질한다.

34 다리 한 짝으로 어깨끈을 만든다.

35 청바지의 윗부분에 어깨끈을 바느질한다.

36 핀이나 단추로 가방을 장식한다.

※ 다음 우리말과 일치하도록 빈칸에 알맞은 말을 쓰시오.

1 _____ Talk _____ Upcycling

2 Hello, _____ _____.

3 _____ _____ _____, this year's Environment Day is _____ _____.

4 _____ we _____ _____ each group's event idea for that day, I want you _____ _____ the meaning of "_____."

5 Can anyone _____ _____?

6 Yes. The word "_____" is a _____ of "upgrade" and "recycling."

7 _____ recycling, upcycling _____ _____ _____ the environment.

8 _____ you _____, you make new and better things _____ _____ _____.

9 Good. Now, _____ _____ _____ each group's idea for the event.

10 _____ _____ _____ with Pei's group.

11 My group wants to _____ _____ trashion _____.

12 "Trashion" is _____ _____ _____ "trash" and "fashion."

13 We'll use trash _____ _____ _____.

14 We want other students to _____ _____ _____ upcycling _____ the show.

15 A trashion show _____ _____ _____!

16 _____ _____ your group, Eric?

17 My group _____ _____ _____ make musical _____ from old things.

1 업사이클링에 대해 이야기해 봅시다

2 동아리 회원 여러분, 안녕하세요.

3 여러분도 알다시피 올해의 환경의 날은 업사이클링에 관한 것입니다.

4 각 그룹이 그날에 할 행사 아이디어를 이야기하기 전에 여러분이 '업사이클링'의 의미를 이해하기를 바랍니다.

5 누가 업사이클링의 뜻을 설명해 줄 수 있나요?

6 네. '업사이클링'이란 단어는 "upgrade"와 "recycling"이 결합한 것입니다.

7 재활용과 마찬가지로 업사이클링도 환경에 좋아요.

8 업사이클링을 하면, 여러분은 오래된 것들로 새롭고 더 좋은 것을 만들어요.

9 좋아요. 이제 각 그룹의 행사 아이디어에 대해 이야기해 봅시다.

10 Pei의 그룹부터 시작하죠.

11 저희 그룹은 트래션 쇼를 하고 싶습니다.

12 "트래션(Trashion)"은 "trash"와 "fashion"이 결합한 말입니다.

13 저희는 옷을 만들기 위해 쓰레기를 이용할 것입니다.

14 저희는 이 쇼를 통해서 다른 학생이 업사이클링에 관심을 갖게 되기를 바랍니다.

15 트래션 쇼라니 멋지겠구나!

16 너희 그룹은 어떠니, Eric?

17 저희 그룹은 낡은 물건으로 악기를 만들려고 합니다.

18 We'll make drums _____ old plastic _____ .

19 We'll _____ make a guitar _____ old boxes and _____

_____ .

20 We _____ _____ _____ the _____ in a mini-concert.

21 Thank you, Eric. Now, _____ _____ _____ Sumi's

group.

22 My group will _____ bags _____ _____ _____ .

23 _____ _____ , we'll use blue _____ .

24 _____ _____ this bag.

25 This _____ _____ _____ Hajun, _____ _____ our

group members.

26 _____ _____ nice?

27 We'll make _____ bags and sell them _____ _____

_____ .

28 We're going to give _____ _____ _____ to a _____

_____ .

29 That's a _____ _____ .

30 _____ ideas are all so _____ .

31 I _____ everyone _____ _____ _____ for Environment

Day.

32 _____ _____ the legs of the _____ _____ .

33 _____ the bottom _____ .

34 Make _____ _____ from _____ of the legs.

35 _____ the straps _____ the top of the jeans.

36 _____ the bag _____ pins and buttons.

18	낡은 플라스틱 양동이로 드럼을 만들 겁니다.
19	또한 저희는 낡은 상자와 고무줄로 기타를 만들 겁니다.
20	저희는 소규모 음악회를 열어 그 악기들로 연주할 계획입니다.
21	고맙다, Eric. 그럼 이제 수미의 그룹 의견을 들어 보자.
22	저희 그룹은 낡은 옷으로 가방을 만들 거예요.
23	예를 들어 청바지를 이용할 거예요.
24	이 가방을 보세요.
25	이것은 저희 모둠원 중 한 명인 하준이가 만들었어요.
26	멋지지 않나요?
27	우리는 가방을 더 많이 만들어서 환경의 날에 팔 거예요.
28	번 돈을 모두 양로원에 줄 예정이에요.
29	훌륭한 생각이구나.
30	너희들의 발상은 모두 아주 창의적이구나.
31	너희들 모두 환경의 날을 위해 열심히 노력하길 바란다.
32	청바지의 다리 부분을 잘라낸다.
33	아래쪽을 붙여서 바느질한다.
34	다리 한 짝으로 어깨끈을 만든다.
35	청바지의 윗부분에 어깨끈을 바느질한다.
36	핀이나 단추로 가방을 장식한다.

※ 다음 문장을 우리말로 쓰시오.

1 ▶ Let's Talk about Upcycling

➡ _____

2 ▶ Hello, club members.

➡ _____

3 ▶ As you know, this year's Environment Day is about upcycling.

➡ _____

4 ▶ Before we talk about each group's event idea for that day, I want you to understand the meaning of "upcycling."

➡ _____

5 ▶ Can anyone explain upcycling?

➡ _____

6 ▶ Yes. The word "upcycling" is a combination of "upgrade" and "recycling."

➡ _____

7 ▶ Like recycling, upcycling is good for the environment.

➡ _____

8 ▶ When you upcycle, you make new and better things from old things.

➡ _____

9 ▶ Good. Now, let's talk about each group's idea for the event.

➡ _____

10 ▶ Let's start with Pei's group.

➡ _____

11 ▶ My group wants to hold a trashion show.

➡ _____

12 ▶ "Trashion" is a combination of "trash" and "fashion."

➡ _____

13 ▶ We'll use trash to make clothes.

➡ _____

14 ▶ We want other students to become interested in upcycling through the show.

➡ _____

15 ▶ A trashion show sounds like fun!

➡ _____

16 ▶ What about your group, Eric?

➡ _____

17 ▶ My group is going to make musical instruments from old things.

➡ _____

18 ▶ We'll make drums from old plastic buckets.

➡ _____

19 ▶ We'll also make a guitar from old boxes and rubber bands.

➡ _____

20 ▶ We plan to play the instruments in a mini-concert.

➡ _____

21 ▶ Thank you, Eric. Now, let's hear from Sumi's group.

➡ _____

22 ▶ My group will make bags from old clothes.

➡ _____

23 ▶ For example, we'll use blue jeans.

➡ _____

24 ▶ Look at this bag.

➡ _____

25 ▶ This was made by Hajun, one of our group members.

➡ _____

26 ▶ Isn't it nice?

➡ _____

27 ▶ We'll make more bags and sell them on Environment Day.

➡ _____

28 ▶ We're going to give all the money to a nursing home.

➡ _____

29 ▶ That's a great idea.

➡ _____

30 ▶ Your ideas are all so creative.

➡ _____

31 ▶ I want everyone to work hard for Environment Day.

➡ _____

32 ▶ Cut off the legs of the blue jeans.

➡ _____

33 ▶ Sew the bottom together.

➡ _____

34 ▶ Make shoulder straps from one of the legs.

➡ _____

35 ▶ Sew the straps to the top of the jeans.

➡ _____

36 ▶ Decorate the bag with pins and buttons.

➡ _____

※ 다음 괄호 안의 단어들을 우리말에 맞도록 바르게 배열하시오.

1 (about / Talk / Upcycling / Let's)
➡ _____

2 (members. / hello, / club)
➡ _____

3 (know, / you / as / Environment / is / this / Day / year's / upcycling. / about)
➡ _____

4 (talk / before / about / we / idea / each / event / group's / day, / that / for / I / to / you / want / "upcycling."/ the / understand / of / meaning)
➡ _____
_____

5 (upcycling? / explain / anyone / can)
➡ _____

6 (yes. / the / "upcycling" / is / word / a / "recycling."/ and / combination / of / and / "upgrade")
➡ _____

7 (recycling, / is / like / upcycling / the / good / environment. / for)
➡ _____

8 (you / upcycle, / when / you / new / make / things / and / old / better / from / things.)
➡ _____

9 (good. / let's / talk / now, / about / each / idea / the / group's / event. / for)
➡ _____

10 (start / group. / let's / Pei's / with)
➡ _____

11 (wants / my / hold / trashion / a / group / show. / to)
➡ _____

12 (is / "trash" / a / "fashion." / combination / and / "trashion" / of)
➡ _____

13 (use / make / we'll / clothes. / to / trash)
➡ _____

14 (other / we / to / want / students / in / become / through / show. / the / interested / upcycling)
➡ _____

15 (show / like / a / trashion / fun! / sounds)
➡ _____

16 (about / Eric? / what / group / your)
➡ _____

17 (group / to / my / is / musical / going / instruments / from / things. / make / old)
➡ _____

1 업사이클링에 대해 이야기해 봅시다

2 동아리 회원 여러분, 안녕하세요.

3 여러분도 알다시피 올해의 환경의 날은 업사이클링에 관한 것입니다.

4 각 그룹이 그날에 할 행사 아이디어를 이야기하기 전에 여러분이 '업사이클링'의 의미를 이해하기를 바랍니다.

5 누가 업사이클링의 뜻을 설명해 줄 수 있나요?

6 네. '업사이클링'이란 단어는 "upgrade"와 "recycling"이 결합한 것입니다.

7 재활용과 마찬가지로 업사이클링도 환경에 좋아요.

8 업사이클링을 하면, 여러분은 오래된 것들로 새롭고 더 좋은 것을 만들어요.

9 좋아요. 이제 각 그룹의 행사 아이디어에 대해 이야기해 봅시다.

10 Pei의 그룹부터 시작하죠.

11 저희 그룹은 트래션 쇼를 하고 싶습니다.

12 "트래션(Trashion)"은 "trash"와 "fashion"이 결합한 말입니다.

13 저희는 옷을 만들기 위해 쓰레기를 이용할 것입니다.

14 저희는 이 쇼를 통해서 다른 학생들이 업사이클링에 관심을 갖게 되기를 바랍니다.

15 트래션 쇼라니 멋지겠구나!

16 너희 그룹은 어떠니, Eric?

17 저희 그룹은 낡은 물건으로 악기를 만들려고 합니다.

18 (drums / we'll / from / plastic / make / buckets. / old)
➡ _____

19 (also / a / we'll / make / boxes / guitar / from / rubber / old / bands. / and)
➡ _____

20 (instruments / plan / the / we / to / play / mini-concert. / in / a)
➡ _____

21 (you, / Eric. / thank // now, / group. / from / let's / hear / Sumi's)
➡ _____

22 (will / my / group / bags / clothes. / make / from / old)
➡ _____

23 (example, / for / use / jeans. / we'll / blue)
➡ _____

24 (this / at / bag. / look)
➡ _____

25 (was / Hajun, / this / made / by / one / our / of / members. / group)
➡ _____

26 (nice? / it / isn't)
➡ _____

27 (we'll / bags / more / make / and / them / Day. / sell / Environment / on)
➡ _____

28 (going / we're / give / to / money / all / to / the / home. / a / nursing)
➡ _____

29 (a / idea. / that's / great)
➡ _____

30 (ideas / all / creative. / so / your / are)
➡ _____

31 (everyone / work / I / to / want / hard / Day. / for / Environment)
➡ _____

32 (the / cut / off / legs / jeans. / the / blue / of)
➡ _____

33 (the / bottom / together. / sew)
➡ _____

34 (shoulder / from / make / straps / the / of / one / legs.)
➡ _____

35 (the / sew / to / straps / the / jeans. / the / top / of)
➡ _____

36 (the / decorate / bag / and / bottons. / pins / with)
➡ _____

18 낡은 플라스틱 양동이로 드럼을 만들 겁니다.

19 또한 저희는 낡은 상자와 고무 줄로 기타를 만들 겁니다.

20 저희는 소규모 음악회를 열어 그 악기들로 연주할 계획입니다.

21 고맙다, Eric. 그럼 이제 수미의 그룹 의견을 들어 보자.

22 저희 그룹은 낡은 옷으로 가방을 만들 거예요.

23 예를 들어 청바지를 이용할 거예요.

24 이 가방을 보세요.

25 이것은 저희 모둠원 중 한 명인 하준이가 만들었어요.

26 멋지지 않나요?

27 우리는 가방을 더 많이 만들어서 환경의 날에 팔 거예요.

28 번 돈을 모두 양로원에 줄 예정이에요.

29 훌륭한 생각이구나.

30 너희들의 발상은 모두 아주 창의적이구나.

31 너희들 모두 환경의 날을 위해 열심히 노력하길 바란다.

32 청바지의 다리 부분을 잘라낸다.

33 아래쪽을 붙여서 바느질한다.

34 다리 한 짝으로 어깨끈을 만든다.

35 청바지의 윗부분에 어깨끈을 바느질한다.

36 핀이나 단추로 가방을 장식한다.

※ 다음 우리말을 영어로 쓰시오.

1 업사이클링에 대해 이야기해 봅시다

➡ _____

2 동아리 회원 여러분, 안녕하세요.

➡ _____

3 여러분도 알다시피 올해의 환경의 날은 업사이클링에 관한 것입니다.

➡ _____

4 각 그룹이 그날에 할 행사 아이디어를 이야기하기 전에 여러분이 '업사이클링'의 의미를 이해하기를 바랍니다.

➡ _____

_____

5 누가 업사이클링의 뜻을 설명해 줄 수 있나요?

➡ _____

6 네. '업사이클링'이란 단어는 "upgrade"와 "recycling"이 결합한 것입니다.

➡ _____

7 재활용과 마찬가지로 업사이클링도 환경에 좋아요.

➡ _____

8 업사이클링을 하면, 여러분은 오래된 것들로 새롭고 더 좋은 것을 만들어요.

➡ _____

9 좋아요. 이제 각 그룹의 행사 아이디어에 대해 이야기해 봅시다.

➡ _____

10 Pei의 그룹부터 시작하죠.

➡ _____

11 저희 그룹은 트래션 쇼를 하고 싶습니다.

➡ _____

12 "트래션(Trashion)"은 "trash"와 "fashion"이 결합한 말입니다.

➡ _____

13 저희는 옷을 만들기 위해 쓰레기를 이용할 것입니다.

➡ _____

14 저희는 이 쇼를 통해서 다른 학생들이 업사이클링에 관심을 갖게 되기를 바랍니다.

➡ _____

15 트래션 쇼라니 멋지겠구나!

➡ _____

16 너희 그룹은 어떠니, Eric?

➡ _____

17 저희 그룹은 낡은 물건으로 악기를 만들려고 합니다.

➡ _____

18 낡은 플라스틱 양동이로 드럼을 만들 겁니다.
➡ _____

19 또한 저희는 낡은 상자와 고무줄로 기타를 만들 겁니다.
➡ _____

20 저희는 소규모 음악회를 열어 그 악기들로 연주할 계획입니다.
➡ _____

21 고맙다, Eric. 그럼 이제 수미의 그룹 의견을 들어 보자.
➡ _____

22 저희 그룹은 낡은 옷으로 가방을 만들 거예요.
➡ _____

23 예를 들어 청바지를 이용할 거예요.
➡ _____

24 이 가방을 보세요.
➡ _____

25 이것은 저희 모둠원 중 한 명인 하준이가 만들었어요.
➡ _____

26 멋지지 않나요?
➡ _____

27 우리는 가방을 더 많이 만들어서 환경의 날에 팔 거예요.
➡ _____

28 번 돈을 모두 양로원에 줄 예정이에요.
➡ _____

29 훌륭한 생각이구나.
➡ _____

30 너희들의 발상은 모두 아주 창의적이구나.
➡ _____

31 너희들 모두 환경의 날을 위해 열심히 노력하길 바란다.
➡ _____

32 청바지의 다리 부분을 잘라낸다.
➡ _____

33 아래쪽을 붙여서 바느질한다.
➡ _____

34 다리 한 짝으로 어깨끈을 만든다.
➡ _____

35 청바지의 윗부분에 어깨끈을 바느질한다.
➡ _____

36 핀이나 단추로 가방을 장식한다.
➡ _____

※ 다음 우리말과 일치하도록 빈칸에 알맞은 말을 쓰시오.

Around the World

1. Kids, I want _____ _____ music _____ _____ you.

2. But we _____ have _____ musical instruments.

3. I _____ _____ you.

4. I _____ a good idea.

5. Oh, _____ you!

6. I _____ _____ musical instruments _____ trash.

7. The world _____ _____ _____.

8. We _____ _____ music.

9. This is the power of _____.

1. 얘들아, 너희에게 음악 수업을 해주고 싶구나.
2. 하지만 우리는 악기가 하나도 없어.
3. 내가 도와줄 수 있어.
4. 나에게 좋은 생각이 있어.
5. 오, 고맙습니다!
6. 나는 쓰레기로 악기를 만들 수 있어.
7. 세상은 우리에게 쓰레기를 보내줬어.
8. 우리는 음악으로 되돌려 준다.
9. 이것이 업사이클링의 힘이란다.

Think and Write

1. _____ _____ Idea: Blue Jeans Basket

2. You _____ : old blue _____, _____ kit, scissors, buttons and pins

3. Step: 1 _____ _____ a leg of the old blue jeans.

4. 2 Cut out a piece _____ make the _____ _____ the basket.

5. 3 _____ the bottom _____ the leg.

6. 4 _____ _____ buttons and pins.

1. 창의적인 업사이클링 아이디어: 청바지 바구니
2. 준비물: 낡은 청바지, 바느질 도구 세트, 가위, 단추와 장식 핀
3. 단계: 1 낡은 청바지의 다리를 자른다.
4. 2 바구니의 바닥을 만들기 위해 한 조각을 자른다.
5. 3 바닥을 다리 부분과 꿰맨다.
6. 4 단추와 핀으로 장식한다.

※ 다음 우리말을 영어로 쓰시오.

Around the World

1. 얘들아, 너희에게 음악 수업을 해주고 싶구나.
   ➡ _____

2. 하지만 우리는 악기가 하나도 없어.
   ➡ _____

3. 내가 도와줄 수 있어.
   ➡ _____

4. 나에게 좋은 생각이 있어.
   ➡ _____

5. 오, 고맙습니다!
   ➡ _____

6. 나는 쓰레기로 악기를 만들 수 있어.
   ➡ _____

7. 세상은 우리에게 쓰레기를 보내줬어.
   ➡ _____

8. 우리는 음악으로 되돌려 준다.
   ➡ _____

9. 이것이 업사이클링의 힘이란다.
   ➡ _____

Think and Write

1. 창의적인 업사이클링 아이디어: 청바지 바구니
   ➡ _____

2. 준비물: 낡은 청바지, 바느질 도구 세트, 가위, 단추와 장식 핀
   ➡ _____

3. 단계: 1. 낡은 청바지의 다리를 자른다.
   ➡ _____

4. 2. 바구니의 바닥을 만들기 위해 한 조각을 자른다.
   ➡ _____

5. 3. 바닥을 다리 부분과 꿰맨다.
   ➡ _____

6. 4. 단추와 핀으로 장식한다.
   ➡ _____

※ 다음 영어를 우리말로 쓰시오.

01	snake	
02	navy	
03	photograph	
04	restroom	
05	gorilla	
06	lucky	
07	succeed	
08	announcement	
09	temple	
10	while	
11	usually	
12	worm	
13	solve	
14	protection	
15	level	
16	parrot	
17	cotton	
18	talent	
19	slowly	
20	record	
21	octopus	

22	shell	
23	male	
24	imagine	
25	crow	
26	pattern	
27	surprise	
28	once	
29	experiment	
30	tail	
31	also	
32	wear	
33	store	
34	not A but B	
35	be good at	
36	pull out	
37	look like	
38	dance to music	
39	watch out for	
40	take a rest	
41	what else	
42	find out	
43	just as	

※ 다음 우리말을 영어로 쓰시오.

01	숨다, 감추다	_____
02	방법, 방식	_____
03	쌓다, 포개다	_____
04	우화, 동화	_____
05	치실질을 하다; 치실	_____
06	~을 두고 가다, 떠나다	_____
07	휴대하다	_____
08	둥근 모양의	_____
09	몸짓, 신호, 표시	_____
10	도구, 수단	_____
11	병, 단지	_____
12	[물체가] (액체 면에) 뜨다	_____
13	줄무늬	_____
14	예, 예제	_____
15	또한	_____
16	코코넛 열매	_____
17	떨어뜨리다	_____
18	독특한	_____
19	실험, 시험	_____
20	보호	_____
21	성공하다	_____

22	무늬, 도안	_____
23	절, 사원	_____
24	천천히	_____
25	사진	_____
26	상상하다	_____
27	면	_____
28	대개, 보통	_____
29	남자의, 수컷의	_____
30	문어	_____
31	앵무새	_____
32	고릴라	_____
33	벌레	_____
34	발표, 소식	_____
35	~ 이상(의)	_____
36	알아내다	_____
37	~의 위에	_____
38	휴식하다	_____
39	A가 아니고 B	_____
40	~을 찾다	_____
41	~을 잘하다	_____
42	~을 뽑다	_____
43	~처럼 보이다, ~와 닮다	_____

※ 다음 영영풀이에 알맞은 단어를 <보기>에서 골라 쓴 후, 우리말 뜻을 쓰시오.

1 _____ : a story that teaches us something: _____

2 _____ : a large brown nut with a hairy shell: _____

3 _____ : to make someone have a feeling of surprise: _____

4 _____ : the hard outside part of a nut or egg: _____

5 _____ : the amount or degree of something: _____

6 _____ : a very dark blue color: _____

7 _____ : an ability to do something well: _____

8 _____ : a picture you take using a camera: _____

9 _____ : a type of cloth made from soft fibres from a particular plant: _____

10 _____ : a scientific test you do to learn about something, or to show if an idea is true: _____

11 _____ : to clean between your teeth with dental floss/special string that you use to clean between your teeth: _____

12 _____ : something important that someone tells people: _____

13 _____ : to put a lot of things on top of each other: _____

14 _____ : to write down information or store it on a computer: _____

15 _____ : a thing that you use for making or doing something: _____

16 _____ : a set of lines, shapes, or colours that are repeated regularly: _____

보기			
pattern	record	cotton	announcement
photograph	navy	surprise	level
tool	experiment	floss	coconut
fable	shell	pile	talent

대화문 Test

※ 다음 우리말과 일치하도록 빈칸에 알맞은 말을 쓰시오.

Listen and Talk A-1

B: Excuse me. I'm _____ _____ my scarf.

W: What does it _____ _____?

B: It's _____ _____ _____ scarf.

W: Can you _____ _____ _____ about it?

B: Well, it's _____.

W: OK. I'll _____ and _____.

B: 실례합니다. 저는 제 스카프를 찾고 있어요.
W: 어떻게 생겼는데요?
B: 그것은 긴 면 스카프에요.
W: 그것에 대해 더 말해 줄래요?
B: 음, 회색이에요.
W: 알겠어요. 가서 확인해 볼게요.

Listen and Talk A-2

W: _____ I _____ you?

B: Yes. I _____ my bag. I _____ I _____ it in the restroom.

W: OK. What _____ it _____ _____?

B: _____ small and _____.

W: _____ _____? _____ me _____ about it.

B: _____ me _____. Oh, it _____ two pockets _____.

W: 도와드릴까요?
B: 네. 저는 제 가방을 잃어버렸어요. 제 생각엔 화장실에 두고 온 것 같아요.
W: 알겠어요. 그것은 어떻게 생겼나요?
B: 작고 노란색이에요.
W: 또 다른 건요? 그것에 대해 더 말해 주세요.
B: 어디 보자. 오, 바깥쪽에 두 개의 주머니가 있어요.

Listen and Talk A-3

W: Do you _____ _____?

B: Yes. I _____ _____ _____.

W: What does it _____ _____?

B: _____ long and _____.

W: Can you _____ _____ _____?

B: Yes. It _____ _____ _____ _____ on it.

W: 도움이 필요하신가요?
B: 네. 저는 제 우산을 잃어버렸어요.
W: 그것은 어떻게 생겼나요?
B: 길고 남색이에요.
W: 더 말해 주시겠어요?
B: 네. 별무늬가 있어요.

Listen and Talk A-4

B: _____ _____ _____ help?

W: Yes. _____ _____ _____ my cat.

B: _____ does it _____ _____?

W: Well, she's not very big and she _____ _____ _____.

B: _____ _____ _____ me more? Is there _____ _____ about her?

W: She has a _____ _____.

B: 도움이 필요하신가요?
W: 네. 저는 고양이를 찾고 있어요.
B: 그것은 어떻게 생겼나요?
W: 음, 그렇게 크지는 않고 털이 검은색이에요.
B: 더 말해 주시겠어요? 특별한 점이 있나요?
W: 그것은 짧은 꼬리를 가지고 있어요.

Listen and Talk B

A: _____ _____ _____ you?

B: Yes. _____ _____ _____ my cat.

A: _____ does it look _____?

B: It's small and it _____ _____ _____.

A: _____ _____ _____ _____ more about it?

B: It has a _____ _____.

Listen and Talk B-2

A: _____ I _____ you?

B: Yes. I'm _____ _____ my _____.

A: _____ does it _____ _____?

B: _____ _____ and red.

A: Can you tell me _____ _____ it?

B: There _____ a card _____ it.

Listen and Talk C

M: May _____ _____ _____?

G: Yes. _____ _____ _____ my dog. _____ name is Prince.

M: _____ does he _____ like?

G: He's very small and has _____ _____ _____.

M: Can you _____ _____ _____?

G: Well, he has a _____ _____ _____.

M: I see. And _____ thing. Where _____ you _____ him?

G: I _____ him _____ the main gate.

M: OK. I'll go and _____ _____ _____. Can you please _____ here?

G: Sure. Thanks _____ _____.

Talk and Play

A: What _____ Amy _____ _____?

B: She's tall and has _____ _____ _____.

A: _____ _____ _____ me more?

B: She's _____ short _____ pants.

A: I _____ her.

Review

G: Hi. I _____ I _____ my umbrella.

M: _____ _____ _____ _____ _____?

G: It's a big _____ umbrella.

M: Can you _____ me _____?

G: It _____ a white flower _____ _____ it.

A: 도와드릴까요?
B: 네. 저는 제 고양이를 찾고 있어요.
A: 그것은 어떻게 생겼나요?
B: 그것은 작고 회색 털을 가지고 있어요.
A: 그것에 대해 더 말해 주실 수 있나요?
B: 그것은 긴 꼬리를 가지고 있어요.

A: 도와드릴까요?
B: 네. 저는 제 지갑을 찾고 있어요.
A: 그것은 어떻게 생겼나요?
B: 그것은 작고 빨간색이에요.
A: 그것에 대해 더 말해 주실 수 있나요?
B: 그것 안에는 카드가 있어요.

M: 도와드릴까요?
G: 네. 제 개를 찾고 있어요. 이름은 Prince 예요.
M: 그가 어떻게 생겼나요?
G: 매우 작고 짧은 흰 털을 가지고 있어요.
M: 더 얘기해 줄 수 있나요?
G: 음, 그는 무척 긴 꼬리를 가지고 있어요.
M: 알겠습니다. 그리고 한 가지 더요. 어디서 잃어버렸나요?
G: 정문 근처에서 잃어버렸어요.
M: 좋아요. 가서 안내 방송을 하겠습니다. 잠시 여기에서 기다려 주시겠어요?
G: 네. 정말 감사합니다.

A: Amy는 어떻게 생겼니?
B: 그녀는 키가 크고 긴 갈색 머리야.
A: 더 말해 주겠니?
B: 그녀는 짧은 남색 바지를 입고 있어.
A: 그녀를 찾았어.

G: 안녕하세요. 제 우산을 잃어버린 것 같아요.
M: 그것은 어떻게 생겼나요?
G: 그것은 큰 남색 우산이에요.
M: 더 말해 주시겠어요?
G: 흰색 꽃무늬가 있어요.

※ 다음 우리말에 맞도록 대화를 영어로 쓰시오.

Listen and Talk A-1

B: _____

W: _____

B: _____

W: _____

B: _____

W: _____

B: 실례합니다. 저는 제 스카프를 찾고
　　있어요.
W: 어떻게 생겼는데요?
B: 그것은 긴 면 스카프에요.
W: 그것에 대해 더 말해 줄래요?
B: 음, 회색이에요.
W: 알겠어요. 가서 확인해 볼게요.

Listen and Talk A-2

W: _____

B: _____

W: _____

B: _____

W: _____

B: _____

W: 도와드릴까요?
B: 네. 저는 제 가방을 잃어버렸어요. 제
　　생각엔 화장실에 두고 온 것 같아요.
W: 알겠어요. 그것은 어떻게 생겼나요?
B: 작고 노란색이에요.
W: 또 다른 건요? 그것에 대해 더 말해
　　주세요.
B: 어디 보자. 오, 바깥쪽에 두 개의 주머
　　니가 있어요.

Listen and Talk A-3

W: _____

B: _____

W: _____

B: _____

W: _____

B: _____

W: 도움이 필요하신가요?
B: 네. 저는 제 우산을 잃어버렸어요.
W: 그것은 어떻게 생겼나요?
B: 길고 남색이에요.
W: 더 말해 주시겠어유?
B: 네. 별무늬가 있어요.

Listen and Talk A-4

B: _____

W: _____

B: _____

W: _____

B: _____

W: _____

B: 도움이 필요하신가요?
W: 네. 저는 고양이를 찾고 있어요.
B: 그것은 어떻게 생겼나요?
W: 음, 그렇게 크지는 않고 털이 검은색
　　이에요.
B: 더 말해 주시겠어요? 특별한 점이 있
　　나요?
W: 그것은 짧은 꼬리를 가지고 있어요.

Listen and Talk B

A: _____
B: _____
A: _____
B: _____
A: _____
B: _____

A: 도와드릴까요?
B: 네. 저는 제 고양이를 찾고 있어요.
A: 그것은 어떻게 생겼나요?
B: 그것은 작고 회색 털을 가지고 있어요.
A: 그것에 대해 더 말해 주실 수 있나요?
B: 그것은 긴 꼬리를 가지고 있어요.

Listen and Talk B-2

A: _____
B: _____
A: _____
B: _____
A: _____
B: _____

A: 도와드릴까요?
B: 네. 저는 제 지갑을 찾고 있어요.
A: 그것은 어떻게 생겼나요?
B: 그것은 작고 빨간색이에요.
A: 그것에 대해 더 말해 주실 수 있나요?
B: 그것 안에는 카드가 있어요.

Listen and Talk C

M: _____
G: _____
M: _____
G: _____
M: _____
G: _____
M: _____
G: _____
M: _____
G: _____

M: 도와드릴까요?
G: 네. 제 개를 찾고 있어요. 이름은 Prince 예요.
M: 그가 어떻게 생겼나요?
G: 매우 작고 짧은 흰 털을 가지고 있어요.
M: 더 얘기해 줄 수 있나요?
G: 음, 그는 무척 긴 꼬리를 가지고 있어요.
M: 알겠습니다. 그리고 한 가지 더. 어디서 잃어버렸나요?
G: 정문 근처에서 잃어버렸어요.
M: 좋아요. 가서 안내 방송을 하겠습니다. 잠시 여기에서 기다려 주시겠어요?
G: 네. 정말 감사합니다.

Talk and Play

A: _____
B: _____
A: _____
B: _____
A: _____

A: Amy는 어떻게 생겼니?
B: 그녀는 키가 크고 긴 갈색 머리야.
A: 더 말해 주겠니?
B: 그녀는 짧은 남색 바지를 입고 있어.
A: 그녀를 찾았어.

Review

G: _____
M: _____
G: _____
M: _____
G: _____

G: 안녕하세요. 제 우산을 잃어버린 것 같아요.
M: 그것은 어떻게 생겼나요?
G: 그것은 큰 남색 우산이에요.
M: 더 말해 주시겠어요?
G: 흰색 꽃무늬가 있어요.

※ 다음 우리말과 일치하도록 빈칸에 알맞은 것을 골라 쓰시오.

1 Animals _____ Use _____

    A. Tools   B. That

2 People _____ _____ that _____ humans can use tools.

    A. thought   B. only   C. once

3 Now, scientists are _____ _____ that many animals can _____ use tools.

    A. out   B. also   C. finding

4 If you go to a Buddhist temple _____ Lop Buri, Thailand, _____ _____ _____ the Macaque monkeys.

    A. out   B. in   C. for   D. watch

5 They _____ come to you and _____ _____ your hair.

    A. out   B. may   C. pull

6 They use human hair _____ _____ their _____.

    A. teeth   B. floss   C. to

7 If you are lucky, you may see _____ monkeys _____ _____ teaching _____ to their babies.

    A. flossing   B. are   C. female   D. that

8 _____ the babies are _____, the female monkeys _____ their _____ very slowly.

    A. floss   B. teeth   C. watching   D. while

9 This _____, the baby monkeys learn _____ _____.

    A. floss   B. way   C. to

10 People _____ _____ _____ that octopuses are smart.

    A. think   B. don't   C. usually

11 _____, octopuses are very smart, and they _____ also _____ tools.

    A. use   B. however   C. can

12 They _____ coconut _____ for _____.

    A. protection   B. shells   C. use

---

1 도구를 사용하는 동물들

2 사람들은 한때 인간만이 도구를 사용할 수 있다고 생각했다.

3 이제 과학자들은 많은 동물들 역시 도구를 사용할 수 있다는 것을 밝혀내고 있다.

4 당신이 태국의 롭부리에 있는 절에 간다면, 마카크 원숭이들을 조심해야 한다.

5 그들이 당신에게 다가와 당신의 머리카락을 뽑을 수도 있다.

6 그들은 이빨을 치실질하기 위해서 사람의 머리카락을 사용한다.

7 만약 당신이 운이 좋으면, 당신은 새끼들에게 치실질하는 것을 가르치고 있는 암컷 원숭이들을 볼 수 있을 것이다.

8 새끼들이 지켜보고 있는 동안, 암컷 원숭이들은 아주 천천히 그들의 이빨을 치실질한다.

9 이런 방식으로, 새끼 원숭이들은 치실질을 배운다.

10 사람들은 대개 문어가 영리하다고 생각하지 않는다.

11 하지만, 문어는 매우 영리하고 또한 도구를 사용할 수 있다.

12 그들은 자신을 보호하기 위해 코코넛 껍데기를 사용한다.

13 When they _____ _____ a good _____ place, they _____ under coconut shells.

A. hide   B. find   C. hiding   D. can't

14 Some octopuses even _____ coconut shells _____ later _____.

A. use   B. store   C. for

15 They _____ the coconut shells and _____ them to use _____.

A. later   B. carry   C. pile

16 _____ _____!

A. smart   B. how

17 In Aesop's fable *The Thirsty Crow*, a crow _____ stones _____ a jar _____ _____ the level of water.

A. to   B. drops   C. into   D. raise

18 You _____ _____ this is _____ a story, but it is not.

A. just   B. think   C. may

19 Scientists who _____ _____ crows did an _____.

A. experiment   B. studying   C. were

20 They _____ a jar _____ water in _____ of a crow.

A. front   B. with   C. put

21 A _____ was _____ on _____ of the water.

A. top   B. floating   C. worm

22 However, the _____ _____ was _____, so the crow _____ not eat the worm.

A. low   B. level   C. could   D. water

23 The crow _____ the problem _____ _____ in the fable.

A. as   B. solved   C. just

24 It _____ stones _____ the jar.

A. into   B. dropped

25 If you think this bird is _____, you are _____.

A. wrong   B. special

26 Scientists did the same _____ _____ other crows, and they all _____ the _____, too.

A. same   B. with   C. experiment   D. did

13 그들이 숨을 만한 좋은 장소를 찾지 못했을 때, 그들은 코코넛 껍데기 아래로 숨는다.

14 어떤 문어들은 심지어 코코넛 껍데기를 나중에 쓰기 위해 모은다.

15 그들은 코코넛 껍데기를 쌓아두고 나중에 쓰기 위해서 가지고 다닌다.

16 얼마나 똑똑한가!

17 이솝 우화 '목마른 까마귀'에서 까마귀는 물 높이를 높이기 위해 항아리 안으로 돌을 떨어뜨린다.

18 당신은 이것이 그저 이야기라고 생각할 수 있지만, 그렇지 않다.

19 까마귀를 연구하던 과학자들이 실험을 했다.

20 그들은 까마귀 앞에 물이 든 항아리를 놓았다.

21 물 위에 벌레가 떠다니고 있었다.

22 하지만, 물 높이가 낮아서, 까마귀는 그 벌레를 먹을 수 없었다.

23 그 까마귀는 우화에서처럼 문제를 해결했다.

24 까마귀는 돌을 항아리 안으로 떨어뜨렸다.

25 만약 당신이 이 새가 특별하다고 생각한다면, 당신이 틀렸다.

26 과학자들은 다른 까마귀들에게도 똑같은 실험을 했고, 그들 모두가 똑같이 그렇게 했다.

※ 다음 우리말을 참고하여 빈칸에 알맞은 것을 고르시오.

1 Animals _____ Use _____

2 People _____ _____ that only humans _____ _____ tools.

3 Now, scientists are _____ _____ that many animals _____ _____ use tools.

4 If you _____ _____ a Buddhist _____ in Lop Buri, Thailand, _____ _____ _____ the Macaque monkeys.

5 They _____ _____ to you and _____ _____ your hair.

6 They use human hair _____ _____ _____ _____ _____ .

7 If you are lucky, you may see _____ monkeys that _____ _____ _____ to their babies.

8 _____ the babies _____ _____ , the female monkeys _____ _____ _____ very slowly.

9 _____ _____ , the baby monkeys _____ _____ _____ .

10 People don't _____ _____ that _____ are smart.

11 _____ , octopuses are very smart, and they _____ _____ _____ tools.

12 They use coconut _____ _____ _____ .

1 도구를 사용하는 동물들

2 사람들은 한때 인간만이 도구를 사용할 수 있다고 생각했다.

3 이제 과학자들은 많은 동물들 역시 도구를 사용할 수 있다는 것을 밝혀내고 있다.

4 당신이 태국의 롭부리에 있는 절에 간다면, 마카크 원숭이들을 조심해야 한다.

5 그들이 당신에게 다가와 당신의 머리카락을 뽑을 수도 있다.

6 그들은 이빨을 치실질하기 위해서 사람의 머리카락을 사용한다.

7 만약 당신이 운이 좋으면, 당신은 새끼들에게 치실질하는 것을 가르치고 있는 암컷 원숭이들을 볼 수 있을 것이다.

8 새끼들이 지켜보고 있는 동안, 암컷 원숭이들은 아주 천천히 그들의 이빨을 치실질한다.

9 이런 방식으로, 새끼 원숭이들은 치실질을 배운다.

10 사람들은 대개 문어가 영리하다고 생각하지 않는다.

11 하지만, 문어는 매우 영리하고 또한 도구를 사용할 수 있다.

12 그들은 자신을 보호하기 위해 코코넛 껍데기를 사용한다.

13 When they _____ find a good _____ _____, they _____ _____ coconut shells.

14 Some octopuses _____ _____ coconut shells _____ _____ _____.

15 They _____ the coconut shells and _____ them _____ _____.

16 _____ smart!

17 In Aesop's _____ *The Thirsty Crow*, a crow _____ stones into a _____ _____ _____ the level of water.

18 You _____ _____ this is _____ a story, _____ it is not.

19 Scientists _____ _____ _____ crows did an _____.

20 They _____ a jar with water _____ _____ _____ a crow.

21 A _____ was floating _____ _____ _____ the water.

22 _____, the water _____ was _____, so the crow _____ _____ eat the worm.

23 The crow _____ the problem _____ _____ in the fable.

24 It _____ stones _____ the jar.

25 _____ you think this bird is _____, you are _____.

26 Scientists did the _____ _____ with _____ crows, and they all did the same, _____.

13 그들이 숨을 만한 좋은 장소를 찾지 못했을 때, 그들은 코코넛 껍데기 아래로 숨는다.

14 어떤 문어들은 심지어 코코넛 껍데기를 나중에 쓰기 위해 모은다.

15 그들은 코코넛 껍데기를 쌓아두고 나중에 쓰기 위해서 가지고 다닌다.

16 얼마나 똑똑한가!

17 이솝 우화 '목마른 까마귀'에서 까마귀는 물 높이를 높이기 위해 항아리 안으로 돌을 떨어뜨린다.

18 당신은 이것이 그저 이야기라고 생각할 수 있지만, 그렇지 않다.

19 까마귀를 연구하던 과학자들이 실험을 했다.

20 그들은 까마귀 앞에 물이 든 항아리를 놓았다.

21 물 위에 벌레가 떠다니고 있었다.

22 하지만, 물 높이가 낮아서, 까마귀는 그 벌레를 먹을 수 없었다.

23 그 까마귀는 우화에서처럼 문제를 해결했다.

24 까마귀는 돌을 항아리 안으로 떨어뜨렸다.

25 만약 당신이 이 새가 특별하다고 생각한다면, 당신이 틀렸다.

26 과학자들은 다른 까마귀들에게도 똑같은 실험을 했고, 그들 모두가 똑같이 그렇게 했다.

※ 다음 문장을 우리말로 쓰시오.

1 ▶ Animals That Use Tools

➡ _____

2 ▶ People once thought that only humans can use tools.

➡ _____

3 ▶ Now, scientists are finding out that many animals can also use tools.

➡ _____

4 ▶ If you go to a Buddhist temple in Lop Buri, Thailand, watch out for the Macaque monkeys.

➡ _____

5 ▶ They may come to you and pull out your hair.

➡ _____

6 ▶ They use human hair to floss their teeth.

➡ _____

7 ▶ If you are lucky, you may see female monkeys that are teaching flossing to their babies.

➡ _____

8 ▶ While the babies are watching, the female monkeys floss their teeth very slowly.

➡ _____

9 ▶ This way, the baby monkeys learn to floss.

➡ _____

10 ▶ People don't usually think that octopuses are smart.

➡ _____

11 ▶ However, octopuses are very smart, and they can also use tools.

➡ _____

12 ▶ They use coconut shells for protection.

➡ _____

13 When they can't find a good hiding place, they hide under coconut shells.

➡ _____

14 Some octopuses even store coconut shells for later use.

➡ _____

15 They pile the coconut shells and carry them to use later.

➡ _____

16 How smart!

➡ _____

17 In Aesop's fable *The Thirsty Crow*, a crow drops stones into a jar to raise the level of water.

➡ _____

18 You may think this is just a story, but it is not.

➡ _____

19 Scientists who were studying crows did an experiment.

➡ _____

20 They put a jar with water in front of a crow.

➡ _____

21 A worm was floating on top of the water.

➡ _____

22 However, the water level was low, so the crow could not eat the worm.

➡ _____

23 The crow solved the problem just as in the fable.

➡ _____

24 It dropped stones into the jar.

➡ _____

25 If you think this bird is special, you are wrong.

➡ _____

26 Scientists did the same experiment with other crows, and they all did the same, too.

➡ _____

※ 다음 괄호 안의 단어들을 우리말에 맞도록 바르게 배열하시오.

1 (Tools / That / Use / Animals)

➡ _____

2 (that / people / thought / once / can / tools. / humans / only / use)

➡ _____

3 (are / now, / out / scientists / finding / animals / also / that / many / tools. / use / can)

➡ _____

4 (Buddhist / you / Lop / go / if / Buri, / in / a / temple / to / Thailand, / for / Macaque / the / watch / monkeys. / out)

➡ _____
_____

5 (come / they / to / you / may / and / your / pull / hair. / out)

➡ _____

6 (use / human / to / they / floss / teeth. / hair / their)

➡ _____

7 (are / you / lucky, / if / may / female / you / monkeys / see / flossing / that / teaching / are / babies. / their / to)

➡ _____
_____

8 (the / babies / watching, / while / are / monkeys / the / floss / female / teeth / slowly. / their / very)

➡ _____
_____

9 (the / way, / monkeys / this / floss. / learn / baby / to)

➡ _____

10 (think / people / usually / that / don't / smart. / are / octopuses)

➡ _____

11 (octopuses / smart, / however, / are / very / they / also / tools. / and / use / can)

➡ _____

12 (for / shells / they / protection. / use / coconut)

➡ _____

1 도구를 사용하는 동물들

2 사람들은 한때 인간만이 도구를 사용할 수 있다고 생각했다.

3 이제 과학자들은 많은 동물들 역시 도구를 사용할 수 있다는 것을 밝혀내고 있다.

4 당신이 태국의 롭부리에 있는 절에 간다면, 마카크 원숭이들을 조심해야 한다.

5 그들이 당신에게 다가와 당신의 머리카락을 뽑을 수도 있다.

6 그들은 이빨을 치실질하기 위해서 사람의 머리카락을 사용한다.

7 만약 당신이 운이 좋으면, 당신은 새끼들에게 치실질하는 것을 가르치고 있는 암컷 원숭이들을 볼 수 있을 것이다.

8 새끼들이 지켜보고 있는 동안, 암컷 원숭이들은 아주 천천히 그들의 이빨을 치실질한다.

9 이런 방식으로, 새끼 원숭이들은 치실질을 배운다.

10 사람들은 대개 문어가 영리하다고 생각하지 않는다.

11 하지만, 문어는 매우 영리하고 또한 도구를 사용할 수 있다.

12 그들은 자신을 보호하기 위해 코코넛 껍데기를 사용한다.

13 > (they / find / when / hiding / can't / place, / good / a / they / shells. / hide / under / coconut)

➡ _____

14 > (even / some / store / octopuses / for / use. / coconut / later / shells)

➡ _____

15 > (the / shells / they / coconut / pile / them / and / later. / to / carry / use)

➡ _____

16 > (smart! / how)

➡ _____

17 > (The / fable / Crow, / Aesop's / Thirsty / in / stones / a / drops / crow / to / jar / into / raise / a / water. / the / of / level)

➡ _____

_____

18 > (think / you / just / may / a / this / story, / is / not. / is / but / it)

➡ _____

19 > (were / crows / did / experiment. / who / scientists / an / studying)

➡ _____

20 > (put / water / they / with / jar / a / front / a / in / crow. / of)

➡ _____

21 > (top / was / worm / water. / a / floating / the / of / on)

➡ _____

22 > (the / level / low, / however, / water / was / crow / so / eat / the / not / worm. / could / the)

➡ _____

23 > (solved / crow / the / problem / as / the / just / in / fable. / the)

➡ _____

24 > (stones / the / dropped / it / jar. / into)

➡ _____

25 > (this / you / if / special, / think / bird / is / wrong. / are / you)

➡ _____

26 > (did / same / scientists / the / experiment / crows, / with / other / and / did / same, / too. / all / they / the)

➡ _____

_____

13 그들이 숨을 만한 좋은 장소를 찾지 못했을 때, 그들은 코코넛 껍데기 아래로 숨는다.

14 어떤 문어들은 심지어 코코넛 껍데기를 나중에 쓰기 위해 모은다.

15 그들은 코코넛 껍데기를 쌓아두고 나중에 쓰기 위해서 가지고 다닌다.

16 얼마나 똑똑한가!

17 이솝 우화 '목마른 까마귀'에서 까마귀는 물 높이를 높이기 위해 항아리 안으로 돌을 떨어뜨린다.

18 당신은 이것이 그저 이야기라고 생각할 수 있지만, 그렇지 않다.

19 까마귀를 연구하던 과학자들이 실험을 했다.

20 그들은 까마귀 앞에 물이 든 항아리를 놓았다.

21 물 위에 벌레가 떠다니고 있었다.

22 하지만, 물 높이가 낮아서, 까마귀는 그 벌레를 먹을 수 없었다.

23 그 까마귀는 우화에서처럼 문제를 해결했다.

24 까마귀는 돌을 항아리 안으로 떨어뜨렸다.

25 만약 당신이 이 새가 특별하다고 생각한다면, 당신이 틀렸다.

26 과학자들은 다른 까마귀들에게도 똑같은 실험을 했고, 그들 모두가 똑같이 그렇게 했다.

※ **다음 우리말을 영어로 쓰시오.**

1 도구를 사용하는 동물들

➡ _____

2 사람들은 한때 인간만이 도구를 사용할 수 있다고 생각했다.

➡ _____

3 이제 과학자들은 많은 동물들 역시 도구를 사용할 수 있다는 것을 밝혀내고 있다.

➡ _____

4 당신이 태국의 롭부리에 있는 절에 간다면, 마카크 원숭이들을 조심해야 한다.

➡ _____

5 그들이 당신에게 다가와 당신의 머리카락을 뽑을 수도 있다.

➡ _____

6 그들은 이빨을 치실질하기 위해서 사람의 머리카락을 사용한다.

➡ _____

7 만약 당신이 운이 좋으면, 당신은 새끼들에게 치실질하는 것을 가르치고 있는 암컷 원숭이들을 볼 수 있을 것이다.

➡ _____

8 새끼들이 지켜보고 있는 동안, 암컷 원숭이들은 아주 천천히 그들의 이빨을 치실질한다.

➡ _____

9 이런 방식으로, 새끼 원숭이들은 치실질을 배운다.

➡ _____

10 사람들은 대개 문어가 영리하다고 생각하지 않는다.

➡ _____

11 하지만, 문어는 매우 영리하고 또한 도구를 사용할 수 있다.

➡ _____

12 그들은 자신을 보호하기 위해 코코넛 껍데기를 사용한다.

본문 ➡ _____

13 그들이 숨을 만한 좋은 장소를 찾지 못했을 때, 그들은 코코넛 껍데기 아래로 숨는다.

➡ _____

14 어떤 문어들은 심지어 코코넛 껍데기를 나중에 쓰기 위해 모은다.

➡ _____

15 그들은 코코넛 껍데기를 쌓아두고 나중에 쓰기 위해서 가지고 다닌다.

➡ _____

16 얼마나 똑똑한가!

➡ _____

17 이솝 우화 '목마른 까마귀'에서 까마귀는 물 높이를 높이기 위해 항아리 안으로 돌을 떨어뜨린다.

➡ _____

18 당신은 이것이 그저 이야기라고 생각할 수 있지만, 그렇지 않다.

➡ _____

19 까마귀를 연구하던 과학자들이 실험을 했다.

➡ _____

20 그들은 까마귀 앞에 물이 든 항아리를 놓았다.

➡ _____

21 물 위에 벌레가 떠다니고 있었다.

➡ _____

22 하지만, 물 높이가 낮아서, 까마귀는 그 벌레를 먹을 수 없었다.

➡ _____

23 그 까마귀는 우화에서처럼 문제를 해결했다.

➡ _____

24 까마귀는 돌을 항아리 안으로 떨어뜨렸다.

➡ _____

25 만약 당신이 이 새가 특별하다고 생각한다면, 당신이 틀렸다.

➡ _____

26 과학자들은 다른 까마귀들에게도 똑같은 실험을 했고, 그들 모두가 똑같이 그렇게 했다.

➡ _____

※ 다음 우리말과 일치하도록 빈칸에 알맞은 말을 쓰시오.

Around the World

1. The _____ snake _____ is Medusa.

2. She is 7.67 meters _____ .

3. Alley _____ the longest jump by a cat.

4. Her _____ was 1.83 meters.

5. _____ _____ pig ever is Ernestine.

6. He _____ _____ 22 years and 359 days.

1. 지금까지 가장 긴 뱀은 Medusa이다.
2. 그것은 길이가 7.67미터이다.
3. Alley는 가장 멀리 뛰는 고양이로 기록되었다.
4. 그녀의 기록은 1.83 미터였다.
3. 지금까지 가장 오래 산 돼지는 Ernestine이다.
5. 그는 22년 359일을 살았다.

Think and Write

1. Animals _____ Special Talents

2. _____ _____ many animals that _____ special talents.

3. An _____ is Einstein.

4. He is an African Grey Parrot _____ can use 200 English words _____ _____ with people.

5. He _____ _____ the "Happy Birthday" song.

6. There _____ many animals _____ have special _____ .

7. _____ _____ is Koko.

8. She is a _____ gorilla which _____ in America.

9. She can _____ _____ people _____ American Sign Language.

10. She knows _____ _____ 1,000 signs.

1. 특별한 재능을 가진 동물들
2. 특별한 재능을 가진 많은 동물들이 있다.
3. 한 예는 Einstein이다.
4. 그는 사람들과 대화를 하기 위해 200개의 영어 단어를 사용할 수 있는 아프리카 회색앵무새이다.
5. 그는 '생일 축하합니다' 노래를 부를 수 있다.
6. 특별한 재능을 가진 많은 동물들이 있다.
7. 한 예는 Koko이다.
8. 그녀는 미국에 살고 있는 암컷 고릴라이다.
9. 그녀는 수화로 사람들과 이야기할 수 있다.
10. 그녀는 1,000개가 넘는 신호를 알고 있다.

※ 다음 우리말을 영어로 쓰시오.

Around the World

1. 지금까지 가장 긴 뱀은 Medusa이다.
   ➡ _____

2. 그것은 길이가 7.67미터이다.
   ➡ _____

3. Alley는 가장 멀리 뛰는 고양이로 기록되었다.
   ➡ _____

4. 그녀의 기록은 1.83 미터였다.
   ➡ _____

5. 지금까지 가장 오래 산 돼지는 Ernestine이다.
   ➡ _____

6. 그는 22년 359일을 살았다.
   ➡ _____

Think and Write

1. 특별한 재능을 가진 동물들
   ➡ _____

2. 특별한 재능을 가진 많은 동물들이 있다.
   ➡ _____

3. 한 예는 Einstein이다.
   ➡ _____

4. 그는 사람들과 대화를 하기 위해 200개의 영어 단어를 사용할 수 있는 아프리카 회색앵무새이다.
   ➡ _____

5. 그는 '생일 축하합니다' 노래를 부를 수 있다.
   ➡ _____

6. 특별한 재능을 가진 많은 동물들이 있다.
   ➡ _____

7. 한 예는 Koko이다.
   ➡ _____

8. 그녀는 미국에 살고 있는 암컷 고릴라이다.
   ➡ _____

9. 그녀는 수화로 사람들과 이야기할 수 있다.
   ➡ _____

10. 그녀는 1,000개가 넘는 신호를 알고 있다.
    ➡ _____

MEMO

MEMO

MEMO

영어 기출 문제집

적중100 plus
1학기 전과정

1학기

정답 및 해설

동아 | 윤정미

중 2

적중100

영어 기출 문제집

적중100

1학기

정답 및 해설

동아 | 윤정미

중 2

My Happy Everyday Life

시험대비 실력평가
p.08

01 boring / uninteresting   02 ②   03 ④
04 ①   05 ②   06 ⑤   07 ④
08 Both, and, be like

01 반의어 관계이다. 일몰 : 일출 = 흥미로운 : 지루한
02 of the day: 하루 중 take good care of ~: ~을 잘 돌보다
03   be proud of ~: ~을 자랑스러워하다 / in your free time: 여가 시간에
04 get together: 모이다 / be on: ~의 일원[소속]이다
05 특히 낮 동안의 짧은 수면
06 사람이나 동물이 가장 빨리 달려서 먼저 끝을 내기 위해 겨루는 경쟁
07 ④의 brush는 동사로 '솔질을 하다'는 뜻이다.
08 both A and B: A와 B 둘 다 / be like: ~처럼 되다. ~와 같다

서술형 시험대비
p.09

01 (1) take   (2) won   (3) care   (4) boring
02 (1) w(W)hen   (2) like   (3) b(B)oth
03 (1) peaceful   (2) boring   (3) usually
04 (1) Minsu likes both soccer and baseball.
   (2) I'm happiest when I play with my friends
   (3) What kind of music do you listen to?
05 (p)ractice, (c)lassical, (g)arden, (d)essert
   (1) classical   (2) practice   (3) dessert   (4) garden

01 (1) take a siesta: 낮잠을 자다 (2) won races: 경기에서 이겼다 (3) take good care of ~: ~을 잘 돌보다 (4) boring: 지루한
02 (1) when: ~할 때; 언제 (2) like: (전치사) ~와 같은; (동사) 좋아하다 (3) both: 둘 다
03 (1) be동사 뒤 보어 자리로 형용사 peaceful이 적절하다, (2) bore는 '지루하게 하다'라는 의미로, 연습 시간이 지루하지 않다는 것은 boring이 적절하다. (3) 동사를 수식하는 부사가 적절하므로 usually가 맞다.
04 (1) both A and B: A와 B 둘 다 (3) what kind of ~: 어떤 종류의 ~

05 (1) 고전적인 (2) 연습하다 (3) 후식 (4) 정원

교과서
Conversation

핵심 Check
p.10~11

1 your free time   2 How, usually   3 kind   4 ③

교과서 대화문 익히기

Check(√) True or False
p.12

1 T   2 F   3 F   4 T

교과서 확인학습
p.14~15

Listen and Talk A-1
what do, usually do / like playing / What kind of / play baduk

Listen and Talk A-2
in your free time / What kind of books / like reading

Listen and Talk A-3
listen to / do you listen to

Listen and Talk A-4
when / baking / What kind of / usually

Listen and Talk B
what, usually do / usually listen to / What kind of / listen to classical

Listen and Talk C
usually do / outside / do you do / play, on / watching / What kind of / fun / sometimes, Why don't we go / That sounds

Review 1
How about you / detective stories

Review 2
when you have / usually watch / kind / favorite

Review 3
1 does, free time
2 What, of

01 ①　　　02 ⑤　　　03 ②　　　04 ③

01 좋아하는 영화의 종류를 묻고 있으므로 ①번이 적절하다.

02 'Why don't we+동사원형?'은 '~하 는 게 어때?'라는 표현이다. ⑤번은 '왜 우리가 함께 영화를 보니?'라는 뜻이다.

03 G의 대답으로 보아 '여가 시간에 무엇을 하니?'의 의미를 가지는 표현이 적절하다.

04 B의 답으로 보아 A에 들어갈 질문은 '어떤 종류의 음식을 먹니?'가 적절하다.

01 ①　　　　　　02 What kind of books do you read?
03 ②　　　　　　04 What do you, do, free time
05 Shall we / How[What] about　　　06 ③
07 ④　　　08 ②　　　09 ④　　　10 ③
11 ⑤　　　　　　12 I usually listen to music.

1 '여가 시간에 무엇을 하니?'라는 표현을 고른다.

2 'What kind of + 명사?'는 '어떤 종류의 ~?'라는 뜻이다. 다음에 일반동사 read의 의문문 형태로 'do+주어+동사원형'을 사용한다.

3 주로 바둑을 둔다고 했으므로 어떤 종류의 게임을 하는지 묻는 것이 자연스럽다.

5 Why don't we+동사원형 ~?과 같이 '~하는 게 어때?'라는 의미를 가진 표현으로 Shall we+동사원형?, How[What] about+-ing?, What do you say to+ing?가 있다.

6 'Andy야, 너는 여가 시간에 주로 무엇을 하니?'라고 묻는 말이므로, '영화 보는 것을 좋아해.'라는 말 앞에 위치하는 것이 자연스럽다.

7 '~할 때'의 의미를 가지는 부사절 접속사 when이 적절하다.

8 enjoy는 동명사를 목적어로 취하는 동사다.

9 여가 시간에 무엇을 하며 어떤 종류의 활동을 하는지 묻는 대화다.

10 ③번은 '너는 무엇을 하고 싶니?'라는 의미로 여가 활동을 묻는 질문으로 어색한 표현이다.

11 Ann은 탐정 소설 읽는 것을 좋아한다고 했기 때문에 액션 배우인 Bruce Lee(이소룡)를 좋아할 것이라고 유추하기는 어렵다.

12 빈도부사 usually는 일반동사 listen 앞에 위치하고, '~을 듣다'는 표현으로 listen to를 사용한다.

01 what do you usually do when you have free time?
02 What kind of movies do you watch?

03 She usually reads books.
04 (1) What kind of exercise do you do
　　(2) playing soccer
05 go shopping

01 의문사 what으로 문장을 시작하고, when은 부사절 접속사로 '~할 때'의 의미를 가지고 있다. 'when+주어+동사'의 어순을 사용한다.

02 What kind of+명사 ~?: 어떤 종류의 ~?, 일반동사 watch의 의문문으로 '조동사(do)+주어(you)+동사 (watch)'의 어순이 적절하다.

03 빈도부사 usually는 일반동사 앞에 위치한다

04 (1)은 What kind of ~? 구문을 이용하여 '어떤 종류의 운동을 하니?'라는 표현이 적절하고, (2)는 동사 enjoy 뒤에 동명사를 이용하여 playing soccer를 쓴다.

05 '-하러 가다'의 의미로 go shopping을 사용한다

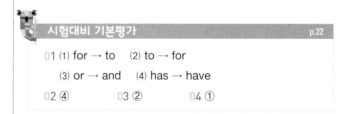
핵심 Check　　　　　　　　　　p.20~21

1 (1) me some pictures　(2) for
2 He made a cake for me.
3 (1) like　(2) have
4 (1) and　(2) or

01 (1) for → to　(2) to → for
　　(3) or → and　(4) has → have
02 ④　　　03 ②　　　04 ①

01 (1) send는 3형식으로 바꿀 때 전치사 to를 쓴다. (2) buy는 3형식으로 바꿀 때 전치사 for를 쓴다. (3) both A and B: A와 B 둘 다 (4) both A and B는 주어로 쓰일 때 복수 취급한다.

02 4형식 문장을 3형식 문장으로 바꿀 때 buy는 전치사 for를 사용한다.

03 B as well as A에서 동사는 B에 일치시킨다.

04 both A and B의 A와 B에는 문법적으로 같은 성질의 것이 와야 하는데 본 문장에서는 형용사가 was의 보어로 와야 한다.

01 ④   02 (1) them math (2) bought (3) and
03 ④   04 (1) bought her son (2) Tell, to
(3) made, for (4) Both, and   05 a bike for me
06 ⑤   07 ①   08 ⑤   09 ②
10 ②   11 ③   12 ④   13 ④
14 for   15 ①   16 (1) both London and
Paris   (2) neither China nor Japan   17 to / of /
for   18 (1) Neither Jacob nor Abe   (2) both
very clean and cute

01 ④ She sent her friend an email. 또는 She sent an email to her friend.가 되어야 한다.

02 (1) 수여동사는 '간접목적어+직접목적어'의 순서이다. (2) buy는 3형식으로 바꿀 때 간접목적어 앞에 전치사 for를 사용한다. (3) both A and B: A와 B 둘 다

03 ④ 4형식 동사인 show는 간접목적어가 직접목적어 뒤로 이동할 때 전치사 to를 사용한다.

04 (1) buy는 4형식 동사일 때 '간접목적어+직접목적어'의 순서이다. (2) tell은 간접목적어 앞에 전치사 to를 사용한다. (3) make는 간접목적어 앞에 전치사 for를 사용한다. (4) both A and B: A와 B 둘 다

05 4형식 문장(주어+수여동사+간접목적어+직접목적어)은 3형식 문장(주어 + 수여동사 + 직접목적어 + 전치사+ 간접목적어)으로 바꿔 쓸 수 있는 데, 이때 수여동사 buy는 전치사 for를 쓴다.

06 ⑤ choose는 3형식 문장으로 바꿀 때 전치사 for를 사용한다.

07 not only A but also B = B as well as A / 주어로 쓰이는 경우 동사는 B에 일치시킨다.

08 ⑤ Sharon sent her friend a pretty long email. 또는 Sharon sent a pretty long email to her friend.가 되어야 한다.

09 both A and B: A와 B 둘 다

10 ②번의 make 동사는 '목적어+목적보어'의 5형식으로 쓰였으나 나머지는 모두 '간접목적어+직접목적어'의 4형식으로 쓰였다.

11 both A and B: A와 B 둘 다

12 want는 4형식으로 쓰이는 동사가 아니다.

13 not only A but (also) B = B as well as A

14 3형식으로 바꿀 때 buy와 choose는 for를 쓴다.

15 Yesterday, it was snowy as well as windy. 상관접속사에 의해 연결되는 어구는 문법적으로 같은 성분이 와야 한다.

16 (1) both A and B: A와 B 둘 다 (2) neither A nor B: A도 B도 아닌

17 3형식 문장으로 바꿀 때 send는 전치사 to를, ask는 of를, cook은 for를 사용한다.

18 (1) neither A nor B: A도 B도 아닌 (2) both A and B: A와 B 둘 다

01 Both Mike and, like
02 (1) Gilbert bought some candies for his daughter.
(2) George sent a card to Mary on her birthday.
(3) Sophie asked the way to the library of Nick.
03 (1) both roses and tulips
(2) not only tigers but (also) cheetahs
04 (1) to → for
(2) was → were
(3) the math teacher → of the math teacher
05 I'll make some cookies for you.
06 (1) Minhee as well as her sisters is very kind and cool.
(2) Annabel likes not only studying history but also playing the computer games. 또는 Annabel likes not only to study history but also to play the computer games.
07 (1) Matthew thought of not only going to the amusement park but (also) enjoying the rides. Matthew thought of enjoying the rides as well as going to the amusement park.
(2) Emily made not only a pancake but (also) some chocolate cookies for me. Emily made some chocolate cookies as well as a pancake for me.
(3) Anna not only enjoyed riding a bike but (also) had a delicious ice cream. Anna had a delicious ice cream as well as enjoyed riding a bike.
08 (1) Mom cooked a delicious dinner for us.
(2) Emma inquired of him when he would come.
09 (1) I as well as you am able to solve the problem.
(2) Both you and Grace are pretty and wise.
(3) Not Sheryll but you know (that) it was wrong.
10 (1) a nice birthday gift for
(2) a letter to
11 gave, brought, sent, bought, made, showed

01 Mike가 친구들과 어울려 노는 것을 좋아하고 Bob도 친구들과 어울려 노는 것을 좋아하는 것이므로 both A and B(A와 B 둘 다)를 이용하고 'both A and B'가 주어로 쓰일 경우 복수로 취급한다는 것에 주의한다.

02 (1) 4형식을 3형식으로 바꿀 때 동사 buy는 간접목적어 앞에 전치사 for를, (2) send는 to를, (3) ask는 전치사 of를 사용한다.

03 (1) both A and B: A와 B 둘 다 (2) not only A but (also) B = B as well as A: A뿐만 아니라 B도

04 (1), (3) 간접목적어가 직접목적어 뒤로 이동할 때 buy는 전치

사 for를, ask는 of를 사용한다. (2) both A and B는 주어로 쓰일 때 복수 취급한다.

05 수여동사 make + 직접목적어 + for + 간접목적어

06 (1) B as well as A: A뿐만 아니라 B도 / 이때 동사는 B에 일치시킨다. (2) 상관접속사에 의해 연결되는 어구는 문법적으로 동일한 것이어야 한다.

07 not only A but also B = B as well as A: A뿐만 아니라 B도 / not only A but also B에서 also는 종종 생략된다.

08 (1) cook은 간접목적어가 직접목적어 뒤로 갈 때 전치사 for를 사용하므로 for를 추가하여야 한다. (2) inquire는 간접목적어 앞에 전치사 of를 사용하므로 of를 추가하여야 한다. 또한 inquire는 'of+간접목적어'가 직접목적어 앞에 오는 일이 많다.

09 (1) B as well as A: A뿐만 아니라 B도 / 이때 동사는 B에 일치시킨다. (2) both A and B: A와 B 둘 다 (3) not A but B: A가 아니라 B

10 간접목적어가 직접목적어 뒤로 이동할 때 buy는 전치사 for를, write는 to를 사용한다.

11 목적어로 간접목적어와 직접목적어를 가지는 동사를 찾는다.

Reading

확인문제   p.28

1 F   2 T   3 T   4 F

확인문제   p.29

1 T   2 F   3 F   4 T   5 T   6 T   7 T   8 F

교과서 확인학습 A   p.30~31

01 Favorite Time   02 I'm   03 15 years old
04 about your favorite time
05 show me some pictures   06 my name
07 of the day   08 usually ends around
09 On most days   10 soup, vegetables, meat
11 have a dessert 12 a short nap   13 Both, and
14 live near   15 when   16 in our culture
17 Almost everyone
18 In fact   19 take good care of
20 often brush, give him some carrots
21 enjoy riding   22 Then, peaceful
23 in Nairobi, Kenya

교과서 확인학습 B   p.32~33

24 our running practice time
25 on the school's running team   26 happiest
27 boring   28 from   29 proud
30 Both, and, be like

1 Teen Talk: My Favorite Time of the Day
2 Hello! I'm Somin.
3 I'm 15 years old, and I live in Korea.
4 Please tell me about your favorite time of the day.
5 You can also show me some pictures.
6 Hi, my name is Diego, and I live in Seville, Spain.
7 My favorite time of the day is lunch time
8 My school usually ends around 2 p.m.
9 On most days, my family gets together and has a big, long lunch.
10 We usually have soup, vegetables, and meat.
11 We also have a dessert like churros.
12 After lunch, we usually take a siesta, a short nap.
13 Both my father and I like to sleep under the tree in our garden.
14 Hi! My name is Tabin, and I live near the Gobi Desert in Mongolia.
15 I'm happy when I ride my horse.
16 Horses are important in our culture.
17 Almost everyone can ride a horse in Mongolia
18 In fact, we say, "We ride horses before we can walk."
19 I take good care of my horse.
20 I often brush him and give him some carrots.
21 I enjoy riding especially in the evening before the sunset.
22 Then the sky is red, and everything is peaceful.
23 Hi! I'm Musa, and I live in Nairobi, Kenya.
24 My favorite time of the day is our running practice time.
25 My friend, Tamu, and I are on the school's running team.
26 I'm happiest when I run with Tamu.
27 Our practice time isn't boring because we can see many animals.
28 Many runners from Kenya won races in the Olympics.
29 I'm so proud of them.
30 Both Tamu and I want to be like them.

01 ④   02 (A) year   (B) lives

03 (1) 하루 중 매우 좋아하는 시간에 대해 자신에게 말해 줄 것
   (2) 자신에게 사진 몇 장을 보여줄 것

04 ②   05 nap   06 ③

07 (A) near   (B) especially   (C) Then   08 ④

09 ⑤   10 ④   11 ⑤

12 many runners from Kenya   13 ⑤

14 (A) has   (B) lunch   (C) I   15 ①, ③   16 ④

17 ①번, bored를 happy 혹은 excited 등 기분이 좋다는
   뜻의 단어로 바꿀 것

18 ③   19 ④   20 ⑤

21 (A) favorite   (B) because   (C) like   22 ④

23 My family   24 ①   25 ②   26 ④

27 ⑤   28 after → before   29 ②

30 ④   31 pride   32 ⑤

33 near to → near   34 ①

35 gives him some carrots   36 ⑤

---

01 위 글은 'SNS 글'이다. ② (신문·잡지의) 글, 기사 ③ 수필

02 명사를 꾸며줄 때는 year에 s를 붙이지 않고 앞뒤에 하이픈을 그어 a 15-year-old girl이라고 해야 한다. 소민이는 '한국'에 사는 '15세' 소녀이다.

03 소민이는 'Please tell me about your favorite time of the day. You can also show me some pictures.'라고 부탁했다.

04 ⓐ 도시 앞에는 in을 쓴다.
ⓑ 날짜 앞에는 on을 쓴다.

05 대체로 낮 동안의 짧은 잠: nap(낮잠)

06 ① He lives in Seville, Spain. ② It is lunch time. ③ Diego의 학교가 대체로 몇 시에 시작하는지는 대답할 수 없다. ④ Yes, they do. ⑤ He likes to sleep under the tree in their garden.

07 (A) 고비 사막 '근처에' 산다고 해야 하므로 near가 적절하다. near: 근처에, nearly: 거의 (B) '특히 저녁에'라고 해야 하므로 especially가 적절하다. especially: 특히, probably: 아마 (C) '그 무렵엔'이라고 해야 하므로 Then이 적절하다. then: 그 무렵에, than: ~보다

08 말은 몽골 문화에서 중요하고 거의 모든 사람들이 말을 탈 수 있다고 한 다음에, 사실은 '걸을 수 있기 전에 말을 탄다.'고 하는 것이 문맥상 적절하다.

09 Tabin은 '해가 지기 전' 저녁에 말 타는 것을 즐긴다.

10 주어진 문장의 Tamu에 주목한다. ④번 앞 문장에서 Tamu를 소개한 다음에 써야 하므로 ④번이 적절하다.

11 ⑤ 많은 동물들을 볼 수 있기 때문에 '지루하지' 않다고 하는 것이 적절하다. ③ 사물이 주어이므로 tiring(피곤하게 만드는, 피곤한)이라고 하는 것이 적절하다.

12 올림픽의 육상 경기에서 우승을 한 '케냐 출신의 많은 선수들'을 가리킨다

13 점심 식사 '후에' 짧게 낮잠을 잔다.

14 (A) gets와 병렬구문을 이루어야 하므로 has가 적절하다.
(B) 일반적으로 식사 이름 앞에는 관사를 붙이지 않는다. 그러나 본문의 a big, long lunch처럼 식사 이름 앞에 형용사가 붙어서 특정한 의미를 갖거나 수식어구가 붙으면 관사를 붙인다.
(C) 주어 자리이므로 주격을 쓰는 것이 적절하다.

15 around, approximately, about, or so는 '대략', '약'이라는 뜻이다. across: 가로질러 / round: ~을 돌아

16 ④ Tabin의 말 이름은 알 수 없다. ① 고비 사막 근처에 산다. ② 몽골에 있다. ③ 종종 털을 빗겨 주고 당근을 준다. ⑤ Tabin은 해가 지기 전 저녁에 말 타는 것을 즐긴다

17 말은 몽골 문화에서 중요하고 거의 모든 사람들이 말을 탈 수 있으며 Tabin도 자신의 말을 잘 돌본다는 내용이므로, Tabin은 말을 탈 때 '지루한' 것이 아니라 '행복하다'고 해야 적절하다.

18 ⓐ와 ③번은 동명사이고, 나머지는 다 현재분사이다.

19 ① Musa는 '케냐의 나이로비'에 산다. ② Musa는 하루 중 달리기 '연습'할 때를 매우 좋아한다. ③ 'Musa의 친구인' Tamu와 Musa는 학교 달리기 팀에 소속되어 있다. (My friend와 Tamu는 동격이다.) ⑤ Musa는 올림픽의 육상경기에서 우승한 케냐 출신의 달리기 선수들을 매우 자랑스러워하고 Tamu와 Musa 둘 다 그들처럼 되고 싶어 한다.

20 on: [소속] ~의 일원으로

21 (A) '매우 좋아하는'이라고 해야 하므로 favorite가 적절하다. terrible: 끔찍한 (B) 뒤에 '주어+동사'가 나오므로 because가 적절하다. 'because of+명사구' (C) '~처럼 되기'를 원한다고 해야 하므로 like가 적절하다. be like: ~와 같다, be different from: ~와 다르다

22 주어진 문장의 also에 주목한다. ④번 앞 문장에서 점심식사 메뉴를 소개한 다음에 '또한 후식도 먹는다'고 하는 것이 적절하므로 ④번이 적절하다.

23 Diego의 가족을 가리킨다. family는 집합체인 가족을 가리킬 때는 단수로, 가족 구성원을 가리킬 때는 복수로 취급한다.

24 ⓑ와 ① 명사적 용법(목적어), ② 부사적 용법(형용사 수식), ③ 형용사적 용법, ④ 부사적 용법(판단의 근거), ⑤ 형용사적 용법

25 (B)는 주어진 글에 대한 설명이므로 제일 먼저 오고 (C)의 Then이 (A)의 in the evening before the sunset을 가리키므로 (A) 다음에 (C)가 와야 한다. 그러므로 (B)-(A)-(C)의 순서가 적절하다.

26 Tabin은 말을 탈 '때' '행복하다'고 하는 것이 적절하다. ① 비록 ~이지만, ③ 그래서

27 ⑤번 다음 문장의 Then에 주목한다. 주어진 문장의 in the

evening before the sunset을 받고 있으므로 ⑤번이 적절하다.

28 걸을 수 있게 된 '후에' 말을 타는 것은 보통의 순서이므로, 말은 몽골 문화에서 중요하고 거의 모든 사람들이 말을 탈 수 있다고 한 다음에 '우리는 걸을 수 있게 된 후에 말을 탄다.'고 하는 것은 어색하다. 우리는 걸을 수 있기 '전에' 말을 탄다고 하는 것이 문맥상 적절하다.

29 ② Musa가 매일 얼마나 오래 동안 달리기를 연습하는지는 대답할 수 없다. ① He lives in Nairobi, Kenya. ③ Yes, he does. ④ He is on the school's running team. ⑤ Yes, he can.

30 Musa는 하루 중 달리기 연습할 때를 매우 좋아한다고 했기 때문에 Tamu와 '달리기'를 할 때 가장 행복하다고 하는 것이 적절하다.

31 나는 그들이 매우 자랑스럽다.(= I'm so proud of them. = I take pride in them very much.)

32 ⓒ, ⑤는 전치사로 쓰였고, 나머지는 동사로 쓰였다.

33 near는 전치사로서 뒤에 바로 목적어를 써서 (장소·시간 따위)의 가까이에, ~에 가깝게(close to)의 뜻으로 쓰인다.

34 take care of: ~을 돌보다

35 그녀는 그에게 '약간의 당근'을 준다.

36 (C)에서 대부분의 날에 가족들이 함께 점심을 먹는다고 한 다음 (B)에서 점심 메뉴를 소개하므로 (C) 다음에 (B)가 이어지고 (A)에서 점심 식사 후의 활동에 대해 설명하고 있으므로 (B) 다음에 (A)가 와야 한다. 그러므로 (C)-(B)-(A)의 순서가 적절하다.

서술형 시험대비
p.40~41

01 your favorite time

02 You can also show some pictures to me.

03 like

04 (A) lunch   (B) short

05 Almost everyone can ride a horse in Mongolia. 혹은 In Mongolia almost everyone can ride a horse.

06 care for, look after

07 riding

08 favorite time of the day is his running practice time

09 am → are

10 Both Tamu and I want to be like them.

11 On most days, my family gets together and has a big, long lunch.

12 sleeping

01 favorite: 가장 좋아하는

02 show는 to를 사용하여 3형식으로 고친다.

03 like: ~와 같은

---

04 거의 매일 Diego의 가족은 함께 '점심'을 먹는다. 점심을 먹은 후에 Diego와 그의 아버지는 보통 정원의 나무 밑에서 '짧은' 낮잠을 잔다.

05 almost를 보충하면 된다.

06 나는 나의 말을 잘 돌본다.(= I take good care of my horse. = I care for my horse well. = I look after my horse well.)

07 enjoy는 목적어로 동명사를 취한다.

08 Musa가 하루 중 가장 좋아하는 시간은 달리기 연습 시간이다.

09 I가 주어가 아니라 My friend, Tamu, and I가 주어이므로 ' are'로 고치는 것이 적절하다.

10 both A and B: A와 B 둘 다 / be like: ~와 같다

11 on most days: 대부분의 날에 / 식사 이름 앞에 형용사가 붙으면 관사를 붙인다.

12 like는 목적어로 to부정사와 동명사를 둘 다 쓸 수 있다.

영역별 핵심문제
p.43~47

01 near   02 ④   03 ⑤   04 ③

05 ⑤   06 ③   07 ④   08 ⑤

09 on, school's   10 ③   11 ⑤

12 ③   13 (1) a scarf to   (2) a nice dress for

14 Paul made Michelle a birthday cake.
Paul made a birthday cake for Michelle.

15 (1) Animals as well as humans need water and air.
(2) Mom bought pork as well as beef.

16 ①   17 ②   18 ③

19 or → and   20 ①   21 ④

22 (1) I will give my pen to you.
(2) Alicia bought a toy robot for her son last weekend.
Alicia bought her son a toy robot last weekend.
(3) The stranger asked the way of the police officer.

23 ⑤   24 ④   25 ④   26 ③

27 ⓑ Both ⓒ and

28 (A) Almost   (B) before   (C) riding   29 ③, ⑤

30 give some carrots to him

31 ④   32 ③번, is → isn't   33 ①

01 반의어 관계이다. 긴 : 짧은 = 먼 : 가까운

02 특정한 사회의 사람들이 공유하고 받아들이는 믿음, 생활 방식, 예술, 관습

03 사람 또는 사물을 돌보다

04 '~의 일원이다, 소속이다'라는 의미로 be on, 동아리는 대가족처럼 되어야 한다는 의미로 전치사 like가 적절하다.

05 바둑을 둔다는 표현으로 동사 play를 사용한다.

06 ③ four or five times는 네다섯 번이라는 뜻이다.

07 여가 시간에 무엇을 하는지에 대한 답으로 (C) 아빠와 게임을

한다. → (A) 어떤 종류의 게임을 하니? → (B) 주로 바둑을 둔다는 말이 이어지는 것이 적절하다.

08 '어떤 종류의 쿠키를 만드니?'라는 질문에 딸기를 좋아한다는 대답은 어색하다.

09 전치사 on이 '~의 일원으로'라는 의미를 가지고 있다

10 액션 영화를 좋아한다고 했으므로 좋아하는 영화의 종류를 묻는 질문이 자연스럽다.

11 Andy가 영화 보는 것보다 운동하는 것을 더 좋아한다는 내용은 본문에 언급되어 있지 않다. prefer A to B: B보다 A를 더 좋아하다

12 (B) 먼저 여가 시간에 무엇을 하는지 묻고 → (D) 쿠키를 만든다 → (C) 어떤 종류의 쿠키를 만드는지 묻고 마지막으로 (A) 주로 딸기 쿠키를 만든다는 내용이 오는 것이 적절하다.

13 3형식으로 바꿀 때 (1) give는 간접목적어 앞에 전치사 to를, (2) make는 전치사 for를 사용한다.

14 3형식으로 바꿀 때 make는 간접목적어 앞에 전치사 for를 사용한다.

15 not only A but also B = B as well as A

16 ①번은 목적어와 목적격 보어가 있는 5형식이고 나머지는 모두 4형식이다.

17 neither A nor B: A도 B도 아니다

18 3형식으로 바꿀 때 ask는 간접목적어 앞에 전치사 of를 사용한다.

19 both A and B: A와 B 둘 다

20 Not only I but also Elizabeth is poor at singing.

21 상관접속사에 의해 연결되는 어구는 문법적으로 동일한 것이어야 한다.

22 3형식으로 바꿀 때 (1) give는 간접목적어 앞에 전치사 to를, (2) buy는 간접목적어 앞에 전치사 for를, (3) ask는 간접목적어 앞에 전치사 of를 사용한다.

23 ⑤ 상관접속사에 의해 연결되는 어구는 문법적으로 동일한 것이어야 한다

24 4형식은 '주어+동사+간접목적어+직접목적어'이다.

25 이 글은 'Diego가 하루 중 가장 좋아하는 시간을 소개'하기 위한 글이다.

26 ⓐ와 ③ [수사와 함께] 대충, 약 ① 사방에서 ② 굴러서 ④ 이리저리, 여기저기 ⑤ 주변에 있는

27 both A and B: A와 B 둘 다

28 (A) '거의' 모든 사람이라고 해야 하므로 almost가 적절하다. almost는 '거의'라는 뜻으로 주로 뒤에 all, every, 숫자가 나온다. most: 대부분의 (B) 걸을 수 있게 된 '후에' 말을 타는 것은 보통의 순서이므로, 말은 몽골 문화에서 중요하고 거의 모든 사람들이 말을 탈 수 있다고 한 다음에 '우리는 걸을 수 있게 된 후에 말을 탄다.'고 하는 것은 어색하다. 사실 우리는 걸을 수 있기 '전에' 말을 탄다고 하는 것이 문맥상 어울리므로 before가 적절하다. (C) enjoy는 목적어로 동명사를 취하므로 riding이 적절

29 Actually = As a matter of fact: 사실은, ① Therefore: 그러므로, ② Instead: 대신에, ④ In other words: 즉, 다시 말해

30 give는 to를 사용하여 3형식으로 고친다.

31 ④ 올림픽의 육상 경기에서 이긴 케냐 선수들의 이름은 알 수 없다. ① 케냐의 나이로비 ② 달리기 팀 ③ Tamu와 함께 달릴 때 ⑤ 자랑스러움

32 많은 동물들을 볼 수 있기 때문에 달리기 연습 시간 동안 지루하지 '않다'고 하는 것이 적절하다.

33 ⓐ Tamu와 '함께' 달릴 때라고 해야 하므로 with가 적절하다. ⓑ 케냐 '출신의' 많은 달리기 선수들이라고 해야 하므로 from이 적절하다.

단원별 예상문제 p.48~51

01 proud   02 ③   03 ④   04 ④
05 southern / riding / runners
06 (1) how do you spend your free time
  (2) Why don't we go see an action movie
07 ③   08 I usually watch movies.   09 ⑤
10 ④   11 ②, ⑤   12 ①   13 ②
14 ③   15 (A) most (B) soup (C) dessert
16 ⑤   17 ③   18 ④
19 my horse   20 ②   21 ⑤   22 ③
23 Neither Tamu nor I → Both Tamu and I   24 ④
25 ⑤번, though → because[as]

01 지루한 : 흥미진진한 = 자랑스러운 : 부끄러운

02 대부분의 경우에 발생하는 일에 관해 말하는 것으로 usually(대개, 일반적으로)가 적절하다.

03 What kind of+명사?: 어떤 종류의 ~?, in your free time: 여가 시간에, Why don't we ~?: ~하는 게 어때?

04 '여가 시간에 무엇을 하니?'의 답으로 대개 영화를 본다는 대답이 적절하다.

05 명사 Europe을 수식하는 형용사로 '남쪽의, 남쪽에 있는'의 뜻을 가진 southern이 적절하고, 동사 enjoy는 동명사를 목적어로 가지기 때문에 riding이 적절하다. 마지막은 Many의 수식을 받는 명사 runners가 와야 한다.

07 'Andy야, 너는 여가 시간에 무엇을 하니?'라고 상대방의 여가 활동을 묻고 있으므로 취미를 묻는 ③이 적절하다.

08 빈도부사 usually는 일반동사 앞에 위치해야 한다.

09 질문 '어떤 종류의 영화를 보니?'에 어울리는 답은 ⑤번이다.

10 위 대화에서 Jenny는 여가 시간에 Chris가 무엇을 하는지 궁금해하고 있다.

11 ① I give my horse some carrots. ③ She bought flowers for me. ④ Both Minsu and Sujin like pizza.

② 4형식을 3형식으로 바꿀 때 동사 write는 간접목적어 앞에 전치사 to를 사용한다. ⑤ not only A but (also) B: A뿐만 아니라 B

12 both A and B: A와 B 둘 다 / either A or B: A 또는 B 둘 중 하나

13 간접목적어 자리이므로 전치사 없이 목적격이 적절하며 buy는 4형식을 3형식으로 바꿀 때 전치사 for를 사용한다.

14 B as well as A에서 동사는 B에 일치시킨다.

15 (A) On most days: '대부분의 날에'라고 해야 하므로 most가 적절하다. almost는 '거의'라는 뜻으로 주로 뒤에 all, every, 숫자가 나온다. (B) 점심식사로 먹는 요리를 나열하고 있으므로 'soup(수프)'가 적절하다. soap: 비누, (C) 추로스와 같은 '후식'이라고 해야 하므로 dessert가 적절하다. desert: 사막

16 take a siesta = have a siesta: 낮잠을 자다

17 ⓑ 명사적 용법(목적어), ① 명사적 용법(진주어), ② 명사적 용법(목적어), ③ 부사적 용법(원인), ④ 명사적 용법(보어), ⑤ 명사적 용법(목적어)

18 ④ 사실 우리는 걸을 수 있기 전에 말을 탄다는 말이 이어지므로 거의 모든 사람들이 '말을 탈 수 있다'고 하는 것이 문맥상 적절하다. ① 말에게 먹이를 주다, ② 경마에 돈을 걸다, ③ 말의 털을 빗겨 주다, ⑤ 말을 타고 곡예를 하다

19 'Tabin의 말'을 가리킨다.

20 ② 몽골의 문화에서 말이 왜 중요한지는 대답할 수 없다.

21 위 글의 마지막 문장의 them은 ④번의 them과 마찬가지로 앞에서 언급한 Many runners from Kenya를 가리키며, 그 사이의 '내가 Tamu보다 더 빨리 달린다.'는 ⑤번 문장은 전체 글의 흐름에서 벗어난다.

22 ③ 경주 ①, ④ 인종, 종족 ② 경주하다(동사) ⑤ 질주하다, 고동치다(동사)

23 Musa는 올림픽의 육상 경기에서 우승을 한 케냐 출신의 달리기 선수들을 매우 자랑스러워한다고 했기 때문에, 'Tamu와 Musa 둘 다 그들처럼 되고 싶어 한다'고 하는 것이 적절하다.

24 위 글은 '하루 중 매우 좋아하는 시간'에 대해 설명하는 글이다.

25 많은 동물들을 볼 수 있기 '때문에' 지루하지 않다고 하는 것이 적절하다.

서술형 실전문제
p.52~53

01 what do you like to do when you have free time?

02 (1) exercise outside (2) What kind of

   (3) play badminton (4) watching movies

   (5) action movies

03 When, favorite, because

04 (1) bought him a necktie

   (2) gave, to them

---

   (3) asked, of

05 (1) works → work

   (2) kindly → kind

06 (1) Liam bought some meat for his family.

   (2) Luna showed some post cards to me

07 Lucas gave her a piece of advice.

   Lucas gave a piece of advice to her.

08 I'm happiest when I run with Tamu.

09 bored   10 runners

11 lunch time 12 such as

13 After lunch, we usually take a siesta, a short nap.

04 (1) buy의 간접목적어로 목적격 him을 쓰고, 직접목적어 a necktie를 쓴다. (2) 직접목적어가 동사 자리 뒤에 있고 give는 전치사 to를 쓰므로 그 뒤에 'to+간접목적어'를 쓴다. (3) ask는 간접목적어 앞에 전치사 of를 사용한다.

05 (1) both A and B는 주어로 쓰일 때 복수 취급한다. (2) 상관접속사에 의해 연결되는 어구는 문법적으로 동일한 것이어야 한다.

06 (1) 4형식을 3형식으로 바꿀 때 동사 buy는 간접목적어 앞에 전치사 for를 사용한다. (2) 동사 show는 간접목적어 앞에 전치사 to를 사용한다.

07 동사 give의 경우 4형식 문장은 '간접목적어+직접목적어'를 이용하고, 3형식 문장은 '직접목적어+to+간접목적어'를 이용한다.

08 happy의 최상급 happiest를 사용하는 것이 적절하다.

09 많은 동물들을 볼 수 있기 때문에 Musa와 Tamu는 달리기 연습 시간 동안 '지루하지' 않다고 하는 것이 적절하다. 사람을 수식하므로 'bored'가 적절하다.

10 케냐 출신의 많은 '달리기 선수들'이 올림픽의 육상 경기에서 우승을 했다고 하는 것이 적절하다. many 다음에 복수명사로 써야 한다.

11 Diego는 스페인 사람이고 그가 하루 중 가장 좋아하는 시간은 '점심시간'이다.

12 such as: ~와 같은

13 usually를 보충하면 된다. 빈도부사는 be동사나 조동사 뒤, 일반동사 앞에 쓰고, 동격 사이에는 콤마를 찍으면 된다.

창의사고력 서술형 문제
p.54

[모범답안]

01 (1) What do you do when you have free time?

   (2) Why don't we go see an action movie this weekend?

   (3) What kind of cookies do you make?

   (4) What do you usually do in your free time?

02 (1) Dad bought a new computer for me.

   (2) Jack sent me some flowers.

   (3) Lily gave a nice wallet to me.

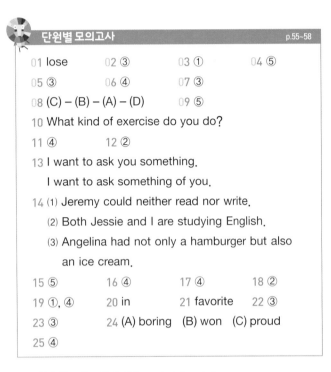

03 (1) I'm Mina. I love playing badminton with my friends after school. That's my favorite time of the day
(2) I'm Minho. My favorite time of the day is night. I love to see the moon and the stars.

단원별 모의고사
p.55~58

01 lose   02 ③   03 ①   04 ⑤
05 ③   06 ④   07 ③
08 (C) – (B) – (A) – (D)   09 ⑤
10 What kind of exercise do you do?
11 ④   12 ②
13 I want to ask you something.
   I want to ask something of you.
14 (1) Jeremy could neither read nor write.
   (2) Both Jessie and I are studying English.
   (3) Angelina had not only a hamburger but also an ice cream.
15 ⑤   16 ④   17 ④   18 ②
19 ①, ④   20 in   21 favorite   22 ③
23 ③   24 (A) boring (B) won (C) proud
25 ④

01 중요한 : 중요하지 않은 = 이기다 : 지다
02 해가 사라지고 밤이 시작되는 시간
03 걱정이나 자극이 없이 조용하고 차분한
04 '~할 때'라는 의미를 가지는 부사절 접속사 when이 적절하다.
05 take care of :~을 돌보다 / be proud of: ~을 자랑스러워하다
06 고전음악을 듣는다고 했으므로, 어떤 종류의 음악을 듣는지 물어보는 것이 적절하다.
07 빵 굽는 것을 즐긴다고 했으므로, 여가 시간에 하는 활동은 쿠키를 만드는 것이 적절하다.
08 여가 시간 활동을 묻는 말에 (C)의 영화를 주로 본다는 내용이 나오고 (B)의 어떤 종류의 영화를 보는지 묻고, 답으로 (A)의 액션영화를 좋아한다는 내용이 적절하다. 마지막으로 (D)의 Bruce Lee를 가장 좋아한다는 추가적인 대답이 오는 것이 옳은 순서다.
09 주어진 문장의 They는 앞에 나온 복수명사를 가리키는 인칭대명사이므로 I like action movies. 다음에 오는 것이 적절하다.
11 '~의 일원이다'라는 의미로 전치사 on을 사용한다.
12 '~하는 게 어때?'라는 표현으로 Why don't we ~?가 적절하다.
13 ask는 4형식 동사이며 3형식으로 바꿀 때 전치사 of를 쓴다.
14 (1) neither A nor B: A도 B도 아닌. 상관접속사에 의해 연결되는 어구는 문법적으로 동일한 것이어야 한다.
   (2) both A and B: A와 B 둘 다. both A and B는 주어로

쓰일 때 복수 취급한다.
(3) not only A but also B: A뿐만 아니라 B도
15 choose는 3형식으로 바꿀 때 전치사 for를 쓴다.
16 ④ Not only Seho but Jinsu wears glasses.
17 ① Charlotte made a cake for her sister. ② Mia sent a text to me. ③ Eric gave some books to Olivia. ⑤ Tom bought Amelia a ring.
18 ⓐ와 ② (예를 들어) ~와 같은, ① ~와 비슷한, ③ ~와 비슷한, (외관·내용 등이) ~을 닮아, ④ ~을 좋아하다, ⑤ ~와 같이, ~처럼
19 both A and B = at once A and B = A and B alike: A와 B 모두, either A or B: A이든가 또는 B이든가, not A but B: A가 아니라 B, neither A nor B: A도 아니고 B도 아니다
20 ⓐ와 ⓒ 국가 이름 앞에 in, ⓑ in our culture: 우리 문화에서, ⓓ in the evening: 저녁에
21 나는 나의 말을 탈 때 행복하다.(= I'm happy when I ride my horse. = My favorite time of the day is my horse riding time.), favorite: 마음에 드는, 매우 좋아하는
22 ③ 사실은, 몽골에서는 거의 모든 사람들이 말을 탈 수 있다고 한 다음에 '사실' 우리는 걸을 수 있기 전에 말을 탄다는 말이 이어지는 것이 문맥상 적절하다. ① 대신에, ② 그러나, ④ 마침내, ⑤ 대조적으로
23 (C)의 Our가 (B)의 My friend, Tamu, and I를 가리키므로 (B) 다음에 (C)가 이어지고 (A)의 them이 (C)의 Many runners from Kenya를 가리키므로 (C) 다음에 (A)가 와야 한다. 그러므로 (B)-(C)-(A)의 순서가 적절하다.
24 (A) 사물을 수식하므로 boring이 적절하다. (B)와 (C) 케냐 출신의 많은 달리기 선수들이 올림픽 경주에서 이겨서 Musa가 그들을 자랑스러워한다고 하는 것이 문맥상 적절하다. give up: 포기하다, ashamed: 부끄러워하는
25 ⓐ와 ④ 명사적 용법(목적어), ① 형용사적 용법, ② 부사적 용법(판단의 근거), ③ 형용사적 용법, ⑤ 부사적 용법(결과)

Enjoying Local Culture

시험대비 실력평가   p.62

| 01 spicy | 02 ④ | 03 ① | 04 ⑤ |
| 05 ② | 06 on | 07 ③ | 08 ④ |

1 둘은 동의어 관계이다. 맛있는 – 매운

2 get to+장소 명사: ~에 도착하다 / have to+동사원형: ~ 해야 한다

3 ① don't have to는 '~할 필요가 없다'라는 뜻이다.

4 무언가에 놀라거나 초조해하는

5 사람들이 구입하거나 사용하거나 즐기는 것을 만들다

6 '~에 있는'의 의미로 전치사 on을 사용한다.

7 '~의 맞은편에'라는 뜻으로 전치사 from과 어울리는 단어는 across이다. '~을 찾다'는 의미로 look for가 적절하다.

8 주어가 3인칭 단수이므로 has to가 적절하고, '~로 유명하다'는 be famous for를 사용한다.

서술형 시험대비   p.63

01 (1) boring   (2) collect

02 (1) bee   (2) moved   (3) tradition   (4) sew

03 (1) amazing   (2) colorful   (3) pieces   (4) tasty

04 (1) The post office is between the bakery and the school.

    (2) How do I get to the police station?

    (3) Jane has to finish her homework by this weekend.

05 (1) getting   (2) going   (3) had to

06 (s)traight, (m)useum

01 (1) 이기다 : 지다 = 흥미진진한 : 지루한 (2) 특별한 : 특별한 = 모으다 : 모으다

02 (1) 모임 (2) '~로 이동하다' 시제가 과거이므로 moved (3) 그 회사는 훌륭한 디자인의 오랜 전통을 가지고 있다. (4) 그녀는 단추를 달려고 바늘과 실을 찾았다.

03 (1) 경관이 놀랍다는 의미로 amaze를 형용사 amazing으로 고친다. (2) 퀼트 경연 대회에서 Eddie는 그의 할머니와 친구분들의 화려한 퀼트를 보았다. 명사 quilt를 수식하는 형용사가 필요하

다. (3) 사람들은 작은 천 조각을 모아서 그것들을 함께 바느질해야 했다. 천 조각은 여러 개의 복수명사가 되어야 하기 때문에 복수형 pieces가 적절하다. (4) 명사 cheese를 수식하는 형용사 형태가 적절하다. 사람들은 맛있는 치즈로 만든 음식을 많이 먹을 수 있다.

04 (1) between A and B: A와 B 사이에 (2) How do I get to+장소?: ~에 어떻게 가나요? (3) have[has] to+동사원형: ~해야 한다 / by this weekend: 이번 주말까지

05 (1) '점점 ~해지다'는 의미로 'get+형용사'를 사용한다. be동사 뒤의 get은 현재분사 getting이 맞다. (2) '~할 예정이다'는 의미로 'be going to+동사원형'을 사용한다. (3) '~해야 한다'는 의미로 'have to+동사원형'을 사용하고, 시제가 과거이면 had to를 사용한다.

06 • 곡선이거나 구부러지지 않은 선이나 방향으로 • 중요한 문화적, 역사적, 과학적인 물건들이 보관되어 있는 건물

교과서
Conversation

핵심 Check   p.64~65

1 show[tell] me the way

2 tell, to / turn, on

3 How, get to

4 ④

교과서 대화문 익히기

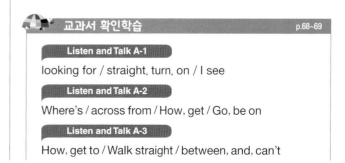

Check(√) True or False   p.66

1 T   2 T   3 T   4 F

교과서 확인학습   p.68~69

Listen and Talk A-1

looking for / straight, turn, on / I see

Listen and Talk A-2

Where's / across from / How, get / Go, be on

Listen and Talk A-3

How, get to / Walk straight / between, and, can't

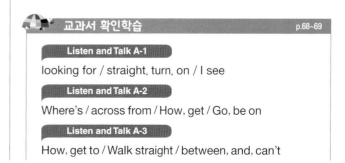

Where / on / How, get / and, next to

Listen and Talk B

Where / on, across from / How do I / Go straight

Listen and Talk C

looking for / look at / get to / straight, across from / going / where / near

Review 1

How, get / turn / sounds easy

Review 2

on, next to

to+장소'를 사용한다. 일반동사 의문문이므로 조동사 do를 의문사 뒤에 쓴다.

11 장소의 위치를 말해주고 마지막으로 '찾기 쉬울 거예요', 또는 '꼭 찾을 거예요'의 의미를 가지는 말이 적절하다. ①번은 안내받은 사람이 할 말로 적절하다.

12 ④번은 '공항에 어떻게 가나요?'라는 질문으로 '너는 너무 늦게 도착했어.'라는 답은 어색하다.

13 ~에 도착하다'는 의미로 동사 get을 사용한다.

14 ~가 하나 있다'는 'there is+단수명사', '~ 옆에'는 전치사구 next to를 이용한다.

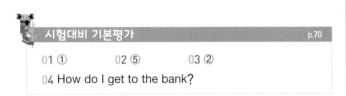

시험대비 기본평가   p.70

01 ①   02 ⑤   03 ②

04 How do I get to the bank?

01 How can I get to ~?는 길을 물을 때 사용하는 표현이다.

02 먼저 (E) 서점이 어디 있는지 묻고, (D) 우체국 맞은편에 있다는 답을 하고, (B) 서점에 어떻게 가는지 묻는다. 그 다음 (A) 길을 안내하는 표현이 나오고 마지막으로 (C) 감사하다는 표현이 적절하다.

03 길을 묻는 질문에 길을 안내하는 표현인 ②가 적절하다.

04 길 묻는 표현으로 'How do I get to + 장소?'가 적절하다.

시험대비 실력평가   p.71~72

01 ③   02 It is next to the bank.   03 ②

04 ④   05 ⑤   06 ②

07 across from   08 ④

09 looking for, look at   10 How do I get to the police station?   11 ②, ⑤   12 ④

13 ③   14 There's one next to the flower shop.

01 B의 대답으로 보아 빈칸에는 길을 물어보는 표현이 적절하다.

03 제시된 대답은 길을 안내하는 표현이므로 길을 물어보는 표현으로 적절한 것은 'How can I get to+장소?' 형태의 ②번이다.

04 길을 묻는 표현이 아닌 것은 ④번으로 '우리 역사박물관에 갈까?'라는 표현이다.

05 도로 상에서 '~에 있는'의 의미로 전치사 on을 사용한다.

06 대화의 흐름상 학교를 어떻게 가는지 묻는 표현이 와야 한다.

08 길을 물어보는 (C)가 오고 길을 안내하는 (A) 다음으로 감사 인사를 하는 (B)가 적절하다.

09 A: 'Green Park를 찾고 있다'는 표현으로 look for를 사용하고, B: '지도를 보세요'의 뜻으로 look at이 적절하다.

10 의문사 how로 문장을 시작하고, '~에 도착하다'는 의미로 'get

서술형 시험대비   p.73

01 Go straight one block and turn right. It'll be on your left.

02 (1) across from   (2) between, and   (3) next to

03 역사 박물관을 찾고 있다.

04 (A) How do I get to the police station?
    (B) It'll be on your right
    (C) It's between the bakery and the school.

05 looking for, two blocks, left, right

01 서점은 출발점에서 한 블록 직진해서 오른쪽으로 돌면 왼쪽 편에 있다.

02 (1) 은행은 가게 맞은편(across from)에 있다. (2) 병원은 경찰서와(and) 박물관 사이에(between) 있다. (3) 극장은 은행 옆에(next to) 있다.

교과서

Grammar

핵심 Check   p.74~75

1 must

2 has   (2) had

3 (1) to win   (2) to find   (3) learn

4 He went to the shop to buy some apples.

시험대비 기본평가   p.76

01 (1) have to → has to   (2) getting → to get
    (3) have to → had to   (4) took → to take

02 (1) had to take   (2) didn't have to finish
    (3) to live   (4) to be   (5) had to do, to take

03 ①

01 (1) have to는 주어가 3인칭 단수 현재일 때 has to가 된다. (2) '~하기 위하여'라는 뜻의 to부정사의 부사적 용법이 적절하다. (3) have to는 과거 시제일 때 had to가 된다. (4) 접속사 없이 동사가 두 개 나올 수 없으므로 took을 '~하기 위하여'라는 뜻의 to부정사의 부사적 용법으로 고치는 것이 적절하다.

02 (1) have to는 과거 시제일 때 had to가 된다. (2) have to의 부정은 do[does] not have to로 '~할 필요가 없다'는 뜻이다. (3), (4) '~하기 위하여'라는 뜻의 to부정사의 부사적 용법이 적절하다. (5) '~하기 위하여'라는 부사적 용법을 이용하고 과거시제이므로 had to를 쓴다.

03 ② Does Mina have to water the plant? ③ Sonya must walk the dog. ④ Cathy didn't have to wash the dishes yesterday. ⑤ She must read the essay. 또는 She has to read the essay.

시험대비 실력평가   p.77~79

01 ④   02 ⑤   03 ②   04 ③
05 ①   06 ③
07 (1) have to → has to   (2) Are → Do
    (3) haven't to → don't have to   (4) have to → had to
08 (1) to live, to eat   (2) to find   (3) to study
    (4) to celebrate
09 ②   10 ④   11 ①   12 ⑤
13 (1) has to solve   (2) don't have to   14 ②, ④
15 to buy a skirt   16 ①, ④
17 doesn't have to finish
18 (1) Bob got up early to catch the first bus.
    (2) Joe was glad to meet her at the party.
19 ②

01 have to의 부정은 'do/does/did not+have to'이고, 의문문은 'do/does/did+주어+have to'이다. 주어가 3인칭 단수 현재일 경우에는 has to를 쓴다.

02 to부정사에는 동사원형이 와야 한다.

03 ② 과거가 아니라 현재의 일이므로 'I have to return it today.'가 적절하다.

04 ③번은 목적격보어로 쓰인 명사적 용법이고, 나머지는 모두 부사적 용법(목적)이다.

05 don't have to: ~하지 않아도 된다, ~할 필요가 없다

06 부사적 용법의 목적(~하기 위하여)에 가장 어울리는 것은 ③번이다.

07 have to는 (1) 주어가 3인칭 단수 현재일 경우에는 has to로, (2) 의문문은 'do/does/did+주어+have to' (3) 부정문은 'do/does/did not+have to' (4) 과거는 had to로 쓴다.

08 모두 to부정사의 부사적 용법의 목적(~하기 위하여)으로 쓰인 것이다.

09 ② at that time이 있으므로 과거형 had to로 썼다.

10 ④번은 부사적 용법의 '원인'이고 나머지는 '목적'이다.

11 <보기>와 ①번은 부사적 용법의 '목적'이다. ② 형용사적 용법 ③ 명사적 용법(주어) ④ 명사적 용법(목적어) ⑤ 부사적 용법의 '결과'

12 부사적 용법의 '목적'으로 쓰는 것이 적절하다.

13 have to는 (1) 주어가 3인칭 단수 현재일 때 has to로, (2) need not은 don't have to로 쓴다.

14 ①에는 at, ③에는 of, ⑤에는 for, ②와 ④에는 to가 적절하다. 전치사 뒤에는 명사나 동명사를 쓰고, to부정사 뒤에는 동사원형을 쓴다.

15 두 번째 문장이 첫 번째 문장의 목적을 나타내므로, 동사 buy를 to부정사로 바꾸어 부사적 용법의 '목적'으로 쓴다.

16 Do I have to ~?로 물었으므로 Yes[No], you do[don't]. 또는 Yes[No], you have to[don't have to].로 대답해야 한다.

17 have to의 부정은 'do/does/did not+have to'로 쓴다.

18 (1)은 to부정사의 부사적 용법으로 '목적'을, (2)는 '(감정의) 원인'을 나타낸다.

19 ②는 명사적 용법이고 나머지는 모두 부사적 용법이다. ①, ④ 목적 ③ 결과 ⑤ (감정의) 원인

서술형 시험대비   p.80~81

01 have to 또는 should

02 (1) Amy was pleased to get A⁺ on the math test.
    (2) Nicole went to France to learn French.
    (3) I study science very hard to be an animal doctor.

03 |모범답안| I don't have to get up early tomorrow. 등 don't have to를 이용해서 어법에 맞게 쓰면 정답임.

04 (1) in order to   (2) so as so   (3) in order that, can

05 (1) Susan didn't have to clean her house yesterday.
    (2) Nick and Dick have to do some more exercise to lose weight.
    (3) Does she have to go see a doctor?

06 (1) to give   (2) to get   (3) to take

07 (1) need to   (2) need not

08 (1) I went to Sophie's house to study with her.
    (2) Amy went to the theater to watch the movie, Avatar.
    (3) Her grandmother lived to be 100.

09 (1) 너는 회의에 참석해서는 안 된다.
    (2) 너는 회의에 참석할 필요가 없다.
    must not은 '~해서는 안 된다'는 금지를 나타내고, don't have to는 '~할 필요가 없다'는 뜻을 나타낸다.

10 (1) to buy   (2) not to be late   (3) to have[eat]

11 (1) You don't have to be rich to help people in need.

(2) Linda went to the shopping mall to meet her friends.

(3) How long does Eddie have to be in hospital?

(4) Abigail had to use the computer to do her homework.

12 The goats in the show don't have to be big, but they have to be healthy. They have to produce a lot of milk to win a prize.

01 의무를 나타내는 must는 have to나 should로 대신할 수 있다.

02 (1)은 부사적 용법의 '(감정의) 원인'을, (2)와 (3)은 '목적'을 나타내는 to부정사를 쓴다.

03 don't have to: ~하지 않아도 된다

04 부사적 용법의 '목적'을 나타내는 to부정사는 (1) 'in order to 부정사', (2) 'so as to부정사', (3) 'in order that 주어+can ~' 으로 바꿔 쓸 수 있다.

05 (1) 과거이므로 didn't have to로 써야 한다. (2) 주어가 3인칭 복수이므로 have to로 써야 하며 to부정사의 부사적 용법의 '목적'이 적절하다. (3) have/has/had to의 의문문은 'do/does/did+주어+have to'이다.

06 to부정사의 부사적 용법의 '목적'을 이용한다.

07 don't have to = don't need to = need not

08 부정사의 부사적 용법 중에서 (1)과 (2)는 '목적', (3)은 '결과' 용법이다.

10 부정사의 부사적 용법의 '목적'을 이용한다. 또한 부정사의 부정은 not을 to부정사 앞에 붙인다는 것에 유의한다.

11 (1) don't have to: ~하지 않아도 된다, ~할 필요가 없다 (2) 부정사의 부사적 용법의 '목적'을 이용한다. (3) have/has/had to의 의문문은 'do/does/did+주어+have to'이다. (4) 부사적 용법의 '목적'을 이용하고 have to의 과거는 'had to'이다.

12 주어가 3인칭 복수 현재일 경우 have to의 부정은 'do not+have to'이고 had to는 과거일 경우에 쓴다. to부정사는 'to+동사원형'의 형태로 여기서는 부정사의 부사적 용법의 '목적'으로 쓰는 것이 적절하다.

교과서
Reading

확인문제   p.82

1 T   2 F   3 F   4 T   5 T   6 F   7 T   8 F

확인문제   p.83

1 F   2 T   3 F   4 T

교과서 확인학습 A   p.84~85

01 at   02 I'm   03 live in
04 are at   05 is over, the biggest fair
06 show, around   07 Follow   08 Look at
09 a goat show   10 entered it
11 don't have to be, have to be   12 to win a prize
13 took good care of   14 won, third prize
15 proud of   16 fair food   17 are eating
18 Tex-Mex food 19 a combination of food
20 is getting red   21 are eating   22 taste great
23 move on to   24 tradition
25 In the past, expensive
26 had to collect, sew   27 a quilting bee
28 work on, for over six months   29 colorful, unique
30 The most exciting   31 Ferris wheel
32 on the top   33 scared, amazing
34 living, going   35 some day

교과서 확인학습 B   p.86~87

1 Fun at the State Fair of Texas!
2 Hi, I'm Eddie Parker.
3 I live in Dallas, Texas.
4 Now, my family and I are at the State Fair of Texas.
5 The fair is over 130 years old, and it's the biggest fair in the USA.
6 I'll show you around.
7 Follow me!
8 Look at the goats here!
9 This is a goat show.
10 My younger brother, Steve, entered it.
11 The goats in the show don't have to be big, but they have to be healthy.
12 They have to produce a lot of milk to win a prize.
13 Steve took good care of his goat, Bonnie.
14 Wow! Steve and Bonnie won a white ribbon, third prize!
15 I'm so proud of them!
16 Now it's lunch time, so we're eating fair food.
17 Mom and Dad are eating nachos and fajitas.
18 They are Tex-Mex food.

19 Tex-Mex food is a combination of food from Texas and Mexico.

20 Dad's face is getting red because his fajita is too spicy.

21 Steve and I are eating corn dogs.

22 They taste great.

23 Let's move on to the quilt contest.

24 Quilting has a long tradition.

25 In the past, fabric was expensive.

26 To make a blanket, people had to collect small pieces of fabric and sew them together.

27 Grandma and her friends had a quilting bee every week.

28 They had to work on the quilt for the contest for over six months.

29 Look! It's very colorful and unique.

30 The most exciting part of the day is riding the Texas Star.

31 It's a tall Ferris wheel.

32 Wow! Steve and I are now on the top.

33 I'm scared, but the view is amazing!

34 I love living in Texas and going to the fair.

35 Come to the fair some day!

시험대비 실력평가

p.88~93

01 the State Fair of Texas
02 (A) more than 또는 over   (B) bigger   03 ④
04 ②   05 ⑤
06 the goat show → Steve and Bonnie   07 ④
08 (A) because   (B) are   (C) great   09 ②
10 ⑤   11 small pieces of fabric   12 ⑤
13 ⑤   14 ①, ④   15 is filled with
16 ⓐ Tongin Market   ⓑ oil Tteokbokki
    ⓒ many traditional Korean houses
17 ① Tongin Market   ② traditional Korean houses
18 ②, ⑤   19 (A) entered   (B) don't   (C) to produce
20 ②, ③   21 ②
22 (A) fair (B) They are (C) combination
23 it → them   24 ②
25 (A) sewed   (B) expensive   26 ①
27 ④   28 (A) are   (B) it's   (C) show
29 ②   30 It's the State Fair of Texas.
31 The goats in the show don't have to be big, but they have to be healthy.
32 ①   33 as → so   34 nachos and fajitas

35 Dad's face is getting red because his fajita is too spicy.

36 short → long

37 people had to collect small pieces of fabric and sew them together

38 (A) a quilting bee   (B) unique

1 '텍사스의 주 품평회'를 가리킨다.

2 (A) over: ~ 이상(= more than) (B) '비교급 than any other 단수명사'는 최상급의 뜻을 가진다.

3 ④ 텍사스 주 품평회를 구경시켜 주겠다고 하면서 '따라와'라고 했기 때문에, 위 글 뒤에는 '텍사스 주 품평회를 소개하는 글'이 이어지는 것이 가장 적절하다.

4 ② '쇼에 참가하기 위해서 염소가 클 필요는 없다.'고 했다.

5 ⑤ 이 글은 '염소 쇼를 소개하기' 위한 글이다. ① introduce: 소개하다, ② advertise: 광고하다, ③ describe: 묘사하다, ④ discuss: 상의[의논/논의]하다

6 Eddie가 자랑스러워하는 것은 'Steve와 Bonnie'이다.

7 ① 그것(앞에 이미 언급되었거나 현재 이야기되고 있는 사물·동물을 가리킴), ② 가주어, ③ It is ~ that의 강조 구문으로 문장의 주어·목적어·부사어구를 강조함. ④ 비인칭 주어(시간·날짜·거리·날씨 등에 대해 말할 때 사용), ⑤ 가목적어

8 (A) 뒤에 주어와 동사가 이어지므로 because가 적절하다. because of 뒤에는 구가 온다. (B) Steve and I가 주어이므로 are가 적절하다. (C) 감각동사 taste 뒤에 형용사보어가 와야 하므로 great가 적절하다.

9 ②번 다음 문장의 내용에 주목한다. 담요를 만들기 위해 작은 천 조각들을 모아 꿰매 붙여야 했다는 내용이므로, 그 앞에 '천이 비쌌다'는 말이 들어가는 것이 알맞다. 그러므로 ②번이 적절하다.

10 ⑤ 할머니와 그녀의 친구들이 퀼트 대회에서 우승했는지는 대답할 수 없다. ① No, it wasn't. ② They had to collect small pieces of fabric. ③ They had it every week. ④ They had to work for over six months.

11 '작은 천 조각들'을 가리킨다.

12 보통 감정을 나타내는 동사가 사람을 수식할 때는 현재분사로, 사물을 수식할 때는 과거분사로 쓴다. ⓐ는 사물을 수식하므로 exciting, ⓒ는 사람을 수식하므로 scared, ⓓ는 사물을 수식하므로 amazing, ⓑ Its는 소유격이므로 It is의 줄임말인 It's로 고쳐야 한다. ⓔ love는 목적어로 to부정사와 동명사 둘 다 쓸 수 있지만, 첫 번째 목적어가 동명사이므로 두 번째 목적어도 동명사로 일치시켜야 한다.

13 ⑤ 텍사스에 사는 것과 축제에 가는 것을 사랑한다고 말하면서 언젠가 축제에 오라고 말하고 있기 때문에 '만족한' 심경임을 알 수 있다. ① 지루한, ② 두려워하는, ③ 불안해[초조해/두려워]하는, ④ 실망한

15

14 (A)와 ②, ③, ⑤는 동명사이고 나머지는 현재분사이다. ① 과 거진행형에 쓰인 현재분사, ② 주어로 쓰인 동명사, ③ 목적어로 쓰인 동명사, ④ 목적격보어로 쓰인 현재분사, ⑤ 전치사의 목적어로 쓰인 동명사

15 be full of= be filled with: ~로 가득 차 있다

16 ⓐ 통인시장, ⓑ 기름 떡볶이, ⓒ 많은 한국의 전통 가옥을 가리킨다.

17 ① '통인시장'에서 기름 떡볶이를 즐길 수 있다. ② 많은 '한국의 전통 가옥'을 보기 위해 걸어다닐 수 있다.

18 (B)와 ①, ③, ④는 부사적 용법(목적)이다. ② 명사적 용법(목적어), ⑤ 형용사적 용법

19 (A) 염소 쇼에 '참가했다'고 해야 하므로 entered가 적절하다. enter into: (논의·처리 등을) 시작하다, (B) The goats가 주어이므로 don't가 적절하다. (C) 많은 우유를 '생산해야 한다'고 해야 하므로 to produce가 적절하다. have to 동사원형: ~해야 한다

20 many와 a number of는 수가 많은 것을 나타내므로, 셀 수 없는 명사 milk와 같이 쓸 수 없다. a lot of = lots of = plenty of: (수나 양이) 많은

21 ② 위 글은 Eddie의 가족이 품평회 음식으로 'Tex-Mex food'를 즐기고 있는 광경에 대해 설명하고 있는 글이므로, 제목으로는 ②번 'Tex-Mex 음식을 즐기세요'가 적절하다.

22 (A) '품평회' 음식이라고 해야 하므로 fair가 적절하다. fare: 요금, (B) nachos and fajitas를 가리키므로 They are가 적절하다. (C) Tex-Mex 음식은 텍사스와 멕시코 음식이 '혼합된 것'이라고 해야 하므로 combination이 적절하다. communication: 의사소통

23 'small pieces of fabric'을 가리키므로 them으로 고쳐야 한다.

24 ③번의 They는 ①번의 Grandma and her friends를 가리키며, 그 사이의 '미국에는 많은 퀼트 모임들이 있다'라는 ②번 문장은 전체 글의 흐름에서 벗어난다.

25 과거에는 천이 '비쌌기' 때문에 사람들은 담요를 만들기 위해 작은 천 조각들을 모아서 '꿰매 붙였다.' sew-sewedsewn[sewed]: 바느질하다

26 ① (C)에서 (A)에서 말한 Tex-Mex food에 대한 설명이 이어지므로 (A) 다음에 (C)가 이어지고, 아빠가 Tex-Mex food인 fajita를 드시고 얼굴이 빨개지는 내용인 (B)가 그 다음에 이어지는 것이 적당하므로 (C) 다음에 (B)가 와야 한다. 그러므로 (A)-(C)(B)의 순서가 적절하다.

27 ④ (A)의 They가 (C)의 The goats를 가리키므로 (C) 다음에 (A)가 이어지고 (A)에서 Bonnie를 언급한 다음에 (B)에서 Steve and Bonnie라고 할 수 있으므로 (A) 다음에 (B)가 와야 한다. 그러므로 (C)-(A)-(B)의 순서가 적절하다.

28 (A) 주어가 my family and I이므로 'are'가 적절하다. (B) '주어+동사'가 와야 하므로 'it's'가 적절하다. its는 it의 소유격이다. (C)

'텍사스 주 품평회를 둘러보도록 안내하겠다.'고 해야 하므로 show가 적절하다. show somebody around/round (something): ~에게 (~을) 둘러보도록 안내하다[구경시켜 주다]

29 ② 품평회 ① 공정한 ③ 금발의 ④ (날씨가) 맑은 ⑤ fair-sized 제법 큰

30 미국에서 가장 큰 품평회는 '텍사스 주 품평회'이다.

31 don't have to: ~할 필요가 없다

32 ⓑ와 ①은 부사적 용법(목적), ② 부사적 용법(원인), ③ 부사적 용법(결과), ④ 부사적 용법(판단의 근거), ⑤ 부사적 용법(조건)

33 '점심시간이라서' 품평회 음식을 먹고 있다고 해야 하기 때문에, as를 so로 고쳐야 한다.

34 '나초'와 '파히타'를 가리킨다.

35 spicy: 양념 맛이 강한

36 '과거에' 천이 비싸서 작은 천 조각들을 모아 그것들을 함께 꿰매어 담요 하나를 만든 내용이 이어지므로, 퀼트하기는 '오랜' 전통을 가지고 있다고 하는 것이 문맥상 알맞다. 그러므로 short를 long으로 고치는 것이 적절하다.

37 sew를 보충하면 된다.

서술형 시험대비
p.94~95

01 (A) need   (B) must

02 took good care of

03 Steve and Bonnie

04 fair

05 Tex-Mex food is a combination of food from Texas and Mexico

06 Tex-Mex food

07 in order that, could

08 They had to work on the quilt for the contest for over six months.

09 colorful

10 ⓐ have to → don't have to
   ⓑ don't have to → have to

11 Steve took good care of his goat, Bonnie.

12 It was a white ribbon.

01 비록 염소 쇼에 출전하는 염소들이 클 '필요는 없지만', 그들은 약해서는 '안 된다.' unhealthy: 건강하지 못한, 건강하지 않아 보이는, 병든 것 같은

02 Steve는 그의 염소 Bonnie를 잘 돌봤다.(Steve took good care of his goat, Bonnie. = Steve looked after his goat, Bonnie, well.)

03 them은 인칭대명사로 앞에 나온 복수명사를 가리킨다.

04 상품과 동물들의 전시, 오락거리, 게임들 그리고 대회들이 있는

행사, fair: 품평회, 박람회

05 combination을 보충하면 된다.

06 Eddie의 가족은 점심으로 nachos, fajitas와 같은 'Tex-Mex' 음식을 먹고 있다.

07 could 대신에 might을 써도 된다. in order to 동사원형 = so as to 동사원형 = (in order) that ~ may[can] = (so) that ~ may[can]

08 for over six months: 6개월 이상

09 color의 형용사형이 온다.

10 염소 쇼에 출전하는 염소들이 클 필요는 없지만, 그들은 건강해야만 한다.

11 good을 보충하면 된다. 동격 사이에 콤마를 찍어야 한다.

12 3등상은 '흰색 리본'이었다.

01 tasty   02 ⑤   03 ④   04 ①
05 ③   06 ④   07 ④   08 ②
09 The African Music Concert   10 ⑤
11 ③   12 ⑤   13 ①   14 ⑤
15 (1) doesn't have to   (2) had to   (3) Does   16 ⑤
17 (1) You don't have to bring your lunch to the picnic.
    (2) Does Melanie have to make a speech in front of other students?
18 ③   19 ②   20 have to put   21 ②
22 has to → must
23 (A) healthy   (B) a lot of   (C) third
24 ③   25 ④   26 ②
27 sweet → spicy 혹은 hot   28 corn dogs   29 ⑤
30 ②   31 cloth
32 They had it every week.

01 유의어 관계이다. 놀라운 : 맛있는

02 '꼭 찾을 수 있을 거예요.'라는 의미로 You can't miss it.을 사용한다.

03 많은 비용이 드는

04 둘 또는 그 이상의 다른 것들이 함께 있거나 조립되는 것

05 '~에 도착하다'라는 의미로 'get to'를 사용한다. '~의 맞은 편에'라는 의미로 'across from'이 적절하다.

06 ④ tradition: 전통

07 길을 안내해 준 다음 대답으로 적절한 말로 '쉽군요(That sounds easy). 감사합니다.'가 적절하다.

08 ②번 뒤에 길을 안내하는 대답이 나오므로 '공원에 어떻게 가나요?'라는 말이 들어갈 위치로 ②가 적절하다.

09 '그것은 오후 4시에 시작할 예정이다'라고 했으므로 앞에 나온 콘서트를 가리킨다는 것을 알 수 있다.

10 Jenny가 Ben과 함께 콘서트를 보러 간다는 내용은 대화에서 언급되어 있지 않다.

11 ③ A: '우체국에 어떻게 가나요?'라는 물음에 B: '그것은 당신 오른쪽에 있을 겁니다'라는 대답은 어색하다. ④ A: '경찰서에 어떻게 가나요?' B: '미안하지만 저도 여기가 처음입니다.'는 표현으로 적절하다.

12 여자가 소녀에게 지도를 주기를 원한다는 내용은 대화에 언급되어 있지 않다.

13 ① Kake has to walk the dog.

14 부사적 용법의 '원인'을 이용하여 쓸 수 있다.

15 (1) have to의 부정은 'do/does/did not+have to'이다. (2) 과거(last week)가 나왔으므로 had to로 써야 한다. (3) have to의 의문문은 'do/does/did+주어+have to'이다.

16 ① 부사적 용법의 '목적' ② '원인' ③ '이유' ④ '결과' ⑤ 형용사적 용법

17 (1) have to의 부정은 'do/does/did not+have to'이다. (2) have to의 의문문은 'do/does/did+주어+have to'이다.

18 <보기>와 ③번은 부사적 용법의 '목적'이다. ① 명사적 용법 (목적어) ② 형용사적 용법 ④ 부사적 용법의 '결과' ⑤ 명사적 용법 (보어)

19 don't need to = don't have to = need not

20 종이와 유리가 분리된 상자에 담겨 있는 그림이므로 have to를 이용한다.

21 ① Cathy visited the library to borrow some books. ③ Minsu goes to the park to play badminton with his friend. ④ Emma got up early to catch the first train. ⑤ I use my smartphone to make a call.

22 have[has] to가 '의무'의 뜻으로 쓰일 때는 must로 바꿔 쓸 수 있지만 have to가 '추측'의 의미로는 쓰일 수 없다.

23 (A) be동사의 보어이므로 형용사 healthy가 적절하다. health: (명사) 건강, (B) 상을 타기 위해서는 '많은' 우유를 생산해야 한다고 해야 하므로 a lot of가 적절하다. a little: 약간의, (C) '3등상'이라고 해야 하므로 third가 적절하다. win (the) third prize: 3등상을 타다

24 Steve와 Bonnie가 3등상을 타서 그들을 '자랑스러워한다.'고 하는 것이 적절하다. ① 부끄러운, ② 불안해[초조해/ 두려워] 하는, ④ 불안해하는, 염려하는, ⑤ 무서워하는, 겁먹은

25 ④ Steve가 염소 쇼에 몇 번 참가했는지는 대답할 수 없다. ① He is at a goat show. ② No, they don't. ③ Yes, they do. ⑤ Yes, he did.

26 ② Eddie의 '엄마와 아빠'가 나초와 파히타를 드시고 계신다.

27 파히타의 '양념 맛이 너무 강해서' 혹은 '너무 매워서' 아빠의 얼굴이 빨개지고 있다고 하는 것이 적절하다. spicy: 양념 맛이 강

한, hot: 매운, 얼얼한

28 '콘도그'를 가리킨다.

29 ⑤ 축제의, 축제 기분의, 흥겨운, ① 지루한, ② 침착한, 차분한, ③ 심각한, ④ 실망스러운

30 move on to: ~로 옮기다[이동하다], work on: ~에 노력을 들이다, for the contest: 콘테스트를 위하여, for over six months: 6개월 이상 동안

31 fabric = cloth: 직물, 천

32 할머니와 친구들은 '매주' 퀼트를 만드는 모임을 가졌다.

단원별 예상문제   p.102~105

01 ④

02 (A) I'm looking for Green Park.
  (B) where is the stage?

03 Go straight two blocks and turn left.

04 ④   05 ⓐ tasty   ⓑ traditional

06 healthy   07 ③

08 How do I get there?   09 ③

10 한 블록 곧장 걸어가서 오른쪽으로 돌면 오른쪽에서 서점을 찾을 수 있다.

11 ③   12 ②   13 ④

14 (1) Vivian didn't need to stand Mike's rudeness.
  (2) What does Steve have to give up?

15 to send   16 ③   17 ①

18 spice → spicy   19 ③   20 ④

21 need not   22 (A) younger brother (B) third

23 cheap → expensive   24 ①

25 (A) had to (B) sew (C) for   26 ④

01 음식이 너무 매워서(spicy) 그의 얼굴이 붉어지고 있다. / 이 주는 버터로 유명하다(famous).

02 (A)는 가고지 히는 구체적인 장소를 묻는 말이 와야 한다.
  (B)는 B의 대답으로 보아 장소를 묻는 말이 와야 한다.

03 '~해라'는 명령문 형태로 동사 go로 문장을 시작하고 두 블록은 복수형이므로 two blocks가 적절하다. 왼쪽으로 돌다는 동사 turn을 사용한다.

04 ④는 이름을 말해달라는 뜻으로, 길을 물어볼 때 사용하는 표현으로 적절하지 않다.

05 ⓐ와 ⓑ는 뒤의 명사를 꾸며주는 형용사 형태가 적절하다.

06 유명한 : 알려지지 않은 = 아픈 : 건강한

07 옷을 만들거나 수선하기 위해 실과 바늘을 사용하다

08 there는 부사이기 때문에 전치사 to를 사용하지 않는다.

09 (B)에는 학교에 가는 길을 안내하는 표현이 와야 한다.
  ③번은 그것은 3층에 있다는 말로 어색하다.

11 ③번은 부사적 용법으로 조건을 나타내고 있다. 나머지는 다 목적을 나타낸다.

12 Does Lilian have to hurry up?

13 부사적 용법의 '목적'은 'in order[so as] to+동사원형'이나 'so[in order] that+주어+can+동사원형'으로 바꿔 쓸 수 있다.

14 (1) don't have to = don't need to = need not
  (2) 의문사+does+주어+have to ~의 어순이다.

15 to부정사의 부사적 용법의 '목적'을 이용한다.

16 ④번의 They는 ②번의 nachos and fajitas를 가리키며, 그 사이의 '몇몇 Tex-Mex 음식은 매우 맵다'는 ③번 문장은 전체 글의 흐름에서 벗어난다.

17 '출처·기원'을 나타내는 from이 적절하다.

18 get 다음에 형용사 보어를 써야 한다. spicy(형용사): 양념 맛이 강한, spice(명사): 양념, 향신료

19 ③ 맛이 ~하다, ~ 한 맛이 나다, 감각동사 taste 뒤에 형용사 보어를 쓴다. ① (음식을) 맛보다, 시식하다, ② (한 입) 먹다, 마시다, ④ 맛을 느끼다, ⑤ 경험하다, 맛보다, 겪다 (=experience)

20 주어진 문장의 They에 주목한다. ④번 앞 문장의 The goats를 받고 있으므로 ④번이 적절하다.

21 don't have to = need not: ~할 필요가 없다

22 Steve는 Eddie의 '남동생'이고 염소 쇼에 참가했다. 그는 자신의 염소인 Bonnie를 잘 돌봤고 그들은 '3등상'을 탔다.

23 담요를 만들기 위해 작은 천 조각들을 모아서 꿰매 붙여야 했으므로 expensive로 고쳐야 한다.

24 ①번은 명사적 용법(주어)이고, ⓑ와 나머지는 다 부사적 용법(목적)이다.

25 (A) 과거의 일이므로 had to가 적절하다.
  (B) collect와 병렬구문을 이루도록 sew를 쓰는 것이 적절하다.
  (C) for+ 숫자, during+기간을 나타내는 명사

26 ④ bee: 사람들이 함께 모여서 공동의 일이나 놀이를 하는 모임, ② 벌레, ③ 박쥐, ⑤ 나비

서술형 실전문제   p.106~107

01 How do[can] I get / straight two, turn left, on, right / across from, miss

02 I'm looking for the zoo. How do[can] I get there?

03 (1) must not (2) don't have to

04 (1) I took the subway to go to school.
  (2) Anne went to the park to walk her dog.

05 (1) Hugh doesn't have to clean his room today.
  (2) Did Bridget have to put off the meeting yesterday?

06 (1) to see (2) to try

07 combination

08 becoming[growing]

09 because of
10 ① 통인 시장에 가서 기름 떡볶이를 먹는 것
　　② 많은 한국의 전통 가옥을 보기 위해 주변을 걷는 것
11 there / There　　　　12 to[and]

02　B가 한 블록 곧장 가서 오른쪽으로 돌면 당신의 왼쪽에 그것을 볼 것이라고 했으므로 A가 가고자 하는 곳은 동물원이다. look for를 이용하여 동물원을 찾고 있다고 말한 다음, 그곳에 어떻게 가는지 물어본다.

03　(1) must not은 '금지'의 의미이다. (2) don't have to는 '~할 필요가 없다'라는 의미이다.

04　to부정사의 부사적 용법의 '목적'을 이용한다

05　have to의 부정은 'do/does/did not+have to'이고, 의문문은 'do/does/did+주어+have to'이다.

06　to부정사의 부사적 용법의 '목적'을 이용한다.

07　combination: 조합, 혼합, mixture: 혼합

08　get, become, grow + 형용사 = ~해지다

09　because of + 명사구, 파히타가 너무 매워서 아빠의 얼굴이 빨개지고 있다.

10　통인 시장에서 기름 떡볶이를 먹을 수 있고, 많은 한국의 전통 가옥을 보기 위해 주변을 걸을 수 있다고 했다.

11　ⓑ 장소부사 there(to Tongin Market), ⓒ 유도부사 There are: ~이 있다

12　Come visit = Come to visit = Come and visit

창의사고력 서술형 문제 p.108

|모범답안|

01 (1) How do I get to the hospital?
　(2) Could you show me the way to the school?
　(3) I am looking for the tourist information center.
　(4) Do you know how to get there?

02 ⓐ (1) I study hard to get a good grade.
　　(2) I want to learn English to achieve my dream.
　ⓑ (1) I have to put out the trash every Saturday.
　　　/ I have to clean my room every day.
　　(2) I don't have to do the dishes every day. / I don't have to take care of my little brother every day.

03 the Beach Festival,
　August 11th – 12th / 10:00 – 20:00,
　Haeundae Beach,
　Why Not Come to the Beach Festival?

단원별 모의고사 p.109~112

01 scared　　02 ③　　03 ①
04 two blocks, left, right　　05 ③
06 one block, turn left, on your right / next to
07 C, the City Hall　　08 B, the Star Mall
09 ⑤　　10 ②
11 It's across from the train station.
12 (C)–(A)–(B)
13 (1) Mom entered my room to wake me up.
　(2) I am pleased to hear that everything is going well.
　(3) Violet grew up to be a doctor.
14 Tim doesn't have to go to work this Sunday.
15 ①　　16 ③
17 (1) have → has
　(2) walking → to walk
　(3) read → to read
18 ⓐ a goat show　ⓑ The goats (in the show)
19 ②　　20 ④　　21 ②　　22 ③, ⑤
23 ①　　24 (A) collect　(B) sew　(C) unique
25 ④

1　유의어 관계이다. 매다 : 무서운

2　곡선이거나 구부러지지 않은 선이나 방향으로

3　무언가에 놀라거나 초조해하는

4　Jenny가 찾고 있는 박물관은 두 블록 곧장 가서 왼쪽으로 돌면 오른쪽에 있다.

5　③은 '서점까지 얼마나 걸립니까?'라는 뜻이다.

6　miss: 놓치다, 그리워하다

7　학교에 가는 길을 묻고 있다. 학교는 경찰서와 시청 사이에 있다고 했으므로 C에는 시청이 있다.

8　Star Mall에 가는 길을 묻고 있다. 두 블록 직전해서 왼쪽으로 돌았을 때 오른쪽의 첫 번째 건물이라고 했으므로 B가 스타 몰이다.

9　(A) Green Park에 가는 길을 묻는 표현으로 look for를 이용하는 것이 적절하다. be동사 am이 있으므로 look은 현재분사 looking을 사용한다. (B) '지도를 보세요.'라는 말이므로 look at이 적절하다.

10　B의 대답으로 보아 (C)는 장소를 묻는 표현이 오는 것이 적절하다.

11　'~의 맞은편에'는 across from을 사용한다.

13　부정사의 부사적 용법의 (1) '목적'을 (2) '원인'을 (3) '결과'를 이용한다.

14　have to의 부정은 'do/does/did not+have to'이다.

15　①번은 동사의 목적어로 쓰인 명사적 용법이고 나머지는 부사적 용법이다.

19

16 주어가 3인칭 단수 현재일 때는 doesn't have to로 써야 한다.

17 (1) 주어가 3인칭 단수 현재일 때는 has to로 써야 한다. (2) 부정사의 부사적 용법의 '목적' (3) 부정사의 부사적 용법의 '원인'이 적절하다.

18 ⓐ는 '염소 쇼'를 ⓑ는 '쇼에 참가한 염소들'을 가리킨다.

19 ② 상을 타기 위해서는 많은 우유를 '생산해야 한다'고 하는 것이 적절하다. ① 붓다, 따르다, ⑤ 더하다

20 ④ 염소 쇼의 1등상 이름은 알 수 없다. ① Steve, ② 클 필요는 없지만 건강해야 한다. ③ Bonnie, ⑤ a white ribbon

21 주어진 문장의 They에 주목한다. ②번 앞 문장의 nachos and fajitas를 받고 있으므로 ②번이 적절하다.

22 ⓐ와 ③번은 현재진행형에 쓰인 현재분사이고, ⑤번은 명사를 꾸며주는 현재분사이다. 나머지는 모두 동명사이다. ① 목적어, ② 주어, ④ 보어

23 ① (A)에서 주어진 글의 내용을 계속 설명하고 있으므로 제일 먼저 오고 (B)의 They가 (C)의 Grandma and her friends를 가리키므로 (C) 다음에 (B)가 와야 한다. 그러므로 (A)-(C)-(B)의 순서가 적절하다.

24 (A) '수집해야만' 했다고 해야 하므로 collect가 적절하다. correct: 바로잡다, 정정하다, (B) 작은 천 조각들을 모아 그것들을 함께 '꿰매어' 담요 하나를 만들었다고 해야 하므로 sew가 적절하다. saw: see의 과거, (C) 할머니께서 출품한 퀼트가 색깔이 다채롭고 '독특하다'고 해야 하므로 unique가 적절하다. common: 흔한, 보통의

25 ④ 6개월 이상 동안 퀼트 대회 출품작을 만드셨다.

Ideas for Saving the Earth

시험대비 실력평가   p.116

01 condition   02 ②   03 ⑤   04 ③
05 ④   06 used[second-hand]   07 ①
08 ③

01 둘은 동의어 관계이다. 할인 – 상태

02 get to+장소: ~에 도착하다 / have to+동사원형: ~ 해야 한다

03 nursing home은 '양로원'이다.

04 음악을 만들어 내기 위해 사용되는 물건

05 어떤 예쁜 것을 위에 놓음으로써 물건을 더 매력적으로 보이게 만들다

06 used = second-hand '중고의'

07 동명사 recycling이 뒤에 있고, 글의 의미상 '~와 같은'의 의미를 가지는 전치사 like가 와야 한다. 야구 글러브를 찾고 있다는 의미로 for가 적절하다.

08 trash와 fashion이 결합한 말이다.

서술형 시험대비   p.117

01 (1) interested   (2) kit   (3) instruments   (4) discount
02 (1) hold, 열다, 개최하다   (2) much, 많은
   (3) explain, 설명하다   (4) creative, 창의적인
03 (1) Cut off   (2) sounds like
   (3) throw, away   (4) take
04 (1) musical   (2) meaning
   (3) combination   (4) take, off
05 (t)rash, (c)ombination
06 (1) different   (2) environment   (3) creative   (4) once
   (5) rubber   (6) almost   (7) through   (8) expensive
   decorate, 장식하다, 꾸미다

01 (1) become 뒤에 형용사가 필요하다. '관심 있는'은 interested가 적절하다. (2) sewing kit 바느질 세트(반짇고리) (3) 콘서트에서 악기를 연주할 계획이다. (4) 할인을 받을 수 있나요?

02 (1) 저희 그룹은 트래션 쇼를 하고 싶습니다. (2) 저 동그란 안경은 얼마인가요? (3) 누가 업사이클링의 의미를 설명할 수 있

나요? (4) 너희들의 발상은 정말 창의적이구나.

03 (1) cut off: ~을 자르다 (2) sound like+명사: ~처럼 들리다 (3) throw away: ~을 버리다 (4) 여기서 take는 '선택하다, 사다'는 의미이다.

04 (1) 명사 instruments(악기)와 어울리는 music의 형용사 형태가 적절하다. (2) 나는 여러분들이 업사이클링의 의미를 이해하길 원합니다. mean의 명사형인 meaning이 적절하다. (3) 동사 combine의 명사형 combination이 적절하다. (4) '할인을 받을 수 있나요?'라는 물음에 '1달러 할인해 줄게요.'라는 의미가 적절하므로 '할인하다'라는 take off가 적절하다.

05 (1) trash: 쓰레기 (2) combination: 조합

교과서 Conversation

핵심 Check p.118~119

1 How much 2 price 3 ① 4 ⑤

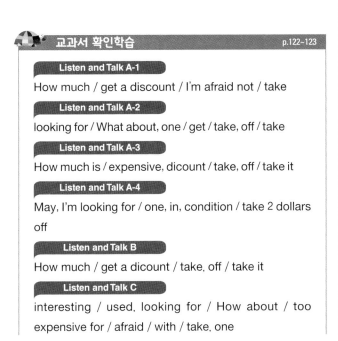

교과서 대화문 익히기

Check(√) True or False p.120

1 F 2 T 3 F 4 T

교과서 확인학습 p.122~123

Listen and Talk A-1
How much / get a discount / I'm afraid not / take

Listen and Talk A-2
looking for / What about, one / get / take, off / take

Listen and Talk A-3
How much is / expensive, dicount / take, off / take it

Listen and Talk A-4
May, I'm looking for / one, in, condition / take 2 dollars off

Listen and Talk B
How much / get a dicount / take, off / take it

Listen and Talk C
interesting / used, looking for / How about / too expensive for / afraid / with / take, one

Review 1
How much / expensive for, How about, one / price, it

Review 2
How much / get / take, off

Review 3
looking for / one, in good condition / get / take, off / take

시험대비 기본평가 p.124

01 looking for 02 ⑤   03 ②   04 get

01 'I'm looking for ~.'는 '나는 ~을 찾고 있다.'라는 뜻으로, 찾고 있는 물건이 무엇인지 말할 때 사용하는 표현이다.

02 밑줄 친 문장은 신발의 가격을 묻는 표현으로 ⑤번 '이 신발의 가격은 얼마인가요?'가 적절하다.

03 B의 마지막 말은 '좋아요'라고 했기 때문에 파란 티셔츠를 구입한다는 말이 오는 것이 가장 적절하다. ①은 '또 다른 셔츠를 보여주세요.'라는 표현으로 처음 본 물건이 마음에 들지 않거나 다른 옷을 보고 싶을 때 사용하는 표현이다. ④의 Here you are.는 물건을 건네줄 때 사용하는 표현으로 '여기 있습니다.'라는 뜻이다.

04 get a discount가 '할인을 받다'라는 뜻이며 '내가 할인을 받을 수 있나요?'라는 표현으로 Can I get a discount?를 사용한다.

시험대비 실력평가 p.125~126

01 ③   02 ⑤   03 ④   04 ②
05 ⑤   06 ④   07 That's expensive for me.
08 backpack 09 ⑤   10 used[second-hand]
11 ②   12 ④

01 B의 대답으로 보아 빈칸에는 둥근 안경의 가격을 묻는 표현이 적절하다. round glasses가 복수명사이므로 복수동사 are가 적절하다.

02 할인해 줄 수 있나요?라는 물음에 대한 답으로 No라고 했기 때문에 '유감스럽지만 안 돼'라는 말이 적절하다.

03 제시된 문장은 가격을 말하는 표현이므로 가격이 얼마인지 묻는 표현이 적절하다. ④번은 '이 책은 할인 중인가요?'라는 뜻이다. on sale은 '할인 중'이라는 의미다.

04 ②번은 '어디서 가방을 살 수 있나요?'라는 표현이고, 나머지는 모두 매장에서 가방을 살 수 있는지 묻는 표현이다.

05 얼마를 할인한다는 의미로 'take+돈+off'를 사용한다.

06 '어서 오세요.'라는 인사말에 (D) 네라고 답하고 신발 가격을 묻는 말이 오고 (A) 신발 가격을 말해주고 (B) 할인 여부를 물어

보는 말이 온다. 마지막으로 (C) 할인을 해주겠다는 말이 오면
된다.

07 주어는 대명사 that이 오고, expensive가 형용사이므로 be동
사가 와야 한다.

08 one은 앞에 나온 명사를 대신하는 부정대명사다.

09 ⑤번의 What are you looking for? 는 사고자 하는 물건이 무
엇인지 물어보는 말이다. look at은 '~ 을 보다'는 의미로 '시계를
보고 있는 중입 니다.'는 어색하다.

10 사용된 결과로 더럽거나 더 이상 좋은 상태에 있지 않은

11 깎아줄 수 있는지 묻는 말에 '일 년 밖에 되지 않아 거의 새 것이
다'라고 했으므로 할인을 해주지 않는다는 표현이 와야 한다.

12 가게 주인은 15달러하는 빨간색 시계를 깎아주지 않아 B는 10
달러하는 파란색 시계를 대신 구입한 것이다.

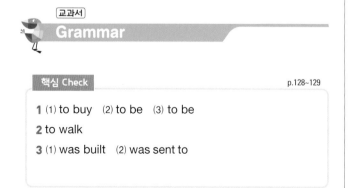

서술형 시험대비
p.127

01 Can I get a discount?

02 She will pay ten dollars.

03 (A) How much is this yellow backpack?
   (B) How[What] about this red one?
   (C) I'll take it.

04 used / How much is it / get a dicount / afraid /
   lage numbers

05 I'll take 3 dollars off.

01 할인을 받는 의미로 get a discount를 사용한다.

02 정상 가격은 12달러인데 남자가 2달러를 할인해 주겠다고 했기
때문에 여자가 지불할 금액은 10달러이다.

03 (A) 가격을 물어볼 때 'How much+동사+주어?' 를 이용한다.
(B) '~은 어때요?'라는 표현은 'How[What] about ~?'을 이
용하고 '빨간색 가방은 어떤가요?'라는 의미이므로 앞에 나온 a
backpack을 대신하는 부정 대명사 one을 이용한다. (C) 물건
을 선택할 때 동사 take를 사용한다.

05 '할인을 하다, 깎아주다'는 표현으로 'take 금액 off'를 사용한다.

교과서
Grammar

핵심 Check
p.128~129

1 (1) to buy   (2) to be   (3) to be
2 to walk
3 (1) was built   (2) was sent to

시험대비 기본평가
p.130

01 (1) cleans → is cleaned   (2) is → was
   (3) sit → to sit   (4) to not play → not to play

02 ⑤

03 were injured / was broken / to be / to exercise

04 (1) to know   (2) was cleaned

01 (1) 바닥이 청소되는 것이므로 수동태가 적절하다. (2) 과거이
므로 was가 적절하다. (3) ask의 목적격보어로 to부정사가 적
절하다. (4) to부정사의 부정형은 'not to+동사원형'으로 쓴다.

02 책이 쓰여지는 것이므로 수동태가 적절하다.

03 (1) 그들이 부상을 입은 것이므로 수동태가 적절하다. (2) 꽃병
이 깨진 것이므로 수동태가 적절하다. (3) want의 목적격보어
로 to부정사가 적절하다. (4) advise의 목적격보어로 to부정사
가 적절하다.

04 (1) want의 목적격보어로 to부정사가 적절하다. (2) 방이 청소
되는 것이므로 수동태가 적절하다.

시험대비 실력평가
p.131~133

01 ③   02 ④   03 (1) to   (2) for   (3) of
04 ⑤   05 ④   06 ①
07 ②   08 ①   09 ⑤   10 ④

11 (1) The Mona Lisa was painted by Leonardo da Vinci.
   (2) The famous player was surprised at her movements.
   (3) The house was not broken by the tornado.
   (4) Ms. Jackson told Tom to clean the windows.
   (5) The teacher expected his students to do their
       best.

12 ⑤   13 to join / to do   14 ③
15 ①   16 ③   17 ②

18 (1) Sujin painted the picture.
   (2) Casa Mila was built by Antonio Gaudi.
   (3) A model plane was made for me by my father.
   (4) Her homework will be finished by Kate by the
       end of this week.
   (5) By whom was the house built?

01 ③ 수동태는 'be+과거분사'의 형태이므로 was built가 되어야
한다.

02 ask의 목적격보어로 to부정사가 적절하다.

03 직접목적어를 주어로 한 수동태에서 간접목적어 앞에 (1)
teach는 전치사 to를, (2) buy는 전치사 for를, (3) ask는 전
치사 of를 쓴다.

04 tell의 목적격보어로 to부정사가 적절하다.

05 Her pictures taken at the party were shown to me by
Mary.

6 make는 목적격보어로 to부정사가 아니라 원형부정사를 쓴다.

7 ① A difficult question was asked of her by them. ③ These books will be sent to you tomorrow morning. ④ The window was broken by Mike yesterday. ⑤ The telephone was invented by Alexander Bell in 1876.

8 ask, tell, advise, want, expect는 모두 목적격보어로 to부정사가 와야 한다

9 cautious: 주의 깊은, 신중한 ⑤ The doctor wanted Harry to get well soon.

10 dust: 먼지 / be covered with: ~로 덮여 있다 / be pleased with: ~에 기뻐하다

11 (1), (3) Mona Lisa가 그려지고, 집이 부서지지 않은 것이므로 수동태가 적절하다. (2) be surprised at: ~에 놀라다 (4), (5) tell과 expect는 목적격보어로 to부정사를 쓴다.

12 turn on은 구동사로 하나의 동사처럼 취급하여 be turned on으로 나타낸다. on을 빠뜨리지 않도록 주의한다.

13 want와 allow는 목적격보어로 to부정사를 쓴다.

14 make는 직접목적어를 주어로 한 수동태에서 간접목적어 앞에 for를 쓴다.

15 시제가 saw로 과거형이므로 was seen으로 쓰고, 목적격 보어 flying은 그대로 써준다. 원형부정사인 경우에는 to부정사로 써야 한다.

16 want는 목적격보어로 to부정사를 쓴다.

17 ② make는 사역동사이므로 목적격보어로 동사원형이 와야 하며, 나머지는 모두 to부정사가 와야 한다.

18 (3) make는 직접목적어를 주어로 하는 수동태만 가능하다. (4) 미래 시제의 수동태는 'will be+과거분사'이다. (5) 의문사 who가 whom으로 바뀌는 것에 주의한다.

서술형 시험대비 p.134~135

01 (1) Angelina was taught English by Williams last year.
   (2) English was taught (to) Angelina by Williams last year.

02 (1) to draw (2) to read (3) to solve
   (4) not to drive (5) to clean

03 (1) The floor was covered with a beautiful carpet.
   (2) The book was not written in Korean.
   (3) Animals there were taken good care of by people.
   (4) The watch was given (to) me two years ago by my father.
   (5) A book was bought for me by her.

04 (1) I made a basket.
   (2) *I and the village* was painted by Marc Chagall in 1911.

(3) A rotten tooth was pulled out by the dentist.
(4) Matthew kindly showed me the way to the National Museum.
(5) Dust covered him while he was walking along the road.

05 (1) She wants Steve to come home early.
   (2) He believed his students to be diligent.
   (3) He asked me to drive a car very carefully.
   (4) My boss forced me to sign the agreement.
   (5) The doctor told me not to do exercise too much.

06 (1) The airplane was invented by the Wright brothers.
   (2) The house was built by him in 1963.
   (3) Handerson is not interested in playing the guitar.
   (4) He will be told of the news by his sister tomorrow.
   (5) Soup was cooked for Christina by John.

07 (1) The woman asked the man to carry her bag.
   (2) Emma advised me to wait till tomorrow.
   (3) Peter told Sylvia to dance with him.
   (4) They expected him to participate in the festival.
   (5) Good health enabled him to finish the plan.

08 (1) study (2) to call

---

01 teach는 직접목적어를 주어로 한 수동태에서 간접목적어 앞에 전치사 to를 쓴다.

02 (1) encourage (2) tell (3) order (4) warn (5) ask는 모두 목적격보어로 to부정사를 쓴다

03 (1) be covered with: ~로 덮여 있다 (2) 수동태의 부정은 'be+not+과거분사'이다. (3) take good care of를 하나의 동사처럼 생각해서 'be taken good care of'로 써야 한다. (4) give 는 직접목적어를 주어로 한 수동태에서는 간접목적어 앞에 전치사 to를 써야 한다. (5) buy 는 직접목적어를 주어로 하는 수동태만 가능하다.

04 (3) pulled out은 하나의 동사로 취급해서 was pulled out으로 써야 한다. (4) show는 직접목적어를 주어로 한 수동태에서 간접목적어 앞에 전치사 to를 쓴다. (5) be covered는 by가 아니라 with를 쓴다.

05 (1) want (2) believe (3) ask (4) force 등의 동사는 목적격보어로 to부정사가 와야 한다. (5) to부정사의 부정형은 'not to+동사원형'으로 쓴다.

06 (1) 비행기가 발명되는 것이므로 수동태 (2) 수동태는 'be+ 과거분사' (3) be interested in: ~에 흥미가 있다 (4) tomorrow가 있는 수동태이므로 미래형 'will be+과거분사'로 써야 한다. (5) cook은 직접목적어를 주어로 한 수동태에서는 간접목적어 앞에 for를 쓴다.

07 ask, advise, tell, expect, enable 등은 모두 목적격보어로 to부정사가 와야 한다.

08 (1) 사역동사 have는 목적격보어로 원형부정사를 쓴다. (2) would like는 목적격보어로 to부정사를 쓴다.

Reading

확인문제
p.136

1 T 2 F 3 F 4 T 5 T 6 F

확인문제
p.137

1 F 2 T 3 T 4 F 5 F 6 T

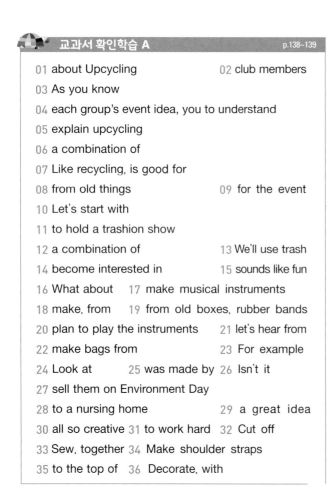

교과서 확인학습 A
p.138~139

01 about Upcycling
02 club members
03 As you know
04 each group's event idea, you to understand
05 explain upcycling
06 a combination of
07 Like recycling, is good for
08 from old things
09 for the event
10 Let's start with
11 to hold a trashion show
12 a combination of
13 We'll use trash
14 become interested in
15 sounds like fun
16 What about
17 make musical instruments
18 make, from
19 from old boxes, rubber bands
20 plan to play the instruments
21 let's hear from
22 make bags from
23 For example
24 Look at
25 was made by
26 Isn't it
27 sell them on Environment Day
28 to a nursing home
29 a great idea
30 all so creative
31 to work hard
32 Cut off
33 Sew, together
34 Make shoulder straps
35 to the top of
36 Decorate, with

교과서 확인학습 B
p.140~141

1 Let's Talk about Upcycling

2 Hello, club members.

3 As you know, this year's Environment Day is about upcycling.

4 Before we talk about each group's event idea for that day, I want you to understand the meaning of "upcycling."

5 Can anyone explain upcycling?

6 Yes. The word "upcycling" is a combination of "upgrade" and "recycling."

7 Like recycling, upcycling is good for the environment.

8 When you upcycle, you make new and better things from old things.

9 Good. Now, let's talk about each group's idea for the event.

10 Let's start with Pei's group.

11 My group wants to hold a trashion show.

12 "Trashion" is a combination of "trash" and "fashion."

13 We'll use trash to make clothes.

14 We want other students to become interested in upcycling through the show.

15 A trashion show sounds like fun!

16 What about your group, Eric?

17 My group is going to make musical instruments from old things.

18 We'll make drums from old plastic buckets.

19 We'll also make a guitar from old boxes and rubber bands.

20 We plan to play the instruments in a mini-concert.

21 Thank you, Eric. Now, let's hear from Sumi's group.

22 My group will make bags from old clothes.

23 For example, we'll use blue jeans.

24 Look at this bag.

25 This was made by Hajun, one of our group members.

26 Isn't it nice?

27 We'll make more bags and sell them on Environment Day.

28 We're going to give all the money to a nursing home.

29 That's a great idea.

30 Your ideas are all so creative.

31 I want everyone to work hard for Environment Day.

32 Cut off the legs of the blue jeans.

33 Sew the bottom together.

34 Make shoulder straps from one of the legs.

35 Sew the straps to the top of the jeans.

36 Decorate the bag with pins and buttons.

시험대비 실력평가
p.142~147

01 ③　　　　02 ⑤　　　　03 ②

04 (A) other (B) through (C) like　　　05 ⑤

06 ③　　　　07 ②　　　　08 more bags

09 the bags → all the money

10 4 → 1 → 3 → 5 → 2　　11 ⓐ with ⓑ to

12 one of the legs　　13 ④　　　14 ③

15 at → for　　　16 ④　　　17 ①, in

18 ②　　　　19 like　　　20 ②

21 I want everyone to work hard for Environment Day.

22 (A) old clothes　(B) Environment Day

　(C) all the money

23 one　　　24 directions

25 ① cut off a leg of the old blue jeans

　② cut out a piece to make the bottom of the basket

　③ sew the bottom to the leg

　④ decorate with pins and buttons

26 ①　　　27 For instance　　28 ④

29 Hajun, one of our group members, made this.

30 for → to　　31 Lastly　　32 decorate

33 To the top of the jeans.　34 ①, ③　　35 ③

36 to become

37 They will make drums and a guitar.

1 recycling과 '마찬가지로' upcycling도 환경에 좋다.

2 ⓐ와 ⑤ 명사적 용법(목적격보어), ①과 ③ 부사적 용법(목적), ②와 ④ 형용사적 용법

3 '오래된 것들로' 새롭고 더 좋은 것들을 만든다고 해야 하므로 from이 적절하다.

4 (A) '다른' 학생들이라고 해야 하므로 other가 적절하다. another + 단수 명사, (B) 이 쇼를 '통해서'라고 해야 하므로 through가 적절하다. though: 비록 ~이지만, (C) '멋지겠구나'라고 해야 하므로 like가 적절하다. sound like fun: 재미있을 것 같다, sound like: ~처럼 들리다, alike: (아주) 비슷한 (명사 앞에는 안 씀)

5 ⑤ 소규모 음악회를 여는 장소는 알 수 없다. ① "trash"와 "fashion"이 결합한 말, ② 쓰레기, ③ 다른 학생들이 업사이클

링에 대해 관심을 가지게 되는 것, ④ 낡은 물건

6 위 글은 '두 그룹의 행사 아이디어'에 관한 글이다.

7 ② 앞의 내용의 예가 나오고 있으므로 For example(예를 들면)이 가장 적절하다. ① 그러나, ③ 그러므로, ④ 게다가, ⑤ 그 결과

8 가방을 더 많이 만들어서 환경의 날에 팔 것이라고 했기 때문에, them은 '더 많은 가방'을 가리킨다.

9 수미의 그룹은 낡은 옷으로 가방을 만들어 팔아서, 번 '돈'을 모두 양로원에 줄 예정이다.

10 4 청바지의 다리 부분을 잘라내기 → 1 아래쪽을 붙여서 바느질하기 → 3 다리 한 짝으로 어깨 끈을 만들기 → 5 청바지의 윗부분에 어깨끈을 바느질하기 → 2 핀과 단추들로 가방을 장식하기

11 ⓐ 'with' pins and buttons: 핀과 단추들로, 핀과 단추들을 가지고, ⓑ 'to' the top of the jeans: 청바지의 윗 부분에

12 어깨 끈을 만들기 위해 청바지의 '다리 한 짝'이 필요하다.

13 ③번의 '업사이클링'의 의미를 이해하기를 바란다는 말과 ⑤번의 누가 업사이클링의 뜻을 설명해 줄 수 있느냐는 말 사이의 '업사이클링'은 새로운 물건을 만들기 위해 폐기물을 사용하는 것이라는 ④번 문장은 전체 글의 흐름에서 벗어난다.

14 upcycling은 upgrade의 'up'과 recycling의 'cycling'을 합친 말이다.

15 재활용과 마찬가지로 upcycling도 '환경에 좋다'고 해야 하므로 at을 for로 고쳐야 한다. be good at: ~을 잘하다, be good for: ~에 좋다

16 ④ 부사적 용법(결과), ⓐ와 나머지는 다 명사적 용법

17 ① be interested in: ~에 관심이 있다. 나머지는 다 from

18 ② 만족한, ① 지루한, ③ 우울한, ④ 부끄러운, ⑤ 실망한

19 sound like: ~처럼 들리다

20 ②번 다음 문장의 This에 주목한다. 주어진 문장의 this bag을 받고 있으므로 ②번이 적절하다.

21 'want+목적어+to부정사' 구문을 사용하면 된다.

22 (A) '낡은 옷'으로 가방을 만들기, (B) '환경의 날'에 가방을 팔아서 (C) '번 돈'을 모두 양로원에 드리기

23 ⓐ 한 가지, ⓑ a basket을 가리키는 부정대명사

24 directions: 지시, 무엇을 할지, 어떻게 할지 혹은 어떤 장소에 어떻게 도착할지를 말해주는 지시, these 뒤이므로 복수 형태로 쓰는 것이 적절하다.

25 ① 낡은 청바지의 다리 부분을 자르기, ② 바구니의 바닥을 만들기 위해 한 조각을 자르기, ③ 바닥을 다리 부분과 꿰매기 ④ 단추와 핀으로 장식하기

26 ① (A)의 drums가 주어진 글의 musical instruments에 해당하므로 제일 먼저 오고 (C)에서 also 로 악기의 예를 계속 설명하므로 (A) 다음에 (C)가 이어지고 (B)의 the instruments가 앞에서 말한 악기들을 가리키므로 (C) 다음에 (B)가 와야 한다. 그러므로 (A)-(C)-(B)의 순서가 적절하다.

27 for example = for instance: 예를 들면

28 ⓑ look at: ~을 보다 ⓓ on+특정한 날

29 by 다음의 행위자를 능동태의 주어로 바꾸고 동격에 해당하는 부분 앞뒤로 콤마를 찍는 것이 적절하다.

30 수여동사 give는 간접목적어 앞에 전치사 to를 쓴다.

31 lastly: 마지막으로, 끝으로(무엇을 열거하면서 마지막 요소 앞에 붙이는 말)

32 뭔가를 덧붙여 어떤 것을 더 매력적으로 만들다: decorate(장식하다)

33 끈을 '청바지의 꼭대기'에 바느질해야 한다.

34 hold[have] a trashion show: 트래션 쇼를 열다

35 문맥상 upcycling이 되어야 한다. / upgrading: 등급상승

36 want+목적어+to부정사를 써야 한다.

---

01 to understand

02 The word "upcycling" is a combination of "upgrade" and "recycling."

03 old → new, new → old

04 trash

05 How about your group

06 드럼: 낡은 플라스틱 양동이 기타: 낡은 상자와 고무줄

07 We're going to give a nursing home all the money.

08 hardly → hard

09 wants to understand → wants club members to understand

10 each groups' → each group's

11 (A) make clothes (B) trashion show

12 (A) drums (B) a guitar

---

01 'want+목적어+to부정사'로 써야 한다.

02 The word와 "upcycling"은 동격이므로 같이 붙여 쓰면 된다.

03 업사이클을 할 때 '오래된' 것들로부터 '새롭고' 더 좋은 것들을 만들게 된다고 하는 것이 적절하다.

04 사용한 종이, 빈 병, 그리고 쓰레기 음식과 같은 원치 않는 물건들 혹은 폐기물, trash: 쓰레기

05 What about ~? = How about ~?: ~은 어때?

06 드럼은 '낡은 플라스틱 양동이'로, 기타는 '낡은 상자와 고무줄'로 만들 것이다.

07 전치사 to를 없애고 간접목적어(a nursing home), 직접 목적어(all the money) 순서로 쓰면 된다.

08 너희들 모두 환경의 날을 위해 열심히 노력하길 바란다고 해야 하기 때문에, hard로 고쳐야 한다. hardly: 거의 ~ 아니다[없다]

09 Mr. Brown은 '동아리 회원들'이 "upcycling"의 의미를 이해하기를 원한다.

---

10 each는 뒤에 단수 명사를 써야 한다.

11 '옷을 만들기' 위해 쓰레기를 사용하고 '트래션 쇼'를 열 것이다.

12 낡은 플라스틱 양동이로 '드럼'을, 낡은 상자와 고무줄로 '기타'를 만들 것이다.

---

01 better 02 ④ 03 ③ 04 ①

05 ② 06 ⑤ 07 ④ 08 ④

09 clock 10 ④ 11 ⑤ 12 ②

13 ①, ③, ④ 14 ⑤

15 (1) was made for me by my mom

  (2) were given to Emily by Jonathan, was given some flowers by Jonathan

  (3) made me wash his car

  (4) painted *Girl in the Woods*

  (5) was put off on account of the rain (by them)

16 (1) These chocolate cookies were baked by me.

  (2) We want to wash our clothes.

  (3) Her sister was taken care of by Judy.

  (4) The thief will be caught by the police.

  (5) She told me to wash my hands before dinner.

17 ⑤ 18 ② 19 ④

20 (1) A doll was made for her by her mother.

  (2) Most of the doors in this building are made of wood.

  (3) I was brought up by my grandparents.

  (4) The teacher warned his students to hand in their homework by Friday.

  (5) I believe Ella to be very smart.

21 ④ 22 As you know 23 ①

24 ③ 25 ⑤ 26 in a mini-concert

27 ③번, of → by 28 ②

---

01 반의어 관계다. 비싼 : 싼 = 더 나은 : 더 나쁜

02 ⓐ는 '~은 어때요?'라는 의미로 How about ~?이 적절하고, ⓑ는 물건을 사겠다는 의미로 take를 사용한다.

03 음악을 만들어 내기 위해 사용되는 물건

04 더 많이 알고 싶기 때문에 어떤 것에 더 많은 관심을 가지는

05 Nancy는 비치백의 끈을 잡았다. / 그녀는 잠옷 끈을 어깨 위로 끌어올렸다.

06 like는 전치사로 '~처럼, ~와 같이'라는 뜻이다.

07 M의 대답으로 보아 할인을 해준다는 말이 온다.

08 '그건 제게 너무 비쌉니다.'라는 말 다음에 '할인을 받을 수 있나요?'라는 말이 오는 것이 자연스럽다.

09 one은 앞에 나온 같은 종류의 명사를 대신하는 부정대명사로 clock을 가리킨다.

10 그것은 단지 일 년 밖에 되지 않았다고 했기 때문에 '거의 새 것이

다'라는 의미가 적절하므로 used를 new로 바꾼다.

11 ②는 '너는 무엇을 할 거니?' '음. 생각해 볼게.'라는 말로 자연스럽다. ⑤는 축구공의 가격을 물어보는 말에 '1달러 할인해 줄게요'라고 하는 말은 어색하다.

12 Andy는 축구공을 1달러 할인받은 가격인 5달러에 구입한다.

13 A의 대답으로 보아 빈칸에는 가격을 물어보는 표현이 자연스럽다.

14 ① We want you to join our club. ② The cookies were cooked by Eric. ③ Mr. Gilbert would like his students to do their best. ④ The airplane was invented by the Wright brothers.

15 (1), (2) 직접목적어를 주어로 한 수동태에서 make는 간접목적어 앞에 전치사 for를, give는 to를 쓴다. (3) make는 사역동사로 목적격보어로 원형부정사를 쓰지만 수동태에서 는 to부정사로 바뀐다. (4) 수동태는 'be+과거분사'의 형태이다. (5) 구동사는 하나의 어휘처럼 취급한다.

16 수동태는 'be+과거분사+by 행위자'의 형태이며, want와 tell은 목적격보어로 to부정사가 온다.

17 'want+목적어+to부정사: (목적어)가 ~하기를 원하다' ②번의 have는 사역동사로 목적격보어로 원형부정사가 온다.

18 The light는 동사 turned off의 행위의 대상이므로 수동태로 써야 적절하다.

19 have는 사역동사이므로 목적격보어로 원형부정사가 온다.

20 (1) make는 간접목적어를 주어로 수동태를 만들 수 없다. (동사의 의미 때문에 만들 수 없는 것임) (2) be made of: ~로 만들어지다(물리적 변화), be made from: ~로 만들어지다(화학적 변화) (3) 구동사는 하나의 동 사처럼 취급한다. 동사와 함께 이어지는 어휘나 전치사 by를 빠뜨리기 쉬우므로 주의한다. (4), (5) warn, believe의 목적격보어로 to부정사가 적절하다.

21 ④ recycling과 upcycling의 차이점은 알 수 없다. ① upcycling, ② '업사이클링'이란 단어는 "upgrade"와 "recycling"이 결합한 것이다. ③ upcycling은 오래된 것들을 이용하여 새롭고 더 좋은 것들을 만들므로 환경에 좋다. ⑤ Pei의 그룹

22 as는 접속사로 '~하다시피[~하듯이]'의 뜻으로 쓰였다.

23 ⓑ와 ①은 '~와 (똑)같이[마찬가지로], ~처럼(전치사)', ②와 ④ ~을 좋아하다(동사), ③ 비슷한 것(명사), ⑤ (예를 들어) ~와 같은

24 ③ 낡은 '플라스틱' 양동이로 드럼을 만들 것이다.

25 Eric의 그룹은 낡은 물건들로 '악기'를 만들 것이다. ① 실험 도구, ② 자동차, ③ 의사소통 기구, ④ 건설장비

26 '소규모 음악회'에서 악기를 연주할 것이다.

27 수동태의 행위자 앞에 'by'를 쓰는 것이 적절하다.

28 ② 창의적인, 앞에서 훌륭한 생각이라고 했기 때문에, 발상이 모두 '창의적'이라고 하는 것이 적절하다. ① 따분한, 재미없는, ③ 흔한, ④ 지루한, ⑤ 구식의

단원별 예상문제   p.156~159

01 creative   02 ③   03 (A) Sew   (B) Decorate
04 ④   05 ②   06 I'll take it.
07 (A) How about this red clock?
   (B) Can I get a discount?
08 how much is this blue clock with the large numbers?
09 ②   10 ③   11 ③   12 ④
13 (1) Were the students taught English by Emma?
       Was English taught to the students by Emma?
   (2) A lot of data can be sent through the Internet (by us).
   (3) The Dance Class was painted by Edgar Degas.
14 (1) give → to give
   (2) to wait → wait
15 (1) was painted by
   (2) was invented by
   (3) was pleased with
16 ②   17 ⑤   18 environment
19 ②   20 ⑤
21 (A) clothes   (B) trashion show   (C) upcycling
22 ③   23 this bag   24 ②
25 (1) Cut off   (2) Sew   (3) from
   (4) Sew   (5) Decorate
26 ④

01 유의어 관계다. 쓰레기 = 창의적인

02 단어나 표현 또는 표시가 나타내는 특정한 생각

03 upcycling은 upgrade와 recycling을 결합한 것이다. 재활용과 마찬가지로 업사이클링도 환경에 좋다. 업사이클링을 하면 여러분은 오래된 것들로 새롭고 더 나은 것을 만든다.

05 ①은 '이 시계는 할인 중 인가요?'라는 뜻으로 yes/no로 대답을 하는 것이 자연스럽다. ③ '돈을 얼마나 가지고 있니?' ④ '이 신발 가격은 얼마인가요?'라는 뜻으로 적절해 보이지만 these shoes는 복수형으로 They are ~로 답해야 한다.

07 (A)는 시계를 찾고 있다는 말에 대해 빨간색 시계가 어떠냐고 제안하는 말이 적절하고, (B)의 앞에 저에게는 너무 비싸다는 말이 있으므로 '할인을 받을 수 있을까요?'라는 말이 자연스럽다.

08 가격을 물어볼 때 'how much is[are] ~?'를 사용하고, 이 파란색 시계(this blue clock)가 주어이므로 단수동사 is를 사용한다.

09 ⓑ everything은 '모든 것'이라는 의미지만 단수 취급한다. are를 is로 바꾸어야 한다.

10 B의 대답이 사지 않겠다고 했기 때문에 할인을 하지 않는다는 표현이 적절하다.

11 ① The key was stolen by Bill. ② Presents were given to all the children. ④ Was her homework finished by

her? ⑤ The spaghetti was made by my dad.

12 Tell them to come to my birthday party.

13 (1) 직접목적어를 주어로 하는 수동태에서 teach는 전치사 to를 간접목적어 앞에 붙여야 한다. (2) 조동사의 수동태는 '조동사+be+과거분사'의 형태로 쓴다. (3) 수동태는 'be+ 과거분사'의 형태로 쓴다.

14 (1) ask의 목적격보어로 to부정사가 와야 한다. (2) make는 사역동사이므로 목적격보어로 동사원형이 와야 한다.

15 (1), (2) 목적어가 주어로 나와 있으므로 수동태로 답을 작성한다. (3) be pleased는 전치사 with를 쓴다.

16 ⓐ와 ② ~하다시피[~하듯이] (접속사), ① (자격, 기능 등이) ~로(서) (전치사), ③ [보통 as ~ as …로 형용사·부사 앞에서] ~와 같은 정도로(지시부사), ④ ~ 때문에(접속사), ⑤ (비례) ~함에 따라(접속사)

17 ⓑ talk about: ~에 대해 말하다, ⓒ event idea for that day: '그날(환경의 날)에 할' 행사 아이디어

18 upcycling은 '환경'에 좋다.

19 hold a show: 쇼를 열다

20 ⑤ 명사적 용법, ⓑ와 나머지는 다 부사적 용법 ① 형용사 수식, ② 원인, ③ 목적, ④ 이유

21 Pei의 그룹은 쓰레기를 사용하여 '옷'을 만들고 '트래션 쇼'를 준비할 것이다. 그들은 그 쇼를 통해 다른 학생들이 '업사이클링'에 관심을 가지게 되기를 바란다.

22 ③ 수미의 그룹이 얼마나 많은 돈을 벌기를 기대하는지는 대답할 수 없다. ① Bags from old clothes. ② On Environment Day. ④ They are going to give all the money to a nursing home. ⑤ He wants everyone to work hard for Environment Day.

23 하준이가 만든 '가방'을 가리킨다.

24 ① 저축하다, ② 기부하다, ③ 간직하다, ④ 저장[보관]하다, ⑤ 재활용하다

25 ① 청바지의 다리 부분을 '자르기', ② 아래쪽을 붙여서 '바느질하기', ③ 다리 '한 짝으로' 어깨 끈을 만들기, ④ 청바지의 윗부분에 어깨끈을 '바느질하기', ⑤ 핀이나 단추로 가방을 '장식하기'

26 '지퍼'는 필요한 재료가 아니다.

서술형 실전문제   p.160~161

01 15 dollars / one year / 10 dallars / the large numbers. He will[is going to] buy the blue clock.

02 (A) How much is this black bag?
   (B) I'll take 2 dollars off.

03 round glasses / 18 dollars / I'm afraid not

04 (1) Ms. Brown asked the students to clean the classroom.

(2) His parents expected him to win the contest.

(3) The boss warned the driver to drive very carefully.

05 The book was not written in Korean.

06 (1) not to be late   (2) not to give up

07 interesting → interested

08 A trashion show sounds like fun!

09 (A) musical instruments   (B) old plastic buckets
   (C) from   (D) the instruments

10 (A) clothes   (B) Isn't   (C) to

11 낡은 옷으로 가방을 만들어 환경의 날에 가방을 판 다음, 번 돈을 양로원에 줄 예정이라는 것

12 wants to work → wants everyone to work

01 소년은 무엇을 살 것인가?

02 (A)는 B의 대답으로 볼 때 검정색 가방의 가격을 묻고 있다는 것을 알 수 있다. (B) 그림에서 15달러를 13달러로 할인해 주고 있다는 것을 알 수 있다. 그래서 2달러 깎아 준다는 표현이 적절하다.

03 Jenny가 사려고 하는 물건은 둥근 안경(round glasses)이고, 가격은 18달러다. 할인을 받을 수 있느냐는 질문에 남자가 No라고 말했으므로 '안 될 것 같아요(I'm afraid not.)'라는 말이 오는 것이 적절하다.

04 ask, expect, warn 등은 목적격보어로 to부정사를 쓴다.

05 그 책이 주어이므로 수동태로 쓴다.

06 ask와 encourage는 목적격보어로 to부정사를 쓰고 부정사의 부정은 not을 앞에 붙인다.

07 '흥미를 가지게 되는 것'이므로 interested가 적절하다.

08 sound like: ~하게 들리다

09 (A) 오래된 물건들로 '악기'를 만들기, (B) '낡은 플라스틱 양동이'로 드럼을 만들기, (C) 낡은 상자와 고무줄'로' 기타를 만들기, (D) 소규모 음악회를 열어 '그 악기들'로 연주하기

10 (A) '낡은 옷'으로 가방을 만들 것이라고 해야 하므로 clothes가 적절하다. cloths: cloth(옷감, 천)의 복수, (B) 그것은 멋지지 '않나요?'라고 해야 하므로 Isn't가 적절하다. (C) give는 to를 사용하여 3형식으로 고친다.

11 ① '낡은 옷으로 가방을 만들 것이다.', ② '환경의 날에 가방을 팔 것이다.', ③ '번 돈을 모두 양로원에 줄 것이다.' 라는 내용을 포함해서 쓰면 정답.

12 Mr. Brown은 '모든 사람들'이 환경의 날을 위해 열심히 노력하길 바란다.

창의사고력 서술형 문제   p.162

|모범답안|

01 (1) A: May I help you?
       B: Yes. How much is this scarf?

A: It's 6 dollars.

B: Can I get a discount?

A: OK. I'll take 2 dollars off.

B: I'll take it.

(2) A: May I help you?

B: Yes. How much is this T-shirt?

A: It's 10 dollars.

B: Can I get a discount?

A: No, I'm afraid not. Sorry.

B: Then, I don't think I'll take it.

02 (1) Mom wants Minsu to clean his room.

(2) Mom wants Mina to do the dishes.

(3) Mom wants me to walk the dog.

03 (A) directions(또는 steps)   (B) cut

(C) Second   (D) decorate

단원별 모의고사

01 ③   02 upgrade   03 ①   04 ⑤

05 (A) How much   (B) It's 20 dallars

(C) take 2 dallars off

06 am looking for / get a discount / take, off / 12

07 (1) How much is this pink skirt?

(2) I'll take 1 dollar off.

08 ④   09 ⑤   10 ⑤   11 ③

12 I'll take the blue one.

13 (1) We made this flower pot from an ice cream bowl.

(2) The song, *Yesterday*, was written by the Beatles.

(3) Some cookies were cooked for us by her.

(4) Picasso was laughed at at first (by people).

14 ②   15 was heard to open the window by me

16 close → to close   17 I believe her to be kind.

18 (this year's) Environment Day   19 ①

20 (A) Pei's group   (B) Environment Day   21 ②

22 ③   23 ⑤   24 member → members

25 Your ideas are all so creative. 혹은 All your ideas are so creative.

01 ③: 물건을 사기 위해 지불해야 하는 금액 = price(가격)

02 반의어 관계다. 비싼 : 값싼 = 격하시키다 : 개선시키다

03 이해하기 쉽고 분명한 방식으로 어떤 것을 말해주다

04 첫 번째 빈칸은 할인을 하다는 의미로 take off를 사용하고, 두 번째 빈칸은 물건을 사다는 의미로 take를 쓴다.

05 (A)는 티셔츠의 가격을 물어보는 표현(How much)이 오고

(B)는 셔츠의 가격이 20달러(It's 20 dollars)라는 말이 오고 (C)는 2달러 깎아 준다(take 금액 off)는 표현이 오는 것이 자연스럽다.

07 (1)은 B의 대답으로 보아 분홍 스커트의 가격을 묻는 말이 오는 것이 자연스럽고 (2)는 '깎아 주실 수 있어요?'라는 물음에 대한 답으로, 그림에서 10달러에서 9달러로 1달러 할인을 해준다는 걸 알 수 있다.

08 ⓐ의 one은 앞에 나온 backpack을 가리키는 부정대명사고, ⓑ의 it은 15달러 하는 the red backpack을 가리킨다.

09 ⑤ 도와 드릴까요?라는 물음에 '좋군요. 그걸 살게요.'라는 답은 적절하지 않다.

10 ① 한정사로 '하나의' ② 강조의 의미로 '단 하나의' ③ 강조의 의미로 '단 하나의' ④ 1을 의미한다. ⑤ 명사를 대신하는 부정대명사

11 ③ 파란색 시계가 얼마나 오래 되었는지는 대화에서 언급되어 있지 않다.

12 take는 물건을 '사다, 선택하다'라는 뜻이다.

13 (1) 보통 We나 They가 주어일 경우 by us나 by them을 생략한다. (3) cook은 직접목적어를 주어로 하는 수동태만 가능하며 간접목적어 앞에 전치사 for를 쓴다. (4) laugh at은 하나의 동사처럼 취급되므로 수동태로 바뀌어도 at을 빠뜨리면 안 된다. by people은 생략할 수 있다.

14 ② ask의 목적격보어로 to부정사가 적절하다.

15 hear는 목적격보어로 원형부정사를 쓰지만, 수동태에서는 원형부정사를 to부정사로 바꿔 주어야 한다.

16 ask의 목적격보어로 to부정사가 적절하다.

17 believe는 목적격보어로 to부정사를 쓴다.

18 '(올해의) 환경의 날'을 가리킨다.

19 start with: ~와 함께 출발하다

20 'Pei의 그룹'이 '환경의 날'을 위한 행사 아이디어에 대해 말할 것이다.

21 ② 몇 명의 학생들이 upcycling에 관심이 있는지는 대답할 수 없다. ① Pei's group. ③ He thinks a trashion show sounds like fun. ④ From old things. ⑤ Sumi.

22 ③ 좋아하다(동사) ⓐ와 나머지는 모두 전치사로 '~와 같은, ~처럼'의 뜻이다.

23 Mr. Brown은 '모든 사람들이' 환경의 날을 위해 열심히 일하기를 원한다.

24 ~ 중의 하나: one of 복수명사

25 all을 소유격 앞에 써도 된다.

The Amazing World of Animals

시험대비 실력평가 p.170

01 ⑤ 02 ⑤ 03 ② 04 ③
05 ① 06 (1) fables (2) unique (3) carried
07 ④ 08 ②

01 have to: ~해야 한다 / wear: 입다 / protection: 보호
02 take a rest: 휴식하다
03 pull out: ~을 뽑다
04 ③ pile: 쌓다, 포개다
05 drop: 떨어뜨리다
06 (1) fable: 우화, 동화 (2) unique: 독특한 (3) carry: 휴대하다
07 ① floss: 치실질을 하다 ② jar: 병, 단지 ③ photograph: 사진 ④ level: 높이, 정도, 수준 ⑤ parrots, parrot: 앵무새
08 fable: 우화

서술형 시험대비 p.171

01 (1) (f)loat (2) female (3) (u)nique (4) lucky
02 (1) hide (2) floss (3) succeeded (4) left
03 (1) look (2) talk
04 (1) She was surprised to see a snake.
   (2) I was dressed in a navy suit.
   (3) The temple is located among the pine trees.
05 (1) a cup[glass] of, experiment (2) male, find
06 (t)alent
07 (n)avy

01 (1) 반의어 관계, subtract: 빼다 add: 더하다 sink: 가라앉다 float: ([물체가] [액체 면에] 뜨다, 떠다니다 (2) 반의어 관계, stupid: 멍청한 smart: 똑똑한 male: 남자의, 수컷의 female: 여성의, 암컷의 (3) 동의어 관계, good: 좋은 nice: 좋은 special: 특별한 unique: 독특한 (4) soft: 부드러운 smooth: 매끄러운 fortunate: 운이 좋은, 행운의 lucky: 운이 좋은
02 (1) hide: 숨다, 감추다 (2) floss: 치실질을 하다 (3) succeed: 성공하다 (4) leave: ~을 두고 가다
03 (1) look for: ~을 찾다 / look like: ~처럼 보이다, ~와 닮다 (2) talk to: ~에게 말하다 / talk with: ~와 이야기하다

04 (1) surprise: 놀라게 하다 (2) navy: 남색 (3) temple: 절, 사원
05 (1) a cup[glass] of ~: 한 컵의 / experiment: 실험, 시험 (2) male: 남자의 / 수컷의 find: 찾다
06 talent: 재능
07 navy: 남색

교과서 Conversation

핵심 Check p.172~173

1 What does, look, long and black
2 (C) → (A) → (D) → (B)
3 Can you explain / has polka dots

교과서 대화문 익히기

Check(√) True or False p.174

1 T 2 T 3 T 4 F

교과서 확인학습 p.176~177

Listen and Talk A-1
looking for / like / cotton / tell me more / grey / go, check

Listen and Talk A-2
I help you / lost, left, restroom / What, like / It's / What else, more / two pockets outside

Listen and Talk A-3
help / lost my umbrella / does it look / long and navy / tell / a star pattern on

Listen and Talk A-4
Do you / I'm looking / it look like / not very big, has / you tell me, anything special / short tail

Listen and Talk B
I'm looking for / does it look like / It's, has grey / Can, about it / has

Listen and Talk B-2
May / I'm looking for, wallet / What, like / tell, about /

There is a card

for, His name / What does he look like / has short
white / Can you / he, really / one more thing, Where /
lost, main / I'll, make an announcement / wait

Talk and Play

look like / tall, brown / Can you tell me more / wearing,
pants / found

Review

lost, umbrella / does it / big navy umbrella / tell me
more / has, flower pattern on

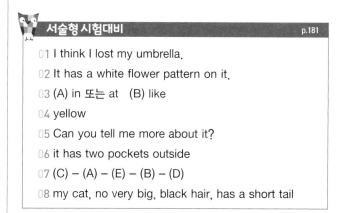

시험대비 기본평가   p.178

01 ⑤   02 ③   03 ④

04 (B) - (A) - (D) - (C)

01 'What does ~ look like?'는 '~는 어떻게 생겼니?'라는 의미
    로 외모나 생김새를 묻는 질문이다.

02 어떻게 생겼는지 질문하고 또 다른 정보를 묻는 상황이므로 ③
    이 어울린다.

03 외모나 형태를 물어보고 있으므로 성격을 나타내고 있는 ④는
    어울리지 않는다.

04 look for: ~을 찾다 / scarf: 스카프, 목도리 / cotton: 면 /
    long: 긴

시험대비 실력평가   p.179~180

01 ①   02 ⑤   03 ③   04 ②
05 ④   06 ① looking → looking for   07 ④
08 ⑤ special anything → anything special 09 ④
10 ④   11 I'm looking for my dog.   12 ②
13 ③   14 (A) has long   (B) wearing short
13 (f)ound

01 ① 다음에 나오는 인칭대명사 it을 사용하기 위해서는 지칭되는
    명사가 나와야 한다.

02 잃어버린 물건을 찾기 위해서 간 장소이므로 분실물 보관소이다.

03 Tell me more about it.: 그것에 대해 더 말해 주세요. ④는
    Talk to me more가 되어야 한다.

04 ② 가방 바깥쪽에 2개의 주머니가 있다.

05 should: ~해야 한다

06 look for: ~을 찾다

07 have: 가지고 있다, she는 3인칭 단수형이므로 has가 적절하다.

08 anything과 같이 -thing으로 끝나는 대명사는 형용사가 뒤에
    서 수식한다.

9   남자아이의 고양이는 꼬리가 짧다.

10 잃어버린 장소를 말하는 문장 앞에 와야 한다.

11 look for: ~을 찾다

12 make an announcement: 방송을 하다

13 ③ main gate: 정문 / near: 근처

14 (1) 명사를 수식하는 형용사가 여러 개 나왔을 경우 '외형(크기,
    형상/길이) + 신구/색깔 + 재료'의 순서로 명사를 수식할 수 있
    다. (2) wear: 입다 / navy: 남색

15 find–found–found: 찾다

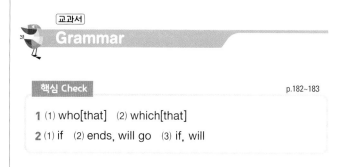

서술형 시험대비   p.181

01 I think I lost my umbrella.

02 It has a white flower pattern on it.

03 (A) in 또는 at   (B) like

04 yellow

05 Can you tell me more about it?

06 it has two pockets outside

07 (C) – (A) – (E) – (B) – (D)

08 my cat, no very big, black hair, has a short tail

02 pattern: 무늬, 도안

03 in[at]: ~에서 / look like: ~처럼 보이다, ~와 닮다

04 yellow: 노란색

05 Can you tell me more?는 '더 말해 주시겠어요?'라는 의미로
    추가적인 정보를 물을 때 사용한다.

06 have: 가지다 / pocket: 주머니 / outside: 바깥

07 May I help you?: 도와드릴까요? / look for: ~을 찾다 /
    look like: ~처럼 보이다, ~와 닮다 / small: 작은

08 look for: ~을 찾다 / cat: 고양이 / lost: 잃어버린 / hair: 털 /
    short: 짧은 / tail: 꼬리

교과서
Grammar

핵심 Check   p.182~183

1 (1) who[that]   (2) which[that]

2 (1) if   (2) ends, will go   (3) if, will

시험대비 기본평가   p.184

01 ③

02 (1) which → who[that]   (2) who → which[that]

31

(3) 뒤에 나오는 don't 삭제 또는 unless → if

(4) will rain → rains

03 (1) If you see my sister

(2) who was wearing a funny hat

04 ②

01 선행사가 The girl로 사람이며 is standing의 주어 역할을 하므로 주격 관계대명사 who나 that이 적절하다.

02 (1) 선행사가 사람이므로 which를 who나 that으로 고쳐야 한다. (2) 선행사가 사물이므로 who를 which나 that으로 고쳐야 한다. (3) unless는 'if ~ not'의 의미이므로 뒤에 나오는 don't를 삭제하거나 unless를 if로 고쳐야 한다. (4) 조건의 접속사가 이끄는 부사절에서는 미래의 의미를 갖더라도 will을 쓰지 않고 현재시제를 쓰므로 will rain을 rains로 고쳐야 한다.

03 (1) if는 '만약 ~한다면'이라는 뜻의 접속사이다. (2) 선행사가 사람이므로 who를 쓴다.

04 조건의 접속사가 이끄는 부사절에서는 미래의 의미를 갖더라도 will을 쓰지 않고 현재시제를 쓴다.

고 사물이면 which나 that을 쓴다. bloom: 꽃이 피(게 하)다, 개화하다

10 의미상 ②, ④가 적절하다. unless = if ~ not

11 선행사가 동물이므로 which나 that을 이용하고 주격이므로 주어로 쓰인 it은 쓰지 말아야 한다.

12 ②번에서는 who를 which나 that으로 바꿔야 하고, ③~ ⑤에서는 관계대명사는 접속사와 대명사 역할을 하므로 it이 없어야 한다.

13 if절은 'if+주어+동사 ~'의 어순으로 쓴다.

14 '이가 아프면 치과 의사에게 가야 한다.'는 말로 조건을 나타내는 if를 이용한다.

15 주격 관계대명사 다음에 동사를 써야 한다.

16 ① What shall we do if it begins snowing?

17 선행사가 사물이므로 which나 that을 써야 한다.

18 unless = if ~ not

19 주어진 문장과 ②, ③번의 who는 주격 관계대명사이다. ①, ⑤번은 목적격 관계대명사, ④번은 의문대명사이다.

20 unless는 'if ~ not'의 의미로 '명령문, or ~(~해라, 그렇지 않으면)'로 바꿔 쓸 수 있다.

01 ③   02 ④

03 (1) who   (2) which   (3) that   (4) if   (5) go

04 You'll feel better if you take a rest.   05 ⑤

06 ②   07 (1) which (2) who is   08 ①

09 ⑤   10 ②, ④   11 ③   12 ①

13 If there is no class today

14 If you have a toothache

15 that is sitting with a boy on the grass

16 ①   17 ⑤   18 ③   19 ②, ③

20 ④

1 모두 주격으로 사용된 관계대명사 that이 들어갈 수 있지만 ③번은 소유격 관계대명사 of which가 들어가야 한다.

2 ④ unless = if ~ not이므로 Unless가 아니라 If가 되어야 한다.

3 (1) 선행사가 사람이므로 who, (2) 선행사가 사물이므로 which, (3) 선행사가 사람이므로 that (4) 의미상 if (5) 조건의 부사절에서는 미래시제 대신에 현재시제를 쓴다.

4 조건의 부사절에서는 미래시제 대신에 현재시제를 쓰므로 if 절은 현재시제로 쓰고, 주절은 미래시제로 쓴다.

5 ⑤번은 접속사이지만 나머지는 모두 관계대명사이다.

6 ②번만 know의 목적절을 이끄는 '~인지 아닌지'로 쓰였다.

7 목적격 관계대명사와 '주격 관계대명사+be동사'는 생략할 수 있다.

8 ① 조건절이 미래의 일을 나타낼 때에도 조건절의 시제는 현재형을 쓴다.

9 관계대명사의 선행사가 사람이면 who, whom이나 that을 쓰

01 (1) This is a great book which[that] gave hope to many people.

(2) Pilots are the persons who[that] fly airplanes.

(3) David has a brother who[that] plays basketball well.

(4) Kate bought some roses which[that] smelled good.

(5) Look at the man and his dog that are sleeping under the tree.

02 (1) If   (2) Unless

03 (1) This is a bird which[that] can talk.

(2) Look at those musicians who[that] are singing on the street.

(3) Alice lives in a house which[that] has a beautiful garden.

(4) She is drawing two pictures that look very similar.

(5) I like Cindy who is very cool.

04 (1) Kathy will go shopping in the afternoon if she is not busy.

(2) If you meet Morina tomorrow, can you tell her to call me?

(3) Unless you study hard, you won't pass the exam. 또는 If you don't study hard, you won't

pass the exam.

  (4) If the weather is bad, I will not go hiking.

05 (1) Don't take the umbrella which I bought last weekend.

  (2) Do you know the girl whom Jack met in the park?

  (3) He is the tour guide who will guide us in New York City.

06 (1) If I go to Jeju-do

  (2) If you finish your homework

  (3) If I go shopping

07 (1) which Diana lives in

  (2) that Diana lives in

  (3) in which Diana lives

  (4) Diana lives in

08 (1) If I meet my favorite actor on the street, I will take pictures with him.

  (2) The work will not be done unless you do it.

09 (1) It can clean my room.

  (2) The girl is my friend, Ann.

  (3) It is famous for traditional Korean food.

  (4) I want to have a friend.

10 If school finishes early today, I will read a book.

01 (1), (4) 선행사가 사물이므로 관계대명사 which나 that을 써야 한다. (2), (3) 선행사가 사람이므로 관계대명사 who나 that을 써야 한다. (5) 선행사가 '사람+동물'이므로 관계대명사 that을 써야 한다.

02 명령문 + and ~: '~해라, 그러면'(= If ~) / 명령문 + or ~: '~해라, 그렇지 않으면'(Unless = If ~ not)

03 (1), (3) 선행사가 사물이므로 관계대명사 which나 that을 써야 한다. (2) 선행사가 사람이므로 관계대명사 who나 that을 써야 한다. (4) two pictures가 선행사이므로 look이 되어야 한다. (5) 관계대명사가 접속사와 대명사의 역할을 하므로 she를 삭제해야 한다.

04 (1), (2) 조건절에서는 현재시제로 미래시제를 대신한다. (3), (4) unless = if ~ not

05 (1) 선행사가 사물이므로 which를 쓴다. (2) 선행사가 사람이고 목적격이므로 whom을 쓴다. (3) 선행사가 사람이고 주격이므로 who를 쓴다.

06 조건절에서는 현재시제로 미래시제를 대신한다.

07 선행사가 사물이므로 which나 that을 쓴다. 전치사를 관계대명사 앞으로 옮길 수 있으나 관계대명사 that은 전치사 다음에 쓸 수 없다. 목적격 관계대명사는 생략 가능하다.

08 조건절에서는 현재시제로 미래시제를 대신하며, unless는 'if ~ not'의 의미이다.

09 주격 관계대명사는 선행사가 사람이면 who나 that, 사물이나 동물이면 which나 that을 쓰고, 관계대명사절에서 주어 역할을 하며 다음에 동사가 나온다.

10 조건절에서는 현재시제로 미래시제를 대신한다.

Reading

확인문제   p.190

1 F 2 T 3 T 4 F

확인문제   p.191

1 T 2 F 3 F 4 T 5 T 6 F 7 T 8 F

교과서 확인학습 A   p.192~193

01 That, Tools   02 once, thought

03 are finding out, also 04 watch out for

05 pull out 06 to floss their teeth

07 that are teaching flossing

08 While, floss their teeth 09 learn to floss

10 don't usually think

11 However, can also use 12 for protection

13 a good hiding place, hide under

14 even store, for later use

15 pile, to use later   16 How

17 drops, into, to raise

18 this is just a story

19 did an experiment   20 with, in front of

21 on top of the 22 However, water level, low

23 just as   24 dropped, into 25 special, wrong

26 with other crows, did the same

교과서 확인학습 B   p.194~195

1 Animals That Use Tools

2 People once thought that only humans can use tools.

3 Now, scientists are finding out that many animals can also use tools.

4 If you go to a Buddhist temple in Lop Buri, Thailand, watch out for the Macaque monkeys.

5 They may come to you and pull out your hair.

6 They use human hair to floss their teeth.

7 If you are lucky, you may see female monkeys that are teaching flossing to their babies.

8 While the babies are watching, the female monkeys floss their teeth very slowly.

9 This way, the baby monkeys learn to floss.

10 People don't usually think that octopuses are smart.

11 However, octopuses are very smart, and they can also use tools.

12 They use coconut shells for protection.

13 When they can't find a good hiding place, they hide under coconut shells.

14 Some octopuses even store coconut shells for later use.

15 They pile the coconut shells and carry them to use later.

16 How smart!

17 In Aesop's fable *The Thirsty Crow*, a crow drops stones into a jar to raise the level of water.

18 You may think this is just a story, but it is not.

19 Scientists who were studying crows did an experiment.

20 They put a jar with water in front of a crow.

21 A worm was floating on top of the water.

22 However, the water level was low, so the crow could not eat the worm.

23 The crow solved the problem just as in the fable.

24 It dropped stones into the jar.

25 If you think this bird is special, you are wrong.

26 Scientists did the same experiment with other crows, and they all did the same, too.

시험대비 실력평가
p.196~201

01 (A) watch (B) to floss (C) are

02 ②

03 ④ 　　04 ⑤ 　　05 ⑤

06 (A) low (B) solved (C) wrong

07 to raise the level of water 　　08 ①, ⑤

09 ④ 　　10 will go → go 　　11 ①, ④

12 ④ 　　13 for 　　14 ⑤ 　　15 (f)able

16 ordinary → special 　　17 ①, ④ / ②, ③, ⑤

18 ④ 　　19 use tools 　　20 ②

21 (A) can't (B) under (C) pile

22 coconut shells 　　23 ③

24 very well 　　25 ④ 　　26 ④

27 The crow solved the problem just as in the fable.

28 ② 　　29 ⑤ 　　30 Scientists

31 (A) dropped (B) into 　　32 ③ 　　33 ②

02 ②번은 허가를 나타내어 '~해도 좋다'라는 뜻이고, ⓐ와 나머지는 다 추측을 나타내어 '~일지도 모른다'라는 뜻이다.

03 ④ 항상 볼 수 있는 것이 아니라, '만약 당신이 운이 좋으면 볼 수 있다.'

04 ⑤ them은 '문어'가 아니라 '코코넛 껍데기'를 지칭한다.

05 ⑤ 문어들이 몇 개의 코코넛 껍데기를 저장하는 지는 대답할 수 없다. ① No. ② Yes. ③ Coconut shells. ④ They hide under coconut shells.

06 (A) 물 높이가 '낮아서' 까마귀는 그 벌레를 먹을 수 없었다고 해야 하므로 low가 적절하다. (B) 그 까마귀는 우화에서처럼 문제를 '해결했다'고 해야 하므로 solved가 적절하다. give up: 포기하다, (C) 이 새가 특별하다고 생각한다면, 당신이 '틀렸다'고 해야 하므로 wrong이 적절하다.

07 까마귀는 '물 높이를 높이기 위해' 항아리 안으로 돌을 떨어 뜨렸다.

08 ⓐ와 ①, ⑤는 부사적 용법,

② 명사적 용법(보어),

③과 ④ 형용사적 용법

09 ④번 다음 문장의 This way에 주목한다. 주어진 문장의 내용을 받고 있으므로 ④번이 적절하다.

10 조건의 부사절에서는 현재시제가 미래시제를 대신한다.

11 ⓑ와 ②, ③, ⑤는 부사적 용법(목적), ① 형용사적 용법, ④ 명사적 용법

12 앞에 나오는 내용과 상반되는 내용이 뒤에 이어지므로 However가 가장 적절하다. ① 그러므로, ② 게다가, ③ 대신에, ⑤ 예를 들면

13 ⓑ for protection: 보호하기 위해,

ⓒ for later use: 나 중에 쓰기 위해서

14 ⑤ 몇몇 문어들은 코코넛 껍데기를 '나중에' 쓰기 위해 가지고 다닌다.

15 fable: 우화, 도덕적 교훈을 가르치고, 가끔 동물을 주인공으로 다루는 이야기

16 이 새가 '특별하다'고 생각한다면 당신이 틀렸다고 해야 하므로, ordinary를 special로 고치는 것이 적절하다. ordinary: 보통의, 평범한

17 ⓐ: 관계대명사, ⓑ: 접속사

18 본문의 끝에서 이제 과학자들은 많은 동물들 역시 도구를 사용할 수 있다는 것을 밝혀내고 있다고 했기 때문에, 다음에 올 내용으로는 ④번이 적절하다.

19 이제 과학자들은 인간들뿐만 아니라 많은 동물들도 '도구를 사용할 수 있다'는 것을 밝혀내고 있다. not only A but also B: A뿐만 아니라 B도

20 ①에서 언급한 protection에 대한 설명이 ③에서 계속되고 있는데, 그 사이의 '코코넛 껍데기는 잠자기에 좋은 장소'라는 ②번 문장은 전체 글의 흐름에서 벗어난다.

21 (A)와 (B) 숨을 만한 좋은 장소를 찾을 수 '없을' 때, 코코넛 껍데기 '아래로' 숨는다고 해야 하므로 각각 can't와 under가 적절하다. (C) 코코넛 껍데기를 '쌓아두고' 나중에 쓰기 위해서 그것들을 가지고 다닌다고 해야 하므로 pile이 적절하다. pile: (물건을 차곡차곡) 쌓다[포개다], file: 서류철

22 그들은 보호를 위한 도구로 '코코넛 껍데기'를 사용한다.

23 ③ 자이언트 판다가 얼마나 빨리 달릴 수 있는지는 대답할 수 없다. ① They grow 1.2m to 1.9m long and weigh up to 135kg. ② They live in the wild, high up in the mountains of China. ④ They eat leaves, fish, and small animals. ⑤ They are very good at climbing trees. They take a rest on trees. They even walk from one tree to another.

24 be good at ~ing: ~을 잘하다

25 (C)의 However가 주어진 글과 반대되는 내용을 이끄는 것이므로 제일 먼저 오고 (C)에서 언급한 protection에 대한 설명이 (A)에서 계속되므로 (C) 다음에 (A)가 이어지고 (B)의 the coconut shells가 (A)의 마지막에 나오는 coconut shells를 가리키므로 (A) 다음에 (B)가 와야 한다. 그러므로 (C)-(A)-(B)의 순서가 적절하다.

26 주어진 문장의 They에 주목한다. ④번 앞 문장의 Scientists를 가리키므로 ④번이 적절하다.

27 just as: 꼭 ~처럼

28 까마귀는 영리한 동물이고 도구를 사용할 줄 안다는 내용의 글이다.

29 위 글은 문어들이 매우 영리하다는 것을 설명하는 글이므로, '문어, 영리한 동물!'이 제목으로 적절하다.

30 '과학자들'을 가리킨다.

31 까마귀가 벌레를 먹을 수 없었을 때, 그것은 이솝 우화 '목마른 까마귀'의 까마귀가 그러는 것처럼 수위를 높이기 위해 항아리 '안으로' '돌'을 떨어뜨렸다.

32 (B)의 They가 주어진 글의 the Macaque monkeys를 가리키므로 제일 먼저 오고 (A)의 the female monkeys가 (C)의 female monkeys를 가리키므로 (C) 다음에 (A)가 와야 한다. 그러므로 (B)-(C)-(A)의 순서가 적절하다.

33 (B)의 this가 주어진 글의 내용을 가리키므로 제일 먼저 오고 (A)의 They가 (B)의 Scientists를 가리키므로 (B) 다음에 (A)가 이어지고 (C)의 It이 (A)의 마지막에 나오는 The crow를 가리키므로 (A) 다음에 (C)가 와야 한다. 그러므로 (B)-(A)-(C)의 순서가 적절하다.

서술형 시험대비 p.202~203

01 Uses → Use 02 that
03 (A) animals (B) humans
04 (A) pull (B) lucky (C) While
05 female monkeys 06 pulling out
07 to prevent accidents → for protection
08 pile 09 stones 10 with
11 과학자들이 다른 까마귀들에게도 똑같은 실험을 했고, 그들 모두가 똑같이 그렇게 했기 때문이다.
12 when they can't find a good hiding place
13 Some octopuses even store coconut shells for later use.
14 to carry → carry

01 선행사인 Animals가 복수이므로 Use가 적절하다.

02 목적어에 해당하는 명사절을 이끄는 접속사 that을 생략할 수 있다.

03 '인간들' 외에도 도구를 사용할 수 있는 많은 '동물들'이 있다. in addition to: ~에 더하여, ~뿐 아니라

04 (A) 당신의 머리카락을 '뽑을 수도' 있다고 해야 하므로 pull이 적절하다. push: 밀다, (B) 만약 네가 '운이 좋으면'이라고 해야 하므로 lucky가 적절하다. unlucky: 불행한, (C) 뒤에 '주어+동사'가 이어지므로 While이 적절하다. during 다음에는 기간을 나타내는 명사가 나온다.

05 새끼들에게 치실질하는 것을 가르치고 있는 '암컷 원숭이들'을 가리킨다.

06 전치사 by 다음에 동명사로 쓰는 것이 적절하다.

07 문어들은 매우 영리하고, 사고를 예방하기 위해서가 아니라 '보호를 위해' 코코넛 껍데기를 사용한다.

08 물건들을 서로 겹쳐 놓다, pile: (물건을 차곡차곡) 쌓다[포개다]

09 까마귀가 낮은 물 높이 때문에 벌레를 먹을 수 없었을 때, 그것은 물 높이를 높이기 위해 항아리 안으로 돌을 떨어뜨렸다.

10 ⓐ a jar with water: 물이 든 항아리, ⓒ with other crows: 다른 까마귀들에게도

11 다른 까마귀들도 똑같이 했기 때문에, 이 새가 특별하다고 생각한다면 당신이 틀렸다.

12 그들을 '숨을 만한 좋은 장소를 찾지 못할 때' 보호를 위해 그들은 코코넛 껍데기 아래로 숨는다.

13 'later'를 보충하면 된다.

14 'pile'과 병렬구문을 이루도록 하는 것이 적절하다.

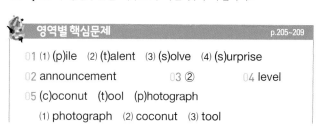

영역별 핵심문제 p.205~209

01 (1) (p)ile (2) (t)alent (3) (s)olve (4) (s)urprise
02 announcement 03 ② 04 level
05 (c)oconut (t)ool (p)hotograph
(1) photograph (2) coconut (3) tool

06 (1) The body of an octopus looks like a bag.

(2) The arms of a gorilla are longer than its legs.

07 (A) big (B) navy (C) flower

08 (A) scarf (B) blue (C) star

09 ③　　　　10 (A) ③ (B) ④ (C) ②

11 the bag which is big and orange

12 ④　　　　13 ④

14 Mr. Kim lives in a house. It has many big windows.

15 ③　　　16 ④　　　17 ②　　　18 ⑤

19 ①　　　20 ③

21 This is the snack shop which[that] is famous for corn dogs.

22 ②　　　23 (A) watching (B) floss[flossing]

24 ⑤　　　25 ②　　　26 to use　　　27 ⑤

28 ①　　　29 that 또는 which

30 그녀는 사람들과 수화로 말할 수 있다. 그녀는 1,000개가 넘는 신호를 안다.

01 주어진 보기는 유의어의 관계이다. (1) stack: 쌓다, 포개다 / pile 쌓다, 포개다 (2) gift: 타고난 재능 / talent: 재능 (3) deal with: ~을 해결하다 / solve: 해결하다, 풀다 (4) amaze: 몹시 놀라게 하다 / surprise: 놀라게 하다

02 announce: 발표하다 / announcement: 발표, 소식

03 ① whale, whale: 고래 ② examples, example: 예, 예제 ③ protection, protection: 보호 ④ pattern, pattern: 무늬, 도안 ⑤ shells, shell: (딱딱한) 껍데기, 껍질

04 level: 높이, 정도, 수준

05 (1) photograph: 사진 (2) coconut: 코코넛 열매 (3) tool: 도구

06 (1) body: 몸 / look like: ~처럼 보이다, ~와 닮다 / bag: 가방 (2) arm: 팔 / loner than ~: ~보다 긴 / gorilla: 고릴라

07 small: 작은 / big: 큰 / pink: 분홍색 / navy: 남색 / cloud pattern: 구름무늬 / flower pattern: 꽃무늬

08 (A) scarf: 스카프, 목도리

(B) blue: 파란색 / grey: 회색

(C) star pattern: 별무늬

09 (B) 화장실에 가방을 두고 와서, 가방을 찾고 있다고 말한다.

(C) 이에 가방의 생김새를 물어본다. (A) 큰 은색 가방이라고 대답한다. (D) (직원이) 가서 확인해 본다고 말한다.

10 (A) May I help you?: 도와드릴까요?

(B) 크기와 색깔이 대답으로 나왔으므로, 생김새를 묻는 질문이 어울린다.

(C) 가방의 다른 특징을 설명하는 대답을 하므로, 또 다른 특징을 묻는 질문이 어울린다.

11 명사+관계대명사 which+동사 ~: ~인 명사

12 어디서 잃어버렸는지 물어보는 질문에, 방송을 하겠다는 대답은

어색하다.

13 ④번은 목적격 관계대명사이고 나머지는 모두 주격 관계대명사이다.

14 선행사가 사물이므로 which로 연결한 문장이다.

15 주어진 문장과 ③번은 조건을 나타내는 부사절을 이끌고 있다. ①, ②, ④번은 '~인지 아닌지'의 뜻으로 명사절을 이끌고 있다. ⑤ 가정법에 쓰인 if이다.

16 조건의 부사절에서는 현재시제로 미래시제를 대신하므로 has가 적절하다.

17 ② I received some flowers yesterday that the boy sent me.

18 조건을 나타내는 부사절을 이끄는 if가 적절하다.

19 선행사가 동물이므로 which나 that이 알맞다.

20 ③ 시간이나 조건을 나타내는 부사절에서는 현재시제가 미래시제를 대신한다.

21 선행사가 사물이므로 which나 that을 이용한다.

22 ⓐ와 ③번 ⑤번은 현재분사, ① 동명사(보어), ② 동명사(목적어), ④ 동명사(주어)

23 새끼 원숭이들은 암컷 원숭이들이 아주 천천히 그들의 이빨을 치실질하는 것을 보면서 치실질을 배운다. (A) 전치사 by 다음에 동명사로 쓰는 것이 적절하다. (B) 지각동사 watch+목적어+동사원형 또는 현재분사

24 문어가 보호를 위해 코코넛 껍데기를 사용하는 것은 '도구'를 사용하는 것에 해당하므로 tools가 적절하다.

25 주어진 문장의 'protection'에 주목한다. ②번 다음 문장의 내용이 'protection'에 대한 설명에 해당하므로 ②번이 적절하다.

26 '나중에 쓰기 위해'라고 해야 하므로, 부사적 용법(목적)의 to부정사로 쓰는 것이 적절하다.

27 ⑤ '이 새가 특별하다고 생각한다면, 당신이 틀렸다'고 했다.

28 ①은 이솝 우화 '목마른 까마귀'에 나오는 까마귀를 가리키고, 나머지는 다 과학자들이 행한 실험 대상인 까마귀를 가리킨다.

29 선행사가 동물이고 주어 자리이므로, 주격 관계대명사 that이나 which를 쓰는 것이 적절하다.

30 Sign Language: 수화

단원별 예상문제　　　p.210~213

01 (1) tool to fix　(2) surprised　(3) floating　02 ③

03 (1) imagine, like　(2) way to solve　　　04 ①

05 ③　　　06 ③　　　07 ②　　　08 ⑤

09 ④　　　10 ③

11 She's not big but her legs are very strong.

12 Coco can stand on two legs and dance to music.

13 ②, ⑤

14 (1) If school finishes early today

(2) If the weather is nice tomorrow

(3) Unless you exercise hard

(4) Unless you try hard

15 ③　　　16 unless　　　17 ③　　　18 ④

19 (1) The students who exercise every day are healthy.

(2) The girl who is eating an ice cream is kind.

(3) She has a machine which makes cotton candy.

(4) If the weather is good tomorrow, we'll go to the park and fly kites.

20 ②　　　21 ④

22 새끼들이 지켜보고 있는 동안, 암컷 원숭이들이 아주 천천히 그들의 이빨을 치실질 함으로써

23 ③　　　24 (A) hiding (B) carry (C) How

25 weight → weigh　　　26 ④

01 (1) tool: 도구, 수단 / to fix: 고치기 위해서(to부정사의 부사적 용법) (2) surprise: 놀라게 하다 (3) float: [물체가] (액체면에) 뜨다, 떠다니다

02 announcement: 발표, 소식 / 사람들에게 말하는 중요한 어떤 것

03 (1) imagine: 상상하다 / like: ~와 같이 (2) way: 방법, 방식 / way to 동사: ~하는 방식 / solve: 해결하다, 풀다

04 tool: 도구, 수단 / equipment: 장치, 설비

05 ③ 'What's ~ like?'는 '~는 어때?'라는 뜻으로 성격, 성품 또는 상태를 묻는 질문이다.

06 ⓐ I'm looking like → I'm looking for, look for: ~을 찾다 ⓒ What does it look like?: 그것은 어떻게 생겼나요? ⓔ It'll → I'll, 사람이 가서 확인하는 것이니, 사물 주어 It이 아니라 사람 주어 I가 나와야 한다.

07 ⓒ They're → It's ⓓ Can you tell me more about it? about이 들어가야 한다.

08 안내 방송을 하는 동안 기다려 달라는 말이 적절하다.

09 ① help ② is ③ look ④ has ⑤ lost

10 잃어버린 개의 크기가 매우 작다고 했다. not very small → very small

11 but: 하지만 / leg: 다리 / very: 매우

12 can: ~할 수 있다 / dance to music: 음악에 맞춰 춤추다

13 선행사가 사람이고 주격이므로 who나 that을 써야 한다.

14 unless = if ~ not

15 ③ 선행사가 사람과 사물이므로 관계대명사는 that을 써야 한다.

16 unless = if ~ not

17 선행사가 사람일 때와 사물일 때 모두 쓰일 수 있는 것은 that이다.

18 조건절이 미래의 일을 나타낼 때에도 조건절의 시제는 현재형을 쓴다.

19 (1)~(3) 선행사가 사람이면 who를, 사물이나 동물이면 which를 쓴다. (4) 조건절에서는 현재시제로 미래시제를 대신한다.

20 ①번에서 마카크 원숭이들이 당신에게 다가와 당신의 머리카락을 뽑을 수도 있다고 한 다음 ③번에서 그 이유를 설명하고 있는데, 그 사이의 '그들은 사람들과 노는 것을 좋아한다.'는 ②번 문장은 전체 글의 흐름에서 벗어난다.

21 ⓐ watch out for: ~을 경계하다[조심하다], ⓑ teach는 to를 사용하여 3형식으로 고친다.

22 암컷 원숭이들은 새끼들이 지켜보고 있는 동안 아주 천천히 그들의 이빨을 치실질함으로써 새끼들에게 치실질을 가르친다.

23 숨을 만한 좋은 장소를 찾지 못할 때, 그들은 코코넛 껍데기 아래로 숨는다는 말이 이어지므로, ③번 '보호'를 위해 코코넛 껍데기를 사용한다고 하는 것이 적절하다. ① 공격, ② 예방, ④ 수리, ⑤ 절약, 저축

24 (A) '숨기에 좋은 장소'라고 해야 하므로 동명사형 hiding이 적절하다. hiding place: 은신처; 은폐 장소, hide를 쓰려면 a good place to hide라고 하는 것이 적절하다. (B) pile과 병렬구문을 이뤄야 하므로 carry가 적절하다. (C) 뒤에 형용사가 나오므로 How가 적절하다. How 형용사 또는 부사 (주어+동사)!, What a[an] 형용사 명사 (주어+동사)!

25 동사를 써야 하므로 weight를 weigh로 고치는 것이 적절하다. weight: (명사) 무게

26 ④ 얼룩말의 수명은 알 수 없다.

01 (1) What does it look like?

(2) How does it look?

02 pattern

03 (1) I teach sign language to gorillas.

(2) They have a black and white stripe on their wings.

04 (1) hurry, will, miss　　　(2) rains, will not go

(3) won't be, see

05 (1) Ann lives in the house which[that] has a beautiful garden.

(2) These are the pictures which[that] were painted by Picasso.

(3) I want to play with the boy who[that] has a new board game.

06 (1) The old lady who is 80 years old still looks healthy.

(2) She has a bird that can repeat after people's words.

(3) If you help me, I will be happy. 또는 I will be happy if you help me.

07 (1) I will see the doctor if I don't feel better tomorrow.

(2) If I get a ticket, I'll go to the concert.

(3) If it snows tomorrow, we will go skiing.

08 they use human hair to floss their teeth

09 which

10 While the babies are watching, the female monkeys floss their teeth very slowly.

11 just a story

12 the water level was low

13 dropped stones into the jar

01 'What does ~ look like?'는 '~는 어떻게 생겼니?'라는 의미로 주어의 외모나 생김새를 묻는 질문이다. 비슷한 표현으로 'How does ~ look?', 'How do you describe ~?', 'Tell me what ~ looks like.' 등이 있다.

02 규칙적으로 반복되는 일련의 선, 모양, 색깔: pattern (무늬, 도안)

03 (1) sign: 몸짓, 신호, 표시 / teach 목적어+to 대상: ~에게 ~을 가르치다 (2) stripe: 줄무늬

04 조건절에서는 현재시제로 미래시제를 대신한다.

05 (1), (2) 선행사가 사람이면 that이나 who를, 사물이나 동물이면 that이나 which를 쓴다. (3) who를 목적격 whom 대신 쓸 수 있지만 whom을 who 대신 쓰지는 않는다.

06 (1), (2) 선행사가 사람이면 that이나 who를, 사물이나 동물이면 that이나 which를 쓴다. (3) 주절이 앞에 나와도 되고 종속절이 앞에 나와도 된다.

07 (1) 'unless = if ~ not'이므로 if로 고쳐야 한다. 보통 unless가 이끄는 절에는 부정어가 나오지 않는다. (2), (3) 조건절에서는 현재시제로 미래시제를 대신한다.

08 마카크 원숭이들은 이빨을 치실질하기 위해서 사람의 머리 카락을 사용하기 때문에, 사람들에게 와서 머리카락을 뽑을지도 모른다.

09 선행사가 동물이므로, 주격 관계대명사 which로 바꿔 쓸 수 있다.

10 While 다음에는 보통 진행형이 나오는 경우가 많다.

11 당신은 이것이 그저 이야기라고 생각할지도 모르지만, 그렇지 않다('단지 이야기가 아니다')

12 '물 높이가 낮아서' 까마귀는 물 위에 떠 있는 벌레를 먹을 수 없었다.

13 다른 까마귀들도 모두 '항아리 안으로 돌을 떨어뜨렸다'는 뜻이다.

창의사고력 서술형 문제 p.216

|모범답안|

01 cat, grey, long

I'm looking for my cat., It's small and it has grey, has a long tail, Where, I lost it near the library.

02 (1) who flies an airplane

(2) who paints pictures

(3) who drives a car

(4) who bakes bread

(5) who teaches students at school

01 그림을 보면, 잃어버린 동물의 종류는 고양이(cat)이고, 이 고양이는 회색 털(grey hair)을 가지고 있다. 이외의 특징으로는 긴 꼬리 (long tail)를 가지고 있다.

단원별 모의고사 p.217~220

01 ④   02 ②

03 (1) out   (2) at   (3) on, of   (4) to

04 (1) record, during   (2) while

(3) the first female   (4) told, fables

05 (A) coin purse (B) a key chain

06 smiley   07 Can you tell me more about it?

08 (1) long brown → short yellow

(2) a racket → a book

(3) her → him

09 ⓐ help   ⓑ is   ⓒ look   ⓓ has   ⓔ has

10 I lost him near the main gate.   11 ④

12 lost, umbrella / yellow / a white flower pattern

13 (1) I have a dog which[that] is eleven years old.

(2) I like the car which[that] won the race.

(3) The boy who[that] has blond hair is my little brother.

(4) If it snows, we won't go to the park.

14 ⑤   15 ①

16 (1) It worked really well.

(2) He drove me to school.

17 ②   18 ④   19 that are   20 ②

21 hide   22 ⑤   23 ⑤

24 항아리에 들어 있는 물 위에 벌레 한 마리가 떠 있지만 물 높이가 낮아서 까마귀가 그 벌레를 먹을 수 없는 것

01 유의어 관계 ① pattern: 무늬, 도안 design: 디자인, 무늬 ② way: 방법 method: 방법, 방식 ③ photograph: 사진 picture: 그림, 사진 ⑤ record: 기록하다, 등록하다; 기록 document: 기록하다; 기록 (물)) ④ 반의어 관계 slowly: 천천히 fast: 빨리

02 try to find: 찾으려고 노력하다 ② look for: ~을 찾다 ③ talk with: ~와 이야기하다 ④ look like: ~처럼 보이다, ~ 와 닮다

03 (1) find out: 알아내다 (2) be good at: ~을 잘하다, ~에 능숙하다 (3) on top of: ~ 위에 (4) dance to music: 음악에 맞춰 춤추다

04 (1) record: 기록하다, 등록하다 / during+기간 명사: ~ 동안 (2) while+주어+동사: ~하는 동안에 (3) female: 여성의, 암

38   정답 및 해설

컷의 (4) fable: 우화, 동화

05 그림에서 표시된 물건은 동전지갑이다. coin purse: 동전 지갑 / key chain: 열쇠고리

06 smiley: 동그라미 속에 눈 두 개와 웃는 입 모양을 그려 넣은 단순한 얼굴 그림 ☺

07 tell(4형식 동사)+me(간접목적어)+more about it(직접목적어): 그것에 대해 더 많은 것을 나에게 말하다

08 그림을 보면, Steve는 짧고 노란색 머리카락을 가지고 있다. 또한 그는 안경을 쓰고, 책 한 권을 들고 있다. short: 짧은 / yellow: 노란색 / glasses: 안경 / hold: 잡고 있다

09 May I help you? 도와드릴까요?, 외모를 묘사할 때에는 'be동사+형용사' 혹은 'have+형용사+명사'의 표현을 사용할 수 있다. look like: ~처럼 보이다, ~와 닮다

10 lose–lost–lost: 잃어버리다 / near: ~ 근처에서

11 ④ announcement: 발표, 소식 / make an announcement: 방송을 하다

12 umbrella: 우산 / yellow: 노란색 / pattern: 무늬 / white: 하얀색

14 a girl이 선행사이고 주격이므로 who나 that을 써야 한다. ③번은 관계대명사나 접속사와 주어가 없어서 잘못되었으며 관계대명사는 접속사와 대명사의 역할을 하므로 ④번에서는 who 다음의 she를 생략해야 한다.

15 조건의 부사절을 이끄는 if가 적절하다.

17 주어진 문장과 ②번은 부사절을 이끌고 있으나 나머지는 명사절을 이끌고 있다.

18 ④ 수컷 원숭이들이 새끼 원숭이들에게 무엇을 가르치는지는 대답할 수 없다. ① Because they may come to you and pull out your hair. ② They use human hair. ③ No. ⑤ By flossing their teeth very slowly while the babies are watching.

19 주격 관계대명사와 be동사를 같이 생략할 수 있다.

20 ⓑ와 ②번은 명사적 용법, ① 형용사적 용법, ③ 부사적 용법(이유), ④ 형용사적 용법, ⑤ 부사적 용법(목적)

21 문어들은 '숨기에' 좋은 장소를 찾을 수 없을 때, 보호를 위해 코코넛 껍데기 아래에 '숨는다'

22 ⓐ와 ⑤ 저장하다, ① 상점, ② 비축[저장]량, ③ 「형용사적으로」기성품인, store clothes: 기성복, ④ (특정한 종류의 상품) 저장고[창고], a grain store: 곡물 저장

23 앞에 나오는 내용과 상반되는 내용이 뒤에 이어지므로 However가 가장 적절하다. ① 예를 들면, ② 게다가, 더욱이, ③ 즉, 다시 말해, ④ 그 결과

24 과학자들이 실험에서 설정한 상황을 가리킨다.

교과서 파헤치기

Lesson 1

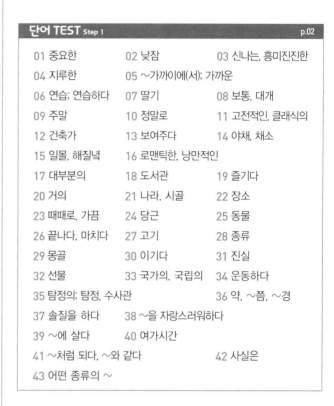

단어 TEST Step 1   p.02

01 중요한	02 낮잠	03 신나는, 흥미진진한
04 지루한	05 ~가까이에(서); 가까운	
06 연습; 연습하다	07 딸기	08 보통, 대개
09 주말	10 정말로	11 고전적인, 클래식의
12 건축가	13 보여주다	14 야채, 채소
15 일몰, 해질녘	16 로맨틱한, 낭만적인	
17 대부분의	18 도서관	19 즐기다
20 거의	21 나라, 시골	22 장소
23 때때로, 가끔	24 당근	25 동물
26 끝나다, 마치다	27 고기	28 종류
29 몽골	30 이기다	31 진실
32 선물	33 국가의, 국립의	34 운동하다
35 탐정의; 탐정, 수사관	36 약, ~쯤, ~경	
37 솔질을 하다	38 ~을 자랑스러워하다	
39 ~에 살다	40 여가시간	
41 ~처럼 되다, ~와 같다	42 사실은	
43 어떤 종류의 ~		

단어 TEST Step 2   p.03

01 when	02 times	03 garden
04 favorite	05 because	06 bake
07 dessert	08 southern	09 sci-fi
10 race	11 ride	12 peaceful
13 novel	14 culture	15 between
16 detective	17 especially	18 free
19 like	20 outside	21 meat
22 horror	23 funny	24 lie
25 sunset	26 boring	27 truth
28 romantic	29 classical	30 exercise
31 sometimes	32 really	33 present
34 architect	35 almost	36 important
37 siesta	38 take care of	39 get together
40 both A and B	41 live in	42 be on
43 be proud of		

1 boring, 지루한   2 nap, 낮잠   3 ride, 타다
4 classical, 고전적인   5 race, 경주
6 practice, 연습하다   7 sunset, 일몰, 해질녘
8 peaceful, 평화로운   9 dessert, 디저트, 후식
10 win, 이기다
11 favorite, 가장 좋아하는   12 usually, 대개, 보통
13 garden, 정원   14 truth, 진실
15 exercise, 운동하다   16 horror, 공포

Listen and Talk A-1

usually, free time / playing games / What kind of / usually play

Listen and Talk A-2

in your free time / go to / read / What kind of / detective stories, really

Listen and Talk A-3

in your free time / listen to / kind of, listen to / Rock

Listen and Talk A-4

when, have free time / enjoy baking / kind, make / usually make, strawberries

Listen and Talk B

usually do / usually listen to / What kind of music / listen to classical

Listen and Talk C

uaually, in / exercise outside / kind of exercise / play, with, usually do, free time / watching movies / What kind of, like / action movies, fun / sometimes watch, Why don't we, action / sounds great

Review 1

uaually, free time / uaually listen to, How about / like detective

Review 2

usually, when, have / watch movies / What kind, watch / action, favorite, star

Review 3

does, free time / games, play

Listen and Talk A-1

G: Hajun, what do you usually do in your free time?
B: I like playing games with my dad.
G: What kind of games do you play?

B: I usually play baduk.

Listen and Talk A-2

G: Hey, Eric. What do you usually do in your free time?
B: I go to the library and read books.
G: What kind of books do you read?
B: I like reading detective stories. I really like Sherlock Holmes' stories.

Listen and Talk A-3

G: Seho, what do you do in your free time?
B: I listen to music.
G: What kind of music do you listen to?
B: Rock music.

Listen and Talk A-4

G: Chris, what do you do when you have free time?
B: I make cookies. I enjoy baking.
G: What kind of cookies do you make?
B: I usually make strawberry cookies. I love strawberries.

Listen and Talk B

A: Minji, what do you usually do in your free time?
B: I usually listen to music.
A: What kind of music do you listen to?
B: I listen to classical music.

Listen and Talk C

B: Subin, what do you usually do in your free time?
G: I exercise outside.
B: What kind of exercise do you do?
G: I play badminton with my brother. I'm on the school's badminton team. What do you usually do in your free time, Andy?
B: I like watching movies.
G: What kind of movies do you like?
B: I like action movies. They're fun.
G: Oh, I sometimes watch action movies, too. Why don't we go see an action movie this weekend?
B: Sure. That sounds great.

Review 1

B: Emma, what do you usually do in your free time?
G: I usually listen to music. How about you, Chris?
B: I read books. I like detective stories.

Review 2

G: Jiho, what do you usually do when you have free time?
B: I usually watch movies.
G: What kind of movies do you watch?
B: I like action movies. Bruce Lee is my favorite movie star.

Review 3

1. W: What does Minho usually do in his free time?
2. W: What kind of games does Sewon play?

01 Favorite, Day   02 Hello, I'm

03 years old, in   04 tell, your favorite

05 show me, pictures   06 my, live in

07 My, of, day   08 usually ends around

09 most, gets together

10 usually have, vegetables   11 also have, like

12 usually take, nap

13 Both, and, under   14 live near, in

15 when, ride my

16 important in, culture

17 Almost everyone, ride   18 In fact, before

19 take, care of   20 brush, give him

21 enjoy riding, before

22 Then, is peaceful

23 in Nairobi, Kenya

24 favorite, running practice

25 on, school's running

26 happiest when, with

27 boring because, can

28 from, won races

29 so proud of   30 and, be like

01 Teen, My Favorite   02 I'm

03 years old, live in

04 tell, about favorite

05 also show, pictures   06 my, live in

07 favorite, lunch 08 usually, around

09 On, gets together

10 usually have, vegetables   11 have, like

12 usually take, nap

13 Both, and, under   14 near, in

15 when I ride   16 important, culture

17 Almost, can ride   18 In fact, before

19 take, care of   20 often brush, carrots

21 enjoy riding, sunset

22 everything peaceful   23 live in

24 favorite, running practice

25 are on, running

26 happiest, run with

27 practice, boring, can

28 runners, won races   29 proud of

30 Both, and, to be

1 십대들의 이야기: 하루 중 내가 가장 좋아하는 시간

2 안녕! 나는 소민이야.

3 나는 15살이고 한국에 살아.

4 너희들이 하루 중 가장 좋아하는 시간에 대해 말해 줘.

5 나에게 사진 몇 장을 보여 줘도 좋아.

6 안녕, 내 이름은 Diego이고, 나는 스페인의 새비야에서 살아.

7 내가 하루 중 가장 좋아하는 시간은 점심시간이야.

8 우리 학교는 보통 오후 2시경에 끝나.

9 대부분의 날에는, 가족들이 모여서 푸짐하고 긴 점심 식사를 해.

10 우리는 보통 수프, 채소 그리고 고기를 먹어.

11 우리는 또한 추로스와 같은 후식도 먹어.

12 점심 식사 후에는 우리는 보통 시에스타, 즉 짧은 낮잠을 자.

13 아빠와 나는 둘 다 우리 정원에 있는 나무 미에서 자는 것을 좋아해.

14 안녕! 내 이름은 Tabin이고, 나는 몽골에 있는 고비 사막 근처에 살아.

15 나는 내 말을 탈 때 행복해.

16 말은 우리 문화에서 중요해.

17 몽골에서는 거의 모든 사람이 말을 탈 수 있어.

18 실제로 우리는 "우리는 걸을 수 있기 전에 말을 탄다."라고 말해.

19 나는 내 말을 잘 돌봐.

20 나는 종종 내 말의 털을 빗겨 주고 당근을 줘.

21 나는 특히 해가 지기 전 저녁에 말 타는 것을 즐겨.

22 그 무렵엔 하늘은 붉고 모든 것이 평화로워.

23 안녕! 나는 Musa이고, 케냐의 나이로비에 살아.

24 내가 하루 중 가장 좋아하는 시간은 달리기 연습 시간이야.

25 내 친구 Tamu와 나는 학교 달리기 팀이야.

26 나는 Tamu와 달리기를 할 때 가장 행복해.

27 우리의 연습 시간은 지루하지 않아, 왜냐하면 우리는 많은 동물들을 볼 수 있기 때문이야.

28 케냐의 많은 달리기 선수들이 올림픽의 육상 경기에서 우승을 했어.

29 나는 그들이 매우 자랑스러워.

30 Tamu와 나는 둘 다 그들처럼 되고 싶어.

1 Teen Talk: My Favorite Time of the Day

2 Hello! I'm Somin.

3 I'm 15 years old, and I live in Korea.

4 Please tell me about your favorite time of the day.

5 You can also show me some pictures.

6 Hi, my name is Diego, and I live in Seville, Spain.

7 My favorite time of the day is lunch time.

8 My school usually ends around 2 p.m.

9 On most days, my family gets together and has a big, long lunch.

10 We usually have soup, vegetables, and meat.

11 We also have a dessert like churros.

12 After lunch, we usually take a siesta, a short nap.

13 Both my father and I like to sleep under the tree in our garden.

14 Hi! My name is Tabin, and I live near the Gobi Desert in Mongolia.

15 I'm happy when I ride my horse.

16 Horses are important in our culture.

17 Almost everyone can ride a horse in Mongolia.

18 In fact, we say, "We ride horses before we can walk."

19 I take good care of my horse.

20 I often brush him and give him some carrots.

21 I enjoy riding especially in the evening before the sunset.

22 Then the sky is red, and everything is peaceful.

23 Hi! I'm Musa, and I live in Nairobi, Kenya.

24 My favorite time of the day is our running practice time.

25 My friend, Tamu, and I are on the school's running team.

26 I'm happiest when I run with Tamu.

27 Our practice time isn't boring because we can see many animals.

28 Many runners from Kenya won races in the Olympics.

29 I'm so proud of them.

30 Both Tamu and I want to be like them.

Before You Read

1. in southern
2. take a short nap
3. is in East
4. Almost everyone, ride
5. in East Africa
6. There are, from

Around the World

1. in, live in, for long
2. move, around
3. usually eat, times a day
4. between
5. national, with, like

Think and Write

1. happiest, exciting
2. when I eat
3. tells me funny jokes
4. when I play with

Before You Read

1. This country is in southern Europe.
2. People here usually take a short nap in the afternoon.
3. This country is in East Asia.
4. Almost everyone can ride a horse here.
5. This country is in East Africa.
6. There are many great runners from here.

Around the World

1. Some people in this country don't live in one place for long.
2. They move around with their animals.
3. People in this country usually eat four or five times a day.
4. They eat tapas between meals.
5. This country has many national parks with animals like lions, zebras, elephants, and giraffes.

Think and Write

1. I'm happiest when I read exciting novels.
2. I'm happiest when I eat candy.
3. I'm happiest when my brother tells me funny jokes.
4. I'm happiest when I play with my friends after school.

단어 TEST Step 1 p.21

01 놀라운	02 서점	03 조합, 결합
04 전망, 경관	05 기차역	06 겁먹은, 무서운
07 건강한	08 취소하다	09 비싼
10 독특한, 특별한	11 (상을) 타다, (경기에서) 이기다	
12 똑바로, 곧장, 곧바로		13 깁다, 바느질하다
14 상	15 영화관	16 전통
17 매운, 양념이 강한	18 경찰서	19 진흙
20 정문	21 작물, 천	22 매다
23 생산하다, 만들다	24 따르다	25 모으다, 수집하다
26 모임	27 바퀴	28 맛있는
29 박물관	30 참가하다, 들어가다	
31 형형색색의, 다채로운		32 담요
33 문, 대문, 출입구	34 조각	
35 ~해야 한다	36 ~을 자랑스러워하다	
37 ~로 이동하다	38 ~할 필요가 없다	39 ~가 되다
40 ~을 돌보다	41 ~에 공들이다, 애쓰다	
42 ~의 맞은편에	43 ~에 도착하다	

단어 TEST Step 2 p.22

01 across	02 goat	03 favorite
04 north	05 stage	06 third
07 state	08 over	09 city hall
10 bakery	11 blanket	12 scared
13 colorful	14 sew	15 expensive
16 collect	17 straight	18 produce
19 wheel	20 cancel	21 fasten
22 gate	23 fair	24 contest
25 exciting	26 quilt	27 block
28 past	29 fabric	30 unique
31 combination	32 tradition	33 piece
34 spicy	35 between A and B	
36 be famous for	37 next to	38 look for
39 on your right	40 take care of	41 wait for
42 across from	43 look at	

단어 TEST Step 3 p.23

1 tasty, 맛있는   2 expensive, 비싼   3 straight, 똑바로
4 unique, 독특한, 특별한   5 healthy, 건강한
6 spicy, 매운, 양념이 강한   7 produce, 만들다, 생산하다
8 collect, 모으다, 수집하다   9 combination, 조합, 결합
10 tradition, 전통   11 sew, 바느질하다
12 scared, 무서운, 두려워하는   13 museum, 박물관
14 gate, 문, 출입구   15 colorful , 형형색색의, 다채로운
16 bakery, 빵집

대화문 TEST Step 1 p.24~25

Listen and Talk A-1
looking for / straight, blocks, turn left, first, on / I see / welcome

Listen and Talk A-2
Excuse, Where's / one across from / How, get / Go straight, turn, on your right

Listen and Talk A-3
How, get to / Walk straight, be on, right / I see / between, and, can't miss / Thank you

Listen and Talk A-4
Where, Museum / on, Street / How, get, straight three blocks, on, next to / so much

Listen and Talk B
Where is / on, across from / How, get / Go straight, turn left, on / Thank

Listen and Talk C
May, help / looking for / look at, are here / see, how, get to / Go straight, left, across from / African, right / it, going to, at / where, stage / near, gate

Review 1
How, get to / Walk straight, on your right / sounds

Review 2
Excuse, Where's / on, next to / Thanks

Listen and Talk A-1

B: Excuse me. I'm looking for the Star Mall.

G: Go straight two blocks and turn left. It'll be the first building on your right.

B: Oh, I see. Thank you.

G: You're welcome.

Listen and Talk A-2

B: Excuse me. Where's the bookstore?

G: There's one across from the post office. `

B: How do I get there?

G: Go straight one block and turn right. It'll be on your right.

B: Thank you!

Listen and Talk A-3

B: Excuse me. How do I get to the police station?

G: Walk straight three blocks and turn left. It'll be on your right.

B: Oh, I see.

G: It's between the bakery and the school. You can't miss it.

B: Thank you!

Listen and Talk A-4

B: Excuse me. Where is the Histroy Museum?

G: It's on Green Street.

B: How do I get there?

G: Go straight three blocks and turn right. You'll see it on your right. It's next to the bank.

B: Thank you so much.

Listen and Talk B

A: Where is the school?

B: It's on Green Street. It's across from the hospital.

A: How do I get there?

B: Go straight three blocks and turn left. It'll be on your right.

A: Thank you.

Listen and Talk C

B: Hello. May I help you?

G: Yes, please. I'm looking for Green Park.

B: OK. Please look at this map. We are here.

G: Oh, I see. So how do I get to the park?

B: Go straight two blocks and turn left. It's across from the train station.

G: I see. The African Music Concert is there, right?

B: Yes, it is. It's going to start at 4 p.m. at the Star Concert Stage.

G: Right, and where is the stage?

B: It's near the north gate of the park.

G: OK, thank you!

Review 1

M: Excuse me. How do I get to the bookstore?

W: Walk straight two blocks and turn left. It'll be on your right.

M: That sounds easy. Thank you..

Review 2

G: Excuse me. Where's Tom's Bakery?

B: It's on Main Street. It's next to the bank.

G: Thanks.

01 at, State Fair　02 I'm Eddie

03 in Dallas, Texas　04 are at, of

05 is over, biggest　　　　　06 show, around

07 Follow me　　08 Look at　　09 goat show

10 younger, entered

11 don't have, be healthy

12 produce, lot, win　　　　13 took, care of

14 won, ribbon, third　　　　15 so proud of

16 it's, fair food　17 are eating, and

18 Tex–Max food 19 combination of, from

20 getting, because, spicy

21 are eating corn　　　　　22 taste great

23 move on, quilt

24 has, long tradition

25 In, past, expensive

26 had to collect, sew

27 quilting bee every

28 work on, for over

29 very colorful, unique

30 most exciting, riding　　　31 a tall, wheel

32 are, on, top　　33 scared, view, amazing

34 living in, going 35 come to, day

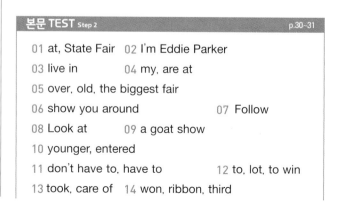

01 at, State Fair　02 I'm Eddie Parker

03 live in　　　　　04 my, are at

05 over, old, the biggest fair

06 show you around　　　　　07 Follow

08 Look at　　　09 a goat show

10 younger, entered

11 don't have to, have to　　　12 to, lot, to win

13 took, care of　14 won, ribbon, third

15 so proud of 16 so, eating fair food

17 are eating 18 Tex-Max food

19 a combination of, from

20 is getting, because, spicy 21 are eating

22 taste great 23 Let's move on

24 a long tradition

25 In the past, expensive

26 To make, had to collect, sew 27 a quilting bee

28 work on, for over 29 colorful, unique

30 most exciting, is riding 31 tall, wheel

32 are, on the top 33 scared, view,

34 love living, going to 35 to, fair

29 봐! 그 퀼트는 매우 색깔이 화려하고 독특해.

30 오늘의 가장 신나는 부분은 Texas Star를 타는 거야.

31 Texas Star는 높은 회전 관람차야.

32 우와! Steve와 나는 지금 꼭대기에 있어.

33 나는 무섭긴 하지만 전망이 멋져!

34 나는 Texas에 살고 지역 축제에 가는 것이 매우 좋아.

35 언젠가 지역 축제에 와라!

1 Texas의 주 품평회를 즐겨요!

2 안녕, 나는 Eddie Parker야.

3 나는 Texas주의 Dallas에 살아.

4 지금 우리 가족과 나는 텍사스 주 품평회에 와 있어.

5 이 품평회는 130년이 넘었고, 미국에서 가장 큰 품평회야.

6 내가 구경시켜 줄게.

7 따라와!

8 여기 염소들을 봐!

9 이건 염소 쇼야.

10 내 남동생 Steve가 이 쇼에 참가했어.

11 이 쇼의 염소들은 클 필요는 없지만 건강해야 해.

12 염소들은 상을 타기 위해서 많은 우유를 생산해야 해.

13 Steave는 자신의 염소인 Bonnie를 잘 돌봤어.

14 와! Steve와 Bonnie는 3등상인 흰색 리본을 탔어.

15 나는 그들이 매우 자랑스러워!

16 지금은 점심시간이어서 우리는 품평회 음식을 먹고 있어.

17 엄마와 아빠는 나초와 파히타를 먹고 있어.

18 그것들은 Tex-Mex 음식이야.

19 Tex-Mex 음식은 텍사스 음식과 멕시코 음식이 혼합된 거야.

20 아빠는 파히타가 너무 매워서 얼굴이 빨개지고 있어.

21 Steve와 나는 콘도그를 먹고 있어.

22 맛이 매우 좋아.

23 퀼트 대회로 이동하자.

24 퀼트 만들기는 오랜 전통을 가지고 있어.

25 과거에는 천이 비쌌어.

26 담요를 만들기 위해서 사람들은 작은 천 조각들을 모아서 꿰매 붙여야 했지.

27 할머니와 할머니의 친구들은 매주 퀼트를 만드는 모임을 가지셨어.

28 그들은 이 대회를 위해서 6개월 이상 퀼트를 만드는 작업을 하셔야 했어.

1 Fun at the State Fair of Texas!

2 Hi, I'm Eddie Parker.

3 I live in Dallas, Texas.

4 Now, my family and I are at the State Fair of Texas.

5 The fair is over 130 years old, and it's the biggest fair in the USA.

6 I'll show you around.

7 Follow me!

8 Look at the goats here!

9 This is a goat show.

10 My younger brother, Steve, entered it.

11 The goats in the show don't have to be big, but they have to be healthy.

12 They have to produce a lot of milk to win a prize.

13 Steve took good care of his goat, Bonnie.

14 Wow! Steve and Bonnie won a white ribbon, third prize!

15 I'm so proud of them!

16 Now it's lunch time, so we're eating fair food

17 Mom and Dad are eating nachos and fajitas.

18 They are Tex-Mex food.

19 Tex-Mex food is a combination of food from Texas and Mexico.

20 Dad's face is getting red because his fajita is too spicy.

21 Steve and I are eating corn dogs.

22 They taste great.

23 Let's move on to the quilt contest.

24 Quilting has a long tradition.

25 In the past, fabric was expensive.

26 To make a blanket, people had to collect small pieces of fabric and sew them together.

27 Grandma and her friends had a quilting bee every week.

28 They had to work on the quilt for the contest for over six months.

29 Look! It's very colorful and unique.

30 The most exciting part of the day is riding the Texas Star.

31 It's a tall Ferris wheel.

32 Wow! Steve and I are now on the top.

33 I'm scared, but the view is amazing!

34 I love living in Texas and going to the fair.

35 Come to the fair some day!

After You Read

1. To, STATE FAIR

2. To win, have to be, lot

3. combination of food

4. Try

5. Come and see, long tradition

6. view, from the top

Around the World

1. popular

2. At, races

3. is famous for

4. For, in this state, from

5. the most, in

6. many tasty, dishes

Think and Write

1. is full of

2. can go to

3. famous for, have to go

4. There are, traditional

5. walk around

6. us in

7. much

Before You Read

1. COME TO THE STATE FAIR OF TEXAS!

2. Goat Show: To win a prize, the goats have to be healthy and produce a lot of milk.

3. Fair Food: Enjoy Tex-Mex food, a combination of food from Texas and Mexico.

4. Try the nachos and fajitas!

5. Quilt Contest: Come and see the beautiful quilts! Quilting has a long tradition.

6. Texas Star: The view is amazing from the top of this tall wheel.

Around the World

1. Maryland State Fair: Horse racing is popular in this state.

2. At the fair in this state, people can see horse races.

3. Iowa State Fair: This state is famous for butter.

4. For the fair in this state, people make a butter cow from about 272 kg of butter.

5. Wisconsin State Fair: This state produces the most cheese in the USA.

6. At the fair in this state people can eat many tasty cheese dishes.

Think and Write

1. Seochon is full of fun things.

2. You can go to Tongin Market.

3. It's famous for oil Tteokbokki, so you have to go there to try it.

4. There are also many traditional Korean houses.

5. You can walk around to see them.

6. Come visit us in Seochon.

7. You'll have so much fun!

8 explain, 설명하다　9 creative, 창의적인
10 decorate, 장식하다　11 backpack, 가방
12 trash, 쓰레기　13 round, 둥근　14 bucket, 양동이
15 purple, 자주색의　16 recycling, 재활용

단어 TEST Step 1　p.40

01 둥근　02 할인
03 두려워하는, 걱정하는　04 자주색의; 자주색
05 비싼　06 상태, 조건　07 중고의
08 거의　09 큰　10 가격
11 던지다　12 양동이　13 가죽 끈
14 악기　15 고무 밴드, 고무줄　16 업사이클링
17 칼　18 환경　19 각각의, 각각
20 이해하다　21 의미　22 누군가, 누가
23 설명하다　24 조합, 결합
25 항상, 개선; 개선하다　26 재활용
27 업사이클하다　28 개최하다, 열다　29 쓰레기
30 옷, 의복　31 ~를 통해　32 창의적인
33 바느질　34 장식하다　35 할인을 받다
36 ~을 할인하다, 깎다　37 버리다
38 잠깐 생각해 볼게　39 ~에 좋다　40 ~에 관한 것이다
41 ~로부터 이야기[소식]을 듣다　42 예를 들어
43 ~을 자르다

단어 TEST Step 2　p.41

01 glasses　02 backpack　03 interesting
04 musical　05 blue jeans　06 event
07 like　08 thing　09 nursing home
10 kit　11 sew　12 bottom
13 shoulder　14 lastly　15 through
16 combination　17 strap　18 understand
19 bucket　20 trash　21 discount
22 expensive　23 throw　24 environment
25 decorate　26 recycling　27 instrument
28 meaning　29 knife　30 almost
31 used　32 price　33 explain
34 hold　35 be made by　36 look for
37 sound like+명사　38 cut off
39 be good for　40 for example　41 throw away
42 get a discount　43 talk about

단어 TEST Step 3　p.42

1 discount, 할인　2 clothes, 옷　3 meaning, 의미
4 environment, 환경　5 combination, 조합, 결합
6 interested, 관심 있는　7 instrument, 악기

대화문 TEST Step 1　p.43~44

Listen and Talk A-1
How much, round glasses / They're / get a discount / afraid not / take

Listen and Talk A-2
May, help / looking for, for / What about / Can I get / take off / sounds, take

Listen and Talk A-3
How much, purple / It's, dollars / expensive, discount / take, off, be / take it

Listen and Talk A-4
May I help / I'm looking for / one, in, condition / get a discount / take, off / take it

Listen and Talk B
May / How much / It's / Can I get / take 1 dollar / be, I'll take it

Listen and Talk C
There are, many / is, used, looking for / looking for / How about / How much / It's / expensive for, discount / afraid, year, almost / how much, with / take, one

Review 1
How much / It's, dollars / expensive for, How about / good price, take it

Review 2
May help / How much / 10 dollars / Can I get / take 2 dollars off / sounds good, take

Review 3
May, help / I'm looking for / on, in good condition / get a discount / take, off / I'll take it

대화문 TEST Step 2　p.45~46

Listen and Talk A-1
G: Excuse me. How much are the round glasses?
M: They're 18 dollars.
G: Hmm. Can I get a discount?
M: No, I'm afraid not. Sorry.
G: That's OK. I'll take them.

M: Hello. May I help you?

G: Yes. I'm looking for a backpack for school.

M: What about this red one? It's 12 dollars.

G: Can I get a discount?

M: OK. I'll take 2 dollars off.

G: That sounds good. I'll take it.

G: Excuse me. How much is this purple T-shirt?

M: It's 10 dollars.

G: That's expensive. Can I get a discount?

M: OK. I'll take 1 dollar off. That'll be 9 dollars.

G: I'll take it, then. Thank you!

M: Hello. May I help you?

G: I'm looking for a baseball glove.

M: This one is 15 dollars and it's in good condition.

G: Can I get a discount?

M: OK. I'll take 2 dollars off.

G: Then it's 13 dollars. I'll take it.

A: May I help you?

B: Yes. How much is this soccer ball?

A: It's 6 dollars.

B: Can I get a discount?

A: OK. I'll take 1 dollar off.

B: Wow! There are so many interesting things here.

W: Everything here is old or used. What are you looking for?

B: I'm looking for a clock.

W: How about this red clock?

B: How much is it?

W: It's 15 dollars.

B: That's too expensive for me. Can I get a discount?

W: No, I'm afraid not. It's only one year old. It's almost new.

B: Then, how much is this blue clock with the large numbers?

W: It's 10 dollars.

B: Then, I'll take the blue one. Thank you.

G: Excuse me. How much is this yellow backpack?

M: It's 18 dollars.

G: Hmm. That's expensive for me. How about this red one?

M: It's 15 dollars.

G: That's a good price. I'll take it.

W: May I help you?

B: Yes. How much is this blue T-shirt?

W: It's 10 dollars.

B: Can I get a discount?

W: OK. I'll take 2 dollars off.

B: That sounds good. I'll take it.

M: Hello. May I help you?

G: I'm looking for a clock.

M: This one is 15 dollars and it's in good condition.

G: Can I get a discount?

M: OK. I'll take 2 dollars off.

G: Then it's 13 dollars. I'll take it.

본문 TEST Step 1   p.47~48

01 Let's about   02 club members

03 As, year's, about

04 each, to understand, meaning   05 Can, explain

06 upcycling, combination, recycling

07 Like, good, environment

08 When, better, from old   09 let's talk, each

10 Let's, with   11 My, to hold

12 combination, trash, fashion   13 trash, clothes

14 other, interested, through   15 sounds like

16 about, group   17 going, make, instruments

18 make, from, buckets

19 also, from, rubber   20 plan, the, in

21 let's hear from

22 will, from, clothes

23 For example, use   24 Look at

25 made by, of   26 Isn't it   27 more, sell, on

28 going, to, nursing   29 That's, great

30 Your, all, creative   31 want, to work

32 Cut off, of   33 Sew, together

34 Make, straps, of   35 sew, straps, top

36 Decorate, with, and

본문 TEST Step 2   p.49~50

01 Let's about   02 club members

03 As you know, about upcycling

04 Before, talk about, to understand, upcycling

05 explain upcycling

06 upcycling, combination

07 Like, is good for

08 When, upcycle, from old things

09 let's talk about

10 Let's start with　　　　　　11 hold a, show

12 a combination of

13 to make clothes

14 become interested in, through

15 sounds like fun　　　　16 What about

17 is going to, instruments　　18 from, buckets

19 also, from, rubber bands

20 plan to play, instruments

21 let's hear from

22 make, from old clothes

23 For example, jeans　　　24 Look at

25 was made by, one of　　26 Isn't it

27 more, on Environment Day

28 all the money, nursing home　29 great idea

30 Your, creative　31 want, to work hard

32 Cut off, blue jeans　　　33 Sew, together

34 shoulder straps, one　　35 Sew, to

36 Decorate, with

18 낡은 플라스틱 양동이로 드럼을 만들 겁니다.

19 또한 저희는 낡은 상자와 고무줄로 기타를 만들 겁니다.

20 저희는 소규모 음악회를 열어 그 악기들로 연주할 계획입니다.

21 고맙다, Eric. 그럼 이제 수미의 그룹 의견을 들어 보자.

22 저희 그룹은 낡은 옷으로 가방을 만들 거예요.

23 예를 들어 청바지를 이용할 거예요.

24 이 가방을 보세요.

25 이것은 저희 모둠원 중 한 명인 하준이가 만들었어요.

26 멋지지 않나요?

27 우리는 가방을 더 많이 만들어서 환경의 날에 팔 거예요.

28 번 돈을 모두 양로원에 줄 예정이에요.

29 훌륭한 생각이구나.

30 너희들의 발상은 모두 아주 창의적이구나.

31 너희들 모두 환경의 날을 위해 열심히 노력하길 바란다.

32 청바지의 다리 부분을 잘라낸다.

33 아래쪽을 붙여서 바느질한다.

34 다리 한 짝으로 어깨끈을 만든다.

35 청바지의 윗부분에 어깨끈을 바느질한다.

36 핀이나 단추로 가방을 장식한다.

1 업사이클링에 대해 이야기해 봅시다

2 동아리 회원 여러분, 안녕하세요.

3 여러분도 알다시피 올해의 환경의 날은 업사이클링에 관한 것입니다.

4 각 그룹이 그날에 할 행사 아이디어를 이야기하기 전에 여러분이 '업사이클링'의 의미를 이해하기를 바랍니다.

5 누가 업사이클링의 뜻을 설명해 줄 수 있나요?

6 네. '업사이클링'이란 단어는 "upgrade"와 "recycling"이 결합한 것입니다.

7 재활용과 마찬가지로 업사이클링도 환경에 좋아요.

8 업사이클링을 하면, 여러분은 오래된 것들로 새롭고 더 좋은 것을 만들어요.

9 좋아요. 이제 각 그룹의 행사 아이디어에 대해 이야기해 봅시다.

10 Pei의 그룹부터 시작하죠

11 저희 그룹은 트래션 쇼를 하고 싶습니다.

12 "트래션(Trashion)"은 "trash"와 "fashion"이 결합한 말입니다.

13 저희는 옷을 만들기 위해 쓰레기를 이용할 것입니다.

14 저희는 이 쇼를 통해서 다른 학생들이 업사이클링에 관심을 갖게 되기를 바랍니다.

15 트래션 쇼라니 멋지겠구나!

16 너희 그룹은 어떠니, Eric?

17 저희 그룹은 낡은 물건으로 악기를 만들려고 합니다.

1 Let's Talk about Upcycling

2 Hello, club members.

3 As you know, this year's Environment Day is about upcycling.

4 Before we talk about each group's event idea for that day, I want you to understand the meaning of "upcycling."

5 Can anyone explain upcycling?

6 Yes. The word "upcycling" is a combination of "upgrade" and "recycling."

7 Like recycling, upcycling is good for the environment.

8 When you upcycle, you make new and better things from old things.

9 Good. Now, let's talk about each group's idea for the event.

10 Let's start with Pei's group.

11 My group wants to hold a trashion show.

12 "Trashion" is a combination of "trash" and "fashion."

13 We'll use trash to make clothes.

14 We want other students to become interested in upcycling through the show.

15 A trashion show sounds like fun!

16 What about your group, Eric?

17 My group is going to make musical instruments from old things.

18 We'll make drums from old plastic buckets.

19 We'll also make a guitar from old boxes and rubber bands.

20 We plan to play the instruments in a mini-concert.

21 Thank you, Eric. Now, let's hear from Sumi's group.

22 My group will make bags from old clothes.

23 For example, we'll use blue jeans.

24 Look at this bag.

25 This was made by Hajun, one of our group members.

26 Isn't it nice?

27 We'll make more bags and sell them on Environment Day.

28 We're going to give all the money to a nursing home.

29 That's a great idea.

30 Your ideas are all so creative.

31 I want everyone to work hard for Environment Day.

32 Cut off the legs of the blue jeans.

33 Sew the bottom together.

34 Make shoulder straps from one of the legs.

35 Sew the straps to the top of the jeans.

36 Decorate the bag with pins and buttons.

Around the World

1. to give, lessons to

2. don't, any

3. can help

4. have

5. thank

6. can make, from

7. sends us trash

8. send back

9. upcycling

Think and Write

1. Creative Upcycling

2. Need, jeans, sewing

3. Cut off

4. to, bottom of

5. sew, to

6. Decorate with

Around the World

1. Kids, I want to give music lessons to you.

2. But we don't have any musical instruments.

3. I can help you.

4. I have a good idea.

5. Oh, thank you!

6. I can make musical instruments from trash.

7. The world sends us trash.

8. We send back music.

9. This is the power of upcycling.

Think and Write

1. Creative Upcycling Idea: Blue Jeans Basket

2. You Need: old blue jeans, sewing kit, scissors, buttons and pins

3. Step: 1 Cut off a leg of the old blue jeans.

4. 2 Cut out a piece to make the bottom of the basket.

5. 3 Sew the bottom to the leg.

6. 4 Decorate with buttons and pins.

단어 TEST Step 1 p.59

01 뱀	02 남색	03 사진
04 화장실	05 고릴라	06 운이 좋은
07 성공하다	08 발표, 소식	09 절, 사원
10 ~하는 동안에	11 대개, 보통	12 벌레
13 해결하다, 풀다	14 보호	15 높이, 정도, 수준
16 앵무새	17 면	18 재능
19 천천히	20 기록하다, 등록하다; 기록	
21 문어	22 (딱딱한) 껍데기, 껍질	
23 남자의, 수컷의	24 상상하다	25 까마귀
26 무늬, 도안	27 놀라게 하다	28 한때, 한동안
29 실험, 시험	30 꼬리	31 또한
32 입다, 신다, 쓰다	33 가게; 저장하다	34 A가 아니고 B
35 ~을 잘하다, ~에 능숙하다		36 ~을 뽑다
37 ~처럼 보이다, ~와 닮다		38 음악에 맞춰 춤추다
39 ~에 대해 조심하다, 경계하다		40 휴식하다
41 그 밖에, 그 외에	42 알아내다	43 꼭 ~처럼

단어 TEST Step 2 p.60

01 hide	02 way	03 pile
04 fable	05 floss	06 leave
07 carry	08 round-shaped	09 sign
10 tool	11 jar	12 float
13 stripe	14 example	15 also
16 coconut	17 drop	18 unique
19 experiment	20 protection	21 succeed
22 pattern	23 temple	24 slowly
25 photograph	26 imagine	27 cotton
28 usually	29 male	30 octopus
31 parrot	32 gorilla	33 worm
34 announcement		35 more than
36 find out	37 on top of	38 take a rest
39 not A but B	40 look for	41 be good at
42 pull out	43 look like	

단어 TEST Step 3 p.61

1 fable, 우화, 동화   2 coconut, 코코넛 열매

3 surprise, 놀라게 하다   4 shell, (딱딱한) 껍데기, 껍질

5 level, 정도, 수준   6 navy, 남색   7 talent, 재능

8 photograph, 사진   9 cotton, 면

10 experiment, 실험, 시험   11 floss, 치실질을 하다, 치실

12 announcement, 발표, 소식   13 pile, 쌓다, 포개다

14 record, 기록하다, 등록하다   15 tool, 도구, 수단

16 pattern, 무늬, 도안

대화문 TEST Step 1 p.62~63

Listen and Talk A-1

looking for / look like / a long cotton / tell me more, grey / go, check

Listen and Talk A-2

May, help / lost, think, left / does, look like / It's, yellow / What else, Tell, more / Let, think, has, outside

Listen and Talk A-3

need help / lost my umbrella / look like / It's, navy / tell me more / has a star pattern

Listen and Talk A-4

Do you need / I'm looking for / What, look like / has black hair / Can you tell, anything special / short tail

Listen and Talk B

May I help / I'm looking for / What, like / has grey hair / Can you tell me / long tail

Listen and Talk B-2

May, help / looking for, wallet / What, look like / It's small / more about / is, in

Listen and Talk C

I help you / I'm looking for, His / What, look / short white hair / tell me more / really long tail / one more, did, lose / lost, near / make an announcement, wait / a lot

Talk and Play

does, look like / long brown hair / Can you tell / wearing, navy / found

Review

think, lost / What does it look like / navy / tell, more / has, pattern on

대화문 TEST Step 2 p.64~65

Listen and Talk A-1

B: Excuse me. I'm looking for my scarf.

W: What does it look like?

B: It's a long cotton scarf.

W: Can you tell me more about it?

B: Well, it's grey.

W: OK. I'll go and check.

Listen and Talk A-2

W: May I help you?

B: Yes. I lost my bag. I think I left it in the restroom.

W: OK. What does it look like?

B: It's small and yellow.

W: What else? Tell me more about it.

B: Let me think. Oh, it has two pockets outside.

Listen and Talk A-3

W: Do you need help?

B: Yes. I lost my umbrella.

W: What does it look like?

B: It's long and navy.

W: Can you tell me more?

B: Yes. It has a star pattern on it.

Listen and Talk A-4

B: Do you need help?

W: Yes. I'm looking for my cat.

B: What does it look like?

W: Well, she's not very big and she has black hair.

B: Can you tell me more? Is there anything special about her?

W: She has a short tail.

Listen and Talk B

A: May I help you?

B: Yes. I'm looking for my cat.

A: What does it look like?

B: It's small and it has grey hair.

A: Can you tell me more about it?

B: It has a long tail.

Listen and Talk B-2

A: May I help you?

B: Yes. I'm looking for my wallet.

A: What does it look like?

B: It's small and red.

A: Can you tell me more about it?

B: There is a card in it.

Listen and Talk C

M: May I help you?

G: Yes. I'm looking for my dog. His name is Prince.

M: What does he look like?

G: He's very small and has short white hair.

M: Can you tell me more?

G: Well, he has a really long tail.

M: I see. And one more thing. Where did you lose him?

G: I lost him near the main gate.

M: OK. I'll go and make an announcement. Can you please wait here?

G: Sure. Thanks a lot.

Talk and Play

A: What does Amy look like?

B: She's tall and has long brown hair.

A: Can you tell me more?

B: She's wearing short navy pants.

A: I found her.

Review

G: Hi. I think I lost my umbrella.

M: What does it look like?

G: It's a big navy umbrella.

M: Can you tell me more?

G: It has a white flower pattern on it.

본문 TEST Step 1   p.66~67

01 That, Tools   02 once thought, only

03 finding out, also

04 in, watch out for   05 may, pull out

06 to floss, teeth 07 female, that are, flossing

08 While, watching, floss, teeth   09 way, to floss

10 don't usually think

11 However, can, use

12 use, shells, protection

13 can't find, hiding, hide   14 store, for, use

15 pile, carry, later   16 How smart

17 drops, into, to raise   18 may think, just

19 were studying, experiment   20 put, with, front

21 worm, floating, top

22 water level, low, could   23 solved, just as

24 dropped, into 25 special, wrong

26 experiment with, did, same

본문 TEST Step 2   p.68~69

01 That, Tools   02 once thought, can use

03 finding out, can also

04 go to, temple, watch out for

05 may come, pull out

06 to floss their teeth

07 female, are teaching flossing

08 While, are watching, floss their teeth

09 This way, learn to floss

10 usually think, octopuses

11 However, can also use

12 shells for protection

13 can't, hiding place, hide under

14 even store, for later use

15 pile, carry, to use later　　　16 How

17 fable, drops, jar to raise

18 may think, just, but

19 who were studying, experiment　20 put, in front of

21 worm, on top of

22 However, level, low, could not　23 solved, just as

24 dropped, into　25 If, special, wrong

26 same experiment, other, too

1 도구를 사용하는 동물들

2 사람들은 한때 인간만이 도구를 사용할 수 있다고 생각했다.

3 이제 과학자들은 많은 동물들 역시 도구를 사용할 수 있다는 것을 밝혀내고 있다.

4 당신이 태국의 롭부리의 절에 간다면, 마카크 원숭이들을 조심해야 한다.

5 그들이 당신에게 다가와 당신의 머리카락을 뽑을 수도 있다.

6 그들은 이빨을 치실질하기 위해서 사람의 머리카락을 사용한다.

7 만약 당신이 운이 좋으면, 당신은 새끼들에게 치실질하는 것을 가르치고 있는 암컷 원숭이들을 볼 수 있을 것이다.

8 새끼들이 지켜보고 있는 동안, 암컷 원숭이들은 아주 천천히 그들의 이빨을 치실질한다.

9 이런 방식으로, 새끼 원숭이들은 치실질을 배운다.

10 사람들은 대개 문어가 영리하다고 생각하지 않는다.

11 하지만, 문어는 매우 영리하고 또한 도구를 사용할 수 있다.

12 그들은 자신을 보호하기 위해 코코넛 껍데기를 사용한다.

13 그들이 숨을 만한 좋은 장소를 찾지 못했을 때, 그들은 코코넛 껍데기 아래로 숨는다.

14 어떤 문어들은 심지어 코코넛 껍데기를 나중에 쓰기 위해 모은다.

15 그들은 코코넛 껍데기를 쌓아두고 나중에 쓰기 위해서 가지고 다닌다.

16 얼마나 똑똑한가!

17 이솝 우화 속 '목마른 까마귀'에서 까마귀는 물 높이를 높이기 위해 항아리 안으로 돌을 떨어뜨린다.

18 당신은 이것이 그저 이야기라고 생각할 수 있지만, 그렇지 않다.

19 까마귀를 연구하던 과학자들이 실험을 했다.

20 그들은 까마귀 앞에 물이 든 항아리를 놓았다.

21 물 위에 벌레가 떠다니고 있었다.

22 하지만, 물 높이가 낮아서, 까마귀는 그 벌레를 먹을 수 없었다.

23 그 까마귀는 우화에서처럼 문제를 해결했다.

24 까마귀는 돌을 항아리 안으로 떨어뜨렸다.

25 만약 당신이 이 새가 특별하다고 생각한다면, 당신이 틀렸다.

26 과학자들은 다른 까마귀들에게도 똑같은 실험을 했고, 그들 모두가 똑같이 그렇게 했다.

1 Animals That Use Tools

2 People once thought that only humans can use tools.

3 Now, scientists are finding out that many animals can also use tools.

4 If you go to a Buddhist temple in Lop Buri, Thailand, watch out for the Macaque monkeys.

5 They may come to you and pull out your hair.

6 They use human hair to floss their teeth.

7 If you are lucky, you may see female monkeys that are teaching flossing to their babies.

8 While the babies are watching, the female monkeys floss their teeth very slowly.

9 This way, the baby monkeys learn to floss.

10 People don't usually think that octopuses are smart.

11 However, octopuses are very smart, and they can also use tools.

12 They use coconut shells for protection.

13 When they can't find a good hiding place, they hide under coconut shells.

14 Some octopuses even store coconut shells for later use.

15 They pile the coconut shells and carry them to use later.

16 How smart!

17 In Aesop's fable The Thirsty Crow , a crow drops stones into a jar to raise the level of water.

18 You may think this is just a story, but it is not.

19 Scientists who were studying crows did an experiment.

20 They put a jar with water in front of a crow.

21 A worm was floating on top of the water.

22 However, the water level was low, so the crow could not eat the worm.

23 The crow solved the problem just as in the fable.

24 It dropped stones into the jar.

25 If you think this bird is special, you are wrong.

26 Scientists did the same experiment with other crows, and they all did the same, too.

Around the World

1. longest, ever

2. long

3. recorded

4. record

5. The oldest

6. lived for

Think and Write

1. with

2. There are, have

3. example

4. which, to talk

5. can sing

6. are, that, talents

7. An example

8. female, lives

9. talk with, in

10. more than

구석구석지문 TEST Step 2 p.77

Around the World

1. The longest snake ever is Medusa.

2. She is 7.67 meters long.

3. Alley recorded the longest jump by a cat.

4. Her record was 1.83 meters.

5. The oldest pig ever is Ernestine.

6. He lived for 22 years and 359 days.

Think and Write

1. Animals with Special Talents

2. There are many animals that have special talents.

3. An example is Einstein.

4. He is an African Grey Parrot which can use 200 English words to talk with people.

5. He can sing the "Happy Birthday" song.

6. There are many animals that have special talents.

7. An example is Koko.

8. She is a female gorilla which lives in America.

9. She can talk with people in American Sign Language.

10. She knows more than 1,000 signs.

MEMO

적중 100 + 특별부록

Plan B

우리학교 최신기출

동아 · 윤정미 교과서를 배우는

학교 시험문제 분석 · 모음 · 해설집

전국단위 학교 시험문제 수집 및 분석
출제 빈도가 높은 문제 위주로 선별
문제 풀이에 필요한 상세한 해설

중2-1
영어

동아 · 윤정미

[광주 ○○중]

◎ 선택형 문항의 답안은 컴퓨터용 수정 싸인펜을 사용하여 OMR 답안지에 바르게 표기하시오.
◎ 서술형 문제는 답을 답안지에 반드시 검정 볼펜으로 쓰시오.
◎ 총 32문항 100점 만점입니다. 문항별 배점은 각 문항에 표시되어 있습니다.

[인천 ○○중]

1. 다음 단어의 영영풀이로 올바른 것은?　(4점)
① dessert: the food that you eat at regular times each day
② jog: something funny that you say or do to make people laugh
③ sci-fi: a book in which the story, characters, and events are not real
④ practice: the activity of doing something regularly so that you can do it better
⑤ architect: a police officer whose job is to find out who has committed a crime

[인천 ○○중]

2. 다음 대화 중 자연스럽게 짝지어진 것은?　(2점)
① A: Do you need any help?
　B: I read books. I like detective stories.
② A: Where's Tom's bakery?
　B: Sure. That sounds great.
③ A: Excuse me. I'm looking for the bookstore.
　B: It's on the main street. It's next to the bank.
④ A: I usually listen to music. How about you?
　B: Oh, I see. Thanks a lot.
⑤ A: Why don't we go see an action movie tonight?
　B: Go straight one block and turn right.

[3~4] 다음 대화를 읽고, 물음에 답하시오.

Andy: Subin. ⓐ여가 시간에 너는 보통 무엇을 하니?
Subin: I exercise outside.
Andy: What kind of exercise do you do?
Subin: I play badminton with my brother. I'm on the school's badminton team. How about you, Andy?
Andy: I like watching movies.
Subin: What kind of movies do you like?
Andy: I like action movies. They're fun.
Subin: Oh, I sometimes watch action movies, too. Why don't we go see an action movie this weekend?
Andy: Sure. That sounds great.

3. 위 대화의 내용과 일치하는 것은?　(3점)
① 수빈이는 여가 시간에 야외 체험 활동을 한다.
② 앤디는 학교 배드민턴 팀의 일원이다.
③ 앤디는 이번 주에 액션 영화를 보러 갔다.
④ 수빈이도 때때로 액션 영화를 본다.
⑤ 수빈이와 앤디는 내일 방과 후에 영화를 보러 가기로 했다.

4. 위 대화의 밑줄 친 우리말에 해당하는 영어 문장을 쓰시오.　(5점)

| ⓐ여가 시간에 너는 보통 무엇을 하니? |

| <조건> |
| 1. 주어와 동사를 포함한 완전한 문장으로 쓰기. |
| 2. 철자와 문법 오류 한 개당 1점 감점. |

→ _____

5. 다음 대화의 내용과 일치하는 것은?　(4점)

Andy: Subin, what do you usually do in your free time?

Subin: I exercise outside.

Andy: What kind of exercise do you do?

Subin: I play badminton with my brother. I'm on the school's badminton team. What do you usually do in your free time, Andy?

Andy: I like watching movies.

Subin: What kind of movies do you like?

Andy: I like action movies. They're fun.

Subin: Oh, I sometimes watch action movies, too. Why don't we go see an action movie this weekend?

Andy: Sure. That sounds great.

① Andy likes to go out and take exercise.

② Subin's brother is on the school's badminton team.

③ Subin watches all kinds of action movies.

④ Andy sometimes plays badminton and he likes to see an action movie with Subin.

⑤ Subin and Andy will watch an action movie this weekend.

6. 다음 빈칸에 들어갈 표현으로 가장 적절한 것은?

(2점)

A: Seho, what do you do in your free time?
B: I listen to music.
A: _____
B: Rock music.

① Who's your favorite singer?

② When do you listen to music?

③ Do you want to be a rock star?

④ Why don't we go to the concert?

⑤ What kind of music do you listen to?

7. 다음 중 짝지어진 대화가 <u>어색한</u> 것은?　(2점)

① A: What do you do in your free time?
　B: I usually do exercise.

② A: What kind of TV show do you watch?
　B: I like to watch cooking shows.

③ A: Can you tell me where the museum is?
　B: Yes. The museum is behind the library.

④ A: Why don't we play badminton today?
　B: Because I was too busy yesterday.

⑤ A: Excuse me. I'm looking for the hospital.
　B: It's across from the National Art Museum.

8. 주어진 우리말을 영어로 바르게 고친 것은?　(4점)

• 나도 David도 교실에 없었다.

① Both I and David were in the classroom.

② Both I and David wasn't in the classroom.

③ Neither I nor David was in the classroom.

④ Neither I nor David weren't in the classroom.

⑤ Neither I nor David wasn't in the classroom.

9. 다음 중 어법상 옳지 <u>않은</u> 것은?　(3점)

① Either you or Susan has the book.

② Both I and he listen to the teacher well.

③ I want both to cook and to water plants.

④ You can either stay home or come with us.

⑤ He is good at neither write nor read English.

10. 다음 두 대화의 빈칸에 공통으로 들어갈 단어는?
(2점)

A: What _____ of sports do you usually play?
B: I play baseball.

A: How can I get to the bus stop?
B: I am on my way to the bus stop. You can come with me.
A: Thank you so much. You are so _____.

① kind   ② ride   ③ plant
④ present   ⑤ question

11. 다음 중 어법상 올바른 문장은?   (3점)
① I'll show you my new dress.
② Don't tell anything about it him.
③ Dad bought a new novel to me.
④ She gave ten thousand won for me.
⑤ Jane sent a birthday gift for Jackson.

12. 다음 대화의 빈칸에 들어갈 말로 적절한 것은? (2점)

A: Younghee, what do you do when you have free time?
B: I make cookies. I like to bake.
A: _____
B: I make blueberry cookies. I love blueberries.

① Do you enjoy baking?
② Which bakery do you go to?
③ What do you do in the bakery?
④ What kind of cookies do you make?
⑤ Do you like to have cookies and blueberries?

13. 다음 대화를 읽고 답할 수 없는 질문은?   (3점)

Subin: What do you usually do in your free time, Andy?
Andy: I like watching movies.
Subin: What kind of movies do you like?
Andy: I like action movies. They're fun.
Subin: Oh, in my free time I sometimes watch action movies, too. Why don't we go see an action movie this weekend?

① What is Subin's favorite movie?
② Why does Andy like action movies?
③ How does Andy spend his free time?
④ What will Subin and Andy do this weekend?
⑤ What does Subin sometimes do in her free time?

14. 다음 중 빈칸에 들어갈 말이 다른 하나는?   (3점)
① My mom made cookies _____ me.
② Please send this letter _____ him.
③ Could you pass the ball _____ me?
④ You should not tell a lie _____ her.
⑤ She will bring some books _____ you tomorrow.

15. 다음 우리말과 일치하도록 주어진 단어를 바르게 배열하시오.   (4점)

• 경찰서는 어떻게 가나요?
(I / how / do / get / the police station / to)

답: _____

[16～17] 다음 글을 읽고 물음에 답하시오.

Hi! I'm Musa, and I live in Nairobi, Kenya. My favorite time of the day is our running practice time. My friend, Tamu, and I are on the school's ⓐrunning team. I'm ⓑhappiest when I run with Tamu. Our practice time isn't ⓒexciting because we can see many animals.
Many runners from Kenya won ⓓraces in the Olympics. I'm so proud of them. Both Tamu and I want to be ⓔlike them.

16. 위 글의 밑줄 친 부분 중, 문맥상 알맞지 않은 것은?　(4점)

① ⓐ　② ⓑ　③ ⓒ　④ ⓓ　⑤ ⓔ

17. 위 글의 Musa에 대한 내용과 일치하지 않는 것은?　(2점)

① Tamu와는 친구 사이다.
② 케냐 나이로비에 살고 있다.
③ 달리기 연습 시간을 좋아한다.
④ 케냐의 달리기 선수들이 자랑스럽다.
⑤ 달리기를 할 때 많은 사람들을 볼 수 있다.

[18～19] 다음 글을 읽고 물음에 답하시오.

Hi! My name is Tabin, and I live near the Gobi Desert in Mongolia. I'm happy when I ride my horse. Horses are ＿＿＿＿＿＿＿ in our culture. Almost everyone can ride a horse in Mongolia. In fact, we say, "We ride horses before we can walk."
I take good care of my horse. I often brush him and give him some carrots. I enjoy riding especially in the evening before the sunset. Then the sky is red, and everything is peaceful.

18. 위 글의 빈칸에 들어갈 말로 가장 적절한 것은?　(4점)

① fast　　　　② cheap
③ healthy　　　④ beautiful
⑤ important

19. 위 글의 Tabin에 관한 내용과 일치하지 않는 것은?　(3점)

① 고비사막으로부터 멀리 산다.
② 말을 탈 때 행복하다.
③ 자신의 말을 잘 돌본다.
④ 말에게 종종 당근을 준다.
⑤ 해 질 무렵 말타기를 즐긴다.

[20～21] 다음 글을 읽고 물음에 답하시오.

Hi, my name is Diego, and I live in Seville, Spain. (A) My favorite time of the day is ＿＿＿＿＿＿ time. (B) On most days, my family gets together and has a big, long ＿＿＿＿＿＿ time. We usually have soup, vegetables, and meat. (D) After ＿＿＿＿＿＿, we usually take a siesta, a short nap. (E) My father and I like to sleep under the tree in our garden.

20. 위 글의 빈칸에 공통으로 들어갈 말은?　(2점)

① lunch　　　　② game
③ shopping　　　④ cooking
⑤ sleeping

21. 위 글의 (A)～(E) 중 다음 문장이 들어갈 위치로 알맞은 것은?　(3점)

We also have a dessert like churros.

① (A)　② (B)　③ (C)　④ (D)　⑤ (E)

[22~23] 다음 글을 읽고 질문에 답하시오.

> Tabin
>
> Hi! My name is Tabin, and I live near the Gobi Desert in Mongolia. I'm happy when I ride my horse. Horses are important in our culture. Almost everyone can ride a horse in Mongolia. In fact, we say, "We ride horses before we can walk."
> I think I take good care of my horse. I often brush him and give him some carrots. (A)I enjoy to ride especially in the evening before the sunset. (B)Then the sky is red, and everything are peaceful.
>
> Musa
>
> Hi! I'm Musa, and I live in Nairobi, Kenya. My favorite time of the day is our running practice time. My friend, Tamu, and I are on the school's running team. I'm happiest when I run with Tamu. (C)Our practice time isn't tiring because we can see many animals.
> Many runners from Kenya won races in the Olympics. (D)I'm so proud with them. (E)Tamu and I wants to become great runners in the future.

22. 위 글에서 (A)~(E) 중 어법상 옳은 것은? (3점)

① (A) ② (B) ③ (C) ④ (D) ⑤ (E)

23. 위 글에서 True/False가 바르게 연결된 것을 고르면? (4점)

① Tabin feels happy when she rides a horse. (False)

② Tabin has no interest in taking care of a horse. (True)

③ Tabin and Musa are talking about their favorite time of the day. (False)

④ Musa likes practice time, so he won races. (False)

⑤ Musa can see animals when he practices running. (False)

[24~26] 다음 글을 읽고 물음에 답하시오.

> Diego
>
> Hi, my name is Diego, and I live in Seville, Spain. My favorite time of the day is lunch time. My school usually ends ⓐaround 2 p.m. On most days, my family ⓑgets together and has a big, long lunch. We usually ⓒhave soup, vegetables, and meat. We also have a dessert ⓓlike churros. After lunch, we usually take a siesta, a short nap. Both my father and I like ⓔto sleep under the tree in our garden.

24. 위 글을 읽고 난 반응으로 적절한 것은? (4점)

① Kate: Diego는 보통 친구들과 점심 때 모이는구나.

② Sam: 스페인 학교에서는 한국처럼 급식을 먹는구나.

③ Amy: Siesta는 점심식사 전에 자는 짧은 낮잠이구나.

④ Tony: Diego의 일상적인 점심식사는 수프, 채소, 고기와 후식이구나.

⑤ Jess: Diego의 가족은 보통 푸짐하고 긴 저녁식사를 먹는구나.

25. 위 글의 ⓐ~ⓔ 중 우리말 뜻이 잘못된 것은? (3점)

① ⓐ: 약, ~쯤 ② ⓑ: 모이다

③ ⓒ: 먹다 ④ ⓓ: 좋아하다

⑤ ⓔ: 자는 것

26. 위 글의 제목으로 가장 적절한 것은? (4점)

① Diego's Diary

② Diego's Lunch Menu

③ Diego's Happy Time

④ A Special Spain Lunch

⑤ The Family Life in Spain

27. 다음 글의 밑줄 친 ⓐ~ⓔ 중 어색한 것은? (3점)

Hi! My name is Tabin, and I live near the Gobi Desert in Mongolia. I'm happy when I ride my horse. Horses ⓐis important in our culture. Almost everyone can ⓑrides a horse in Mongolia. In fact, we say, "We ride horses ⓒbefore we can walk." I ⓓtake good care of my horse. I often brush him and give him some carrots. I enjoy ⓔriding especially in the evening before the sunset. Then the sky is red, and everything is peaceful.

① ⓐ ② ⓑ ③ ⓒ ④ ⓓ ⑤ ⓔ

[28~30] 다음 글을 읽고 물음에 답하시오.

Musa

Hi! I'm Musa, and I live in Nairobi, Kenya. My favorite time of the day is our running practice time. ⓐMy friend, Tamu, and I are on the school's running team. ⓑI'm happiest when I run with Tamu. ⓒOur practice time isn't boring because we can see many animals.
ⓓMany runners from Kenya won races in the Olympics. ⓔI so proud of them. Both Tamu and I want to be like (A)them.

28. 위 글을 읽고 답할 수 없는 질문은? (4점)

① What does Musa want to be?

② How does Musa go to school?

③ Is Tamu on the school's running team?

④ Does Musa like his running practice time?

⑤ Why is practice time not boring for Musa?

29. 위 글의 ⓐ~ⓔ 중 어법상 옳지 않은 문장은? (3점)

① ⓐ ② ⓑ ③ ⓒ ④ ⓓ ⑤ ⓔ

30. 위 글의 밑줄 친 (A)의 의미는? (3점)

① Musa의 학교 친구들

② 케냐 나이로비의 주민들

③ Musa의 학교 달리기 팀

④ 달리기 연습 시간에 보는 동물들

⑤ 올림픽 경기에서 우승한 케냐의 육상 선수들

[31~32] 다음 글을 읽고 물음에 답하시오.

Hi, my name is Diego, and I live in Seville, Spain. My favorite time of the day is lunch time. My school usually ⓐends around 2 p.m. On most days, my family ⓑgets together and ⓒhave a big, long lunch. We usually have soup, vegetables, and meat. After lunch, we usually ⓓtake a siesta, a short nap. Both my father and I ⓔlike to sleep under the tree in our garden.

31. 위 글의 밑줄 친 ⓐ~ⓔ 중 어법에 맞지 않는 것은? (2점)

① ⓐ ② ⓑ ③ ⓒ ④ ⓓ ⑤ ⓔ

32. 위 글을 읽고 답할 수 없는 질문은? (3점)

① Where does Diego live?

② When is Diego's favorite time of the day?

③ What does Diego's family have for dinner?

④ What does Diego's family usually do after lunch?

⑤ Where do Diego and his father like to sleep after lunch?

2학년 영어 1학기 중간고사(1과) 2회

문항수 : 선택형(27문항) 서술형(6문항)   20 . . .

◎ 선택형 문항의 답안은 컴퓨터용 수정 싸인펜을 사용하여 OMR 답안지에 바르게 표기하시오.
◎ 서술형 문제는 답을 답안지에 반드시 검정 볼펜으로 쓰시오.
◎ 총 33문항 100점 만점입니다. 문항별 배점은 각 문항에 표시되어 있습니다.

[충북 ○○중]

1. 다음 빈칸에 들어갈 말로 가장 적절한 것은? (2점)

• When we want to do something perfect, we need to _____.

① fix   ② take care of
③ look after   ④ invent
⑤ practice

[경기 ○○중]

[2~3] 다음 대화를 읽고 물음에 답하시오.

B: Subin, (A)what (a) do (b) you (c) do (d) in (e) your free time?
G: I exercise outside.
B: (B)_____
G: I play badminton with my brother. I'm on the school's badminton team. How about you, Andy?
B: I like watching movies.

2. 위 대화에서 (A)에 'usually'를 넣을 때 가장 알맞은 곳은? (3점)

① (a)   ② (b)   ③ (c)   ④ (d)   ⑤ (e)

3. 위 대화의 (B)에 들어갈 말로 가장 적절한 것은? (2점)

① When do you play badminton?
② What kind of exercise do you do?
③ Do you play badminton with your brother?
④ What kind of game do you like to watch?
⑤ Which do you like better, playing badminton or watching movies?

[인천 ○○중]

4. 다음 중 우리말 뜻과 일치하며 어법상 옳은 것은?

(4점)

① Jane과 William은 둘 다 캐나다 출신이다.
→ Both Jane and William is from Canada.
② 그것은 숟가락이나 포크로 쓸 수 있다.
→ It can be used as both a spoon and a fork.
③ 형과 나는 모두 축구를 잘한다.
→ Both my brother and I am good at soccer.
④ 우리는 그 사건에 대해 속도 상하고 화도 났다.
→ We were either sad and angry about the accident.
⑤ 선생님도 학생들도 모두 교실에 없었다.
→ Neither the teacher nor the students were in the classroom.

[대구 ○○중]

5. 다음 중 짝지어진 대화가 가장 자연스러운 것은?

(3점)

① A: What time do I have to come?
   B: By 9 a.m. You don't have to be late.
② A: What's the weather like today?
   B: It's raining. You don't have to take an umbrella.
③ A: What time is it? We have to catch the train.
   B: We have enough time. You had better hurry up.
④ A: Do you need Mike's help? I can tell him.
   B: Mike should come. Robby will come to help me.
⑤ A: Hey, where are you going now?
   B: To the library. I must return this book by today.

[6~7] 다음 대화를 읽고 물음에 답하시오.

A: Subin, what do you usually do in your free time?

B: ⓐI exercise outside.

A: ⓑWhat kind of exercise do you do?

B: I play badminton with my brother. I'm on the school's badminton team. ⓒWhat do you usually do in your free time, Andy?

A: ⓓI like watching movies.

B: What kind of movies do you like?

A: ⓔI like novels. They're fun.

B: Oh, I sometimes watch action movies, too. Why don't we go see an action movie this weekend?

A: Sure. That sounds great.

A: Andy B: Subin

6. 위 대화의 ⓐ~ⓔ 중 흐름상 어색한 문장은? (2점)

① ⓐ ② ⓑ ③ ⓒ ④ ⓓ ⑤ ⓔ

7. 위 대화를 읽고 질문에 답할 수 없는 것은? (3점)

① What does Subin do in her free time?

② How often does Andy watch movies?

③ What does Andy do in his free time?

④ Who does Subin play badminton with?

⑤ What are Subin and Andy going to do this weekend?

8. 다음 중 짝지어진 대화가 어울리지 않는 것은? (3점)

① A: What kind of games do you play?

B: I usually play games.

② A: What do you do when you have free time?

B: I usually watch movies.

③ A: Why don't we play basketball after school?

B: OK. That sounds great.

④ A: May I help you?

B: Yes, please. I'm looking for the museum.

⑤ A: I'm looking for the bank.

B: Walk straight one block and turn left. It's on your right.

9. 다음 대화를 완성하시오. (5점)

<조 건>
• 빈칸에 한 단어씩 쓸 것.

G: What do you usually do in your free time?

B: I read books.

G: _____ _____ _____ books _____ _____ _____?

B: I like reading detective stories. I really like Sherlock Holmes' stories.

10. 다음 중 빈칸에 들어갈 전치사가 같은 것끼리 짝 지어진 것은? (3점)

<보기>
a. Jake made a cake _____ me.

b. Could you tell the secret _____ me?

c. Mom bought a bag _____ my brother.

d. Let's give this bag _____ your mother.

e. My old friend, Jane sent flowers _____ me.

① a, b ② a, c, d

③ b, c, d ④ b, d, e

⑤ c, d, e

11. 다음 대화의 빈칸에 들어갈 말로 가장 적절한 것은? (2점)

A: Subin, _____
B: I exercise outside.
A: What kind of exercise do you do?
B: I play badminton with my brother. What about you?
A: I like watching movies. I like action movies.

① what do you do in your free time?
② what time does the exercise start?
③ when do you usually exercise?
④ how often do you exercise?
⑤ what did you do yesterday?

12. 다음 대화의 흐름상 <u>어색한</u> 문장을 있는 대로 고른 것은? (2점)

B: Subin, what do you usually do when you have free time?
G: ⓐI exercise outside.
B: ⓑWhat kind of exercise do you do?
G: I play badminton. ⓒI'm on the school's swimming team. I am happy when I play badminton with my brother. What do you usually do in your free time, Andy?
B: ⓓI like watching movies.
G: ⓔWhat kind of novels do you like?
B: I like action movies. They're fun.
G: Oh, I sometimes watch action movies, too.

① ⓐ
② ⓐ, ⓑ
③ ⓒ, ⓔ
④ ⓒ, ⓓ
⑤ ⓒ, ⓓ, ⓔ

13. 다음 문장을 'A와 B 둘 다'라는 표현의 어구를 사용하여 완전한 영어 문장으로 완성하시오. (4점)

• Tamu는 영어와 과학 둘 다 좋아한다.

→ Tamu _____.

14. '나의 할아버지는 우리들에게 재미있는 이야기를 하나 말씀해 주셨다.'라는 의미가 되도록 영어 문장을 완성하시오. (7 단어) (5점)

정답: _____

[15~16] 다음 글을 읽고 물음에 답하시오.

Hi, my name is Diego, and I live in Seville, Spain. My favorite time of the day is lunch time. My school usually ends around 2 p.m. On most days, my family gets together and has a big lunch. We usually have soup, vegetables, and meat. We also have dessert (A)_____ churros. After lunch, we usually take a siesta, a short nap. Both my father and I (B)_____ to sleep under the tree in our garden.

15. 위 글을 읽고 답할 수 없는 질문은? (3점)
① What does a 'siesta' mean?
② How long is Diego's lunch time?
③ What time does Diego's school end?
④ Where does Diego like to take a nap?
⑤ What does Diego's family usually eat for lunch?

16. 위 글의 빈칸 (A), (B)에 공통으로 들어갈 말로 가장 적절한 것은? (3점)
① like
② take
③ exercise
④ guess
⑤ practice

- 9 -

[17~24] 다음 글을 읽고 질문에 답하시오.

(A) Somin
Hello! I'm Somin. I'm 15 years old, and I live in Korea. Please tell me about your favorite time of the day.
(B) Diego
Hi, my name is Diego, and I live in Seville, Spain. My favorite time of the day is lunch time. My school usually ends around 2 p.m. ⓐWe usually have soup, vegetables, and meat. ⓑOn most days, my family gets together and has a big, long lunch. ⓒAfter lunch, we usually take a siesta, a short nap. ⓓWe also have a dessert like churros. My father and I like to sleep under the tree in our garden.
(C) Tabin
Hi! My name is Tabin, and I live near the Gobi Desert in Mongolia. I'm happy when I ride my horse. Horses are important in our culture. Almost everyone can ride a horse in Mongolia. In fact, we say, "We ride horses before we can walk." ⓔI take good care with my horse. ⓕI often give some carrots him. ⓖI enjoy to ride especially in the evening before the sunset. ⓗThen the sky is red, ⓘ and everything is peace.
(D) Musa
Hi! I'm Musa, and I live in Nairobi, Kenya. My favorite time of the day is our running practice time. My friend, Tamu, and I are ㉠_____ the school's running team. I'm ㉡_____ when I run with Tamu. Our practice time isn't ㉢_____ because we can see many animals.
Many runners from Kenya won races in the Olympics. I'm so proud of them. Both Tamu and I want to be ㉣like them.

17. 위 글에 대한 설명 중 옳은 것은?   (3점)
① Somin은 자신이 가장 좋아하는 것을 소개하고 있다.
② Diego는 학교에서 점심을 먹는다.
③ Diego는 점심 식사 후 산책을 한다.
④ Musa는 그의 친구 Tamu를 자랑스러워한다.
⑤ Musa와 Tamu는 올림픽 경기에서 우승하기를 원한다.

18. 위 글에서 (B)의 ⓐ~ⓓ를 글의 흐름에 맞게 배열한 것은?   (3점)
① ⓐ-ⓑ-ⓒ-ⓓ   ② ⓐ-ⓒ-ⓑ-ⓓ
③ ⓑ-ⓐ-ⓓ-ⓒ   ④ ⓑ-ⓓ-ⓒ-ⓐ
⑤ ⓒ-ⓑ-ⓐ-ⓓ

19. 위 글에서 (C)의 ⓔ~ⓘ 중 내용 또는 어법상 오류가 없는 것은?   (3점)
① ⓔ   ② ⓕ   ③ ⓖ   ④ ⓗ   ⑤ ⓘ

20. 위 글에서 (D)의 ㉠과 보기의 빈칸에 둘 다 어울리는 것은?   (2점)

• My family has special dinner with my grandparents _____ Sundays.

① on   ② at   ③ with
④ to   ⑤ by

21. 위 글에서 (D)의 글의 흐름상 ㉡과 ㉢에 알맞은 말로 짝지어진 것은?   (3점)

	㉡	㉢
①	happy	bored
②	most happy	boring
③	most happy	bored
④	happiest	boring
⑤	happiest	bored

22. 위 글에서 (D)의 ㉣like와 같은 의미로 쓰인 것은? (3점)

① I don't like sad movies.
② Do you like spicy food?
③ He doesn't like playing outside.
④ He runs like the wind.
⑤ I like to read books in my free time.

23. 위 글에서 답을 찾을 수 없는 질문은? (2점)

① Where does Musa live?
② What does Diego do after lunch?
③ How old is Tabin's horse?
④ What does Diego's family have for lunch?
⑤ When is Musa's favorite time of the day?

24. Answer the question in a full sentence. (4점)

Q: When does Tabin feel happy?
A: _____

[25~26] 다음 글을 읽고 물음에 답하시오.

> Hi! My name is Tabin, and I live near the Gobi Desert in Mongolia. I'm happy when I ride my horse. Horses are important in our culture. Almost everyone can ride a horse in Mongolia. In fact, we say "(A)_____"
> I take good care of my horse. I often brush him and give him some carrots. I enjoy riding especially in the evening before the sunset. Then the sky is red, and everything is peaceful.

25. 위 글의 빈칸 (A)에 들어갈 알맞은 표현은? (3점)

pack 짐 / lead 데려가다

① Every horse thinks his pack heavy.
② Don't put the cart before the horse.
③ We ride horses before we can walk.
④ If you can't get a horse, ride a cow.
⑤ You can lead a horse to water but you can't make him drink.

26. 위 글의 내용과 일치하는 것은? (2점)

① Tabin lives in Kenya.
② Tabin is happy when she reads books.
③ Horses are important in Tabin's culture.
④ Tabin enjoys riding a horse especially in the morning.
⑤ Tabin often brushes her horse and gives him some apples.

27. 다음을 읽고 대답할 수 있는 질문이 아닌 것은? (3점)

> Hi, my name is Diego, and I live in Seville, Spain. My favorite time of the day is lunch time. My school usually ends around 2 p.m. On most days, my family gets together and has a big, long lunch. We usually have soup, vegetables, and meat. We also have a dessert like churros. After lunch, we usually take a siesta, a short nap. Both my father and I like to sleep under the tree in our garden.

① Where does Diego live?
② What do they usually do in their weekend?
③ When is Diego's favorite time of the day?
④ What does Diego's family have for lunch?
⑤ Where do Diego and his father like to sleep after lunch?

28. 다음 글의 밑줄 친 ⓐthem에 대해 글쓴이가 가지고 있는 감정을 가장 잘 나타내는 단어는?   (4점)

Musa
Hi! I'm Musa, and I live in Nairobi, Kenya. My favorite time of the day is our running practice time. My friend, Tamu, and I are on the school's running team. Our practice time isn't boring because we can see many animals. Many runners from Kenya won races in the Olympics. I'm so proud of them. Tamu and I want to be like ⓐthem.

① relaxed   ② annoyed   ③ confused
④ respectful   ⑤ disappointed

[29~32] 다음 글을 읽고 물음에 답하시오.

Tabin
Hi! My name is Tabin, and I live near the Gobi Desert in Mongolia. I'm happy when I ride my horse. Horses are important in our culture. Almost everyone can ride a horse in Mongolia. (A)[At / In] fact, we say, "We ride horses before we can walk."
I take good care of my horse. ⓐI often brush him and give him some carrots. I enjoy (B)[ride / riding] especially in the evening before the sunset. ⓑThen the sky is red, and everything (C)[is / are] peaceful.

29. 위 글의 내용과 일치하는 것은?   (3점)
① Tabin은 고비 사막에 산다.
② Tabin은 소유하고 있는 말이 있다.
③ 몽골에서 말을 못 타는 사람은 없다.
④ 몽골 사람들은 "우리는 말을 타기 전에 걷는다."라고 한다.
⑤ Tabin이 승마를 좋아하는 이유는 몽골 문화에서 말이 중요하기 때문이다.

30. 위 글의 문장 ⓐ와 의미가 일치하는 올바른 어법의 문장은?   (2점)
① I often brush him and give some carrots him.
② I often brush him and give some carrots of him.
③ I often brush him and give some carrots to him.
④ I often brush him and give some carrots on him.
⑤ I often brush him and give some carrots for him.

31. 위 글의 (A)~(C)에 들어갈 말을 순서대로 짝지은 것은?   (3점)

	(A)	(B)	(C)
①	At	ride	is
②	At	riding	are
③	In	ride	is
④	In	riding	is
⑤	In	riding	are

32. 위 글의 ⓑ가 가리키는 때를 구체적으로 본문에서 찾아 영어로 서술하시오.   (4점)
→ _____

33. 다음 주어진 우리말과 같은 뜻이 되도록 〈조건〉에 맞게 완전한 영어 문장으로 쓰시오. (축약형은 1 단어로 인정.)   (4점)

(1) 나의 아빠와 나는 둘 다 나무 밑에서 자는 것을 좋아해.
(2) Tom 아니면 James가 학교에 늦었다.

〈조건〉
• (1) 문장: 총 11 단어, both를 사용할 것
• (2) 문장: 총 8 단어, either를 사용할 것

답 (1) _____
   (2) _____

◎ 선택형 문항의 답안은 컴퓨터용 수정 싸인펜을
사용하여 OMR 답안지에 바르게 표기하시오.
◎ 서술형 문제는 답을 답안지에 반드시 검정
볼펜으로 쓰시오.
◎ 총 31문항 100점 만점입니다. 문항별 배점
은 각 문항에 표시되어 있습니다.

[대전 ○○중]

1. 다음 〈보기〉의 영영풀이에 해당되지 <u>않는</u> 단어는?

(3점)

<보기>
• more than other things or people
• to state or decide that something will not
happen
• to treat something carefully so that it stays
in good condition
• the activity of doing something regularly
so that you can do it better

① cancel   ② fasten   ③ practice
④ especially   ⑤ take care of

[경기 ○○중]

2. 다음 글의 문맥상 밑줄 친 문장의 의미로 가장 적절
한 것은?

(3점)

Rose Bakery is my favorite place near school.
From the school's main gate, first turn right.
Then walk straight on Hana-ro. When you
see Sun Bank on your right, turn left. <u>You
can't miss it.</u>

① You can't see it.
② It's near Sun Bank.
③ It's right over there.
④ You can find it easily.
⑤ You can't understand directions.

[대구 ○○중]

3. 다음 대화가 자연스러운 대화가 되도록 (A)~(D)를
바르게 배열한 것은?

(2점)

(A) I make cookies.
(B) I usually make strawberry cookies.
(C) Are there any cookies you like to make?
(D) What do you usually do in your free
time?

① (A)-(C)-(B)-(D)   ② (B)-(A)-(D)-(C)
③ (B)-(D)-(C)-(A)   ④ (D)-(A)-(C)-(B)
⑤ (D)-(C)-(B)-(A)

[광주 ○○중]

[4~5] 다음 지도를 보고 물음에 답하시오.

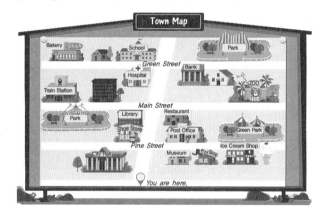

4. 빈칸에 알맞은 것은?

(3점)

B: Excuse me. How do I get to _____?
G: Walk straight three blocks and turn left.
It'll be on your right.
B: Oh, I see.

① the School   ② the Bank
③ the Post office   ④ the Hospital
⑤ the Toy Shop

5. Which building is across from the restaurant?

(3점)

① the Hospital   ② the School
③ the Shoe Store   ④ the Library
⑤ City hall

[6~8] 다음 지도와 대화를 보고 질문에 답하시오.

Town Map

Tom: Hello. May I help you?

Sue: Yes, please. I'm looking for Green Park.

Tom: OK. Please look at this map. We are here.

Sue: Oh, I see. So how do I get to the park?

Tom: Go straight two blocks and turn (A)_____. It's (B)_____ _____ the train station. It is next to the library.

Sue: I see. The African Music Concert is there, right?

Tom: Yes, it is. It's going to start at 4 p.m. at the Star Concert Stage.

Sue: Right, and where is the stage?

Tom: It's near the north gate of the park. ⓐ 반드시 찾으실 겁니다.

Sue: OK, thank you!

6. 위 대화의 내용과 일치하는 것은? (3점)

① Green Park is on Green Street.

② Sue is giving directions to Tom.

③ Sue wants to go to the Asian Music Concert.

④ Tom doesn't know where the Star Concert Stage is.

⑤ Sue has to be near the north gate of the park around 4 p.m. to see the concert.

7. 위 대화의 빈칸 (A), (B)에 적절한 단어를 쓰시오. (5점)

<조 건>
• (B)는 두 단어 모두 맞아야 점수 부여함.

(A) _____

(B) _____ _____

8. 위 대화의 ⓐ의 우리말을 영어로 옮기시오. (3점)

ⓐ _____ can't _____ _____.

9. 주어진 우리말을 영어로 바꿀 때, 5번째로 오는 단어들을 순서대로 나열한 것은? (4점)

조건: 주어진 단어들을 꼭 사용할 것.

(A) 그 재킷은 겨울에 입어도 될 정도로 충분히 따뜻해 보인다. (The / jacket / looks / warm)

(B) 그녀는 너무 빨리 걸어서 따라잡을 수가 없다. (She / follow / fast)

(C) 그 개는 시각장애인을 안내할 만큼 충분히 똑똑하다. (The / dog / the blind / guide)

	(A)	(B)	(C)
①	to	to	enough
②	to	to	to
③	to	too	to
④	enough	to	enough
⑤	enough	to	to

10. 제시된 단어를 활용하여 우리말과 의미가 일치하도록 자연스러운 문장을 완성하시오. (5점)

• 지구를 지키기 위해서 종이컵을 사용해서는 안 된다. (paper cups / save the earth)

We _____.

11. 다음 (A)~(C)에 들어갈 말로 바르게 짝지은 것은? (4점)

The most (A)[exciting / excited] part of the day is riding the Texas Star. It's a tall Ferris wheel. Wow! Steve and I are now on the top. I'm scared, but the view is (B)[amazing / amazed]! I love living in Texas and (C)[going / to go] to the fair. Come to the fair some day!

	(A)	(B)	(C)
①	exciting	amazed	to go
②	excited	amazing	to go
③	excited	amazed	going
④	excited	amazing	going
⑤	exciting	amazing	going

12. 다음 대화에서 ⓐ~ⓔ 각각이 가리키는 대상이 바르지 않은 것은? (4점)

B: Hello. What can I do for you?
G: I'm looking for Green Park.
B: OK. Please look at this map. We are here.
G: Oh, I see. So how do I get to the park?
B: Go straight two blocks and turn left. ⓐIt's across from the train station. You can't miss ⓑit.
G: I see. The African Music Concert is there, right?
B: Yes, it is. ⓒIt's going to start at 4 p.m. at the Star Concert Stage.
G: Right, and where is ⓓit?
B: ⓔIt's near the north gate of the park.
G: OK, thank you!

① ⓐ It → The park
② ⓑ it → the park
③ ⓒ It → The African Music Concert
④ ⓓ it → the park
⑤ ⓔ It → The stage

13. 다음 중 밑줄 친 to 부정사 중 용법이 다른 하나는? (2점)

① I listen to music to feel good.
② I study hard to get good grades.
③ I use the computer to play games.
④ I want to travel around the world.
⑤ I exercise every day to get healthier.

14. 다음 주어진 우리말을 조건에 맞게 영어로 쓰시오. (4점)

• 우리 가족은 5명이다.

<조건>
• 5 단어로 쓸 것.
• in을 반드시 사용할 것.
• 숫자도 영어로 쓸 것.

정답: There are _____.

15. 다음 글을 읽고 글의 흐름상 빈칸 ⓐ에 들어갈 말은? (3점)

Look at the goats here! This is a goat show. My younger brother, Steve, entered it. The goats in the show ⓐ_____ be big, but they have to be healthy. They have to produce much milk to win a prize. Steve took good care of his goat, Bonnie. Wow! Steve and Bonnie won a white ribbon, third prize!

① has to   ② have to
③ should   ④ don't have to
⑤ doesn't have to

[16~18] 다음 글을 읽고 물음에 답하시오.

Now, it's lunch time, so we're eating fair food. Mom and Dad are eating nachos and fajitas. They are Tex-Mex food. Tex-Mex food is a combination of food from Texas and Mexico. Dad's face is getting red because his fajita is too spicy. Steve and I are eating corn dogs. They taste great.

Let's move on to the quilt contest. Quilting has a long tradition. In the past, fabric was _____, so to make a blanket, people had to collect small pieces of fabric and sew them together.

Grandma and her friends had a quilting bee every week. They had to work on the quilt for the contest for over six months. Look! It's very colorful and unique.

The most exciting part of the day is riding the Texas Star. It's a tall Ferris wheel. Wow! Steve and I are now on the top. I'm scared, but the view is amazing!

I love living in Texas and going to the fair. Come to the fair some day!

16. 위 글의 빈칸에 들어갈 말로 가장 적절한 것은?

(3점)

① expensive   ② cheap   ③ common
④ unique   ⑤ long

17. 위 글의 밑줄 친 부분과 쓰임이 같은 것은? (2점)
① I'm glad to meet you.
② I have to wash the dishes.
③ I want to go there with you.
④ He grew up to be a musician.
⑤ I got up early to help my mom.

18. 위 글에 관한 내용으로 올바른 것은? (4점)
① The history of quilting wasn't that long.
② Fajitas and nachos are food from Texas.
③ Fajitas are too spicy for the writer's mom.
④ They went to the quilt contest before lunch.
⑤ The view on the top of the Texas Star is great.

[19~21] 다음 글을 읽고 물음에 답하시오.

Now, it's lunch time, so we're eating fair food. Mom and Dad are eating nachos and fajitas. ⓐThey are Tex-Mex food. Tex-Mex food is a combination of food from Texas and Mexico. Dad's face is getting red ⓑ_____ his fajita is too spicy. Steve and I are eating corn dogs. They taste great.

19. 위 글의 밑줄 친 ⓐThey가 가리키는 것은? (3점)
① fair foods
② corn dogs
③ Mexican foods
④ mom and dad
⑤ nachos and fajitas

20. 위 글의 빈칸 ⓑ에 들어갈 말로 알맞은 것은? (2점)
① so   ② or   ③ but
④ because   ⑤ therefore

21. 위 글을 읽고 답할 수 없는 질문은? (3점)
① How are the corn dogs made?
② What does Tex-Mex food mean?
③ What are the writer's mom and dad doing?
④ Why is the writer's father's face getting red?
⑤ According to the writer's father, how does his fajita taste?

[22~24] 다음 글을 읽고 물음에 답하시오.

Let's move (A)[on to / in to] the quilt contest. Quilting has a long tradition. In the past, fabric was expensive. To make a blanket, people had to collect small pieces of fabric and (B)[sew / sewed] them together. Grandma and her friends had a quilting bee every week. They had to work on the quilt for the contest (C)[for / during] over six months. Look! It's very colorful and unique. The most exciting part of the day is riding the Texas Star. It's a tall Ferris wheel. Wow! Steve and I are now on the top. I'm scared, but the view is amazing!
I love living in Texas and going to the fair. Come to the fair some day!

22. 위 글을 통해 알 수 <u>없는</u> 내용은? (3점)

① Grandma's quilting meeting has a long tradition.

② Grandma worked on the quilt for more than 6 months.

③ The Texas Star is a tall Ferris wheel.

④ The view on the top of the Texas Star is great.

⑤ People had to collect small pieces of fabric because of its high price.

23. 위 글의 괄호 (A)~(C)에서 어법상 알맞은 것끼리 순서대로 바르게 짝지어진 것은? (3점)

① on to – sew – during

② in to – sew – for

③ on to – sewed – during

④ in to – sewed – during

⑤ on to – sew - for

24. 위 글에서 다음 빈칸에 알맞은 단어를 찾는다면? (3점)

> • A _____ is a custom or belief that has existed for a long time.

① contest   ② tradition   ③ fabric
④ view   ⑤ fair

[25~26] 다음 글을 읽고 물음에 답하시오.

Hi, I'm Eddie Parker. I live in ⓐ<u>Texas, Dallas</u>. Now, my family and I are at the State Fair of Texas. The fair is over 130 ⓑ<u>years</u> old, and it's the biggest fair in the USA. I'll show you around. Follow me!
Look at the goats here! This is a goat show. My younger brother, Steve, entered it. The goats in the show ⓒ<u>doesn't</u> have to be big, but they have to be ⓓ<u>healthy</u>. They have to ⓔ<u>product</u> a lot of milk to win a prize. Steve took good care of his goat, Bonnie. Wow! Steve and Bonnie won a white ribbon, third prize! I'm so proud of them!

25. 위 글을 읽고 질문에 답할 수 <u>없는</u> 것은? (3점)

① Who entered the goat show?

② How old is the State Fair of Texas?

③ What is the biggest fair in the world?

④ What prize did Steve and Bonnie win?

⑤ Where are Eddie and his family now?

26. 위 글의 밑줄 친 ⓐ~ⓔ 중에서 어법에 맞는 것은? (4점)

① ⓐ, ⓑ   ② ⓑ, ⓒ   ③ ⓒ, ⓔ
④ ⓑ, ⓓ   ⑤ ⓓ, ⓔ

[27~28] 다음 글을 읽고 물음에 답하시오.

Look at the goats here! This is a goat show. My younger brother, Steve, entered it. The goats in the show don't have to be big, but they have to be healthy. They have to produce a lot of milk <u>to win</u> a prize. Steve took good care of his goat, Bonnie. Wow! Steve and Bonnie won a white ribbon, third prize!

27. 위 글을 읽고 대답할 수 <u>없는</u> 질문은? (3점)

① What is the writer talking about?
② What is the brother's name of the writer?
③ Who entered the goat show?
④ How much milk does Bonnie produce?
⑤ What prize did Steve and his goat win?

28. 위 글의 밑줄 친 부분과 쓰임이 같은 것은? (3점)

① I like <u>to sleep</u> after lunch.
② My hobby is <u>to play</u> the piano.
③ He studied really hard <u>to pass</u> the test.
④ You went <u>to school</u> during the winter vacation.
⑤ <u>To study</u> English is important for your future.

[29~30] 다음 글을 읽고 물음에 답하시오.

Let's move on to the quilt contest. (A) Quilting has a long tradition. (B) To make a blanket, people had to collect small pieces of fabric and sew them together. (C) Grandma and her friends had a quilting bee every week. (D) They had to work on the quilt for the contest for over six months. (E) Look! It's very colorful and unique.

29. 위 글에서 주어진 문장이 들어갈 위치로 가장 알맞은 곳은? (3점)

In the past, fabric was expensive.

① (A)   ② (B)   ③ (C)   ④ (D)   ⑤ (E)

30. What did people have to do to make a blanket? (3점)

① 오랫동안 바느질을 배워야만 했다.
② 퀼트 대회에 나가서 상을 받아야만 했다.
③ 작은 천 조각들을 모아서 꿰매 붙여야만 했다.
④ 비싼 천 값 때문에 담요를 만드는 일은 불가능했다.
⑤ 화려하고 독특한 천을 사기 위해 전국을 돌아다녀야 했다.

31. 주어진 글 다음에 이어질 글의 순서로 가장 적절한 것은? (4점)

It was lunch time, so Eddie's family had fair food.

(A) His dad's face got red because of his spicy fajita.
(B) Eddie's mom and dad ate nachos and fajitas.
(C) Steve and Eddie ate corn dogs. They tasted less spicy than his dad's fajita.
(D) They are Tex-Mex food. It is a combination of food from Texas and Mexico.

① (A)-(B)-(C)-(D)   ② (A)-(C)-(B)-(D)
③ (A)-(D)-(B)-(C)   ④ (B)-(C)-(D)-(A)
⑤ (B)-(D)-(A)-(C)

◎ 선택형 문항의 답안은 컴퓨터용 수정 싸인펜을
사용하여 OMR 답안지에 바르게 표기하시오.
◎ 서술형 문제는 답을 답안지에 반드시 검정
볼펜으로 쓰시오.
◎ 총 29문항(선택형 22문항, 서술형 7문항)
100점 만점입니다. 문항별 배점은 각 문항
에 표시되어 있습니다.

[인천 ○○중]

1. 다음 글에서 글쓴이가 쓴 목적으로 가장 알맞은 것
은? (3점)

Seochon is full of fun things. You can go to
Tongin Market. It's famous for oil
Tteokbokki, so you have to go there to try
it. There are also many traditional Korean
houses. You can walk around to see them.
Come visit us in Seochon. You'll have so
much fun!

① To visit   ② To warn
③ To celebrate   ④ To complain
⑤ To advertise

[부산 ○○중]

2. 다음 대화의 흐름상 밑줄 친 (A)에 들어갈 가장 알
맞은 영어 표현은? (3점)

B: Hello. May I help you?
G: Yes, please. I'm looking for Green Park.
B: OK. Please look at this map. We are here.
G: Oh, I see. (A)_____
B: Go straight two blocks and turn left. It's
across from the train station.
G: I see. The African Music Concert is there,
right?
B: Yes, it is.

① So I agree.
② So I can't find it.
③ So how do I get to the park?
④ So I know where Green Park is.
⑤ So what about going to the park?

[경기 ○○중]

[3~4] 다음 지도를 보고, 아래 각 대화의 빈칸에 들어
갈 말을 조건에 맞게 완전한 영어 문장으로 완성하시오.

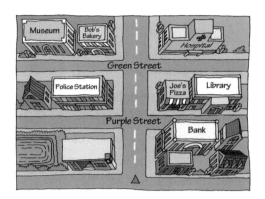

<조건>

• 주어진 단어나 철자로 시작하고 필요하면 새로운
단어를 추가할 것.

3. (4점)

A: Excuse me. W_____?
B: It's on the Purple Street. It's next to
Joe's Pizza.

→ _____

4. (5점)

A: How do I get to Bob's Bakery?
B: Go _____ and _____.
It'll _____.

→ _____

[경기 ○○중]

5. 다음 제시된 단어들을 순서대로 배열하여 자연스러
운 문장을 완성하시오. (4점)

• 너는 안전벨트를 매야 한다.
[seat belt / you / to / your / have / fasten]

→ _____

6. 다음 글의 밑줄 친 부분 중, 문맥상 낱말의 쓰임이
   적절한 것은?   (4점)

Quilting has a long tradition. In the ⓐfuture, fabric was expensive. To make a blanket, people had to collect small pieces of fabric and sew ⓑit together.

Grandma and her friends had a quilting bee every week. They had to work ⓒon the quilt for the contest for over six months. Look! It is very colorful and unique.

The most exciting part of the day is riding the Texas Star. It is a ⓓshort Ferris wheel. Steve and I are now on the top of it. I am scared, but the view is ⓔamazed.

① ⓐ   ② ⓑ   ③ ⓒ   ④ ⓓ   ⑤ ⓔ

7. 다음 대화의 내용과 일치하는 것은?   (3점)

A: How can I get to Green Concert Hall?
B: OK. Please look at this map. We are here.
A: Oh, I see. So how do I get to the concert hall?
B: Go straight three blocks and turn left. It's across from the bakery.
A: I see. The African Music Concert is there, right?
B: Yes, it is. It's going to start at 4 p.m. at the Star Concert Stage.
A: Right, and where is the stage?
B: It's near the north gate of the concert hall.
A: OK, thank you!

① Speaker A wants to go to the bakery.
② Green Concert Hall is far from the bakery.
③ The two speakers are looking at the map together.
④ The African Music Concert will end around 4 p.m.
⑤ The stage is near the south gate of the concert hall.

8. 다음 밑줄 친 부분과 쓰임이 같은 것은?   (3점)

• To stay healthy, I exercise every day.

① They have a lot of work to do.
② I want to go to America next year.
③ To learn Korean history is important.
④ I have something to tell you before you go.
⑤ I went to the park to take a walk with Mom.

9. 다음 지도를 보고 길을 잘못 설명한 것을 고르면?
                                            (3점)

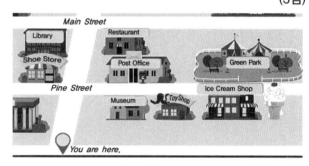

① A: Excuse me, where's the restaurant?
   B: It's across from the library.
② A: Excuse me. I'm looking for the library.
   B: Go straight two blocks and turn left. It'll be on your left.
③ A: Where is the toy shop?
   B: It's between the museum and the ice cream shop.
④ A: Excuse me. I'm looking for the post office.
   B: Go straight one block and turn right. It's next to Green Park.
⑤ A: Excuse me, where is the shoe store?
   B: It's on Main Street. It's across from the library.

[10~13] 다음 글을 읽고 물음에 답하시오.

Hi, I'm Eddie Parker. I live in Dallas, Texas. Now, my family and I are at the State Fair of Texas. The fair is over 130 years old, and it's the biggest fair in the USA. I'll show you around. Follow me!

Look at the goats here! This is a goat show. My younger brother, Steve entered ⓐit. The goats in the show don't have to be big, ⓑ_____ they have to be healthy. They have to produce a lot of milk to win a prize. Steve took good care of his goat, Bonnie. Wow! Steve and Bonnie won a white ribbon, third prize! I'm so proud of them!

10. 위 글을 통해 알 수 없는 내용은? (3점)

① Eddie Parker and his family live in Texas.

② The State Fair of Texas is the biggest fair in the world.

③ There is a goat show at the State Fair of Texas.

④ The goats must produce much milk to get a prize.

⑤ Steve's goat won third prize at the State Fair.

11. 위 글의 밑줄 친 ⓐit이 가리키는 것으로 가장 알맞은 것은? (2점)

① the fair　　　　② a goat

③ a lot of milk　　④ a goat show

⑤ a white ribbon

12. 위 글의 ⓑ에 들어갈 가장 알맞은 말은? (3점)

① and　　② before　　③ but

④ so　　　⑤ then

13. 위 글에서 다음 질문에 알맞은 답을 찾아 7 단어로 쓰시오. (4점)

Q: How old is the State Fair of Texas?

A: _____

14. 다음 제시된 단어를 활용하여 우리말과 의미가 일치하도록 자연스러운 문장을 완성하시오. (4점)

> • 그 바지는 너무나 꽉 조여서 입을 수 없어요.
> [tight / too]

답: The pants _____.

15. 다음 우리말과 의미가 같도록 주어진 단어의 순서를 바르게 나열한 것은? (3점)

> • 너는 너무 빨리 걸어서 따라잡을 수가 없다.
> • (A)follow (B)walk (C)to (D)too (E)fast
> = You _____.

① (A)-(B)-(C)-(D)-(E)

② (A)-(C)-(E)-(D)-(B)

③ (B)-(C)-(E)-(D)-(A)

④ (B)-(D)-(E)-(C)-(A)

⑤ (E)-(D)-(A)-(C)-(B)

16. 다음 주어진 조건에 맞게 우리말을 영어로 옮기시오. (5점)

> • 나는 전기 자전거를 사기 위해 돈을 저축하고 있다.

> <조건>
> • 현재진행형을 이용할 것.
> • 8 단어로 쓸 것. (축약형 이용)
> • to부정사를 사용할 것.

→ _____

[17~18] 다음 글을 읽고, 물음에 답하시오.

Let's move on to the quilt contest. Quilting has a long tradition. (A)_____ the past, fabric was expensive. To make a blanket, people had to collect small pieces of fabric and sew them together.

Grandma and her friends had a quilting bee every week. They had to work (B)_____ the quilt for the contest for over six months. Look! It's very colorful and unique.

The most exciting part of the day is riding the Texas Star. It's a tall Ferris wheel. Wow! Steve and I are now (C)_____ the top. I'm scared, but the view is amazing!

I love living in Texas and going to the fair. Come to the fair some day!

17. 위 글의 내용과 일치하지 <u>않는</u> 것은? (3점)

① 퀼트 만들기는 오랜 전통이 있다.

② 과거에는 천이 비싸서 작은 천을 모아 담요를 만들었다.

③ 나의 할머니와 할머니 친구들은 여러 달 동안 대회 준비를 했다.

④ 나는 회전 관람차를 타는 것이 가장 신났다.

⑤ 나는 관람차가 꼭대기에 도달했을 때 무서워서 밖을 못 봤다.

18. 위 글의 빈칸 (A), (B), (C)에 가장 적절한 말을 차례대로 나열한 것은? (3점)

	(A)	(B)	(C)
①	In	on	on
②	On	at	in
③	In	at	on
④	On	in	in
⑤	In	on	in

[19~20] 다음 글을 읽고 물음에 답하시오.

Look at the goats here! This is a goat show. My younger brother, Steve, entered it. The goats in the show don't have to be big, (A)_____ they have to be healthy. They have to produce a lot of milk to win a prize. Steve took good care of his goat, Bonnie. Wow! Steve and Bonnie won a white ribbon, third prize! I'm so proud of them!

Now, it's lunch time, (B)_____ we're eating fair food. Mom and Dad are eating nachos and fajitas. They are Tex-Mex food. Tex-Mex food is a combination of food from Texas and Mexico. Dad's face is getting red because his fajita is too spicy. Steve and I are eating corn dogs. They taste great.

19. 위 글의 흐름상 빈칸 (A), (B)에 들어갈 가장 적절한 말이 순서대로 짝지어진 것은? (3점)

① so - so   ② but - so

③ so - and   ④ but - but

⑤ and - but

20. 위 글의 내용과 일치하는 것은? (4점)

① The writer is older than Steve.

② Mom doesn't like Tex-Mex food.

③ Corn dog is a kind of Tex-Mex food.

④ The spicy nacho is making Dad's face red.

⑤ Only the big goats can enter the goat show.

[21~23] 다음 글을 읽고 물음에 답하시오.

Hi, I'm Eddie Parker. I live in Dallas, Texas. Now, my family and I are at the State Fair of Texas. The fair is over 130 years old, and ⓐit's the biggest fair in the USA. I'll show you around. Follow me!

Look at the goats here! This is a goat show. My younger brother, Steve, entered it. The goats in the show don't have to be big, but they have to be healthy. ⓑThey have to produce a lot of milk to win a prize. Steve took good care of his goat, Bonnie. Wow! Steve and Bonnie won a white ribbon, third prize! I'm so proud of ⓒthem!

Now, it's lunch time, so we're eating fair food. Mom and Dad are eating nachos and fajitas. ⓓThey are Tex-Mex food. Dad's face is getting red because his fajita is too spicy. Steve and I are eating corn dogs. ⓔThey taste great.

21. 위 글에서 ⓐ~ⓔ가 의미하는 것으로 알맞지 않은 것은? (3점)

① ⓐ State Fair of Texas
② ⓑ Steve and his goat
③ ⓒ Steve and Bonnie
④ ⓓ nachos and fajitas
⑤ ⓔ corn dogs

22. 위 글을 읽고 답할 수 없는 질문은? (3점)

① What color is Bonnie?
② Who entered a goat show?
③ Why is Dad's face getting red?
④ How old is the State Fair of Texas?
⑤ What do the goats have to do to win a prize?

23. 위 글의 내용과 일치하는 것은? (3점)

① The State Fair of Texas is the biggest Fair in the world.
② Steve entered the goat show with his friend, Eddie Parker.
③ The goats have to be big to win a prize in the goat show.
④ Nachos, fajitas, and corn dogs are fair food.
⑤ Steve is so proud of himself and his dog.

24. 다음 문장의 의미가 통하도록 (A), (B)에서 알맞은 말을 1개씩 고른 후, 'to+동사원형'을 사용하여 <보기>와 같이 한 문장으로 완성하여 쓰시오. (5점)

(A)
• I learn English.
• Tom went to the shopping mall.
• <u>I use a smartphone.</u>
• I study hard.
• I went to the park.

(B)
• travel abroad
• take a walk
• <u>make a call</u>
• buy shoes
• pass the exam

⇩

<보기>
• I use a smartphone to make a call.

(1) _____

(2) _____

25. 다음 글의 빈칸에 들어갈 말로 알맞게 짝지어진 것은? (4점)

> Hi, I'm Eddie Parker. I live in Dallas, Texas. Now, my family and I are (A)_____ the State Fair of Texas. The fair is (B)_____ 130 years old, and it's the (C)_____ fair in the USA. I'll show you (D)_____. Follow me!

	(A)	(B)	(C)	(D)
①	in	over	bigger	down
②	at	over	biggest	around
③	at	in	bigger	right
④	on	around	biggest	around
⑤	in	more	bigger	more

[26~28] 다음 글을 읽고 물음에 답하시오.

> Let's move on to the quilt contest. Quilting has a long ⓐ_____. ⓑ과거에는, fabric was expensive.
> To make a blanket, people had to collect small pieces of fabric and sew ⓒthem together.
> Grandma and her friends had a quilting bee ⓓevery week. They had to work on the quilt for the contest for over six months. Look! It's very colorful.
> The most exciting part of the day is ⓔride the Texas Star. It's a tall Ferris wheel. Wow! Steve and I are now on the top. (A)_____

26. 위 글의 ⓐ~ⓕ에 대한 설명이 옳지 않은 것은? (4점)

① ⓐ에 적당한 말은 tradition이다.
② ⓑ를 영어로 옮기면 In the present이다.
③ ⓒ는 small pieces of fabric을 가리킨다.
④ ⓓ는 '매주'라는 뜻이다.
⑤ ⓔ에 알맞은 형태는 'riding'이다.

27. 위 글을 읽고 대답할 수 없는 질문은? (3점)

① What is the Texas Star?
② When did Grandma start quilting?
③ Who is on the top of the Texas Star?
④ How often did Grandma have a quilting bee with her friends?
⑤ How long did it take for Grandma and her friends to complete the quilt for the contest?

28. 위 글의 (A)에 들어갈 문장으로 가장 적절한 것은? (3점)

① I'll show you around. Follow me!
② Which fair food do you want to try?
③ I'm scared, but the view is amazing!
④ I'm Eddie Parker and I live in Dallas, Texas.
⑤ The State Fair of Texas is the biggest fair in the USA.

29. 다음 대화의 내용이 어색한 것은? (3점)

① A: May I help you?
   B: Oh, thank you. Where's Green Park?
② A: Where's the History Museum?
   B: Yes, please. You can't miss it.
③ A: Excuse me, where's the bookstore?
   B: There's one across from the post office.
④ A: How do I get to the police station?
   B: Walk straight three blocks and turn left.
⑤ A: Turn left at the corner and it'll be on your right.
   B: Oh, I see. Thank you.

◎ 선택형 문항의 답안은 컴퓨터용 수정 싸인펜을
　사용하여 OMR 답안지에 바르게 표기하시오.
◎ 서술형 문제는 답을 답안지에 반드시 검정
　볼펜으로 쓰시오.
◎ 총 28문항 100점 만점입니다. 문항별 배점
　은 각 문항에 표시되어 있습니다.

[대구 ○○중]

1. 다음 단어의 영영풀이가 바르게 짝지어진 것은? (4점)

① shell: the hard inner part of a nut or egg

② raise: to put something to a lower position

③ bucket: a deep round container with a handle on the top

④ throw: to make something go through the air by moving your leg

⑤ pile: to put something somewhere and not use it until you need it

[대구 ○○중]

2. 다음 영어 단어와 우리말 뜻이 바르게 연결된 것은?

(2점)

① invent - 발명가　　② signature - 실험

③ meaning - 뜻하다　④ explain - 설명하다

⑤ relationship - 상태

[광주 ○○중]

3. 다음 대화가 자연스러운 대화가 되도록 (A)~(C)를 바르게 연결한 것은? (3점)

Seller: Hello. May I help you?
(A) It's 10 dollars but I can take 2 dollars off.
(B) How much is this blue clock?
(C) It's nice. Then, I'll take it.

① (A)-(B)-(C)　　　② (B)-(A)-(C)

③ (B)-(C)-(A)　　　④ (C)-(A)-(B)

⑤ (C)-(B)-(A)

[종로구 ○○중]

4. 다음 대화 중 어색한 것은? (4점)

① A: I'll take 2 dollars off.
　 B: That sounds good. I'll take it.

② A: Do you want to dance?
　 B: No. You got the wrong person.

③ A: How much is this soccer ball?
　 B: It's 12 dollars and it's in good condition.

④ A: Hello. May I help you?
　 B: Yes, please. I'm just looking around.

⑤ A: What is special about it?
　 B: It can stand on one leg and dance to music.

[광진구 ○○중]

5. 다음 대화의 흐름에 맞도록 빈칸에 들어갈 문장으로 가장 적합한 것은? (3점)

G: Excuse me. How much are the round glasses?
M: They're 18 dollars.
G: Hmm. Can I get a discount?
M: ＿＿＿＿＿＿＿＿＿＿＿＿ Sorry.
G: That's OK. I'll take them.

① Yes, you can.

② No, I'm afraid not.

③ That sounds good.

④ I can't get a discount.

⑤ Everything here is old and used.

- 25 -

[6~8] 다음 대화를 읽고 물음에 답하시오.

Andy: Wow! There are so many interesting things here.
Woman: We sell old or used things to give all the money to a nursing home. What are you looking for?
Andy: I'm looking for a clock.
Woman: How about this red clock?
Andy: How much is it?
Woman: It's 15 dollars.
Andy: That's too expensive for me. (A)_____
_____
Woman: No, I'm (B)_____ not. It's only one year old. It's almost new.
Andy: Then, how much is this blue clock with the large numbers?
Woman: It's 10 dollars.
Andy: Then, I'll take the blue one. Thank you.

6. 위 대화를 읽고 답할 수 없는 질문은? (4점)

① What is Andy looking for?
② What is Andy going to buy?
③ How much is the blue clock?
④ How much money does Andy have?
⑤ What is she going to do after she sells old and used things?

7. 위 대화의 흐름상, 빈칸 (A)에 들어갈 말로 가장 적절한 것은? (4점)

① How are you?
② May I help you?
③ Will you take it?
④ Can I get a discount?
⑤ What do you usually do?

8. 위 대화의 흐름상, 빈칸 (B)에 들어갈 말로 가장 적절한 것은? (3점)

① fear   ② scared   ③ angry
④ afraid   ⑤ nervous

[9~10] 다음 대화를 읽고 물음에 답하시오.

G: How much are the jeans?
M: They're 18 dollars.
G: Hmm. Can I get a discount?
M: No, I'm afraid not. Sorry.
G: Then how much is this purple T-shirt?
M: It's 10 dollars.
G: That's too _____. Can I get a discount?
M: OK. I'll take 1 dollar off. That'll be 9 dollars.
G: I'll take it, then. Thank you!
*G: Girl, M: Man

9. 위 대화의 내용과 일치하지 않는 것은? (4점)

① The jeans are 18 dollars.
② The girl bought the purple T-shirt.
③ The purple T-shirt was 9 dollars at first.
④ The girl asked for a discount on the items.
⑤ The man did not give a discount on the jeans.

10. 위 대화의 빈칸에 들어갈 말로 가장 적절한 것은? (3점)

① big   ② cheap
③ creative   ④ expensive
⑤ interesting

[11~12] 다음 대화를 읽고 물음에 답하시오.

Boy: Wow! There are so many interesting things here.

Woman: Everything here is old or used. What are you looking for?

Boy: I'm looking for a clock.

Woman: How about this red clock?

Boy: How much is it?

Woman: It's 15 dollars.

Boy: Hmm. Can I get a discount?

Woman: (A)_____
It's only one year old. It's almost new.

Boy: Then, how much is this blue clock with the large numbers?

Woman: It's 10 dollars.

Boy: Then, I'll take the blue one. Thank you.

11. 위 대화의 빈칸 (A)에 들어갈 말로 가장 알맞은 것은? (3점)

① No, I'm afraid not.

② Wow. That's surprising.

③ I hope you can't miss it.

④ No, thanks. I had enough.

⑤ Don't worry. You will be fine.

12. 위 대화의 내용과 일치하는 것은? (4점)

① The woman is looking for a clock.

② The red clock has the large numbers.

③ The boy got a discount on the blue clock.

④ The boy bought the blue clock for 10 dollars.

⑤ The blue clock is more expensive than the red one.

13. 다음 문장 중 어법상 옳은 것은? (3점)

① The pizza was ate by Sue.

② English is spoken in Australia.

③ This report were written by Mary.

④ The pictures was taken at school.

⑤ This book is read by me yesterday.

14. 다음 글의 (A)의 단어들을 배열하여 문장을 완성하고자 할 때 다섯 번째로 써야 할 것은? (4점)

Pei: My group wants to hold a trashion show. "Trashion" is a combination of "trash" and "fashion." We'll use trash to make clothes. (A)[become / want / other / in / to / students / we / upcycling / interested] through the show.

Mr. Brown: A trashion show sounds like fun!

① to   ② want

③ become   ④ students

⑤ interested

15. 다음 중 동사의 변화형이 잘못 연결된 것은? (3점)

원형	과거형	과거분사형
① cut	cut	cut
② say	said	said
③ run	ran	ran
④ eat	ate	eaten
⑤ write	wrote	written

[16~17] 다음 글을 읽고, 물음에 답하시오.

Sumi: My group will make bags from old clothes. For example, we'll use blue jeans. Look at this bag. This (A)_____ Hajun, one of our group members. Isn't it nice? We'll make more bags and sell them on Environment Day. We're going to give all the money to a nursing home.

Mr. Brown: That's a great idea. Your ideas are all so creative. I want everyone to work hard for Environment Day.

<Blue Jeans Bag>

You Need: old blue jeans, sewing kit, scissors pins and buttons

Step

1. Cut off the legs of the blue jeans.
2. Sew the bottom together.
3. Make shoulder straps from one of the legs.
4. Sew the straps to the top of the jeans.
5. Decorate the bag with pins and buttons.

16. 위 글의 (A)에 알맞은 말은? (3점)

① made
② is made
③ was made by
④ made by
⑤ was made

17. 위 글의 'Blue Jeans Bag'을 만드는 순서를 위 글에서 설명한 순서대로 나열한 것은? (4점)

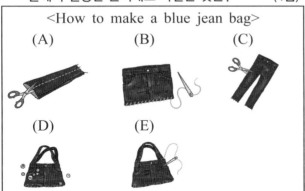

<How to make a blue jean bag>

(A) (B) (C)

(D) (E)

① (C)-(A)-(B)-(D)-(E)
② (C)-(B)-(A)-(E)-(D)
③ (C)-(B)-(A)-(D)-(E)
④ (A)-(C)-(D)-(E)-(B)
⑤ (A)-(D)-(C)-(B)-(E)

[18~19] 다음 글을 읽고, 물음에 답하시오.

Mr. Brown: Hello, club members. As you know, this year's Environment Day is about upcycling. Before we talk about each group's event idea for that day, I want you to understand the meaning of "upcycling." Can anyone explain upcycling?

Sumi: Yes, The word "upcycling" is a (A)_____ of "upgrade" and "recycling."

Eric: Like recycling, upcycling is good for the environment. When you upcycle, you make new and better things from old things.

Mr. Brown: Good. Now, let's talk about each group's idea for the event. Let's start with Pei's group.

18. 위 글 다음에 이어질 내용으로 알맞은 것은? (4점)
① 환경의 날에 대한 소개
② 자연 환경 보호의 중요성
③ 'Upcycling'의 뜻
④ 'Upcycling'의 좋은 점
⑤ 각 모둠의 행사 아이디어 소개

19. 위 글에서 (A)에 알맞은 말은? (3점)
① couple
② combination
③ pair
④ protect
⑤ instrument

[20～22] 다음 글을 읽고 물음에 답하시오.

Mr. Brown: Hello, club members. As you know, this year's Environment Day is about upcycling. Before we talk about each group's event idea for that day, (A)나는 너희가 업사이클링의 의미를 이해하기 원한다. Can anyone explain upcycling?

Sumi: Yes, The word "upcycling" is a combination of "upgrade" and "recycling."

Eric: Like recycling, upcycling is good for the environment. When you upcycle, you make new and better things from old things.

Mr. Brown: Good. Now, let's talk about each group's idea for the event. Let's start with Pei's group.

Pei: My group wants to hold a ⓐtrashion show. "Trashion" is a combination of "trash" and "fashion." We'll use trash to make clothes. We want other students to become interested in upcycling through the show.

Mr. Brown: A trashion show sounds like fun!

20. 위 글의 내용과 일치하지 <u>않는</u> 것은?　(3점)

① 올해 환경의 날의 주제는 업사이클링이다.

② 재활용과 달리 업사이클링은 환경에 좋다.

③ Pei의 모둠부터 아이디어를 소개하기 시작했다.

④ 각각의 동아리가 아이디어를 소개할 것이다.

⑤ Pei는 트래션 쇼를 통해 다른 학생들이 업사이클링에 관심을 갖기를 원한다.

21. 위 글의 밑줄 친 (A)를 〈보기〉의 단어를 배열하여 영어로 옮길 때 다섯 번째에 위치할 단어는?　(4점)

> ＜보기＞
> of / you / the / upcycling / want /
> I / meaning / understand / to

① to　　　② you　　　③ meaning

④ upcycling　　⑤ understand

22. 위 글의 밑줄 친 ⓐ에 전시될 상품과 가장 거리가 먼 것은?　(4점)

① gloves made from new fabric

② pants made from bottle caps

③ T-shirts made from used CDs

④ shoes made from old newspaper

⑤ dresses made from used coffee filters

23. 다음은 청바지를 이용하여 바구니를 만드는 방법이다. 빈칸 (A)～(C)에 알맞은 것은?　(4점)

> **Blue Jeans Basket**
>
> You need: old blue jeans, a sewing kit, scissors, and pins and buttons.
>
> Step
> First, (A)_____ a leg of the old blue jeans.
> Second, cut out a piece to make the bottom of the basket.
> Third, (B)_____ the bottom to the leg.
> Lastly, (C)_____ with pins and buttons.

	(A)	(B)	(C)
①	cut off	sew	decorate
②	cut down	make	practice
③	cut off	make	practice
④	cut down	sew	practice
⑤	cut off	make	decorate

[24~26] 다음 글을 읽고 물음에 답하시오.

Pei: My group wants to hold a trashion show. "Trashion" is a combination of "trash" and "fashion." We'll use trash to make clothes. We would like other students to become interested in upcycling through the show.

Mr. Brown: A trashion show sounds like fun! What about your group, Eric?

Eric: (A) We'll make drums from old plastic buckets. (B) We'll also make a guitar from old boxes and rubber bands. (C) We plan to play the instruments in a mini-concert. (D)

Mr. Brown: Thank you, Eric. (E) Now, let's hear from Sumi's group.

24. 위 글의 주제로 알맞은 것은? (4점)

① Upcycling ideas
② Holding a trashion show
③ Making clothes from trash
④ A mini-concert for teenagers
⑤ Upcycled musical instruments

25. Why does Pei's group want to hold a trashion show? (3점)

① Her group is interested in fashion design.
② Her group wants to make cloth bags from trash.
③ Her group wants to share how to make clothes from trash.
④ Her group would like other students to get interested in upcycling.
⑤ Her group would like other students to become interested in trash problem.

26. 위 글의 (A)~(E) 중 주어진 문장이 들어갈 위치로 알맞은 것은? (4점)

Our group members are going to make musical instruments from old things.

① (A)　② (B)　③ (C)　④ (D)　⑤ (E)

[27~28] 다음 글을 읽고 물음에 답하시오.

Sumi: My group will make bags from old clothes. (A) Look at this bag. ⓐ이것은 Hajun에 의해서 만들어졌다, one of our group members. Isn't it nice? (B) We'll make more bags and sell them on Environment Day. (C) We're going to give all the money to a nursing home. (D)

Mr. Brown: That's a great idea. Your idea are all so creative. (E) I want everyone to work hard for Environment Day.

27. 위 글에서 주어진 문장이 들어가기에 가장 적절한 곳은? (4점)

For example, we'll use blue jeans.

① (A)　② (B)　③ (C)　④ (D)　⑤ (E)

28. 위 글의 밑줄 친 ⓐ의 우리말을 〈조건〉에 맞게 완성하시오. (5점)

〈조건〉
1. 수동태 표현을 사용할 것.
2. 5개의 영어 단어로 완성할 것.

답: _____

◎ 선택형 문항의 답안은 컴퓨터용 수정 싸인펜을
  사용하여 OMR 답안지에 바르게 표기하시오.
◎ 서술형 문제는 답을 답안지에 반드시 검정
  볼펜으로 쓰시오.
◎ 총 28문항 100점 만점입니다. 문항별 배점
  은 각 문항에 표시되어 있습니다.

[종로구 ㅇㅇ중]

1. 다음 밑줄 친 hold와 같은 의미를 가진 것은? (4점)

• Our school will hold a fashion show next month.

① I was holding a baby in my arms.
② I think the branch will hold your weight.
③ The boy tried to hold his mother's hand.
④ He wants to hold a birthday party for his son.
⑤ Could you hold my bag for me?

[영등포구 ㅇㅇ중]

2. 다음 중 두 단어의 관계가 나머지와 다른 것은? (3점)

① clothes – blue jeans
② trash – waste paper
③ nature – tree
④ upcycling – recycling
⑤ musical instrument – piano

[양천구 ㅇㅇ중]

3. 다음 중 대화가 자연스러운 것은? (3점)

① A: May I help you?
   B: Thank you. I'll take it.
② A: Can I get a discount?
   B: Sorry. I'll take 3 dollars off.
③ A: How much are these shoes?
   B: They are too expensive.
④ A: Are these on sale?
   B: Yes, they are 20% off.
⑤ A: Can you help me with my homework now?
   B: No. I'm afraid not. I'll help you.

[대구 ㅇㅇ중]

4. 다음 빈칸에 들어갈 말로 가장 알맞은 것은? (3점)

A: Excuse me. _____
B: How about this? It'll look great on you.
A: It looks OK, but I think it's a little small for me.

① How do I look?
② Can you help me?
③ Is this T-shirt on sale?
④ I'm looking for a bank.
⑤ I'm looking for a T-shirt.

[인천 ㅇㅇ중]

5. 다음 두 사람의 관계로 알맞은 것은? (3점)

A: May I help you?
B: Yes. How much is this yellow backpack?
A: It's 18 dollars.
B: That's expensive for me. How about this red one?
A: It's 15 dollars.
B: That's a good price. I'll take it.

① fan – actor   ② guide – tourist
③ son – mother   ④ seller – customer
⑤ teacher – student

[6~8] 다음 대화를 읽고 물음에 답하시오.

B: Wow! There are so many interesting things here.

W: Everything here is old or used. What are you looking for?

B: I'm looking for an umbrella.

W: How about this red one?

B: How much is it?

W: It's 15 dollars.

B: That's too expensive for me. Can I get a discount?

W: No, I'm afraid not. It's only one year old. It's almost new.

B: Then, how much is this navy one with stripe patterns?

W: It's 10 dollars. I can give you a discount for this one. I will (A)_____ two dollars off.

B: Wow, good! Then, I'll (A)_____ this one. Thank you.

6. 위 대화의 빈칸 (A)에 공통으로 들어갈 것은? (3점)

① get   ② buy   ③ pay
④ give   ⑤ take

7. 위 대화에 나오는 화자 간의 관계로 가장 알맞은 것은? (2점)

① student – teacher
② assistant – manager
③ clerk – storekeeper
④ designer   buyer
⑤ customer – salesperson

8. 위 대화의 내용과 일치하는 것은? (4점)

① B did window-shopping for an umbrella.

② Not all the items in this store are used or old.

③ W can't give B a discount for the red umbrella because it is new.

④ B is satisfied with the navy umbrella's price after a discount.

⑤ B will pay 7 dollars for the navy umbrella.

9. 다음 대화의 흐름에 맞게 (A)~(D)를 알맞게 배열하시오. (3점)

Luke: Hello. May I help you?

(A) This one is 15 dollars and it's in a good condition.
(B) I'm looking for a baseball glove.
(C) Can you give me a discount?
(D) OK. I'll take 2 dollars off.

Maya: Then it's 13 dollars. I'll take it.

→ _____

10. 다음 중 어법상 옳은 문장은? (3점)

① I want to have a robot which can talks.

② The girl who is standing next to him are my sister.

③ I want to live in a house that have a big garden.

④ If you will see my sister, please give her this book.

⑤ They can catch the train if they leave now.

[11~12] 다음 대화를 읽고, 물음에 답하시오.

> A: Wow! There are so many interesting things here.
> B: Everything here is old or used. What are you looking for?
> A: I'm looking for a clock.
> B: How about this red clock?
> A: How much is it?
> B: It's 15 dollars.
> A: That's too expensive for me. Can I get a discount?
> B: (A)_____ It's only one year old. It's almost new.
> A: Then, how much is this blue clock with the large numbers?
> B: It's 10 dollars.
> A: Then, I'll take the blue one. Thank you.

11. 위 대화에서 밑줄 친 (A)에 들어갈 말로 옳은 것은? (3점)

① Yes, you can.
② Yes, I'll give you a discount.
③ OK, I'll take 5 dollars off.
④ No, I'm afraid not.
⑤ No problem.

12. 위 대화의 대화 내용과 일치하지 않는 것은? (4점)

① A는 중고품 가게에 왔다.
② B는 상점에서 일하는 사람이다.
③ B는 파란 시계를 추천했다.
④ A는 시계를 사려고 한다.
⑤ A는 파란 시계를 살 것이다.

13. 다음 중 밑줄 친 부분의 형태가 어법상 올바른 것은? (4점)

① The book <u>was writen</u> by Shakespeare.
② The radio <u>turned on</u> by Tom.
③ These cookies <u>made</u> by my sister.
④ The pictures <u>was painted</u> by Mina.
⑤ The computer <u>was used</u> by Jason.

14. 다음 문장을 어법에 맞게 영작한 것은? (4점)

> • 나는 즐기기에 충분히 흥미로울 그 콘서트에 네가 늦지 않기를 원한다.

① I want you to not late for the concert which will be too exciting to enjoy.
② I don't want you to coming late for the concert which will be exciting enough to enjoy.
③ I don't want you to late for the concert which will be exciting enough to enjoy.
④ I don't want to you to be late for the concert which will be exciting enough to enjoy.
⑤ I don't want you to be late for the concert which will be exciting enough to enjoy.

15. 다음 중 어법상 올바른 문장은? (4점)

① I wasn't woke up by the noise.
② Who told you come to the party?
③ Tom wants me not to play games.
④ This word doesn't used very often.
⑤ The doctor advised him stop smoking.

[16~17] 다음 글을 읽고 물음에 답하시오.

Mr. Brown: Hello, club members. As you know, this year's Environment Day is about upcycling. Before we talk about each group's event idea for that day, I want you (A)[understand / to understand] the meaning of "upcycling." Can (B)[anyone / someone] explain upcycling?

Sumi: Yes, The word "upcycling" is a combination of "upgrade" and "recycling."

Eric: Like recycling, upcycling is good (C)[at / for] the environment. When you upcycle, you make new and better things from old things.

16. 위 글의 괄호 (A), (B), (C) 안에서 적절한 표현으로 연결된 것은? (3점)

	(A)	(B)	(C)
①	understand	anyone	at
②	to understand	anyone	for
③	understand	someone	for
④	to understand	someone	at
⑤	understand	someone	at

17. 위 글의 제목으로 가장 적절한 것은? (4점)

① The Origin of Environment Day

② Some Wonderful Upcycling Ideas

③ Upcycling: A Great Way to Reuse Old Things

④ Recycling VS. Upcycling: What Is the Difference?

⑤ Many Event Ideas for This Year's Environment Day

18. 다음 그림의 청바지 가방을 만드는 방법에 대한 그림과 일치하지 않는 설명은? (4점)

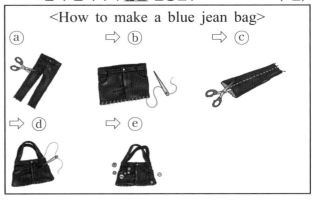

<How to make a blue jean bag>

① ⓐ Cut off the legs of the blue jeans.

② ⓑ Sew the bottom together.

③ ⓒ Make shoulder straps from one of the pockets.

④ ⓓ Sew the straps to the top of the jeans.

⑤ ⓔ Decorate the bag with pins and buttons.

19. What is Eric talking about? (4점)

Mr. Brown: A trashion show sounds like fun! What about your group, Eric?

Eric: My group is going to make musical instruments from old things. We'll make drums from old plastic buckets. We'll also make a guitar from old boxes and rubber bands. We plan to play the instruments in a mini-concert.

Mr. Brown: Thank you, Eric. Now, let's hear from Sumi's group.

① the importance of saving the earth

② the plan of having a trashion show

③ three steps to make musical instruments

④ changing old things into musical instruments

⑤ good points of using old things in a mini-concert

[20~22] 다음 글을 읽고 물음에 답하시오.

> Pei: ⓐMy group wants to held a trashion show. "Trashion" is a combination of "trash" and "fashion" We'll use trash (A)to make clothes. ⓑWe want other students to become interesting in upcycling through the show.
>
> Mr. Brown: ⓒA trashion show sounds like fun! What about your group, Eric?
>
> Eric: ⓓMy group is going to make musical instruments to old things. We'll make drums from old plastic buckets. We'll also make a guitar from old boxes and rubber bands. ⓔWe planning to play the instruments in a mini-concert.
>
> Mr. Brown: Thank you, Eric.

20. 위 글의 밑줄 친 (A)와 쓰임이 같은 것은? (3점)

① I decided to be a painter.

② To ride a bike here is dangerous.

③ She didn't expect to see him again.

④ She wants to sell the old tablet PC.

⑤ He went to the bookstore to buy books.

21. 위 글의 밑줄 친 ⓐ~ⓔ 중 어법상 바르게 사용된 것은? (4점)

① ⓐ   ② ⓑ   ③ ⓒ   ④ ⓓ   ⑤ ⓔ

22. 위 글의 내용과 일치하지 <u>않은</u> 것은? (4점)

① Pei's group will open a trashion show.

② Mr. Brown thinks a trashion show will be fun.

③ Eric's group will make old boxes and rubber bands.

④ Pei's group will design new clothes by using trash.

⑤ Eric's group is going to hold a mini-concert with the upcycled instruments.

[23~24] 다음 글을 읽고 물음에 답하시오.

> Mr. Brown: Hello, club members. ⓐAs you know, this year's Environment Day is about upcycling. Before we talk about ⓑeach group's event idea for that day, I want you ⓒto understand the meaning of "upcycling." Can anyone explain upcycling?
>
> Sumi: Yes. The word "upcycling" is ⓓa combination of "upgrade" and "recycling."
>
> Eric: Like recycling, upcycling ⓔis bad for the environment. When you upcycle, you make new and better things from old things.

23. 위 글의 밑줄 친 부분 중 글의 흐름상 옳지 <u>않은</u> 것은? (3점)

① ⓐ   ② ⓑ   ③ ⓒ   ④ ⓓ   ⑤ ⓔ

24. 위 글을 읽고 'upcycling'에 대해 가장 <u>잘못</u> 이해한 사람은? (4점)

① 문광: 업사이클링은 재활용에 개선한다는 개념이 합해진 신조어구나.

② 기우: 쓰레기 입장에서는 재활용보다는 업사이클링하는 게 좋겠어.

③ 기택: 업사이클링을 하면 환경을 보호할 수 있겠다.

④ 기정: 재활용하는 것보다는 비용이 많이 드니 그냥 버리는 게 낫겠어.

⑤ 근세: 버려지는 것들을 새롭게 활용하는 건 참 가치 있는 일 같아.

[25~28] 다음 글을 읽고, 물음에 답하시오.

Mr. Brown: Hello, club members. As you know, this year's Environment Day is about upcycling. Before we talk about each group's event idea for that day, I want you to understand the meaning of "upcycling." Can anyone explain upcycling?

Sumi: Yes. The word "upcycling" is a combination ⓐof "upgrade" and "recycling."

Eric: Like recycling, upcycling is good ⓑwith the environment. When you upcycle, you make new and better things from old things.

Mr. Brown: Good. Now, let's talk about each group's idea for the event. Let's start ⓒwith Pei's group.

Pei: My group wants to hold a trashion show. "Trashion" is a combination ⓐof "trash" and "fashion." We'll use trash to make clothes. (A)저희는 다른 학생들이 업사이클링에 관심을 갖게 되기를 바랍니다.

Mr. Brown: A trashion show sounds like fun! What about your group, Eric?

Eric: My group is going to make musical instruments from old things. We'll make drums from old plastic buckets. We'll also make a guitar from old boxes and rubber bands. We plan to play the instruments in a mini-concert.

Mr. Brown: Thank you, Eric. Now, let's hear ⓓfrom Sumi's group.

Sumi: My group will make bags from old clothes. For example, we'll use blue jeans. Look at this bag. This was made by Hajun, one of our group members. Isn't it nice? We'll make more bags and sell them on Environment Day. We're going to give all the money ⓔto a nursing home.

25. 위 글의 ⓐ~ⓔ 중 쓰임이 <u>어색한</u> 것을 고르시오.

(4점)

→ _____

26. 위 글의 (A)를 아래 〈보기〉에 주어진 단어를 모두 활용하여 영어로 쓸 때 6번째에 오는 단어는? (4점)

<보기>
want, become, upcycling, in, students, we, to, other, interested

① in   ② want   ③ other
④ become   ⑤ interested

27. 다음은 위 글의 내용을 요약한 요약문이다. 위 글의 내용과 <u>다른</u> 부분은 모두 몇 군데인가? (5점)

Mr. Brown and club members are talking about each group's event idea for this year's Upcycling Day. When you recycle, you can make new and better things from old things. Pei's group will hold a trashion show. They will use trash to make clothes. Eric's group will make musical instruments from old things. For example, they will make a guitar from old plastic buckets and rubber bands. Sumi's group will make bags from new blue jeans. They plan to sell blue jeans bags and give a nursing home all the money.

① 1군데   ② 2군데   ③ 3군데
④ 4군데   ⑤ 5군데

28. 위 글을 읽고 답할 수 없는 질문은? (4점)

① 올해 환경의 날은 무엇에 관한 것인가?
② 'Upcycling'의 의미는 무엇인가?
③ 'Pei'의 모둠이 옷을 만들기 위해 어떤 종류의 쓰레기를 이용하였는가?
④ Eric의 모둠은 자신들이 만든 악기로 무엇을 할 예정인가?
⑤ Sumi의 모둠은 환경에 날에 무엇을 할 예정인가?

[용산구 ○○중]

1. 다음 단어 중 종류가 나머지 넷과 <u>다른</u> 것은?　(2점)

① panda　　　　② monkey
③ octopus　　　④ gorilla
⑤ elephant

[부산 ○○중]

2. 다음 중 단어의 영영풀이로 바르게 짝지어지지 <u>않</u>은 것은?　(3점)

① jar: a glass container
② female: someone that is a girl or woman
③ temple: a building used for the worship for gods　　　*worship: 숭배
④ talent: a natural ability to do well
⑤ hide: to put something in a place where they can be seen

[광진구 ○○중]

3. 다음 중 대화의 흐름이 <u>어색한</u> 것은?　(2점)

① A: What does your cat look like?
　 B: It's a long tail.
② A: Do you need any help?
　 B: Yes. I lost my book.
③ A: I'm looking for my bag.
　 B: What does it look like?
④ A: I lost my wallet.
　 B: OK. I'll go and check.
⑤ A: Is there anything special about him?
　 B: Hmm. Let me think.

[인천 ○○중]

[4~5] 다음 대화를 읽고 물음에 답하시오.

M: May I help you?
G: Yes. I'm looking for my dog. His name is Prince.
M: What does he look like?
G: He's very small and has short white hair.
M: Can you tell me more?
G: Well, he has a really long tail.
M: I see. And one more thing. Where did you lose him?
G: I lost him near the main gate.
M: OK. I'll go and make an announcement. Can you please wait here?
G: Sure. Thanks a lot.

4. 위 대화가 이루어지는 장소로 가장 알맞은 것은?　(3점)

① Hospital　　　　② Toy Shop
③ Book Store　　　④ Post Office
⑤ Lost and Found Office

5. 위 대화의 내용과 다음 보고서의 내용이 일치하지 <u>않는</u> 것은?　(2점)

Lost Pet Report: Prince	
Type of Animal	ⓐ dog
Size	ⓑ very small
Color	ⓒ white hair
Lost Place	ⓓ near the main gate
Anything Special	ⓔ short tail

① ⓐ　　② ⓑ　　③ ⓒ　　④ ⓓ　　⑤ ⓔ

[6~7] 다음 대화를 읽고 물음에 답하시오.

M: May I help you?
G: Yes. I lost my dog, Prince.
M: Is there anything special about your dog?
G: He has short white hair.
M: What else?
G: Well, he has a really long tail.
M: I see. Where did you lose him?
G: I think I lost him near the main gate.
M: OK. I'll go and make an announcement. Can you please wait here?
G: Sure. Thanks a lot.

6. 위 대화를 통해서 알 수 없는 정보는? (2점)

① pet's name
② pet's size
③ kind of pet
④ pet's color
⑤ lost place

7. 위 대화에서 추론한 내용 중 가장 알맞은 것은? (3점)

① G is not asking M for help.
② M works at the Lost and Found office.
③ G is visiting the office for a volunteer work.
④ M is interviewing G to get her information.
⑤ G will leave the office before making an announcement.

8. 다음 대화의 빈칸에 들어갈 말로 알맞은 것은? (3점)

A: What does he look like?
B: _____

① He is sick.
② I like him very much.
③ He has short black hair.
④ He is very kind and active.
⑤ He doesn't look good today.

9. 다음 주어진 표현 뒤에 이어질 대화로 자연스러운 것은? (3점)

Excuse me. I'm looking for my scarf.
(A) Can you tell me more about it?
(B) It is a long cotton scarf.
(C) OK. I will go and check.
(D) What does it look like?
(E) Sure. It's gray.

① (A)-(B)-(D)-(E)-(C)
② (A)-(E)-(C)-(D)-(B)
③ (C)-(A)-(B)-(D)-(E)
④ (D)-(B)-(A)-(E)-(C)
⑤ (D)-(E)-(C)-(A)-(B)

10. What will the boy do right after the conversation according the dialogue below? (4점)

M: May I help you?
B: Yes. I'm looking for my dog. His name is Prince.
M: What does he look like?
B: He's very small and has short white hair. And, he has a really long tail.
M: I see. And one more thing. Where did you lose him?
B: I lost him near the main gate.
M: OK. I'll go and make an announcement. Can you please wait here?
B: Sure. Thanks a lot.
M: man B: boy

① He will make an announcement.
② He will go out to look for his dog.
③ He will wait for Prince near the gate.
④ He will tell the man about his lost pet.
⑤ He will stay at the Lost and Found Office.

[11~12] 다음 대화를 읽고 물음에 답하시오.

A: Do you need help?
B: Yes. I'm looking for <u>my pet.</u>
A: What does it look like?
B: Well, she is brown and she is very pretty.
A: (가)_____ Is there anything special about her?
B: She has antlers and hooves.

11. 위 대화의 밑줄 친 <u>my pet</u>에 해당하는 것은? (4점)

① 　② 　③

④ 　⑤

12. 위 대화의 문맥상 (가)에 들어갈 말로 가장 적절한 것은? (3점)
① When did you lose her?
② What are you looking for?
③ Can you please wait here?
④ What are you waiting for?
⑤ Can you tell me more about her?

13. 다음 밑줄 친 that 중 관계대명사로 쓰인 것은? (3점)
① We know the person <u>that</u> donated it.
② They didn't think <u>that</u> he was smart.
③ It was necessary for me to do <u>that</u>.
④ They found out <u>that</u> dolphins can't sing.
⑤ He thought <u>that</u> only humans can use tools.

14. 다음 중 if의 위치가 내용상 가장 <u>어색한</u> 것은? (4점)
① Please call me <u>if</u> you have any problems.
② <u>If</u> she exercises every day, she will get fit.
③ <u>If</u> you get some fresh air, you'll feel better.
④ I will go to the concert <u>if</u> I can get a ticket.
⑤ <u>If</u> he can get there in 20 minutes, he takes the subway.

15. 다음 중 어법상 올바른 문장의 개수는? (4점)

- James has a brother who play the piano well.
- I saw a picture who was drawn last night.
- Did you clean the dishes I bought yesterday?
- I like the students whom are polite.
- The movies I want to watch is very famous.
- Children love vegetables are not common.
- The songs I listened to were beautiful.

① 1개　② 2개　③ 3개　④ 4개　⑤ 5개

16. 다음은 상수가 주말에 할 일들을 생각해 본 것들이다. 어법상 오류가 있는 문장은? (3점)
① I will go hiking unless it rain.
② If I meet Tom, I will take a picture with him.
③ If I feel tired, I'll sleep a lot.
④ If I get up late, I won't have breakfast.
⑤ If I'm not busy, I can watch a movie.

[17~18] 다음 글을 읽고 물음에 답하시오.

In Aesop's fable *The Thirsty Crow*, a crow drops stones into a jar to raise the level of water. You may think this is just a story, but it is not. Scientists who were studying crows did an experiment. They put a jar with water in front of a crow. A worm was floating on top of the water. However, the water level was low, so the crow could not eat the worm. The crow solved the problem just as in the fable. It dropped stones into the jar. If you think this bird is special, you are wrong. Scientists did the same experiment with other crows, and they all did the same, too.

17. 위 글의 요지로 가장 알맞은 것은?　　(4점)

① All animals are smart.

② Crows can solve problems.

③ Scientists like to do the same experiment.

④ There are many animals in Aesop's fables.

⑤ Crows are the smartest animal in the world.

18. Why couldn't the crow eat the worm in a jar?

(3점)

① It's because the water level was low.

② It's because the worm was not fresh.

③ It's because the bird was not hungry.

④ It's because there was a stone in a jar.

⑤ It's because the crow didn't want to eat it.

19. 다음 글의 아래 문장이 들어갈 위치로 가장 적절한 것은?　　(4점)

If you go to a Buddhist temple in Lop Buri, Thailand, watch out for the Macaque monkeys. (A) They may come to you and pull out your hair. (B) They use human hair to floss their teeth. (C) If you are lucky, you may see female monkeys that are teaching flossing to their babies. (D) This way, the baby monkeys learn to floss. (E)

While the babies are watching, the female monkeys floss their teeth very slowly.

① (A) ② (B) ③ (C) ④ (D) ⑤ (E)

[20~21] 다음 글을 읽고 물음에 답하시오.

People don't usually think that octopuses are smart. However, octopuses are very smart, and they can also use tools. They use coconut shells for protection. When they can't find a good hiding place, they hide under coconut shells. Some octopuses (A)_____ store coconut shells for later use. They pile the coconut shells and carry them to use later. How smart!

20. 위 글의 빈칸 (A)에 들어갈 말로 가장 알맞은 것은?　　(3점)

① so　　　　② also　　　　③ even

④ very　　　⑤ too

21. 위 글의 내용과 일치하는 것은?　　(4점)

① 문어는 조개 껍데기를 도구로 사용한다.

② 문어는 도구를 사용할 만큼 영리하지 못하다.

③ 문어는 자신을 보호하기 위해 코코넛 껍데기를 사용한다.

④ 코코넛 껍데기는 바위 틈 다음으로 숨기에 좋은 장소이다.

⑤ 문어는 코코넛을 먹고 껍데기는 나중에 사용하기 위해 저장한다.

[22~24] 다음 글을 읽고, 물음에 답하시오.

In Aesop's _fable_ *The Thirsty Crow*, a crow drops stones into a jar to raise the level of water. You may think this is just a story, but it is not. Scientists (A)_____ were studying crows did an experiment. They put a jar with water in front of a crow. A worm was floating on top of the water. However, the water _level_ was low, so the crow could not eat the worm. The crow solved the problem just as in the fable. It dropped stones into the _jar_. If you think this bird is special, you are wrong. Scientists did the same _experiment_ with other crows, and they all did the same, too.

22. 위 글의 밑줄 친 단어의 영영풀이가 잘못된 것은?

(4점)

① fable – a story that teaches us a moral lesson

② crow – a large sea animal that makes a loud sound

③ level – the amount or degree of something

④ jar – a glass container with a lid

⑤ experiment – a scientific test you do to learn about something

23. 위 글의 (A)에 들어갈 말로 알맞은 것은?   (2점)

① who   ② what   ③ whom

④ which   ⑤ whose

24. 위 글의 내용과 일치하지 <u>않는</u> 것은?   (3점)

① 다른 까마귀들도 돌을 이용하였다.

② 물 위에는 벌레가 떠다니고 있었다.

③ 이솝우화의 까마귀 이야기는 사실이다.

④ 까마귀는 돌을 사용하여 문제를 해결했다.

⑤ 과학자들은 특별한 까마귀로 실험을 하였다.

[25~27] 다음 글을 읽고, 물음에 답하시오.

People don't usually think that octopuses are smart. (A)_____, octopuses are very smart, and they can also use tools. They use coconut shells for protection. When they can't find a good ⓐ_____ place, they ⓑ_____ under coconut shells. Some octopuses even store coconut shells for later use. They pile the coconut shells and carry them to use later. How smart!

25. 위 글의 빈칸 (A)에 들어갈 말로 가장 알맞은 것은?

(2점)

① So   ② And   ③ Also

④ However   ⑤ For example

26. 위 글의 내용과 일치하지 <u>않는</u> 것은?   (3점)

① 문어는 매우 영리하다.

② 문어는 코코넛 껍질을 운반할 수 있다.

③ 문어는 코코넛 껍질을 도구로 사용한다.

④ 문어는 나중에 쓰기 위해 코코넛 껍질을 저장한다.

⑤ 문어는 음식을 저장하기 위해 코코넛 껍질을 사용한다.

27. 위 글의 빈칸 ⓐ, ⓑ에 들어갈 단어로 옳은 것은?

(3점)

	ⓐ	ⓑ
①	hide	hiding
②	hiding	hide
③	hiding	to hide
④	to hide	hiding
⑤	hid	hidden

[28~29] 다음 글을 읽고 물음에 답하시오.

People once thought that only humans can use tools. Now, scientists are finding out that many animals can also use tools.
Macaque Monkeys
If you go to a Buddhist temple in Lop Buri, Thailand, watch out for the Macaque monkeys. (A) They may come to you and pull out your hair. (B) They use human hair to floss their teeth. (C) If you are lucky, you may see female monkeys that are teaching flossing to their babies. (D) While the babies are watching, the female monkeys floss their teeth very slowly. (E)

28. 위 글을 읽고 답할 수 있는 것을 고르면? (3점)

① How many Buddhist temples are there in Thailand?

② What do female monkeys teach to their babies?

③ Why did people think that only humans can use tools?

④ How did the scientists find out the animals that used tools.

⑤ How did the monkeys brush their hair?

29. 위 글의 흐름으로 보아 주어진 문장이 들어가기에 가장 적절한 곳은? (3점)

This way, the baby monkeys learn to floss.

① (A)　② (B)　③ (C)　④ (D)　⑤ (E)

[30~32] 다음 글을 읽고 물음에 답하시오.

Crows
In Aesop's fable *The Thirsty Crow*, a crow drops stones into a jar to raise the level of water. (A) You may think this is just a story, but it is not.
ⓐ까마귀를 연구하고 있던 과학자들이 실험을 하나 했다. (B) They put a jar with water in front of a crow. A worm was floating on top of the water. (C) However, the water level was low, so the crow could not eat the worm. The crow solved the problem just as in the fable. (D) It dropped stones into the jar. (E) Scientists did the same experiment with other crows, and they all did the same, too.

30. 위 글의 내용상 (A)~(E) 중 〈보기〉 문장이 들어가기에 가장 알맞은 곳은? (3점)

〈보기〉
If you think this bird is special, you are wrong.

① (A)　② (B)　③ (C)　④ (D)　⑤ (E)

31. According to the passage, which is true? (3점)

① The crow in the experiment did not do the same as the crow in the fable.

② Scientists found out that only special crows can use stones to raise the level of the water in a jar.

③ The name of Aesop's fable is *The Thirsty Crow*.

④ Scientists put a worm into a jar with sand.

⑤ When they did the same experiment with other crows, the scientists didn't find the same result.

32. 위 글의 ⓐ의 우리말과 의미가 같도록 〈보기〉에 주어진 단어들을 활용하여 문장을 완성하시오. (5점)

〈보기〉
study / do / be (필요시 변형 가능, 8 단어)

→ _____

2학년 영어 1학기 기말고사(4과) 2회

문항수 : 선택형(31문항) 서술형(1문항)   20 . . .

◎ 선택형 문항의 답안은 컴퓨터용 수정 싸인펜을
   사용하여 OMR 답안지에 바르게 표기하시오.
◎ 서술형 문제는 답을 답안지에 반드시 검정
   볼펜으로 쓰시오.
◎ 총 32문항 100점 만점입니다. 문항별 배점
   은 각 문항에 표시되어 있습니다.

[경북 ○○중]

1. 다음 빈칸에 공통으로 들어갈 말로 알맞은 것은? (2점)

- If you know the answer, _____ your hand.
- Many stores will _____ prices of milk.

① buy   ② make   ③ raise
④ sew   ⑤ decorate

[종로구 ○○중]

2. 다음 각 문장의 빈칸에 들어갈 수 <u>없는</u> 것은? (3점)

- People brush and _____ their teeth.
- The Buddhist _____ is located among the pine trees.
- They _____ the room with balloons for her party.
- Let us _____ that dogs can talk like us.

① imagine   ② floss   ③ creative
④ decorate   ⑤ temple

[인천 ○○중]

3. 다음 대화가 이루어지는 장소로 가장 알맞은 것은? (2점)

A: May I help you?
B: Yes. I'm looking for my cat.
A: What does it look like?
B: She's not very big and she has black hair.
A: Is there anything special about her?
B: She has a short hair.

① library   ② museum
③ bookstore   ④ shopping mall
⑤ lost and found office

[영등포구 ○○중]

[4~5] 다음 대화를 읽고 질문에 답하시오.

Man: (A)_____
Girl: Yes. I'm looking for my dog. His name is Prince.
Man: (B)_____
Girl: He's very small and has short white hair.
Man: (C)_____
Girl: Well, he has a really long tail.
Man: I see. And one more thing. (D)_____
   _____
Girl: I lost him near the main gate.
Man: OK. I'll go and make an announcement.
   (E)_____
Girl: Sure. Thanks a lot.

4. 위 대화에 등장하는 개의 'Lost Dog Report' 설명이다. 내용이 일치하지 <u>않는</u> 것은? (3점)

① size   very small
② color   white hair
③ name   Prince
④ lost place   announcement office
⑤ something special long tail

5. 위 대화의 흐름상 (A)~(E)에 어울리는 말이 바르게 연결된 것을 2개 고르면? (4점)

① (A) - Can you help me?
② (B) - What does he like?
③ (C) - Can you tell me more?
④ (D) - Where did you get it?
⑤ (E) - Can you please wait here?

[6~9] 다음 대화를 읽고, 물음에 답하시오.

> A: May I help you?
> B: Yes. I'm looking for my dog. His name is Prince.
> A: What does he look like?
> B: ⓐ_____
> A: ⓑ_____
> B: Well, he has a really long tail.
> A: I see. And one more thing. ⓒ_____
> B: I lost him near the main gate.
> A: OK. I'll go and make an announcement. Can you please wait here?
> B: Sure. Thanks a lot.

6. 위 대화의 ⓐ에 <u>어색한</u> 대답을 고르면? (3점)
① He's very small.
② He has short hair.
③ He has black dots.
④ He's very friendly.
⑤ He has short white hair.

7. 위 대화의 ⓑ의 빈칸에 들어갈 질문으로 <u>어색한</u> 것은? (2점)
① What else?
② Can you tell me more?
③ Can you give me some advice?
④ Tell me more about him, please.
⑤ Is there anything special about him?

8. 위 대화의 ⓒ에 들어갈 수 있는 질문은? (3점)
① What is it?
② Where is he?
③ Why was he lost?
④ What were you doing?
⑤ Where did you lose him?

9. 위 대화의 내용과 일치하는 것은? (2점)
① B가 잃어버린 동물은 암컷이다.
② B는 작은 고양이를 가지고 있다.
③ B가 잃어버린 동물은 긴 꼬리가 있다.
④ B는 정문에서 잃어버린 동물을 찾았다.
⑤ B가 잃어버린 동물은 긴 털을 가지고 있다.

10. 다음 대화의 빈칸에 들어갈 말로 가장 알맞은 것은? (3점)

> A: _____
> B: He's very small and has short white hair.

① What is he doing?
② What is he look?
③ How is he look like?
④ What does he feel like?
⑤ What does he look like?

11. 다음 중 대화가 <u>어색한</u> 것은? (3점)
① A: I think I lost my cat.
　 B: Where did you last see it?
② A: May I help you? I'm looking for a nice bag.
　 B: What does it look like?
③ A: Hello. Do you need my help?
　 B: No, thank you. I can deal with it.
④ A: I lost my son in blue jeans and a yellow hat.
　 B: I'll go and make an announcement.
⑤ A: I left my backpack at the subway station.
　 B: That's too bad.

[12~13] 다음 대화를 읽고, 물음에 답하시오.

M: May I help you?
S: Yes. I'm looking for my dog. His name is Prince.
M: (A)_____
S: He's very small and has short white hair.
M: Can you tell me more?
S: Well, he has a really long tail.
M: I see. And one more thing. Where did you lose him?
S: I lost him near the main gate.
M: OK. I'll go and make an announcement. Can you please wait here?
S: Sure. Thanks a lot.

12. 위 대화의 밑줄 친 (A)에 들어갈 알맞은 말은? (3점)

① What does he like?
② What does he look for?
③ What does he look like?
④ How does he meet my dog?
⑤ Why are you looking for my dog?

13. 위 대화의 내용과 일치하지 않는 표의 내용은? (4점)

Lost Pet Report	
Type of Animal	ⓐ dog
Name	ⓑ Prince
Size	ⓒ very small
Color	ⓓ white hair
Lost Place	near the main gate
Something Special	ⓔ short tail

① ⓐ　　② ⓑ　　③ ⓒ　　④ ⓓ　　⑤ ⓔ

14. 다음 중 어법상 바르지 않은 문장은? (3점)

① If you find my dad, please give him this book.
② They can catch the train unless they wake up late.
③ She will be tired unless she goes to bed earlier.
④ I will give my money to the poor if I make a lot of money.
⑤ You cannot go out if you will be busy.

15. 다음 중 밑줄 친 단어 중 주격 관계대명사가 아닌 것은? (2점)

① I want a friend who is kind.
② She was a spy who loved me.
③ He is the painter who painted it.
④ This is a story which I told to him.
⑤ Mike has a brother who plays soccer well.

16. 다음 주어진 단어와 접속사 'if'를 사용하여 우리말을 영작하시오. (5점)

(1) 만약 네가 지금 떠난다면 너는 기차를 탈 수 있다. (catch, leave) → _____ (2) 만약 내가 달걀들을 판다면 나는 돈을 벌 수 있다. (sell, make) → _____

(1) _____

(2) _____

[17~23] 다음 글을 읽고 물음에 답하시오.

People once thought ⓐthat only humans can use tools. Now, scientists are finding out ⓑthat many animals can also use tools.

(A) If you go to a Buddhist temple in Lop Buri, Thailand, watch ㉠_____ for the Macaque monkeys. They may come to you and pull ㉠_____ your hair. They use human hair to floss their teeth. If you are lucky, you may see female monkeys ⓒthat are teaching flossing to their babies. While the babies are watching, the female monkeys floss their teeth very slowly. This way, the baby monkeys learn to floss.

(B) People don't usually think ⓓthat octopuses are smart. However, octopuses are very smart, and they can also use tools. They use coconut shells for protection. When they can't find a good hiding place, they hide under coconut shells. Some octopuses even store coconut shells for later use. They pile the coconut shells and carry them to use later. How smart!

(C) In Aesop's fable *The Thirsty Crow*, a crow drops stones into a jar to raise the level of water. You may think ⓔthat this is just a story, but it is not. ㉡(who, crows, scientists, studying, experiment, an, did, were) (가)They put a jar with water in front of a crow. (나)A worm was floating on top of the water. (다)However, the water level was low, so the crow could not eat the worm. The crow solved the problem just as in the fable. (라)It dropped stones into the jar. (마)If you think this bird is special, you are right. Scientists did the same experiment with other crows, and they all did the same, too.

17. 위 글의 전체 제목으로 가장 적절한 것은? (4점)
① Clever Octopuses
② Animals That Use Tools
③ Monkeys Flossing Their Teeth
④ Why Can Only Humans Use Tools?
⑤ Scientists' Experiments on Animals

18. 위 글의 빈칸 ㉠에 공통으로 들어갈 표현으로 알맞은 것은? (3점)
① on   ② at   ③ of
④ off   ⑤ out

19. 위 글의 단락 (A)와 (B)를 읽고 답할 수 없는 질문은? (3점)
① Why do octopuses store coconut shells?
② Why do Macaque monkeys floss their teeth?
③ What do octopuses use coconut shells for?
④ What do Macaque monkeys use human hair for?
⑤ How do female Macaque monkeys teach flossing to baby monkeys?

20. 다음은 위 글의 내용을 요약한 글이다. 빈칸에 들어갈 표현으로 적절하지 않은 단어는? (4점)

Scientists are now finding out that many animals can use ⓐ_____. Macaque monkeys use human hair to ⓑ_____ their teeth. Octopuses hide under coconut shells when they can't find a good ⓒ_____ place. Crows can drop stones into a jar to ⓓ_____ the level of water to eat the worm that is ⓔ_____ on top of the water.

① ⓐ tools   ② ⓑ floss   ③ ⓒ pile
④ ⓓ raise   ⑤ ⓔ floating

21. 위 글의 밑줄 친 ⓐ~ⓔ 중 that의 쓰임이 나머지와 다른 것은? (3점)

① ⓐ   ② ⓑ   ③ ⓒ   ④ ⓓ   ⑤ ⓔ

22. 위 글의 빈칸 ⓛ의 단어를 아래 문장이 되도록 옳게 배열한 것은? (3점)

• 까마귀를 연구하는 과학자들이 실험을 했다.

① Studying crows who were scientists did an experiment.
② Crows who were studying scientists did an experiment.
③ Crows who did an experiment were studying scientists.
④ Scientists who were studying crows did an experiment.
⑤ Scientists were studying crows who did an experiment.

23. 위 글의 단락 (C)의 (가)~(마) 중 내용상 흐름에 적절하지 않은 문장은? (3점)

① (가)   ② (나)   ③ (다)
④ (라)   ⑤ (마)

[24~25] 다음 글을 읽고 물음에 답하시오.

Octopuses
People don't usually think that octopuses are smart. However, (A)_____,
and they can also use tools. They use coconut shells for protection. When they can't find a good hiding place, they hide under coconut shells. Some octopuses even store coconut shells for later use. They pile the coconut shells and carry them to use later. ⓐHow smart!

24. 위 글의 문맥상 빈칸 (A)에 들어갈 문장으로 옳은 것은? (3점)

① octopuses use tools
② octopuses aren't smart
③ octopuses are very smart
④ octopuses can't use tools
⑤ octopuses cannot be smart

25. 위 글의 글쓴이가 밑줄 친 ⓐ와 같이 말한 이유로 옳지 않은 것은? (4점)

① Because octopuses can use tools.
② Because octopuses can hide under coconut shells.
③ Because octopuses use coconut shells for protection.
④ Because octopuses cannot find a good hiding place.
⑤ Because octopuses pile coconut shells to use them later.

26. 다음 글의 빈칸에 들어갈 말로 가장 적절한 것은? (4점)

In Aesop's fable *The Thirsty Crow,* a crow drops stones into a jar to raise the level of water. You may think that this is just a story, but it is not. Scientists did an experiment with some crows. They put a jar with water in front of a crow. A worm was floating on top of the water. However, the water level was low, so the crow could not eat the worm. The crow solved the problem _____. It dropped stones into the jar.

① just as in the fable
② by adding more water
③ by picking up the worm
④ by the opposite of the fable
⑤ following the scientists' directions

[27~29] 다음 글을 읽고, 물음에 답하시오.

People don't usually think that octopuses are smart. ⓐ_____, octopuses are very smart, and they can also use tools. They use coconut shells (A)_____ protection. When they can't find a good hiding place, they hide under coconut shells. Some octopuses even store coconut shells (B)_____ later use. They pile the coconut shells and carry them (C)_____ use later. How smart!

27. 위 글의 ⓐ에 들어갈 말로 알맞은 것은? (3점)
① So ② And ③ Then
④ However ⑤ For example

28. 위 글의 (A)~(C)에 알맞은 것은? (4점)

	(A)	(B)	(C)
①	for	to	for
②	to	for	for
③	to	to	for
④	for	to	to
⑤	for	for	to

29. 위 글의 내용과 일치하지 않는 것은? (3점)
① 문어는 도구를 사용한다.
② 문어는 매우 머리가 좋다.
③ 문어는 코코넛 껍질을 보관한다.
④ 문어는 음식을 코코넛 껍질에 저장한다.
⑤ 문어는 코코넛 껍질을 피난처로 사용한다.

30. 다음 글의 뒤에 이어질 내용으로 가장 알맞은 것은? (3점)

People once thought that only humans can use tools. Now, scientists are finding out that many animals can also use tools.

① 인간과 동물의 차이점
② 도구를 사용하는 동물들
③ 인간에게 도움을 주는 동물
④ 과학 실험 대상이 되는 동물들
⑤ 새로운 기술을 연구하는 과학자들

[31~32] 다음 글을 읽고, 물음에 답하시오.

In Aesop's fable *The Thirsty Crow*, a crow drops stones into a jar to raise the level of water. You may think this is just a story, but it is not. Scientists who were studying crows did an experiment. ⓐThey put a jar with water in front of a crow. A worm was floating on top of the water. (A)_____, the water level was low, so the crow could not eat the worm. The crow solved ⓑthe problem just as in the fable. ⓒIt dropped stones into the jar. If you think this bird is special, you are wrong. Scientists did the same experiment with other crows, and ⓓthey all did ⓔthe same, too.

31. 위 글의 밑줄 친 (A)에 들어갈 단어로 적절한 것은? (3점)
① If ② So ③ After
④ Before ⑤ However

32. 위 글의 ⓐ~ⓔ가 가리키는 것으로 올바르게 짝지은 것은? (3점)
① ⓐ: the crows
② ⓑ: the crow could not eat the worm
③ ⓒ: the worm
④ ⓓ: scientists
⑤ ⓔ: to do some experiment

정답 및 해설

Lesson 1 (중간) 1회

> 01 ④ 02 ③ 03 ④
>
> 04 What do you usually do in your free time?
>
> 05 ⑤ 06 ⑤ 07 ④ 08 ③ 09 ⑤ 10 ① 11 ①
>
> 12 ④ 13 ① 14 ①
>
> 15 How do I get to the police station?
>
> 16 ③ 17 ⑤ 18 ⑤ 19 ① 20 ① 21 ④ 22 ③
>
> 23 ④ 24 ④ 25 ④ 26 ③ 27 ② 28 ② 29 ⑤
>
> 30 ⑤ 31 ③ 32 ③

01 각각 ① meal, ② joke, ③ novel, ⑤ detective에 대한 풀이이다.

02 서점을 찾는다고 하자 위치를 알려주고 있다.

03 수빈이는 'I sometimes watch action movies, too.'라고 했다.

04 'What do you usually do in your free time?'은 어떤 여가 활동을 하는지 묻는 표현이다. 'What do you enjoy doing in your free time?', 'What do you like to do in your free time?', 'How do you spend your free time?' 등으로 물을 수도 있다.

05 'Why don't we go see an action movie this weekend?'에 'Sure.'라고 답하고 있다.

06 'Rock music.'이라고 답하는 것으로 보아 어떤 종류의 음악을 듣는지 묻는 것이 적절하다.

07 배드민턴 치자고 제안하고 있는데 이유를 답하고 있다.

08 both A and B: A와 B 둘 다, neither A nor B: A도 B도 아닌. 'neither A nor B'가 주어이면 B에 수를 일치시킨다.

09 He is good at neither writing nor reading English.

10 kind는 명사로 '종류', 형용사로 '친절한'이라는 뜻이다.

11 ② him → to him, ③ to → for, ④, ⑤ for → to

12 'blueberry cookies'를 만든다는 답으로 보아 어떤 종류의 과자를 만드는지 묻는 것이 적절하다.

13 Subin이 가장 좋아하는 영화가 무엇인지는 알 수 없다.

14 ①번은 for가 들어가야 하지만 나머지는 모두 to가 들어간다.

15 의문사 How로 시작하고 '~에 도착하다'라는 의미의 'get to'를 이용한다.

16 '많은 동물을 볼 수 있기 때문에 지루하지 않다.'가 적절하다.

17 많은 동물들을 볼 수 있다.

18 거의 모든 사람이 말을 탈 수 있고, "우리는 걷기도 전에 말을 탄다."라고 말하는 것으로 보아 '중요하다'가 적절하다.

19 'I live near the Gobi Desert in Mongolia.'라고 했다.

20 'a short nap'으로 보아 'lunch'가 적절하다.

21 also로 보아 추가하는 문장이므로 (D)가 적절하다.

22 (A) to ride → riding (B) are → is
(D) proud with → proud of (E) wants → want

23 Musa가 우승했다는 언급은 없다.

24 'We usually have soup, vegetables, and meat. We also have a dessert like churros.'라고 했다.

25 ⓓ의 like는 전치사로 '~ 같은'이라는 뜻이다.

26 'My favorite time of the day is lunch time.'이 주제문이다.

27 조동사 can이 앞에 있으므로 ⓑ의 rides는 원형 ride로 고쳐야 한다.

28 Musa가 '학교에 어떻게 가는지'는 알 수 없다.

29 'I so'를 'I'm so'로 고쳐야 한다. be proud of: ~를 자랑스러워하다

30 '올림픽 경기에서 우승한 케냐의 육상 선수들'을 가리킨다.

31 'gets'와 병렬로 'has'가 되어야 한다.

32 저녁으로 무엇을 먹는지는 나와 있지 않다.

Lesson 1 (중간) 2회

> 01 ⑤ 02 ③ 03 ② 04 ⑤ 05 ⑤ 06 ⑤ 07 ②
>
> 08 ① 09 What kind of, do you like 10 ④ 11 ①
>
> 12 ③ 13 (Tamu) likes both English and science.
>
> 14 My grandfather told us an interesting story.
>
> 15 ② 16 ① 17 ⑤ 18 ③ 19 ④ 20 ① 21 ④
>
> 22 ④ 23 ③
>
> 24 Tabin feels happy when she rides her horse.
>
> 25 ③ 26 ③ 27 ② 28 ④ 29 ② 30 ③ 31 ④
>
> 32 In the evening before the sunset
>
> 33 (1) Both my dad and I like to sleep under the tree.
> (2) Either Tom or James was late for school.

01 우리가 완벽해지려면 '연습'할 필요가 있다.

02 빈도부사는 보통 be동사나 조동사 뒤에, 일반동사 앞에 나온다.

03 '나는 남동생과 배드민턴을 쳐.'라는 답으로 보아 '어떤 종

류의 운동을 하는지' 묻는 것이 적절하다.

04 ① is → are ② both ~ and → either ~ or
③ am → are ④ either → both

05 '어디 가고 있는지' 묻는 질문에 '도서관'이라고 답하고 있다.

06 좋아하는 영화를 물었는데 소설을 좋아한다고 답했다.

07 Andy가 얼마나 자주 영화를 보는지는 언급되지 않았다.

08 무슨 게임을 하는지 물었는데 게임을 한다고 답하는 것은 어색하다.

09 '탐정 소설 읽는 것을 좋아한다.'는 답으로 보아 어떤 종류의 책을 좋아하는지 묻는 것이 적절하다.

10 각각 a. for b. to c. for d. to e. to가 들어가야 한다. 간접목적어를 직접목적어 뒤에 둘 때 동사 make와 buy는 전치사 for를 쓴다.

11 '나는 밖에서 운동을 해.'라는 답으로 보아 '여가 시간에 주로 무엇을 하는지' 묻는 것이 가장 적절하다. 다른 선택지들은 답이 될 수 없음을 확인한다.

12 ⓒ swimming → badminton ⓔ novels → movies

13 both A and B: A와 B 둘 다

14 수여동사는 '동사+간접목적어+직접목적어'의 어순으로 쓴다.

15 Diego의 점심 시간이 얼마 동안인지는 알 수 없다.

16 like는 전치사로 '~같이', 동사로 '좋아하다'라는 뜻이다.

17 'Both Tamu and I want to be like them(올림픽 경기에서 우승한 케냐 육상 선수들).'으로 보아 ⑤번이 옳다.

18 2시쯤 점심을 먹는다는 말에 이어 ⓑ에서 설명을 시작하고 ⓐ에서 무엇을 먹는지 언급하고 ⓓ에서 also로 디저트도 먹는 것을 언급한 후 ⓒ에서 식사 후의 시에스타로 이어진다.

19 ⓔ with → of ⓕ him → to him ⓖ to ride → riding ⓘ peace → peaceful

20 on [종사·소속] ~에 관계하고 (있다), ~에 종사하고, ~의 일원으로. be on a team: 팀에 속해 있다. [날·때·기회] ~에, ~때에. on Sundays: 일요일에

21 ⓛ 가장 좋아하는 시간은 달리기 연습 시간이라고 했으므로 happiest ⓒ 많은 동물들을 볼 수 있다고 했으므로 boring

22 ⓔ과 ④는 '~ 같이(전치사)' 나머지는 모두 '좋아하다(동사)'라는 뜻이다.

23 Tabin의 말이 몇 살인지는 알 수 없다.

24 'I'm happy when I ride my horse.'라고 했다.

25 거의 모든 사람이 말을 탈 수 있다고 했으므로 '우리는 걷기도 전에 말을 탄다.'가 적절하다.

26 'Horses are important in our culture.'라고 했다.

27 주말에 무엇을 하는지는 알 수 없다.

28 'I'm so proud of them.'으로 보아 respectful이 적절하다.

29 'I'm happy when I ride my horse.'와 'I take good care of my horse.'로 보아 말을 갖고 있음을 알 수 있다.

30 간접목적어를 직접목적어 뒤에 둘 때 동사 give는 전치사 to를 쓴다.

31 (A) In fact: 사실(은) (B) enjoy는 목적어로 동명사를 취한다. (C) everything은 단수로 받는다.

32 그때는 'in the evening before the sunset'을 의미한다.

33 (1) both A and B: A와 B 둘 다
(2) either A or B: A 또는 B

Lesson 2 (중간) 1회

01 ②	02 ④	03 ④	04 ①	05 ④	06 ⑤

07 (A) left (B) across from   **08** You, miss it
09 ④   **10** must not use paper cups to save the earth
11 ⑤   **12** ④   **13** ④   **14** five people in my family
15 ④   **16** ①   **17** ⑤   **18** ⑤   **19** ⑤   **20** ④   **21** ①
22 ①   **23** ⑤   **24** ②   **25** ③   **26** ④   **27** ④   **28** ③
29 ②   **30** ③   **31** ⑤

01 순서대로 especially, cancel, take care of, practice 이다.

02 'You can't miss it.'은 '찾기 쉽다.'라는 말이다.

03 (D) 여가 시간에 무엇을 하는지 묻고 (A) 과자를 만든다고 답하자 (C) 만들기 좋아하는 과자가 있는지 묻고 (B) 딸기 과자라고 답하는 순서가 자연스럽다.

04 세 블록 곧장 가서 왼쪽으로 돌면 오른쪽에 있는 것은 학교이다.

05 식당 맞은편에 있는 것은 library(도서관)이다.

06 African Music Concert는 공원 북문 근처에 있는 Star Concert 무대에서 오후 4시에 시작한다.

07 두 블록 곧장 가서 왼쪽으로 돌이 기차역 맞은편에 공원이 있다. across from: ~의 바로 맞은편에

08 You can't miss it.: 찾기 쉽다, 꼭 찾을 것이다

09 각각을 영작하면 (A) The jacket looks warm enough to wear in winter. (B) She walks too fast to follow. (C) The dog is smart enough to guide the blind.이다.

10 'must not(~해서는 안 된다)'와 to부정사의 부사적 용법 중 '목적(~하기 위하여)'을 이용한다.

11 (A), (B) 감정을 유발하는 경우 현재분사를 쓴다.
(C) love의 목적어로 living이 나왔으므로 going을 써야 한다.

12 ⓓ의 it은 'the Star Concert Stage'를 가리킨다.

13 ④: 명사적 용법(목적어) ①, ②, ③, ⑤: 부사적 용법(목적)

14 5명은 'five people'로 쓰고 in을 사용해서 'in my family'로 쓴다.

15 뒤에 나오는 'but they have to'로 보아 상반되는 'don't have to'가 적절하다.

16 'to make a blanket, people had to collect small pieces of fabric and sew them together'로 보아 'expensive'가 적절하다.

17 to make와 ⑤번: 부사적 용법 '목적' ① 부사적 용법 '원인' ② have to 동사원형 ③ 명사적 용법, ④ 부사적 용법 '결과'

18 'I'm scared, but the view is amazing!'이라고 했다.

19 엄마와 아빠가 먹고 있는 'nachos and fajitas'를 가리킨다.

20 뒤에 이유가 나오고 있으므로 'because'가 적절하다.

21 corn dogs가 어떻게 만들어지는지는 알 수 없다.

22 할머니의 퀼트 모임이 오랜 전통을 갖고 있는지는 알 수 없다.

23 (A) move on to: ~로 옮기다, 이동하다 (B) had to collect와 병렬로 sew (C) 뒤에 'over six months'가 이어지므로 for가 적절하다.

24 '오랫동안 존재해 온 관습이나 믿음'은 'tradition(전통)'이다.

25 세상에서 가장 큰 fair가 무엇인지는 알 수 없다.

26 ⓐ Dallas, Texas, ⓒ don't, ⓔ produce

27 Bonnie가 얼마나 많은 우유를 생산하는지는 알 수 없다.

28 to win과 ③: 부사적 용법 '목적' ①, ②, ⑤: 명사적 용법 ④ 부사구

29 주어진 문장은 '과거에는 천이 비쌌다'라는 것으로 그 결과에 해당하는 내용이 (B) 다음에 나오므로 (B)가 적절하다.

30 'To make a blanket, people had to collect small pieces of fabric and sew them together.'라고 했다.

31 축제 음식을 먹는 주어진 글에 이어 (D)의 They가 (B)의 nachos and fajitas이므로 (B) 다음에 (D)가 나오고, (D)의 fajita를 먹은 아빠가 매운 fajita로 인해 얼굴이 빨개지는 (A)가 이어진 후 (C) Steve와 Eddie가 먹은 것을

아빠가 먹은 것과 비교하는 (C)가 이어지는 것이 자연스럽다.

Lesson 2 (중간)

01 ⑤ 02 ③ 03 Where is the library
04 straight 2 blocks, turn left, be on your right
05 You have to fasten your seat belt. 06 ③ 07 ③
08 ⑤ 09 ⑤ 10 ② 11 ④ 12 ③
13 The fair is over 130 years old.
14 are too tight to wear   15 ④
16 I'm saving money to buy an electric bike[bicycle].
17 ⑤ 18 ① 19 ② 20 ① 21 ② 22 ① 23 ④
24 (1) I learn English to travel abroad. (2) I study hard to pass the exam. (그 외 Tom went to the shopping mall to buy shoes. / I went to the park to take a walk.)
25 ② 26 ② 27 ② 28 ③ 29 ②

01 'Come visit us in Seochon.'으로 보아 서촌으로 오라고 광고하는 글임을 알 수 있다.

02 뒤에서 찾아가는 길을 안내하고 있으므로 '길을 묻는 표현'이 적절하다.

03 B가 library에 가는 길을 설명하고 있다.

04 Bob's Bakery는 두 블록 가서 왼쪽으로 돌면 오른쪽에 있다.

05 have to+동사원형: ~해야 한다

06 ⓐ future → past ⓑ it → them ⓓ short → tall ⓔ amazed → amazing

07 B가 Please look at this map.이라고 했다.

08 To stay와 ⑤는 부사적 용법(목적)이다. ①, ④ 형용사적 용법 ②, ③ 명사적 용법

09 'shoe store'는 Pine Street에 있으며 library 앞에 있다.

10 'it's the biggest fair in the USA'라고 했다.

11 앞에서 언급한 'a goat show'를 가리킨다.

12 'don't have to'와 'have to'로 서로 상반되고 있으므로 but이 적절하다.

13 'The fair is over 130 years old.'라고 했다.

14 too ~ to … : 너무 ~해서 …할 수 없다

15 영작하면 'You (B)walk (D)too (E)fast (C)to (A)follow.'이다.

16 to부정사의 부사적 용법의 '목적'을 이용한다.

17 'I'm scared, but the view is amazing!'라고 했다.

18 (A) In the past: 과거에는 (B) work on: ~에 노력을 들이다/~을 작업하다 (C) on the top: 꼭대기에

19 (A) 'don't have to'와 'have to'로 서로 상반되고 있으므로 but이 적절하다. (B) 뒤에 '결과'가 이어지고 있으므로 'so'가 적절하다.

20 'My younger brother, Steve, entered it.'이라고 했다.

21 ⓑ는 'The goats'를 의미한다.

22 Bonnie가 무슨 색인지는 알 수 없다.

23 'we're eating fair food.'라고 한 후, 'Mom and Dad are eating nachos and fajitas.'라고 했고 'Steve and I are eating corn dogs.'라고 했다.

24 to부정사의 '부사적 용법' 중 '목적: ~하기 위하여'를 이용한다.

25 (A) at: 비교적 좁은 장소 앞이나 건물 이름, 단체 이름 같은 고유명사 앞에 쓰이는 전치사 (B) over: ~이 넘는, ~ 이상의 (C) the+최상급+in+장소/집단: …에서 가장 ~한 (D) show ~ around: ~에게 (…을) 둘러보도록 안내하다

26 In the past: 과거에는. present: 현재, past: 과거

27 할머니는 언제 퀼트 만드는 작업을 하셨는지는 나와 있지 않다.

28 a tall Ferris wheel인 Texas Star 꼭대기에서 할 수 있는 말로 ③번이 적절하다.

29 길을 묻는데 '틀림없이 찾을 것'이라고 하는 것은 어색하다.

Lesson 3 (기말)

01 ③	**02** ④	**03** ②	**04** ④	**05** ②	**06** ④	**07** ④
08 ④	**09** ③	**10** ④	**11** ①	**12** ④	**13** ②	**14** ①
15 ③	**16** ③	**17** ②	**18** ⑤	**19** ②	**20** ②	**21** ⑤
22 ①	**23** ①	**24** ①	**25** ④	**26** ①	**27** ①	

28 This was made by Hajun.

01 ① inner → outer ② lower → higher ④ leg → arm ⑤ pile → store

02 ① 발명하다 ② 서명 ③ 뜻 ⑤ 관계

03 도움이 필요한지 묻는 질문에 이어 (B) 가격을 묻고 (A) 답하며 할인해 주겠다고 하자 (C) 좋다며 샀다고 하는 순서이다.

04 도움이 필요한지 묻는 질문에 '긍정'으로 답한 후 '그냥 둘러보고 있다'는 말은 어색하다.

05 할인을 받을 수 있는지 묻는 질문에 답을 하며 '미안하다'고 하는 것으로 보아 할인이 안 된다는 말이 적절하다.

06 Andy가 돈을 얼마나 많이 갖고 있는지는 알 수 없다.

07 질문에 'not'으로 답을 하며 '거의 새 것과 다름없다'고 하는 것으로 보아 할인을 받을 수 있는지 묻는 말이 적절하다.

08 'I'm afraid not.'은 상대방에게 정중하게 '안 된다'고 말할 때 쓰는 표현이다.

09 The purple T-shirt는 원래 10달러였다.

10 뒤에서 할인해 달라고 한 것으로 보아 'expensive(비싼)'가 적절하다.

11 할인을 받을 수 있는지 묻는 질문에 답을 하며 '겨우 일 년 됐다며 새것과 다름없다.'고 하는 것으로 보아 '할인이 안 된다.'는 말이 적절하다.

12 Woman이 'It's 10 dollars.'라고 하자 Boy는 'Then, I'll take the blue one.'이라고 했다.

13 ① ate → eaten ③ were → was ④ was → were ⑤ is → was

14 어법에 맞게 배열하면 'We want other students to become interested in upcycling.'이다.

15 'run - ran - run'이 적절하다.

16 This가 주어로 앞에 나와 있고 Hajun이 마지막에 있으므로 수동태가 적절하며 과거시제로 쓴다.

17 청바지의 다리 부분을 잘라내는 (C), 맨 아랫부분을 바느질하여 붙이는 (B), 다리 중 한 쪽으로 어깨끈들을 만드는 (A), 청바지의 맨 윗부분에 끈들을 바느질하여 붙이는 (E), 핀과 단추로 가방을 장식하는 (D)의 순서이다.

18 마지막에 'Let's talk about each group's idea for the event.'라고 했으므로 ⑤번이 적절하다.

19 "upcycling"은 "upgrade"와 "recycling"의 "combination(결합)"이다.

20 재활용'처럼' 업사이클링은 환경에 좋다.

21 어법에 맞게 배열하면 'I want you to understand the meaning of upcycling.'이다.

22 "Trashion"은 "trash"와 "fashion"을 결합한 것이다.

23 (A) cut off: 잘라내다 (B) sew: 꿰매다, 바느질하다 (C) decorate: 장식하다

24 각 그룹이 Upcycling 아이디어에 대해 이야기하고 있다.

25 'We would like other students to become interested in upcycling through the show.'라고 했다.

26 '낡은 물건으로 악기를 만들려고 한다.'라는 주어진 글 다음에 어떻게 만들지에 대한 설명이 이어지는 것이 자연스러우므로 (A)가 적절하다.

27 'For example'로 (A) 앞 문장의 예를 들고 있으므로 (A)가 적절하다.

Lesson 3 (기말)

01 ④	**02** ④	**03** ④	**04** ⑤	**05** ④	**06** ⑤	**07** ⑤
08 ④	**09** (B)-(A)-(C)-(D)		**10** ⑤	**11** ④	**12** ③	
13 ⑤	**14** ⑤	**15** ③	**16** ②	**17** ③	**18** ③	**19** ④
20 ⑤	**21** ③	**22** ③	**23** ⑤	**24** ④		
25 ⓑ with → for			**26** ④	**27** ④	**28** ③	

01 주어진 문장과 ④번의 'hold'는 '개최하다'라는 의미이다. ① 갖고[안고] 있다 ② 견디다[지탱하다] ③ 잡다 ⑤ 들고 있다

02 모두 앞에 있는 단어의 뜻에 뒤에 있는 단어의 뜻이 포함되지만 ④번은 '업사이클링 - 재활용'으로 엄밀한 의미에서 뒤에 있는 단어에 앞의 단어가 포함된다고 할 수 있다.

03 할인 중인지 묻는 질문에 20% 할인이라고 답하고 있다.

04 답으로 나온 '이건 어때요?'로 보아 ⑤번이 적절하다.

05 가격을 묻고 답하며 가방을 사는 것으로 보아 '판매원 - 고객'이 적절하다.

06 'I'll take+할인 금액/할인율+off'는 '~ 만큼 깎아 주겠다'라는 표현이다. 'I'll take ~'는 '~을 사겠다'라는 표현이다.

07 우산을 찾으며 가격을 묻고 답하며 할인을 받고 있으므로 '고객 - 판매원'이 적절하다.

08 B는 W가 2달러를 깎아 주겠다고 하자 그럼 사겠다고 했다.

09 도와드릴까요?라는 물음에 (B) 답으로 야구 장갑을 찾고 있다고 하고 (A) 15달러라고 답하자 (C) 할인해 줄 수 있는지 묻고 (D) 2달러 깎아 주겠다고 하자 사겠다는 순서가 적절하다.

10 ① talks → talk ② are → is ③ have → has ④ will see → see

11 할인을 받을 수 있는지 묻는 질문에 답을 하며 '거의 새것과 다름없다.'고 하는 것으로 보아 할인이 안 된다는 말이 적절하다.

12 B는 빨간 시계를 추천했다.

13 각각 ① was written ② was turned on ③ were made ④ were painted가 되어야 한다.

14 want의 목적격보어로 to부정사를 써야 하며, enough를 형용사 exciting 다음에 써야 한다는 것에 주의한다.

15 ① woke → woken ② come → to come ④ doesn't

→ isn't ⑤ stop → to stop ③ 'not+to부정사'에 주의한다.

16 (A) want의 목적격보어로 to부정사, (B) 의문문이므로 anyone, (C) be good for: ~에 좋다, be good at: ~을 잘하다

17 'upcycling'의 뜻에 대해 묻고 다양하게 답하고 있으므로 ③번이 적절하다.

18 pockets가 아니라 legs이다.

19 'My group is going to make musical instruments from old things.'라고 했다.

20 (A)와 ⑤는 부사적 용법(목적)이고 나머지는 모두 명사적 용법이다. ①, ③, ④: 동사의 목적어 ②: 주어

21 각각 ⓐ held → hold ⓑ interesting → interested ⓓ to → from ⓔ planning → are planning으로 고쳐야 한다.

22 'We'll also make a guitar from old boxes and rubber bands.'라고 했다.

23 ⓔ는 is good for가 되어야 한다.

24 'When you upcycle, you make new and better things from old things.'라고 했으므로 그냥 버리면 안 된다.

25 be good for: ~에 좋다

26 어법에 맞게 배열하면 'We want other students to become interested in upcycling.'이다.

27 Upcycling day → Environment Day, recycle → upcycle, a guitar from old plastic buckets and rubber bands → drums from old plastic buckets and a guitar from old boxes and rubber bands, new blue jeans → old clothes

28 쓰레기를 이용한다고만 했지 그 종류에 대한 언급은 없다.

Lesson 4 (기말)

01 ③	**02** ⑤	**03** ①	**04** ⑤	**05** ⑤	**06** ②	**07** ②
08 ③	**09** ④	**10** ⑤	**11** ①	**12** ⑤	**13** ①	**14** ⑤
15 ②	**16** ①	**17** ②	**18** ①	**19** ④	**20** ③	**21** ③
22 ②	**23** ①	**24** ⑤	**25** ④	**26** ⑤	**27** ②	**28** ②
29 ⑤	**30** ⑤	**31** ③				
32 Scientists who were studying crows did an experiment.						

01 모두 육지에 사는 동물이지만 ③번 '문어'는 바다에서 산다.

02 can을 can not으로 바꿔야 한다.

03 'It has a long tail.'이 적절하다.

04 잃어버린 개를 찾고 있다. '분실물 취급소'가 적절하다.

05 'he has a really long tail'이라고 했다.

06 잃어버린 pet의 크기에 대한 언급은 없다.

07 개를 잃어버려 '분실물 취급소'에서 찾고 있다.

08 'What do/does ~ look like?'는 '~은 어떻게 생겼니?'라는 의미로 생김새를 물을 때 사용한다.

09 스카프를 찾고 있다는 말에 이어 (D) 어떻게 생겼는지 묻자 (B) 긴 면 스카프라고 답하고 (A) 그것에 대해 더 말해 달라고 하자 (E) 회색이라고 말하고 (C) 가서 확인해보겠다고 하는 순서가 자연스럽다.

10 M이 'Can you please wait here?'라고 하자 B가 'Sure.'라고 답했으므로 기다릴 것이다.

11 갈색이며, 뿔과 발굽이 있는 동물은 사슴이다. antler: (사슴의) 가지친 뿔, hoof: (말 등의) 발굽

12 '뿔과 발굽이 있다'는 답으로 보아 그것에 대해 더 말해 달라고 하면서 '특별한 점'을 묻는 것이 자연스럽다.

13 ①번은 the person을 선행사로 하는 주격 관계대명사이다. ②, ④, ⑤ 접속사 ③ 지시대명사

14 ⑤번은 '20분 안에 그곳에 도착할 수 있다면 지하철을 탄다'로 어색하다. 'He can get there in 20 minutes if he takes the subway.'가 적절하다.

15 • play → plays • who → which • (○)
• whom → who • is → are
• Children love → Children who love • (○)

16 I will go hiking unless it rains. 조건의 부사절에서는 미래시제를 현재로 나타낸다.

17 까마귀가 항아리 안으로 돌을 넣어 물의 높이를 높여 벌레를 먹었다는 내용으로 ②번이 요지로 적절하다.

18 'the water level was low, so the crow could not eat the worm.'이라고 했다.

19 (D) 다음의 'This way'가 가리키는 것이 주어진 문장의 내용이므로 (D)가 적절하다.

20 '심지어, ~조차'의 뜻으로 'even'이 적절하다.

21 'When they can't find a good hiding place, they hide under coconut shells.'라고 했다.

22 crow: a large black bird that makes a loud sound

23 사람인 Scientists를 선행사로 하는 주격 관계대명사 who나 that이 적절하다.

24 'Scientists did the same experiment with other crows, and they all did the same, too.'라고 했다.

25 서로 상반되는 내용이 나오므로 'However'가 적절하다.

26 'Some octopuses even store coconut shells for later use.'라고 했다.

27 ⓐ place를 수식해야 하므로 동명사 hiding이, ⓑ 동사가 있어야 하므로 hide가 들어가야 한다.

28 'If you are lucky, you may see female monkeys that are teaching flossing to their babies.'라고 했다.

29 주어진 문장의 'This way'가 (E) 앞 문장의 내용을 가리키므로 (E)가 적절하다.

30 주어진 문장의 'this bird'가 (E) 앞 문장의 'It'을 가리키고 (E) 다음에 'other crows'가 나오므로 (E)가 적절하다.

31 'In Aesop's fable *The Thirsty Crow*'라고 했다.

32 동사가 3개 주어졌으므로 접속사가 필요한데 진행형으로 쓰고 관계대명사로 접속사와 대명사의 역할을 하도록 한다.

Lesson 4 (기말)

01 ③	**02** ③	**03** ⑤	**04** ④	**05** ③, ⑤	**06** ④
07 ③	**08** ⑤	**09** ③	**10** ⑤	**11** ②	**12** ③	**13** ⑤
14 ⑤	**15** ④				

16 (1) If you leave now, you can catch the train.
(2) If I sell the eggs, I can make money.

17 ②	**18** ⑤	**19** ②	**20** ③	**21** ③	**22** ④	**23** ⑤
24 ③	**25** ④	**26** ①	**27** ④	**28** ⑤	**29** ④	**30** ②
31 ⑤	**32** ②				

01 raise: (위로) 올리다

02 순서대로 floss, temple, decorate, imagine이 들어간다.

03 잃어버린 고양이를 찾고 있다. '분실물 취급소'가 적절하다.

04 'I lost him near the main gate.'라고 했다.

05 (A) - Can I help you? (B) - What does he look like? (D) - Where did you lose it?이 적절하다.

06 생김새를 묻고 있으므로 생김새에 대한 답이 적절하다.

07 긴 꼬리를 갖고 있다고 '추가'로 답하고 있으므로 '추가적인 것을 묻는 질문'이 자연스럽다.

08 잃어버린 곳을 답하고 있으므로 '어디서 잃어버렸는지 묻는 것'이 적절하다.

09 'Well, he has a really long tail.'이라고 했다.

10 생김새를 묻는 질문이 적절하다.

11 가방을 찾고 있다고 했는데 '어떻게 생겼는지' 묻는 것은 어색하다.

12 '작고 짧은 희색 털을 갖고 있다'라고 생김새를 답하고 있으므로 생김새에 대해 묻는 것이 적절하다.

13 'Well, he has a really long tail.'이라고 했다.

14 You cannot go out if you are busy. 조건의 부사절에서는 미래시제를 현재로 나타낸다.

15 ④번은 told의 직접목적어로 쓰인 story를 관계대명사로 연결한 목적격 관계대명사이다.

16 조건의 부사절에서는 미래시제를 현재로 나타낸다.

17 Macaque monkeys, octopuses, crows 모두 도구를 쓴다는 내용의 글이다.

18 watch out for: ~을 주의하다, 조심하다 pull out: 뽑다

19 마카크 원숭이가 왜 치실질을 하는지는 알 수 없다.

20 ⓒ에는 hiding이 들어가야 한다.

21 ⓒ는 주격 관계대명사이고 나머지는 모두 접속사이다.

22 선행사 Scientists를 관계대명사절 who were studying crows가 수식하도록 하고 did an experiment로 쓴다.

23 뒤에서 '다른 까마귀들에게도 똑같은 실험을 했고, 그 까마귀들도 모두 똑같이 행동했다'라고 했으므로 (마)는 'you are wrong.(당신은 틀렸다.)'이 되어야 한다.

24 'However'가 있으므로 앞의 내용과 상반되는 내용이어야 한다.

25 문어들이 똑똑한 이유로 적절하지 않은 것은 ④번이다.

26 까마귀가 '우화에서처럼' 돌을 항아리 안으로 떨어뜨렸다.

27 서로 상반되는 내용이 나오므로 'However'가 적절하다.

28 (A) for protection: 보호하기 위해 (목적, 용도를 나타내는 전치사 for) (B) for later use: 나중에 사용하기 위해 (C) to use: 사용하기 위해서 (to부정사의 부사적 용법 '목적')

29 '음식을 코코넛 껍질에 저장한다'는 언급은 없다.

30 '이제는 과학자들이 많은 동물들 역시 도구를 사용할 수 있다는 것을 알아내고 있다.'고 했으므로 '도구를 사용하는 동물들'의 이야기가 이어질 것으로 추론할 수 있다.

31 '물 위에는 벌레 한 마리가 떠 있었지만' '물 높이가 낮아서 그 까마귀는 그 벌레를 먹을 수 없었다.'로 'However'로 연결하는 것이 자연스럽다.

32 ⓐ They: Scientists, ⓒ It: the crow, ⓓ they: other crows, ⓔ the same: dropping stones into the jar